BALDWIN

Books by
H. MONTGOMERY HYDE

The Rise of Castlereagh
The Russian Journals of Martha and Catherine Wilmot
  (with the Marchioness of Londonderry)
More Letters from Martha Wilmot: Impressions of Vienna
  (with the Marchioness of Londonderry)
The Empress Catherine and Princess Dashkov
Air Defence and the Civil Population
  (with G. R. Falkiner Nuttall)
Londonderry House and its Pictures
Princess Lieven
Judge Jeffreys
Mexican Empire
A Victorian Historian: Letters of W. E. H. Lecky
Privacy and the Press
John Law
The Trials of Oscar Wilde
Mr and Mrs Beeton
Cases that Changed the Law
Carson
The Trial of Craig and Bentley
United in Crime
The Strange Death of Lord Castlereagh
The Trial of Sir Roger Casement
Sir Patrick Hastings: His Life and Cases
Recent Developments in Historical Method and Interpretation
Simla and the Simla Hill States Under British Protection
An International Case Book of Crime
The Quiet Canadian
Oscar Wilde: The Aftermath
A History of Pornography
Norman Birkett
Cynthia
The Story of Lamb House
Lord Reading
Henry James at Home
Strong for Service: The Life of Lord Nathan of Churt
The Other Love
Their Good Names
Stalin

Baldwin by Sir William Rothenstein   *National Portrait Gallery*

H. MONTGOMERY HYDE

BALDWIN

The Unexpected Prime Minister

Hart-Davis, MacGibbon   London

Granada Publishing Limited
First published in Great Britain 1973 by Hart-Davis, MacGibbon Ltd, Frogmore,
St Albans, Hertfordshire AL2 2NF and 3 Upper James Street, London W1R 4BP

Copyright © 1973 by Harford Productions Ltd

ISBN 0 246 64093 6

Printed in Great Britain by Richard Clay (The Chaucer Press) Ltd, Bungay, Suffolk

There is only one thing which I feel is worth giving one's whole strength to, and that is the binding together of all classes of our people in an effort to make life in this country better in every sense of the word. That is the main end and object of my life in politics.

Stanley Baldwin at Stourport-on-Severn   12 January 1925

The position of leader came to me when I was inexperienced, before I was really fitted for it, by a succession of curious chances that could not have been foreseen. I had never expected it: I was in no way trained for it.

Stanley Baldwin to the Earl of Oxford and Asquith   23 October 1926

I tried hard in those confused years immediately following the [Great] War to get a re-orientation as it were of the Tory party and in Disraeli's words to make it national, i.e. to give it a national rather than a party outlook. If such a spirit should animate those who undertake the great adventure of government after the [present] war, then I could feel that I had not worked in vain.

Earl Baldwin of Bewdley to Mr D. Pepys-Whiteley   15 February 1941

To ROBBIE

who has done so much for this book and its author.

CONTENTS

ILLUSTRATIONS

Between pages 178 and 179

ACKNOWLEDGEMENTS

My first duty is to thank Her Majesty the Queen for her gracious permission to see and quote from the papers of her grandfather King George V in the Royal Archives, and also for similar permission in respect of the royal correspondence in the Baldwin Papers, particularly concerning the Abdication of King Edward VIII, the use of which is at present restricted. In this context I am greatly indebted to Mr R. C. Mackworth-Young, CVO, the Queen's Librarian, and the library staff in Windsor Castle for their invariable help and courtesy.

The present Earl Baldwin of Bewdley has kindly verified certain details of his father's early life contained in the first two chapters. I am also grateful to him for his ready encouragement and advice at all times and for allowing me to draw upon his own books *My Father: The True Story* and *The Macdonald Sisters*, as well as the material in the Baldwin Papers and elsewhere in which he controls the copyright. I also acknowledge with gratitude the assistance which I have received from other members of the Baldwin family, namely, Lady Lorna Howard, Lady Margaret Huntington-Whiteley, Mr Miles Huntington-Whiteley, Lady Diana Kemp-Welch and Mr Colin Munro. My debt to them as well as to Lord Baldwin is considerable.

I am glad to acknowledge the help I have had from Joan Viscountess Davidson who with her late husband was very close to Stanley Baldwin throughout his political life. I am obliged to her for being able to use the Davidson Papers, now in the Beaverbrook Library, and more particularly the documents reproduced or abstracted by Mr Robert Rhodes James in his *Memoirs of a Conservative: J. C. C. Davidson's Memoirs and Papers 1910–1937*, published by Weidenfeld and Nicolson.

I have derived similar benefit from the published diaries and letters of another of Baldwin's close friends, the late Dr Thomas Jones, and I wish to thank Lady White and Mr Tristan Jones for permission to quote from the three volumes of Dr Jones's *Whitehall Diary* edited by Keith Middlemas, and the later *Diary with Letters*, both published by the Oxford University Press.

For authorising the use I have been able to make of the Chamberlain Papers, now preserved in Birmingham University Library, I have to thank Colonel and Mrs Terence Maxwell and Mr and Mrs Stephen Lloyd.

I am grateful to Mr Nigel Nicolson and to his publishers William Collins & Co. Ltd for allowing quotations from his edition of his father the late Sir Harold Nicolson's *Diaries and Letters*. I have also to thank the following publishers for similar permission in respect of the undermentioned works – Cassell & Co. Ltd: *A King's Story* (Duke of Windsor), *The Eden Memoirs* (Earl of Avon) and *The Gathering Storm* (Sir Winston Churchill); Hutchinson & Co. (Publishers) Ltd: *Reminiscences* (Marchioness Curzon of Kedleston); Weidenfeld & Nicolson Ltd: *Walter Monckton* (Earl of Birkenhead).

I am especially grateful to Mr Robert Somervell for allowing me to make the fullest use of the unpublished diaries and papers of his uncle the late Lord Somervell of Harrow, who as Sir Donald Somervell was Attorney-General at the time of the Abdication of King Edward VIII.

Mr Michael Howard of Jonathan Cape Ltd was good enough to afford me access to the file in the Jonathan Cape archives relating to the controversial publication in 1942 of *Private and Confidential* by Nourah (Lady) Waterhouse.

I have to thank the Prime Minister, the Rt Hon. Edward Heath MP, for kindly arranging for me to visit Chequers under the guidance of the Secretary of the Chequers Trust, Mr C. F. Penruddock, and to see over this historic property which Mr Heath's predecessor enjoyed so much and where he and Mrs Baldwin spent so much of their time during nearly fifteen years. However, Mr Heath did not feel able to accede to my request to be allowed to examine the Chequers Visitors' Book for the period of Baldwin's three tenancies of the house between 1923 and 1937. Fortunately I later ascertained that Lord Lee of Fareham, the donor with Lady Lee of Chequers to the nation, had had photocopies made of every page of the Visitors' Book from the time he acquired the property in 1910 to the end of Sir Winston Churchill's tenancy in 1945. These photocopies have been bound into a single volume, which is now preserved with the rest of the Lee collection in the Beaverbrook Library in London where it can be seen without restriction. I have found it of the greatest value, as will be seen from the references to its contents in the following pages.

Baldwin's old country home, Astley Hall, near Stourport-on-Severn, is now a school administered by the Birmingham Education Authority. I am grateful to the Headmistress, Miss B. M. Smith, for sparing the time to show me the house and grounds and for answering my questions.

To the librarians and staffs of the University Libraries of Oxford, Cambridge and Birmingham; Nuffield College, Oxford; Churchill College, Cambridge; the Public Record Office in London; the Public Record Office of Northern Ireland in Belfast; the National Register of Archives; the London Library; the Beaverbrook Library; and the India Office Library, I take this opportunity of expressing my thanks for the generous help they have given me in facilitating my researches.

My thanks are likewise due to the following for advice and information of various kinds about my subject: the Rt Hon. Julian Amery MP, the Earl of Birkenhead, Lord Blake, Mr G. D. M. Block, Lord Boothby, Sir Arthur Bryant, Mr Richard Bullock, Lady Mairi Bury, Dr Alistair Cooke, Mr Maurice Cowling, the Rt Hon. Lord Crathorne, Miss Mary Crozier, Mr D. H. Elletson, Mr Nigel Fisher MP, Mr Neville Ford, Dr Martin Gilbert, Sir James Harford, Professor R. F. V. Heuston, Dr M. A. Hoskins, Mr Robert Rhodes James, Mrs Margaret Kircham, the Rt Hon. Malcolm MacDonald, Mr David Marquand MP, the Dowager Lady Monckton of Brenchley, Sir Oswald Mosley, Mr Keith Middlemas, Sir Gerald Nabarro MP, Mr A. E. B. Owen, Mr Derek Pepys-Whiteley, Mr Michael Pick, Captain Stephen Roskill RN, Mrs David Somervell, Mr A. J. P. Taylor, Sir William Teeling, Viscount Trenchard, and Mrs Christine Woodland.

Mr Robert Mackworth-Young has read the text in typescript, and Dr Cameron Hazlehurst, currently Research Fellow at the Australian National University in Canberra, has read the proofs in part. I am grateful to them for their suggestions and corrections which I have been glad to adopt.

The sources of the illustrations where necessary for copyright purposes have been acknowledged beneath each picture. I apologise to any copyright owners of pictures or other material whom I have failed to trace or identify.

Lastly, as ever, I am under the greatest sense of obligation to my wife for typing this book from my original draft, as well as for the unfailing patience she has shown throughout its composition.

H. M. H.

Westwell House,
Tenterden, Kent
June 1973

ONE

FATHER AND SON

I

For generations the Baldwins or Baldwyns (as their name was alternatively spelled) were yeomen and small tenant farmers in Shropshire cultivating the land on the hills and in the valleys between the river Severn and the Welsh border. A collateral ancestor of Stanley Baldwin, Thomas Baldwin of Diddlebury, was imprisoned for four years in the Tower of London for his part in a plot to free Mary Queen of Scots. His name, with an inscription and the date July 1585, can still be seen on the wall of his cell in Beauchamp Tower where he carved it. He later succeeded in effecting his own escape from the Tower, an event which he was to commemorate in the motto *Per Deum meum transilio murum* (Through the help of my God I leap over the wall). The motto has been used by the family ever since.

These Shropshire Baldwins generally favoured the royalist cause during the Civil War. Some of them became country parsons, others were apprenticed to industry, including one who had an iron forge near Cleobury Mortimer in Charles II's time. Thomas Baldwin (1751–1823) was an ironfounder who migrated from Shrewsbury to Stourport in Worcestershire during the Industrial Revolution and laid the foundations of a successful family business on the banks of the Severn. Stourport was the first of the industrial towns to spring up in the Severn Valley and owed its existence to the local system of inland waterways constructed by James Brindley in the third quarter of the eighteenth century. 'How many people in London, where they know so much, realise that Stourport was lighted with gas before the City of London was?' The question was posed by Stanley Baldwin when he received the Freedom of the Borough shortly after becoming Prime Minister for the second time in 1924. 'Indeed, had it not been for the railways – and as an old Tory I am against all that kind of progress,' he added jocularly, 'Stourport would have been a very large town by now.

We are essentially a creation of those days when people looked to the canals as being the principal method of England's navigation, and for that purpose the site of this town was chosen, I think, with uncommon skill.' [1]

Stanley Baldwin was Thomas's great-grandson. He took a keen interest in his antecedents and in his later years he liked to poke about churches and graveyards searching for ancestral remains. He had to admit that none of his forbears, with the possible exception of Thomas Baldwin of Diddlebury, had made any great stir in the world, but he was pleased whenever he came across a lapidary inscription referring to any of them. Once, while talking to Thomas Jones, the Deputy Secretary of the Cabinet, he read out a Latin epitaph he had discovered on the grave of one of Thomas Baldwin's uncles in Shrewsbury. 'I'd like to have that sort of thing said about me,' he remarked. 'I should have liked to have known him, shouldn't you?' [2]*

Stanley's researches also revealed that his lineal ancestor Richard Baldwin of Munslow, near Church Stretton on the border with Herefordshire, was a yeoman of the Crown in the reign of Henry VII; in other words, he held his land in freehold direct from the King. At the same time he was charged with the duty as Collector of Subsidies, to which office he was appointed in 1523, of going round the district and collecting the special taxes levied by Parliament to defray the costs of foreign wars and the like. Richard Cecil, a contemporary of Richard Baldwin and father of the Elizabethan statesman William Cecil Lord Burleigh, was also a yeoman of the Crown, and Stanley thought that they might have known each other. According to Stanley, Thomas Baldwin of Diddlebury, who was a cousin of Richard of Munslow, could not have been shut up in the Tower without Cecil's knowledge. [3]

Unlike the Cecils, the Baldwins made no effort to advance their fortunes at Court, but carried on quietly with their farming. According to a local survey made in 1595, we learn that Richard's great-great-grandson, 'William Baldwyn gent., had the custody of the hundred of Munslow for the term of twenty-one years, paying the yearly rent of fifty-three shillings.' [4] Such genealogical details before the middle of the seventeenth century as Stanley was able to glean came from the pedigree recorded by William's son Edward Baldwin of Much Wenlock during the Heralds' Visitation of Shropshire in 1663. 'There is no greater tribute to the want of energy in one's family,' Stanley observed of his ancestors, 'than that for six or seven hundred years they had not moved twenty miles from Corvedale and the

* Thomas's uncle Edward Baldwin, who died in 1735 aged fifty-three, is buried in the south aisle of the Abbey Church of the Holy Cross in Shrewsbury beneath 'a very handsome plain monument' with Ionic columns. The inscription reads in part: *Ab omni perturbatione Animi Alienus, Judicio perspicax Agendo efficax. Ut omnes Amicum sibi certatim Arripuerint. Amplissimis Clientelis Bonorum Amicitiis Opibus non exiguis Beatus vixit, desideratus obiit.* H. Owen and J. B. Blakeway, *A History of Shrewsbury* (1825), II, p. 157.

sight of the Clee Hills and through the Reformation had not added an acre to their estate.' In this respect they were very different from families like the Cecils and Russells who became courtiers and ended up Marquesses and Dukes as well as great landowners.

In 1788 Thomas Baldwin set up an iron foundry at Stourport, near where the canal constructor Brindley's 'stinking ditch' entered the Severn. It was a small concern at first and only survived the trade depression in 1803 with the aid of a loan of £500 from the old bank in Worcester, later the Capital and Counties Bank, which was again to come to the firm's assistance on several occasions later in the century. It was left to Thomas's eldest surviving son George Pearce Baldwin (1789–1840) to raise the firm to affluence, which he did by a series of skilful amalgamations and the purchase of collieries in South Wales. G. P. Baldwin was twice married, having two sons by his first wife and five sons and four daughters by his second wife Sarah, whose father was a Methodist Minister, the Rev. Jacob Stanley of Alnwick, Northumberland. It was Alfred Baldwin (1841–1908), George's youngest son by his marriage to Sarah Stanley, who made the business wealthy and at his death was worth a quarter of a million pounds. As Alfred's only child and heir, Stanley Baldwin was thus to come in for a considerable patrimony, inheriting not only the bulk of his father's fortune but his seat in Parliament as well.

By all accounts Alfred Baldwin was an outstandingly successful ironmaster. His father had died of scarlet fever eight months before his birth, and he was brought up a good Methodist by his mother who sent him to school at the Wesley Collegiate Institution in Taunton. He did not go to university but on leaving school was apprenticed to the family business in which he was made a partner at the age of sixteen, along with seven other members of the family including his two elder half-brothers Pearce and William, his two full brothers George and Stanley (the latter being referred to here as the elder Stanley so as to distinguish him from Alfred's son), and his cousin Enoch Baldwin, later MP for Bewdley. 'My father, who was enormously respected and loved,' the younger son Stanley has recalled, 'would have gone to Oxford if his half-brother [William] had lived, but he died at forty-six of drink. My father, then barely twenty, had to buckle to because of his blood-brothers who did little or no work and drank.' [5]

In addition to the foundry at Stourport, a forge at Wilden, a mile or so to the east, was built in 1849 for the production of wrought-iron, while the family's business interests included worsted spinning mills at Stourport, a carpet factory at Bridgnorth and a tin-plate works at Wolverhampton. Giving evidence before the parliamentary committee on the Severn Valley Railway Bill in 1853, Pearce Baldwin stated that he employed 250 men in his ironworks and that they consumed 1,000 tons of raw iron and 2,500 tons of coal and coke every year. He favoured the construction of the proposed new line which would link Hartlebury and Stourport, by a junction with the Oxford, Worcester and Wolverhampton Railway, with Shrewsbury and the Shrewsbury and Hereford Railway and the Shropshire and South Wales coalfields, thus enabling him to obtain better and cheaper coal more quickly than hitherto. At a dinner given at the George Hotel in Bewdley to mark the opening of the Severn Valley Line in 1862, William Baldwin responded to the toast of 'The Town and Trade of Stourport', remarking that as the owner of one of the largest businesses in the area he anticipated that he would be as great a customer of the new line as he was of the existing railway system to the south and east.[6]

William died in the following year at the age of forty-six – his elder brother Pearce was already dead by this date – so that William's expectation of the advantages of the new line were realised for his nephew Alfred. In 1872, the Severn Valley Railway was taken over by the Great Western, after which Alfred was elected to the board of the latter, eventually in 1903 becoming chairman – 'a tremendous responsibility', he called it. ('My election to the chair of the GWR is the strangest thing that has happened to me, and I can't understand why I was chosen.')[7]

About 1860 a division of interest in the ironworks took place, Enoch Baldwin continuing in charge of the Stourport foundry under the name of Baldwin, Son & Co., while Alfred's half-brothers and brothers ran the forge at Wilden under the name of E. P. and W. Baldwin, by which style the firm was known until it amalgamated with others and 'went public' as Baldwins Ltd. in 1902. Thus, with the death of Pearce and William, effective control of the forge passed to the two younger brothers. Unfortunately George's and the elder Stanley's inclinations towards good living and extravagance soon brought the firm to the verge of bankruptcy, the process being accelerated by the serious financial crisis and bank failures of 1866. Although he got on well enough with his brothers and their wives, Alfred became despondent at the mismanagement of the business for which he rightly considered that George and the elder Stanley were responsible, and he determined to buy them out and dissolve the partnership. How he was able to do this is not clear, but he succeeded in raising £20,000 for this purpose in 1870 and also paid off the brothers' indebtedness to the firm at Wilden, probably with the help of a loan from the Capital and Counties Bank. 'This is a good instance of the element of luck in life,' his son Stanley later remarked. 'One dies before the business is made safe, another lifts them up and saves them.'[8] Meanwhile

Alfred Baldwin had found a wife, Louisa Macdonald, whose parents lived in Wolverhampton where her father was a Wesleyan minister.

2

The Macdonalds were a remarkable family, whose forbears came from the Isle of Skye and after the '45 Rebellion settled near Enniskillen in Northern Ireland. Thus the future Prime Minister was able to boast that his ancestry on one side was entirely Celtic. 'My mother's family fled from the Highlands after having been out with Prince Charles in 1745,' he once told the House of Commons. 'I remember that, in my early days, it was with very great difficulty that we could stand up while the band was playing *God Save the King*, because we had a Hanoverian and not a Jacobite King.' [9] The Rev. James Macdonald (1761–1833) was ordained by Wesley himself and sent over to England to preach. According to his great-grandson, the preacher taught himself six languages and educated his elder brother to take a scholarship at Cambridge University. ('I mention that as something peculiarly typical of the race from which he sprang – that love of an almost divine individualism, coupled with the ambition to get learning, not for the sake of money but for its own sake.') The son, George Browne Macdonald (1805–68), was also a Wesleyan Methodist and a strong temperance advocate, but this did not prevent him from being friendly with George Baldwin and his brother Stanley, who had them and one of their daughters as guests during a troublesome period of moving house in Wolverhampton. 'Alice goes to [the elder] Stanley Baldwin's tomorrow,' Mrs Macdonald wrote to Louisa in 1863. 'Mr and Mrs George are so kind to us, as if we were their parents, we could not have been more favourably situated.' At this time George and his wife Amy were living in Wilden House beside the forge. Mrs Hannah Macdonald, *née* Jones, was a Welsh girl from the Vale of Clwyd, and met her husband while he was preaching in Manchester. She bore him eleven children, of whom two sons and five daughters survived to adulthood. Four of the girls proved exceptionally gifted and were married to equally distinguished husbands – Alice, the eldest, to John Lockwood Kipling (their son was the novelist and poet Rudyard); Georgiana ('Georgie') to Sir Edward Burne-Jones, the Pre-Raphaelite painter and friend of William Morris; Agnes ('Aggie') to another artist Sir Edward Poynter, President of the Royal Academy; and Louisa ('Louie') to Alfred Baldwin, father of the future Prime Minister.

Alfred and Louie first met when Louie, then aged twenty, was on a visit to the elder Stanley Baldwin and his wife Mary at Stourport in the autumn of 1865. It is said that Alfred was not pleased when he heard that the Macdonald girl was coming to stay, but that when he caught sight of her reading by a window he immediately lost his heart to the visitor.

She was a sweet, pretty girl with literary leanings, and during the month she spent with the Baldwins she wrote a short story which was later published in the *Victoria Magazine*. Afterwards she was to produce four full-sized novels, a volume of ghost stories and several books of poems and tales for children. Her good looks were matched by Alfred's, although his beard and habitually serious demeanour made him look older than his years. In face and figure, so it was said, he was 'something between a Spanish grandee and a Hebrew prophet'.

A few days after Louie's return home, Alfred wrote to her mother informing her of his feelings and asking that they might become engaged. After a short delay, Mrs Macdonald replied as a typical mid-Victorian mama might be expected to do.

> Waterloo Road,
> Wolverhampton
> [September, 1865]

My dear Mr Alfred,

You were right in thinking I should be surprised at hearing from you, indeed few things could have surprised me more than the contents of your note. The state of solicitude and perplexity in which my mind has been must be my apology for not replying at an earlier period to your very important communication.

The subject is a very serious one and is engaging our very careful consideration as no hasty conclusion could be arrived at that would be favourable to your request. Mr Macdonald and I think that we should have some conversation with you before coming to any decision, and therefore we should be glad to see you, if you will call upon us, any time after noon on Wednesday next.

In conclusion allow me to assure you that, while I am deeply concerned for my daughter's happiness, I am by no means indifferent to your own.

> I remain,
> Yours sincerely,
> HANNAH MACDONALD

The earnest young man of twenty-four seems to have made a good initial impression, and permission for the engagement was given provided that Louie herself was agreeable. At first she seems to have had some doubts about casting her lot with such an extremely serious young man. 'I cannot make your people love me,' Alfred wrote to her at this time, 'but your people shall be my people: and I will love them first for your sake and then I am sure for their own. Is there any other trouble or cloud of any kind I can lighten for you? . . . You will not keep me waiting very long?' Louie did not, and the engagement was duly announced. When he gave his mother the news, 'she expressed herself very thankful for one thing, that I was not going to marry for money, which she was always afraid I should do. Just fancy that idea coming into her head!'

During the courtship, Alfred unburdened himself to Louie on a number of subjects. A few passages deserve quotation as throwing light on the formation of his character and intellectual interests. For instance, he happened to be in Birmingham on business in October 1865 when the news of the death of the Prime Minister Lord Palmerston caused 'general gloom' among everyone with whom he talked.

> I cannot help, and you would not have it otherwise, taking an interest in these things; and the old Lord was a favourite of mine because he was such an Englishman. And I am prouder of being one of this country than of anything else . . . It seems to me that in the Reformation times the great truths that had been lost were laid hold of again: that a man to be a good man must be a lover of his country and hold above all things to purity of life. And it seems to me that in these days people are forgetting these things, and I want you to help me to live up to what I know is right and which I have tried to put to you as it has presented itself to me at various times.

'From the day I went to business first,' he told his fiancée, 'I was taught, by example at any rate and by mouth too a good deal, to estimate first of all this world and its belongings and to let nothing interfere with work. This last part of my teaching is right enough if once a proper motive had been supplied to me. Well, time went on and the lessons took effect; but I knew very well that I was wrong; and the older I got and the more experience I got, I felt that none of the sophistries with which I tried to quiet myself were worth a button.' At this time in the matter of religion he described himself as 'what is called an extreme High Churchman', having begun as 'a strong dissenter, a Methodist, a rationalist; but at last I fell in with Charles Kingsley's writings; and, although I tie myself to no man, the principles which he first spoke to my heart have been my mainstay for over six years'.

On New Year's Eve, when his mother and the rest of his family were at a

'Watch Night' service, Alfred Baldwin penned another letter to his future bride:

The year that is nearly gone has been the most important of my life: naturally. Twelve months ago I was settling my mind, or rather trying to, to all kinds of worldly maxims as my guide: I was hardening myself, until the autumn day that you came here. Then the current of my life was changed. I knew when I first saw you how great an influence you would soon have over me; I am ashamed to write it now, but I will tell you the truth. I fought against it; but my love would not listen to those deceits of the devil which I had harboured before; I told my love to you; and the rest you know . . .

If it be well for us, I would like a long life: that we may always be learning of one another how to live (though you will be the principal teacher); and then if riches come, well; if we are poor, it shall still be well. Our love will be strong and the love of Christ toward us will be stronger. I can picture myself how for many a year we shall grow together; how I may share your plans and your books; your hopes and your fears; and I can see how I shall try to shield you from care and from sorrow, and to be always a joy to your eyes. I will be a true husband to you, God helping me; and your love too will much repay me.

These words were destined to be fulfilled to the great joy of Louie's parents, as both were to testify. 'He was a man of business,' wrote Louie's brother Frederic Macdonald of his future brother-in-law, 'and if I said he was the finest specimen of his order I ever knew, I should not be saying too much. Few men carried heavier responsibility and duty, yet I do not know that I ever saw him irritable, or greatly depressed, or so engrossed as to close his mind to religion, or books, or the happy interests of his home. By conviction an Anglican, he represented to me the Church of England layman, in a form that had my admiration.' In her own way Hannah Macdonald thought just as highly of Alfred Baldwin. 'He could not give an inferior article, nor do a shabby thing,' she once confided in her daughter, 'and if he was minded to try, he would not experiment upon my Louie.'

The prospective bridegroom was already busy house-hunting, and some months passed before he was able to find anything suitable in the neighbourhood. 'It will be a relief to him to have a local habitation to offer you as well as a name!' her mother wrote to Louie in the spring of 1866, when Louie was away with her sister Aggie on a shopping expedition to London. Eventually, Lower Park House, a three-storeyed brick dwelling, was found in Bewdley, at the corner of the narrow High Street and Lax Lane in the southern part of the town known as Lower Park, near the river. Incidentally, the name of the lane was a curious survival from the days of the Vikings, since *lax* is the Norse word for salmon, and the lane led down to the old salmon ford across the Severn which was in use before the river was bridged in the eighteenth century. The house had a small garden.

Agnes Macdonald was now engaged to Edward Poynter, and so it was arranged that there should be a double wedding. The ceremony took place on 9 August 1866 in Wolverhampton parish church. Since their father was in too frail health to attend, the girls were given away by their brother Fred, the third generation of his family to be a Wesleyan Minister. So the Rev. Frederic Macdonald walked up the centre aisle with a bride on each arm, and after the wedding breakfast duly despatched the two couples on their respective honeymoons. Next day Louie wrote to her mother from Liverpool *en route* for Scotland to say how well and happy she was. 'I didn't want to leave you,' she added dutifully, 'but also I don't want to come home again yet.'

In Edinburgh, they found themselves in 'a rush of grouse shooters' – it was 12 August – and after some days spent seeing the local sights they went north to Aberdeen where Louie celebrated her twenty-first birthday. Then on to Inverness, where Alfred, to compensate his bride for her identity being 'hidden under the lesser name of Baldwin', gave her a Macdonald tartan shawl 'with a silver brooch engraved with the Macdonald arms and crest on it to fasten the shawl with'. Alfred's ancestry was, of course, just as much a matter of pride as Louie's Highland antecedents, and on settling into their new home at Bewdley, Louie was quite happy to use the crested writing paper which Alfred had ordered; for the Baldwins had an authentic coat of arms, whose crest was a 'cockatrice sejant, wings addorsed argent, combed wattled and beaked or'. It was on a sheet of paper thus adorned that Louie wrote to 'Darling Pal Aggie' to tell her of their homecoming: 'Tho' they tried to keep it quiet, little dear Bewdley got to know when we came home, and peals of old bells were rung on our account. We wouldn't go to church next day as that would lay me open to callers at once, but next Sunday we go, which is a fiery ordeal in the country and like opening the floodgates to everyone.'

It was a matter of some family speculation whether the Baldwins or the Poynters would be the first in the race to become parents. Indeed at one moment Louie thought that her child would be born prematurely and she engaged a temporary 'gamp', as she called the local monthly nurse. 'The nearer it comes,' she told Aggie, 'the more one's spirits rise to the event.' Everything was ready, 'pins, powder, and brush; this last affects me much, tho' I reflect with the cookery book, first catch your hare'. The infant she was carrying gave every promise of lustiness, and we are told he once gave a kick which knocked a plate of cherries off her lap. In the event the Baldwins beat the Poynters by two months with an August baby.

3

The forge at Wilden was three miles south-east of Bewdley. Alfred Baldwin would leave Lower Park House about seven each morning and drive in his carriage or dog-cart to the ironworks. Sometimes he would walk when the weather was good. When he said good-bye to his wife on the morning of 3 August 1867, she felt her pains coming on; but, wishing to spare Alfred anxiety, she did not tell him so. Thus when he returned home in the evening he found that his wife had been safely delivered of a boy. The day being warm, so we are told, the baby had already been carried through the garden to be proudly displayed to his Macdonald grandparents, who had recently arrived from Wolverhampton to live near by in Lower Park. He was also taken by Emma, the cook, to the top of the house, where in accordance with a local superstition he was held up high on a chair, since infants thus exhibited immediately after being born were certain to rise in the world. A month later he was baptised in the beautiful old parish church of Ribbesford near by which dates from Norman times. The godparents were his uncle and aunt the elder Stanley and Mary Baldwin, also his maternal uncle Harry Macdonald on whose behalf one of the others stood proxy, since Harry was far away in New York seeking his fortune. 'We christened the dear thing yesterday at Ribbesford by the name of Stanley,' his mother wrote afterwards, 'and he behaved sublimely, was wide awake the whole time and never cried a note, only saying "Amen" once.' The boy was named after his great-grandfather Jacob Stanley, the Methodist minister of Alnwick. Stanley soon became abbreviated to Stan, by which he was always known in the family.*

The first General Election to be held under the new Reform Bill, which had been introduced by Disraeli and extended the franchise to the borough householder, took place in the autumn of 1868. It was the last election at which the candidates were nominated and spoke from the hustings, while the electors cast their votes in public very much on the model of Eatanswill. Things were often pretty rough, and for this reason Alfred sent his wife

* A plaque on the front of Lower Park House (67 High Street, Bewdley) records the fact that Stanley Baldwin, who was born there, did rise in the world to become his country's Prime Minister.

and child away from Bewdley for the week that polling continued. On the eve of the election, Louie wrote to her sister Aggie Poynter in London:

> The election will be early next week and we are getting wrought up to a terrible degree. Alfred is so determined I shan't be either in Bewdley or alone during the next terrible week that he and baby and I are going to spend the week with Stanley and Mary at Wilden, where they removed last Thursday. This will be very nice for both Mary and me, as both our husbands will be out on election business all the time, so we shall keep each other company.
>
> We are in sad fears the Tories will win, their beer and money are so wildly flying, and the people they have bribed are getting so fearfully impudent now and demanded spirits and cigars, they are so tired of beer. Poor Papa is so very poorly it would be impossible for him to be carried to the poll, so if Mr Lloyd's chances hinge on Papa I fear they must go to the wall . . .*
>
> My little Stanley can say his own name in quite an impudent voice now, and can walk the whole length of our garden and back again hold of a hand, but dare not take a step alone, such is his timidity.

The election was fought on the specific issue of whether the Irish Church should be disestablished and more generally on the merits of the new Liberalism embodied in Gladstone and his Radical policies which had now been given an appearance of respectability. Although Alfred Baldwin later came out as a supporter of Disraeli and proclaimed himself 'a Progressive Conservative, opposed to Home Rule for Ireland and the Disestablishment of the Church', he is known to have favoured Gladstone at this election. It was otherwise with his infant son. 'I wore the Tory colours in my pram in the 1868 election,' he was to confess many years later. 'My father voted Whig then, but our cook was a Tory and she saw to my politics.' Alfred's cousin Enoch Baldwin was also for Gladstone; he was to be returned as Liberal member for Bewdley in 1880, after his Conservative opponent had been unseated on petition for corrupt practices. (On this occasion Alfred voted for the Conservative, but this gesture does not seem to have disturbed the otherwise harmonious fraternal relations.) As in 1880, the 1868 election was a resounding victory for the Liberals. Alfred's father-in-law George Macdonald died in his sleep during the night of 12/13 November, a few days before the local results were known.

According to Stanley Baldwin, his earliest childhood memory – he

* T. Lloyd, the Liberal candidate, was defeated by 518 to 418 votes. The total electorate of Bewdley at this time was 1,043.

cannot have been more than three years old at the time – he was looking up the river Severn from the bridge at Bewdley 'into that mysterious and romantic land of Shropshire, so close to us, from which my people came only three generations before, and watching the smoke of the train running along the little railway through places bearing names like Wyre Forest, Cleobury Mortimer, Neen Sollars and Tenbury – names steeped in romance and redolent of the springtime of an England long ago passed, but whose heritage is ours'. [10]

In September 1870 Alfred Baldwin bought out his two brothers' shares in E. P. and W. Baldwin and became sole proprietor of the business. This meant that the elder Stanley Baldwin moved out of Wilden House opposite the works and went to live in Lancashire, while Alfred and Louie left Bewdley and took over Wilden House, a large Victorian villa with a big garden. It was a commodious enough dwelling, though when the wind blew from the direction of the forge it was liable to cover everything with smuts and dirt, a disadvantage which Alfred willingly put up with since (as he said) it represented their bread and butter. It stood across Wilden Lane which separated it from the works, and the top of the hillside garden at the back commanded a fine view of the Welsh hills. Here young Stan grew into a strong, healthy lad, but because his father was away a good deal on business and his mother was a confirmed invalid, spending much of her time lying in a darkened room with the blinds drawn, he was left much to his own resources. No little brothers or sisters followed his birth, since Louie's health was considered too delicate to risk having another baby, and so Stan remained the only child.

His father had collected a fair-sized library, particularly of the classics and history, and the boy soon learned to enjoy their companionship, being usually found with an open volume on the hearth rug before the winter fire or in summer time stretched out in the orchard at the back of the house. Sometimes his imagination would run riot. When he was about five, his grandmother Hannah Macdonald wrote of him: 'He told me last evening, while we were taking tea together, that he had seen Queen Elizabeth, Sir Walter Raleigh, the Earl of Essex and other lords and gentlemen, in the gallery of the church at Ribbesford on Sunday! He knew the Queen by her ruff, and something like a coronet for a bonnet. What a whole seething romance there must be in his history-ridden brain!' His grandmother was also much taken with his droll and affectionate manners. 'I never saw so young a child with so much of the comic element in him in my life,' she wrote at this time to another of her daughters. 'You know Miss Amies's gentle manner of speaking. She was trying some coats on Stanley the other day, and she said something to him about his being so good, to which he replied in a voice as dulcet as her own: "Thanks, dear love." It was both funny and pretty.'

His fifth birthday was celebrated in traditional country style. When the family appeared in the village after breakfast, 'the place was changed into quite a bower, ropes of evergreen hung across the road, and wreaths and posies, and banners with strange devices everywhere, most touchingly kind we thought', wrote his mother afterwards. 'The wives of all the workmen clubbed together and gave little Stan a beautiful Church Service.' Other presents included a cider cup, a glass jug and cup, a sugared cake and a basket of apples. In the afternoon there was a birthday party in the meadow where a marquee had been erected and the local Temperance Band performed 'banging and tootling its utmost'. Afterwards there was the greasy pole, sack and three-legged races and everyone had 'as much tea and cake as they could eat in the tent'. Finally Mr Felton, the works manager, inflated about two hundred balloons, most of which caught fire as they rose in the air. 'I am happy to think little Stan behaved sweetly and went quietly to bed and was left alone after a most exciting day.' [11]

Sometimes the Kipling, Burne-Jones and Poynter cousins would come to stay at Wilden, and these visits would occasionally lead to lively exchanges. On one occasion when young Ambrose Poynter, two months Stanley's junior, was playing with Stanley on the veranda at Wilden, a quarrel arose. As Ambrose shrieked louder and louder, Stanley's voice grew correspondingly lower. 'Why do you speak like that?' asked Ambrose. 'Why don't you speak louder, Stan?' According to one of their elders who witnessed the incident, Stanley replied, 'Because, if I spoke any louder, I should hit you.' If this is an example of self-control, Stanley Baldwin learned to cultivate the quality at an early age. In fact, the two boys were the greatest friends and Stanley would visit the Poynters from time to time in London, where he appreciated what he called the atmosphere of art and culture, of wit and humour, which he found in the Poynter household, and he would watch Ambrose's father at work in his studio at Beaumont Lodge, Wood Green. Edward Poynter was now regularly exhibiting his pictures at the Royal Academy and had just been elected ARA.

When the Kiplings stayed at Wilden during one of their leaves from Bombay, where John taught art, Alfred took a great fancy to their daughter Trix, whom he treated with grave courtesy, strewing May blossom outside her bedroom door to watch her delight at finding it. He would have liked Trix to live with them at Wilden, while her brother Rudyard went to the Burne-Joneses, until they were old enough to rejoin their parents in India; but arrangements had already been made for them to go as paying guests to the home of a retired naval officer in Southsea, an experience which they were both to detest. Trix was particularly disappointed; she wrote long afterwards: 'It would have been a lovely life – with the garden and the pony and the dear people – and I was quite sharp enough to have shared Stan's early lessons.' But it was not to be. However, the Wilden household did receive a welcome addition in March 1875, when Louie's mother died in Bewdley and her only surviving unmarried daughter Edith, who had been living with her, came to Wilden as companion and mother's help. Edie was a lively girl of twenty-seven with a sharp tongue but an affectionate nature.

Hannah Macdonald was laid to rest beside her husband in Ribbesford churchyard and beneath a headstone which bore the appropriate inscription: 'Her children arise up and call her blessed.' Afterwards a memorial window was painted by William Morris at the west end of the church from a design by Edward Burne-Jones and erected to her memory by Alfred Baldwin. It showed two angels on either side of Dorcas, the disciple also known as Tabitha and described in *The Acts of the Apostles* as a woman 'full of good works and alms deeds which she did', whom Peter raised from the dead. If this description fitted Hannah Macdonald, the window was, as her daughter Edith put it, 'perhaps a unique instance of a memorial window being erected to the memory of a mother-in-law' by two sons-in-law. [12]

Alfred Baldwin later met the cost of building the church at Wilden, to which contributions were also made by Morris and Burne-Jones, as well as by Louie, Aggie and Georgie who together embroidered the altar frontal. But it was the older church at Ribbesford that Stanley particularly remembered. The male members of the congregation appeared in tall hats and some of the older workers from the nearby farms still wore the smocks of an earlier age. Years later he liked to recall the scene on a Sunday morning:

> I can see once again the pony cart and the landau on the road, people in knots of two or three coming down the lanes, and the little crowd that gathered in the churchyard, discussing the events of the past week, while the peal of bells, whose music had been the companion of the last half-hour of our walk, yielded to the urgent shriller note of the five minutes' bell. Then the smell of freshly baked loaves in the porch, waiting for distribution after the service, the baize door, and we passed into the church to the big pew in which I spent so much time counting the ten torteaux in the pile of the Episcopal arms in the east window, and trying to catch the wandering eye of one of our servants in the gallery. [13]

The reading of the lessons, to which he listened Sunday after Sunday in the text of the authorised version of King James I, also left an indelible impression. 'The language of the English Bible leaves its mark on you for life,' he was to observe in one of his speeches as Prime Minister. It certainly left its mark on the small Worcestershire boy, and to it in the course of time Stanley Baldwin was to owe in great measure the good, homely English which he habitually employed and which was to appeal so much to his fellow-countrymen when he became a political leader.

In later years he liked to recall how he had lived as a child in the heart of Worcestershire, by the side of one of the last of the iron forges that were left in the rural districts of England.

Among the chief friends that I had in those days – they represented two sides of life, the industrial and the agricultural – one was a shepherd who could neither read nor write, but like many men of those days who could neither read nor write, he was a great deal more intelligent than many who can do both now. He had a face like an old pippin, and he talked the undiluted tongue of our fathers. I learned much from him. Another man that I learned much from was one who had been a workman, and who rose to be a manager, and who went to work at ten years old on a twelve-hours' night shift, thus being a link with an industrial past which, thank God, has passed away for ever. But with such friends of one's childhood, it is little wonder that one learned a profound sympathy with and affection for the common man, of whom I am one, which has never deserted me and never will.[14]

4

'Don't send little Stan to school, Louie,' the gentle Edward Burne-Jones wrote to his sister-in-law when the boy was seven. 'It's much worse than you would think, and I don't feel sure at all of the compensating good. It is really a constant blank and source of small heartache losing one's little companion.'[15] No doubt Burne-Jones had heard tales of the frightful beatings and bullying which sometimes went on at private boarding schools of the period; possibly he may have regretted having parted with his son Philip at an early age. At all events the plea had some effect, since Stanley did not leave home until within three months of his eleventh birthday, much later than boys usually did in those days. The institution chosen for him was Hawtrey's Preparatory School, Aldin House, Slough, where the boys were prepared for Eton. His mother's physique was too weak to endure fitting him out with his school kit and this task was entrusted to his aunt Alice Kipling, who was again on leave from India. However, both parents were able to accompany him to the school where, with twenty-two other new boys including his cousin Ambrose Poynter, he was deposited on 8 May 1878. 'You were a very good brave boy this afternoon,' his father wrote to him the same evening, 'and I was very pleased with your manly way. If you will be as good in your work and as brave in your play while you are at school, you will indeed do well.' [16]

As a parting present, his parents had given him a parcel of books to be opened after their departure. This turned out to be a pocket set of the Waverley novels and a volume of Leech's cartoons which had appeared in *Punch*, heavy enough reading for a ten-year-old. After a couple of days he confessed to being surprised that none of the other boys he spoke to had ever heard of Sir Walter Scott. 'Being one who liked going his own way with as little friction as possible,' he afterwards admitted, 'I dreamed my own dreams and kept my own counsel.'

His school reports were consistently good for the three years he spent at Hawtrey's; but otherwise there was nothing particularly remarkable about his activities which were reflected in his letters home and ran pretty true to the form of most schoolboys. 'A postal order for 5s., or 10s., please, as I have only 1s. and I want to put something in the collection; thirty or forty stamps, please, as I write a great many letters.' 'I try not to nibble my nails and I wash better than I ever did: the loopha is lovely.' There were enthusiastic descriptions of plays and fireworks and conjuring tricks; he also expressed a keen interest in party political affairs and begged for news on this score. ('I want to talk to papa about politics, there is no one here to.') The Conservatives had been in power for several years under Disraeli, now Lord Beaconsfield, but the country was beginning to tire of his policies, particularly his foreign entanglements, and was also disturbed by the growing agricultural depression, a development which the Conservative leader had foretold in his youth was bound to happen sooner or later after the repeal of the Corn Laws. The mood of the country was reflected in the loss of by-elections, although the Tories held an important seat in Ireland at this time. 'We have had a great victory in County Down,' wrote Alfred Baldwin to his son. 'Lord Castlereagh won by a large majority . . . This will balance the loss of Tamworth.' * *The Illustrated*

* Lord Castlereagh, who defeated a Liberal in a by-election in May 1878 in County Down where his family owned considerable property, succeeded his father as 6th Marquess of Londonderry in 1884. He was later Lord Lieutenant of Ireland and sat in Balfour's Cabinet between 1900 and 1905. The Conservative who lost Tamworth, the Hon. F. C. Bridgeman, son of the Earl of Bradford, was afterwards elected for Bolton.

London News had been specially ordered for Stanley while he was at school and he was told not to forget to ask for it 'and then you will know what is going on in the great world outside'.

During one of his holidays, he was taken, wearing a new top hat and Eton jacket, to Lord's cricket ground, where he watched the Harrow XI winning a great victory. Forty years later he could still remember that at the tail of the team there walked to the wicket the largest schoolboy he had ever seen. 'The first ball that boy got he put well into the old pavilion.' His name was Ronald McNeill (later Lord Cushendun) and he was among the Harrovians whom Stanley Baldwin as Prime Minister was to include in his Cabinet.[17] Baldwin was later to witness a dramatic incident during the Irish Home Rule debates in the House of Commons in 1912, when McNeill threw a book at Winston Churchill and hit him on the forehead.

'Top of the class is the place you must always try for,' his mother had written to Stan in his first term. 'You can't always be top, but *always be top if you can* . . . Be a good boy: stick to work and cricket.' The boy conscientiously followed this advice, in due course rising to top of the school and winning no less than eighteen prizes of books with the school crest stamped in gilt on their leather-bound covers. 'Abilities decidedly above the average' set the tone of his reports, and he was confidently expected to win a scholarship to a public school, although it was noted in one report that 'he does not do himself justice in examinations'. He shone particularly in classics, geography, history and scripture, and in his early days at Hawtrey's he won the Lower School arithmetic prize. Yet when the time came, he failed to win a scholarship, greatly to the surprise of both his teachers and his parents.

Since the school was designed to prepare its pupils for Eton, the boy might have been expected to go there in due course. But in his last year his father happened to meet the Rev. Dr Montagu Butler, the great headmaster of Harrow, who had been appointed to this post at the unusually early age of twenty-six and whose reign had lasted for more than twenty years. Alfred Baldwin was impressed by him and decided to send his son to the celebrated school on 'the Hill'. The boy duly sat for the entrance scholarship examination in the famous Fourth Form Room, where delinquents used to be flogged by the headmaster before breakfast. 'Stan did not win a scholarship at Harrow,' his father wrote when he returned home for the holidays. 'I have tried today to realise what happened more than I ever tried before, but with only ill success.' The reasons for his failure are obscure; possibly he suffered from nerves. 'I remember so well my disappointment at finding myself among the rejected,' Stanley afterwards recalled, remarking at the same time, 'Happy the school whose outcasts and rejected can yet make good in after life!'

He was then able to console himself with the knowledge that three other outstanding men with whom he came into close contact had been similarly ploughed; they were F. E. Smith, who became Lord Chancellor as Lord Birkenhead; L. S. Amery who gained a Double First at Oxford and a Fellowship at All Souls and like Birkenhead was to sit in Baldwin's Cabinet; and A. B. Ramsay, Master of Magdalene College, Cambridge, and Vice-Chancellor of the University when Baldwin was Chancellor. 'In those days,' Birkenhead would recall bitterly, 'the examiners rejected what were known as the half-wits after two days' examination, making it plain that those who were so rejected were cumbering up the ground to the embarrassment of really promising youngsters. I was among the half-wits.' But the setback never rankled with Baldwin as it did with Birkenhead, who used to declare that he had succeeded in everything he had undertaken in life except on this one occasion.[18]

In Baldwin's case, there were no financial reasons to prevent him going to Harrow without the assistance of a scholarship, and so he entered the school in the ordinary way in the autumn term of 1881, a month after his fourteenth birthday, being put in Dr Butler's house. At this period Harrow was still in the country. The view towards London from the Headmaster's House revealed a succession of green fields, while from the churchyard there was an uninterrupted vista of English landscape as far as Windsor, which could be seen on a clear day. Here Baldwin was to spend the next four years, most of the first three happily and successfully, but in the last year nursing a sense of grievance and considerably disillusioned. He was remembered by the manager of the school bookshop, who retired in 1931 after fifty-three years' service, as 'a boy of retiring disposition', compared with another boy named Winston Churchill, who arrived in the school shortly after Baldwin left and who 'would argue in the shop on any subject'. Among Baldwin's Harrow contemporaries, who also frequented the bookshop, was John Galsworthy, 'a thoughtful boy', who 'walked about looking at the ground, as if thinking deeply'.[19] Baldwin was to admire the latter's novels and plays, and one day in the distant future Galsworthy was to be offered and to accept the honorary degree of Doctor of Literature at Baldwin's hands as Chancellor of Cambridge University.

The first half of his time at Harrow was largely one of success as Baldwin made his way up the scholastic and athletic ladder. At the end of his second term he came top of his form and brought home two prizes, and when he returned for the summer term his father proudly noted that 'he has his double remove, and so goes into Tails'. When he was fifteen, he got into his house football XI and was reported as also playing well at cricket and squash, and distinguishing himself as a jumper on the sports ground. He took up music and wrote home to say that he had bought 'a very good collection of Gregorian chants' for four shillings. Politics continued to engross his attention, and he was greatly interested in the details of the new Reform Bill which was to effect a redistribution of parliamentary seats as well as enfranchising the agricultural labourers and other rural industrial workers. ('I am sorry Bewdley is going to be disfranchised and our cousin will thereby lose his seat.')* He was happy, too, because his mother who had spent much of the time since her marriage in visiting a succession of continental spas and specialists, suddenly came home a new person, completely cured. Her son happened to be at Wilden as it was during the holidays. Instead of being carried into the house in an invalid chair as had happened in the past, we are told that a pretty woman got out of the carriage and ran up the steps to greet him. Stanley is said to have been so surprised that 'he turned as white as a sheet and looked as though he was going to faint'.

That same summer of 1883, the family spent a month in a cottage in Rottingdean by the Sussex Downs, next door to Ned and Georgie Burne-Jones. The Poynters and Kiplings were also there with their children. Such was the wonderful improvement in his wife's health that Alfred Baldwin could write: 'Aggie and Louie actually went with the youngsters on the roundabout!'

By the middle of his third year, Stan was in the Fifth Form at Harrow. 'He is very well and has done well,' his father noted. Then misfortune struck on 8 June 1884, when Alfred Baldwin received a telegram from Dr Butler followed by an indignant letter complaining of young Baldwin's conduct, which the headmaster felt had brought disgrace upon his house. It appears that the boy had indulged in a piece of juvenile pornography, probably no worse than the interest shown by many schoolboys before and since. Unfortunately for Stan he had sent an example of his composition in this genre to his cousin Ambrose Poynter at Eton, and this action was detected. What increased the gravity of the offence in the headmaster's eyes was that the boy had chosen to pollute the rival school with his filth. Punishment followed swiftly in the form of a birching performed by the headmaster according to the time-honoured ritual before breakfast in the Fourth Form Room. The infliction was no doubt not particularly severe,

* Enoch Baldwin, who ran the family ironworks at Stourport, represented Bewdley from 1880 to 1885 in the Liberal interest. He voted for Gladstone's Reform Act of 1885 which by redistribution of seats and assimilating the borough and county franchise eliminated his constituency. He died in 1905, aged eighty-two. There is a stained glass window to his memory in Wilden Church.

since Dr Butler was known to wield the birch lightly and to comfort the culprit as he lay across the bench with such expressions as: 'Please be brave,' 'I'm sorry' and 'It hurt me so'.

Alfred Baldwin hurried off to Harrow on receiving the news and saw the headmaster. After listening to the full story, he wrote to his wife that 'the whole affair was much exaggerated and far more folly than anything else . . . the upshot is a flogging, which is now over and done with'.[20] If the flogging was over and done with, the shame of the punishment and its cause lingered on to infect the relations between pupil and head. Although he spent his fourth and final year in the Upper Sixth and made some mark in the school debating society, Baldwin was never made a monitor, as the prefects at Harrow were known, and for the rest of his time at the school he smarted under what he felt was an injustice, concealing his feelings behind a façade of studied indolence. As a senior boy, he was entitled to have a fag, and the junior who performed these characteristic chores for him was Jack Seely, the future soldier and Liberal politician who in the performance of his tasks, according to his fagmaster, 'combined immaculate cleanliness with an immaculate manner'. The extent to which the school, like Eton, was expected to provide the country's future rulers, may be gauged from the fact that, of Baldwin's contemporaries at Harrow, four became viceroys, ten became bishops, twelve became colonial governors, another dozen became ambassadors, seventeen became judges, thirty-three became privy councillors and sixty-four became generals. Baldwin himself was to become Prime Minister, the first Old Harrovian to do so since Palmerston. In spite of the set-back he suffered in his third year and the resulting disillusion, he was always to retain a warm affection for his old school and he could never hear the famous school song 'Forty Years On', with which every Harrow function traditionally ends, without a lump in his throat. Yet he seldom wore the Old Harrovian tie, preferring the colours of the I Zingari cricketers.

Three incidents remained in Baldwin's mind during his last year. The first was when Dr Butler summoned the whole school together and gave them the news of General Gordon's death at Khartoum. The second was when Gladstone paid the school a visit and addressed the boys. 'Politically opposed to him as I was, I waited eagerly for the message,' Baldwin later recalled in humorous vein. 'When Mr Gladstone opened with the words, "Your admirable Headmaster," I felt that the Prime Minister was so out of touch with the whole of the life I was leading that I never listened to another word.' Finally, when the time came to say a rather embarrassing and stiff good-bye to the headmaster at the end of his last term, Dr Butler asked Baldwin what he was going to do as a career. 'I am going first into business and then to the House of Commons,' said the lad confidently. However, the headmaster did not have a very high opinion of Parliament as a legislative body. 'I doubt if it will be worth entering,' he said discouragingly.

Baldwin thus left Harrow a year earlier than he otherwise might have done. He did not go into the family business immediately, as his father thought it would be as well if he were to go on to university. A place was found for him in Cambridge, at Trinity College, and he went up after the summer holidays in 1885. Soon after he arrived, he discovered to his chagrin that Dr Butler had likewise left Harrow and taken up residence in the Master's Lodgings at Trinity on his appointment to the headship of the college. This may have had something to do with Baldwin's decision to drop classics and take the easier discipline of history for his degree course. Thereafter the three years which Baldwin spent as an undergraduate were undistinguished except for idleness, and the fact that in his very first week at Cambridge he told his father that he was thinking of going into the Church. 'I don't know that I am surprised,' commented Alfred Baldwin. However, nothing was to come of the idea, although Baldwin did spend most of one Easter vacation with the Trinity Church mission in Camberwell. He also joined the Magpie and Stump, the college debating society, but was afterwards asked to resign on the ground that he never spoke. As he grew older, he regretted more and more that he had 'wasted so much time when I was at University and failed to follow in the footsteps of those who had gone before me, with far less advantages'. On the other hand, there was something to be said for the easy life he led at Cambridge. 'I attribute such faculties as I have,' he later remarked, 'to the fact that I did not overstrain them in youth.'[21]

Baldwin's closest friend of his own age at Cambridge, as also at home, was his cousin Harold, a son of George Baldwin, one of the improvident brothers who had nearly ruined the family business and since died. Alfred took pity on his nephew, had him to live at Wilden and sent him to Cambridge with Stanley. He hoped that Harold would also enter the business in due course. Unfortunately Harold turned out to be an epileptic and in a fit fell thirty feet from the window of his rooms in college on to the flagged quadrangle below; he later became a chronic invalid and practically useless for business or any other form of active life. Nevertheless the two cousins remained devoted to each other, and Harold, although he was debarred from going into the business, was later responsible for some vivid pen pictures of Stanley as an apprentice ironmaster.*

Stanley Baldwin's academic career at Cambridge can be briefly stated.

* Harold Baldwin later married his nurse. He died in 1920.

After getting a First in Part I of the History Tripos, probably without any great effort due to the grounding he had had at school, he deteriorated progressively. In Part II of the Tripos he was placed in the Second Class but in the Finals he only managed to scrape a Third. 'I hope you won't have a Third in life,' his father wrote to him on hearing the news.[22]

5

Before entering the family business, which he did in the autumn of 1888, Stanley Baldwin spent a month or two learning to become a gunner with the Artillery Volunteers. His twenty-first birthday found him in camp at Malvern and the birthday celebrations at Wilden had to be postponed. 'I am sorry he is away, and the village doesn't like it,' noted his father, although Alfred Baldwin was bound to admit that his son was doing the right thing. 'I could have picked your being with us,' he wrote to him at the time, 'but you are in your right place and I hope you are enjoying it. I know you will do your best to make a good officer.' Master Stan, as he was affectionately known in the works, was duly fêted with banners and garlands and the usual sports on his return from camp and was called upon for a speech. 'Stan spoke very well and to the point,' his father remarked. He then went off to Woolwich for a gunnery course, returning home at the beginning of October with a certificate of efficiency. He was to keep up his connection with the Volunteers and spent many a winter's evening drilling with them. But the social side of the army did not appeal to him, as evidenced by his cousin Harold's remark at this time that Stan was going to a mess dinner in Worcester 'which he cordially dreaded as the officers are hardly his style'.

Alfred Baldwin was determined that his son should begin at the bottom and work his way up in the business according to the well-established Victorian practice. His starting salary was £2 a week, and he shared his father's office above the entrance to the works at Wilden. 'I am very thankful you have chosen to be my help and partner in business,' Alfred Baldwin had told him before he joined.

You have had the best education I could give you, and it remains for you to apply it. What I sometimes fear is that you may inherit some of my faults and so may miss the front rank into which you ought with your advantages to get. You ought to be a first-class man, and it is entirely in your own hands . . . I want you to aim at being a complete master of the business and not a half one; this can only be done by sheer hard work from day to day; and if only you will do this, I believe, starting where you do, you will be able to take an independent position early in life. There are great chances in your favour, if you will avail yourself of them.

The father added a pious hope as to the course his son's future would take:

I hope we shall live to see you full of honours as a public man, if your choice lies that way; and in all things a Christian gentleman. I hope no stain will ever be on your life. You know the way to walk in; and I have full trust in you. I am very glad you will be with us at home for a while; we shall have time I hope to cultivate our friend-ship . . . I am anxious to be your helper and to save you from the troubles I have passed through, and to warn you against the points where I have gone wrong.

Harold Baldwin, who in spite of his disability had started work in an-other of his uncle's works, is an interesting source of information on his cousin's progress as a man of business. 'He hates it cordially,' noted Harold, 'but of course as a sensible man he will stick to it and do his level best. Uncle is telling him pretty well everything, and no doubt he'll soon have all at his fingers' ends.' Two months later, Harold wrote again: 'Stan was in great form; he's evidently awfully depressed by this damnably dull business life, and he hates it as cordially as I do; poor old chap, it is terrible for him, and as one looks forward the view is gloomier still.' After a year or so, the picture was rather different. 'Walked across to Wilden and saw my beloved Stan, looking a little older, but otherwise the same as ever . . . He is quite the man of business when in the office, but once out-side the same dear merry soul he has ever been . . . The way in which he has settled down to business amazes me; he's almost as keen on it as his father, and at the same time from the bottom of his heart he detests it; he's wonderfully quick and grasps a situation in no time.' [23]

In the summer of 1899, his first after entering the family business, his artist uncle Edward Poynter took him on a holiday to Switzerland and Italy. 'The friendship which I enjoyed with my uncle,' he recalled long afterwards, 'was one which lasted from the earliest days I can remember to the day of his death.' *

It is strange and curious to look back on those days, and to remember

* Sir Edward Poynter ARA died in 1919.

that atmosphere of art and culture, of wit and humour, and to recognise what one owes to it. One learns, in having the privilege of mixing with men like that, and their friends, the inestimable value of such an association for after life, even for one who has taken a far different career . . . I learnt there, all unconsciously, the value of work. The men I am thinking of were workmen, first and foremost. They were men who worked at what they loved and who felt that it was due to the art they loved to give it every power that God had given them. If, at any time, they went for holidays they painted all the time, because they liked it. That is the secret of good work, and the secret, incidentally, of happiness.[24]

One incident during this holiday he particularly remembered, 'standing on the terrace of a beautiful villa near Florence', and he was to describe it many years later in a speech to the Classical Association.

It was a September evening, and the valley below was transfigured in the long horizontal rays of the declining sun. And then I heard a bell, such a bell as never was on land or sea, a bell whose very vibration found an echo in my innermost heart. I said to my hostess, 'That is the most beautiful bell I have ever heard.' 'Yes,' she replied, 'it is an English bell.' And so it was. For generations its sound had gone out over English fields, giving the hours of work and prayer to English folk from the tower of an English abbey, and then came the Reformation, and some wise Italian bought the bell whose work at home was done and sent it to the Valley of the Arno, where after four centuries it stirred the heart of a wandering Englishman and made him sick for home.[25]

After two years at the Wilden iron forge, Alfred Baldwin despatched his son across the Atlantic on a tour of Canada and the United States in order to make contact with the firm's customers in North America. Accompanied by an old school friend, James Fyfe-Jamieson, he arrived in the St Lawrence river by steamer and after visiting Quebec and Montreal travelled south to Boston, New York, Philadelphia, Washington and Richmond, then east to Chicago and finally to New Orleans. In Boston his uncle Edward Burne-Jones had given him a letter of introduction to a prominent art collector who happened to be out of town when the visitors arrived. On learning of this the collector immediately returned to Boston to show them his pictures, an example of American courtesy which Stanley Baldwin never forgot. From Boston an excursion was made forty miles west to Worcester. This town had been established by settlers from its English namesake early in the eighteenth century; among the more recent settlers was a Stourport weaver, who had married Stanley's old nurse and had emigrated with her to become a successful carpet manufacturer in this former colonial outpost. There was a happy reunion in Worcester, Mass.

Baldwin's tour coincided with the debates in Congress on the tariff measure known as the McKinley Bill from the name of its sponsor, the Republican leader in the House of Representatives; this measure with its high and in some cases almost prohibitive import duties, although it passed Congress and became law, was extremely unpopular both in the United States and abroad, and was responsible for William McKinley being defeated in the Congressional elections later the same year. Among the infant industries which the McKinley Tariff was designed to protect was the manufacture of tin-plate, and as a result of the heavy duties imposed on imports of this and other engineering products the Baldwin business lost its American market and had to find new outlets. It would probably be too much to say that his visit to America converted Stanley Baldwin to the policy of protection at home, but it certainly brought to his attention for the first time the salient factors of the Free Trade versus Fair Trade controversy, which was to come to a head a decade later through the tariff reform campaign of Joseph Chamberlain.[26]

The traveller returned home to a 'splendidly kind welcome' from the works people at Wilden. 'Stan is wonderfully well, and has enjoyed his trip thoroughly,' his father noted. 'It is pleasant to see him here again, God be thanked.' He was next sent off to Manchester to take a course in metallurgy at Owens College, which was the nucleus of the university there, after which his father pronounced him to be 'a satisfactory son in every way', and he was promoted to managerial status. This was a source of much comfort to Alfred Baldwin, who had been persuaded at this time to accept adoption as Conservative candidate for the West Worcestershire or the Bewdley Division of the county, as it was generally known. ('It had come naturally and I hope I am in some ways ready for it.') At the General Election in 1892, he was returned unopposed. The event was the occasion for considerable jubilation at Wilden; but it was unfortunately tinged with tragedy, since one of the workpeople was killed loading a cannon and another was seriously injured.

For the next fifteen years Alfred Baldwin was to spend each parliamentary session in London, where he took a flat in Kensington Palace Mansions and joined the Carlton, Athenaeum, St Stephen's and City of London Clubs. During his absence he was content to leave his son in charge, which suited

'Master Stan' who was more interested in the administrative than the technical side of the business. 'Higgledy-piggledy' was how the new works manager described the Wilden forge, where 'charcoal' iron was still made with charcoal burned in the Wyre Forest. ('The boilers appeared to have been thrown down from the skies, and where they fell foundations built up, and steam pipe connections made to the nearest venerable beam engine.')[27] Looking back thirty years later, Stanley Baldwin admitted that when he was first in business he was working under a system that was already passing. Nevertheless it had its endearing side.

> It was a place where I knew, and had known from childhood, every man on the ground; a place where I was able to talk with the men not only about the troubles in the works, but troubles at home and their wives. It was a place where strikes and lockouts were unknown. It was a place where the fathers and grandfathers of the men then working there had worked, and where their sons went automatically into the business. It was also a place where nobody ever 'got the sack', and where we had a natural sympathy for those who were less concerned in efficiency than is this generation, and where a large number of old gentlemen used to spend their days sitting on the handles of wheel-barrows, smoking their pipes.
>
> Oddly enough it was not an inefficient community. It was the last survival of that type of works which ultimately became swallowed up in one of those great combinations towards which the industries of today are tending.[28]

6

In January 1892 Stanley Baldwin came up to London for a luncheon at Brown's Hotel to celebrate the wedding of his cousin Rudyard Kipling to Caroline Balestier. By this date, Kipling, who was eighteen months older than Baldwin, had already achieved success as a short story writer and novelist, notably with *Plain Tales from the Hills* and *The Light that Failed*. Henry James, who gave the bride away 'in a dreary little wedding with an attendance of simply four men', wrote at this time: 'Kipling strikes me personally as the most complete man of genius (as distinct from fine intelligence) that I have ever known.' Baldwin was proud of their common puritan stock and he thoroughly agreed with what his cousin once said to him – indeed he had come to the same conclusion himself: 'When you have two courses open to you and you thoroughly dislike one of them, that is the one you must choose, for it is sure to be the right one.'[29]

Three months later Baldwin announced that he was following his cousin's example by becoming engaged to be married. His fiancée was a robust, cheerful, forthright, extrovert girl named Lucy Ridsdale, who excelled at cricket and hockey, and whom he had met while staying with the Burne-Joneses at Rottingdean in the previous summer. The Ridsdales lived in The Dene, opposite North End House, inhabited by the Burne-Joneses and flanking the village green. Lucy's father, Edward Lucas Jenks Ridsdale, a former Master of the Mint, was as different from Alfred Baldwin as could be imagined – a scientist, atheist and Liberal. The young Baldwin's interest in Lucy Ridsdale, known as Cissy in the family circle, is said to have been first aroused when he saw her score a half-century at a Ladies' cricket match. If his courtship was slow, the speed with which he lost his heart to her was remarkable. On his way home after another visit, he sent her a telegram from every station at which his train stopped between Brighton and Worcester. Inland telegrams were delivered eighty years ago more rapidly than they are today, with the result that Lucy received the stream of affectionate greetings at intervals throughout dinner, much to her embarrassment and the amusement of her family, who included a younger sister and three brothers. The latter would also tease Stanley on his visits. Once when he was caught sight of reading a book in the corner of the sitting-room at The Dene, one of her brothers inquired: 'Got the hump, old man?'

The news of the engagement was conveyed in a letter which Stanley wrote to his mother from Penzance where he and the Ridsdales were holidaying in April 1892:

> You and father have often said you wanted a nice daughter-in-law; so I have carried out your wishes to the letter and trust you will take Cissy Ridsdale for a daughter to make up for never having had one of your own. It seems a big jump now the step is taken, but it was one I meant to take since September . . .
>
> The things that first attracted me to Cissy were her absolute innocence and unworldliness and the strong loyalty she felt towards every member of her own family. I felt that in so many ways her influence could only be wholly for good with me; for whereas in one or two things I may know more than she does, she is far before me in all the virtues of daily life that combine to make a lovely and lovable character.[30]

'It was a love match between him and Cissy,' wrote Angela Thirkell, the novelist daughter of Stanley's first cousin Margaret Burne-Jones who married the classical scholar J. W. Mackail. 'Her parents, Londoners and South of England, did not wish their elder daughter to go to remote Worcestershire to live among industrial people; the Baldwins would greatly have preferred their only son to "marry into the county". The event proved that both sets of parents were wrong. The marriage was of love, enduring affection and splendid team work.'

The wedding took place in the parish church of Rottingdean on 12 September 1892, being officially witnessed according to the register by the bridegroom's father and both the bride's parents. (Alfred Baldwin no longer gave his rank of profession as 'Ironmaster' as he had done at Stanley's birth, but as 'Gentleman', as also did both the bridegroom and his father-in-law.) The first night of the honeymoon was spent at Chichester, after which the young couple toured the cities and cathedrals in the West Country, ending up in the New Forest. They then returned to Wilden for a few months while Dunley Hall, the rambling, red-brick, Georgian house which Stanley had rented about two miles from Stourport and which was to be their home for the next ten years, was being redecorated. Baldwin's official biographer G. M. Young has written that 'there was not much passion in their mating', and it is no surprise that this statement should have given considerable offence to the Baldwin family, since the biographer cites no evidence in support of it: in the circumstances he could hardly be expected to.[31] However that may be, Stanley and Lucy Baldwin were to be united throughout the whole term of their lives by a deep and lasting affection, as indeed Young himself admits. If she was not her husband's intellectual equal and did not share all his interests – she was not musical nor was she such an enthusiast for walking as her husband – nevertheless there was something very refreshing and down-to-earth about Lucy, and a certain astringent quality about her, which delighted her family and her friends. Her unconscious humour, too, could at times be striking. For instance, on one occasion her male listeners at a charity meeting which she addressed were convulsed when she told them: 'I want every one of you in this audience to be responsible for one unmarried mother!'

In January 1894, after an abnormally long labour, Lucy Baldwin gave birth to a still-born son in London. Her husband took the blow much harder than she did and became ill himself, for many weeks being unable to sleep. Moreover, he had to return to the daily grind at Wilden, leaving Lucy to recover in London without him at her side. But the nursery at Dunley Hall was not destined to remain empty for long. Three daughters arrived during the next three years, Diana, Leonora (Lorna) and Margaret

(Margot). They were followed in 1899 by a son and heir, who was named Oliver. A fourth daughter, Esther, always called Betty, appeared three years later, and finally another son Windham, nicknamed 'Little', two years after Betty. By producing six children who grew to adulthood, Lucy Baldwin certainly did her duty as a wife and mother. But, with the exception of the initial tragedy of the still-born son and the death of another child shortly after birth, these were happy years for husband and wife. There were annual visits to stay with Cissy's people at Rottingdean, where they would be joined by the Kiplings and their children. Rudyard afterwards recalled 'packing farm-carts filled with mixed babies – Stanley Baldwin's and ours – and despatching them into the same clean heart of the motherly Downs for jam-smeared picnics'.[32]

By now the course of Alfred Baldwin's life had also entered calmer waters. 'How thankful I ought to be for all the blessings with which God has surrounded my life,' he wrote on his fifty-second birthday: 'Louie first of all; then Stan, and now there is Cissy, who will I hope become more and more our own daughter. Blessings innumerable.'[33]

Every morning 'Master Stan' would reach the Wilden forge punctually at 8.45 a.m., and would stay until five or six, walking home when he could through the fields by the Stour river past its confluence with the Severn at Lower Mitton. The sympathetic ear with which he listened to the ironworkers who took their problems to him, domestic as well as works, and his suggestions for their solution, made him a prime favourite at the forge. One example is worth quoting for its humorous side. A worker came to him with a troubled expression and looking rather sheepish. 'You know, Master Stan,' he began, 'last week I got married.' 'Yes, of course,' was the reply, 'but what of it?' 'Well, you see this is very awkward: last night the bed broke!' It was the custom of the firm that any ironwork which the men needed for their homes should be done at cost price in the forge, and the embarrassed bridegroom, wishing to avoid the ribald laughter of his mates if he brought along the bed for repair, hit on the happy expedient of asking his employer to have it mended in his name. So it came to pass that one night when nobody was around to see, a broken iron bedstead was carried to Dunley Hall, whence it was conveyed by 'Master Stan' to Wilden for the necessary attention which was duly bestowed upon it in the repair shop, after which it was unobtrusively returned to its owner.[34]

On Sundays he would sing in the choir at Wilden church, and in the summer would play cricket at Areley King's, the next village to Dunley. His first experience of political responsibility occurred shortly after his marriage when he was elected to the Areley King's parish council. Here he took his duties seriously and was so punctual that on one occasion the entire agenda was completed by the chairman and himself with the help of the secretary before the other members, 'with native slowness and deliberation', deigned to put in an appearance. Later he served on the Worcestershire County Council, making his first speech while Queen Victoria was still on the throne in opposition to an overdue local sewage scheme – 'a thoroughly reactionary proceeding', as he was lightheartedly to recall. He also became a magistrate on the local bench of justices, as well as Chairman of the Wilden School Managers. Then he joined various Friendly Societies and similar bodies like the Foresters and the Oddfellows, whose gatherings he attended for their rustic good cheer. At the General Election in 1895 and again in 1900, he canvassed and addressed meetings for his father throughout the fifty miles of the West Worcestershire Division which extended from the Malvern Hills to the Wyre Forest, becoming known in every bar parlour where he would stop to drink cider and beer and smoke a clay pipe with the locals. There was no better apprenticeship to national politics than getting to know everyone in this way and everyone getting to know him.

In 1902, thanks largely to Alfred Baldwin's foresight, Baldwins Ltd came into being as a public company through the amalgamation of the various Baldwin concerns, including two tin-plate works in South Wales, with the Blackwall Galvanised Iron Co. of London, the Bryn Navigation Colliery, and Wright Butler & Co., of Pontypool. The moving spirit in the latter firm was Colonel John Roper Wright, who had worked as an assistant to Sir William Siemens, the great metallurgist and inventor of the open-hearth process for the manufacture of sheet steel through the melting of wrought-iron scrap with pig iron in an open-hearth furnace, important for railways and ships' boiler plates. Thus the amalgamation brought together works whose roots went back to the early development of iron manufacture in the Midlands and South Wales with those who had pioneered the Siemens open hearth steel and its successful use for tin-plate and sheet steel. Alfred Baldwin became chairman of the new company, while Roper Wright, who was thoroughly familiar with the Siemens techniques, became a director along with the chairman's son. Four years later the important Port Talbot Steel Co. under the management of Roper Wright's son Charles joined the combine, which now covered all the stages in the production of iron and steel from the raw materials to tin-plate and galvanised sheets.[35]

In the same year as Baldwins came into being, the successful young director of thirty-five moved into a larger house. This was Astley Hall, which at first he rented and later bought; it was situated about a mile from Dunley, on a hill above the Severn, and set in a small estate of one hundred acres, about eighty of which were farmed by tenants. Here he kept a few cows and pigs and some poultry, for he had come to relish the sights and sounds and smells of the countryside, although he wisely left the mechanics of farming to his wife and his one cowman, preferring merely to contemplate what his cousin Rudyard Kipling called the 'common, honest, decent swine'. He used to say that the view from the garden at Astley presented a circle of beauty which he defied any part of England to match, embracing as it did the whole length of the Cotswolds, cut only by Bredon in the middle and the Malverns at the end.

It is indeed a chosen and favoured spot. The great beauty of these high places is that there can have been but little change in the outline of the landscape in the face of the [Severn] valley since the [Roman] legions piled their arms almost on this spot, after their long march to relieve those who were keeping watch and ward over that Welsh frontier – the frontier which my people further up the valley in Shropshire watched and helped to guard for centuries and centuries.[36]

Later on his critics were wont to say that his professed love of the countryside was really a pose and that his pretended 'Englishness' was 'sheer propaganda'. But this was not so. 'He really did like leaning over a gate and scratching a pig,' said his friend J. C. C. Davidson. 'He liked talking to farmers and to farm labourers, he was of the country and of the people, not only the industrial people. One of the things which he was at pains to explain to his own people in Worcestershire was that, although they were now working in a factory, they all stemmed from the land, which was really their spiritual home; that is why he talked about himself, and re-garded himself, in that vein. He was the son of an industrialist and had run an ironworks, but it was really the land which he came from, the oldest and biggest industry of all.' Indeed in the early days Rudyard Kipling once introduced his cousin to an agriculturalist of his acquaintance as one who 'hopes one day to make a name for himself in the farming world'.[37]

'I think of Stan,' wrote Angela Thirkell of him at this period, 'sitting at one end of the big dinner table at Astley, blowing a kiss to Cissy and saying, "My Queen! you are the most beautiful woman in Europe." A joke of course – but from the heart. And it was Cissy's proud boast that she had had eight children . . . If this did not mean passion (to use Mr Young's word), the only other meaning could be that Stan was a brute; which is impossible.'[38]

TWO

THE POLITICAL APPRENTICE

I

It had always been a fond hope of Alfred Baldwin that his only son would one day join him on the Conservative benches of the House of Commons. With the exception of the Droitwich or Mid-Worcestershire Division, which was won for the Liberals at the General Election in 1900 by Cecil Harmsworth, a younger brother of the newspaper magnate Lord Northcliffe, the county and county boroughs were solidly Conservative; and although the tide began to run against the Tories after the Liberal-Unionist Joseph Chamberlain, rich Birmingham industrialist and Colonial Secretary, came out strongly in favour of the policy of Tariff Reform (as Protection was euphemistically called by its protagonists) in the spring of 1903, the elder Baldwin looked forward to his son being chosen for the next Worcestershire seat which became vacant and that his return would follow as a matter of course. The chance came in 1904, when Sir Frederick Godson, the sitting MP for Kidderminster, for long the centre of English carpet manufacture, announced that he would not contest the constituency at the next election, and Stanley Baldwin was invited to stand in his place.

Even before his adoption for Kidderminster, Stanley Baldwin used to dine regularly with his father in the House of Commons and listen to the debates. In this way he met his father's political friends, notably Joseph Chamberlain, his son Austen, the Chancellor of the Exchequer, who sat for East Worcestershire, and Andrew Bonar Law, a successful Canadian businessman of Ulster ancestry who had entered Parliament at the 1900 Election and after only eighteen months on the back benches had been appointed Parliamentary Secretary to the Board of Trade at the age of forty-four. ('Yours is an admirable appointment,' Alfred Baldwin had written to him when he heard the news of his promotion. 'I wish you many years of prosperity.')[1] Alfred Baldwin and his son, like Bonar Law and Austen Chamberlain, supported Joseph Chamberlain on the tariff issue. On the other hand, there were powerful Free Traders in the Government and the Party, and Arthur Balfour's task as Prime Minister in holding both together and preventing an irreconcilable split was becoming increasingly difficult.

In June 1905, Stanley Baldwin received a disconcerting letter from an anonymous well-wisher. The writer did not sign the letter, because, as he remarked, 'if I did I should get the Party leaders down upon me and they would charge me with trying to do the party an injury, but such is not the case – it is only that I admire you and think what a pity it is that you should be sacrificed that I take the trouble to write'. The fact was that there was an exceptionally strong Liberal Association in Kidderminster with an active agent, while the Liberal candidate, Edmund Barnard, although he was not a local man, had been assiduously nursing the constituency for the past five years, having fought the seat in 1900 when he was only defeated by 146 votes. 'If I give you my honest conviction, I do not think you have the slightest chance of winning, nor has any other Unionist, and therefore I think it is a great pity that you should fight a hopeless battle here when you might go elsewhere and win.' The writer concluded by begging Baldwin instead to contest Mid-Worcester, where (according to him) the local Liberals did not like Cecil Harmsworth and a good Tariff Reform candidate could hold the seat easily.[2] Apparently the writer had a good deal of influence with the Conservative Committee at Droitwich and on the face of it the suggestion seemed a tempting one. But Baldwin rightly felt that he could not abandon the Kidderminster Conservatives, however discouraging his electoral prospects might be, and that he should stick to his guns, which in the event he did.

Hoping to score a tactical victory over the Liberals, who were divided over a number of issues such as Home Rule for Ireland, Balfour suddenly resigned in December 1905 without asking the King to dissolve Parliament. He was succeeded by the elderly Liberal leader Sir Henry Campbell-Bannerman, who immediately obtained a dissolution followed by a General Election.

A few days after Christmas, Stanley Baldwin opened his campaign in a Kidderminster school on a depressingly wet night. 'I think I ought to begin by expressing my gratitude to all of you who have been good enough to turn out on such a night as this to come to this schoolroom to listen to me and my friends,' he told his audience. 'At the same time I think it is only fair to add that I have been tramping the streets of Kidderminster all day; so perhaps it is a fair reward that you should sacrifice some part of your pleasant evenings at home in coming to meet me here.' He went on to examine the most controversial question of the hour, the effect of tariff reform on food prices. He explained that a tariff on imported foodstuffs, with preferential treatment for Empire imports, would not raise food prices, as its Liberal opponents claimed; it would merely give the home farmer an opportunity to sell his products and divert the source of imported supplies from foreign dumpers to the overseas Empire. When he mentioned the recently increased duty on beer, which he claimed, in support of his main argument, had not raised the retail price of that commodity, the audience began to show some interest.

'They put more water in it!' someone shouted.

'I should be sorry to take such a low opinion of the publicans as my friend in the corner,' the speaker retorted, 'but perhaps he knows more about Kidderminster beer than I do.'

This sally was loudly cheered by the candidate's supporters, and the chairman rubbed in the point in his concluding remarks when he stated that the candidate had given 'the most able exposition of the subject of food taxation that I have ever heard'. He thereupon asked the meeting to pass a vote of confidence in him. This was duly done, although the vote does not appear to have been unanimous, since Baldwin in returning thanks to the chairman politely acknowledged 'the courteous hearing given me by the gentlemen who have held up their hands against the resolution'.[3]

At another meeting a day or two later, appropriately held in a schoolroom, he dealt with a second controversial subject, religious instruction, taking his cue from a framed text hanging on the wall which caught his eye as he entered the room – 'Fear of the Lord is the beginning of wisdom'. That text summarised his view of the subject, which still remains the official Tory formula for appeasing Church of England, Nonconformists and Roman Catholic partisans alike: 'I entirely agree that, if possible, the child should be instructed in the religious knowledge which would be satisfactory to the child's parents.'

The rival candidates' election addresses reached the 4,697 registered electors of Kidderminster in the first week of the New Year. 'I have acceded to a request made to me by several of my old friends in Kidderminster that I would (*sic*)* come forward as the Conservative and Unionist candidate at the General Election,' proclaimed Baldwin. 'Having lived all my life in the neighbourhood, I am spared having to speak of myself, but I will put before you briefly my views on the principal controversial subjects of the day.'

He proceeded to proclaim his opposition to the policy of Home Rule for

---

* This was a misprint for 'should', as appears from Baldwin's autograph correction of the address preserved in the Baldwin Papers.

Ireland, the disestablishment of the Welsh church and the secularisation of the schools. ('I still hope that in a Christian country it may be possible to come to an agreement on a matter of such vital importance as the religious education of their children.') On the positive side, he was in favour of 'tariff reform' and his attitude was conditioned by his personal experience in the iron and steel industry.

I have always been interested in whatever tends to the bettering of life for those who have to earn their daily bread. These conditions of life can only be permanently improved by securing more employment for the people, so that regular wages may be earned and the ranks of the unemployed reduced to a comparatively small number of those who cannot work.

How can we secure the necessary employment as long as we expose our own labour to the unrestricted competition of the labour of the world? We rightly try to protect our wages from being reduced by free competition amongst our own countrymen, and yet we neutralise all our efforts in this direction by admitting into our markets the products of the cheapest Continental and Eastern labour.

I am convinced that this is not wise, and that the time is now ripe for ending that era of unrestricted competition which has brought so much suffering on the working classes of these islands and has driven so many to seek in other lands a livelihood which has been denied them at home.

In his election address, Baldwin's Liberal opponent was scarcely more eloquent. Fifty-year-old Edmund Broughton Barnard, who came from Hertfordshire, where he was a member of the local county council and was an expert on water undertakings – he was later Chairman of the Metropolitan Water Board – belonged to the Radical wing of the Liberal Party and declared his adherence to Free Trade, religious equality in education, Old Age Pensions and the reform of local government and trade union law. Somewhat vaguely he also stated that he would 'support any proposal which appears to me to offer a permanent remedy for the present deplorable condition of affairs'.

Kidderminster had the reputation of being as corrupt a borough as any in the country at election time. Years later Baldwin described the occasion euphemistically as 'what was called an old-fashioned election in an ancient borough now disenfranchised'. A canvasser on knocking at an elector's house would commonly be told: 'Call at a quarter to eight,' when he would guide the elector to the polling station and literally tell him how to vote.

One incident at this election Baldwin liked to relate as an illustration of how an injudicious remark by a Conservative supporter could be turned against him. The Conservative had accused the Liberal candidate of having been warned off the racecourse at Nice for pulling his horse. 'And why shouldn't he?' asked a Liberal from the body of the meeting. 'It was his own horse, wasn't it?'[4] The candidates, as Baldwin also recalled, were expected to spend three evenings a week during the election 'in one or another of the public houses which jostled each other through the constituency, listening to and vociferously applauding what, for want of a better name, was called, on the *lucus a non lucendo* principle, comic or humorous song'. After a time, he confessed, his soul needed something between a moral purge and a literary sedative. 'When I came home at night from these orgies I seldom went to bed without reading something of the *Odyssey*, the *Aeneid*, or the *Odes* of Horace. By the date of the election I had read all the last named, and most of the others, not without labour in the dictionaries, not always with ease, but with care and increasing joy . . .'[5]

Electioneering in the open air was chilly work in January. 'I never saw a better prescription for catching cold than these meetings,' the candidate told the few curious spectators who had gathered at the street corners, 'but I hope that not too many of you will be too ill to vote.' At one indoor meeting the chairman presented an image which was to become familiar in after years. 'We have in Mr Stanley Baldwin a plain, straightforward man in whose speeches there is a ring of honesty which will appeal most forcibly to the intelligent electors of this borough.' At the same meeting a speaker held up a strip of inferior Belgian-made bedside carpet, complaining that it sold in England for 2s. 11d. a yard, while the price of the superior Kidderminster product, a specimen of which he also exhibited, was 5s. 1d. 'If you elect me to Parliament,' said Baldwin when asked for his views on the difference in price and quality, 'you will find that I wear like the Kidderminster "bedside" that has been produced, and not like the Belgian article.'[6]

The climax to the campaign was the eve-of-the-poll meeting in Kidderminster Town Hall. 'Stanley Baldwin is a man well known to us from his youth, of great intellectual capacity and of high culture,' the chairman assured the audience with understandable hyperbole. 'He is ready of speech and full of energy, pleasant and tactful in his manners and of unblemished reputation, thoroughly conversant with commercial life, and like his father before him, he takes a personal interest in the welfare of the workpeople he employs.' This flattering opinion was not unnaturally endorsed by Alfred Baldwin who was present. 'If my son is returned to

Parliament, he will be an honest representative,' declared the candidate's father. 'I am glad to say that my son has followed me in one thing; he has not made promises all over the country. If he did, people would call round at Wilden, whereas,' he added, in a delicate allusion to Mr Barnard's home, 'Hertfordshire is far away.' [7]

In those days, voting at parliamentary elections took place on different days in different constituencies at the discretion of the Returning Officer, who in this instance was the Mayor of Kidderminster. The latter gentleman, with the approval of both candidates, chose the first appointed polling day, which happened to be a Saturday, because, he said, 'the electors of this borough should not have their minds burdened on Sunday with the thought of an impending parliamentary election on the morrow'. In the event, the poll was an exceptionally heavy one, even for those days, no less than 97 per cent. But the result, which the Mayor declared from the steps of the Town Hall the same night, came as an unpleasant surprise to Stanley Baldwin and also to his agent, who had prophesied a Conservative victory of 500.

S. Baldwin (Unionist)	2,083
E. B. Barnard (Liberal)	2,354
Liberal majority	271

Since polling in the Bewdley division was not due to take place until the following week, Alfred Baldwin was present to hear the result at Kidderminster. It is said that the crowd parted outside the Town Hall and made a passage for him as he walked down the street after hearing Mr Barnard declared elected, 'his great bearded head bowed in sorrow for his son's defeat'. Later that night the son rallied his dejected supporters in the Lion Hotel, showing the Englishman's traditional stiff upper lip. 'We have been beaten but not disgraced,' he said. 'Gentlemen, if we had won, we would have won as gentlemen, and, as we have been beaten, let us take our defeat as gentlemen.' [8]

A day or two later, he went off by himself on a walking tour through the Cotswolds, talking to all and sundry and drinking ale in the local pubs in Burford and Minster Lovell and tramping through the rain from Witney to Oxford where he ran into his Mackail cousins, eventually making his way home by rail at the end of the week and, as he put it, 'arriving a new man and purged of my humours'. [9]

2

The 1906 General Election was a landslide for the Liberals, who gained 377 seats in all. Thus they had a majority of 88 over the other combined parties, which consisted of 157 Conservatives, 83 Irish Nationalists and 53 Labour members. The Liberal triumph was largely due to the success of the old party cry, 'Hands off the People's Food', and the conjuring up of the bogey of the 'Hungry Forties' of the previous century, when it was said that English people had starved and Irish had died because a Conservative Government had refused to allow the free import of corn. Among the Liberals elected for the first time was Lucy Baldwin's brother Aurelian Ridsdale, who captured Brighton. Besides her husband, the Conservative casualties included Bonar Law and Balfour himself. 'Yours is no slight loss to our party,' wrote one Tory survivor to the former. 'No one has done better work than you have; and if your constituents do not value it, your friends do. None more than yours sincerely Alfred Baldwin.'[10] Incidentally, the forecast of a majority of 3,250 made by Alfred Baldwin's election agent in Bewdley for his candidate was much nearer the mark than his son's in Kidderminster – in fact, the Conservative majority in West Worcestershire was 3,194.*

Shortly afterwards the son's hopes revived on learning that the elected member for Worcester City had been unseated for corrupt practices during the election following an election petition. 'I thought I was certain to be chosen at once,' Stanley Baldwin later recalled. But 'a venomous Radical' moved the suspension of the new writ for a year and his motion was agreed to.

I was thirty-nine and felt that if I didn't get in quickly it would be too late. The year passed and I went before the selection committee holding my head high. And they chose an Irishman whom I thought – and still think – to be vastly my inferior. So I was turned down in my own county town in favour of a stranger, and bang went all my hopes . . . I remember vividly how I felt. One's friends know, understand and sympathise. The world don't care a damn. And one has to bite on it and go about one's job with a cheerful face.[11]

The outsider preferred to the local man in Worcester was Edward ('Paddy') Goulding, afterwards Lord Wargrave, a wealthy bachelor and

* The Liberal candidate whom Alfred Baldwin defeated was G. R. Benson, afterwards Lord Charnwood.

company director – he was chairman of Rolls-Royce – and a man of considerable influence behind the political scenes, who already had ten years' experience in the House of Commons and was the owner of a luxurious house on the Thames near Henley, where he liked to entertain the people who counted in politics. Baldwin never cared for him, no doubt considering him to be an intriguer; but if 'Paddy' Goulding intrigued, it was certainly not for himself, as he never aspired to any government office. Later on he was to play an inconspicuous but significant part in the choice of Bonar Law as Conservative leader.

In those days the statutory life of a Parliament extended to seven years, and with the huge Liberal majority in the House of Commons there was no immediately apparent reason why the Liberal Premier should not allow the Parliament which had been elected in 1906 to run its full term. Thus in the normal course of events the next General Election would not take place until 1913 when Stanley Baldwin would be getting on for fifty, too advanced an age at which to begin a political career. A further twelve months passed after his rejection by the Worcester Conservatives and his prospects of entering Parliament remained as bleak as ever. Then another chance suddenly and unexpectedly presented itself, although the circumstances were not what Stanley Baldwin would have wished.

A few days after the opening of the new session of Parliament at the end of January 1908, Alfred Baldwin travelled up to London from Wilden with his wife and they stayed as usual in their flat in Kensington Palace Mansions. While on his way to the flat in a cab after attending the half-yearly board meeting of the Great Western Railway in Paddington in the afternoon of 13 February, he suddenly felt a violent internal pain. On reaching Kensington Palace Mansions, he managed to stagger into the hall, where he collapsed in a chair. He was helped into bed, murmuring, 'I am very ill.' Unfortunately his wife was out at the time and had not returned twenty minutes later when he died from the heart attack. His last words were to remind the porter to pay the cabman. 'In the mercy of God,' wrote his bereaved widow afterwards, 'he was saved pain, illness, apprehension of death, and the sorrow of parting. He did not ask for me, he did not miss me. We were both mercifully led blindfold to our parting.'

Stanley was immediately summoned by telegram and he brought his father's remains back to Wilden, where in the pretty red-brick church which Alfred Baldwin had built he and his cousins took turns in keeping vigil beside the coffin throughout the night before the funeral. Louisa Baldwin was not present at the funeral service, having gone for comfort in her grief to her sister Georgiana Burne-Jones in Rottingdean. Then, in the words of her brother-in-law John Kipling, 'Georgie and Stan have held her up and carried her in their arms sharing her sorrow in the most marvellous way.' Yet nineteen months passed before Louie could bring herself to look on Alfred's grave in Wilden churchyard, while there were to be fifteen years of widowhood before she was eventually laid beside him. Her son never failed to write to her on the anniversary of Alfred Baldwin's death. 'I must look on each anniversary as a great inspiration,' he told her, 'as Father's life has been to me since his own work was done.'[12]

The Times paid a formal tribute in its obituary columns, but it revealed nothing of Alfred's character and personality. A local Worcester paper published a more perceptive appreciation of the Wilden ironmaster.

It was perhaps his chief glory in the eyes of the villagers that Mr Baldwin dwelt among his own people . . . The youngest child in the village was known to him, and there was not a man in the place who was not addressed by Mr Baldwin by his Christian name and whose life story was not known to him . . . It was not only that he secured for them well-provided and comfortable homes . . . or even that he built schools for their children, and a church for them to worship in, and in a hundred other ways promoted their well-being. Others have done that for their workpeople, but have not gained for themselves the esteem, amounting to love and veneration, which was felt for Mr Baldwin. The secret of it all was his own personality, his unaffected goodness and his love for his people. Never did a cloud darken the home of the humblest dweller on the happy hillside than there came the silver lining of sympathy and help from Wilden House.

A few days after the funeral, the West Worcestershire Conservatives met to decide on a successor to the late member and unanimously decided to invite his son to allow his name to go forward as the official Party candidate. They accordingly invited him to a meeting in Worcester to discuss the prospect. Recalling the occasion when he took leave of the constituency twenty-nine years later, Stanley Baldwin remarked: 'When I came to Worcester in February 1908 to meet the Selection Committee who I knew were going to interview me to stand in my father's place, I drove in with a pair of horses from Astley, and took over an hour to do it . . . I really knew most people in the Division because I had been about the whole countryside for my father. Since 1892 there was not a village or hamlet I did not know, or a Friendly Society with which I had not dined. I knew them all, and by my side were my father's friends.' His selection was a foregone conclusion. He accepted it with characteristic humility and a sense of filial pride.[13]

He had a second stroke of luck when the local Liberals decided not to put up a candidate against him. No doubt they realised that it would have been a futile exercise to do so, since the late Alfred Baldwin had been returned by a majority of over two to one and in the event of a contest his son would have been found to attract a powerful wave of sympathy from his supporters. Thus it came about that the first speech which Stanley Baldwin delivered as an MP was on the steps of the Shire Hall at Worcester. After thanking the Returning Officer for having declared him duly elected as the member for West Worcestershire, he continued:

I thank my political opponents for the kindly courtesy they have extended to me at a time when a contest would have been almost impossible for me. Their forbearance will for years soften the asperities of political life in this division. This division of Bewdley, in which I was born and have lived all my life, has been a singularly fortunate one, for, during the twenty-three years it has had a separate existence, it has been represented in Parliament by the highest type of Englishman. It has had only two representatives, and both have been men who placed the common weal above their own interests, and to whom public honours were as nothing beside the maintenance of their own private honour.*

If it is an honour you have done me today, I feel that it entails on me an immense responsibility. I assure you that with the help of God I shall follow the example of my predecessors.[14]

It is the custom of the House of Commons that newly elected MPs at by-elections have to be introduced by two sponsors. It gave Baldwin considerable pleasure when Austen Chamberlain, who represented the neighbouring division of East Worcestershire and whom he had known slightly for some years, wrote and asked whether he might act as his principal sponsor. 'I need not tell the House,' Baldwin recalled on the occasion of Chamberlain's death in 1937, 'with what gratitude I, a young and unknown Member, accepted that compliment from one who had already held high office as Chancellor of the Exchequer.'[15] His other sponsor was Lord Quenington, MP for Tewkesbury, whose family name was Hicks Beach. The ceremony took place after Questions on 8 March 1908.

'It was a quarter to four when I was introduced, marching up between

* The other member, who represented the Bewdley division from 1885 to 1892, was Sir Edmund Lechmere, 3rd Baronet, of Hanley Castle, a large landowner in the county, whose property dated back to William the Conqueror.

Austen Chamberlain and Hicks Beach,' he wrote after taking the oath of allegiance to the sovereign, signing the Roll of Members and shaking hands with Mr Speaker Lowther, who gave him a warm welcome. 'People were very kind, both Members and attendants. One of the latter has just been up to me and offered to show me anything and he said how much they all liked Father.' [16]

3

Then as now, the British House of Commons was probably the most friendly and at the same time most critical assembly of its kind in the world. It also had the reputation of being the best club in Europe. MPs received no salaries from the state and membership was consequently regarded as very much of a part-time occupation. Fortunately for the new member, he had come in for a comfortable patrimony, becoming Vice-Chairman of Baldwins while Colonel Roper Wright succeeded to the chair at the head of the boardroom table. Baldwin also inherited his father's place as a director of the Great Western Railway, so that he was now financially independent and free to devote as much or as little of his time as he pleased to national politics. Since his father's flat was too small for him and his growing family, he bought a fair-sized house in South Kensington, 27 Queen's Gate, to which the family would migrate for the parliamentary session three times a year with a retinue of servants and governesses in a private railway coach of the GWR. This was to be his London home for the next five years, after which he moved to 93 Eaton Square, a substantial town dwelling more conveniently situated for the House and better suited for political entertaining.

Baldwin's younger daughter Margaret,* then a girl of eleven, has recalled for the benefit of the present writer some of her memories of her parents at this period:

I was always terrified of my Father. My earliest recollection of him was when we moved to Queen's Gate when he first became a Member of Parliament, and he used to take us three girls out on a Saturday afternoon. I always heard he was wonderful with other people's children, but nervous of his own.

On Sundays, we all walked to Astley Church and walked back again and then ate hot roast beef and apple tart (or whatever fruit was in season) and junket, followed by a fruit luncheon cake or

* Now Lady Margaret Huntington-Whiteley.

cheese. I tried to go walks with my Father but it was not a success: the paths (cross-country) were too narrow for me to walk by his side, and he got annoyed with me if I walked in front of him, as I was unable to walk fast enough, and he got annoyed with me if I walked behind, as I had to keep on running to catch up with him. I once travelled down in the same compartment as he did from Paddington Station to Worcester (he got into the train after I did), but he never spoke a word to me the whole way down, and I was much too frightened to speak to him. He couldn't bear grumblers or grumbling, particularly over food, and he said we should be grateful for what was provided for us. Religion meant a lot to both of them in their different ways.

My Mother was a most remarkable woman. Two people could not have been more unlike than she and my Father, but I never heard them quarrel or shout at one another; should they ever differ, it was always done quietly and politely. She loved gaiety, entertaining and parties, and my Father had to put a good face on it. He was terrified of big receptions and always tried to keep near the wall in case the floor gave way! (He was always apprehensive of the future and always feared the worst.) They both abhorred noise and shouting, and we were always told: 'Don't shout, go and look for the person.' He also had a horror of being asked questions, and always became non-committal and stupid when asked them, especially when asked the obvious. He did not care to be next to a silent person at meals: 'they' were not playing their part in helping their host and hostess to make the party 'go'.

If it hadn't been for my Mother, my Father would have remained quite happily where he was in Worcestershire, going daily to the office and back. He had no ambition, push or drive. My Mother supplied them all: he was her first concern, and she always saw he had every comfort in his library, especially in his London library, as *she* preferred London to the country. But by present-day standards of comfort, they neither of them knew what a comfortable bed, chair or sofa was like, nor did they know what labour saving devices meant. I well remember, after my Father's death, seeing his old wooden, single bedstead, with the chain-wires sagging to within inches of the floor. His bedroom faced north, with a big window and a very small one on the west wall: he never felt the cold.

A few weeks after Baldwin took his seat at Westminster, Campbell-Bannerman resigned on medical advice and died following a sudden heart attack before he was able to move out of No. 10 Downing Street. He was succeeded by Herbert Henry Asquith, who in reconstructing the Liberal Government promoted the thirty-four-year-old Winston Churchill to be President of the Board of Trade. This post was of Cabinet rank, but as the law then stood it necessitated its newly appointed holder resigning his seat in North-West Manchester and submitting himself for re-election. The Conservative candidate whom he had defeated at the General Election was a London solicitor named William Joynson-Hicks, noted for his strict sabbatarian and temperance views as well as being the part-author of a pioneer work on the law relating to motor vehicles. Churchill was again opposed by Joynson-Hicks, who incidentally gained the soubriquet of 'Jix' during this by-election. Because of his father's prominence as a supporter of tariff reform and the fact that he was known to share Joseph Chamberlain's views, Stanley Baldwin was asked to campaign for Joynson-Hicks. Thus it came about that his first political speeches after his own election were not made in the House of Commons but in Free Trade Manchester. The contest proved to be extremely hard fought and in the event resulted in Churchill failing to hold the seat by 476 votes, a setback which the defeated candidate attributed not to the electors being converted to the Protectionist cause but rather to 'those sulky Irish Catholics changing sides at the last moment under priestly pressure', since Asquith was considered to be much less enthusiastic for Home Rule than Campbell-Bannerman. No one who heard the newly elected and relatively unknown MP for West Worcestershire speak on the eve-of-the-poll meeting in Manchester, least of all Baldwin himself, could have foreseen that seventeen years later both 'Jix' and Churchill would be sitting in the same Conservative Cabinet presided over by Baldwin as Prime Minister.

On 16 June 1908, he was one of a dozen Conservatives who voted for the second reading of the Government's Old Age Pensions Bill, the first measure of its kind in English parliamentary history to reach the statute book. He was to remind his constituents of his record in this respect at the next General Election, adding that he had also supported, by his votes in the Committee stage, 'various amendments, which, if they had been accepted by the Government, would have given more relief to the aged poor'.[17]

Six days later, he made his maiden speech. The occasion was a debate on a Government Bill limiting work in the coal mines to eight hours a day. The Bill was the result of pressure from the Government's Labour supporters in the Commons; it was by no means generally endorsed from the government benches and among those who spoke against it was Baldwin's brother-in-law Aurelian Ridsdale and another backbencher named Russell Rea, who sat for the town of Gloucester. When Baldwin caught the Speaker's eye in the afternoon, it was near the dinner hour and he spoke to largely empty benches. He began by saying that he spoke for a class which he and his family had represented for four or five generations, 'a class which today is thought little of, though it has played some part in the State, a class once called "masters", then "employers of labour", and now "capitalists" – and, in the stress of elections, "capitalists" with an epithet in front of it'. After this mildly humorous beginning he complained that, standing as a Tariff Reformer at Kidderminster at the last General Election, he had been beaten by 'the cry from one end of the constituency to the other that the country should take care of the consumer, and the producer would take care of himself', whereas now the miners' representatives were asking the House 'to take care of the producer and let the consumer go to' – here he paused deliberately before completing the sentence which got him a laugh – 'to the textbooks of political economy!'[18]

He went on to twit Liberals like Ridsdale and Rea for what they had said in the debate. 'It may seem hardly necessary for Members on the Opposition side to rise and oppose the Bill when we have had such admirable diatribes against it from honourable gentlemen sitting behind the right honourable mover of the Bill. I am not yet sufficiently acquainted with the procedure of the House of Commons to understand how the honourable Member for Gloucester proposes, after his admirable speech, to vote for the Bill, but no doubt, when I have been a member as long as he has, I shall understand this and many other things likewise.'

This jest raised a further laugh, which encouraged the maiden speaker to continue on a more serious note:

> If it isn't egotistical, I should like to say that, in speaking of any question where capital and labour are involved, the personal equation must be considered. I may mention, not as of any interest to the House but merely as showing what the House may expect from me in the way of fair debate, that, though my family has been engaged for a hundred and thirty years in trade, the disputes we have had with our men can be numbered on the fingers of one hand. I myself have been in active business for twenty years, and I have never had the shadow of a dispute with any of my men.

Moreover, he added, Baldwins had long since given one section of their employees an eight-hour day, so that he 'might be acquitted of speaking as a man who is constitutionally against the interests of working men' and might 'claim to speak as honestly against the Bill as I believe others support it'.

He opposed the Bill, he said, because he believed it would raise the price of coal. The coal trade might not lose by this, though it might be plunged into 'a very serious state of strife'. But what of the rest of the country? 'It seems to me that a great many men, whose entire sympathies have been with Trade Unionists in the past, will look at it in this way: they will say that the miners are pushing this measure without any consideration for the interests of the commonwealth and only in the interest of their own Unions, and they may feel that they are benefiting the members of a rich and prosperous Union at the expense of other people less fortunately circumstanced.'

To ironical cheers from the Labour Members who belonged to the Miners' Federation, Baldwin retorted that he did not expect these gentlemen to agree with him. 'That is my belief,' he concluded, 'and I would not be acting honestly to the House if I did not give expression to it.'

The speech seems to have made remarkably little impression. No subsequent speaker in the debate, which eventually petered out with the adjournment of the House, thought it worth while congratulating Baldwin on his maiden effort. Nor did *The Times* lobby correspondent give it any mention, although its content was briefly reported in what was then the leading national newspaper. Baldwin himself dismissed it as a failure. 'I thought the speech a poor one,' he wrote at the time. 'It took twenty minutes and it was a deadly experience, but people have been extraordinarily kind about it.'[19]

He seems to have quickly settled down to the routine of the average backbencher, voting when required by the Party Whips, sitting on committees ('I have just sat on my first committee: it was a curious performance . . .'), and answering letters from constituents ('I have done over thirty letters today! The stream continues. So many people think I am interested in their views on the Licensing Bill but I am not.'). Much of Baldwin's first parliamentary session was indeed devoted to the contentious Licensing Bill, a government measure designed to reduce the numbers of licences to sell alcoholic drinks and at the same time to limit the compensation to dispossessed publicans. It was vigorously denounced from the Opposition benches, on which the brewing interests were well represented, as a step towards Socialism. Although Baldwin did not immediately realise its significance, the Licensing Bill was in effect the first stage in the impending constitutional struggle between the two Houses of Parliament, or 'peers against people', as it was popularly called. In the event, it was the rejection of the Licensing Bill by the Lords towards the end of the session in 1908 which encouraged the peers to throw out Mr Lloyd George's Budget in the following year.

There would have been no difficulty in Baldwin following up his maiden speech with as many other speeches as he cared to make during his first session, since there were relatively so few Conservatives in the House, and the Opposition Whips were only too glad for the members of their flock to intervene in debate as frequently as they could. But he preferred to bide his time and go slowly. He did not speak again during his first session and in the following session he only did so twice. The first occasion was the result of what he called 'a great stroke of luck' when he drew first place in the ballot for Private Members' Motions. 'I have chosen the question of the investment of British capital in foreign countries,' he wrote to his mother, 'and I only trust I shall do justice to the subject, for it is a great opportunity. A really good speech would give me a good lift, so I shall work hard at it.'[20]

He was well briefed by W. A. S. Hewins, the first director of the London School of Economics, who had become secretary of the Tariff Commission, a body of industrialists whose aim was to promote Joseph Chamberlain's Protectionist policies and encourage imperial economic unity through a system of preferential tariffs. Hewins, like Baldwin, was the son of an ironmaster, and had filled the chair of modern economic history at London University, but he never held any political office, although he was near to it on one occasion. His role, by no means unimportant, was to help ministers and backbenchers as a researcher.[21]

Baldwin's motion duly appeared on the Order Paper and the Hon. Member for West Worcestershire duly moved it in a poorly attended House at 8.30 in the evening of 17 March 1909. It read as follows:

That, in the opinion of this House, the feeling of insecurity due to the policy of His Majesty's Government, to the unfair competition of foreign producers in British markets, and to the high tariffs of foreign countries, has caused capital to be employed abroad which might have been used at home to the great advantage of the wage-earning population of the country.[22]

In his speech Baldwin contended that capital had been driven out of the country by the Government's financial policies declared through the mouth of Mr Lloyd George, the Chancellor of the Exchequer, whom he described as 'a mere shadow of his former self, wandering in a sort of Celtic twilight among figures'. The Chancellor, he went on, had expressed his intention to 'rob hen-roosts'. This in itself was 'enough to strike a chill into the heart of the studious working-man', because 'a hen-roost is possessed by nearly every man, every working-man, in the Kingdom'.

It is not your millionaire who is frightened by the Government's rash words. He is a mere episode. There are not many of them. They don't count. The people who are frightened are the hundreds of thousands of people with a little. If you put any difficulty in the way of the thrifty people of all classes, if they are not encouraged to invest, it is a bad thing for the industries of the country, and all your efforts to raise and improve the position of the working-classes, whether with regard to hours of labour or wages, will come to nothing unless you can guarantee for the industries of the country an environment of security and an ample amount of capital for the use of those industries.

Baldwin's speech showed a considerable improvement on his maiden performance and was listened to attentively, among others by the former Chancellor of the Exchequer Austen Chamberlain, who referred to it as 'remarkable both for its form and matter' and expressed his regret that 'our old friend his father could not be here to listen to it'. In winding up for the Government, Winston Churchill, President of the Board of Trade, spoke of the mover's 'good and careful speech', but like most of the other speakers he did not waste much time on it. The minister did not deny that British capital was going abroad, but he thought this on the whole a good thing. Since much of it was in the Empire, it helped to bind Canada and Australia more closely to the Mother country. As for Baldwin's motion, Churchill supported a hostile amendment which had been moved by Mr Russell Rea disapproving of tariffs and approving the export of capital 'as an important instrument for maintaining cheap supplies of food for the people and raw materials for the manufacturers of this country'. The amendment was carried by 230 to 72 votes, and this in effect ended the debate.

'I got through all right and my friends were very kind in their congratulations,' he wrote to his mother when it was over. 'But it is difficult work making one's way in a place like the House of Commons. Keep on pounding at 'em is the only thing. I shall gain a little confidence each time.'[23]

One gratifying result of his speech was an invitation from Mr Balfour to lunch. To his surprise he found himself placed on his Party leader's right, where he seems to have been sounded out about possible future contributions to parliamentary discussion. But he was in no hurry to be called again by the Speaker and in fact did not rise again from his place for another four months when he spoke briefly on a railway bill after an all-night sitting.[24] 'There was no time for bed,' he wrote to his mother having returned home at 9.30 a.m. for breakfast, 'so I went straight on, and in the evening fired off a speech on behalf of the North Eastern Railway which I am told was all right.' At a constituency meeting in Bewdley at this time he stressed what he considered the only alternative to the latest example of 'Cobdenite finance' in the Budget.

Accordingly a campaign is entered upon by which an attempt is made to stir up the envy and hatred of the poorer people against the richer people – not realising that the only way to increase the permanent prosperity of the country is not by threatening industry and spoiling individuals but by taking steps to protect trade that will increase the amount available for wages. This of course will alone make money filter through to the people. I am against the Budget as a whole because it is brought in as an alternative to tariff reform, which I believe is the only policy that will save the industries of this country and the wages of the people in the years of international competition that are ahead.[25]

The Budget controversy came to a head on 30 November 1909, when the Finance Bill which embodied its provisions was thrown out in its entirety by the House of Lords, the voting against it being 350 to 75. Asquith immediately determined to appeal to the country, Parliament was dissolved, and Baldwin among others went down to his constituency to fight another General Election.

This time he was opposed by a Liberal, apparently not with any intention of dislodging him, since the Bewdley seat was quite safe, but in order to prevent him campaigning in support of other Tory candidates elsewhere. His election address, which he composed during the last week of December, to some extent repeated what he had said in 1906 with the addition of a reminder about his record on the Old Age Pensions Act and a brief statement of his attitude on the burning issue of the day. 'The Radical Party wish to take away the power of the House of Lords,' he wrote, 'in order to facilitate, amongst other things, the passage of a Home Rule Bill [for Ireland] knowing that this is a policy which for twenty years the people of England have refused to support. I am opposed to any alteration of the Constitution that will give power to one House alone to pass Measures which are not in accord with the *Will of the People* and the best interests of the Empire.'[26] Polling took place on 21 January 1910, and Baldwin was returned by a comfortable majority of 4,240, which so pleased the constituency party that they presented the candidate's wife with a diamond brooch as a token of the victory.

The result of the Election in January 1910 was a serious loss of strength to the Government. The commanding Liberal majority of 1906 over all parties in the House of Commons disappeared, the Liberals coming back only 275 strong as against 273 Conservatives and Unionists, while the Irish Nationalists won 82 seats and the Labour Party 40. Thus the Irish Nationalists once again held the balance of power at Westminster and were in a good position to enforce their leader John Redmond's threat to make Asquith 'toe the line' on the Home Rule issue. In return for this they were prepared to support the Government's plan to curb the powers of the Lords and vote with the Liberals generally.

In an attempt to rid himself of the irritating and humiliating dependence on the Redmond faction, Asquith called another General Election in December of the same year. Unfortunately for the Liberal Premier, this left things in terms of party strengths in the Commons almost exactly what they had been before.

Although he was returned unopposed at the second election of 1910, Baldwin found what he called the 'infernal electioneering' a burden. 'It would all be unbearable if it wasn't one's rather obvious duty and if one hadn't the love of friends all around,' he wrote to his aunt Edith Macdonald with his father's record in mind. 'And when one of the generation in front of me drops out of the ranks, it acts as a stimulus to me to push on, for the time is short, so that I may not be ashamed when I meet once more those who fought a good fight while they were with us.' [27]

4

'I had the good fortune to hear Stan speak,' Lucy Baldwin wrote in February 1911, 'and he spoke very well and so distinctly it was a pleasure to listen to such a change from some of the mumblers. He is getting over his nervousness.' Yet he remained a relatively silent backbencher, making only four speeches during the next three years in the House of Commons, apart from several brief interventions in the standing committee on the National Insurance Bill, a measure of which he approved in principle.

A few days after Bonar Law's election as Conservative and Unionist leader in November 1911, following Balfour's resignation, Baldwin was described as 'a railway magnate' in a list of MPs submitted to the new leader who were expected to respond to a motion by the Labour member Ramsay MacDonald, 'in effect a vote of censure on the railway companies'.[28] But Baldwin did not intervene on this occasion. Nor did he harry ministers with parliamentary questions designed to embarrass them, but restricted himself to such mild topics as post office savings and the quality of the horse rugs and the fodder provided for the Worcester-shire Yeomanry on manoeuvres. Indeed there was a certain unconscious prophetic insight in a photograph taken of Stanley Baldwin playing tennis at this time and about to receive his opponent's service. Underneath the picture his wife wrote: 'He also serves who only stands and waits.'

The Irish Nationalist MP and journalist, T. P. O'Connor, described how Baldwin impressed him in those days:

> For a long time after his entrance into the House he was probably unknown even by sight to the majority of his colleagues. He sought the obscure seats, and avoided the seats of the mighty. He did not try, as so many of the young and ambitious do, even the comparatively small conspicuousness of the corner seat . . .
>
> He wasn't playing a game – there is nothing in him that suggests a man playing a game – but that was just his temperament. He did not crave for notoriety or for plaudits; he almost exaggerated the part of the humdrum Englishman of business who had his job to do and did it unostentatiously and thoroughly and left the rest to fortune.[29]

In June 1912, he intervened in a debate initiated by Austen Chamberlain on the great dock strike in the Port of London. He spoke, he said, as a businessman who was proud to think that, during the twenty years he had been directly responsible for the management of a large number of men, there had never been any question of a lock-out or strike. He took the opportunity to criticise the Government for what he felt was their in-effective interference in the dispute particularly in not stopping intimi-dating forms of picketing and waiting until a breach of the peace had oc-curred. While he approved of the principle of collective bargaining be-tween trade unions and employers, he expressed the opinion that 'the great tragedy of these strikes is that, when so many of the men's leaders think to promote the interests of their own class and to elevate them and raise their wages . . . the only result of those strikes must be . . . to depress it, because the harm that is done and the damage that is done to the commerce of the country is far greater than anything the men can hope to get back, and any temporary advantage they may obtain'.[30]

The miners came out in sympathy with the dockers and the strike in coalfields spread throughout the country. As a result many industrial employers who depended upon coal, including Baldwins, were obliged to lay off their workers. This is how Stanley Baldwin later described what happened at his works and how he dealt with the situation.

We tried to carry on as long as we could, but, of course, it became more and more difficult to carry on, and gradually furnace after furnace was damped down and the chimneys ceased to smoke, and about 1,000 men, who had no interest in the dispute that was going on, were thrown out of work, through no fault of their own, at a time when there was no unemployment benefit . . .

It seemed to me at that time a monstrous injustice to these men, because I looked upon them as my own family, and it hit me very hard . . . and I made an allowance to them, not a large one, but something for six weeks to carry them along, because I felt they were being so unfairly treated.[31]*

The plight of the labourer in the fields likewise enlisted Baldwin's sympathy. In November 1912, he joined several other Tory backbenchers, including the future Lords Astor, Halifax, Mountemple and Swinton, in addressing a letter to Bonar Law, who had by this time succeeded Balfour as Leader of the Opposition, on the need for an inquiry to ascertain the best way of raising the wages of agricultural workers, especially 'in those districts where wages are notoriously low'.[32]

The Baldwin children were now growing up. Oliver, the elder boy, was already at Eton, to which his father sent him no doubt remembering his own unhappy experience of Harrow, though Oliver seems to have liked Eton even less. Years later when he was filling in his entry in *Who's Who*, Oliver was to write of his education: 'in football at Eton; in other things beginning to learn'. The children relished the long, hot summers at Astley, the regular visits from friends and relations, and the dances at Christmas for fifty to a hundred guests. The Kipling cousins were frequent visitors, as also were Bonar Law's children who had recently lost their mother. 'You have been much in my mind,' wrote Baldwin to the future Tory leader with 'sincerest sympathy'.[33] If the Baldwins' country house entertaining was modest by some Edwardian standards, it was made possible by a domestic staff, which included a butler and eight other indoor servants, as well as ten gardeners and a boy. After the children had gone back to school, Baldwin and his wife would usually have a short winter sports holiday in Switzerland, skiing and skating and taking German lessons. Politics apart, it was a happy and largely carefree life.

The new intake of Conservative members in the second election in 1910 included the young Canadian millionaire Max Aitken, who was a particular

* He gave this account to the House of Commons in his so-called 'peace in industry' speech during the debate on the Second Reading of the Trade Union (Political Fund) Bill on 6 March 1925.

friend of Bonar Law and whose acquaintance Baldwin made at this time. Soon they were lunching together, the beginning of a long and by no means harmonious association. Aitken owed his initial appearance on the English political scene partly to Bonar Law and partly to R. D. Blumenfeld, the editor and chairman of the *Daily Express*, a newspaper which the new Canadian MP, who at the time of his return for Ashton-under-Lyme was not even eligible to vote in a parliamentary election, was shortly to acquire and revitalise, although he was to retain Blumenfeld as editor. Baldwin also became on good terms with 'R.D.B.', whom he met at the Carlton Club, when (as he was subsequently to remind the newspaperman) he was 'innocent of office and . . . inclined to think Cabinet Ministers great men'.[34] During this Parliament the Opposition backbenchers were also joined by an old friend of Baldwin's, William Hewins, the secretary of the Tariff Commission, who came in at a by-election for Hereford City.

In 1913, Baldwin opposed the disestablishment and disendowment of the Welsh Church, because, he said, 'it is one thing to do good to your own soul by renouncing your own earthly goods, but it is quite another to do good to another man's soul by taking away *his* goods'. He was surprised by the congratulations which he received not only from members of his own Party but from the Government Front Bench. 'It has been very interesting to see the result of an unpretending little speech,' he told his mother, 'just because the point of view had not been put before and because people felt one believed what one said. It will encourage me to try again and I shall try again to say what I really think.'[35]

In fact, eleven months elapsed before he did try again. This was perhaps his most statesmanlike utterance to date, when he spoke on the Budget of 1914, castigating Lloyd George, the Chancellor, for rushing about the country making propaganda speeches and taking Asquith, the Prime Minister, to task for declaring that 'we could look for no remission of taxation in future', and that the constant pressure of public opinion would not only keep public expenditure high but force it still higher.

It is of the very highest importance that men who occupy great positions in public life, and who call themselves leaders of the people, should really be leaders of the people, and not wait for pressure to be exercised on them from the outside. In other words, I think it ought to be an integral part of a statesman's duty today, when speaking on platforms, not only to point out to the people the benefits that may accrue to them by expenditure on social legislation, but to point out with equal candour and fairness what the charges on the nation will be for such benefits, so that the people, who have not got the necessary training to form a judgement in these matters, may be able to form some reasoned judgement as to whether . . . the net result of legis- lation for social purposes is going to be a gain or a loss to the community as a whole.[36]

Among those who listened to this speech was the Prime Minister who was in his usual place on the Treasury Bench. Sir John Simon, the youthful Solicitor-General – he was only thirty-seven at the time of his appointment in 1910 – happened to be sitting beside Asquith, who did not know who the speaker was. Asquith whispered to Simon: 'Do you notice what good English this man talks?' On learning Baldwin's identity, Asquith reached for a copy of *Dod's Parliamentary Companion*, that invaluable little work of parliamentary biography, which was lying on the table in front of him, and which Baldwin himself was frequently to consult. Simon was afterwards to recall how the Prime Minister immediately recognised the name and pointed out to him that the speaker was the son of a former Member, who had been Chairman of the Great Western Railway.[37]

5

Apart from recording his vote in the Opposition Lobby in response to the Whips, Baldwin made no other contribution to the Home Rule Bill, which having passed the Commons three times and been three times rejected by the Lords was due to become law in accordance with the provisions of the Parliament Act, which had only reached the statute book in the face of Asquith's threat to create a sufficient number of peers to swamp the Tory opposition in the Upper House. The Ulster Unionists were advocat- ing the use of arms rather than submit to the rule of a Dublin Parliament and to this end their leaders had indulged in some spectacular gun- running. The feeling at Westminster, where there was a desire to reach an all-party solution, was reflected in a letter which Baldwin wrote to his mother in March 1914.

Certain it is that never in our lives have we been standing on such a perilous brink. There is a move among moderate men on both sides to get some compromise that will make for peace, the one idea being at any cost to save the country either from civil war or from a wild campaign against the army. [Sir Edward] Grey [the Foreign Secretary] is in charge today and neither [Lloyd] George nor Winston [Churchill] is in the House, with the result that the debate is proceeding in a calmer air, and Grey has said in effect that the Government will consider almost any suggestion from our side. Ordinarily it would not be for us to suggest, but I hope we may now: things are much too serious for us to hold our hands and wait.[38]

In the event King George V intervened by calling the various Party leaders to a conference at Buckingham Palace. It was not long before the conference was deadlocked, and civil war was only averted by the greater world conflict which began a few days later.

Britain went to war with Germany on the day after Baldwin's forty-seventh birthday. 'I think Germany has suddenly gone mad,' he wrote to his mother on 4 August. 'I can't think of any other explanation that fits the case.' He remembered seeing a group of 'men walking down Kensington Gore, being splashed by the mud from taxi-cabs as they went on their way to drill. They were the first volunteers to join Kitchener's Army, and, as I saw them, I wished that I was with them. I wanted to do service for my country . . .'[39]

He was too old for active military service. He might have been accepted, it is true, if he had lied to the recruiting officer about his age, but this would have been out of character, and he never consciously told a lie. Most of those who did so in this instance might have been better employed elsewhere. In Baldwin's case the chance of rendering useful war service came in June 1915 when he was appointed a lay member of a judicial committee, which sat in Westminster Hall and was presided over by Mr Justice Sankey, for the purpose of reviewing the cases of enemy aliens who had been arrested and interned under Regulation 14B of the Defence of the Realm Act. Two manuscript notebooks filled by Baldwin's neat hand with details of the cases testify to the care with which he discharged his unpaid task.[40]

'We did our twelve thousandth case yesterday,' he wrote to his mother after six months on this committee, 'and I put in a really good day, eight hours in committee and nearly three writing up cases at the Athenaeum in the evening. We have nearly finished the internments.'[41] In fact, internment orders continued to be made and appeals to be heard for virtually the duration of the war, and Baldwin was to continue to serve on the committee for a further eighteen months. The majority of the cases were straightforward, concerning enemy subjects who were interned automatically and former enemy nationals who had become naturalised British subjects. In addition there were British subjects of proved enemy or anti-British sympathies. One of these was Ernest Blythe, the well-known Sinn Fein organiser, who was subsequently to hold several ministerial posts in the

Irish Free State Government. Another was J. B. Askew, an old Etonian and Oxford graduate, who had married a German and had spent many years in Germany; he was also a Socialist and belonged to a Communist club. At the hearing of his appeal, several prominent Labour Party members including Ramsay MacDonald and Philip Snowden spoke on his behalf, but in spite of their testimonials the internment order was confirmed in his case.

Occasionally the appeals succeeded and the internees were released. Among the latter was Harold Fraser, a journalist of Scottish parentage, who had been born in Chicago where his father was Professor of English Literature at the University there. On account of his Scottish antecedents, he asked for his appeal to be heard in Scotland. ('A patriotic bugger,' observed Mr Justice Sankey.) His request was refused, but after the editor of the *Daily Chronicle* and others had testified for him, the committee ordered his release. Another successful appellant was a naturalised German named J. W. Gruban, whose engineering firm had been one of the first to produce machine tools for use in the manufacture of munitions on the outbreak of war. Unfortunately for him an unscrupulous Liberal MP, Frederick Handel Booth, had got himself on to the board of Gruban's company by falsely representing that he had such influence with the Ministry of Munitions as to protect Gruban from attack on account of his German origin, also that unless Gruban resigned as managing director of the company and handed over all his interest in it to Handel Booth he would be interned. In fact, Gruban was interned as the direct result of a letter which the Ministry received from Booth. No doubt Booth hoped that Gruban would be kept in internment for the rest of the war, but Gruban fought back and appealed. Not only was his appeal allowed when the committee had heard his story, but he was advised on his release to seek the advice of the best solicitor he could find with a view to taking proceedings in the courts. The result was that Gruban brought an action against Handel Booth for fraudulent misrepresentation and was awarded damages amounting to £4,750, after a trial which attracted the greatest publicity, exposing Handel Booth for the rogue that he was and bringing his career as an MP to an ignominious end.*

The sinking of the *Lusitania*, which occurred in the month before Baldwin joined the committee, led to an outbreak of spy-mania in the country, and some internment orders seem to have been made on the merest sus-

---

* For a detailed account of the whole case, see the present writer's *Sir Patrick Hastings* (1960), pp. 57–67. Hastings, who appeared for Gruban afterwards wrote: 'If I wished to quote one particular example of impartiality and strict fair play, I should choose the jury who tried the case of Gruban against Booth.' Booth, who described himself in the later editions of *Who's Who* as a 'retired ironmaster', died in 1947.

picion. One such order was made in the case of a journalist named Graham Scott, who worked for *The Globe*. At the hearing in Westminster Hall he told 'an extraordinary story' to the effect that his editor had commissioned him to act as English correspondent with the Germany Army, that the Foreign Office was aware of this assignment and had actually provided him with a passport for the purpose about ten days after the war had begun. 'The Committee believed this whole story to be a hallucination,' wrote Baldwin in his notes, 'but they have sent for the documents which Scott alleges are in the custody of his solicitor.' But the story turned out to be quite true, and the passport dated 13 August 1914 and describing the holder as 'Correspondent-in-chief *Globe* with the Germany Army' was actually produced to the committee. This enterprising journalist, who seems to have been arrested on attempting to leave the country, was recommended for release 'under conditions', one of which presumably was that he should not try to do it again.

Another good spy story, which Baldwin liked to recall in later years, derived from his experience on the Aliens Committee at this time.

> Several transports leaving Malta had been destroyed by submarines. Four enemy spies were working in collaboration, and one of them, a monk of English origin, living in Barcelona, split, and with his assistance a member of our Secret Service was sent out by the most devious route, and with the aid of destroyers, to a house in Malta where he asked for a Madame X. He was told she had left on the previous day, but forced his way in and found a lady upstairs packing, demanded from her a copy of Larousse's Dictionary (underlined words in the Dictionary had been used as a code) but she denied possessing a copy, and invited the visitor to search her trunks. He found nothing, watched her movements for some time, and then announced the Dictionary was in her bustle. The game was up and she produced it.[42]

One of the most interesting and difficult cases under Regulation 14B, which Baldwin had to consider, was that of Philip Alexius László de Lombos, otherwise the fashionable portrait painter Philip de László. A Hungarian Jew by birth, the son of a Budapest tailor, de László had come as a young man to England, where he married into the wealthy Guinness family, eventually settling in this country in 1907 and painting many well-known society figures including King Edward VII. He retained his Austro-Hungarian nationality until the eve of the outbreak of the war, when he applied for a certificate of naturalisation, his application being supported among others by A. J. Balfour; it was rushed through shortly afterwards as the result of pressure from de László on the Home Secretary Reginald McKenna. He was known to have strong pro-Hungarian sympathies, which he made no attempt to conceal from some of the distinguished sitters in his studio. He also admitted to having infringed various war-time regulations in sending money to his family in Hungary and communicating with his relatives and friends there through the Dutch diplomatic bag; he likewise pleaded guilty to helping a fugitive Hungarian officer to escape.

According to some allied intelligence reports, based largely on intercepted correspondence, there were grounds for believing that he was employed as an Austrian spy. This he denied, and it is only fair to add that the authorities, which decided after the war not to revoke his naturalisation certificate, were satisfied that there was no credible evidence of disaffection or disloyalty on his part. However, the Sankey Committee decided that his Hungarian connections justified his being no longer allowed to remain at liberty and he was consequently interned, although by the time the order was made in this case, in September 1917, Baldwin had ceased to be a member of the committee.

During the two years that he served on the committee, Baldwin would sometimes complain of 'having to get to Westminster Hall with a long and dull list of cases', with the feeling that his work was all on top of him, as if he were wrestling with an infinite amount of 'bedclothes' that were slowly suffocating him. 'I always have a double prayer about my work – ability to do it, whatever and wherever it is, and to do it with cheerfulness,' he wrote at the end of 1916. 'Every day for eight years have I asked for those two things.' [43] Soon his sphere of endeavour was to be unexpectedly enlarged.

6

Besides the Aliens Committee, Baldwin's war work involved service on two other government committees, one on War Office contracts and the other on post-war trade problems in the light of German economic penetration. These additional assignments were due to the activities of a Conservative 'ginger group' of backbenchers which included Baldwin and originated in a meeting early in 1915 at the offices of the Irish Unionist Alliance under the chairmanship of Walter Long, MP, who had been Chief Secretary for Ireland in the Balfour Government and was a leading anti-Home Ruler. Known as the Unionist Business Committee, the group which rapidly grew in membership and came to include nearly all those backbench Conservative MPs who were not at the front, aimed at a more efficient prosecution of the war and advocated such measures as conscription and the government control of merchant shipping.[44]

The Business Committee also had a good deal to do with compelling Asquith to take a number of the Opposition Front Bench Conservatives into the Government in May 1915, thus forming the First Coalition, in which the Liberals retained the principal posts and which, in spite of this fact, the group helped to sustain throughout most of 1916. When news of an intrigue between some right-wing Conservatives and left-wing Liberals to upset the Government reached the Business Committee in March 1916, it says something for Baldwin's standing and influence that his house in Eaton Square was chosen as the venue for a meeting of about seventy rank-and-file Conservatives in order to counter what Lucy Baldwin called a 'gunpowder plot'. 'Great fun watching them come in,' she noted in her diary for 20 March, 'some furtively, some more excitedly.' The outcome was that the plot came to nothing, principally because Bonar Law, with whom the Business Committee kept closely in touch, saw no alternative to Asquith's resignation but a General Election which was unthinkable in war-time. Yet Baldwin wondered whether he would not be better employed in doing local work for the war effort in Worcestershire and at one time he seriously thought of giving up national politics altogether and retiring to Astley. 'I'm no good here,' he told his wife: 'better go back.' She thought he might be right, but after talking it over persuaded him to stay on. 'Let's give it ten years,' she said, and he agreed.[45]

With each passing month, opposition to Asquith's leadership continued to grow among the disgruntled Conservatives and Unionists, who found a powerful and influential spokesman in Sir Edward Carson, the Irish Unionist leader, who had been a member of the Asquith Coalition in its early days but had resigned towards the end of 1915. This development placed an increasing strain on Bonar Law's loyalty to the Prime Minister, not to mention an increasing difficulty with the Conservative Whips in supporting the Government with the votes of their followers. In November 1916, Baldwin breakfasted with his cousin Rudyard Kipling in Brown's Hotel and they talked politics for two hours. ('I was highly pleased to find that he had come to the same conclusion about the Government as I had, and by the same road, after almost as long and as anxious a cogitation.') They both agreed that Asquith did not appear to realise the extent of his unpopularity in Parliament and the country and that sooner or later there must be a political crisis of the first magnitude.

It was touched off in the same month by a debate in the House of Commons initiated by Carson on the sale of certain enemy properties engaged mainly in the production of palm kernels in Nigeria. Bonar Law, who was Colonial Secretary, proposed to allow neutrals to bid for these properties. Carson and his friends, who claimed to have information that some at least of the neutrals interested were really acting on behalf of the enemy, moved that the purchasers be confined to British-born subjects or wholly British companies. Stung by Carson's reproaches that he was playing the enemy's game, Bonar Law declared that the issue was one of confidence in the Government and warned Carson that it would be the end of the Coalition in its present form if the motion were carried to a successful division. Baldwin supported his Conservative leader by speaking and voting against Carson's motion, but he seems to have had some struggle with his conscience as he justified his action solely on economic grounds.[46] When the division bells rang, only 73 out of 286 Conservative and Unionist members went into the Government lobby. It was the beginning of the break-up of the Asquith Coalition, since the Government majority of 114 in this debate was largely secured by Liberal, Labour and Irish Nationalist votes. Bonar Law's friend and fellow-Canadian, Sir Max Aitken, thereupon urged the Conservative leader to resign, but this Bonar Law refused to do, since by doing so he foresaw the total withdrawal of Conservative support from the Coalition and the return to party polemics to which in the circumstances of the war he could not reconcile himself.

Within a month Asquith had resigned and Lloyd George had become Prime Minister. The story of this dramatic change has been often told, among others by the present writer in his biography of Carson, and there is no need to repeat the details here, except to record that immediately after Asquith left Buckingham Palace the King sent for Bonar Law as Conservative leader and invited him to form a government. While Lloyd George was prepared to serve under Bonar Law, Asquith was not, and neither Bonar Law nor Balfour, who was also consulted, felt that he could head an administration in which Asquith was not included. In the end, Bonar Law advised the King to send for the man whose leadership in his view 'was most likely to win the war'. This was done and Lloyd George moved into Downing Street where he quickly formed a new Coalition. In this Bonar Law agreed to serve as Chancellor of the Exchequer and Leader of the House of Commons. He also agreed to join the four-man War Cabinet, whose members with the exception of himself were to be free from departmental duties so as to enable them to concentrate upon the direction of the war.*

---

* The other two members were Lord Curzon, the Lord President of the Council and Leader of the House of Lords, and Arthur Henderson, Secretary of the Labour Party. Carson attended initially but soon dropped out.

Bonar Law thus occupied a position of power second only to that of Lloyd George himself. Much depended for his success as a minister on his Parliamentary Private Secretary. John Baird (later Lord Stonehaven), who had served his chief in this capacity ever since the latter's election as Conservative leader in 1911, was anxious for a change which would enable him to take a more active part in the war, and in fact had been invited to join the Air Board. Bonar Law accordingly agreed to let him go after he had found a suitable replacement. Then, after some discussion and reflection, he sent for Baldwin and offered him the job. But he did so with a noticeable lack of enthusiasm, telling Baldwin 'in his usual modest way' that 'he did not suppose I should care for it' and furthermore that it was unpaid.[47] He went on to say that the new Financial Secretary to the Treasury, Mr Hardman Lever, a chartered accountant who had been of considerable help to Lloyd George at the Ministry of Munitions, was an unorthodox and questionable appointment, since he had no seat in the House of Commons and, although he was an expert in cost accountancy, he did not know much about national finance and parliamentary procedure. Baldwin would therefore be expected when necessary to answer for Lever's office in the Commons.

After talking it over with Bonar Law's Private Secretary John Davidson, Baldwin decided to accept, 'because', as he was to put it, 'I believed that at my time of life, having already sufficient means to be independent of the active business in which I had passed my life up to then, I had the opportunity of giving my services to the country without any feeling that it was necessary to be remunerated for them'.[48] He gave his wife the news on 15 December 1916 when he and John Davidson saw Bonar Law into the Chancellor's official residence at 11 Downing Street.

Several individuals subsequently claimed the credit for having persuaded Bonar Law to make this appointment. One of them was Max Aitken, soon to become Lord Beaverbrook. ('I recommended Mr Baldwin to Mr Bonar Law as his Parliamentary [Private] Secretary – the first step in his upward career. I admit I did not foresee in any way the remarkable talents he was going to develop. He seemed simply a sound, steady man who could be absolutely depended upon by his parliamentary chief.')[49] Another friend of Bonar Law's who certainly spoke up for Baldwin was Ralph Blumenfeld, the editor of Beaverbrook's newspaper *The Daily Express*, since Baldwin is on record for having thanked the editor afterwards for his efforts on his behalf. ('I admire your courage in backing a rank outsider, it doesn't often come off.')[50] However, the decisive voice, as usually happens in appointments of this kind, particularly when the minister holds a key post in the Cabinet, was the Conservative Chief Whip Lord Edmund Talbot, since the prime duty of a PPS, apart from the usual 'fetching and carrying' for his master within the precincts of the House, is to act as liaison between him and the Party backbenchers and to reflect backbench opinion to the minister. For this reason the PPS is expected to work closely with the Whips' office.

The precise manner in which Baldwin came to be appointed has been described by John Davidson in an undated memorandum:

> Ned Talbot and Sir George Younger [Conservative Party Chairman], with whom I had already become close friends, came one day to have a talk about a successor to Baird as Bonar's PPS. I suggested he should be an older man who would not be likely to be taken for military service, and who could give his full time to the job, and above all keep his mouth shut. Having gone through several names, we decided that Stanley Baldwin, a Worcestershire Member with a long Parliamentary tradition and a reputation for taciturnity, who was doing good work on the 14B Committee and whose children had met the Laws socially, would be the best candidate. Younger was doubtful, but Ned Talbot backed me and the result was that Baldwin was invited to play tennis at Pembroke Lodge* in order that Bonar should have a look at him, and I suggested that he should have a talk with him himself, which he did. Baldwin was somewhat taken aback, but after an hour's talk with me at the Colonial Office, when I explained to him the nature of his duties, his modesty gave way to his sense of duty, and he accepted.[51]†

As Bonar Law's PPS, Baldwin was given a room opening off his chief's in the House of Commons, while in the mornings, and at other times when his presence was not required in the Commons, he worked with Lever in the Treasury. However, the latter arrangement only lasted for a few weeks, since Lloyd George decided to send the Financial Secretary to New York to represent the Treasury in the purchase of war supplies. Lever, who had worked there for many years and knew the leading American industrialists and financiers, consequently departed with a knighthood to boost his ego, and Baldwin moved into his room at the Treasury and took over his work. On 30 January 1917, it was announced that in addition to being Bonar

---

* Bonar Law's house in Kensington.
† According to Wickham Steed, then foreign editor of *The Times*, the choice was not due to any belief in Baldwin's 'cleverness'. 'It was made on the assumption that he was discreet enough to be "safe" and "stupid" enough not to intrigue.' Wickham Steed, *The Real Stanley Baldwin* (1930), p. 26.

Law's PPS, Mr Stanley Baldwin had been appointed a Junior Lord of the Treasury (unpaid). This office is usually occupied by an Assistant Whip, but in this instance it was stated to be an exceptional arrangement to enable Baldwin to act in effect as Under-Secretary to the Chancellor of the Exchequer, 'answering parliamentary questions on points of detail and rendering the sort of assistance given by the Financial Secretary to the Treasury when he was a Member of the House of Commons'.[52] In the event Sir Hardman Lever never again occupied his old room, since the United States came into the war shortly afterwards and he stayed on as principal Treasury representative in North America for the duration.

'It is all exceedingly interesting,' Baldwin wrote to his mother on the eve of Lever's departure: 'one is in the very centre of the spider's web and, as I always wanted a full-time job, I can't complain now I have got one!'[53]

THREE

ASCENT TO THE CABINET

I

One result of becoming a junior member of the Government, even though his post carried no salary, was that Stanley Baldwin had to give up his remunerative company directorships, and to cease attending board meetings and drawing directors' fees, although he was still able to benefit from the dividends which in the case of his holding in Baldwins, the family business, were by no means inconsiderable. Here he owned 180,000 shares on his own account, as well as a number of preference shares. The ordinary £1 shares, which in 1913 were quoted on the London Stock Exchange as only a little above par, stood at 55s. when Baldwin joined the Government; they were eventually to rise above £3, due to the great demand during the war for steel in the manufacture of arms and munitions. Baldwin, it may be noted here, never sold out any portion of his holding in this period which he might have done at great profit to himself. Indeed he was to live to see the shares one day touch a record low level of 1s. 8d., which they did in 1931. Meanwhile in 1916 and 1917 Baldwins paid a dividend of 12½ per cent, of which 2½ per cent was a tax-free bonus, so that the junior minister found both his capital and his income from this business greatly increased by its war-time trading.[1]

Baldwin made his first appearance on the Government Front Bench on 13 February 1917, when he was in charge of a small group of Supplementary Estimates. The date was the anniversary of his father's death and on the previous day he wrote to his mother at Wilden:

He would have been so pleased, and if there is any knowledge with him of what we do, the knowledge that in our several ways we try to do our duty must be a joy to him.

I wish I could look in on you on Tuesday [the 13th] and indeed often, but I am sure I am right in undertaking this work here. We both believe there is guidance in these things. I never sought a place, never expected it, and suddenly a way opened and an offer of wider service was made. If one tackles public life in the right spirit, it is an unselfish service . . . If we are returned again and I am offered a post, then I shall have to decide finally between commerce and public life. And if I live, the experience of the next six months should enable me to choose.[2]

'My peaceful life is a thing of the past,' he wrote when his first ordeal on the Treasury Bench was over: 'it is all alarums and excursions, and in the House, when I am not the butt of that assembly, I am cornered and button-holed by all and sundry from T. P. O'Connor to Mr Outhwaite. The hen is not hatched that can out-sit me.' * And again: 'I am still enjoying the work, and after a month's experience I don't feel that I shall fail. I am gaining in a modest confidence!'[3]

The first five per cent War Loan had been launched by Bonar Law the previous month in a blaze of publicity, against the advice of the financial experts who favoured a higher interest rate, and it now fell to Baldwin to help his chief to get the necessary legislation through the House. Thus, he had to defend the inclusion in the prospectus of provision for a depreciation fund to allow the Treasury to intervene and support the price of the stock, so as to protect the capital value of the investment. On the whole he put up a creditable performance. Incidentally the flotation of this loan, redeemable after twelve years, was a remarkable success, £100 million being subscribed by the time the lists closed on 16 February, and it abundantly confirmed the Chancellor's estimate of public patriotism, in which Baldwin concurred. Then came the record Budget of nearly £2,200 million, which Bonar Law opened on 2 May, leaving it to Baldwin to wind up the ensuing debate. The principal change was to raise the Excess Profits Duty from 60 to 80 per cent, but owing to the lack of effective price control even this heavy tax did not prevent large profiteering by unscrupulous manufacturers of war material.

At the end of June 1917, Baldwin's services in handling the Finance Bill were rewarded by the formal appointment of Financial Secretary to the Treasury at a salary of £2,000 a year. He wrote on hearing the news: 'It is a compliment that I appreciate; though I have been doing the work since January, it is nice to have the office. I have really been extraordinarily lucky.'[4]

---

* R. L. Outhwaite, a native of Tasmania, represented one of the Birmingham divisions as a Liberal and had the reputation of being a great bore.

The new minister appeared to be a regular glutton for work and thought nothing of spending thirteen or fourteen hours without a break on the Front Bench piloting the Finance Bill through the committee stage. ('I don't feel a penny the worse . . .') But he yearned for his Worcestershire home, as he sat cooped up in Treasury Chambers during the hot summer. 'I can't tell you how much I miss Astley,' he wrote to one of his daughters at this time. 'I had such a lovely holiday last year I was spoilt. I can see you all drifting out into the garden to breakfast and the line of hills over the lavender bushes. Well, well, I am not the only one at work, and if I had been younger I should have been in France and probably under the ground by now. I have no cause to grumble.' His son Oliver, now eighteen, had already joined the Army, which worried him, since Bonar Law had just lost one of his sons in the fighting in France.

When the House rose for the summer recess in August, the Financial Secretary began to show some signs of strain as he laboured on at his desk in Whitehall. 'My work gets more instead of less: I don't quite know how to stop it . . . I get quite stupid by Sunday . . . Two mornings a week I leave at a quarter to ten for my office, and three mornings I go first to the Bank of England, which is an odd start for the day, isn't it?'[5]

Baldwin's tri-weekly visits to Threadneedle Street were the outcome of a violent quarrel between the Chancellor and the Bank's autocratic and choleric Governor Lord Cunliffe, who complained that the Treasury advisers, particularly Sir Robert Chalmers, the Permanent Secretary, and the brilliant and unorthodox economist and head of the external finance department, John Maynard Keynes, were continuing to meddle in City matters contrary to a promise made by Bonar Law's predecessor Reginald McKenna. Cunliffe also complained that the London Exchange Committee, which had been set up by McKenna under Cunliffe's chairmanship to deal with questions of foreign currency, was being bypassed by the Treasury officials, and he went so far as to demand that Chalmers should be dismissed. Bonar Law, who wished to co-operate amicably with the Bank, now proposed that the Exchange Committee should meet at the Treasury to ensure closer co-operation, and that Mr Baldwin, the Joint Financial Secretary, should be a member of it. But this did not satisfy Cunliffe. The very next day he informed Bonar Law that on his own initiative he had instructed the Canadian Government not to hand over to the Treasury any of the Bank's gold, of which large quantities had been sent to Canada as a precaution in the event of German invasion, if asked to do so by Sir Hardman Lever, the other Joint Financial Secretary, who represented the Treasury in Ottawa as well as New York. It is unnecessary to describe the quarrel in further detail. Suffice it that Bonar Law threatened to transfer the Government account to some of the joint stock banks and appealed to Lloyd George, with whom he insisted that the Bank must act in all things on his direction as Chancellor for the duration of the war and must consult him on all matters affecting credit. Although he had no wish to humiliate Cunliffe, Bonar Law also insisted that the Governor should retire if called upon to do so and should give him a written undertaking to this effect. In the event the Prime Minister supported Bonar Law and the Governor gave in. A few weeks later Cunliffe resigned and was succeeded by the Deputy-Governor Sir Brian Cockayne, with whom the Treasury's relations were quite harmonious. Thus the Treasury's authority over the Bank of England was successfully exerted, and it was to remain paramount until the two departments were in effect amalgamated on the nationalisation of the Bank in 1946.[6]

The only holiday Baldwin had in 1917 was a long week-end late in September when he succeeded in walking sixty miles in three days in the Cotswolds. On his twenty-fifth wedding anniversary earlier the same month he presented the Worcester Infirmary with a 'silver wedding' gift of £1,100 War Loan stock to endow a bed in memory of a young officer who had died in the war, and following his father's example during the Boer campaign, he paid the Friendly Society dues of all his workpeople who joined the forces. Another example of his generosity, which for long remained anonymous, occurred during his brief walking tour of the Cotswolds. His young friend Joan Dickinson, who was shortly to marry Bonar Law's private secretary John Davidson, had told him about the good work being done in a home for mentally retarded girls by two elderly ladies in a Gloucestershire village, one of the first of its kind, and they were in need of help to enable them to carry on. When he reached Stroud he is said to have collected two hundred dirty and crumpled £1 notes – another account puts the number at a hundred – and stuffed them into a cardboard box which he tipped a yokel to deliver at the home with a letter written in the style of an illiterate tramp:

> from one who once saw S. Mary's Home, and having been feble-minded from the cradle regarded it with simpathy and under-standing.
>
> Passing thro' this valley of shaddoes as a useless 'Fantum' himself he desires to be the humble means of bringing a ray of light to kindrid unfortunates.[7]

Baldwin returned to face a series of Zeppelin attacks on London. 'The raids have not been pleasant. Monday night was beastly. A bomb fell in South Eaton Place, just out of our square, and another in Lupus Street, and another back of Ebury Street. The row was appalling in our basement and I thought for one horrible moment that the top of the house was falling in.' He spent most evenings during the raids with the Chancellor at 11 Downing Street, and some years later when he paid an obituary tribute to Bonar Law in the House of Commons he recalled his chief's characteristic reaction on these occasions.

I can see him now, with his family around him – and he was never happy at these times unless they were around him – sitting in the middle of them, working away with the deafening noise outside, paying not the slightest attention to it. The only time that I remember when he failed to work during an air raid was when one of his children was absent, and was reported to be making her way to Downing Street from some other part of London. We lost Mr Bonar Law, and we discovered that he had wandered out in his slippers to the Horse Guards' Parade, in the middle of a heavy barrage, to look for his own child.[8]

'Today I made my first appearance at the War Cabinet, which was amusing,' he wrote to Miss Dickinson from Treasury Chambers on 4 October 1917. 'Never a politician out for his own hand, or a profiteer for his own pocket, or the anarchist workman for chaos and topsy-turvydom, but we know all about it in this office. I can tell you some strange stories some day.'

The Financial Secretary had not only to deputise for his chief as Chancellor of the Exchequer, which resulted in his summons to the War Cabinet, but also in Bonar Law's role of Leader of the House of Commons responsible for arranging daily business. 'When I have finished breakfast to eleven at night I am hunted like a hart in the mountains,' he told Miss Dickinson at the beginning of November. 'Every hand is against this noble but unhappy office and I am looked upon and treated as a cross between the Kaiser and Ferdinand of Bulgaria.' And again from the House a few days later: 'I had a dose on the [Government Front] Bench yesterday evening, and had all the pestiferous elements to listen to. Coming out of the dining room some radical member said to a man I know: ''That's the hardest worked man in the House of Commons!'' meaning me!! It ain't true, but I preened myself and did the goose-step to the smoking room.'[9]

2

'S.B. proved to be a very good Financial Secretary to the Treasury,' Davidson wrote of him at this time: 'he had business experience, he could read a balance sheet and he was very quick with figures. He wasn't at all controversial, and the Treasury liked him very much . . . The House liked him and he never tried a fast one on it.'

Soon he was being invited to the breakfast parties at Derby House given by the immensely wealthy War Minister Lord Derby – his household expenses alone amounted to £50,000 a year – to meet Lloyd George. 'They are very agreeable meetings,' noted Baldwin, 'and give me a good opportunity of studying that strange little genius who presides over us. He is an extraordinary compound.' At the first of these breakfasts which he attended they all sat round the table until nearly eleven o'clock.

> The talk was on Ireland. Events in this war are bringing home to some
> of us an understanding of the attitude of our rude forefathers in regard
> to the Church of Rome. If the hopes of an Irish settlement are broken
> it will be owing to the Roman Bishop at the Vatican . . . The Vatican
> influence has been against us in Europe all the time.[10]

That Baldwin at first got on well with the Prime Minister appears from an incident which took place just before what came to be known as the Maurice Debate, probably at 11 Downing Street where Lloyd George would come in most mornings by the indoor passage from No. 10 and have a few words with Bonar Law. On 7 May 1918 Major-General Sir Frederick Maurice, a former Director of Military Operations at the War Office, wrote a letter to *The Times* in which he charged Lloyd George and Bonar Law with making inaccurate and misleading statements in Parliament on military matters. Public opinion at this time was extremely sensitive owing to the heavy losses in France following the big enemy offensive in March, and also to the tightening pressure of manpower conscription at home. Asquith proposed an inquiry by a Select Committee of the House of Commons, but Lloyd George forced an immediate debate and scored a parliamentary triumph.

Happening to meet Lloyd George on the morning of the debate Baldwin remarked that doubtless the humour of the situation had not escaped him. 'You know, PM, that for ten years we have been trying to catch you deviating by an inch from the strict path of veracity and pin you down,' Baldwin went on. 'We never succeeded. Now others think they have got you and they will find out this afternoon that they have caught you speaking the truth. They will have the shock of their lives.'

According to Baldwin's account, Lloyd George roared with laughter and afterwards went about telling the Cabinet that 'he had been caught telling the truth'. The Prime Minister also sympathised with Bonar Law, who wanted a judicial inquiry. 'Poor old Bonar, he felt it very much. He doesn't like being called a liar. I don't mind it. I've been called a liar all my life. I've had more of the rough and tumble of life than he has.' [11]

'As for the Budget,' the Financial Secretary wrote to his mother in the same month, 'your poor son has been doing rather well and at the moment is suffering from a surfeit of compliments; but that won't last! Still, I am finding my feet in the House, and making a small, modest position for myself. And high time too, you will say.' While successfully resisting a move to increase the Excess Profits Tax on the ground that with rapid inflation of prices and costs the 20 per cent of profits which a firm was allowed to retain barely sufficed to carry on current business, he forecast that income tax 'must remain at a very high level' for many years. At the same time he was pleased when his wife was awarded the Order of the British Empire for her war work, but was naturally worried when his son Oliver sailed for France and was posted to the Arras front where he heard that 'the Bosche' had just bombed a hospital behind the allied lines. 'More and more one feels that Kaiserdom has got to be rolled in the dust if it takes a generation to do it, if the whole world is ever to progress to something better.' [12]

Baldwin's most publicised parliamentary performance to date was when he was put up to defend Lord Beaverbrook's conduct of the Ministry of Information which was strongly criticised in the annual debate on the Consolidated Fund, before the House rose for the summer recess in August 1918, when it is in order to raise any subject. On this occasion several private members gave examples of what they considered the Ministry's waste and excessive spending, besides which it was suggested that the Minister and his various departmental heads were 'capitalists' who mixed private business with public service, although Beaverbrook himself received no salary. Bonar Law, who might have been expected as Chancellor to speak for the Minister, declined to do so since he felt that his friendship with Beaverbrook was so close that his remarks might not seem impartial. His action in deputing the Financial Secretary to undertake the business did not please Beaverbrook, who had no confidence in Baldwin's parliamentary experience. Afterwards Beaverbrook admitted that he was wrong, 'for Baldwin made a very good speech in my defence'. This is how he concluded it:

The Minister of Information is a man of very strong personality. Men with strong personalities have this in common, that the magnetism which comes with that personality either attracts or repels . . . I want to say this in all seriousness. Lord Beaverbrook has taken on a most difficult, delicate and thankless task. Do not let his pitch be queered. Give him a fair chance and judge him by results. Do let us, in time of war, pull together to this extent, that we do not allow the personality of an individual to warp our judgment as to the value of the work he is doing or the means he employs in doing it . . . I do feel this very strongly. Lord Beaverbrook is not an intimate friend of mine, and therefore I can speak with perfect freedom in this matter.[13]

After Baldwin had finished, the attention of the House was neatly diverted by Beaverbrook's friend the Irish Nationalist Tim Healy to Irish affairs; a regular Irish squabble ensued, and the supposed iniquities of the Information Minister were temporarily forgotten by the time the House adjourned. 'Give me some pea soup and a steak and a bottle of beer, and I will tell you the fun,' said Healy when he joined the Minister in the Hyde Park Hotel where he was then living. Thus was Beaverbrook's reputation at a crucial period in his career saved by the combined efforts of the Financial Secretary and a most experienced and astute parliamentary tactician.

Baldwin told his mother that he had achieved what was called a 'parliamentary success', but had found his job 'a really rather difficult' one. 'It was the first thing of the kind I have had to do and I was lucky to have the opportunity. People whose criticism I value were very kind and Bonar said it was a very good performance. All of which seems very odd, and I am glad I am too old to get my head turned over a thing like that.'

Some years later Beaverbrook wrote a character sketch of Baldwin at this period which deserves quotation here:

He was stout and sturdy, pipe-smoking frequently, and then rubbing the bowl of the pipe on his nose, possibly to polish it (the pipe).

His home life was happy, and he had a passion for a mechanical piano-player. A contented middle-class millionaire, he was not widely read, but he had literary associations and would stroll round his library, picking up a volume at random and reading out those passages which caught his eye. His simple jokes endeared him to his friends, and he was much liked and greatly respected.

Up to the outbreak of war he showed not the slightest trace of political push or ambition. He had given no sign of his great oratorical

talents and immense political prescience. He was busy with the directorships of various important companies. His contemporaries regarded
him as a man of affairs who had all the characteristics of a country
squire. His conversation turned on the beauty of the mountain rose,
and the splendour of the hawthorn buds in spring.

In 1917 he began to ascend the political ladder; he had placed a foot
on the first rung when he became Bonar Law's Joint Financial Secretary to the Treasury. His appointment was due to no past performance,
but to the fact that he was rich enough to entertain among Members
of Parliament, and popular enough to win friends for himself and his
chief.

On attaining Junior office his character changed. Ambition marked
him. Thereafter came a steady development of growing powers.[14]

3

'I find three impressions strongest,' wrote Baldwin in November 1918, a
few days after the Armistice. 'Thankfulness that the slaughter is stopped,
the thought of the millions of dead and the vision of Europe in ruins. And
now to work. Pick up the bits.'[15] Parliament was immediately dissolved
and preparations were made for a General Election under a new franchise.
This practically amounted to universal suffrage and admitted women both
as voters and candidates for the first time. Lloyd George and Bonar Law
issued a joint manifesto for the continuance of the Coalition and sent a
letter to all those candidates – about 150 Liberals and 450 Conservatives –
of whom they approved endorsing their candidatures. The test for getting
the 'coupon', as Asquith described the letter in a word suggested by the
war-time ration book, was long believed to be whether or not the candidate had supported Lloyd George in the Maurice debate; but this was not
so, since recent research has established that the selection was made on
quite an arbitrary basis. The Financial Secretary was naturally one of the
favoured, although in the event he was returned unopposed at Bewdley.
Certainly the possession of the 'coupon' proved a most effective passport
to Westminster, since 338 Conservatives and Unionists and 136 Liberals
to whom it had been addressed were elected. Only 26 Asquithian Liberals
survived, without their leader who was defeated, although the Coalition
leaders had refused his Tory opponent the 'coupon'. The residue of the
Opposition included 59 Labour members. The only woman to be returned
in the 'Coupon Election' was the Irish Sinn Fein Countess Markiewicz,
who with 72 other Sinn Feiners refused to take their seats as this would

have involved them in swearing the customary oath of allegiance to the British Crown; instead they formed their own legislative assembly in Dublin styled Dail Eireann.

Meanwhile Baldwin carried quietly on with his work in Treasury Chambers. 'It has been an interregnum, and things get held up until a new ministry is formed,' he wrote to his mother in the first days of January 1919. 'I am pretty certain I shall be left where I am, which is what I wanted, for the only promotion I should care about would be the Exchequer itself which would never be given to a Minister of only two years' experience. I anticipate that Austen [Chamberlain] will be my new chief, an appointment that will meet with a good deal of criticism. The weak point about him is his health: he is in that sort of condition that he may crack up, so I shall feel like an understudy at the pantomime (or in a tragedy according to one's mood!).'[16]

The composition of the new Government, which engaged Lloyd George's attention for the best part of a month, contained few surprises and almost no newcomers. Of the seventy-seven names in the list all but ten had been members of the old administration and most of the ten had held office before. Baldwin's forecast so far as he and his new chief were concerned proved correct. Bonar Law relinquished the Exchequer and became Lord Privy Seal, but continued as Leader of the House of Commons. Balfour returned to the Foreign Office and Winston Churchill became Secretary of State for War and Air. Carson refused the office of Lord Chancellor for the second time, with the result that F. E. Smith at forty-six became the youngest occupant of the Woolsack in modern times, being raised to the peerage as Lord Birkenhead, in spite of the King's expressed doubts as to the suitability of his appointment. Somewhat to Chamberlain's annoyance, Lloyd George insisted that Bonar Law should remain in occupation of 11 Downing Street, the official residence of the Chancellor of the Exchequer, on the ground that 'so long as the leadership of the House is treated as an office by itself, it is necessary that the holder of it should have constant access to me'.

The small War Cabinet, which Chamberlain had joined the previous year, was carried over into peace-time, but Chamberlain, while giving way over the Downing Street house, insisted as a condition of his going back to the Treasury – he had been Chancellor in Balfour's Government from 1903 to 1905 – that there should be an early return to the pre-war Cabinet system. To this Lloyd George agreed. (In fact, the old system was restored ten months later.) 'One might as well be Chancellor of the Exchequer as a gardener!' Chamberlain remarked at the time. 'Both are at the mercy of elemental forces.'[17]

His father's only son by his first wife, Joseph Austen Chamberlain was fifty-five when he became Chancellor for the second time, being thus four years older than his subordinate Stanley Baldwin. They were both graduates of the same Cambridge college but had missed each other there by a term. However, they had known each other for many years, representing neighbouring constituencies as they did, and it will be remembered that Chamberlain had been one of Baldwin's sponsors when he took his seat in 1908. They were both nature lovers and shared an interest in country things, particularly flowers. Like his father 'Joe', Austen habitually wore a monocle, since his eyesight was poor, and this accompanied by a rather stiff manner gave strangers an impression of austerity, which was by no means the case. He was happily married with two young sons and one daughter and he always appeared immaculately dressed. He had an even temper and an inborn generosity of spirit which did not make him diffident about acknowledging his mistakes. 'About him gathered glowing affections; there were no hatreds,' Lord Beaverbrook has written of him. 'He was trusted and respected and he always told the truth, rare gifts for a man born to public affairs.' Lord Birkenhead, who also knew him well, summed him up and his career in an incomparable phrase: 'Austen always played the game and he always lost it.' [18]

Baldwin got on well with his new chief. 'Austen is very pleasant to work with; slower than Bonar but thorough and conscientious and with plenty of courage,' was his impression after their first fortnight together in the office. This impression was mutual and to be confirmed over the next two years, although at times Chamberlain could be very demanding; there was a certain primness about him and he was easily shocked on occasion. 'You were Financial Secretary under Austen, I think?' Baldwin's official biographer G. M. Young once asked him. '*Under* is a well-chosen word,' replied Baldwin, who proceeded to give an illustration of what he meant. He had to wind up a debate for the Government on Irish affairs. Chamberlain, who had previously seen his subordinate in action at the Despatch Box, sent for him and said: 'Remember, this is not an occasion for levity.' On a later occasion, when the Conservative Central Office proposed to make a film of Ministers at work, with officials in their shirtsleeves carrying files and boxes, Chamberlain was aghast. 'Bovril may do this,' he remonstrated, 'but should Baldwins?' [19]

On the other hand, Chamberlain was quick to praise Baldwin when he deserved it. An instance of this occurred during a Budget debate when the Financial Secretary was suddenly called upon to speak on the complexities of currency exchange control. Afterwards the Chancellor wrote to him:

A word of grateful thanks for the quite admirable speech which you made on Tuesday. The House cannot know as I do at what short notice you undertook the task, but had you had unlimited time for preparation it could not have been better. I find it difficult to express my sense of what I owe to you for the immense burden which you take off my shoulders and for the perfect confidence which you give me that any work which you undertake will be thoroughly well done.[20]*

'We have started at last with the new House of Commons,' Baldwin wrote to his mother on 12 February 1919. 'They look much as usual; not so young as I had expected. The prevailing type is a rather successful-looking business kind which is not very attractive.' A variant of the latter phrase, attributed to him by the Treasury official Maynard Keynes, was that the new MPs consisted for the most part of 'hard-faced men who looked as if they had done well out of the war'. While the Prime Minister was busy in Paris with the Peace Conference, Bonar Law was 'in charge of things' at home and was 'keeping his head well'. Meanwhile Baldwin's young friend John Davidson continued to serve Law as his private secretary and in addition announced his engagement to Miss Joan ('Mimi') Dickinson after having proposed once and been turned down. Baldwin was delighted and wrote to reassure the bride's mother who seems to have had some doubts about the match. ('Dear Lady, there is no need for anxiety, believe me. I know them both and love them both, and I believe that in a few years you will look back and bless this day, and, who knows, you may even have a kind word for the man who brought them together!')

As a wedding present Baldwin joined with Bonar Law, and others whom Davidson had served, including Lord Crewe, Lord Harcourt and Lord Edmund Talbot, the Government Chief Whip, in giving him a silver salver. The presentation was made by Talbot in the presence of the others with a few appropriate words. 'I think that little gift tonight must have given you a very real satisfaction,' wrote Baldwin to the prospective bridegroom immediately afterwards.

Leave me out, and it's a rather remarkable group of men from whom to have received such a token of appreciation, and appreciation accompanied with regard and genuine affection. It's a great thing at your age and if it had happened to me at thirty I should have walked six inches higher! And the best of it is that you deserve it and everything

* 13 March 1920. 'The ruin which has been wrought in the world,' Baldwin remarked in this speech, 'can only be made good in time, and with toil and with tears.' A. W. Baldwin, *My Father*, p. 94.

that Ned Talbot said – every word of it . . . Never has a man had such a friend as you have been to me. You can't tell yourself, nor can any other: but I know it and I shall never forget it. I could have fought through alone but I should have been a soured, embittered devil . . .[21]

After their wedding, the Davidsons took a house in Barton Street, Westminster, near enough to the House of Commons to have a division bell installed, and this became Baldwin's second home. Davidson has described their relations thus:

Mimi gave him much affection, understanding and companionship, and he depended on me for advice of an entirely different kind. I often used to tell her the things that he ought to be doing and wasn't inclined to do, and she would tell him. She has always been like that, and S.B. adored her because of it. It was an extraordinary friendship for us both . . .

S.B. loved music. He was a pretty good accompanist, and my wife used to sing. This was a great relaxation for him. Usually he could only take a short break at dinner time from the House of Commons, when he would slip across to our house.[22]

Their relations were further cemented in the following year when Davidson entered the House of Commons at a by-election and was introduced by Bonar Law and Baldwin as his sponsors. They became even closer after Law's temporary retirement from political life for health reasons in 1921 and Davidson became Baldwin's PPS. 'If my life ever comes to be written,' Baldwin was to tell the Davidsons some years later, 'no one can express in it what you both are to me nor can I ever repay you for the never ending, all comprehending love you give me; yet talk about repayment is unseemly where we are concerned with a friendship devoted, unselfish and unalloyed.'[23]

It was at this time that Baldwin joined the Travellers' Club in Pall Mall. 'I have found a really peaceful club at last where no one talks to you unless you want it,' he told his mother. It was supposed to be 'the original club of which the old story was told that a member sat for three days dead in an armchair before anyone noticed him!' And, he added with a touch of regret, 'there are few places left now where such a thing is possible'. He was also a regular visitor to Bateman's, his cousin Rudyard Kipling's house at Burwash, one of the most attractive of Sussex villages. ('For more than one reason it is the completest haven to me that the world affords.') On one of these visits, he recorded without comment that Kipling had shown him a letter which he had received from Theodore Roosevelt, in which the former American President referred to the nascent League of Nations as 'the product of men who want everyone to float to heaven on a sloppy sea of universal mush'.[24]

At this time Baldwin made a remarkable public gesture, which for the time being remained anonymous. He had been disturbed by the amount of money his investments in Baldwins and its associated companies had brought him from the production of war materials, and discussing it with his son Oliver, who had fortunately returned from France unscathed, he told him that he felt it to be 'blood money'. He had therefore made calculations and decided to hand over to the State every penny he had made in excess of what he was receiving before the slaughter began. He reckoned this came to £120,000. He revealed his intention in a letter which he addressed to the editor of *The Times*, and which he asked John Davidson to despatch, enclosing his card and signing himself with the initials of his political office. The letter reached the editor, then Wickham Steed, on 23 June; but so little did Steed know about the writer that he had to inquire, presumably of the paper's parliamentary correspondent, whether the Financial Secretary to the Treasury was 'really a man of weight'. On being told that 'Baldwin is a good fellow', he published the letter on the following day, accompanied by a leader describing his action as 'noble'.[25]

Sir, – It is now a truism to say that in August, 1914, the nation was face to face with the greatest crisis in her history. She was saved by the free-will offerings of her people. The best of her men rushed to the colours; the best of her women left their homes to spend and be spent; the best of her older men worked as they had never worked before, to a common end, and with a sense of unity and fellowship as new as it was exhilarating. It may be that in four and a half years the ideals of many became dim, but the spiritual impetus of those early days carried the country through to the end.

Today, on the eve of peace,* we are faced with another crisis, less obvious, but none the less searching. The whole country is exhausted. By a natural reaction, not unlike that which led to the excesses of the Restoration after the reign of the Puritans, all classes are in danger of being submerged by a wave of extravagance and materialism. It is so easy to live on borrowed money; so difficult to realise that you are doing so.

It is so easy to play; so hard to learn that you cannot play for long without work. A fool's paradise is only the ante-room to a fool's hell.

* The Peace Treaty was about to be signed in the Hall of Mirrors at Versailles (28 June 1919).

How can the nation be made to understand the gravity of the financial situation; that love of country is better than love of money?

This can only be done by example, and the wealthy classes have today an opportunity of service which can never recur.

They know the danger of the present debt; they know the weight of it in the years to come. They know the practical difficulties of a universal statutory capital levy. Let them impose upon themselves, each as he is able, a voluntary levy. It should be possible to pay to the Exchequer within twelve months such a sum as would save the taxpayer 50 millions a year.

I have been considering this matter for nearly two years, but my mind moves slowly; I dislike publicity, and I hoped that someone else might lead the way. I have made as accurate an estimate as I am able of the value of my own estate and have arrived at a total of about £580,000. I have decided to realise 20 per cent. of that amount or, say, £120,000, which will purchase £150,000 of the new War Loan, and present it to the Government for cancellation.

I give this portion of my estate as a thank offering in the firm conviction that never again shall we have such a chance of giving our country that form of help which is so vital at the present time.

Yours etc.,
F.S.T.

The letter was typed by Davidson's private secretary Miss Watson, and so well was the secret kept that not even Austen Chamberlain realised that the initials concealed the identity of his own Financial Secretary. 'You and I and Miss Watson have done it with a vengeance!' Baldwin wrote to Davidson, who had gone to Paris with Bonar Law for the signing of the Peace Treaty. 'I don't know what you said to the *Times* man, but when I opened the paper in bed (*ut mea mos est*) wondering whether my letter would find a place at all – well I dived under the bedclothes and went pink all over – as pink as you! I feel like a criminal in momentary fear of detection . . .' Eventually the secret did leak out, but neither Davidson nor Baldwin was responsible, although Davidson was suspected in spite of repeated denials.[26]*

In due course the Chancellor of the Exchequer publicly acknowledged the receipt of £150,000 of loan stock for cancellation. This was followed by smaller amounts from other patriotic donors, but in all only some

* The culprit, if culprit he can be called, was Wickham Steed, who published the story in the *Review of Reviews* which he took over and edited after leaving *The Times* in 1922.

£500,000 reached the Treasury instead of the £1,000 million which Baldwin had hoped would be raised. One of his official duties was to witness the burning of the bonds, so that when he saw a substantial part of his personal fortune literally going up in smoke, he was tempted for a moment to recover it from the flames. 'I have never been nearer to doing a wrong action!' he admitted afterwards.[27]

4

The year 1919 was marked by a considerable measure of industrial unrest in Great Britain, while in Ireland civil war raged between the Irish Republican army and the British security forces. In September the railwaymen, encouraged by the miners and dockers, struck against a threatened reduction of wages and there was talk of a general strike. A Cabinet committee, which Baldwin joined, was set up to prepare against such a contingency, and some Cabinet ministers favoured a tough line with the unions. During the negotiations, which were mishandled by the Minister of Transport Sir Eric Geddes, Baldwin lunched at the Carlton Club with his old friend W. A. S. Hewins and told him that 'Winston and F.E. [Lord Birkenhead] had wished to confiscate the funds of the unions, but the committee would have nothing to do with such ideas'.[28] Eventually Lloyd George stepped in and settled the strike on the railwaymen's terms as demanded by their leader J. H. Thomas, who had driven a locomotive on the Great Western Railway when Baldwin was a director. Baldwin was also officially concerned with the financing of unemployment insurance which was put on a joint contributory basis as between employers and workers and extended to cover all categories of the latter except domestics, agricultural labourers and civil servants.

'There is no job which brings you in such close and constant touch with the House as mine,' Baldwin wrote to his mother at this time, 'and so far I think I am getting on all right.' During 1919, for example, the subjects with which he had to deal at the despatch box ranged from totalisators for horse-racing and the wages of the employees in Kew Gardens to the hours of opening at the British Museum and the liability of cricket clubs to amusement tax. But he sometimes found difficulty in speaking when he had to wind up a debate and finish precisely at a given time. 'It wants a lot of practice to speak to the clock,' he told his mother after one such experience in May 1919. 'I got up at 7.40 and had to finish and get the Bill [through] at 8.15. I did pretty well till five past eight and then I got muddled and talked nonsense. A first-class debater makes his points to the end and manages to finish to the tick whether he has an hour or only ten minutes. But it takes such a lot of practice.' [29]

Bonar Law's confidence in Stanley Baldwin was reflected in a conversation which took place between them in May 1920 when the Leader of the House of Commons inquired whether he would be interested in accepting a governorship of one of the dominions.

'Would you like to go to South Africa?'

'No, I don't think so,' replied Baldwin. 'In what capacity?'

'To succeed Buxton.'*

'Are you joking?'

'No,' said Bonar Law in all seriousness.

'Well,' Baldwin rejoined, 'there are plenty of men who would do that job as well or better than I. I think I am more use at home.'

'Would you like Australia?'

'Not a bit!'

'Well, I thought you wouldn't look at it!' [30]

'Not in my line, but it is a compliment,' was how he described these offers to his mother. He added: 'You can rely on me carrying on Father's tradition so long as I can carry on anything in this slippery world of government. And I can tell you it is a curious world.'

A few days later, Lloyd George gave Baldwin the welcome news that the King had approved his appointment as a Privy Councillor, which meant that henceforth he would be officially styled 'Right Honourable'. Again he lost no time in telling his mother. 'I hadn't worried about it for a second, but am pleased that it has come.' The announcement in the King's Birthday Honours brought a number of letters of congratulation including one which he particularly appreciated from Sir John Bradbury, the well-known former Permanent Secretary to the Treasury.† 'I have seen many Financial Secretaries to the Treasury raised to that dignity, but none with more satisfaction than yourself,' wrote Bradbury. 'If it has been longer in coming to you than some, that is due to that absence of pushfulness which is one of your most amiable traits.' [31] ‡

* Lord Noel-Buxton, a Liberal, had been High Commissioner and Governor-General of South Africa since 1914 and was about to retire. He was previously President of the Board of Trade and as such responsible for the Copyright Act of 1911.
† Later Lord Bradbury. The facsimile of his signature on the war-time currency notes had made his name familiar in every home and led to the notes themselves being popularly known as 'Bradburys'.
‡ Baldwin took the oath of allegiance to the King along with another new Privy Councillor, Frederick Kellaway, Secretary for Overseas Trade. The Clerk of the Privy Council noted the occasion in the entry to his diary for 11 June 1920. 'Council at Buckingham Palace at 10.30 much to the Lord President [Lord Balfour]'s disgust at so early an hour . . . Stanley Baldwin and Mr

It was rumoured at this time that Baldwin might be chosen as Speaker of the House of Commons in succession to James Lowther, who had occupied the chair for the past sixteen years in the most difficult circumstances and was about to retire.* The rumour got into the press and someone sent him a cutting about it when he was on holiday in August. 'It is funny how the odd rumour of the Speakership keeps cropping up,' was his immediate reaction. 'I don't know whether there is anything in it, and if I were offered it I haven't an idea what I should do. Sufficient unto the day.' In all probability Baldwin's name was canvassed by a group of Conservative backbenchers as an alternative to Lloyd George's nominee J. H. Whitley, who was a Liberal. The latter had been Deputy Speaker and Chairman of Committees since 1911, and the Conservatives may have feared that his formal election to the chair would establish a precedent. However that may be, nothing came of the rumour, since the opposition had died down by the time Parliament met in the autumn and Whitley was duly elected.

It is extremely doubtful if Baldwin would have been at all happy in the Speaker's chair and being tied for such long periods to the Palace of Westminster, since at heart he was a countryman. On the same day as he wrote about the rumour he unburdened himself in a letter to Mrs Davidson.

> This is the first time for years that I have been long enough away from work really to forget it and I feel I should like never to come back to London.
>
> Country folk are my own folk: in London I am a stranger, in the country at home.
>
> On my tramps I sometimes feel I am not at all a bad companion, and I say to myself as I roll along with waistcoat open and bareheaded, 'And is this the —— fool that walks every morning along the Buckingham Palace Road in a black coat?'[32]

In February 1921, Lord Lee of Fareham, who with his wife had recently presented the Chequers estate in Buckinghamshire to a trust for the use of successive Prime Ministers in perpetuity, became First Lord of the Admiralty. The Parliamentary and Financial Secretary, Sir James Craig,

---

Kellaway were sworn on introduction. The King was very kind to Kellaway, who has an artificial leg, and had some difficulty in kneeling.' Sir Almeric Fitzroy, *Memoirs* (1925), II, 732.
* J. C. Lowther, who was created Viscount Ullswater on his retirement, survived his two immediate successors as Speaker and died in 1949, a few days before his ninety-fourth birthday.

was about to leave to become the first Prime Minister of Northern Ireland, and Lee was much exercised in his mind about a successor. 'It would be, in present circumstances, a particularly responsible and difficult job and one which will require real financial ability,' he wrote to Bonar Law. 'Would Baldwin be out of the question? It would be, in a sense, a promotion for him as he would have no Chief in the Commons.' [33] But Bonar Law had something bigger in mind for Baldwin, who had now been more than four years at the Treasury and was in any event due for a move. The Conservative Party leader planned to withdraw altogether from the political scene on medical advice and he knew that this was bound to bring about a reshuffle of government posts.

Baldwin was so depressed when he heard the news of Law's retirement that he seriously thought of giving up himself. But before he could take any step in this direction, Lloyd George told him that Sir Robert Horne, the President of the Board of Trade, was being appointed Chancellor of the Exchequer in place of Austen Chamberlain, who was to succeed Bonar Law as Lord Privy Seal and Leader of the House of Commons (and also as Conservative Party Leader), and he offered Baldwin the Board of Trade with a seat in the Cabinet.* According to Lord Beaverbrook, the offer was made under pressure from Bonar Law, who insisted on the continuance of parity between the respective parties in the Coalition. This may well be true. It is difficult to escape the conclusion that Bonar Law had a hand in the appointment to the Board of Trade which Baldwin after a short hesitation accepted. 'You have what I am told is one of my defects – too much modesty,' wrote Bonar Law in congratulating him; 'so my advice to you is to get rid of that defect as soon as possible.' [34] The promotion involved an increase of salary from £2,000 to £5,000 a year.

'I cannot tell you what pleasure your letter gave me,' Baldwin replied to his old chief; 'my whole heart was in my work with you, and I don't mind confessing to you that I nearly took advantage of the shuffle to go back to private life and to business. But it came over me that were I to do that I should have fallen far from the standard that you set for so long, and I should have felt later as ashamed of myself as you would have been of me. I owe you a great deal and I still marvel at your patience with me on the [Front] Bench at the beginning of 1917 when I was all at sea. Our friendship indeed remains, for it was welded and tested in stern years.' [35]

His last letter from Treasury Chambers – 'this place which has been my

---

* Baldwin was mentioned by *The Times* parliamentary correspondent as a possible candidate for Chancellor of the Exchequer, although 'all the signs were that Horne' would succeed Chamberlain. 'He [Baldwin] knows more about the Treasury than any member of Parliament and has no black marks against him.' *The Times*, 18 March 1921.

home for four eventful years' – was written to Davidson on 31 March. 'I am just off to Astley and return on Monday to start at the Board of Trade. The writ will be moved on Monday for my re-election so I shall not be in the House next week. Perhaps you will let me dine at Barton Street one evening. I shall be alone. I am feeling rather sad and helpless, but it will pass . . . Some of the new appointments will make you shy all across the road!' [36]*

Unexpectedly he was opposed by an Independent so-called Popular People's candidate at the by-election which was still necessary in the case of a minister accepting a post of Cabinet rank. His opponent Mr Henry Mills, who lived at Oxshott, Surrey, was a republican and if not a Communist certainly a 'fellow-traveller', being a fervent admirer of the Soviet experiment in Russia, which he seemed to wish to be introduced in Britain. He talked a great deal about idle capitalists, parasites and 'the order of the capitalists'. Such attacks as these made a poor impression on the Bewdley electors who had little but contempt for the Popular People's candidate. As one of Baldwin's supporters put it at a campaign meeting, they had heard a great deal from Mr Mills about the shirker and the good-for-nothing: but in Mr Baldwin they had 'one who could be one of the most leisured men in the kingdom if he chose, yet who never sought ease but was out to serve his country and to save it'. How they cheered Baldwin too when he told his constituents that 'many times in the life of any one who is working in Parliament and in the Government in times like these, one feels that one would like to throw the whole thing up'. In the result Mr Mills was duly trounced by a large majority, polling only 1,680 votes against Baldwin's 14,537. It was very different from the Kidderminster poll of fifteen years before.

As usual the figures were declared on the steps of the Shire Hall in Worcester, and there were some lively scenes caused by the sight of the defeated candidate's car, which stood near the statue of Queen Victoria and ostentatiously displayed the red flag of the Bolshevists. Baldwin's supporters, regarding this as an insult, sprayed the flag with petrol and burnt it, after which they proceeded to slash the tyres. Mr Mills, who had some difficulty in getting away, protested vigorously, but his protests were drowned by the singing of the National Anthem.

Meanwhile the victor went on with the customary speech of thanks to

* Baldwin did not specify any of these appointments, but he may have been thinking among others of Lord Edmund Talbot, ex-Unionist Chief Whip, who became Lord Lieutenant of Ireland as Lord Fitzalan (the first and last Roman Catholic to hold that historic office), Captain F. E. Guest, who left the Whip's Office to become Air Minister, and C. A. McCurdy, KC, who became Liberal Chief Whip: the latter, according to *The Times* (2 April 1921), possessed 'few of the social qualities which are the most useful attributes of a Chief Whip'.

the Returning Officer. 'And now let me get back to my job,' he concluded simply.[37]

5

The Board of Trade, to which Baldwin now applied his energies, was one of the older departments of government in Whitehall. Originally a committee of the Privy Council, it was reconstituted as a Board in 1696 with a President and about a dozen members for 'promoting the trade of our kingdom and improving our plantations in America and elsewhere'. By the middle of the nineteenth century the Board had ceased to meet as such, the President having become in effect minister of commerce, while the Vice-President was transformed into the Parliamentary Secretary. Indeed it was generally forgotten that there ever had been a Board at all, as we learn from a contemporary jingle about the President:

> This highly-placed official
> Is grossly overpaid,
> There never was a Board; and now
> There isn't any trade.

Besides trade and industry, the Board was responsible for a variety of subjects including merchant shipping, mines, gas, weights and measures, patents, trade marks and copyright.[38]

When he arrived for the first time at his new offices in Great George Street, Baldwin found his Parliamentary Secretary already installed in the person of Sir Philip Lloyd-Greame, a thirty-seven-year-old Conservative MP, who had been knighted in the previous year on Lloyd George's recommendation. (The son of a Yorkshire landowner, Lloyd-Greame was to change his name twice, in 1924 to Cunliffe-Lister on inheriting a fortune and in 1935 to Swinton on becoming a peer.) John Davidson, who had recently entered the House of Commons at a by-election, was appointed by Baldwin to be his PPS and thus he had a good opportunity of observing how his chief and Lloyd-Greame worked together. 'Lloyd-Greame was never very popular in the House of Commons,' Davidson afterwards recalled. 'This was partly because of his manner of speech; it was very much Oxford, and the Oxford manners of his generation were somewhat hectoring. They all seemed to have long upper lips and they were always lecturing the House of Commons, but Lloyd-Greame made a perfect foil for the Cambridge yokel Baldwin, and they were a formidable combination.' The Permanent Secretary to the Board of Trade at this time was Sir Sydney Chapman, an outstanding economist and former university professor who had been drafted into the civil service during the war.* Besides John Davidson he had as his private secretary Patrick Duff, an able young civil servant, who was later to render a similar service to successive Prime Ministers.†

As for Baldwin himself, Davidson considered him to be 'a very good President of the Board of Trade'.

> He understood trade, he understood both sides of industry. Lloyd George was much too tricky, and Baldwin believed in honesty and hated professional negotiators. He disliked most emphatically both the paid organiser of the men and the paid spokesman of the employers – especially the latter, because they worked for a salary and in their approach to life they had the worst attributes of the shop steward – they had to keep differences boiling in order to justify their salary. Peace in industry, which was Baldwin's goal, was the last thing they wanted; that is why Baldwin was not very popular with the Employers' Federation and other organisations, and still less with their paid organisers or secretaries.[39]

The first Cabinet Meeting which Baldwin attended was summoned for 4 April to consider a major crisis in the coal industry. The colliery owners on resuming control of the mines had proposed cuts in wages and a return to the old system of district rates, which gave miners at inferior pits less than those working on richer seams. The miners demanded a 'national pool' which would equalise wages. The owners refused and began a lock-out as from 1 April. It was feared that the coal strike would develop into a general strike, backed by the railwaymen and transport workers as well as the miners, and there were prolonged discussions during the next fortnight when the Cabinet met daily to decide how the army could best be used to deal with the situation. However, owing to divided counsels, the railwaymen and transport workers called off their strikes which had been

---

* Davidson's memory was at fault when he stated in his memoirs that Horace Wilson was Permanent Secretary to the Board of Trade when Baldwin was President. In fact Wilson was Permanent Secretary to the Ministry of Labour, in which capacity he frequently came into touch with Baldwin. 'Baldwin and he became great friends because their attitude towards industrial relations were very much the same. Wilson felt that friendship and understanding, not hostility, were vital and with these views Baldwin entirely agreed . . . Wilson's attitude on industrial conciliation at home was one that warmly attracted him to a man like Baldwin.' Robert Rhodes James, *Memoirs of a Conservative*, p. 106.

† Later Sir Patrick Duff, UK High Commissioner in New Zealand. He died in 1972.

planned to take place in sympathy with the miners; this was due to the miners' executive turning down the acceptance by their moderate General Secretary Frank Hodges of the owners' offer of a standstill on wages while negotiations went on for a national pool, an offer which J. H. Thomas and Ernest Bevin for the railwaymen and transport workers felt that the miners should have taken up. Thus, as Tom Jones put it, 'the Red Revolution was postponed once more. It was the most exciting day since the Armistice – three Cabinet meetings and endless comings and goings, the PM in great form as the day went on in his favour. The Strike Committee very sick. They had been waiting for two years to press the button. They had pressed it . . . But Jim Thomas upset it all . . . and was being damned as a traitor by the miners . . .' In the event, when the miners could hold out no longer, they were compelled to accept worse terms than they could have obtained if they had negotiated in the early days of the dispute as Hodges wished.

The Government's role as mediator was played by Lloyd George with Horne, the Chancellor of the Exchequer, as his understudy. Baldwin was compelled to be a silent spectator, while both in the Cabinet and at the various ministerial conferences his voice was seldom raised. According to Jones, Baldwin only opened his mouth once during the initial Cabinet when he remarked: 'What a fool!' on hearing the Prime Minister say that Hodges had communicated with all the local secretaries in the Miners' Federation 'to the effect that a subsidy can be forced from the Government'.[40]* In a letter to Bonar Law about the reconstituted Cabinet at work, Jones referred to 'the long silences of Stanley Baldwin'. Sir Arthur Griffith-Boscawen, the Minister of Agriculture, whose garrulity made up for Baldwin's lack of it, described the President of the Board of Trade as 'the most silent member of the Coalition Cabinet'. On the other hand, as Baldwin's younger son has pointed out, while silence with him did not always mean consent, vocal dissent did not always come easily to him. But when it did come, it was clear and decisive. On one occasion, when some Budget adjustment had been under discussion for some time, Lloyd George said: 'But we have not heard what the President of the Board of Trade has to say.' 'Perhaps, you will not like what he is going to say,' said Baldwin. 'He feels as if he were a director of a fraudulent company engaged in cooking the balance sheet.' No more was heard of the adjustment.[41]

The historian Sir Arthur Bryant, in a tribute to Baldwin, has written of him at this time:

* Hodges, whom Baldwin was to get to like and respect, proved right, since the Cabinet eventually agreed to a subsidy of £10 million.

In the Cabinet he seldom spoke. Like Brer Rabbit he lay low and said nothing. But he was a good listener. Consequently he came to know more about his brilliant colleagues than they ever learnt about him. He was not favourably impressed. There seemed to be an absence of principle in the way in which they dealt with the problems of a great nation, postulating ten future problems for every one they solved, and a looseness in the presentation of fact that shocked a man who had been brought up to conduct his own business on lines of strict and literal probity. Brilliance, he began to think, was synonymous with a rapid capacity for changing one's ground to suit one's convenience. He found that he disliked it very much.

Only when the affairs of his Department were concerned did he make his presence felt. He fought for weeks over the duty on fabric gloves and carried his point. He made it clear that, were he unable to do so, he was quite ready to go. He never made any pretence of personal friendship with the Prime Minister. He was in the Coalition Government to represent his Party: that was all. His colleagues found it hard to temporise with a man who had no desire to retain office for its own sake. He might be a fool, but he could not be disregarded. And his reputation for sincerity and honesty in his own Party made it unsafe to discard him.[42]

'The business of a Minister is different from that of Financial Secretary,' he wrote to his mother shortly after his appointment to the Board of Trade. 'I have less work in the House except when I have a Bill . . . so I am off to Surrey to a little house I have taken to put in two hard days work preparing a difficult speech, for my bill which I have inherited is THE controversial Bill of the Session.' The measure in question was the Safeguarding of Industries Bill, 'safeguarding' being a euphemism for Protection; it had been drafted by Baldwin's predecessor and was designed to implement the principle of Imperial Preference announced by Chamberlain in the budget of 1919. The Bill provided for two rates of duty – $33\frac{1}{3}$ per cent on certain 'key' articles, mostly produced in Germany, such as fabric gloves, and an additional $33\frac{1}{3}$ per cent on goods dumped in Britain below the cost of production abroad and sold at less than the British price for similar manufactures through the advantages of depreciated currencies. Food was exempted contrary to Dominion wishes, otherwise the public outcry would have been too great for even Lloyd George to assuage. (Instead he convened an Imperial Conference as a gesture of goodwill towards the Dominion Prime Ministers.) Male unemployment in Britain was approaching the two million mark and it was hoped that the antidumping duties in particular would reduce the number of jobless. Although the Bill had been produced by a ministerial committee presided over by the Conservative elder statesman Lord Balfour, some of the Liberals in the Cabinet such as Churchill were far from enthusiastic about it. Even Baldwin, who had moved away in some degree from the protectionist views of his younger days, did not find it wholly satisfactory, although he conceded that a system of low tariffs might help the economic development of the Dominions and colonies, besides being an effective form of retaliation for the discrimination against British goods practised by foreign countries. 'A Free Trade country, such as we still are,' he told the House of Commons, 'finds it very difficult to argue with a country that has a tariff weapon in its hand.' [43]

The Bill had quite a stormy passage through its various stages and was to some extent amended in committee, but Baldwin stuck to his guns and he had the advantage of the guillotine procedure which limited the hours of discussion in committee. Only once did he put a foot wrong. Anxious that protection should not be used as a device to conceal industrial inefficiency, he introduced a clause which stipulated that if, after two years, an industry had made no progress towards establishing itself as a going concern, it should lose its protection. That such a matter should be decided by a government department raised a storm of protest from all sides of the House, notably from Austen Chamberlain's younger half-brother Neville, then a backbencher, who pointed out somewhat caustically that the proper course to pursue was to impose a higher tariff. The offending clause was withdrawn and Baldwin moved another, which required industries seeking protection to prove that they were reasonably efficient in operation. This was duly adopted.

The Safeguarding of Industries Bill passed its Third Reading in the Commons on 12 August and immediately afterwards Baldwin indulged in a characteristic gesture. 'My dear Philip,' he wrote to his Parliamentary Secretary, who had shared the burden of debate with him, 'before the sun goes down I must write and thank you for the invaluable help you have given me throughout the passage of our Bill. I could not have done it without you. You will know in time what it means to the man in charge to have someone by his side on whom he can depend absolutely and entirely. I hope indeed that your first experience may be as happy as mine has been.' [44] It may be noted in passing that the use of Christian names between parliamentary and official colleagues was practically unknown before this time and largely owed its practice to Baldwin's example.

'It [the Bill] has been very little altered,' noted W. A. S. Hewins in his diary on the same day it was sent to the Lords. 'The Free Trade opposition has been noisy, but ineffective through being uninformed.' Somewhat foolishly the Lords amended the measure, although they were constitutionally not entitled to do this since it had been certified by the Commons Speaker as a 'Money Bill'. In the result the Lords gave way and rescinded the amendments under threat of the operation of the Parliament Act, which through prolonging the session would have enabled the Bill to be passed automatically, much to Baldwin's relief, since by this time he was both physically and mentally quite exhausted. Hewins's comment on the situation showed how far Lloyd George had moved away from the traditional Liberal support for Free Trade principles as expressed at the 'Coupon Election'. 'I had a talk with Stanley Baldwin about his bill and asked him whether he did not think it remarkable that a Government formed to prevent the adoption of a tariff should not only end by doing so, but should actually use a drastic closure and the Parliament Act to bring it about.'[45]

When Parliament rose for the summer recess, the Baldwins went to Aix-les-Bains so that Mrs Baldwin could 'take the cure'. They were charmed with the little spa in the Savoy mountains a mile or so from the picturesque Lac du Bourget and they were to revisit it summer after summer thereafter. 'I walk whenever possible for hours and hours,' was how Baldwin described his main activity while his wife was in the *établissement thermal*. 'Up, up and ever up. Chestnuts, walnuts, acacias, vines everywhere, Indian corn, heavenly patches of pasture with the aftermath of being cut, and the scent of the fresh grass mingled with that of cows and wood smoke.' His broodings on these solitary walks after five months of Cabinet office were often far from happy as he ruminated over the less endearing qualities of some of his colleagues including the Prime Minister himself. Still it was a time when he could, as it were, recharge his batteries, and the peaceful surroundings of Aix-les-Bains were to make him look forward more and more to his annual holiday there. To his younger son he wrote a few weeks after his fifty-fifth birthday:

The lake has all the colours of Italy, varying its shades of blue from pale turquoise to aquamarine, while away to the south there stands the line of Alps with their everlasting snows catching and reflecting all the lights of heaven. My walks are a daily joy and I am rapidly getting into some sort of condition. I find I can now do six hours, climbing to a couple of thousand feet, with ease, and though I am very happy by myself I often feel I want someone for a minute to enjoy the beauty of it all and shout 'Thank God!'[46]

Baldwin's main achievement at the Board of Trade was in piloting the Safeguarding Bill to the statute book and administering it afterwards, since the department had to draw up lists of articles amounting to some 6,500 items covered by 'key' industries. His other noteworthy piece of legislation was the Merchandise Marks Act which extended and revised the existing law and gave the Board power to require the country of origin to be marked on imported goods, while prohibiting the use of British emblems by foreign importers to disguise the true origin. He seems to have been generally liked within the department as well as outside it in the City and with industry. As he put it, 'they were delighted to find a Minister who knew what a trial balance was'. Also his style of speaking in the House endeared him to the lobby journalists. 'It was a pretty Balfourian performance,' the Labour *Daily Herald* man remarked when the Minister came to defend his department's record on the Supply Vote at the end of his first year in office. 'Instead of statistics, he quoted the witticism of a lady with whom he had dined, an epigram by Lord Melbourne and the motto he had read that morning on his calendar.'[47]

From time to time he was received in audience by King George V, usually after a Privy Council meeting. During one of these audiences the King told Baldwin that he could relate 'the most extraordinary things' that had been said to him by other ministers during these audiences if he chose. 'I hope, Sir,' Baldwin replied, 'that you will not write autobiographical articles in the Press?' 'Not till I'm broke!' His Majesty laughingly rejoined.

Probably the most difficult matter he had to handle was the proposed duty on fabric gloves, which aroused opposition on the part of the Lancashire cotton manufacturers, who felt that the enforcement of the order might result in the Germans turning to another source of supply for cotton yarn. When Lloyd George announced that the order would be postponed until the cotton trade had a chance to present a written case against it, *The Times* quoted the opinion of an influential Tory backbencher to the effect that if the Cabinet reversed the decision to enforce the order, there would be an end to the Coalition. However, Lloyd George was only flying a kite and the order was eventually approved with two others almost as controversial, although seventy-six Coalition Liberals either voted against the orders or else abstained.

Baldwin's parliamentary performances as President of the Board of Trade considerably increased his standing in the eyes of the Tory backbenchers and the Conservative Party generally. 'Mr Stanley Baldwin is not leaving the Board of Trade, much as the Prime Minister and the Coalition Liberals dislike his handling of the Safeguarding of Industries Act,' wrote the outspoken weekly *John Bull*. 'What worries them is that Mr Baldwin is an honest politician.'[48]*

6

Baldwin was obliged to cut short his first two holidays in Aix-les-Bains owing to political crises at home. The first blew up over Ireland; it nearly split the Conservative Party and bitterly disillusioned its Unionist element led by Carson. For the past two years the history of Ireland had been largely one of murders, ambushes, burnings, torturings and other outrages committed by both sides in the struggle for political independence. The Sinn Fein terror was matched by the counter-terror of the 'Black-and-Tans', a paramilitary force mainly recruited from British ex-servicemen and so called because owing to a shortage of police uniforms they were clothed temporarily in military khaki with a black hat and armband. Speaking at the Lord Mayor's Banquet in November 1920, Lloyd George boasted that 'we have murder by the throat', while as late as May 1921, the Chief Secretary for Ireland, Sir Hamar Greenwood, assured the House of Commons that the Government would 'hunt down the murder gang' and 'pluck the last revolver out of the last assassin's hand'. Within a few weeks the goal had abruptly changed to 'a lasting reconciliation with the Irish people'. As Winston Churchill was to put it later, 'no British Government in modern times has ever appeared to make so complete and sudden a reversal of policy as that which ensued'.

Hoping to turn to account the good impression created by the visit of King George and Queen Mary to Belfast for the opening of the Parliament of Northern Ireland in June 1921, Lloyd George addressed a letter to the Sinn Fein leader Eamonn de Valera as 'the chosen leader of the great majority of Southern Ireland', inviting him to attend a conference in London 'to explore to the utmost the possibility of a settlement' and bring with him for the purpose any colleagues he might select. Sir James Craig, the Northern Irish Prime Minister, who had recently met Mr de Valera, at a secret rendez-vous near Dublin, was also invited.† The invitations were accepted at the beginning of July and a 'truce', which had previously been agreed to by both sides, was proclaimed.

---

* *John Bull* was rather sensitive on the subject of political honesty, since its editor Horatio Bottomley, MP, had just been convicted of fraud and sentenced to seven years penal servitude.
† Craig's secret mission had proved abortive. 'At the end of four hours Mr de Valera's recital of Irish grievances had only reached the iniquities of Poyning's Act in the days of Henry VII. There were by that time various reasonable excuses for terminating not a discussion but a lecture.' Winston Churchill, *The World Crisis: The Aftermath* (1929), p. 292.

The parleys initiated with de Valera and his colleagues nearly foundered when the Southern Irish leader insisted that when the respective plenipotentiaries met formally to frame a 'treaty', they must be 'untrammelled by any conditions'. This was opposed by a minority of the Cabinet which did not include Baldwin: it was led by Birkenhead and Churchill, and eventually they gave way under the threat of renewed civil war. The formal negotiations opened in Downing Street on 11 October 1921 with Lloyd George in the chair. It was the need for Cabinet approval of the composition of the British delegation which necessitated Baldwin's early return from Aix-les-Bains. This was agreed as follows: Lloyd George (chairman), Austen Chamberlain (Leader of the House of Commons), Birkenhead (Lord Chancellor), Churchill (Colonial Secretary), Sir Laming Worthington-Evans (War Minister), Sir Hamar Greenwood (Chief Secretary for Ireland) and Sir Gordon Hewart (Attorney-General). Lionel Curtis and Tom Jones acted as secretaries. The Irish delegation was led by Arthur Griffith, a pioneer of the Sinn Fein movement, whom Churchill described as 'that unique figure, a silent Irishman'. His principal lieutenant was Michael Collins, the romantic gunman whom Lloyd George was to call 'one of the most courageous leaders ever produced by a valiant race', but whom Greenwood regarded as 'the head of the murder gang' in Ireland. This ill-assorted group included two lawyers, Eamonn Duggan and Charles Gavan Duffy, and an economic expert, Robert Barton, who was the only Protestant. The two secretaries were both Englishmen, who had been converted to the Sinn Fein cause – John Chartres, a barrister, and Erskine Childers, author of the thrilling adventure story *The Riddle of the Sands*.

This is not the place to traverse the course of the conference which continued intermittently during the next two months. As a member of the Coalition Cabinet, Baldwin approved the final draft of the 'Treaty', having at the last moment to cancel a visit to Cambridge for a reunion in his old college. 'It is rather a depressed S.B. this afternoon,' he wrote on 5 December, 'for I have been done out of my dinner at Trinity (and a stay at the Lodge, if you please!). We had a Cabinet on Ireland at noon, sitting till half past one: at half past two Griffith and Collins were to be interviewed again, and a second Cabinet is expected about six. It is now a quarter past four and no news yet.' When it came the news was good. Griffith had agreed on behalf of his delegation to sign. Southern Ireland was to be known henceforth as the 'Irish Free State' and to enjoy the status and rights of a self-governing Dominion, with control of her finances and defence arrangements. Northern Ireland, whose Prime Minister had not been invited to participate in the conference, was to be given the choice either of coming into an all-Ireland Parliament, with certain safeguards, or else of remaining an integral part of the United Kingdom with her local Parliament in Belfast and also submitting to a Boundary Commission designed to redraw her boundary with the south as nearly as possible on nationalist and sectarian lines.

The 'Treaty' was duly signed in the early hours of 6 December 1921, and its terms were immediately published to the world. 'I never thought I should live to see the day of such abject humiliation for Great Britain,' Carson remarked when he read them.[49]

However, this was not the view of Lloyd George and the Cabinet. In public Baldwin took the line that the Irish settlement was not a surrender to murder and that it had prevented further bloodshed which there would have been if the civil war had been resumed and the British forces had persisted in a policy of conquest. Bonar Law, who supported it, spoke for Baldwin and the majority of the Conservatives at this time when he said: 'When I say that I am in favour of this Agreement, I do not pretend to like it. I am sure the Government do not like it in many particulars. I do not pretend to like it, but I ask myself this. What is the alternative? Are we going back to the condition of things which prevailed over the last two years?' This feeling was shared by the great majority of Conservatives. Although only fifty-eight voted against the motion when the 'Treaty' was approved by the House of Commons, there was a general feeling of uneasiness and even resentment about the manner in which the matter had been handled by Lloyd George, particularly on the part of several junior ministers who were friends of Baldwin, such as his parliamentary secretary Lloyd-Greame, as well as other rising Tories like Leopold Amery and Edward Wood. Some leading Liberals also felt strongly that the Prime Minister was moving towards a presidential form of government. One of these was Edwin Montagu, the Secretary of State for India, who wrote at this time to the Viceroy Lord Reading:

Politics here at home are in an awful state. We are governed by the Prime Minister who has confidence only in Chamberlain, F.E. [Smith] and Horne and carries with him Winston because of the necessity for doing so. F.E. has become a very much larger figure and is really the Prime Minister's right-hand man. The Cabinet is hardly ever called together and then only to register decisions. Everything that wants doing is given to one of these people to do . . .[50]

There was even talk of 'F.E.' becoming Prime Minister if anything should happen to Lloyd George.* At this time Birkenhead was very close to Lloyd George and he suggested to him the holding of another 'Coupon Election' with a view to getting rid of the Tory dissidents and perpetuating the Coalition as a kind of 'Middle Party'. Lloyd George jumped at the idea, but with the exception of Birkenhead he found the Tories lukewarm if not hostile, notably Chamberlain.

On 13 January 1922, Davidson wrote to Bonar Law, who was greatly recovered in health and looked to some as if he might make a political come-back:

> I was talking to S.B. the other day (he is against an election) and he is inclined to share the opinion that our people fervently desire to know where they stand and what they stand for. The re-establishment of a great Conservative Party with: Honest Government; Drastic Economy; National Security; and *No* adventures abroad or at home, would carry great weight in the country.
>
> Derby in the Lords and you as Leader and PM in the Commons has been mooted pretty widely. Naturally it is what I should like though I don't know whether D. is to be trusted. Birkenhead doesn't cut any ice with the public in the same way as D.
>
> I hope that the election will be postponed, but if it comes the Tories must go separately to the country . . .
>
> Stanley B. has had some fun with the Economy Millionaires Committee. On being ushered in he surveyed Maclay and Inchcape with a smile and remarked: 'I feel as if I had come to arrange an overdraft. I expect you are good for a million, aren't you?' Upon which they each one buttoned up his trousers pocket.[51]

The press was seething with rumours and *The Times* regarded a February election as a virtual certainty. 'How they are all intriguing,' Baldwin wrote to Mrs Davidson. 'I am so sick of it all sometimes. I want a cleaner atmosphere. Cowardice. Does the pig make the sty or "t'other way on"?' In an attempt to dissipate the Conservative opposition to an immediate election, Lloyd George offered Bonar Law the post of Foreign Secretary in a reconstructed government, and when he turned down the offer the Prime Minister bowed to the inevitable. On 21 January, Lloyd George announced that there would be no election, at least for the time being. 'The little PM is very busy and I don't know what he is up to,'

---

* William Hewins mentions this possibility in his diary under date 3 November 1921: 'I saw Walter Long. He thought that if L.G. resigned Birkenhead would have to be Prime Minister.' W. A. S. Hewins, *The Apologia of an Imperialist*, II, 243.

noted Baldwin when he heard the news. 'I think he was trying to get the old Liberal party united under his leadership and then throw us all out. But he has failed in that enterprise and I have no idea where he will break out next!' [52]

Lloyd George's next move was to offer to retire in favour of Austen Chamberlain and even to serve under him. 'I have always felt the anomaly of holding the first position in a Government the majority of whose supporters belong to another Party,' he wrote to the Conservative leader on 27 February. 'I have repeatedly offered Mr Bonar Law, and I renewed the offer to you when you succeeded him, to go out and give independent and loyal support to a government formed by either of you to carry out the policy upon which I knew we were in complete agreement. I suggest in all sincerity to you that the time has come for you to accept that offer.' Lloyd George, on whom the strain of work was beginning to tell, had been in office for the past sixteen years without a break, over five of them as Prime Minister, and not surprisingly he was about to go sick. However, Austen Chamberlain, who was having trouble with his 'Diehard' followers, begged Lloyd George to remain in Downing Street, remarking that his resignation would be a disaster.

Whether Chamberlain thought he could form a Government at this time is unclear, but he certainly threw away the chance of doing so, as in the event of Lloyd George's resignation the King would have been bound to send for him as the leader of the largest separate Party in the House of Commons. How Chamberlain saw things in the Party appears from what he told his sister. 'I know what I want,' he wrote to her the day before he got Lloyd George's letter. 'My colleagues are agreed with me and Younger intends to carry out my policy; yet they all seem to conspire to prevent it. Younger humiliates the PM publicly, F.E. attacks Younger personally; Bonar Law tries on the crown, but can't make up his mind to attempt to seize it, won't join us and share the load, but watches not without pleasure the trouble of his friends, and the Diehards instead of responding to my advances harden in their resistance.' [53]

A few days later, the Government's reputation suffered a severe blow through the enforced resignation from the India Office of Edwin Montagu, who was in fact peremptorily dismissed by Lloyd George for having published a telegram from the Viceroy Lord Reading about certain moves in the Middle East designed to placate Indian Moslem aspirations. Montagu's ultra-liberal policies were detested by the majority of Conservatives and his departure was hailed with savage glee. Chamberlain insisted that Montagu's successor must be a Tory, to which the Prime Minister agreed, and Chamberlain undertook to sound out his colleagues. The first approach was made to Lord Derby, but he declined, as also did the Duke of Devonshire. According to Chamberlain's official biographer Sir Charles Petrie, Chamberlain then suggested Baldwin but 'the Prime Minister demurred on account of his lack of decision'.

On the other hand, according to Lord Beaverbrook, 'Lloyd George, strange though it seems, favoured Baldwin for the vacancy, but Chamberlain rejected this recommendation.'* What is certain, in the face of a conflict of evidence, is that Baldwin's name was considered for the vacancy and turned down.[54] The post was eventually accepted by another Tory peer Lord Peel, whose great-grandfather Sir Robert Peel had been Queen Victoria's Prime Minister and is regarded as the founder of the modern Conservative Party. However, the fact that men of the standing of Derby and Devonshire had refused to enter the Cabinet was another nail in the coffin of the Coalition.

'As he explained to his intimates,' Wickham Steed wrote of Baldwin at this time, 'he had seen one decent fellow after another go to pieces under the influence of the Lloyd George group. In his own phrase, the morality had been "sucked out of them"; and he began to fear that, if he remained much longer in the Government a like fate might befall him.' The nickname of 'the Goat' bestowed upon Lloyd George originated when he was Chancellor of the Exchequer before the war, because of the Premier's reputation for capriciousness or, as some would have it, for amorousness. 'He who lies in the bosom of the goat spends his remaining years plucking out the fleas' was a proverb, allegedly Afghan, which Baldwin liked to quote *à propos* of the Prime Minister at this period.

'I think it is true that, although Baldwin fully appreciated the genius of Lloyd George,' Davidson has written, 'he so mistrusted his political and moral conduct of affairs that he reacted at once to any proposal or policy of Lloyd George's in a very negative and critical light. They were so entirely different in their mental and moral outlook on life that it was not surprising that they instinctively disliked each other. Although Baldwin appreciated the speed and subtlety of Lloyd George's mental processes, when it came to fundamentals they were poles apart.'[55] An example of this difference occurred during the Cabinet meeting on the question of according full diplomatic recognition to the new state of Soviet Russia, which Lloyd George was anxious to concede when he met the Russians at the forthcoming international conference at Genoa. After Churchill had threatened to resign rather than accept *de jure* recognition, Baldwin

---

* The Beaverbrook version is supported by the Lloyd George Papers, from which it appears that Lloyd George was at this time courting the 'old Tories', of whom Baldwin was considered to be one. See Maurice Cowling, *The Impact of Labour* (1971), pp. 162, 202, 484, 495.

urged that, while he agreed to *de facto* recognition in the interests of getting Anglo-Russian trade moving again, it would help to minimise criticism of the Government if Lloyd George would make it clear that full recognition would be conceded only after a probationary period when experience had shown that the Russians would honour their under-takings and that anything agreed in this sense at Genoa should be subject to ratification by Parliament. In the event nothing came of recognition at the conference since the question of the Russian imperial debt which had been repudiated by the Soviets proved a stumbling block and this was referred to another conference at The Hague before anything else should be decided.

The Irish Treaty was ultimately to prove fatal to the survival of the Coalition. If it had been a success, the Conservatives might have accepted it, albeit with reluctance, in the interests of peace, but it was immediately repudiated by de Valera and a cruel civil war broke out between the 'Free Staters' and the 'Republicans', as the respective supporters of Griffith and de Valera were styled, while Griffith and Collins were powerless to prevent Republican gunmen from invading the north. They even invaded England, and in June Field-Marshal Sir Henry Wilson was fatally shot down outside his London house, a few doors from Baldwin's in Eaton Square. For these tragic developments Birkenhead and Chamberlain in-curred considerable odium among the Unionist rank and file who felt that their leaders had been hoodwinked by 'the dirty little Welsh attorney' (as Neville Chamberlain privately called Lloyd George) and they themselves betrayed. Further discontent was occasioned by Lloyd George's reckless handing out of political honours, culminating in the award of peerages to three businessmen of dubious commercial morality, of whom one had been guilty of trading with the enemy during the war, as Baldwin was no doubt aware. As a result largely of Bonar Law's intervention, Lloyd George was forced to agree to the appointment of a Royal Commission to consider the whole procedure of honours awards in the future, although he would not admit that his own conduct hitherto had been in any way remiss. Mean-while Bonar Law was waiting restlessly in the wings. Baldwin, who lunched with him on 9 June about the time the honours scandal broke, found him 'in excellent fettle', though he thought that time hung heavily on his hands. 'He is singularly resourceless and after his six strenuous years in office he seems able to think of nothing else than politics except when he is playing chess or bridge.' By way of contrast, Baldwin added, 'the little PM returned from Genoa looking as if he had had a long holiday'.[56]

Shortly afterwards, the Conservative Junior Ministers, among them Lord Winterton, the Under-Secretary for India, asked for a meeting with

Chamberlain, and when this took place they let him know the disquiet in the constituencies about the leadership in general and the honours scandal in particular. 'What's all this I hear about you and other junior Ministers intriguing against the Prime Minister because you don't like his Honours List?' Birkenhead asked Winterton whom he happened to meet afterwards. 'It is both disloyal and foolish. Winston, Austen and I are behind him. We four are the most powerful combination in political life. Who is going to lead you to victory if you smash the Coalition? Someone like Bonar or Baldwin? You would not stand a chance.' Winterton, who was profoundly disturbed by this outburst, could only reply that they were entitled to state their views to the Party leader.[57]

Chamberlain, who promised to pass on these views to the other Conservatives in the Cabinet, subsequently wrote:

> I had previously seen the Under-Secretaries who were for the most part very restless about the continuation of the Coalition under Lloyd George and I placed their views before the Cabinet Ministers. They probably knew this but without expressing them I invited my colleagues to speak. They *unanimously* advised that it would be madness to break up the Coalition. I agreed but we decided to meet in October to see if there was any change in the situation. This was conveyed to the Under-Secretaries who asked to meet the Cabinet Ministers. They repeated their doubts and dislikes. Then F.E. scolded them with an intellectual arrogance which nearly produced a row there and then and did infinite harm. (I remonstrated very courteously but very strongly with him next day.) Balfour spoke persuasively, but it is astonishing how little weight he now carries with the Party. I spoke gravely in the same sense.[58]

'Mr Baldwin sat, *more suo*, silent and aloof,' noted Lord Winterton, who had vigorously counter-attacked Birkenhead, 'but I detected a gleam of sympathy for us in his face.' Amery, who could see his colleagues 'bristling more and more with every sentence', afterwards observed that 'whatever chances F.E. may have had of the Unionist leadership of the future they are not likely to have survived this unfortunate performance'. Chamberlain, in promising to convey their feelings to the Prime Minister, 'wound up with a few pontifical sentences', in Amery's words, 'and we dispersed, most of the juniors spluttering with indignation'.[59]

Balfour, whom Winterton asked what he thought of the meeting, remarked: 'It was not a very happy occasion, nor one that was very tactfully handled on either side.' From which Winterton concluded that 'with his great discernment and experience' the elder statesman of the Tory Party considered that the Coalition was doomed.[60]

Lloyd George carried on seemingly unconcerned by the volcano on which he was sitting. 'Our Goat is well,' noted Baldwin at the end of August; 'clad in a light suit, brown of face, he presided for two hours at a sort of bastard Cabinet this afternoon.' A few days later Baldwin and his wife left for their annual holiday in Aix-les-Bains.

FOUR

CHANCELLOR OF THE EXCHEQUER

I

Baldwin and his wife arrived at Aix-les-Bains on 10 September 1922. Before leaving London, he had seen his doctor who told him that he was suffering from pronounced fatigue and that he should not read any newspapers, so that, in his wife's words, 'his mind should have as much rest from public affairs as possible'. A week later he wrote to Mrs Davidson: 'I only want rest and I was awfully tired when I came out. I have been for two or three months. Age, I suppose . . . I walk wherever possible for hours and hours.' For another week, he carried out his doctor's orders and did not look at any papers. Then his eye caught a French news poster suggesting that England might go to war as the result of trouble with the Turks. He promptly bought a French paper and as many English ones as he could lay hands on. 'Such a surfeit on a clean stomach made me quite ill,' he noted. 'We seem to have messed up everything in the Near East, from the years preceding the war till today.'

Encouraged by Lloyd George, who was fanatically anti-Turk, the Greeks had undertaken to put down the rebellion led by the nationalist Turkish leader Mustapha Kemal, who had repudiated the peace treaty concluded between Turkey and the Allies at Sèvres in 1920. Unfortunately for them, the Greeks were driven out of Asia Minor, while the Kemalist forces seized and sacked Smyrna on the same day as the Baldwins reached Aix. It immediately began to look as if the Kemalists might now take the Dardanelles and cross into Europe, thus coming into conflict with the British troops at Chanak who were part of the small international force guarding the Straits. On 17 September the British Cabinet, largely at Churchill's instigation, issued a communiqué announcing that the British occupation troops under General Sir Charles Harington at Chanak would be reinforced and that they would act with the British Mediterranean Fleet in opposing any infraction of the neutralised zone of the Straits by the Kemalists or any attempt on their part to cross into Europe. France reacted by withdrawing French troops from the area, not wishing to be involved in an Anglo-Turkish war, while the Italians announced that in such an event they would likewise remain neutral.

These developments were reported in the local press and noted by Baldwin with an increasing sense of alarm, although his wife tried to reassure him that 'things could not be as bad as the French papers made out or he would have been wired for'. On 28 September he went for a twenty-mile walk by himself, during which, according to Lucy Baldwin, 'he did a good deal of clear thinking in the mountains'. Next morning, he wrote to Mrs Davidson: 'I have got into training again and yesterday I did a 5,000 feet little mountain, to the top and back on my own legs in about seven hours and fit as a fiddle after it. I couldn't have done it three weeks ago to save my life. My agility in the descent surprised me and I can only conclude that living with *goats* made me sure-footed among rocks.'[1]

In the afternoon of 29 September Baldwin took a shorter walk, this time with his wife, and on their way back to the hotel they bought another paper; from this they learned that 'things seemed to be getting worse instead of better'. Lucy Baldwin then went to her room for a rest before changing for dinner, while her husband sat down in another room to play patience. As he was thus engaged, one of the hotel staff brought him a telegram. 'It has come,' he exclaimed as he burst into his wife's room holding the telegram in his hand. 'I have been expecting it. There is some devilment afoot and I must get back to back up poor dear old Austen.' They then talked over the matter and it was decided that he should return to London next morning, while his wife should stay on for another week at Aix to complete her cure, and that they should meet again in Paris.[2]

By travelling overnight, Baldwin reached Downing Street in time for the Cabinet Meeting on the morning of 1 October. He then discovered that it was not 'poor dear old Austen' who needed support, but that two days previously the majority of the Cabinet, bent on a showdown with the Turks, had agreed to the despatch of a telegram to General Harington instructing him to deliver an ultimatum threatening war unless the Kemalists halted their advance and withdrew their forces from the Chanak area. Lord Curzon, the Foreign Secretary, had asked for a delay of at least twenty-four hours so that he could consult with Raymond Poincaré, his opposite number in Paris, but the war party in the Cabinet led by Churchill and Birkenhead with the Prime Minister's backing had brushed aside Curzon's request. Curzon's strongest supporter in the Cabinet was Sir Arthur Griffith-Boscawen, the Minister of Agriculture, who brought Baldwin up to date as to what had been happening in his absence at Aix.

'I am greatly alarmed at the situation generally, the terrible risks of war which some of our friends appear prepared to take and their distrust of diplomatic methods,' Griffith-Boscawen summarised his view which was shared by Baldwin. 'I am certain the country does not want war and will not have it, unless it is convinced that every effort has been made to avoid it.'[3] It was clear to Baldwin, as he later told his wife, that 'Winston and L.G. had been all for war and had schemed to make this country go to war with Turkey so that they should have a "Christian" (save the mark) war *v*. the Mahomedan and turn the Turks out of Europe. On the strength of that, they would call a General Election at once and go to the country, which, they calculated, would return them to office for another period of years.' Indeed the decision to seek a dissolution of Parliament had been taken at a week-end meeting at Chequers of the inner circle of the Cabinet, at which Austen Chamberlain warned Lloyd George that, while he was willing to take the risk of going to the country, he might fail to carry the Conservative Party with him and thus be 'unable to deliver the goods' at another 'coupon election'.

The Cabinet was in almost continuous session throughout 1 October, expecting to hear from Harington that hostilities had broken out. Fortunately the General with the support of Sir Horace Rumbold, the British High Commissioner in Constantinople, ignored his instructions and did not deliver the ultimatum. His reply to the 'Chanak telegram' intimated that strong-arm methods were unnecessary to resolve the trouble and that a cease-fire between the Turks and the Greeks was imminent. Negotiations thereupon began between Harington and the Turks on the spot and between Curzon and Poincaré in Paris. As a result, the Greeks agreed to withdraw to the line of the Maritza and Allied detachments proceeded to occupy Eastern Thrace pending its restoration to the Turks. Meanwhile the ex-Conservative leader Bonar Law wrote a letter to *The Times* stating in effect that he was not prepared to support a policy of intervention abroad on issues which had no direct connection with British interests, although he supported the principle of a 'decisive warning' to the Turks as reflected in the Chanak telegram. 'We cannot alone act as the policemen of the world,' he stressed. 'The financial and social condition of this country makes that impossible. It seems to me, therefore, that our duty is to say plainly to our French Allies that the position in Constantinople and the Straits is as essential a part of the Peace settlement as the arrangement with Germany, and that if they are not prepared to support us there, we shall not be able to bear the burden alone . . .'[4]

This letter, which Beaverbrook saw was also given prominence in the *Daily Express*, initiated a strong movement among the growing body of anti-Coalition Conservatives in favour of Bonar Law resuming the Party leadership, and he was bombarded with letters in this sense. The annual Party Conference was due to take place in November and Lloyd George sensed that this would result in the bulk of the rank-and-file Tories refusing any longer to support the Coalition. At a meeting of Unionist Cabinet ministers on 10 October it was agreed with one dissentient that the Coalition should continue under Lloyd George, but to hold a General Election as soon as possible on a Coalition ticket. The dissenting voice was Baldwin's. 'I arose and spoke and told them that I for one could not and would not do it,' he afterwards described the scene to his wife. 'I must be free and stand as a Conservative: I could not serve under L.G. again. The rest of the Unionist ministers were aghast and they were all apparently against me.'

Later the same day, it appears, Churchill called at the Board of Trade to discuss some departmental matter with Baldwin. He then went on to harangue his Cabinet colleague upon 'the disloyalty of anyone daring to leave the PM'. Baldwin listened in silence until Churchill said: 'There'll be some pretty mudslinging.' To which Baldwin replied quietly: 'That would be a pity because some pretty big chunks could come from the other side!'

By this time Baldwin had given up hope of finishing his holiday with his wife, and he wrote to her suggesting that she might like to complete it at Folkestone where he might be able to join her at the week-end. But she preferred to come back to London, which she did on 12 October. Baldwin met her off the boat train at Victoria Station. It was a pleasant evening, so they decided to walk to Eaton Square which was quite near the station, while Mrs Baldwin's maid, who had travelled with her, went ahead in a taxi with the luggage.

'I have done something dreadful without consulting you,' Baldwin began as they set out on their walk home. 'I do hope you won't mind. I have been fearfully worried, but I felt that it had to come. I am resigning from the Cabinet. I do hope you won't mind fearfully, but I've said I cannot continue to serve under the Goat any longer. Do tell me what you think.'

'You did quite right, I am absolutely with you,' his wife told him after he had brought her up to date on the rapidly developing political crisis. He added that the Unionist ministers had met again earlier in the

day and that Griffith-Boscawen had definitely thrown in his lot with
Baldwin. Otherwise the prospect was bleak. 'Curzon was sympathetic,
but that was all. So there it is. They will follow the Goat and I can't, so
it means that I shall drop out of politics altogether.'[5]

Lucy Baldwin summed up the position in a letter which she wrote to
her mother-in-law at this time:

> I knew Stan wasn't happy at the way things were going under the
> PM's leadership, but up to the present he had no real reason to
> break with him. But just this last peril [of war with Turkey] and the
> way it had been brought about was too much for him. So we decided
> we must make our protest knowing that we should of course go
> under and of course Stan would not get office again as long as the
> [present] PM was Prime Minister . . .
>
> Dear old Bonar's inclination was to remain as he is in peace and
> quiet, but I am glad that his sense of duty to his country won and
> he came out strong. He is such an odd being that one really didn't
> know up till the last if he really would come out and [give a] lead,
> though one knows which way his sympathies were.

She added that her husband told several of his political friends and
colleagues that he always consulted her with the result that 'they talked
to me as though I was a Cabinet Minister too!'[6]

2

Next day Baldwin went to see Bonar Law at his house in Onslow Gardens,
already the scene of much coming and going occasioned by Bonar Law's
recent letter in *The Times* and the growing feeling among the Tories in
the country egged on by Beaverbrook that he should come out of his
retirement and lead the Party again. Baldwin added his voice to the
others, but Bonar Law was not encouraging, although he did agree to
see his doctor. He also counselled Baldwin to hold his hand about
resigning, or at least to take no precipitate step until the next Unionist
ministerial meeting which Chamberlain had called for the 16th. Amery,
one of the junior ministers who also saw Bonar Law on 13 October,
advised Baldwin in like sense. At the same time Bonar Law told Davidson
that he was by no means certain that he could reunite the Conservative
Party or that his health could stand the strain. It would also mean a
battle with old friends and he shrank from such unpleasantness.

Meanwhile on 13 October Chamberlain urged in a public speech in Birmingham that the Conservatives and Liberals should together fight the coming election on an anti-Socialist platform, although he feared some Tory backsliding. 'I am not sure that it may not now be necessary to call a Party meeting,' he had written to Birkenhead on the eve of his Birmingham speech, 'and to tell them bluntly that they must either follow our advice or do without us in which case they must find their own Chief and form a Government at once. They would be in a d——d fix! . . . I am not willing to step into L.G.'s shoes and to take any post in a Government formed in personal opposition to him. The malcontents assume that they can reject our advice and use us for their own purposes. They make a mistake and it may be well to prove it to them.'[7]

This is the first hint of such a meeting which in the event was to take place just a week later at the Carlton Club.

On Saturday the 14th, Baldwin met his wife for lunch at her club and told her that 'things were beginning to move', that the Under-Secretaries thought of joining him in the stand he had taken and that he had invited three of them to have tea at 93 Eaton Square that afternoon. They walked back to the house, in Lucy Baldwin's words, 'buying cakes on the way as the household wasn't yet up and we were only camping there until they came'. Only Lloyd-Greame and Amery were able to come, as Sir John Baird, whom Amery had hoped to bring along with him, could not be reached. Edward Wood was also out of town. Nevertheless it was clear from what Baldwin learned that most of the Under-Secretaries were seriously thinking of coming out against the Coalition. The impression gathered strength when they read the details of a speech delivered by Lloyd George the same afternoon in Manchester, in which the Prime Minister spoke of the Turks as cut-throats and barbarians and implied that the French were treacherous and lacked courage. It was this speech which is said to have finally turned Curzon against Lloyd George for his meddling in foreign policy.[8]

The Conservative backbenchers in the Commons were also getting restive. One of the most respected of these was Sir Samuel Hoare, MP for Chelsea, a middle-of-the-road man who used to play tennis regularly with Bonar Law and was also in touch with Beaverbrook and Davidson. He spent the morning of Sunday, 15 October, drafting a letter to *The Times*, a copy of which he sent to Davidson.[9] In it he wrote:

The Coalition of 1918 was a temporary expedient based upon the general acceptance of the Conservatives and the Lloyd Georgian

Liberals. As long as the Conservative Party continued to accept the expedient, the majority of the Conservative Members of the House of Commons were prepared to support it. It is now certain that the rank-and-file of the Conservative Party have withdrawn this general acceptance. It is useless, therefore, for Mr Chamberlain or any other Conservative leader to attempt to impose from above the continuance of an arrangement which nine out of ten of the party desire to see ended.

What Conservatives are demanding is a means to close the divisions in their own ranks. Mr Chamberlain's policy would only dig them deeper. Fortunately, as there seems to be general agreement amongst the rank-and-file, it is hoped that a bridge for restoring unity will soon be found.

As Baldwin's PPS, Davidson undertook to show the letter to his master. But he was unable to do this until the evening, since Baldwin and his wife had gone off to Brighton for the day. ('S. very worried,' noted Lucy, 'and he thought a walk on the Downs would help him.') When he saw the letter, Baldwin approved of it and its publication at once. Meanwhile Hoare had taken it round to *The Times* offices, where Wickham Steed agreed to run it next morning with a supporting editorial. Another significant development took place on Sunday evening when Churchill gave a dinner at his house in Sussex Square for the Prime Minister and a number of other ministers including Chamberlain, Birkenhead and Balfour. The Chief Whip Leslie Wilson was also present. The only one of the leading Coalitionists who was conspicuous by his absence was Curzon who had now broken with the Prime Minister on account of his Manchester speech and had written to Churchill earlier in the day excusing himself.

For some time past Wilson had been urging Chamberlain to await the Party Conference in November before agreeing to a General Election and he repeated his plea at the dinner. Chamberlain refused, but he offered a compromise in the shape of a meeting of all Conservative Members of the House of Commons for the following Thursday the 19th at the Carlton Club. 'Leslie, do you accept that?' Chamberlain asked the Chief Whip. 'Yes, I do,' replied Wilson, adding that he had not changed his own opinion.[10] Next day telegrams were sent by Wilson to all Conservative MPs summoning them to meet Chamberlain and the Conservative Ministers. The invitation did not include Conservative peers, unless like Balfour and Birkenhead they also happened to be members of the Government, since the majority of the peers were thought to be more opposed to the continuance of the Coalition than their colleagues in the Commons.

'S. hardly slept he was so worried,' Baldwin's wife recorded on the 16th. 'The telephone is getting very active.' Unlike Curzon, Baldwin disliked this instrument, but he had to endure its more or less incessant ringing during the next few days. Curzon was particularly busy in this regard, and he would ring up quite early when Baldwin was in his bath, 'such an early bird was his Lordship'. On the same Monday morning Chamberlain again met the Unionist members of the Cabinet, after which Chamberlain wrote: 'Baldwin this time definitely declared his policy to be to tell L.G. that he must go.' Baldwin evidently repeated this view at lunch when he and Griffith-Boscawen met Amery and the Under-Secretaries as well as the Chief Whip. Amery acted as spokesman on this occasion and in the afternoon they all went off to another meeting with Chamberlain. Baldwin, Amery and the others were unanimous in recommending that the Conservatives should fight the election as an independent Party and if returned with a majority they should accept the responsibility of forming a Government. This was rejected by Chamberlain who appealed for unity and advocated the continuance of the Coalition. Amery has recalled that, as he walked away from this meeting with Baldwin, he told him that 'everything now depended on whether Bonar Law's doctor would agree that he was well enough to undertake the strain of leadership if called upon'.[11]

That night Davidson telephoned Hoare and suggested a meeting with his master. Hoare had not previously seen Baldwin, as he 'wished to act independently of the dissentient ministers', but on being told that Baldwin would like to sound him out on the subject of backbench opinion, Hoare invited them both to lunch with him next day, the 17th, at his house in Cadogan Gardens.

In the morning, before the luncheon, the Under-Secretaries met again, this time with Baldwin, Griffith-Boscawen and Sir George Younger, the Party chairman. 'A good deal of excitement seemed to be in the air,' noted Lucy Baldwin, 'and Stan was rather depressed.' His anxiety was shared by Amery who has recorded that at the meeting 'Baldwin spoke briefly, but with great feeling, to say that nothing would induce him ever to serve under Lloyd George again. Others were doubtful as to the use of going into the wilderness, unless Bonar Law were available to lead us. We know that support for our attitude was growing . . . All the same I remained anxious that the unity of the Party should somehow be preserved.'[12]

After the lunch at Hoare's house, when Baldwin described in detail the attitude of each Conservative minister in the Government, Baldwin was due to attend the opening of a new building of the Port of London Authority at 2.30. He was reluctant to keep the engagement since he did not wish to find himself placed next to the Prime Minister which as President of the Board of Trade he was most likely to be. Accordingly he seized the opportunity of going on with the discussion with Hoare and Davidson by sending a telephone message to say that he was prevented from keeping the engagement. 'We were therefore able to continue our talk without interruption,' Hoare afterwards recalled. 'This was very fortunate, for out of it emerged a proposal that may well have had a decisive effect on the crisis.'

As Parliament was still in recess, it was difficult to estimate at all accurately the up-to-the-moment opinion of the Tory backbenchers. Hence it was agreed, apparently at Hoare's suggestion, to pick out about a hundred typical Conservatives who sat on the back benches of the House of Commons and ask them to attend a meeting at the host's house the following afternoon. The three of them then sat round the dining table with Vacher's *Parliamentary Guide* before them and marked off eighty names, chosen not for their known views, but for the impression they would make on the country. When they had finished, Hoare went off to Ashworth's, the House of Commons typists, and telegrams were immediately despatched inviting the selected members to meet in Cadogan Gardens at 5.0 p.m. next day, Wednesday, 18 October. Meanwhile Baldwin went back to his own house in Eaton Square.[13]

Shortly afterwards Bonar Law called and they had a short talk. When Law left, Baldwin went into his wife, looking very gloomy. 'It's no go,' he told her. 'Bonar can't join us.' In fact, the verdict was the reverse in the sense that Law had been pronounced fit to resume work, although the medical opinion seems to have been that he probably could not carry on for more than two years. What disturbed him now was the prospect of breaking with Lloyd George with whom he had formerly worked so well. 'We must never let the little man go,' he had said to a prominent Conservative at the time of the Coupon Election in 1918. 'His way and ours lie side by side in the future.'[14]

That night Baldwin dined at home with his wife and Sir John Baird, one of the dissident Under-Secretaries. According to Lucy Baldwin, Baird's 'one anxiety seemed to be that Stan should not send in his resignation five minutes before he did'. After dinner Davidson came in and 'put quite a different complexion on affairs'. He reported that Bonar Law's sister Mary, upon whose judgement Law set great store, was pressing him to come out and lead the Party. She had seen Sir Thomas

Horder, Law's physician, Davidson went on, and had said that 'the report was good and that he can work again and that was what had depressed Bonar so much'. Law did not want to come out, Davidson added, but was beginning to feel that he might have to respond to the call of duty, although he had written (but not yet sent) his letter of resignation to the chairman of his constituency association in Glasgow.

Again Baldwin 'had hardly any sleep', so his wife tells us, 'but was cheered next morning by hearing that Bonar and Austen Chamberlain also had hardly slept'. So far the leading Conservative Coalition ministers had remained faithful to Lloyd George, but Chamberlain was growing increasingly uneasy about Curzon since he had failed to turn up at Churchill's dinner on 15 October. 'My Lord Curzon appears to be playing a sort of puss-in-the-corner much to our amusement,' noted Lucy Baldwin. For her, as for her husband, it was 'a most agitating time'.

3

After breakfast on 18 October, Baldwin briefly saw two of the Conservative Under-Secretaries, Baird and Wood, who were strongly anti-Coalition, and they consented to come to a meeting with their like-minded colleagues after dinner that night at 93 Eaton Square. It was agreed that Younger and Wilson should also be invited. Baldwin and the two Under-Secretaries then went together to Whitehall, where Baldwin spent the morning as usual at the Board of Trade before going off with Davidson to lunch with Bonar Law in Onslow Gardens. Among Baldwin's callers that morning was Samuel Hoare, who had come straight from seeing Bonar Law at his home. Law, said Hoare, had confirmed that he had definitely decided not to come out and so far from leading the Party that he intended to resign his seat. 'His refusal was all the more devastating,' wrote Hoare afterwards, 'as it came on the very morning of the meeting at my house. It seemed to put an end to all our plans.' Baldwin agreed with Hoare that 'everything was finished'. Hoare then remarked that, 'if Bonar Law still made personal considerations his main reason, his friends must also insist on their personal considerations. They had staked everything upon Bonar Law, and would lose it all if Bonar Law ran out.' He was telling Baldwin this, said Hoare, because he had gathered from Law that Baldwin and Davidson were lunching with him that day and the arguments of such old and trusted friends might be persuasive.[15]

The luncheon in Onslow Gardens lasted for three hours. But nothing that Baldwin or his PPS said could move Bonar Law from his declared intention of resigning his seat in the Commons and retiring from political life for good. 'Well,' said Baldwin as they took their departure, 'you are leaving all the white men on the beach. They can't get on without you to lead and it means that we shall just all sink out of politics and we shall leave it to those who are not so honest.'[16]

Baldwin went back to the Board of Trade and shortly afterwards received a note from Amery setting out a formula which he had devised for a compromise with Chamberlain. 'There are really two points,' wrote Amery from the Admiralty; 'firstly to find a solution which will secure unity at tomorrow's meeting and really leave things open after the election; secondly, if unity is secured, how to preserve the position of Ministers, who feel as you and I do, with the least embarrassment to Austen.' The gist of the proposed formula was that the Conservatives, while co-operating with the Coalition Liberals during and after the election, should go to the country as a separate Party, and that Chamberlain as Leader should convene a Party meeting of members of the new House of Commons before joining any fresh coalition. Wilson, the Chief Whip, had already submitted this formula to Chamberlain, and even as Amery was dictating his note to Baldwin, Wilson telephoned him to say that Chamberlain had accepted it. However, his acceptance was conditional upon his consulting his colleagues, and in the event the formula was turned down by Birkenhead and Balfour. Chamberlain consequently felt that it was his duty to stand by them.[17]

Before this development Chamberlain called at Onslow Gardens where he saw Bonar Law who told him that he might plead his health as a means of avoiding the issue, but that if he did come to the meeting at the Carlton Club he must speak against him. 'It's a hateful position,' he told Chamberlain as they parted. 'I expect that if I had remained in your place I should have acted like you.'[18]

He was still undecided when Davidson went to see him again about six o'clock. 'All my efforts were now devoted to persuading Bonar to attend,' Davidson recalled afterwards. 'In this I was ably supported by Lady Sykes – Bonar's eldest daughter – and by her husband Sir Frederick, but in my opinion the most decisive voice was that of Mary Law.'[19] Law told Davidson that he had been particularly struck by Baldwin's parting shot at lunch about the white men on the beach. Then, while they were talking, Samuel Hoare was shown in. The meeting of backbenchers at his house was just over, he said. Out of the eighty invitations sent out, seventy-four MPs had turned up. There was unanimous agreement that three of their number, Ernest Pretyman, a Privy Councillor and former minister, together with George Lane Fox, and Hoare himself, should immediately see Chamberlain on behalf of them all and inform him that a substantial body of Conservative backbench opinion was 'in favour of independent Conservative action, an independent programme, and an independent leader'.

Bonar Law looked at the lists of MPs which Hoare showed him and was evidently much impressed. 'These are very good names,' he repeated.

Hoare and his two colleagues then went on to Downing Street where they saw Chamberlain who rebuffed them stiffly. 'This is an astonishing list,' he said when he saw it. 'Inskip's name is on it. Inskip wrote to me this morning to say that he was strongly in favour of my policy of Coalition.' Lane Fox thereupon answered that Inskip had certainly made an inconclusive speech at the meeting, but he had not demurred in any way to the general conclusions.

After a diatribe from Chamberlain on the merits of continuing the Coalition, Hoare replied that they had not come to argue the respective cases, but merely to give him information which they thought that, as leader of the Party, he ought to have. Chamberlain reacted angrily by saying that he would fight them at the Party meeting, as he regarded the policy approved by the backbench group which they represented as a direct attack on himself. If their view prevailed at the meeting, he went on, or even if they were in a substantial minority, he would resign.

When Hoare returned with this news to Onslow Gardens, he found that the die had been cast. Bonar Law was at dinner when he arrived, but he immediately left the table and took Hoare into the adjoining billiards room. According to Hoare, it was the first time he had seen him smile during the whole crisis. 'I have decided to go to the meeting,' he said simply, 'and I shall make a speech at it.' [20]

The first to hear this important news had been his friend Beaverbrook, to whom Law had telephoned asking him to come to his house. With his usual sense of a good news story, Beaverbrook had promptly telephoned the Press Association to make sure that it was given a prominent place in next morning's papers. There is some evidence that Bonar Law considered that he had been rushed into this fateful decision – 'he hated being bounced', said Davidson – but it was now too late to retract. [21]

Bonar Law's next visitor was Sir Archibald Salvidge, the politically powerful Lord Mayor of Liverpool and a staunch Coalitionist. While Salvidge was putting the case for the Coalition and appealing to Bonar Law's sense of gratitude and loyalty to Lloyd George, the butler entered the room and whispered something in his master's ear. To Bonar Law's remark that there was a bigger issue at stake, the unity of the Conservative Party, Salvidge retorted that Lloyd George retained the unswerving support of every one of his principal Conservative colleagues in the Cabinet.

Bonar Law puffed at his pipe for a few moments. At last he said, almost regretfully, without the slightest note of triumph in his voice: 'I may as well tell you that Lord Curzon is here. He is waiting in another room.' *

Salvidge was flabbergasted. So the much-vaunted loyalty of Lloyd George's Cabinet was a myth, he reflected. Already the Coalition's Foreign Minister had a foot in the other camp! There was no more to be said and he rose to go. Bonar Law called him back. 'Tell Austen and F.E. [Birkenhead] to be moderate,' he said. 'Do you think I or Curzon imagine we can rule the country with the sort of people that will be left to make up a Cabinet after the break tomorrow? I must have Austen and F.E. back at the first possible opportunity. But there will have to be an interval. Tell them not to let it be protracted by unnecessary bitterness.' 22

Meanwhile Davidson had stayed on for a while in Onslow Gardens, answering the telephone and making himself generally useful. About ten o'clock there was a call from Lord Derby who told Davidson that he was 'sick of Lloyd George's manipulations and was prepared to come out in support of Law and the Tory Party fighting the election independently'. At this time Derby did not hold any political office, but he was immensely influential particularly in the industrial north. 'I suggested to Bonar that it would be necessary to keep a careful watch on Derby lest he be influenced to change his mind,' noted Davidson afterwards. 'I knew that, if they knew his change of attitude, F.E. and Salvidge would put great pressure upon him. I therefore arranged that Bonar should ask Derby to call at Onslow Gardens the following morning to take him to the Carlton Club in his car. Perhaps I was over-cautious, and perhaps I underestimated Derby's resolution, but I believed that if he was seen arriving with Bonar Law he would have less difficulty in resisting pressure from the pro-Coalitionists. Bonar Law, who had little faith in Derby's strength of character, acquiesced.' 23

A little later Davidson went back to Eaton Square and briefed Baldwin on the latest developments. The Under-Secretaries together with Younger and Wilson were meeting in the dining-room to discuss the

---

* At their subsequent interview Curzon intimated that he would be willing to carry on as Foreign Secretary and Leader of the House of Lords under Bonar Law but that 'out of loyalty to Chamberlain' he would stay away from the Party meeting next day.

Amery formula. This was now rejected – in any case it was abortive – after Hoare, who had also been invited, had described the meeting earlier in the day at his house and had indicated that Pretyman would move a resolution at the Party meeting next day in the sense of what he had already told Chamberlain, namely that 'the Conservative Party, whilst willing to co-operate with the Coalition Liberals, should fight the election as an independent party with its own leader and its own programme'. It was after midnight when Baldwin went up to bed. 'He seemed happier,' noted his wife, 'and David[son]'s optimism about our winning tomorrow had cheered him.'

Meanwhile back in Onslow Gardens, Bonar Law had been having second thoughts. At 10.30, so he subsequently told Sir Maurice Hankey, the Secretary to the Cabinet, he 'had been on the point of telegraphing to his constituency to resign his seat, and his [sister and his] children had been the principal influence' in persuading him to hold his hand and take what was coming to him. Yet he even hesitated again when, as *The Times* was going to press, he telephoned to Wickham Steed, the editor, to ask whether there was 'anything new' and was told that the paper would carry a lead story in the morning that he would attend the Carlton Club meeting and oppose the Government. He remarked: 'But I have not yet decided to go.' The editor then pressed him to attend in the interests of a return to 'straightforward party government' and promised him the backing of *The Times*. This seems to have been decisive.[24]

The final act on this long and dramatic day was played out in the Cabinet Room in Downing Street. When Salvidge arrived to report the outcome of his encounter with Bonar Law, he found an informal meeting of ministers was in progress. Lloyd George called him in and Salvidge sat down with the others at the historic table. The news of Bonar Law's decision to attend the Carlton Club meeting was not unexpected, but when Salvidge spoke of Curzon's defection there was a gasp of consternation all round. Someone said, 'So our punctilious Proconsul has ratted, has he?' Salvidge realised they knew then that 'their whole position had been given away. Bonar would not be acting now merely on the advice of Baldwin of the Board of Trade, obscure and ineffective Diehards and ambitious Under-Secretaries anxious for their masters' jobs.'

To Salvidge the biggest surprise was Lord Balfour. He banged his fist on the table and shouted: 'I say fight them, fight them, fight them! The thing is wrong. The Conservative Party has always acted on the advice of its leaders. Is the lead of Law and Curzon to count as everything, and the advice of the rest of us as nothing? This is a revolt and it should be crushed.'

Birkenhead came in. He had been speaking at some function and was resplendent in full evening dress on which his orders and decorations shone. He looked extraordinarily youthful and handsome. The others made Salvidge repeat his story. Birkenhead sat with his hands thrust deep into his trousers pockets and his long legs stuck out. 'I have always wanted to make a trip round the world,' he said when Salvidge had finished. 'I think I've got a thousand pounds. I'll be able to go now. The Coalition will not survive tomorrow.'

Lloyd George spoke without bitterness. Personal ambition had undoubtedly played some part in Bonar Law's decision, he remarked, but it had been less of a factor in Bonar's career than in that of any man he knew, and anyhow it was a perfectly laudable ambition. As soon as Chamberlain had reported an adverse Carlton Club decision to him – and there could be little doubt that it would be adverse (Lloyd George went on) – he intended to go to Buckingham Palace, tender his resignation and advise the King to send for Bonar Law. He regretted Law's decision, he said, not because of their historic partnership during the war – every man must take his own view of what his duty required – but because Bonar had allowed his judgement to be rushed. It had been rushed, not by the best brains of his party, but by the least in experience and ability.

The Prime Minister paused and looked round the table at the others. He concluded with a characteristic flourish: 'I have with me the official leader of the Conservative Party in Joseph Chamberlain's worthy son; I have the most distinguished of the elder Conservative statesmen and the only living Conservative ex-Premier in Lord Balfour; I have the most brilliant Conservative figure of modern times in Lord Birkenhead; and, as a mouthpiece of the rank-and-file, the most successful organiser of Tory democracy in Salvidge of Liverpool. But the Conservative Party must settle its own affairs. It is not for me to decide.'[25]

4

Baldwin's first caller on the morning of 19 October was his PPS John Davidson. The morning papers, besides headlining the news that Bonar Law would go to the Carlton Club, carried the result of a parliamentary by-election at Newport, at which an independent Conservative had soundly beaten the Coalition candidate. This augured well for the meeting. Then, while Davidson and Baldwin were talking about it, the telephone rang. It was Hoare, who gave them the terms of the motion which it had been agreed that E. G. Pretyman should propose at the meeting timed to start in the Carlton Club at eleven o'clock. Davidson hurried round to Onslow Gardens where he found Derby waiting with his car as arranged to take Bonar Law to the meeting. Davidson and Sykes, Law's son-in-law, got into the car with them and they were among the first to enter the club. Outside in Pall Mall and in the side street leading to Carlton Gardens, a curious crowd had collected, alternately cheering and booing the arrivals. A cold wind was blowing as Beaverbrook with his accustomed news sense mingled with the onlookers. When Bonar Law walked up the club steps with Davidson, the lobby correspondent of the *Yorkshire Post* called out: 'What is going to happen?' 'A slice off the top,' answered Davidson – with remarkable accuracy as it turned out. Austen Chamberlain arrived with Sir Robert Horne and Lord Lee of Fareham. A woman in the crowd shouted 'Judas!' A similarly hostile reception was accorded Lord Birkenhead when he appeared a little later. Baldwin arrived alone, having told his wife that he would telephone her at home as soon as he knew the result.

The 274 MPs who attended this historic gathering did so in un-expectedly genial and indeed mirthful mood. Bonar Law was cheered much more loudly than Chamberlain when they made their appearance in the Club room. When most of the members had taken their places facing the long table at which Chamberlain was to preside, flanked by his principal supporters among the Conservative Cabinet ministers, an MP, who had a taste for practical jokes, beckoned one of the club servants and told him to bring a couple of glasses of brandy and place them in front of Chamberlain and Birkenhead. The servant did so and then withdrew to the accompaniment of loud laughter from the younger MPs present. According to Beaverbrook, 'Chamberlain eyed the liquid through his hastily-adjusted monocle, gave a start and with a gesture he hid the tumbler behind a chair.' On the other hand, Birkenhead took a 'perfectly sensible attitude', that is, presumably, he drained his glass, a gesture to which he was by no means unaccustomed.[26]

The meeting began with the reading of a letter from Curzon in which the Foreign Secretary sought to explain his absence on the ground that it was a meeting of MPs and although he could attend and speak he could not vote. In any event, he explained: 'I would not speak against my colleagues.' ('But he would intrigue against them,' was Beaverbrook's acid comment.) Chamberlain then led off with a lecture lasting half an hour in which he put the case for the continuance of a Coalition Govern-ment as the only alternative to Labour rule. It was a schoolmasterish performance which grated on his listeners and coming immediately after the result of the Newport by-election carried little conviction. While he was speaking, an unfortunate interruption occurred; someone shouted 'Traitor' and the cry was taken up by several others. Chamberlain thought it was intended for him, whereas it was really meant for Birkenhead with whom the Under-Secretaries were still feeling angry for his attempt to bully them.

The Conservative leader was immediately followed by Baldwin who spoke for only eight minutes, but long enough to put before the meeting with most forcible impact 'the views of the minority in the Cabinet – that is, of myself and Sir Arthur [Griffith-] Boscawen'.[27] He purposely did not mention Curzon whom he considered might be hedging his bet on Bonar Law. He made three points. The first was that 'a fatal mistake was made in agreeing to an election without consulting the Party as to whether they were willing or not to continue the arrangement which they entered into in 1918'. Baldwin's second point was that the Prime Minister was 'a dynamic force', as Birkenhead had described him. 'I accept those words,' said Baldwin. 'He *is* a dynamic force, and it is from that very fact that our troubles, in our opinion, arise. A dynamic force is a very terrible thing; it may crush you and it is not necessarily right.' He went on to make this third point:

It is owing to that dynamic force and that remarkable personality that the Liberal Party, to which he formerly belonged, has been smashed to pieces; and it is my firm conviction that, in time, the same thing will happen to our party. I do not propose to elaborate, in an assembly like this, the dangers and perils of that happening. We have already seen, during our association with him during the past four years, a section of our party hopelessly alienated.* I think that if the present association is continued, and if this meeting agrees that it should be continued, you will see some more breaking up, and I believe the process must go on inevitably until the old Conservative Party is smashed to atoms and lost in ruins.

It was a measure of Lloyd George's disintegrating influence, Baldwin concluded, that he and Chamberlain – 'men who I believe, certainly on my side, have esteem and perhaps I may add affection for each other' – who held the same political principles, should be so divided that one was prepared to go into the wilderness rather than stay with the Prime Minister and the other to go into the wilderness rather than forsake him.

* Baldwin was referring to the Diehards led by Salisbury and Carson who had bitterly opposed the Irish Treaty, which they considered to be a betrayal of the Conservative anti-Home Rule principles.

'It was for that reason that I took the stand that I did. I do not know what the majority here or in the country may think about it. I said at the time what I thought was right, and I stick all through to what I believe to be right.'

In even shorter speeches, Pretyman and Lane Fox then respectively moved and seconded the motion which Hoare had drafted and which Chamberlain was eventually to put to the meeting:

> That this meeting of Conservative Members of the House of Commons declares its opinion that the Conservative Party, whilst willing to co-operate with the Coalition Liberals, should fight the election as an independent party with its own leader and its own programme.

Some desultory discussion followed, after which there was a general cry for Bonar Law. He rose somewhat reluctantly and at first spoke with considerable hesitation, but he eventually made it clear that he supported Pretyman's motion. 'I confess frankly that in the immediate crisis in front of us,' he said, 'I do personally attach more importance to keeping our party a united body than to winning the next election.' Like Baldwin, he felt that if they followed Chamberlain's advice the party would be broken and a new party would be formed. 'Therefore if you agree with Mr Chamberlain in this crisis, I will tell you what I think will be the result. It will be a repetition of what happened after Peel passed the Corn Bill. The body that is cast off will slowly become the Conservative Party, but it will take a generation before it gets back to the influence which the Party ought to have.' He concluded by declaring that he would, though very reluctantly, vote for ending the Coalition. His speech was received with much enthusiasm.

Balfour followed with a philosophic analysis of the principles of a party accustomed to accept the advice of its leaders, insisting that no substantial differences of policy divided the Party from the Coalition Liberals. This dissertation was heard politely, but it cut little ice. Birkenhead remained silent, as also did Horne and Worthington-Evans, the two other leading Conservative ministers who supported the Coalition. Leslie Wilson, the Chief Whip, speaking 'he believed for a certain number of junior ministers', repeated Baldwin's arguments, much to Chamberlain's annoyance. Then, in reply to a question, the chairman emphasised that in his view those who voted in favour of Pretyman's motion would 'exclude the possibility of any but a Tory Prime Minister . . . if there was a Tory majority' at the election. Thus he rejected the compromise which had earlier been suggested.

The meeting then proceeded to a card vote. The result was officially declared as follows:

For the motion	185
Against	88
Abstentions	1

In all 14 Conservative Ministers in the Commons supported the motion, 12 were against it, and there were in fact 4 abstentions. In addition to Baldwin and Griffith-Boscawen, the Ayes included Amery, Baird, Lloyd-Greame, Wilson and Wood; the Noes, in addition to Chamberlain, included Horne, Worthington-Evans, the two Law Officers (Sir Ernest Pollock and Sir Leslie Scott), and Sir William Mitchell-Thompson, who was one of Baldwin's Parliamentary Secretaries at the Board of Trade. Several MPs, such as Lord Winterton and the chairman's brother Neville Chamberlain, did not vote owing to absence abroad. Some others, in Lucy Baldwin's words, 'nailed their colours firmly to the fence' and abstained.

Afterwards Lloyd George sedulously spread the view that the result was due to an intrigue carried out by a clique of reactionary Tory Die-hards, and the fact that the meeting was held in a West End Tory Club gave some currency to this version of events. In fact, the Diehards only formed a small proportion of the anti-Coalition vote, and many of the majority such as Hoare and Baldwin himself were anything but reactionary in their political outlook. Nor, of course, as has sometimes been suggested, was the meeting engineered by the dissident Tories. As has been seen, it was called by Austen Chamberlain himself, and in the event rebounded against him.

Lucy Baldwin's account of how she spent the time waiting for the result of the meeting is worth quoting:

I had arranged with Mimi Davidson to go and sit outside the Carlton Club so that we should hear the verdict as soon as possible. I did not tell Stan as I thought that it would fuss him knowing I was outside; so I arranged that he was to ring me up as to the result. Betty was too nervous and declined to come with me but stayed at home.

The morning was very long, and I walked and I walked and I walked to pass the time and at 12.30 started to call for Mimi Davidson, picked her up, and then we waited with other cars in the side street by the Carlton which leads to Carlton Gardens. Such a crowd outside the Carlton – photographers, cinema men, policemen among others. We were the only occupants of a car; all the others were empty waiting for their owners. It was a most exciting time.

We caught sight of Geoffrey Fry* and he came and sat with us a little and then, excitement needing action, he walked about, reporting to us every now and again. Then Sykes, Bonar's son-in-law, joined us and the excitement grew more and more tense. It was now 1.30 . . .

Opposite our car was stationed a rather unwholesome-looking Rolls-Royce car with a smart but 'bookie'-looking chauffeur and with a snake about to strike as its mascot. Suddenly there burst through the crowd a yellowish-white drawn face and the slight figure of a man who jumped into this car and was off in a flash.

It was Sir Philip Sassoon, Lloyd George's wealthy PPS, on his way to convey the news to his chief. 'Look at Philip,' exclaimed Mrs Davidson, clutching the other's arm, 'we must have won!'

At the same time Sykes brought us news that the figures were 187–86. Mimi Davidson and I said in one breath: 'What's the good of that?' Then I saw Sir Arthur Griffith-Boscawen hurrying away (afterwards I heard to report to Lord Curzon) and I called to him and asked the figures. '186–87,' he replied and hurried off. Still we didn't know which was which. Then we saw David emerging with Geoffrey Fry on one side and Sykes on the other, looking as though he was emerging from a football scrimmage, and he told us that our side had won by 99, and that Bonar Law had come down plump on our side and carried the room with him . . .

Mimi Davidson and I were nearly off our heads with excitement. I took her home to luncheon at 2 p.m. and heard that Stan had already rung me up and that Betty had got the result. Next followed the resignations. Stan sent in his at once, followed by all the Under-Secretaries who had thrown in their lot with Stan. Later in the afternoon, according to the evening papers, all the rest of the Cabinet resigned, and the PM went to see the King who had come up unexpectedly. Then Bonar Law was sent for and asked to form a Government which he said he'd do.

* Sir Geoffrey Fry (1888–1960) was employed in the Treasury under Keynes when Baldwin was Financial Secretary. He later served Bonar Law and also Baldwin as Private Secretary. He was created a baronet in 1929. A man of considerable private means, he used to entertain Baldwin at Oare House, his country home in Wiltshire.

Baldwin received many congratulations on his performance, including some from those who hoped to jump on the Bonar Law bandwaggon. 'They say he has saved the Tory Party,' noted his wife. 'Everyone is most kind and says he spoke excellently. Just the right length, etc. But of course it was Bonar's weight that won us the day.'[28]

5

Lucy Baldwin's account of the crisis suggests that after the Carlton Club meeting Bonar Law immediately agreed to form a new government. This was not so. Although Lord Stamfordham, the King's Private Secretary, telephoned Onslow Gardens and asked Bonar Law to come to Buckingham Palace in the afternoon of 19 October, Bonar Law demurred on the ground that he was not the leader of the Conservative Party and he politely but firmly refused to take office until he had been formally elected leader. Whether Bonar Law's reluctance was due to his respect for constitutional niceties or whether he hoped that something would intervene at the last moment to relieve him of the duty of assuming supreme political responsibility is unclear. Certainly other potential Prime Ministers have not been deterred from accepting the sovereign's invitation to form an administration by any such scruples or hesitation. However, Bonar Law did consent to have an interim audience with the King at which he explained his position and he also sounded out a number of ex-ministers as to whether they would serve in any Government that he might be able to form.

In view of most of the leading Coalition Unionists being ruled out, Bonar Law's task was far from easy. Curzon's last-minute defection from Lloyd George ensured that he should continue as Foreign Secretary. Otherwise, with the exception of Baldwin and Griffith-Boscawen, there were to be none who had been in the Lloyd George Cabinet. Bonar Law immediately offered Baldwin the post of Chancellor of the Exchequer, which had been vacated by Sir Robert Horne. According to Lucy Baldwin, her husband 'had a feeling that he didn't want to make anything out of the *bouleversement* and said he thought McKenna, if he'd take it, would be the stronger and more experienced for the country, and so Stan was empowered to ask McKenna'. Reginald McKenna, who was four years older than Baldwin, had been Chancellor in the Asquith Coalition during the war and had previously served as Home Secretary. He was an Asquithian Liberal who did not get along with Lloyd George; furthermore he had lost his seat in the 1918 Election and had been out of the Commons since that time. He was now chairman of the Midland Bank. Although he was willing publicly to support a Conservative Government, McKenna realised that to take office in it would alienate many Liberals who might otherwise vote for it. There was also the problem of finding another seat. Accordingly, after he had taken three days to think it over, he told Baldwin that he felt he must decline the offer, but added that if Baldwin went to the Treasury instead he would give him all the help he could through his powerful connections in the City.[29]

It is clear from the diary of the Cabinet Secretary Sir Maurice Hankey, who saw the new Prime Minister for the first time on Saturday morning 21 October, that Bonar Law had as yet made no ministerial appointments. Hankey pointed out to him the need for filling the principal offices without delay such as those of the Lord Chancellor, Lord President, Foreign Secretary and Colonial Secretary. Hankey felt it hardly necessary to add 'how important it was to have a Chancellor of the Exchequer'. While he was talking to Bonar Law, the latter sent for Baldwin who, Hankey gathered, was 'to be his right-hand man, and who stood in the corner of the room ''belching'' – for some time he has had a distressing stomach trouble'.[30]*

On Monday 23 October, at a meeting of Conservative peers, MPs and parliamentary candidates held in the Hotel Cecil, Bonar Law was unanimously re-elected leader of the Party, being proposed by Curzon who presided, and seconded by Baldwin. 'In Mr Bonar Law,' remarked Baldwin, 'we have a man whose wisdom, tolerance, freedom from all kinds of pettiness of nature, make him the one man who in these circumstances can bring the whole party united round him.'[31] Bonar Law immediately went to Buckingham Palace to kiss hands on his formal appointment as Prime Minister. The rest of the day he spent in settling the final details of his Cabinet, upon which he had been working for the past three days. His method of choosing his Cabinet seems to have been quite unusual. Having taken over John Davidson as his PPS from Baldwin, he asked Davidson to draw up a list of vacant offices. It was rather like an application form, Davidson later recalled, 'the vacant offices on the left hand, and on the right hand the various candidates in order of preference. We then started off interviewing people. It was really rather awkward because Bonar always had in his hand the paper with the names written in.'[32]

Lucy Baldwin has also recalled that during this period of Cabinet-making, the Davidsons and John Baird visited her in the evenings, 'all

---

* It has been suggested that Baldwin was suffering from peptic ulcers at the time, but there is no evidence of this. He probably had nothing more than an attack of indigestion.

of us suggesting names for the future Cabinet. I was fortunate to name Lord Cave for the Woolsack; doubtless Bonar Law had thought of him before but I was very pleased at the appointment being made and accepted.' Thus George Cave, an unobtrusive Chancery lawyer of great academic distinction and learning, who was already a law lord, became Lord Chancellor in succession to the brilliant and flamboyant Birkenhead. Besides Cave and Curzon, the Cabinet was to include five other peers, altogether an unusually large number.* The Commoners included Amery (Admiralty), Bridgeman (Home Office), Griffith-Boscawen (Health), Lloyd-Greame (Board of Trade) and Wood (Education), all, with the exception of Griffith-Boscawen, newcomers to Cabinet rank.

There remained the question of Baldwin's office. As soon as Bonar Law heard that McKenna had declined the offer of the Treasury, he called to see Baldwin at his house in Eaton Square. According to Lucy Baldwin, who was waiting with her daughter Betty 'in a fever upstairs', Bonar Law and Baldwin talked together for a little. Then Bonar Law got up and said, 'I must get home.'

'But what about the Exchequer?' asked Baldwin. 'Am I to go there?'

'Why, of course.'

A few minutes later, Baldwin walked into his wife's room and said, 'Treat me with respect, I am the Chancellor of the Exchequer!'

6

As might be expected, the new Government met with a mixed reception from the press and public. While the rank-and-file Tories accepted it as the best in the circumstances, it was attacked by the leading Coalitionists such as Churchill as a 'Government of the Second Eleven', and Birkenhead contemptuously referred to its 'second-class brains'. In fact, Bonar Law's Cabinet contained three Fellows of All Souls (Amery, Curzon and Wood), so that it could hardly be said to be so weak intellectually, while there were several promising newcomers to ministerial posts outside the Cabinet, notably Sir Douglas Hogg (Attorney-General), Sir Samuel Hoare (Air Minister) and Austen Chamberlain's fifty-three-year-old younger half-brother Neville who became Postmaster-General. ('I was not surprised by Neville's decision but it *hurt* awfully,' Austen remarked at the time. 'But we both cared more for one another than anything politics could

* Salisbury (Lord President), Devonshire (Colonies), Peel (India), Derby (War), Novar (Scotland).

bring.') Birkenhead also criticised the new Premier's inclusion of so many peers in his Cabinet, and this was taken up by the left-wing newspapers such as the *Daily Herald*. Austen Chamberlain's criticism was more restrained than Birkenhead's and nearer the mark.

> Bonar Law's health is none too good. He has never before gone into action without a stronger man beside him. There is the first uncertainty. Then his young men may blossom out, but Curzon is weak and ill; Baldwin has the reputation both in business and the Treasury of being unable to take a decision; Amery is a poor Parliamentarian, very unhandy so far in spite of his brains; Peel is good, Salisbury and Devonshire are good too in their separate ways, but it is rather of the House of Commons that I am thinking. Lloyd-Greame is the most promising of his Cabinet and Neville outside it, but they do not look a strong team.[33]

Nevertheless, Bonar Law and his policies, together with the men whom he had chosen to carry them out, were clearly endorsed at the General Election when the voters went to the polls on 15 November 1922 and returned 344 Conservatives to the House of Commons, which gave Bonar Law a majority of 77 over all the other parties combined – Labour (138), Asquithian Liberals (60) and Coalition Liberals (57) – although the Conservatives actually received a minority of the total votes cast. 'Tranquillity and stability at home and abroad so that free scope should be given to the initiative and enterprise of our citizens', constituted the low-pitched keynote of his appeal to the country. Specifically he undertook, presumably in agreement with his Chancellor, that there should be drastic economies in Government expenditure in order to reduce taxation, revive trade and bring down unemployment. He also pledged that there should be no change in the fiscal system in the present Parliament. Baldwin, who was returned for Bewdley with a majority of 5,443 over a Liberal, repeated his chief's pledge of financial economy in his own election address. He also promised to pay 'to the last penny' the debt incurred to the United States during the recent war, a pledge which he was soon to be called upon by the Cabinet to redeem. As regards foreign relations he undertook to promote better relations with France than had existed under Lloyd George. It was the first time that he had played a major part in an election. 'Now in a new position, as second man in the Government,' as Lord Beaverbrook was to write, 'he had had to venture forth throughout the land. He spoke with success. He said nothing sensational. He made no spectacular promises. He went before the electorate as a plain businessman representing a plain business Government out to do a solid job of work. And the electorate liked it.'[34]

Baldwin received over 150 letters of congratulation on his new appointment. Three from members of his family he particularly treasured. 'You can't tell how proud I am of my son,' wrote old Louisa Baldwin from Wilden House. 'I feel sure your father rejoices over you in whatever distant sphere he lives, for what dear Cissy tells me today is news of a spiritual victory that makes me grateful indeed that I am your mother.' His cousin Philip Burne-Jones wrote: 'Dear old man, I'm so delighted about you, *you're the best of the bunch* . . . If anyone can steer the Financial Ship of his country into calmer waters, you will.' Another kinsman, Denis Mackail, was equally enthusiastic. 'Once again I am delighted to see the right relation in the right place. I shall do my very best to pay my income tax as regularly as funds will allow and it will be a great comfort to know that you will be laying it out to the best advantage.'[35]

Baldwin was no stranger to the Chancellor's spacious room in the Treasury overlooking Parliament Square, with its William and Mary inkstands and Georgian chairs, which he now proceeded to occupy officially. He had been in it almost daily when he was Financial Secretary under Bonar Law and later Austen Chamberlain. Besides the furniture, he took over from the previous Chancellor Sir Robert Horne his Principal Private Secretary, Percy James Grigg, who thus continued in charge of the minister's private office. Grigg, whose origins were humble – his father had been a carpenter and his mother a children's nurse – was an industrious but somewhat humourless and intellectually intolerant young Treasury official at this time. John Davidson remarked that he had behaved in a 'very superior' manner to Baldwin when the latter was Financial Secretary. Davidson resented this, since Baldwin 'had lived in the world a little longer than he, and had a culture that was not purely experience but was inherent'. Davidson's conclusion was that 'P.J. wasn't a really attractive person, because he lacked human sympathy and was intolerant, and the greatest of the people whom I met in the Civil Service were the people who had tolerance. However superior they were, they never gave you that impression.' No doubt Baldwin was to find this out for himself, since five months later when he moved from 11 Downing Street to No. 10, he did not take Grigg with him as Principal Private Secretary much to the latter's disappointment.*

---

* Grigg afterwards served three successive Chancellors as Principal Private Secretary – Neville Chamberlain, Philip Snowden and Winston Churchill. He was knighted in 1932 and in 1942 entered Parliament when he became Secretary of State for War and was made a Privy Councillor. In 1948 he published his autobiography, *Prejudice and Judgement*. He died in 1966.

One of the time-honoured duties of the Chancellor of the Exchequer was to draw up in conjunction with the Lord Chief Justice the annual list of sheriffs or 'high sheriffs', as these county executive officers are usually known, since the expenses of the office were partly met by the treasury. The ceremony takes place every November in the Lord Chief Justice's court with the Chancellor presiding and is attended by the Clerk of the Privy Council, since the list has subsequently to be approved in council by the sovereign 'pricking the roll'. Sir Almeric Fitzroy, who as Clerk had witnessed nine previous Chancellors in action, noted with satisfaction that on this occasion 'Baldwin acquitted himself with dignity and readiness'.[36]

Weightier matters than this picturesque ceremony in the Law Courts now claimed the Chancellor's attention. The new Prime Minister had instructed his PPS to 'clean up Downing Street', which the faithful Davidson did with Baldwin's enthusiastic support. In the process the economy axe fell heavily both on the swollen Cabinet Secretariat and Lloyd George's team of personal advisers known as the 'Garden Suburb', headed by Philip Kerr (later Lord Lothian) and originally accommodated in the basement of 10 Downing Street, later overflowing into a temporary annexe in the garden. The 'Garden Suburb' had been particularly resented by Curzon on account of its interference in foreign affairs; it now disappeared altogether, while the Cabinet Secretariat was drastically reduced in numbers. Although Maurice Hankey and Thomas Jones kept their jobs in the Secretariat, the staff was cut from 129 to 37, resulting in an annual saving of £23,000. 'Of secretaries Lloyd George never could have enough,' wrote Jones, who was one of them.[37]

Besides the Budget, which Baldwin was expected to begin planning, his predecessor had left behind an important piece of unfinished business for him to complete. This was the settlement of the £978 million war debt to the United States. The debt had largely been incurred in the purchase of arms and munitions much of which had been supplied to France, Italy and the other European allies. Two years previously, Balfour, then temporarily in charge of the Foreign Office, had informed Britain's debtors, who owed her about four times what she owed America, that Britain would only expect them to pay enough to cover the Anglo-American debt. The Balfour Note, as it was called, had not gone down at all well in the United States, which rejected the idea of an all-round settlement involving any cancellation of indebtedness and demanded that Britain should honour her legal obligation and that the debt should be funded as soon as possible. Horne was on the point of leaving for Washington when the Conservative revolt against the Coalition took place, and

Horne, who remained faithful to Lloyd George, resigned. The Americans agreed to a short postponement of the negotiations while the Bonar Law government got settled in, and in the event it was arranged that a small British delegation headed by the new Chancellor should sail for New York immediately after Christmas.

Baldwin embarked on board the *Majestic* on 27 December, accompanied by Montagu Norman, the Governor of the Bank of England, who with the brilliant and erudite Scot Sir Auckland Geddes, then British Ambassador in Washington and a former President of the Board of Trade in Lloyd George's Cabinet, completed the delegation. Also in the party were Baldwin's wife and their daughter Betty, besides James Grigg and Mrs Grigg. Norman, who had been appointed Governor of the Bank in 1920 and was to hold the appointment for the unprecedented period of twenty-two years, was a leading exponent of the gospel of financial orthodoxy, unlike Maynard Keynes; he was eager for Britain to return to the gold standard, as well as for settling the debt in the interests of his country's credit standing abroad. With his broad forehead, striking eyes and pointed beard, Norman looked like the Commendatore in *Don Giovanni*. He had known Baldwin slightly since the time of the Chancellor's first stint at the Treasury. Now on this voyage they came to know each other well which resulted in a mutual friendship cemented by a love of classical music and the English countryside. 'He is a quiet homely sort of countryman who thinks there is no place in the world quite like Worcestershire and who seems to be where he is more from duty or necessity than from real choice,' Norman thus described the new Chancellor in a letter to his mother from the ship. 'But here again,' he added cautiously, 'appearances may well be deceivable.'[38]

The weather in the Atlantic was extremely rough and a fog followed the gales with the result that the crossing took eight days instead of the usual four or five. Many of the passengers were seasick, but 'Mr Baldwin never turned a hair', noted Grigg; 'indeed I remember having been told while I was utterly prostrate, that he had even paid a visit to the engine room during the storm!'[39] Baldwin himself wrote to the Davidsons when they were nearing New York:

We are completing a record passage, the longest ever taken by this ship. On six days out of seven we have logged gales, from moderate gales to strong gales and whole gales, and all the time with head seas. One day we ran 202 miles in 24 hours! But with all that, it has been a wonderful rest and I feel as fit as a whole orchestra of fiddles . . .

We have about half our complement of passengers: no one of note except Backhaus the pianist who played gloriously for us on New Year's night. He gave us five Chopins, a beautiful Schumann and two Liszts, including the 2nd Rhapsody. I like him, he is entirely un-affected and free from pose . . .

The ship, of course, is the last word and her steadiness in rough weather beyond belief, and everyone has been kindness itself. Our party is very happy. The Griggs disappeared for three days or so: Betty ditto. The Governor like me enjoyed the rest so much and looks pounds better already. I haven't worried a bit; in fact, I successfully dismissed all thoughts of working, but I am beginning to wonder now whether we shall have any luck. It would give such a fillip all round if we could bring off a decent deal. I am anxious to get news of Paris which I suppose I shall find waiting for me in Washington.[40]

The news which Baldwin was expecting from Paris concerned the progress of the Reparations Conference. In fact the conference had broken down, and it was announced that the French intended to occupy the industrial Ruhr, as Baldwin and his party learned on 4 January 1923 when they were on their way by train to Washington. Reporters and journalists crowded into the Pullman coach, which had been reserved for the visitors; here the newspapermen were kept at arm's length by Grigg who informed them that the Chancellor was not available for comment and then proceeded somewhat rashly to beguile them with his own views which were highly critical of French policy. Unfortunately these views were attributed to Baldwin in the newspapers and the French Ambassador in Washington was instructed by the Quai d'Orsay to take up the matter with the Chancellor. The Ambassador did so with what Grigg thought was 'undue *empressement*' at a reception given for the Baldwin delegation at the British Embassy. 'This issue of a denial that he had ever made the remarks was demanded,' Grigg noted afterwards 'and Mr Baldwin immediately complied with a light heart and a perfectly clear conscience.' Grigg did not then confess to his part in the incident and it was only later that Baldwin learned the truth.[41]

The delegates had no written instructions, but Bonar Law had given the Chancellor verbal authority to settle with the Americans as he thought fit, provided that Britain's payments did not exceed an annuity of £25 million a year.

The first few days were spent in informal discussions, calling on various Washington notabilities and becoming acquainted with the members of the American Debt Commission, who were all leading

Republicans. They consisted of Andrew Mellon, multi-millionaire Secretary of the US Treasury, who was to act as chairman, Charles Evans Hughes, Secretary of State and former Chief Justice, and Herbert Hoover, Secretary of Commerce, together with two Republican members of Congress. Hoover impressed Grigg as being the ablest member of the commission, although anti-British; Hughes, on the other hand, was 'just an able lawyer'.

The British mission was very well entertained, so much so that Grigg commented disapprovingly on 'the vulgar display of luxury'. In spite of Prohibition, there was a lavish display of liquor in private houses, the only 'dry' host being Secretary of State Hughes. 'At Mr Mellon's apartment we were done extremely well,' noted Grigg, 'and we were surrounded by old masters from the collection he afterwards presented to the American nation. He did not appear to be a man who was a connoisseur of painting, and I remember being told many years later that his real interest was in the process of acquiring the pictures, especially if there was any element of outwitting an alternative buyer.' On his return to London, Grigg described the occasion to Tom Jones:

> There were vast bowls of solid silver, filled with the most exotic flowers which come daily from Pittsburg of all places, where Mellon laid the basis of his fortune. There were bowls of strawberries out of season, and all the rest in keeping. Mrs Marshall Field and the other ladies were covered with ropes of pearls. The remains of the dinner would be enough to feed scores of hungry people.[42]

The first formal session opened with a welcome from Mellon and Baldwin reading a carefully prepared statement calculated to appeal to American public opinion. 'This debt is not a debt for dollars sent to Europe,' the British Chancellor declared. 'The money was all expended here, most of it for cotton, wheat, food products and munitions of war. Every cent used for the purchase of these goods was spent in America . . . These goods were supplied in war-time at war prices. Prices have fallen so far that thus to repay four billion dollars Great Britain would have to send America a far greater bulk of goods than she originally purchased with the money loaned . . .' What Britain wanted, said Baldwin, was 'a fair business settlement, a settlement that will secure for America repayment to the last cent . . . on such terms as will produce the least possible disturbance in the trade relations of the two countries. Our wish is to approach discussion as businessmen seeking a business solution of what is fundamentally a business problem.'[43]

The details of the negotiations properly belong to the international financial history of the times, and it is only possible to describe them briefly here. Fearing that Congress would disapprove of any settlement considered 'soft', the Commissioners felt that they had to drive a fairly hard bargain. The best that they would agree to, after one offer had been turned down flat by the British Cabinet, was 3 per cent for the first ten years and $3\frac{1}{2}$ per cent for the remaining fifty-two, with the arrears of interest at $4\frac{1}{4}$ per cent. 'We are all three convinced that these are the best terms we can obtain,' Baldwin cabled the Prime Minister on 14 January. 'They represent a tremendous advance in American opinion.' On 15 January Bonar Law cabled Baldwin that he had discussed the matter confidentially with McKenna who 'in spite of all the risks is quite definitely of opinion that we ought not to accept'. To them the worst feature 'from the point of view of the spirit of the negotiations' was the recalculation of the interest on the arrears at such a high rate. 'Is it not possible that you are too much under the influence of Washington which is not even the New York atmosphere? What would you have thought of such proposals before you left?'[44]

By this time the latest American offer had been 'leaked' to the American press. Norman and Geddes were still for accepting it as the best that could be got, particularly in view of the fact that Congress was due to rise early in March and failure to ratify before that date would involve postponement until December when the question would be bedevilled by the next Presidential election. Even Grigg's former chief Horne, whom the British party met on their last day in New York, volunteered 'rather nobly for one who had been supplanted', in Grigg's words, to cable the Prime Minister advising acceptance of the American terms. In fact Horne did sign a private telegram to this effect which had been drafted by Geddes and also bore the signature of Lord Burnham, the proprietor of the influential London *Daily Telegraph*, who like Horne happened to be in New York at the time.[45]

It has sometimes been thought that Baldwin clinched the deal before he left America without further reference to Bonar Law and the rest of the Cabinet. This is not so. He kept in touch throughout by cable with Whitehall, and after the Commission had put forward their ultimate offer he had hoped that a simple statement would be issued to the effect that he was returning to London for personal consultation and that his return was to be regarded as an adjournment of the negotiations. Unfortunately this hope was dashed by the premature publication in the newspapers and this gave the impression that the offer had crystallised into a 'take it or leave it' proposition. In addition there was an ominous warning from Hughes at the final meeting that if the offer were not promptly accepted and if the negotiations were allowed to drag on so that the debt became an issue at the Presidential election, any chance of American help in the financial reconstruction of Europe must be considered at an end. Such was the Chancellor's final and abiding memory of what the ex-Liberal Prime Minister Asquith, for whom he had promised to bring back some maps, described as 'the land of the long-winded and the short-sighted'.[46]

7

The Baldwin mission sailed from New York on 20 January 1923 in the *Olympic*, and after a relatively calm voyage the vessel docked at Southampton early in the morning of the 29th. A bevy of reporters swarmed on board while Baldwin and the others were still having breakfast. The Chancellor's initial reaction was to send them away, but on being pressed to say something he relented and agreed to hold a press conference. What he was subsequently reported as saying – and the reports do not appear to have been wholly accurate – was to get him into serious trouble on both sides of the Atlantic. He emphasised that the matter of the debt was in the hands of Congress, which represented 'the people of America from one end of America to the other'. He continued:

> We have got men of our way of thinking in the eastern states of America, but that does not cut any ice at all in regard to other parts of America. If you look at the Senate, you will find that the majority come from the agricultural and pastoral communities, and they do not realise the position which exists in regard to the meaning of our international debt. The bulk of the people of America have no acquaintance with international trade. A great many people in America think that all we have to do is to send the money over. The debt can only be funded on such terms as can be got through Congress and the Senate, and that is the root of the difficulty with which we are now faced.[47]

Questioned about the terms of the Commission's latest offer, which he confirmed, the Chancellor admitted that what he called 'the provisional settlement' would be considered very severe and even ungenerous by the British people. But, he went on, it would be useless to put forward any further counter-proposals, since the Americans 'have gone to the limit of what they are likely to propose'. He left no doubt in the minds of his hearers, who duly reported him to this effect, that he was in favour of the American offer as the best which could be obtained. On the other hand, he seems to have regarded this admission as a piece of background information which would be treated as 'off the record'. He was consequently disagreeably surprised when he was quoted more or less verbatim. Afterwards he admitted that he would rather his tongue had been torn out.

In America, where his remarks appear to have been somewhat garbled in the course of transmission, Baldwin was represented as describing the average Senator and Congressman as a 'hick from way back', which naturally aroused considerable resentment, especially in the Middle West. At home the King remonstrated with Bonar Law, asking him through his Private Secretary Lord Stamfordham why his Chancellor of the Exchequer had publicly recommended a settlement before it had received Cabinet approval.

His Majesty, knowing and respecting as he does Mr Baldwin, is at a loss to understand how the latter came even to be interviewed and still less to make any communication to the public before having seen and reported to you – especially when the question involved was of so delicate a character *vis-à-vis* to the United States Government.

'I am very sorry that His Majesty should have noticed Mr Baldwin's remarks to the Press,' Bonar Law replied to Stamfordham. 'They were intended of course for consumption at home and he fully realises the harm they may have done in America.'

'I don't see how I could very well help noticing the remarks, as I always read the papers,' the King commented sharply. 'He [Bonar Law] owns it has done harm in America and Baldwin realises it too. Surely that was a pity and ought to have been avoided . . . I fear the harm is done and the Congress will be very annoyed and no wonder.'

On reaching London, Baldwin immediately went to Downing Street to report to the Prime Minister, bringing with him the American Ambassador, Colonel George Harvey, who had also travelled on the *Olympic*. He found Bonar Law as adamant as ever. 'I should be the most cursed Prime Minister that ever held office in England if I accepted those terms,' he said. During the next two hours the matter was debated in all its aspects between Prime Minister and Ambassador, while Baldwin, conscious that his political future hung in the balance, remained silent. 'Not the slightest attempt did he make to defend the settlement he had accepted,' the Ambassador said afterwards. After the meeting, Colonel Harvey told a friend that he 'felt pretty good'. On the other hand, Baldwin, when the ambassador's remark was reported to him, remarked that for his part 'he had never felt so miserable in his life'.[48]

The Cabinet met at four o'clock the following afternoon to discuss the issue. While the members were in session, Keynes told Davidson, Bonar Law's PPS, that he hoped on the whole they would refuse the American offer, 'in order to give them time to discover that they are at our mercy as we are at France's, France at Germany's. It is the debtor who has the last word in these cases.' But the brilliant young economist ignored the political arguments in favour of the proposed settlement which were advanced in the Cabinet room at 10 Downing Street.[49] According to Derby, who was present and who had talked with the Prime Minister on the previous day: 'Baldwin stated his case for acceptance very clearly, very concisely and with a very strong recommendation that we should accept.' Much as he resented the attitude of America – so run the Cabinet minutes – Baldwin felt that they were in honour bound in the matter of making a settlement. ('If we let this chance go we might get none other for years. It would be a blunder we should regret later.')

'Bonar Law then did an extraordinary thing. Instead of asking for expression by each of us of our opinions he produced the same arguments as he had used to me the day before, said his mind was quite made up and that nothing would induce him to remain the head of a Government which consented to sign.' ('The Americans thought they had us in their pocket. They made the rate of interest and left us to take it or leave it . . . To treat us as badly as that must strike anyone as absurd . . . If it were decided to accept, this would have to be without him.') Derby's account continues:

> We were all aghast at this, and the Lord Chancellor [Cave] really voiced our opinions when he made in a very tactful way a remonstrance against a pistol being put to our heads. Bonar agreed that he had done this but thought it best to let us know his views, but he then proceeded to ask each of us what we thought. With the exception of Lloyd-Greame we were absolutely unanimous in saying that we ought to accept the terms, and it looked at the moment as if there would be a break of the Government there and then, but luckily somebody – I cannot remember who – suggested that we might adjourn and meet the next day.

In fact, the suggestion for an adjournment which was adopted came from Lord Cave, who with Bonar Law's agreement also invited the rest of the Cabinet with the exception of the Prime Minister to meet him privately at his room in the House of Lords next morning so as to review the position.[50]

After the Cabinet, Derby had a talk with the Duke of Devonshire, who was Colonial Secretary and whom Derby found more indignant than he was, saying that he thought 'we had all been put in an extremely false position and it practically meant that there was not a Cabinet but a Dictator, the one thing we had all complained of with regard to the last Government'. Devonshire's inclination was to resign, the timing depending upon what Baldwin did. 'I told him that was very much my feeling too,' Derby noted at the time, 'and I did not see how I could remain a member of a Government which repudiated a debt.'*

Every member of the Cabinet apart from the Prime Minister attended the meeting in the Lord Chancellor's room next morning. All present agreed that it would, as Cave put it, be 'fatal for Bonar Law to go' after barely three months in office; at the same time everyone except Lloyd-Greame and Lord Novar, the Secretary for Scotland, agreed that the latest American terms should be accepted. Finally, three ministers – Cave, Baldwin and Devonshire – were deputed by the majority to see the Prime Minister before the Cabinet meeting in the afternoon, inform him that the majority view about acceptance was unchanged and try to persuade him to change his mind about resigning. This they duly did.

Lloyd-Greame also saw Bonar Law, and while he was with him Reginald McKenna was shown in. According to Lloyd-Greame, McKenna, while still being opposed in principle to the terms, now took the view that 'matters had gone so far that there was no alternative to acceptance, and that Bonar's resignation would be a national disaster, a view which all his colleagues shared to the full'. Eventually, in the face of this accumulated pressure, the Prime Minister yielded. Thus, when the Cabinet met at 4 p.m., the proceedings only lasted a few minutes. The Prime Minister

* Devonshire went on to ask Derby whether he had noticed an anonymous article in *The Times* (27 January 1923) signed 'A Colonial' which 'embodied word for word and almost phrase for phrase . . . the arguments Bonar had used at the Cabinet'. Derby had not noticed the article, and Devonshire admitted to an uncomfortable feeling that the Prime Minister might have instigated Beaverbrook to write it or perhaps had even done so himself. 'I can hardly credit that,' noted Derby in his diary, 'when I remember that it was only at the last Cabinet that Bonar put an obligation on all of us not to write letters or articles to the press.' See R. Churchill, *Lord Derby*, p. 496. In fact, Bonar Law did write the article, but the secret was so well kept that it was apparently unknown to Law's official biographer Robert Blake, who does not mention it. The secret was disclosed for the first time in 1955, by Sir Evelyn Wrench in his life of Geoffrey Dawson, *The Times* editor, who had recently succeeded Wickham Steed: *Geoffrey Dawson and Our Times*, p. 215.

said that he had come to the conclusion that he was asking his colleagues to make too great a sacrifice, and although he held the same opinion he was prepared to give way and agree to the American proposal. 'A great relief to all of us,' wrote Derby in his diary that night.

The crisis of the American debt caused a temporary coolness between Baldwin and Bonar Law, and for a time Baldwin ceased to pay his usual morning call on the Prime Minister in his official residence which was next door to his own and connected by an internal passage. Then one morning, Baldwin looked in at the Private Secretary's room and asked Ronald Waterhouse, 'How is he?' Formerly, according to Waterhouse, he would have gone into Bonar Law's room without waiting to inquire. 'Go up and see him,' Waterhouse replied. Afterwards Waterhouse wrote:

> Ten minutes later I found Bonar with his legs crossed over the arm of his chair, and the Chancellor pulling moodily at his pipe, as he polar-beared up and down the opposite side of the room, but temperamentally they had drifted miles apart. I don't believe that either had spoken a word. My entry opened the door to Mr Baldwin's escape.[51]

While the cloud between them soon passed away, their personal relations were never quite so cordial and intimate as they had been, although Baldwin did his best to restore them to their old footing. But to Waterhouse, who was an observant Private Secretary and was later to serve Baldwin in a similar capacity, they never appeared to be at ease together again.

Baldwin was sustained by the knowledge that the Treasury officials with the notable exception of Keynes supported him, as did the City and banking circles generally apart from McKenna. The press too was favourable except for the Beaverbrook newspapers. The opinion of the man-in-the-street was that the settlement was in the nature of a book transaction since Britain had debtors of her own who owed her more than she owed America, and the bankers would no doubt eventually sort out the whole business between them. The idea that Britain always kept her word in the matter of international agreements was still prevalent, and no one foresaw that this particular settlement would be vitiated barely a dozen years later when the country defaulted on future payments.

'We got the thing settled at the psychological moment,' Colonel Harvey, the American Ambassador, afterwards declared. 'If the settlement had been delayed we shouldn't have got a cent . . . Bonar Law said he couldn't see his way to pay, but the Cabinet pushed it through.'[52] Meanwhile Baldwin defended his action in Parliament in words which gained him widespread approval at the time. When he went to America, so he told the House of Commons, the one thing more than any other that made him anxious to obtain a settlement was that he was convinced that a settlement 'assuring the world that one country, at least, in the midst of all this maelstrom, stood by the sanctity of contracts and by its bond, might be some help to the countries of the world to face the difficulties in front of them instead of ignoring them or trying to slip round them'.*

Even more applauded round the country as well as in the House itself was Baldwin's peroration to this speech, in which he replied to the Labour leader Ramsay MacDonald in the customary debate on the Address following the opening of the new Parliamentary session in February 1923. What he said had the characteristic ring of honesty and sincerity which the country was to come to associate with Baldwin's public utterances. This particular effort, which was carefully thought out and was designed for a much larger audience than the House of Commons, earned him many congratulations, among others from an ex-Lord Chancellor (Haldane) and the Vice-Provost of Eton. The Dean of Bristol even made it the theme of a sermon which he preached to businessmen. Baldwin's official biographer G. M. Young, who had opportunities for studying his subject at first hand, felt that at this relatively early date the speech showed to those nearest to him that Baldwin was ready to accept the succession to the Premiership, even if he was not actually aiming at it. Here at least was an authentic note of leadership – so much so that *The Times* made it the subject of a leading article.

When the Labour Party sit on these benches, we shall all wish them well in their effort to govern the country. But I am quite certain that whether they succeed or fail there will never in this country be a Communist Government and for this reason: that no gospel founded on hate will ever seize the hearts of our people . . .

* According to Davidson, writing many years later, Baldwin 'was upset that Bonar should feel that he hadn't been able to get the Americans to virtually wipe out the debt . . . Baldwin was also very hurt that the Americans, who had made immense fortunes out of the war, should not have reduced the interest on the debt to an even greater extent than they did; I remember that he made the passing comment that he would have liked to send a British cruiser to the United States with a replica of the Golden Calf in the bows just to let the Americans know what he was feeling about their putting money before all else . . . It was a reflection on what he believed to be the worship of the God-Almighty dollar in the United States. But that does not mean that he believed we could avoid our obligation.' James, *Memoirs of a Conservative*, p. 143.

It is no good trying to cure the world by spreading out oceans of bloodshed. It is no good trying to cure the world by repeating that pentasyllabic word 'Proletariat'. The English language is the richest in the world in monosyllables. Four words of one syllable each, are words which contain salvation for this country and for the whole world, and they are 'Faith', 'Hope', 'Love', and 'Work'. No government in this country today, which has not faith in the people, hope in the future, love for its fellow-men, and which will not work and work and work, will ever bring this country through into better days and better times, or will ever bring Europe through, or the world through.[53]

8

In addition to the Chancellor's official residence at 11 Downing Street, Baldwin also became the tenant of Chequers, previously the country home of Lord and Lady Lee of Fareham who had generously presented it to the nation in 1921 as a 'thank-offering' for England's 'deliverance in the Great War 1914–1918, and as a place of rest and recreation for her Prime Ministers for ever'. Under the terms of the trust set up by the donors, should the Prime Minister of the day not require it for his own use, the place should then be available to the Chancellor of the Exchequer, this minister being expressly designated next in the line of succession, since Lord Lee was under the impression, apparently a mistaken one, that there was some ancient association of the property with the holder of the Chancellor's office.[54]*

After the Bonar Law Government had been confirmed in power by the General Election, the Prime Minister informed the trustees that he did not wish to occupy Chequers in the immediate future, although he seems to have thought he might go there occasionally during the summer. On 29 November 1922, Lady Lee noted in her diary:

Bonar Law has decided that he does not wish to take advantage of his

* Some of the earlier owners had been clerks of the Exchequer, being referred to in official documents by their first names with the addition of the Latin words '*de Scaccario*' from the chequered table or board on which public accounts were settled. The Norman-French variant of the Latin was '*del Chekers*' or '*del Checkers*', from which it can be seen how the house got its name. In the nineteenth century it was known as Chequers Court. In 1912, Mr H. J. Delaval Astley, the last owner by inheritance in the direct line from 1173, was killed in a flying accident. At this date the Lees were living at Chequers as tenants under a lease; in 1917 they acquired the property by outright purchase and it was conveyed to the nation in the same year, although it was not until 1921 that the Lees vacated possession and handed over to Lloyd George.

right, and we are not altogether surprised, as, apart from his feeling about us, he seems to have a definite and ineradicable dislike of anything that is beautiful. A[rthur Lord Lee] is rather relieved than otherwise, as he does not like B.L. and always had the lowest opinion of him, but it is of course a breach of the principle which we had endeavoured to establish – that Chequers should be occupied by the PM of the day. Stanley Baldwin who is 'heir apparent', as C of the E, is to go instead.[55]

The following week-end the Baldwins went to Chequers for the first time. They were enchanted with everything they saw, and at the next meeting of the trustees which he attended Baldwin told them that in his opinion the place had a quality which could only be described as the 'Peace of God'. He added that his wife could not express what she felt – 'that nothing has made such an impression upon her'. Indeed Lucy Baldwin wrote to Lady Lee ecstatically about 'how perfectly wonderful we thought it was and what delight the air of peace and rest gave us. If it should happen that we are to be the fortunate tenants I can only assure you that we appreciate all the loving care that has been spent in bringing the house to its wonderful perfection.' Her words were echoed by her husband's seventy-eight-year-old mother who was able to spend the Whitsun holiday with her son at Chequers in May 1923. Louisa Baldwin likewise wrote to Lady Lee afterwards:

On crossing the threshold I was conscious of an atmosphere of kindly welcome as of unseen hands extended to greet me. No spooky feeling in the slightest degree, but as if in the many generations of inmates of the beautiful old house good men and women have lived benevolent and harmonious lives and gone gently and trustfully to their rest, leaving sweet influences behind them.[56]

The house, which is Elizabethan in style with some later additions, was largely rebuilt in 1565 by its then owner William Hawtrey, who incorporated some parts of the original medieval structure. One melancholy domestic association resulted from the ill-fated Lady Jane Grey's sister Mary having incurred Queen Elizabeth's displeasure by reason of her marrying a servant in the royal household and in consequence being confined for two years in a garret at the top of the house, Hawtrey being made responsible for her custody. If any spirit has particularly haunted the house, no doubt it has been that of Lady Mary. Perhaps the most remarkable association has been provided by Oliver Cromwell, whose grandson John Russell (son of Oliver's daughter Frances and her husband Sir John Russell, 3rd Baronet) married Joanna Rivett, who had inherited Chequers in 1715 through a previous marriage. In this way the estate passed into the possession of Cromwell's descendants who were to live there for the next two centuries and incidentally to bring with them the collection of Cromwell family portraits and relics of the Protector, including his watch, slippers and two swords, which adorn the Long Gallery today. As for the estate itself, which is mentioned in Domesday Book, it consisted of about twelve hundred acres comprising several farms as well as the mansion house, and is about an hour's drive from London, being intersected by the road from Great Missenden to Aylesbury. The park surrounding the house was quite thickly wooded with beech trees, interspersed with larch, holly and box, which with the addition of a pleasing garden and fine lawns make Chequers just about as attractive a property as can be imagined within easy reach of London. Baldwin relished the quiet of the Long Gallery with its conventional country house library of calf-bound volumes consisting of standard editions of eighteenth-century writers, among which he looked in vain for Boswell's life of Dr Johnson. He also enjoyed the walks, particularly to Combe Hill and Beacon Hill, which enclosed the house in a hollow, and from the top of which on a clear day he could see places as far apart as the Cotswolds, Salisbury Plain, the Berkshire Downs and even the Welsh mountains.

Except when he had to go to his constituency, Baldwin hardly missed a week-end at Chequers where he felt that he could think much more clearly than in his confined domestic quarters in Downing Street where he was often interrupted. The first week-end which he spent at Chequers (2–4 December 1922) was a purely family affair, the party besides himself and his wife consisting of their daughters Betty and Diana, the latter's husband Gordon Munro, and the Kiplings' daughter Elsie.* Apart from members of the family and close relatives like the Kiplings, Mackails and Philip Burne-Jones, the most frequent guests were John and Joan Davidson, and later on Thomas Jones, the Deputy Secretary of the Cabinet, and Ronald Waterhouse, the Prime Minister's Private Secretary. Baldwin's only Cabinet colleagues whose names appear in the Chequers Visitors' Book at this period were Edward Wood, William Bridgeman, Neville Chamberlain and Leo Amery with their respective wives. Montagu Norman paid his first visit in February 1923 and shortly afterwards received an open invitation to come down any week-end he could get away from the Bank and was not otherwise engaged. A remark-

* Now Mrs George Bambridge.

able intimacy developed between them following their American visit, which was to last for the remainder of Baldwin's life. 'Your friendship is one of the greatest possessions I have,' he told Norman, 'and I value it.'

Both men shared a love of walking and music. There was a ramblers' club made up of Treasury officials and known as 'The Tramps', whom Baldwin encouraged to explore the Chilterns, because, as he put it, 'open air exercise blows away the mental cobwebs'; he and Norman would sometimes meet them in a local pub for a pint of ale on these occasions. The Treasury staff also provided a group of singers, who would appear at Chequers from time to time and entertain them with madrigals. 'No shop was ever talked,' Davidson later recalled. 'It was a case of two intensely patriotic and romantic individuals who enjoyed the English countryside and music at week-ends in all seasons.'[57]

Baldwin's cousin, the artist Philip Burne-Jones, was also moved to write to Lord and Lady Lee at this time:

> I can think of no man living who is more actually alive to that benignant atmosphere – in which those beloved walls are steeped – than the present Chancellor of the Exchequer. If you could have seen him and his wife, as I did, this week-end, regaining strength and health after the exhaustion of the Budget days, I think you would have acknowledged that in this case at all events the noble object of your hospitality had been more than fulfilled.[58]

The Budget – Baldwin's only one, as events turned out – received its finishing touches at Chequers during the Easter holidays. The occasion inspired the cartoonist Bernard Partridge to publish his first drawing of Baldwin in *Punch*. This so pleased its subject that he immediately got in touch with the artist and bought the original from him. The cartoon which appeared three days after Easter depicted 'Farmer Baldwin' holding a tin of wool restorer, while the taxpayer in the guise of a shorn lamb says: 'If you could see your way, sir, to treating me with a little of that mixture in preference to going over me with a razor, I venture to think it would be to our mutual advantage.' In the event the shorn lamb was not altogether disappointed when Baldwin opened his Budget a fortnight later, on 16 April 1923, in a speech which only took him one hour and twenty minutes to deliver and was shorter than any of his predecessors' during the previous half century, although he was dealing with accounts totalling nearly £810 million.

An unexpected revenue surplus of £100 million the Chancellor largely devoted to the redemption of the national debt, thereby saving the taxpayer £750,000 a year in interest. The rather lower surplus which he estimated for the following financial year enabled him to take sixpence off the standard rate of income tax, which then stood at six shillings in the pound, and a penny off beer. In short, it was a safe and sound Budget on conventional lines, which earned him praise among others from Sir John Bradbury, who told him that it went far 'towards re-establishing that faith in human nature which was so gravely jeopardised' by his experience as a senior Treasury official under the financially heterodox Lloyd George when he was Chancellor. Besides this, Asquith told a friend of Baldwin's that the Budget speech was 'one of the best done things he had ever heard in the House. He was much impressed.' But Baldwin took it all with a grain of salt. 'I am going through that dangerous time when all men speak well of me,' was his characteristic reaction. 'But it won't turn my head, nor will it last. So that's that!' [59]

9

By this date Bonar Law's health was visibly failing. His voice had never been very strong and it now became progressively weaker. There was a painful scene in the House when the Prime Minister was at the Despatch Box and a member shouted to him to speak up. 'I cannot,' Law muttered in a hoarse whisper. Baldwin took his place, thereafter answering at Question Time for his chief. Then, on medical advice, Law took a short sea cruise, leaving Southampton on 1 May in the Dutch liner *Princess Juliana*. In his absence, it was arranged that Curzon should preside at Cabinet meetings and Baldwin should act as Leader of the House of Commons. Baldwin also kept Law posted with current parliamentary news. 'The House has been uncannily calm all week,' he wrote to him on 4 May. Neville Chamberlain, who had recently been promoted from the Post Office to the Ministry of Health, had so far done 'extraordinarily well in his new post and the Labour men are beginning to appreciate him'. With the exception of Lloyd-Greame, who was away ill, 'the rest of the team are happy and contented and doing their jobs in the House effectively. The Party as a whole are full of beans. In fact they are very good boys in the absence of the headmaster.' Baldwin concluded by assuring his chief that he would be 'very welcome back'.

This letter together with other correspondence and papers were delivered personally by Davidson, who travelled overland so as to meet the *Princess Juliana* at Genoa. Here he found to his dismay that the voyage had done the sick man little if any good and that he had decided to leave the boat and go to Baldwin's favourite holiday resort of Aix-les-Bains where the Kiplings were staying. Rudyard was shocked by the Prime Minister's appearance and immmediately telephoned Beaverbrook in London to come out, a plea reinforced by Law himself, whose throat was now giving him considerable pain. Beaverbrook promptly alerted Law's doctor, Sir Thomas Horder, whom he arranged should cross over to Paris and examine the Prime Minister as soon as he and his party reached the Hotel Crillon. By this time the unfortunate Law was already under heavy sedation which increased his habitual depression to a mood of hopeless despair.

Meanwhile Baldwin continued to write about the progress of House of Commons business. Among other things, there was to be a luncheon to T. P. O'Connor, the 'Father' of the House, at which 'Asquith, L.G., MacDonald and I are to lay pats of butter on his head', and Baldwin asked for a congratulatory telegram which was duly sent. The luncheon took place as planned on 15 May and in his speech on the occasion, far from seeking to follow O'Connor's long record of parliamentary membership, Baldwin expressed the hope that he might soon be allowed to go back to Worcestershire 'to read the books I want to read, to live a decent life, and to keep pigs'.[60] Seen in the light of the dramatic political changes which were barely a week distant in point of time, it was a remarkable wish for a man in Baldwin's public position. In the event it was not to be realised for nearly fifteen more years.

On 17 May Horder examined the Prime Minister in his sitting-room at the Crillon. After making some non-committal remarks, the doctor left the room and told Beaverbrook, who was waiting outside to hear the verdict, that the Prime Minister was suffering from incurable cancer of the throat and could not be expected to live for more than another six months. Beaverbrook was horrified, as he had hitherto been strongly opposed to the idea of Bonar Law resigning. It is uncertain whether the Prime Minister realised how gravely ill he was, but he knew that he was not fit to carry on and that he should relinquish the burden of office as soon as possible. What worried him particularly was the question of his successor, and he was greatly relieved when Lord Crewe, the British Ambassador, told him that the choice rested constitutionally with the King and that he was not obliged to tender any advice at all to the sovereign on the succession.

Davidson received the Prime Minister's permission to return to London immediately to prepare the way for his resignation. On his arrival, on the afternoon of Friday, 18 May, he immediately telegraphed Baldwin, who by this time had left for Chequers for the week-end, asking him to come back to London as soon as he could. Then, after dinner, he went round to Downing Street and telephoned Lord Stamfordham, the King's Private Secretary, with the news of Bonar Law's imminent resignation; he asked Stamfordham to warn the King what to expect, adding that the Prime Minister did not wish to be consulted on the question of his successor. According to his own account, Davidson did not hide his view that 'the day when a peer could be Prime Minister had passed, and that resistance to Lord Curzon – who was the obvious peer – would not only come from the Labour Opposition, but from a very large percentage of the Conservative Party also'. Asked by Stamfordham whom the King should consult, Davidson replied that of course His Majesty could ask advice from anyone he liked, but two individuals immediately came to mind. These were Balfour, who was an ex-Premier and Conservative Party leader, and Salisbury, who was a former Conservative Leader of the House of Lords.

Baldwin came up from Chequers next day and dined with Davidson at his club. Over dinner Davidson broke the news about Bonar Law and told his friend that it was 'almost inevitable' that he should be nominated the successor. To Davidson's surprise, Baldwin was alarmed at the prospect – in fact, 'he was genuinely frightened'.

> I think that Baldwin hoped that his promotion to the Premiership would be put off, and that Curzon would succeed Law [Davidson's account continues]. He realised that Curzon, for all his foibles, had an immense amount of experience . . . In the last analysis he was conscious that he [Baldwin] was ill-equipped in experience for the higher atmosphere of politics . . . I told him that the choice was not his, and that if he were sent for by the King he must accept as a duty to his country and to his party.[61]

This view was confirmed by Bonar Law's Private Secretary, Lieutenant-Colonel (later Sir) Ronald Waterhouse, whom Baldwin also talked with that evening.

The Prime Minister had arrived in London the same evening from Paris and had gone not to Downing Street but to his private house in Onslow Gardens. Next morning, which was Whit Sunday, Baldwin called on him there, as he was about to write out his letter of resignation to the King, who was then at Aldershot for a military review. The letter, in which he would make no recommendation as to his successor, so Bonar Law told Baldwin, would be delivered personally in the afternoon by his son-in-law Sir Frederick Sykes, and Waterhouse would accompany him to Aldershot. Later the same day, he wrote to Curzon, who was spending the holiday at Montacute, his country house in Somerset:

> I understand that it is not customary for the King to ask the Prime Minister to recommend his successor in circumstances like the present and I presume he will not do so; but if, as I hope, he accepts my resignation at once, he will have to take immediate steps about my successor.[62]

During the Sunday morning meeting between Bonar Law and Baldwin, a third person was present at least for part of the time. This was Lord Beaverbrook, whose testimony as to what passed on this occasion there is no reason to doubt. Beaverbrook subsequently recorded it in an anonymous article in the *Evening Standard*, which he inspired if he did not actually write himself, and which he afterwards confirmed in conversation with Bonar Law's biographer Robert Blake.

> Mr Bonar Law's own judgement was that Lord Curzon ought to succeed of right, though his personal preference was for Mr Baldwin . . .
>
> The Prime Minister explained to the Chancellor of the Exchequer that, as he was unable for physical reasons to consult with his colleagues on the Leadership, he did not intend to make any recommendation at all, now that the doctors insisted on his immediate retirement.
>
> For his own part, setting his own personal feelings aside, he regarded the fact that, as he was making no recommendation, it would be equivalent to the automatic succession of Lord Curzon, as the acting head of the Cabinet, appointed to this post by himself during his tour abroad, and as the Leader of the House of Lords. He felt sure that his colleagues would have taken the same view. Mr Baldwin replied, very properly, that he was perfectly ready to serve under any man who would carry a united Unionist party with him, even if he were not chosen himself.
>
> Mr Bonar Law then said to him, in a kindly fashion, that a decision in Lord Curzon's favour might really prove to the Chancellor's ultimate advantage. It would give him the opportunity of gaining experience in the management of the House of Commons – so that, if and when an opening for the Leadership occurred, he would have a far better chance of obtaining and retaining it, as the result of his added knowledge and skill.[63]

According to Robert Blake, Bonar Law went on to warn Baldwin that he should, from the outset, come to a clear understanding with Curzon about the division of power between them. In particular Baldwin should keep in his own hands all patronage, appointments and promotions within the House of Commons. Otherwise his position as Leader of the House, to which he had a prescriptive right, would be intolerable.[64]

Baldwin took note of all this and then departed for Chequers, which he reached about noon. He spent most of the remainder of the day as well as much of Whit Monday playing patience in the Long Gallery. The Davidsons motored down from London on the Monday afternoon. Eventually a telephone message came from the King's Private Secretary, Lord Stamfordham, suggesting that he should come up to London and see him the same evening. However, as Stamfordham noted afterwards, 'he begged to be allowed to put off his arrival till the following morning (the 22nd)'.[65]

As already stated, Mrs Louisa Baldwin was staying with her son at Chequers over the Whitsun holiday. 'What does he want me for so early?' he asked her.

The old lady, who had a shrewd notion of what was afoot, answered: 'You don't think he would command you to be in town so early to discuss someone else's prospects of being Prime Minister, do you?'[66]

FIVE

PRIME MINISTER

I

Baldwin and the rest of the week-end house party at Chequers, with the exception of his mother, who stayed behind for a few days longer, left early on Tuesday, 22 May 1923. The morning papers, which they read on the journey to London, all canvassed the rival claims of the Foreign Secretary and the Chancellor of the Exchequer to succeed Bonar Law. The Conservative *Morning Post* came out strongly in Baldwin's favour, the *Daily Express*, voicing the opinion of its proprietor Lord Beaverbrook, less so. The *Daily Telegraph* backed Curzon. *The Times*, on the other hand, in a leader entitled 'The King's Choice', observed that in sending for either Curzon or Baldwin, 'the King would be acting strictly in accordance with constitutional precedents and with the facts of the situation'; but the paper went on to point out that the days had gone by when the position of Prime Minister could be held to the public advantage by a member of the House of Lords. Such qualified support for Baldwin was put forward with the advantage of hindsight, since the editor, Geoffrey Dawson, who had seen Lord Stamfordham on the previous evening before the paper went to press, had learned from him that 'the King (on the telephone from Aldershot) had come down on the side of Baldwin'.[1]

Apparently the King wished to be satisfied on one point, which Stamfordham put to Baldwin immediately they met at 10.30 a.m. on 22 May. If His Majesty were to entrust him with the carrying on of the Government, would Baldwin be prepared to retain Lord Curzon as Foreign Minister? Baldwin replied that he 'would welcome such an arrangement', but that he had been told that 'Lord Curzon had declared that he would not be able to serve under him'. If he were sent for, he went on, and Curzon resigned, which Baldwin quite expected, he would try to persuade Austen Chamberlain to come back and become Foreign

Secretary, failing him perhaps Lord Robert Cecil. As for himself he said he could not continue to be Chancellor of the Exchequer as well as Prime Minister and would try to secure the return of Sir Robert Horne to that office. However, he asked Stamfordham to believe that 'he had no ambition to be Prime Minister' and would have gladly served under Curzon. 'He loved his present job and would have liked to continue it under a Prime Minister in the Commons.' [2]

Like Salisbury, the King's Private Secretary personally inclined towards Curzon. However, when Stamfordham met Colonel Stanley Jackson, the new Conservative Party chairman and a well-known cricketer, at noon, he heard from him that the feeling in the constituencies as relayed by the area agents was largely for Baldwin; Jackson added that, although he personally respected Curzon, he doubted if more than fifty Conservative MPs would vote for him. When he returned to Buckingham Palace shortly afterwards, Stamfordham found that the King's mind was made up and nothing that he might say on Curzon's behalf could alter it. Thinking that it would be kinder to warn Curzon in advance of his decision, the King told his Private Secretary to see Curzon at 2.30 and explain the position to him. He was also to summon Baldwin to the Palace at 3.15. [3]

At this point it may be convenient to look briefly at the factors which operated in Baldwin's favour and eventually led the King to this decision. On their journey to Aldershot on the Sunday afternoon, Sykes and Waterhouse carried two documents. One was Bonar Law's letter of resignation, which his son-in-law handed over to the King during his audience. The other document was a memorandum setting out the case for each of the 'only two possible alternatives' to the succession. Although the memorandum was unsigned, it is now known to have been written by Davidson, who had previously told Stamfordham on the telephone that he would let him have it. It was anything but impartial, being heavily biased towards Baldwin, whose only disadvantage was stated to be that his official life was short, while Curzon's drawbacks in the way of temperament, the lack of confidence in him on the part of his colleagues, his embodiment in himself of 'privileged Conservatism' and the fact that he was not a commoner, were all underlined. Thus Baldwin was represented as the ideal choice:

Mr Stanley Baldwin has had a very rapid promotion and has, by his gathering strength, exceeded the expectation of his most fervent friends. He is very much liked by all shades of political opinion in the House of Commons and has the complete confidence of the

City and the commercial world generally. He, in fact, typifies, both the spirit of the Government which the people of this country elected last autumn and also the same characteristics which won the people's confidence for Mr Bonar Law, i.e. honesty, simplicity and balance.

This cogently worded memorandum, of which it is safe to say that Baldwin had no knowledge, was given to the King at the same time as Bonar Law's letter of resignation. It was contained in a sealed envelope, and Davidson afterwards declared that there was no question of Waterhouse having seen it before he handed it over to Stamfordham. Nevertheless Waterhouse assured Stamfordham that it *'practically expressed the views of Mr Bonar Law'*, and Stamfordham endorsed the document in this sense before putting it away in the Royal Archives. In acting as he did, Waterhouse certainly exceeded his instructions. He also violated his chief's confidence, since he told the King during his audience that at heart the Prime Minister preferred Baldwin to Curzon as Prime Minister. Writing many years later in her book *Private and Official*, Waterhouse's wife Nourah described the difficult decision her husband had to make on the journey to Aldershot: 'He found himself being driven fatefully to an immediate choice between unqualified service to the State and the silence imposed by his word of honour given that morning to Bonar. The two were diametrically opposed but the former prevailed . . .'[4]*

In stating as he did that the Davidson memorandum 'practically expressed the views of Mr Bonar Law', Waterhouse misled both Stamfordham and the King besides betraying Bonar Law's trust. He was probably motivated by self-interest, since he had every reason to suppose that Baldwin, with whom his relations were good, would keep him on as Principal Private Secretary if he became Prime Minister, whereas Curzon would lose no time in dispensing with his services. At this date

* In the first draft of her book, Lady Waterhouse wrote a detailed account of her husband's audience with the King at Aldershot on 20 May 1923. 'These passages,' she wrote to the publishers on 26 November 1941, 'are not a verbatim reproduction from a brief but from an *aide-mémoire* made by Ronald immediately after his audience with the King, and based substantially on the brief. The original of this latter document is in my possession and formed the background of the case which Ronald had to present.' However, the relevant chapter was objected to by Court officials and the Treasury Solicitor to whom the draft was submitted for clearance, and Lord Wigram went so far as to state that the conversation as described never took place. Waterhouse took strong exception to the implications of this refutation, and put on record a categorical affirmation that his wife had accurately reported the events as they had taken place. This statement, together with the letter quoted above, is now in the archives of Jonathan Cape, who published the book in 1942 after the controversial chapter had been rewritten by Lady Waterhouse in abbreviated form and with numerous amendments. For further details of this curious episode, see Michael Howard, *Jonathan Cape, Publisher* (1971), pp. 192–5.

Waterhouse was in his early forties. A former Guards officer, he had first met Bonar Law through Sir Frederick Sykes, whom he had served as Private Secretary at the Air Ministry when Sykes was Chief of the Air Staff. Seconded to Bonar Law's secretariat during the temporary absence of John Davidson, Waterhouse had been kept on after Davidson's return, eventually stepping into his shoes when Davidson left to enter the House of Commons. It was an odd choice, since Bonar Law was said personally to dislike Waterhouse and could not bear to be in the same room with him. Nor was Waterhouse particularly good at his job, at least in dealing with paper work. However he seems to have got on well with Sykes, to whom he quite likely owed his position. When Bonar Law retired for a time from politics due to the state of his health, Waterhouse served the Duke of York, later King George VI, as equerry; but he went back to Downing Street when Bonar Law became Prime Minister. In the event he was to serve both Baldwin and Ramsay MacDonald in the same capacity, while his wife Nourah, whom he met while working in Downing Street, was Mrs Baldwin's secretary.

On Whit Monday morning Bonar Law saw Salisbury, who had come up from the country in the milk train, sitting in the guard's van, in order to discuss the question of the succession. Later that day Salisbury met Stamfordham and told him that Bonar Law had given him the impression that 'in this very complex and grave situation he would not on the whole be disinclined to pass over Curzon', but begged that he should not be quoted to the King, 'as it must be remembered they were the expressions of a very sick man'. This disclosure caused Stamfordham to send for Waterhouse, who came to Buckingham Palace early on 22 May. Asked whether Bonar Law's family 'considered that, had he been asked, Bonar Law would have advised the King to appoint Mr Baldwin', Waterhouse replied that he would, adding that indeed he had been so informed by Bonar Law when he breakfasted with him on Sunday morning in Onslow Gardens. He went on to say that Sir Frederick Sykes had read the Davidson memorandum and considered that it embodied his father-in-law's views, a fact which Sykes subsequently denied. Bonar Law's sister was also said to be strongly pro-Baldwin, but if she did say anything on the subject to Waterhouse it was probably no more than that Bonar Law personally preferred Baldwin to Curzon. This was confirmed by Tom Jones who called at Onslow Gardens on Sunday evening when Bonar Law told him in a loud whisper that 'if the King asked for his advice he would put Baldwin first'. Hence, after he had seen Waterhouse for the second time, Stamfordham told Salisbury that, leaving aside the personal factor, what he had learned directly or indirectly from Bonar

Law's family was that 'he would, if asked to advise the King, have been in favour of the Premiership remaining in the House of Commons'.

In fact, this was the identical advice given by Lord Balfour, and it was this advice rather than the Davidson memorandum which ultimately determined the King to come down in Baldwin's favour. In response to an urgent message from Buckingham Palace, the Conservative elder statesman left his sick-bed in Norfolk, to which he had been confined by an attack of phlebitis, and came up to London where Stamfordham met him at his house in Carlton Gardens.

Lord Balfour said he was speaking regardless of the individuals in question, for whereas, on one side, his opinion of Lord Curzon is based upon an intimate, life-long friendship, and the recognition of his exceptional qualifications; on the other, his knowledge of Mr Baldwin is slight and, so far, his public career has been more or less uneventful and without any signs of special gifts or exceptional ability.

However, Balfour went on, to have a Premier in the House of Lords was an anachronism in a democratic age. He told Stamfordham that his uncle, the late Lord Salisbury, 'had found it very difficult to lead the Conservative Party from the House of Lords' in the eighteen-nineties, even though he had Balfour's assistance as Leader of the House of Commons, 'and the Opposition then was the Liberal Party, with an equal representation in the Upper House'. The difficulty today would be insuperable, he added, since the Labour Opposition was completely unrepresented in the Lords. Nor does Balfour appear to have had any doubts as to the effect his advice would have upon the King. When he returned to Norfolk, a friend asked him: 'And will dear George be chosen?' To which Balfour confidently replied: 'No, dear George will not.'[5]

In response to a telegram from Stamfordham, specially delivered by the village policeman to Montacute, since Curzon refused to have a telephone in the house, the Foreign Secretary and his wife travelled up to London by train on Tuesday morning, as the Baldwins were making a similar journey from Chequers. The difference between them was that, whereas Baldwin was still uncertain whether he would be chosen, Curzon was quite confident that the matter had already been settled in his favour. Else why should he have been summoned? His terrible disappointment, which followed when Stamfordham called on him at his house in Carlton House Terrace and informed him that Baldwin was already on his way to the Palace, has often been described, notably by Harold

Nicolson in his *Curzon: The Last Phase*, so that it is unnecessary to repeat it here except to recall that he broke down and wept when he heard the shattering news that 'a man of no experience, and of the utmost insignificance', as he described Baldwin between sobs, had been preferred to him. 'Not even a public figure,' he added pitifully.[6]

Baldwin, who had donned a frock-coat for the occasion, returned to Downing Street after he had been received by the King and had accepted His Majesty's invitation to become Prime Minister. As soon as they heard the news, Tom Jones and several others who happened to be in No. 10 went next door to offer their congratulations. Meanwhile in Printing House Square, a suitable leading article for next day's issue of *The Times* was being composed by the editor, who observed: 'Mr Baldwin's political career has been without exception the most amazing of modern times.'[7] Tom Jones wrote in his diary the same night:

All of us astonished at the swiftness of his ascent. Six years in office. Very nearly becoming Speaker when Whitley was appointed. A plain man, domesticated like B[onar] L[aw], fond of books and music and walks in the country. Nothing like B.L.'s brain – much slower and always eager to consult one or two others before coming to a decision; but stands by his decision once taken . . .

We found the new PM very self-conscious in his frock-coat, surrounded by his wife and daughters. 'Thank God,' shouted Warren Fisher with the fervour of an Archdeacon. I shook hands and the PM said: 'I shall want you to hold my hand, Tom.' 'I'll be a cabin boy with pleasure,' I replied and we all trooped out again. I crossed to tell Hankey the news and to arrange to ring up private secretaries and ask them to send in the resignations of their respective chiefs.

I hear tonight that a great effort is to be made to get [Austen] Chamberlain and Horne back to office, Chamberlain as Foreign Secretary if Curzon does not continue and Horne at the Treasury.[8]

'My first letter shall be to you,' Baldwin wrote to his mother, echoing what he told the journalists who were waiting for him when he got back to Downing Street from Buckingham Palace. 'Prayers and not congratulations for anyone called to this particular post. The King was very friendly but worried by Curzon's grief at being passed over. I don't think he'll serve with me. Anyway I shall have a couple of busy days trying to form a Government, and I hope to get it completed by Friday . . . I am not a bit excited and don't realise it in the least.'[9]

2

Baldwin's next letter was at Stamfordham's suggestion addressed to the man whom he did not think would serve with him; but he felt that he must write to him in view of the undertaking he had given the King. The letter was sent round to Carlton House Terrace by hand the same evening.[10]

11 Downing Street, SW 1

My dear Curzon,

I hope, both on personal and public grounds, that you will feel able to continue your great work at the Foreign Office in the new administration.

There never was a time when foreign affairs caused more anxiety than they do at present, and your unrivalled experience is today one of the greatest assets of the Empire.

Yours very sincerely,
STANLEY BALDWIN

Curzon, still smarting under a sense of bitter disappointment, hesitated before replying. He had not done so by noon next day when Geoffrey Dawson called on Davidson at Downing Street and was shown in to Baldwin whom he found 'very composed, if rather subdued and waiting for the Marquess's reply'. The new Premier told Dawson something of his plans for reuniting the Conservative Party; but he gave no hint of his intention to offer Austen Chamberlain the Foreign Secretaryship in the event of Curzon refusing to continue. The expected letter arrived shortly after Dawson had left. It put an end to any possibility of Austen Chamberlain becoming Foreign Secretary. 'I have every desire to retire,' wrote Curzon. 'But, as there are certain things which in the public interest I ought, perhaps, to endeavour to carry through, and as my retirement at this moment might be thought to involve distrust in your administration which would be a quite unfounded suspicion, I will for the present continue at the Foreign Office.'[11]

Austen Chamberlain's brother Neville had recently succeeded the unfortunate Minister of Health Griffith-Boscawen, who had twice failed to secure re-election to the House of Commons on his appointment and had consequently dropped out of politics. Neville Chamberlain, who confessed to his sister Ida at this time that he 'had rather hoped that Curzon would have been PM, but had not realised the extent of his unpopularity in the country', made haste to congratulate the new Premier 'on the general recognition of your own great qualities which have brought you so quickly to the top'. He also told his sister that in his opinion Baldwin was 'the nearest man we have to Bonar in the qualities of straightforwardness and sincerity'. Later the same day (2 May), when Neville Chamberlain saw Baldwin and agreed to carry on at the Ministry of Health, the Prime Minister repeated what he had already said to Dawson about healing the breach in the Party, but added that 'he did not think he ought to press for Austen if it meant the resignation of some of those who had stuck by the ship in difficult times'.[12] Baldwin did not mention anyone by name in this context, but his mind seems to have been inclining towards the view that if he brought in Austen Chamberlain, even as a minister without portfolio such as Lord Privy Seal, he would lose the services of men like Amery, Salisbury and Devonshire, who could not forgive Austen Chamberlain for the part he had played as a signatory of the Irish 'Treaty'.

The same night Neville Chamberlain noted in his diary that 'S.B. seemed in good spirits'.

He declared himself by no means overwhelmed by his responsibilities. He was convinced something must be done to get a move on in Europe – we could not go on drifting. As to domestic politics, we could not think about them till we had got through the next nine weeks. We should not have time. He was going to the theatre tonight![13]

The business of Government had to be carried on, and at a small ministerial meeting held in the Cabinet Room on 24 May, in order to deal with the urgent matter of relations with Russia, before the Cabinet had been fully constituted and the Prime Minister had 'kissed hands' on his formal appointment as First Lord of the Treasury, Curzon, in the words of the official Minutes, 'as the Minister present who had longest held office, took advantage of the opportunity to offer the Prime Minister, on behalf of his colleagues and himself, their congratulations on his appointment and their assurance of loyal and unfaltering support'.[14]

The post which Baldwin had most difficulty in filling was the Exchequer. Horne, whom Baldwin saw twice on 24 May, refused unless Austen Chamberlain was also in the Cabinet, and to this Baldwin would not agree. Reginald McKenna, who had turned it down before, was again approached and once more declined, as he was recovering from a serious attack of paratyphoid and his doctor said that he would not be fit to resume work for several months. Finally Baldwin agreed to hold open the post for him and in the meantime to continue himself as Chancellor as well as Prime Minister. To this end as understudy he appointed Sir William Joynson-Hicks Financial Secretary to the Treasury with a seat in the Cabinet. Joynson-Hicks's successor as Postmaster-General, also in the Cabinet, was Sir Laming Worthington-Evans ('Worthy'), the only Coalition Conservative to take a job under Baldwin, much to the annoyance of Austen Chamberlain. Salisbury's brother Lord Robert Cecil (later Viscount Cecil of Chelwood) became Lord Privy Seal with the object of helping Curzon at the Foreign Office. Otherwise the mixture was very much as before, with the ministers who had served under Bonar Law carrying on under Baldwin. Hoare, who remained Air Minister, was advanced to Cabinet rank, and the thirty-four-year-old John Davidson joined the Government as Chancellor of the Duchy of Lancaster, a largely sinecure office 'with few departmental duties and no parliamentary responsibilities' which enabled him to continue as the Prime Minister's Parliamentary Private Secretary and closest confidant.*

The existing Private Secretaries at 10 Downing Street, including Ronald Waterhouse and Geoffrey Fry, Baldwin took over from Bonar Law, leaving James Grigg in charge of the Private Office at the Treasury.

Baldwin was formally sworn First Lord of the Treasury at a Privy Council in Buckingham Palace on the morning of 25 May. In conversation with Sir Almeric Fitzroy, the Clerk of the Council, 'he admitted that his position in regard to the Exchequer was, as Horne said, a difficult one, short of retaining it temporarily himself, but he evidently felt his old colleague's failure to respond to his invitation rather bitterly, and there came out . . . that the difficulty lay with an agreement between those who acted together last October [the Coalition Conservatives] in no case to take office separately'. Fitzroy also recorded that on this occasion he 'was much struck by the high pitch he [Baldwin] gave to the standards of political life and by the obvious sincerity of his regret to find it meet so little sympathy'.[15]

As he expected, Baldwin was able to complete the principal posts in his Ministry the same afternoon. He and his wife then went off for the week-end to Chequers, where they were joined by the Davidsons and Sir Eyre Crowe, the permanent head of the Foreign Office. His mother

---

* 'I was not in the Cabinet,' Davidson later recalled, 'but I saw the papers circulated, and most of the other Cabinet Ministers talked to me as though I were a colleague. I had deliberately refused any chance of Cabinet rank because I wished my relationship with S.B. to continue on the former basis.'

was waiting at Chequers to welcome him. 'God be with our dear Premier,' she wrote to her sister. 'I never saw the nobility, calmness and
modesty of his character to more splendid advantage.'[16]

3

Old Mrs Baldwin's view of her son's merits was not shared for one by
Austen Chamberlain, who had heard nothing from the new Premier until
after all the ministerial appointments had been filled. He thus considered
that as an ex-Party leader with some contribution to make to Party
unity he had been treated with gross discourtesy. It was not until the
Friday evening that he received a telephone message from Baldwin asking
if he could come to Chequers on the following day. Chamberlain replied
that he would be there in the afternoon.

The Prime Minister was on the look-out for him when he arrived and
met him at the door. Asked by his visitor how he was standing the strain
of the Premiership, Baldwin replied that he was standing it pretty well
'*thanks to Chequers*, and without the peace and rest that he got there he
did not believe he could carry on at all'.[17] Although he greeted Chamberlain with marked cordiality, agreeing that they were friends still even
when they differed, the meeting, which took place in the ground-floor
study, got off to a bad start. After filling him in on the events of the
week, which corresponded broadly with what Chamberlain had already
gathered from his own friends such as Horne and Birkenhead, Baldwin
'with considerable hesitation' and, as Chamberlain thought, 'choosing
his words rather carefully', said he wished to ask him a question. He did
not want an immediate answer, Chamberlain noted in an account of the
meeting which he wrote next day, but he wished him to 'have it in
mind'.[18]

If the position changed and he was able – say in three months' time –
to offer me office, would I then be able to accept? And there was
another question which he wished to put, to which again he did
not want an immediate answer, but he would like me to think it
over and perhaps at some future date we might discuss it again. The
Washington Embassy was shortly to be vacant. There was no position
of greater consequence to the British Empire and it was a very
difficult one to fill, because not only must the man have the necessary
qualifications but the qualifications of the wife were equally important. He thought that I was admirably suited for the post: that

my appointment would be most acceptable to the Americans, and Mrs Chamberlain would be a perfect Ambassadress. He repeated that he did not ask for any answer now but would like me to think this over.

Chamberlain's immediate reaction was to ask Baldwin whether he had mentioned this idea to Curzon. Baldwin replied that he had, whereupon to the Prime Minister's astonishment Chamberlain informed him that he had previously been offered this post by Curzon, and also the Paris Embassy, 'which I believe was considered the best diplomatic appointment', and had turned down both offers, as well as that of the Viceroyalty of India.

'I am not very easily made angry,' Chamberlain spoke his mind to Baldwin, 'but when I heard, as I did from my colleagues, that you intended to make me this offer, I frankly say that I lost my temper. You have made it, however, with such consideration and evident good-will and sincerity that I cannot be angry with you now. But of course I refuse absolutely, and that not only because having given the best years of my life to Parliament I am not prepared to take up an appointment abroad, but because it would neither be to your credit nor to mine that the offer should be made or accepted. You would have the appearance of trying to buy off possible opposition and I of accepting a fat salary as compensation for the discourtesy shown to me.'

Baldwin assured Chamberlain that he had known nothing of his previous refusals of the Embassies and he would at once withdraw the proposal. ('Let us treat it as not having been made.') According to Chamberlain's account, the Prime Minister rather naïvely went on to explain that whether he could carry on and make a success of the job or not, he was Prime Minister, he was a younger man than Chamberlain, and if he succeeded then he would block Chamberlain's path, and he thought that 'perhaps under these circumstances' Chamberlain would like a diplomatic appointment. 'It is perhaps to my credit,' noted Chamberlain afterwards, 'that I did not lose my temper again.'

I then turned to his question about my contingent willingness to accept office in the future. I said that I was sorry that he had put that question. It was not a question that I could answer, and, indeed, it was not a suggestion that ought to have been made. What assurance could he have that the obstacles which he had been unable to overcome at the present time would not be equally strong three months hence?

He interjected that he would tell me why he thought the position would be changed, but I said that I did not wish to know, for, as I had already said, I was sorry that he had even put the question to me. I was not prepared to be treated as a boy on probation who was told that if he behaved well he might get a remove next term or to have a bundle of carrots dangled before my nose to induce me to gallop. I intimated that any approach on those lines was offensive. It could only alienate me and drive me into opposition.

He at once disclaimed any such idea, to which I replied that this was exactly what was being said by a section of his supporters and by some of his colleagues.

'My dear Stanley, why didn't you send for me?' Chamberlain asked. 'If you wanted to offer me office with some of my colleagues in order to restore the unity of the party, why didn't you ask me to come and see you? I should have come at once at any moment if you had sent for me, and I think agreement might have been secured.'

Baldwin replied that this was what he had wished to do, but, as he had already explained, he was prevented by the resistance of colleagues.

'But even so, Stanley,' Chamberlain repeated, 'why didn't you send for me? We are old friends. You could have talked to me with the same frankness that you have shown today. You could have explained your difficulty and made your appeal to me to help you with my colleagues. I can tell you that there would have been no insistence by any of them on personal claims – as it was, I had set them free as far as lay in my power from any sense of obligation to myself . . . Suppose the position had been reversed and I had tried to secure your services whilst excluding Bonar Law and without communicating with him. You know you would not have accepted. No man of honour would. How could you think that Horne would do differently? Why, my dear Stanley, why didn't you send for me?'

'I am very sorry,' the Prime Minister said slowly, and, as Chamberlain thought, sadly. 'I never thought of it. I am very sorry. I never thought of it,' he repeated.

Baldwin went on to emphasise that he had not offered the Exchequer to McKenna until Horne had refused it. Then, after Chamberlain put some questions about what McKenna, an ex-Liberal, might be expected to do as Chancellor in a Conservative ministry – 'I could not help feeling that there was a certain humour in the attitude of his Government who were so jealous of the purity of the Conservative faith that they proscribed me and accepted McKenna' – Chamberlain was asked whether he thought that if Horne were offered the same post in three months' time he would then accept.

> I replied that that was a question that I was absolutely unable to answer. Nobody could answer except Horne, and I doubted whether Horne himself could answer it in advance. But, I said, I will tell you my attitude in regard to your offer to 'Worthy'. He has not answered you and I don't know what his answer is going to be. I have made it clear to Worthington that I do not wish him to refuse on my account if he thinks it right to accept. But I say to you, Stanley, what I have not said to Worthington – that if I could eliminate myself from the question and give my advice to Worthington as a friend, I should tell him not to accept; for if he now goes in alone after all that has passed you will have no respect for him and he will lose all credit with others . . . To this he made no reply.

Although they 'parted most cordially' and Chamberlain 'was left with the impression that Baldwin sincerely regretted that he had not communicated with me at once, even if he had felt unable to invite me to join his ministry', nevertheless the matter rankled with the former Conservative leader. 'To so good and intimate a friend as yourself,' he wrote to Birkenhead after the meeting, 'I may say without being afraid of misconception that I have been deeply wounded. I feel some contempt for Baldwin's weakness, which does not, however, remove my sense of his discourtesy, and his blundering approaches to me with the suggestions that I can be bribed to good behaviour or bought off by a lucrative appointment are galling to a proud man. But I have suppressed these feelings and I shall not allow them to influence my public conduct.'

Neville Chamberlain did his best to convince his brother that Baldwin never intended to show him discourtesy:

> He may have blundered, indeed he did, through lack of full appreciation of your position, but I am sure he did it unintentionally. You must make some allowance for the fact that he had suddenly come into his position, that he was in a hurry to complete his Cabinet, that he did not anticipate serious opposition and that Horne was at hand and you were not . . . and it never occurred to him till you or Horne pointed it out that you were the first person he should have seen.

But Austen Chamberlain refused to be mollified. Although he hid his resentment in public, he pointedly absented himself from the Party meeting on 28 May in the Hotel Cecil at which Baldwin on Curzon's proposal was elected Leader, as also did Birkenhead.[19]

Yet there was no doubt of Baldwin's popularity with the Conservative backbenchers in the House of Commons, and he was loudly cheered as he entered the chamber and took his place on the Treasury Bench for the first time as Prime Minister. 'These are difficult times,' he told the veteran Irish Unionist Lord Carson who had written to congratulate him, 'but I shall try to run straight and keep the affection of my friends which has always been my main support and my strength.'

4

When Bonar Law went abroad at the beginning of May, Baldwin had taken over from him the duty, which customarily devolves on a Prime Minister, of writing an account of the day's proceedings in the Commons for the information of the King. His own initial contribution as Prime Minister may be conveniently quoted here:

> *House of Commons, 29 May 1923* . . . The House met yesterday in the shadow of a great loss. There can have been few instances in the past in which the resignation of a Prime Minister evoked such unanimous expressions of genuine regret as in the case of Mr Bonar Law. He had won for himself the respect, admiration, and affection not only of his own followers but also of his political opponents including even those who, owing to their fanatical intolerance and vehement emotions, tend to attribute nothing but evil motives and sinister designs to those who disagree with them on fundamental principles.
>
> There were few, if any, Members in the House yesterday who did not feel a sense of personal loss, and Mr Ramsay MacDonald, Mr Asquith, Mr Lloyd George and Mr Austen Chamberlain were giving expression to a universal feeling when, in very happily worded speeches, they paid a warm tribute to Mr Bonar Law's great services and ability, and expressed sympathy with him in the circumstances which led to his resignation. It was one of those occasions when the House of Commons appears at its best.[20]

These daily reports while Parliament was sitting were usually character-ised by a lighter note, and on at least one occasion, as will be seen, the King was to rebuke his Prime Minister for what he considered unseemly levity in his description of a scene in the Commons chamber. Probably no Prime Minister, at any rate in modern times, was to spend more time on the Front Bench than Baldwin, so that in his case he was usually well placed to observe what was going on and to report it at first hand. He would constantly be seen reading *Dod's Parliamentary Companion*, an indispensable work of reference containing the biographies and details of the constituencies and majorities of all MPs. If a Member whom he did not know rose to speak, he would immediately consult *Dod* for the relevant background information. He would sometimes also do this for other purposes. Once, when he was particularly engrossed, a junior colleague slid across the bench to find that the page he was perusing referred to none other than Lloyd George and his constituency record. 'I think if the Old Man goes,' said Baldwin, looking up for a moment, 'we should stand a very good chance of winning Caernarvon Boroughs.' [21]*

Although he was later to be helped by his private secretaries in the composition of his parliamentary reports for the King, at first Baldwin invariably wrote them himself. A good example of style occurred a few days after the one already quoted, in which he described the speech by Edward Wood, the President of the Board of Education, in moving the departmental vote.

1 June 1923 . . . In referring to suggestions which had been made in certain quarters that the whole blame for any defects in the present system should be placed on the permanent officials of the Board, he recalled to mind an illustration which was used by a young tutor at Oxford when lecturing his students on the possible fallacies of logic. This illustration was as follows: – a young undergraduate had been intoxicated on three successive nights, the first night on whisky and soda, the second on brandy and soda, and the third night on gin and soda. With a disregard of logic he had ascribed his downfall to the only constant factor of the soda and had accordingly decided to forswear the beverage for the rest of his life.

Applying that illustration to the present case, Mr Wood suggested that the permanent officials of the Board of Education filled the role of the soda water and the Ministers in charge of the Department were the alcohol concomitants at whose door the responsibility for the actions of the Board should be laid.

Baldwin met his Cabinet for the first time at 11.30 a.m. on 30 May, taking the Prime Minister's traditional place in the sole armchair at the

* Lloyd George had been Liberal MP for Caernarvon Boroughs since 1890.

middle of the long table, with his back to the fireplace above which hangs a portrait of Sir Robert Walpole, the first occupant of the office in the modern constitutional sense. After he had greeted the new members, the Cabinet agreed 'that the Prime Minister should send on their behalf a message of condolence and affection to Mr Bonar Law'.[22]

'Baldwin always had a great trust in his departmental chiefs,' Davidson was to recall. 'It came out again and again in the Cabinet. He deliberately did not dominate the Cabinet, but sat there quietly listening, entering the arena only at the end of a discussion or when the Prime Minister's views were particularly needed. He wasn't – nor did he attempt to be – a Winston or a Lloyd George, but the Chairman of a competent Board of Managers, and if the Board wasn't competent, then he'd made some bad choices . . . He often said that he had put so-and-so into such-and-such a Ministry and if he couldn't hold the job down then he'd better clear out. He was extremely nice to his Ministers, but never showed the slightest inclination to come to decisions on their behalf. It seemed to me then, and it seems to me now, a very good and wise attitude. Either you trust your Ministers or you don't.'[23]

An illustration of how Baldwin worked, though it belongs to a later period, may be given here. When Derby's son Oliver Stanley was Minister of Labour, a problem arose over unemployment insurance and Stanley went to see Baldwin about it. 'Of course the old man has thrown the ball back into my court,' Stanley told Davidson when he came out of the Cabinet Room.

> I wanted his advice and he listened very attentively and I found myself talking faster and faster until at last I ran out of words. I'd finished my case in ten minutes, and then he said: 'Well, we've had a very interesting conversation, Oliver. Always remember you can come at any time to see me when you've a problem to discuss. Now go away and make your decision for yourself and I'll back you.'

There were nineteen ministers in Baldwin's Cabinet, and it formed a team which he drove on an easy rein. 'If Stanley Baldwin would give a lead, go ahead and keep his Cabinet in order, his position would be impregnable,' Asquith remarked to a friend. 'But if he goes on doing nothing, he will not be able to save himself. He will be bound to fall – and the trouble is that there will be little chance of anything much better coming after him.' During the period of a little short of eight months that Baldwin's ministry lasted, the Cabinet met on thirty-one occasions, usually in Downing Street at 11.30 a.m. but occasionally in the Prime Minister's room in the House of Commons. Baldwin did not miss a single meeting. Reparations and unemployment figured most prominently and frequently on the agenda. Another question which caused animated argument centred on whether the Royal Air Force should remain an independent service or whether its components should be handed over to the other two service departments to be run as a part of their own establishments. As the minister responsible Hoare had to fight hard for the survival of this service. Fortunately a Cabinet committee under Balfour's chairmanship recommended that the Fleet Air Units should remain an integral part of the Air Force, and although this produced an acute clash with the Admiralty and several senior admirals threatened to resign, the Cabinet accepted the committee's recommend- ations and the Admiralty reluctantly followed suit, although it continued to hope that the decision would one day be reversed. The army co- operation squadrons were similarly retained by the Air Ministry in spite of Derby's protests from the War Office.

It should be noted here that the Balfour committee was in fact a sub- committee of a committee chaired by Lord Salisbury, the Lord President of the Council. The Salisbury committee, which Baldwin had joined when he was Chancellor of the Exchequer, was in turn a sub-committee of the Committee of Imperial Defence; it had been set up by Bonar Law early in 1923 to consider the whole question of co-operation between the armed forces and the service ministries including the question of establishing some co-ordinating authority such as a Ministry of Defence. Perhaps the Salisbury committee's most important recommendation which it fell to Baldwin to implement when he became Prime Minister was the creation of the Chiefs of Staff Committee. John Davidson regarded this as one of Baldwin's most important decisions. 'I used to have long talks with him about it while he was thinking it all out talking on the mountains at Aix,' Davidson afterwards wrote, claiming that he had converted Baldwin to his way of thinking.

I held the view very strongly that we should be left behind unless we had much closer integration of [the] Services. The only way that we could get good advice was to get the three expert advisers into a room by themselves rather than have them mingle with the politicians of the CID. By the latter way we never got a combined view, because they had never discussed it among themselves before- hand. Meeting and speaking frankly together they did not have to commit themselves in front of other Ministers, including the

Chancellor of the Exchequer. Between themselves they could clear the air and make a joint recommendation.[24]

Unfortunately the early years of the Chiefs of Staff Committee were to be embittered by the dispute over the Fleet Air Arm, which was to flare up again in 1926. But the COS Committee was fully justified in the long term and its annual reviews of defence policy were to prove of great value. Another innovation for which Baldwin secured Cabinet approval in 1923 was the creation of a joint staff college located in London which in the event came to be known as the Imperial Defence College.

Of all the Cabinet Ministers the Foreign Secretary gave Baldwin the most trouble. At an early stage Curzon complained to the Prime Minister at the way foreign policy was carried on in the Cabinet. ('Any member may make any suggestion he pleases and the discussion wanders off into helpless irrelevancies. No decision is arrived at and no policy prepared.') At times Baldwin found him a sore trial. 'Curzon is difficult,' he confessed to Tom Jones, 'very bad-tempered in the forenoon but better as the day advances. He gets on Eyre Crowe's nerves, but Sir William Tyrell [the Assistant Under-Secretary] has humour and can handle him better. If anything happened to Curzon, I should try to bring Grey back as Foreign Secretary.'[25] This bi-partisan approach on Baldwin's part to foreign affairs is remarkable, since Grey was always a Liberal.

Jones had his first meeting alone with the Prime Minister on the day he was elected party leader. 'There are three things I want to do,' Baldwin told him. 'We've got to settle Europe. We can't wait for Emigration and Empire Development. We live by our export trade and can't afford to let Europe go to pieces with all the serious economic consequences.' Here he particularly had in mind the need to stabilise the German mark, which had completely collapsed. 'Secondly, we must try to avoid a break with Russia.'* Thirdly, there was the implementation of Disraeli's canon – 'the welfare of the people'. At this time there were 1,300,000 unemployed and they urgently needed help.

As he was speaking, Jones noticed that Baldwin exhibited several peculiar mannerisms. His face started twitching, he rolled his tongue about, and he looked away into space.[26]

---

* Curzon had threatened to denounce the existing Anglo-Soviet trade agreement unless the government in Moscow gave full satisfaction for outrages committed against British subjects in the Soviet Union and also ceased anti-British propaganda in the Middle East.

5

'I do not envy Baldwin his job,' wrote the veteran Liberal lawyer Lord Haldane at this time, 'but I am glad that it is he and not Curzon. I think that Baldwin is a shrewd manager of men and that Curzon certainly is not.' The fact that Baldwin was most accessible, particularly to colleagues and senior civil servants, may have had something to do with his success as a manager. Indeed Davidson thought that there never had been a Prime Minister, even Bonar Law, who could be seen so easily. This had its drawbacks and before many months had passed the Prime Minister was complaining to Tom Jones, whom he was coming to employ more and more as a speech writer, that he had no energy available for serious reading. ('A PM was bothered all day with someone or other reporting discontent here, there and everywhere.') As Baldwin put it to his mother, 'when you are at the beck and call of everyone for fourteen hours a day for four days and for eight hours on the fifth day each week you want a short space in which you relax and do just what you like'. According to Davidson, 'anyone could go into his room, and he wasn't at all shy of people coming up to him in the Smoking Room' of the House of Commons. At the same time he realised his handicap. 'I am in-experienced and new to this job,' he frankly admitted to Jones. And, looking back some years later, he elaborated on this to Asquith: 'The position of leader came to me when I was inexperienced, before I was really fitted for it, by a succession of curious chances that could not have been foreseen. I had never expected it: I was in no way trained for it.'[27]

Baldwin was sometimes to be accused of laziness, but there was certainly no evidence of it at this period. 'The work goes on, one week like another, and pretty incessant till Friday night,' he wrote to his mother after he had been at it six weeks, 'and then the break which gives one time to get one's breath again. So far, I am thankful to say, it is not too heavy. Of course there are things that always cause anxiety, but I don't worry. The French settlement is the most difficult and that worried Bonar frightfully.' He said something similar to Bonar Law, who was surprised at what he considered Baldwin's 'nonchalance' in 'a sea of trouble' and told him that he thought he '*ought* to be worried'.[28]

The Prime Minister's private quarters were on the second floor of 10 Downing Street, and Mrs Baldwin found them even less satisfactory than the living-rooms in No. 11 when they moved in. She complained that there was nobody to look after the linen and blankets; she had to use the same curtains as Mrs Gladstone, and as they had been repeatedly washed instead of being cleaned, they had shrunk and were thus too short for the long Georgian windows of the house. Furthermore, there was only one bath, which had been put in for Disraeli and had a lid on it, being 'deep and narrow and dangerous'.[29] Like her husband, Lucy Baldwin much preferred Chequers, which had been so tastefully furnished by Lord and Lady Lee. But Lucy did her best with No. 10, redecorating the sitting-room in a pleasing light shade and substituting gay chintzes for the dark plush which the Office of Works had used for soft furnishings.

Stanley and Lucy Baldwin gave the impression, on being suddenly thrust before the public eye, of a devoted, homely couple with all the domestic virtues, who were sustained by a simple, religious faith. Geoffrey Dawson, the editor of *The Times*, recalled spending a Sunday with them at Chequers at this time and leaving them 'puddling off over the fields' to Ellesborough Church for evensong. To Baron Palmstierna, the Swedish Ambassador, who once asked Mrs Baldwin whether she was 'a believer', she answered: 'I am indeed, and I must tell you that every morning when we rise we kneel together before God and commend our day to Him, praying that some good work may be done in it by us. It is not for ourselves that we are working, but for the country and for God's sake. How else could we live?' According to the Swede, she looked at him so 'sincerely and naturally' that he immediately realised what he called 'the simple earnestness of their conception of life'. This, Tom Jones thought, was perhaps the 'truest clue' to Baldwin's personality.[30]

Until Parliament rose for the summer recess and they went to Worcestershire, the Baldwins did not miss a single week-end at Chequers. There were guests most times, but these did not include any of the Prime Minister's Cabinet colleagues. Only Baird and Davidson, who had posts outside the Cabinet, went with their wives, also the Private Secretaries Ronald Waterhouse and Geoffrey Fry. Rudyard Kipling, and his wife and daughter were there in July, also Reginald McKenna, who told his host that after all he did not think he could take on the Exchequer, which Baldwin had been holding open for him, since he had been unable to find a parliamentary seat. Other guests in the same month included Andrew Mellon, the American Secretary of the Treasury, and his wife, who were on a visit to England; they were also joined by Montagu Norman.[31]

Lloyd George, said Baldwin in one of his first speeches as Prime Minister, had described Bonar Law as being 'honest to the point of simplicity'. He (Baldwin) thought the British people felt that that was just 'what we have been looking for', and it was the public image which he himself consistently tried to put across. 'Although I cannot hope to emulate my late leader,' he told an audience of young Conservatives at the undergraduate Chatham Club in Oxford, 'if those six words can be uttered of me when the General Election takes place, I shall be a proud man as an individual and I shall have every confidence in the success of the party I am leading.'* Lloyd George, by contrast, he regarded as 'a real corrupter of public life and couldn't understand the spell'. Unlike Bonar Law, he shared Geoffrey Dawson's view that 'the Welsh wizard' was unlikely to make a quick political come-back. In this context Baldwin was contemptuous of 'oratory' and 'first-class brains'. As he told a meeting of Conservatives in Glasgow, he 'had never yet known a good workman who could talk' nor 'a good talker who was a good work-man'.[32]

A Prime Minister has to make frequent speeches to large audiences outside Parliament, and Baldwin soon felt the strain both in their preparation and their delivery. Fortunately he had Tom Jones to help him with the former, while in the first few months in office he admitted that he drank more champagne than he had done for many years, since he found that it 'bucked him up' for the effort of delivery. 'In the happy pre-war days,' he told his mother, 'our statesmen could lock themselves up for days before a big speech, and now you have to prepare in odd moments. And a big speech means a lot of brain sweat. You can't expect to hold five thousand people for an hour unless you have something to say and arrange it in proper sequence, and give out the nervous force all the time that rivets them.'[33]

During the two months which elapsed before Parliament rose for the summer recess, one major piece of legislation was passed. This was a Housing Act, providing for state subsidies to encourage private rather than municipal building. Baldwin was much impressed by the way in which Neville Chamberlain, the responsible minister, piloted it through the Commons. Consequently, after McKenna had refused the Exchequer for the second time, Baldwin wrote to Neville Chamberlain, who was then enjoying a fishing holiday in Scotland, and asked him whether he would now become Chancellor. 'What a day!' Chamberlain replied. 'Two salmon this morning and the offer of the Exchequer this afternoon!' However, although he regarded it as 'the greatest compliment I ever received in my life', he asked the Prime Minister not to press it. 'I do not feel that I have any gift for finance which I have never been able to

---

* When the Chatham Club first invited Baldwin to its annual Dinner, he was Chancellor of the Exchequer, which accounts for the fact that this was the first political speech (8 June 1923) he made outside the House of Commons. Asked by the Club Secretary, William Teeling, later MP, what he was doing the following day, he replied: 'I am going over to Chequers for the week-end and I want to go cross-country by the slowest train. I love looking out at the countryside and it gives me time to think.' Sir William Teeling, *Corridors of Frustration* (1970), p. 24.

understand,' he explained, 'and I feel that as Chancellor I should not fulfil your expectations.' But, on the offer being repeated, Chamberlain cut short his fishing holiday and agreed after a long interview. The consideration which eventually broke down his resistance was the Prime Minister's admission that he felt the need of a colleague with whom he could discuss affairs as he used to do with Bonar Law at their morning talks when he himself was Chancellor and was on his way to the Treasury. He added that McKenna had himself suggested Neville Chamberlain for the post. Nevertheless, Chamberlain, who was looking forward to two more years as Minister of Health, thought that it revealed 'a certain weakness in the government, since the PM feels there is no choice open to him'.[34]

Baldwin found time to attend the 'Fourth of June' celebrations at Eton and also Harrow Speech Day. He was the guest of honour at the Harrovian Association dinner, when he spoke to a large gathering, noting that one of those present, whose name was Yates Thompson, had been Head Boy sixty years earlier in the time of Palmerston, the last Old Harrovian to become Prime Minister before Baldwin. One jocular allusion in Baldwin's speech on this occasion went down particularly well with the Old Boys. 'When the call came to me to form a Government,' he told them, 'one of my first thoughts was that it should be a Government of which Harrow should not be ashamed. I remembered how in previous Governments there had been four or, perhaps, five Harrovians and I determined to have six. To make a Cabinet is like making a jig-saw puzzle fit, and I managed to make my six fit by keeping the post of Chancellor of the Exchequer for myself. I think we have good reason to be content.'

He concluded on a more serious note:

I realise as well as anyone here that the kindness you have shown me and the welcome you have given me are not so much a tribute to achievement – that, please God! may come later – but as holding out the hand to one from the same School who is now taking on himself the heaviest burden in the world. You mean by your greeting to assure me that you wish me well, as I know you do, and that whether I succeed or fail you have the belief in me that as a son of the Hill I will run straight; that if I fail I will not whine; that if success is mine I will not be puffed up; but that I will try in all things to follow in the footsteps of those who have trodden the same difficult path before me; and that I will, with God's help, do nothing in the course of an arduous and a difficult career which will cause any Harrovian to say of me that I have failed to do my best to live up to the highest ideals of the School.[35]

Perhaps the most important statement which Baldwin made during his early days in office, although its significance was not fully appreciated at the time, was to the House of Commons on the subject of air defence. It laid down the principle that Britain must not be left in a position of inferiority in air strength to any country within bombing range of her shores. As will be seen, the principle was to be reaffirmed in another House of Commons speech eleven years later in circumstances which attracted considerably more publicity, when it was regarded by many people as a novel one. Its origin can be traced to a Sub-Committee of the Committee of Imperial Defence, which had been appointed in March 1923 when Bonar Law was Prime Minister to investigate how the country's essential air power requirements could best be met. It was a high-powered committee which sat under the chairmanship of Lord Salisbury and included Baldwin, Curzon, the three service ministers, and the secretaries for India and the colonies, as well as Lord Balfour and Lord Weir, a prominent industrialist who had been the first Air Minister. At the end of three months, the committee reported to the Cabinet which endorsed the opinion of its members that 'British air power must include a Home Defence Air Force of sufficient strength adequately to protect us against air attack by the strongest air force within striking distance of this country'. It was agreed by the Cabinet that Salisbury and Hoare, the Secretary of State for Air, should draw up the terms of a statement which should be made by the Prime Minister in the Commons and Curzon in the Lords and that this should 'contain an affirmation of the desire of the Government to secure a reduction of aerial as well as other armaments by means of an international agreement'.[36]

Baldwin's statements announcing that a Home Defence Force of fifty-two squadrons should be created 'with as little delay as possible' as a defence against 'attack from the strongest air force within striking distance' was made on 26 June 1923. He concluded, as the Cabinet had done, by expressing the Government's readiness to co-operate with other Governments in limiting the strength of air armaments. It was widely and correctly deduced, among others by the Trades Union Congress, that the country 'within striking distance' which the Prime Minister and the Cabinet had in mind could only be France, which was credited with having six hundred first-line aircraft. In fact, the figure of six hundred was a considerable exaggeration, but it so alarmed the TUC, now convinced that 'the fifty-two squadron scheme' heralded the start of a new arms race, that it instructed all Labour MPs to oppose the scheme as vigorously as they could.

'We must remember that our island story is told and that with the advent of the aeroplane we shall cease to be an island,' said Baldwin. '*Whether we like it or not, we are indissolubly bound to Europe.*'[37]

6

The questions of unemployment and German reparations were much on Baldwin's mind as he and his wife left London on 26 August 1923 for their annual holiday at Aix-les-Bains. 'I shall do a lot of quiet thinking at Aix,' he told Davidson on the eve of his departure. As usual they stayed at the Albion Hotel, where a private telegraph wire had been specially installed for the British Prime Minister's use, while the Union Jack and the French tricolour flew side by side over all public buildings in the town, as a compliment to the distinguished visitor. Before leaving home Baldwin had intimated through the Foreign Office that if Poincaré, his opposite number in Paris, wished to see him privately he would be glad to meet him. The matter was settled through the Prime Minister's cousin Philip Burne-Jones, who was holidaying with the Baldwins at Aix and invited a friend in the French Government, the Marquis de Chambrun, to talk it over with the Prime Minister at lunch. 'It seems a unique chance brought about by fortuitous circumstances,' remarked Burne-Jones, 'for the statesmen of two great nations to meet absolutely inform-ally and discuss their differences of opinion.' This amateur diplomacy on the part of Burne-Jones quickly bore fruit when Poincaré responded favourably and it was arranged that Baldwin should break his homeward journey three weeks later in Paris and that the meeting should take place in the British Embassy.

As things turned out, Baldwin's holiday did not remain undisturbed and the telegraph wire in his hotel was kept extremely busy. The crisis which led to this unexpected activity was caused by the murder of an Italian general by brigands in the Greek mountains on the very day that Baldwin arrived in Aix.

One of the problems left over from the Peace Conference was the de-limitation of the frontier between Greece and Albania. This had been entrusted to an inter-allied commission working under the direction of the so-called Ambassadors' Conference, which consisted of representa-tives of the Great Powers meeting in more or less continuous session in the Quai d'Orsay for the purpose of carrying on the executive functions of the Peace Conference on its termination in 1920. The Italian Premier Benito Mussolini was now in process of consolidating his dictatorial power. His reaction to the murder of General Tellini, who was the principal Italian member of the commission, was to send a humiliating ultimatum to Athens and to follow this up by bombarding and occupying the Greek island of Corfu. Greece promptly appealed to the League of Nations. The Assembly opened on 1 September, and Lord Robert Cecil, who had been appointed to the vacant office of Lord Privy Seal by Baldwin in order to keep a watching eye on League affairs, now requested permission from Baldwin and Curzon to take a strong line in the Assembly. This permission was immediately forthcoming. Thus Cecil was able not only to support the League's competence to decide the affair, but when his view was challenged to have the relevant articles of the Treaty of Versailles read out in the Assembly, much to the discomfiture of Poincaré who had sided with Mussolini. So, in the words of Harold Nicolson, 'the prestige of England had been affirmed in full Assembly'.[38]

Baldwin's presence at Aix, with its rapid communications with Geneva and Paris, may well have averted a greater disaster. This was the view taken by John Davidson, who had joined his chief during the crisis. 'Had there been greater delay in enabling Bob Cecil to take his stand with the full authority of his Government behind him on the Treaty,' he noted at this time, 'the French Government might have gone so far in Paris in supporting the Italians as to have made war inevitable.' However, if the fact of Cecil's stand was creditable to the British Government, the sequel was not, being the result of Mussolini's overt refusal to surrender to any dictation from Geneva. To save the Italian Government's face, a compromise was proposed by France, whereby the matter should be transferred to the Ambassadors' Conference in Paris. On 10 September, Curzon withdrew his support of Cecil and the League, and the League was consequently obliged to accept the compromise solution worked out by the Ambassadors' Conference, under which the Greek Government paid a fine of £1 million, although it was never established that they were in any sense responsible for the assassination, and the Italians undertook to evacuate Corfu.

Through this gesture of appeasement, destined to be the first in a long series marking the period between the two World Wars, the League suffered a severe blow, from which some observers of the international scene consider that it never really recovered. However, Baldwin did not see the matter in this light, taking the view that the peace had been preserved by a generally acceptable compromise, and congratulating Curzon on his contribution to the settlement. 'If you get Mussolini out of Corfu this month, you will have done a great thing,' he wrote to the Foreign Secretary on 14 September. 'I saw Bob [Cecil] last Sunday, we lunched together at Talloires and from all I have seen and heard I think he has done admirably in Geneva. I am delighted with your direction of affairs in a most difficult situation and I hope the country will realise what an awkward corner you have got them round.' Yet it was barely three weeks previously that Baldwin had remarked to Derby that 'in his opinion Curzon's four years as Foreign Minister had been more harmful to this country than any previous Foreign Secretary. It was thanks to him that foreign nations had not only lost confidence in us but no longer believed in our honesty or truthfulness.' [39]

The Baldwin–Poincaré confrontation, much publicised in advance by the French press, took place in the British Embassy after a luncheon to which Lord Crewe, the Ambassador, also invited President Millerand and various other guests including Davidson and Sir William Tyrell, who had come over from London to brief Baldwin on the latest developments. With the exception of one interpreter nobody else was present at the talk which lasted for three hours. Baldwin began by expressing his feeling that 'most of the trouble came from the fact that France had lost confidence in Mr Lloyd George and did not trust him'. Considerable discussion followed on the state of public opinion in England, which the British Prime Minister was anxious that the Frenchman should appreciate. Baldwin put it very clearly:

> English temperament was peculiar in certain respects and was doubt-less difficult to French understanding; but the average Englishman pre-eminently disliked the military occupation of a civilian district; it antagonised and roused him. This might appear difficult to understand, but was none the less a fact that had to be reckoned with, and no British Government would be able to co-operate fully in order to make the Entente what it ought to be as long as the military character of the Ruhr appeared unchanged.

Only a few days previously, Baldwin went on, the British Foreign Office had pressed Germany, not for the first time, to abandon passive resistance and try to come to terms with France.

In his reply the French Premier emphasised that his Ruhr policy was approved by at least 99 per cent of the French people. At the same time he indicated that France had no designs for the territorial dismember-ment of Germany. When passive resistance ceased, he would, he said, be quite prepared to permit 'a certain latitude, subject to conditions, in order to allow Germany to stabilise her position'. In view of this assurance, Baldwin did not insist on immediate evacuation. He felt that he had got what he principally wanted, namely that the negotiations which Poincaré undertook to open with Germany should be confined to the technical aspects of reparations, and, as Davidson put it, 'any question of annexation or the breaking up of Germany is far from the intention of the French Government', notwithstanding France's encouragement of separatist movements in the Rhineland.

When the two Premiers parted, Poincaré embraced Baldwin in true Gallic fashion, kissing him on both cheeks. A somewhat non-committal communiqué was then issued, stating that 'on no question is there any difference or divergence of principle that would impair the co-operation of the two countries'.

A few days later, the new German Government, presided over by Gustaf Stresemann, unconditionally abandoned passive resistance and withdrew the ordinance suspending reparation deliveries. But the French persisted in their previous refusal to negotiate and strongly supported the separatist movement all over the left bank of the Rhine. Baldwin was bitterly disillusioned. When Tom Jones remarked to him that it was 'not enough to have one honest man at an interview', Baldwin agreed. 'Poincaré has lied,' he said. 'I was led to believe that when passive resistance ceased he'd negotiate with the Germans.' [40]

Some months previously, Charles E. Hughes, the US Secretary of State, had suggested the appointment of an expert commission with American participation to assess what Germany could pay in the way of reparations. This had been rejected by Poincaré, but Baldwin now reverted to it. This time, after some hesitation, the French Premier announced that he would accept in what he claimed to be a gesture of personal goodwill to Baldwin, although he insisted that the occupation of the Ruhr must continue for the time being. The result was the establishment of two committees of experts, one on the means of balancing the German budget and stabilising her currency and the other on the export of German capital. The chairman selected for the first was General Charles G. Dawes, an able American lawyer with considerable experience of public finance; the chairman of the second committee was the British banker Reginald McKenna. Although not generally recognised at the time, this was a considerable achievement on Baldwin's part, particularly in view of the fact that at this time Britain was in no position to impose her will on France by *force majeure*. The view of the British Foreign Office, privately expressed at this time by Tyrell, was that 'S.B. might legitimately claim great credit for the agreement just arrived at with the

French to set up committees to go into the question of Germany's capacity to pay. It is a triumph for his patient policy of securing the co-operation of the Allies.'[41]

7

When Bonar Law was still in Downing Street, he had convened an Imperial Economic Conference of Dominion and Colonial Premiers, and their senior ministers and advisers for the beginning of October 1923. Thus it fell to Baldwin to preside at this gathering, mainly concerned with the question of trade preferences, almost immediately after his return from France. The previous week-end he spent at Chequers working on his opening speech which he rehearsed to his wife. It contained the following paragraph which he wrote into the draft which Tom Jones and the other civil servants concerned had prepared for him:

> The economic condition of Europe makes it essential that we should turn our eyes elsewhere. The resources of our Empire are boundless and the need for rapid development is clamant. I trust that we shall not separate before we have agreed upon the first steps to be taken to create in the not too distant future an ample supply of those raw materials on which the trade of the world depends. Population necessarily follows such extensions, and that in its turn leads to a general expansion of business from which alone can come an improvement in the material condition of the people.

As the conference got under way, various new preferences were proposed by Lloyd-Greame, the President of the Board of Trade, who undertook on behalf of the Government to bring them forward in Parliament in due course. Meanwhile Baldwin was thinking how he might best embody this in a statement of Party policy which he planned to give at the annual Conservative Party Conference at Plymouth later the same month. He revealed something of what was in his mind to Neville Chamberlain who spent a week-end with him at Chequers. This was passed on by Chamberlain to his sister Hilda to whom he wrote from Chequers on 7 October:

> I find the PM very seriously considering the party policy and disposed to go a long way in the direction of new duties with preference designed to help the Dominions and to develop Empire sugar, cotton

and tobacco, all of which we now have to buy from the USA. I need hardly say that I warmly welcome this disposition and believe that it will be the salvation of the country and incidentally of the party . . . Look out for Baldwin's speech to the Party Conference on October 25th. [42]

Besides pressing for the imposition of a preferential tariff, the Dominion Premiers advanced new claims for participation in imperial defence. They resented Curzon sending telegrams in their names on the subject of reparations to Paris and Washington without prior consultation, and Baldwin was to some extent blamed for this. At all events Tom Jones, who had his ear to the ground, urged him to take the Premiers into fuller confidence. 'It was no use trying to fob them off and then table a lot of resolutions at the last moment,' Jones noted in his diary. 'He appeared to agree. I then asked had he taken advantage of their visit to Chequers to talk over the French and Ruhr situation. He said ''No!'' but it was plain that his attitude to Poincaré was hardening.' [43] Most outstanding of the Dominion Premiers was the South African General Jan Smuts, who delivered a speech on reparations towards the end of the conference, advocating a firm line with France even to the extent of Britain renouncing the Entente. Smuts also advocated what he called 'the newer conception of the British Empire as a smaller League of Nations, as a partnership of free and equal nations under a common hereditary sovereign', what in fact was to become known as the Commonwealth when the next Imperial Conference met three years later. It was a developing process which Baldwin welcomed, although his enthusiasm was not shared by the diehards in the Conservative Party. 'Nothing can exceed the cheerfulness, good temper and courtesy of Baldwin, except his impotence,' Curzon remarked at this time. 'At the Imperial Conference he never opens his mouth and leaves the entire lead to me.' [44]

Bonar Law, who carefully followed the course of the conference in the newspapers, barely survived the dispersal of the assembly which he had convened. He died on 20 October 1923 and after being cremated his remains were laid to rest in Westminster Abbey. Baldwin went to the funeral service where he acted as one of the pallbearers; he was thus among those who heard its conclusion with the singing of the 'Recessional' composed by his cousin Rudyard Kipling, who had been one of Bonar Law's early admirers. But Tom Jones was not so favourably impressed. ('All these prayers and hymn singing very alien to the B.L. known to me.') Nor was Curzon who described the scene to his wife: 'Of course cremation has the advantage of saving a great deal of space and thereby of admitting of many future interments. But it has its ridiculous side. For a sham coffin was carried under a great white pall and deposited on a catafalque in the Sanctuary in the earlier part of the service and subsequently borne to the grave, where it was put on one side and disappeared, everyone knowing it was empty.'[45]

Baldwin afterwards paid his tribute in the House of Commons 'to the memory of a very great leader', as he put it. 'There is no doubt that Mr Bonar Law gave his life for the country, just as if he had fallen in the Great War.' Or, as Asquith was reported to have said on a less formal occasion, 'it is fitting that we should have buried the Unknown Prime Minister by the side of the Unknown Soldier'.[46]

8

'I think Baldwin has gone mad,' Birkenhead wrote to Austen Chamberlain at this time. 'He simply takes one jump in the dark: looks round, and then takes another. And all around him there are yawning pitfalls in which he might find his own destruction, which would matter little at any time. What is serious is that he takes our fortunes with him.'[47]

Chamberlain agreed with his friend. Indeed this view appeared to them both to be proved up to the hilt by the Prime Minister's sudden and (so far as the general public were concerned) totally unexpected announcement in the House of Commons on 13 November 1923 that he had decided to dissolve Parliament at once and hold a General Election on the tariff issue.

There is some doubt as to exactly when Baldwin reached this decision which was to put at risk the comfortable majority he had inherited from Bonar Law. To a friend who asked him at the end of October what he intended to do, according to Wickham Steed, 'Mr Baldwin replied that he would hang on until he was kicked out; and he added that, in any case, to have been Prime Minister was an interesting experience to have had.' In the event he was to be kicked out much sooner than he expected. It was during his solitary walks in the mountains above Aix that he began to give serious consideration to appealing to the country, although he does not seem to have definitely made up his mind until some weeks later. 'I came to the decision by myself,' he admitted many years later to Tom Jones, 'and how I drove that Cabinet to take the plunge I shall never know. I must have more push than people think . . . I wanted it because I saw no other weapon then to fight against unemployment.'[48]

He gave no hint of it during Neville Chamberlain's visit to Chequers in early October. Indeed, he said to Auckland Geddes, who was the only other guest that week-end: 'I have quite made up my mind that we shall have to go very slowly with the question of tariffs and under no circumstances will I be rushed into having an election for another twelve months.' However, when Amery and Lloyd-Greame went down for the following week-end (13–15 October) to discuss his forthcoming speech at Plymouth, Baldwin raised for the first time with any of his Cabinet colleagues the question of an appeal to the country and its timing. Afterwards he denied that he was 'pushed by Amery and cabal'. This has been confirmed by Amery himself in his memoirs. 'Our main conclusion,' wrote Amery, 'was that Baldwin should take the opportunity of the annual meeting of the Conservative Party at Plymouth on the 25th to announce a whole-hearted policy of protection and preference, but to give the country time to understand the issues by postponing the election – forced on us by Bonar Law's pledge – until at any rate after the middle of January.' [49]

Speculation as to Baldwin's intentions was widespread in the press and the clubs. Austen Chamberlain, who had been told by his brother what was afoot, while sympathetic by training and conviction, counselled caution. 'I think that any extension of individual protection may very probably bring the storm about your ears, and that before Baldwin speaks at Plymouth he ought to know very clearly how far he is going,' he told Neville on 15 October. 'The worst possible for him, for you, and for the Party, would be that he should seem to indicate a new and very bold policy and that then nothing should come of it.' [50]

Baldwin first broached his ideas to Geoffrey Dawson on 16 October. 'He put them rather vaguely,' *The Times* editor recalled a little later, 'but very much as they afterwards took shape in his speeches – the hopeless problem of Europe, the difficulties for him personally of Bonar Law's pledge, his own belief in more general protection, the development of the Empire and its markets. A General Election would no doubt be necessary sooner or later.' Dawson thought Baldwin's policy and plans far too immature for immediate action and that it was unwarrantable to risk upsetting the British Government, 'the only fixed point in Europe'. This was strongly pressed in *The Times* on 20 October. The same day Joynson-Hicks, the Financial Secretary to the Treasury, wrote to Baldwin pointing out how unpopular an election would be in the City and commercial circles, also with Conservatives in the House of Commons. 'They have all paid one thousand pounds to get there, and their wives do not want them to pay another thousand with a risk of being thrown out.' [51]

On 23 October there was a three-hour meeting of the Cabinet, at which Baldwin told his colleagues what he intended to say at Plymouth on imperial development and protectionist remedies together with the advantages of obtaining cheap raw materials as a cure for unemployment. He realised that he was bound by the Bonar Law pledge and he would, he said, be prepared 'to take the verdict of the country in six months'. According to Tom Jones, what he said 'came as a bolt from the blue' to most of his colleagues, while Hankey, the Cabinet Secretary who recorded the Minutes, was even more explicit in his diary:

Poor Bonar [Law] never had the nerve for the job of Prime Minister. The responsibility preyed on his mind, and I feel sure hastened on his cancer. Baldwin has nerve but scant capacity and I fear will not last long. He is astonishingly maladroit with the Cabinet. For example he sprang his protectionist policy on them only a day or two before he announced it at Plymouth. Half his colleagues were Free Traders by conviction and were horribly shocked. This was straining loyalty too far.[52]

There is an element of exaggeration here. Baldwin's announcement did not come as a complete surprise, as during the previous week he had sounded out most of his colleagues. But this was the first time that the matter had been put to them collectively, and Free Traders like Salisbury, Devonshire, Cecil, Wood and Novar were certainly taken aback and registered protests. So much so, that on the motion of the Lord Chancellor (Cave) the following formula was agreed and incorporated in the Minutes:

(a) that in announcing his policy the Prime Minister should endeavour to avoid committing the Cabinet as a whole and embarrassing those of his colleagues who, owing to election pledges or other reasons, required time to consider their attitude;
(b) that this might be effected by the Prime Minister announcing at Plymouth that the Government realised that the steps already decided on in the relief of unemployment were only palliatives, that owing to Bonar Law's pledge they were prevented from going further in the present Parliament, but that speaking for himself, he thought they might have to go further and apply a tariff.

So that there could be no doubt as to the measure of his agreement with this formula, it is significant that Baldwin signed the Minutes, and that a copy was sent to the King for his information. After the meeting ended, Neville Chamberlain, Lloyd-Greame and Wood lunched together, the consensus of opinion being that 'after the ball had been started at Plymouth an election would not be necessary before the spring of 1924'.[53]

Baldwin travelled down to Plymouth in the afternoon of 25 October. Before the meeting he dined with Lord and Lady Astor in their house on the Hoe. Here he also put the finishing touches to his speech, scribbling the notes for a peroration on a piece of paper which contained the words: 'Fight against unemployment is vital.' It had been arranged that Neville Chamberlain, who accompanied him along with Amery and Davidson, should address an overflow meeting the same evening in the Guildhall. The main meeting took place in the New Palladium Theatre, where the Conservative conference had been holding its sessions.

His speech was on the whole politely rather than enthusiastically received, although he was cheered when he told his audience that he had come to the conclusion that the only way of fighting unemployment, 'the most critical problem of our country', was by protecting the home market. On the question of the Bonar Law pledge he had this to say:

Mr Bonar Law's pledge, given a year ago, was that there should be no fundamental change in the fiscal arrangements of the country. That pledge binds me, and in this Parliament there will be no fundamental change, and I take those words strictly. I am not a man to play with a pledge. But I cannot see myself that any slight extension or adoption of principles hitherto sanctioned in the Legislature is a breach of that pledge. But at any time I am challenged, I am willing to take a verdict.

Meanwhile at the overflow meeting Neville Chamberlain went further and stated that if the unemployment situation were to be dealt with adequately 'next winter', it would be necessary 'that we should ask to be released from that pledge'. This was taken by *The Times* to imply 'a definite decision on the part of the Cabinet to go to the country on the question of tariff reform, and it is already obvious that there is to be a great struggle between those who want an early election and those who believe that the appeal to the country should be deferred until as late as possible next year'.[54]

9

A few days later, on 29 October, Austen Chamberlain wrote despondently to his brother after he had gauged some of the reactions to the Prime Minister's speech:

> I assume that he means business – but it is not the way to hunt a pack of hounds . . . He himself makes the declaration – not on behalf of his Government, but expressly and with twice repeated emphasis – for himself only. The Unionist Press is puzzled and half-hearted, and unless in one of this week's speeches he makes his position plain and definite I think we shall go to destruction. I will take my stand on your side, but I do not conceal from myself that the campaign has not been opened in the spirit or form that makes for success.

To his sister he complained in similar terms:

> The impression left on everyone's mind is one of doubt and perplexity . . . I have written to both Neville and Amery urging decision and definiteness. We have had six columns and more of speeches from the PM in less than a week and no one knows what he means.[55]

The same day there was a Cabinet meeting at which Baldwin indicated that as the country appeared to be opposed to 'stomach taxes', so the Government did not intend any tax on wheat or meat. According to the Minutes, the Cabinet took note in the course of a long discussion that 'the Prime Minister intended to make clear that he had no desire to rush the country into a General Election, but wished to give the electorate time to examine the Government's economic policy carefully before they were called to vote on it, and that the Lord President [Salisbury] also proposed to develop the case against an early election'.

Baldwin's next major speech was on the following Friday, 2 November, in Manchester, and on this occasion he was much more specific than he had been at Plymouth, proposing that imported foreign goods which caused the greatest amount of unemployment should be taxed, but specifically excluding wheat and meat and granting preferences to the dominions and colonies. The meeting, ironically enough, was held in Manchester's famous Free Trade Hall with a somewhat embarrassed

Stanley Baldwin's mother and the title page of one of her books.

Wilden House *from a photograph by courtesy of Lady Lorna Howard.*

Stanley Baldwin aged 4, with his mother.

Aged 7.

Harrow schoolboy.

Cambridge undergraduate.

Wedding group with Stanley and Lucy Baldwin at
Rottingdean, 12 September 1892. Lilly Ridsdale is on
the bride's left. The back row includes (left to right)
Julian Ridsdale, Ambrose Poynter, Askew Ridsdale,
Aurelian Ridsdale, and Philip Burne-Jones. *From a
photograph by courtesy of Lady Lorna Howard.*

Lucy and Stanley Baldwin on
their honeymoon. *From a
photograph by courtesy of Earl
Baldwin of Bewdley.*

Astley Hall *from a
photograph by courtesy
of Lady Lorna
Howard.*

The directors of Baldwin's at the time of the amalgamation with Wright Butler & Co. of Pontypool and other companies in 1902.
Back row: Stanley Baldwin, Charles Wright, Roger Beck, Samuel Dore, Aubrey Butler.
Front Row: Col. Roper Wright, Alfred Baldwin, M.P., Isaac Butler.

Father and son outside the House of Commons. *From photographs by courtesy of Earl Baldwin of Bewdley.*

cousins having tea. Left to right:
p Burne-Jones, Rudyard Kipling,
Carrie Kipling, Stanley Baldwin,
got Baldwin, Diana Baldwin,
Kipling.

stley in 1912.
also serves who only stands and
s.' Lucy Baldwin. *From photographs
ourtesy of Earl Baldwin of Bewdley.*

Lloyd George.

Asquith.

Bonar Law leaving the Carlton Club
with J.C.C. Davidson, 19 October 1922.

The Chancellor of the Exchequer in his private office in the Treasury Chambers at the time of the General Election, 1922.

The American Debt negotiators in Washington, January 1923. Stanley Baldwin (Chancellor of the Exchequer) and Montagu Norman (Governor of the Bank of England) are seated at the table on the left. Charles Evans Hughes (U.S. Secretary of State) and Andrew William Mellon (Secretary of the Treasury) are sitting on the right.

BUCKINGHAM PALACE

Memorandum by Lord Stamfordham.

This is the memorandum handed to the
King on Sunday, 20th. May: and which
Colonel Waterhouse stated practically
expressed the views of Mr. Bonar Law.

The resignation of the Prime Minister
makes it necessary for the Crown to
exercise its prerogative in the choice of
Mr. Bonar Law's successor. There appears
to be only two possible alternatives--
Mr. Stanley Baldwin and Lord Curzon.
The case for each is very strong.
Lord Curzon has, during a long life,
held high office almost continuously, and
is therefore possessed of wide experience
of government. His industry and mental
equipment are of the very highest order.
His grasp of the international situation
is great.
Mr. Stanley Baldwin has had a very
rapid promotion, and has, by his
gathering strength, exceeded the
expectation of his most fervent friends.
He is very much liked by all shades
of political opinion in the House of
Commons, and has the complete confidence
of the city and the commercial world
generally. He, in fact, typifies both
the spirit of the Government which the
people of this country elected last
autumn and also the same characteristics
which won the people's confidence for
Mr. Bonar Law, i.e., honesty,
simplicity, and balance. There is,

1.

The first page of the unsigned memorandum by
J. C. C. Davidson setting out Baldwin's claims t[o]
become Prime Minister in preference to Curzon
It was given by Bonar Law's Private Secretary
Ronald Waterhouse to King George V at
Aldershot, 20 May 1923.
*From the original in the Royal Archives by gracio[us]
permission of Her Majesty the Queen.*

With Curzon outside
10 Downing Street.

Arriving with Leo Amery at Oxford
railway station to address the Chatham
Club of Conservative undergraduates.
Baldwin is being welcomed by the club
secretary William Teeling, later M.P.,
June 1923.
*From a photograph by courtesy of Sir
William Teeling.*

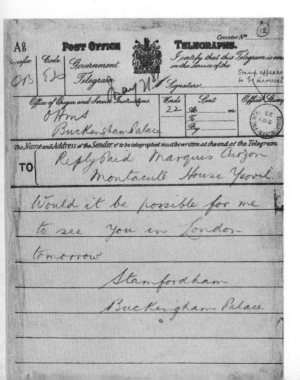

The telegram (mistakenly dated two days late[r])
sent by King George V's Private Secretary to
Curzon on 21 May 1923, which led Curzon to
suppose that he was to be appointed Prime
Minister on Bonar Law's resignation.
*From the original in the Royal Archives reprod[uced]
by gracious permission of Her Majesty the Que[en.]*

Posing with Austen Chamberlain outside Chequers, 26 May 1923, after Baldwin had told Chamberlain that he was unable to offer him a place in the new government.

The Baldwins and the Davidsons at Aix-les-Bains, August 1923.

With Tom Jones (left) and Windham Baldwin at Astley, November 1923.

THE PRACTICAL VISIONARY.
Cartoon by Sir Bernard Partridge.
Punch, 18 March 1925. *From the artist's
proof in the possession of Mr D. Pepys-
Whiteley.*

The Old and the Young Self.
Young self: "Prime Minister? You?
Good Lord!!"
*From the drawing by Max Beerbohm in
the Athenaeum Club, published in the
artist's* Observations *by William
Heinemann Ltd. (1925).*

Press Club Luncheon, St. Bride's House, London.
Left to right: Birkenhead, Baldwin, Edgar Wallace (Chairman), M. Fleuriau (French Ambassador), Churchill.

With the Chancellor of the Exchequer in the Cabinet Room.

Beaverbrook addressing a public meeting on 'Empire Free Trade'.

Baldwin with his son Windham, his Private Secretary Ronald Waterhouse and Lucy Baldwin watching a meet of hounds at Chequers.

'This may be your last chance to photograph me.' Baldwin outside Caxton Hall 30 October 1930.

Derby in the chair. While describing himself as a Free Trader, though not a bigoted one, Derby cautiously admitted that protection as expounded by the Prime Minister was 'a policy which I do not hasten to adopt; but it is a policy which I do not exclude as a policy I can support'. With Baldwin's approval, he concluded by assuring the audience that there was no question of an immediate election and thanking the Prime Minister for 'his honest advice, to which earnest thought would be given in the hope of arriving at a right solution'.[56]

Baldwin and his wife, who was with him on the platform, went on to spend the week-end as Derby's guests at Knowsley Hall, the chairman's palatial property on the way to Liverpool. On the Sunday, Sir Archibald Salvidge came to lunch, having been invited 'in an endeavour to gather from Mr Baldwin some idea of what he actually contemplated doing'. Should his opinion be invited, Salvidge intended to say 'how precarious it seemed to us in Lancashire for a Tory Government to give up a comfortable majority in Parliament for the purpose of letting our opponents raise the old "dear food" cry in the constituencies', and adding that, 'though I was a Tariff Reformer just as Derby had always been a Free Trader, this was our joint view in the light of our past experience of electioneering in the North'.

Things did not go at all as Derby and Salvidge expected. During most of the meal the Prime Minister talked about how to grow raspberries. He said that the raspberry was 'a jolly little fellow' and provided an interesting hobby for anyone who took the trouble to cultivate him. According to Salvidge, 'Mrs Baldwin listened with rapt attention, and from time to time beamed in appreciation of the Prime Minister's remarks.' Later, over coffee in the library, Derby and Salvidge were alone with Baldwin. Salvidge afterwards described what happened there.

He [Baldwin] was fairly definite about his conviction that to fight unemployment properly he must have weapons, and that the only effective weapon was the tariff. But as to whether such a policy would carry the country he asked for no opinion, and never allowed the conversation to get down to practical politics from the point of view of the electioneering.

There seemed nothing to be gained by prolonging the conversation, and when Derby came out to see me off I told him my impression was that the PM hardly contemplated an appeal to the country before next year, thus giving some chance of educating the new electorate, especially the women, on the subject of Protection. As it turned out, I was hopelessly wrong . . .[57]

Some time during the next day or two, Devonshire confided in Salisbury that he had heard from the King that 'the PM meant to ask him to dissolve Parliament at once', and rumours that a dissolution was imminent were repeated in the newspapers. On 7 November Salisbury invited Devonshire to meet him at his house in Arlington Street along with his brother Cecil, Novar and Wood. According to the latter, 'they were all very uneasy both about general policy and the way it was being brought forward, and the proposal to dissolve Parliament at once'. Each member of the group agreed to write to Baldwin deprecating a December election. Wood sent off his letter next day. 'There are, no doubt, a good many reasons (January fox-hunting among them) which support having an election, which is inevitable, as early as possible,' he wrote. 'But I think it is vital that we should give Parliament, and through Parliament the country, an adequate opportunity of examining the question on which they are being asked to pronounce.'[58]

Curzon raised the matter in Cabinet on 9 November. He strongly deprecated an immediate election, so he afterwards told his wife, 'as savouring of trickery at the expense of the electorate and of our opponents, as fatal to the proper or resolute conduct of foreign affairs during the very serious foreign crisis through which we are passing, and as likely to lead to electoral disaster. The majority of the Cabinet were in my favour, but there was a strong minority (Lloyd-Greame, Chamberlain, Hoare, Sanders, Bridgeman, Worthington-Evans) who were on the other side. The PM as usual did not utter – but promised to think carefully over the matter before Parliament meets next week.'[59]

Discussion in the Cabinet turned on whether the dissolution of Parliament should take place immediately, or in January or later in the spring when the economic proposals of the Government might be laid before the country in the form of a Finance Bill. Strangely enough, considering that he was the leading Protectionist in the Cabinet, only Amery seems to have been in favour of postponing the election until after the spring Budget in order, as he put it, 'to secure more time for educating our public'. It was clear that the majority in the Cabinet, realising that the Prime Minister's Plymouth speech had made an election inevitable, were in favour of January. Nevertheless, before breaking up, the Cabinet appointed a small committee consisting of Cave, Bridgeman, Worthington-Evans and Joynson-Hicks to examine and report as to whether it would be preferable to dissolve Parliament during the forthcoming session or let the session run its normal course before doing so.[60]

'He is not so simple as he makes out,' noted Neville Chamberlain of

Baldwin at this time. This assessment was confirmed by a note which the Prime Minister sent Birkenhead after the Cabinet, asking if he could see him at Chequers next morning, which was a Saturday. Baldwin significantly began his note 'My dear F.E.', although he had completely held aloof from Birkenhead since the Carlton Club meeting. Birkenhead could only interpret this, as his friend Austen Chamberlain put it, 'as a signal of distress on the Prime Minister's part and as indicating that he intended to ask for F.E.'s assistance on whatever terms might be most likely to secure it'. Austen's surmise was correct. Baldwin hoped to secure the support of the Coalition Conservatives on his election platform and to do this effectively it was necessary to reach an accommodation with their two leading figures. Birkenhead replied that he could not come to Chequers as he had just returned from America and had engagements in London which he was unable to put off. However, he agreed to come to Downing Street first thing on Monday morning, 12 November.[61]

Baldwin spent the week-end alone with his wife at Chequers, the only one on which there had not been any guests since he took office as Prime Minister. Thus he had ample time for undisturbed reflection. He decided that he must see the King on Monday and ask for an immediate dissolution.

What finally led him to this decision, which he later admitted to Tom Jones was 'a long-calculated and not a sudden' one? The most plausible explanation is what he described to Jones as the prospect of having 'dished the Goat'. At this time Lloyd George was on his way back from America where he had been on a lecture tour. 'I had information that he was going protectionist and I had to get in quick,' Baldwin confided in Jones some years later. 'Otherwise he would have got the Party with Austen and F.E. and there would have been an end to the Tory Party as we know it.'[62]

SIX

OPPOSITION
LEADER

I

While Baldwin was ruminating quietly at Chequers, Austen Chamberlain learned that Birkenhead was spending Sunday night (11 November) with Beaverbrook at Cherkley, the latter's house near Leatherhead. He telephoned Beaverbrook and asked if he could join them and was invited to do so. On reaching Cherkley about tea-time, he discovered to his surprise and rather to his regret that Lloyd George and Churchill were also expected for the night. He had already discussed with Birkenhead what decision they ought to take if they were asked by Baldwin to join the Government. Chamberlain was at first opposed to any idea of assuming direct personal responsibility in the election which now seemed inevitable 'for a policy on which we had not been consulted and a situation which we had not helped to create'. But he had been persuaded by Birkenhead that if a suitable offer was made they should in the interests of Party unity be obliged to join. This view was confirmed in the course of the talk which they had with their host before dinner and before the arrival of the other two guests.[1]

No mention is made by Chamberlain in the notes which he kept at the time of what passed in the way of conversation after Lloyd George and Churchill joined the party. Lloyd George was still in favour of a Centre Party with himself, Churchill, Chamberlain and Birkenhead as principals, particularly if Baldwin should lose the election. However, although attracted to Protection as a possible cure for unemployment, he could not come out and take charge of Baldwin's policy, as his friend Hamar Greenwood had been urging him to do. 'If it had been one of the men who stood by me . . .' he said. 'But Baldwin knifed me and I shall knife Baldwin.' Thus he now proceeded to stigmatise Baldwin's policy as 'unutterable folly' and 'an insult to an intelligent but starving people'.[2]

Next morning Birkenhead motored up to London with Chamberlain and after dropping him at his flat went on to Downing Street for his appointment with Baldwin. The Prime Minister began by asking about his American visit and 'talked of the relative merits of different hotels and steamship companies like a man who was rather diffident about approaching the real object of his meeting. Some allusion, however, to American agriculture brought Baldwin to the point.' Baldwin went on to give some account of the reasons which had prompted him to go for Protection and now that the Liberals were reuniting he wondered whether the time had not come for a similar move to reunite the Conservative Party. On Birkenhead observing that this was his wish also, Baldwin suggested that he should come back after lunch with Chamberlain when they could take the matter a step further. The appointment was originally made for three o'clock but had to be advanced by a quarter of an hour because the King wished to see Baldwin at 3.45. When they heard this, Chamberlain and Birkenhead were certain that Parliament would be dissolved during the next few days.

'What do you mean by reuniting the Party?' Chamberlain asked Baldwin when they met. 'Do you mean merely that we are to fight together, or that we are to join your Government?' He paused for a moment, and before Baldwin could reply, he added: 'Let me say at once, whatever the result of our interview, I shall, as I have already publicly stated, fight by your side.' Whereupon Birkenhead interjected: 'So shall I.'

Baldwin then said [Chamberlain's account continues] that his hope was that if we fought together in the elections it might be found possible afterwards that we should become colleagues, but on my repeating that I still did not understand exactly what was in his mind, he said, 'I want to know what is in *your* minds.'

I therefore said that I would speak with perfect frankness; that I could not profess to know exactly what his policy was, and must have further explanations of it before I could take the responsibility of joining the Government; but that under no circumstances would I come under any conditional engagement to join at a future date. I hoped I had made it clear to him in our Chequers conversation that I was not prepared to be put on probation or to have it intimated to me that if I ran well in the race there would perhaps be a bunch of carrots at the other end. The Prime Minister said: 'Oh, do not put it that way!'

I replied that that was how it inevitably appeared and it was in any case an impossible position. He was contemplating that we should take ministerial responsibility for a policy about which we had not been consulted and which I must frankly say I thought went either too far or not far enough . . .

If we were to join at all, we ought to join at once: that I did not suggest that there should be any displacement of existing ministers at the moment, but that if he wished it F.E. and I could join temporarily as ministers without portfolio and without salary. But . . . I was not prepared to join the Government myself, nor could I ask or advise F.E. to join, except in positions which would show clearly that we returned to the counsels of the party on the same footing of influence and authority as we had previously held . . .

We had some discussion as to the date of the election which both of us held ought now to take place at the earliest possible moment . . . Baldwin concluded by saying that he must now go to the King, but that he was very glad to feel that he knew exactly my mind which even after the Chequers conversation he was not quite sure that he understood . . . Whether I was wise under these circumstances to talk so frankly depends upon whether he is genuinely anxious for reunion or only manoeuvring for position.[3]

On being received by the King in Buckingham Palace, Baldwin asked for an immediate dissolution which he proposed to announce in the House of Commons on the following day. The King was at first most reluctant to give his consent, pointing out that he had implicit confidence in the Prime Minister and the Conservative Party and that he 'considered that, as most countries in Europe, if not in the world, were in a chaotic and indeed dangerous state, it would be a pity if this country were to be plunged into the turmoil of a General Election on a question of domestic policy which will arouse all the traditional bitterness of the hard-fought battles between Protection and Free Trade; also that it was quite possible that his majority might be reduced, or that he might not get a majority at all'. The King added that he was therefore prepared to take the responsibility of advising the Prime Minister to change his mind and that he was also prepared for Baldwin to tell his friends that he had done so.

Baldwin replied that he had gone too far and that it was impossible for him to change his mind, that the country expected a dissolution and that he would appeal to the country at once, and that he was ready to stand or fall by the result. In the face of this pressure the King yielded. The Prime Minister then told the King about his meeting with Austen

Chamberlain and Birkenhead and their promise of support during the election; he asked the King for his approval of their appointment as ministers without portfolio, to which the King also assented. 'I also asked him,' noted the King, 'if he did not think that this would unite the Liberal Party and he said yes, probably it would, and it would be a very good thing if it did.'[4]

The Prime Minister returned to Downing Street and immediately instructed Tom Jones to prepare a draft of the King's Speech dissolving Parliament.* At the same time he sent telephone messages to Derby, Austen Chamberlain and Birkenhead to come and see him. He asked Derby, who arrived first, whether he had any objection to the other two rejoining the Cabinet, and on Derby replying that this had always been his wish, Baldwin said: 'Very well then, I will bring them in.' A few minutes later both men entered the room, as Baldwin remarked to Derby, 'Here are your two new colleagues.'

Derby was in favour of postponing the election, and it was now clear to Chamberlain that the reason why he and Birkenhead had been sent for was to persuade Derby in the contrary sense, which in the event they did. In fact, Birkenhead and Derby agreed to meet for lunch next day and work out a plan of campaign for Lancashire. 'The Prime Minister took no part in the conversation,' noted Chamberlain, 'except to say that he entirely agreed with what we had said.'

As Derby took his leave, he turned to Chamberlain and Birkenhead and said: 'We shall meet at the Cabinet tomorrow.' But they were not there, and in answer to Derby's surprised query, Baldwin replied that 'there were some difficulties'. Derby was not to discover what these were until some time later, since immediately after the Cabinet he went off to Lancashire to organise the election there.[5]

It was at this Cabinet, which met in the morning of 13 November, that Baldwin announced that 'the march of events had compelled him to decide to recommend to the King the immediate dissolution of Parliament'. He went on to say that since his speech at Plymouth it had become inevitable that there should be a General Election before the next Budget, and so as to curtail the dislocation of commercial business which this would involve, he had decided that the Election should take place with the minimum of delay, actually on or about 6 December.[6]

Later the same day Curzon described the general reaction of the Cabinet to Baldwin's announcement in a letter to his wife:

* Jones informed Wood of this the same night and Wood, according to his own account 'felt very much disposed to resign'. See E. F. L. Wood, 'Record of some events preceding the dissolution and General Election Nov.–Dec. 1923'. Baldwin Papers 35 f. 9.

There was I think a general feeling that he has gone so far with his preliminary steps that there was probably no other way out, and that a postponed election would be fraught with even worse disaster. But I think the Cabinet were profoundly shocked and incensed at the way in which they have been treated, and at the recklessness with which the Government and the country, entirely contrary to the will and wish of either, have been plunged into a General Election by the arbitrary fiat of one weak and ignorant man.

Jim Salisbury is thinking of resigning and I think will. He declined to attend [the] H[ouse of] L[ords] this afternoon. Derby is furious, and says Europe is dominated by madmen – Poincaré and Mussolini – and England is ruled by a damned idiot (Baldwin). This is the man whom he assisted to put into power in May last and for whom he helped to turn me down. I wonder what all the men who clamoured for Baldwin then think now.[7]

Immediately after the Cabinet, Salisbury and the other Free Trade members lunched together at his house. Wood afterwards recorded what happened:

They were all in favour of resigning, partly on general grounds, partly because they were convinced that the PM wanted to get rid of them to make room for Austen Chamberlain and Birkenhead. I deprecated any immediate decision.

I had some talk with Salisbury on the way down to the House of Commons, and tried to impress upon him the danger of breaking the party on the eve of an election in view of the certain damage that must ensue, and emphasising my view that however clumsy the PM had been about it they were the mistakes of inexperience rather than vice!

In the evening I went to see the PM at the House of Commons, and asked him point blank whether he wished to get rid of Salisbury and Co. He said he certainly did not, and I told him that in that case he was proceeding very much as if he did, and that if he wished to keep them it was imperative that he should see Salisbury, explain his position, and make it as easy for Salisbury and Co. to stay as he could.

He was evidently impressed with this new point of view. He said the reason he had taken no action was that he thought when he saw people wrestling with their consciences it was indecent for a third party to intervene.[8]

Besides infuriating his Free Trade colleagues, Baldwin's statement to the House of Commons, in which he persistently used the first person singular, upset the constitutional pundits. 'In my view,' he had said, 'it was essential that the election should be taken in such time that, if the country decided to release me from the pledge and give me a mandate, I could incorporate in next year's Budget the measures that I believe to be necessary.'

J. G. Swift MacNeill, who had been first elected to Parliament in Gladstone's time, pointed out in *The Times* that Gladstone had twice wanted a dissolution but was prevented by the opposition of his colleagues. Thus MacNeill contested the apparently novel doctrine as exemplified in Baldwin's action that a Premier could advise the dissolution of Parliament whenever he pleased irrespective of the wishes of his Cabinet colleagues. He was supported by G. E. Buckle, a former editor of *The Times* and biographer of Disraeli. 'Mr Baldwin we know is a modest and unassuming man,' he wrote, 'being in this as in other things in direct line of succession to Bonar Law. Are we to attribute his language to inexperience? Or is it rather typical of the enormously exaggerated importance acquired during Mr Lloyd George's War Dictatorship of the office of Prime Minister? Once he was *primus inter pares*; now even when he himself is far from courting the limelight, his Cabinet have become lieutenants rather than colleagues.' [9]

2

Besides the incipient revolt of Salisbury and his friends, strong opposition to the inclusion of Birkenhead in the Government now began to develop, particularly among the junior ministers who had not forgotten his hectoring behaviour towards them in the previous year. Indeed, three of the Under-Secretaries told the Prime Minister that they would resign if Birkenhead were brought in before the election.* Their reaction was reinforced by Davidson and Sidney Herbert; the latter had succeeded Davidson as Baldwin's PPS and could be expected to reflect backbench Conservative opinion. They addressed a memorandum to Baldwin setting out the objections to Birkenhead particularly among the women in the Party and the constituencies. Davidson's wife, for example, thought that Birkenhead's return would 'offend all decent people'. The memorandum concluded as follows:

---

* They are believed to have been William Ormsby-Gore, Walter Elliot and Lord Wolmer.

We gather the impression that the possibility of F.E. joining the Government before the Election was impossible to contemplate, and that there was a feeling that one of the greatest assets among the non-party electorate is your good name and high reputation which would suffer a most serious blow if you were to come to terms with F.E., especially if it were believed that you had been blackmailed by him. Thus, in the view of the righteous, it would be regarded as natural for you to refuse to deal on those terms.[10]

Birkenhead had recently been elected Rector of Glasgow University. His rectorial address, which he delivered to the students on 7 November 1923, added fuel to the flames of opposition to his immediate inclusion in the Government. In this controversial allocution, the ex-Lord Chancellor expressed the belief that Jesus Christ did not really intend the man who was assaulted to turn the other cheek or the rich to give away their possessions to the poor, that the motive of self-interest was and ought to be the mainspring of human conduct, and that since '*the world continues to offer glittering prizes to those who have stout hearts and sharp swords*, it is for us who in our history have proved ourselves a martial people to maintain in our hands the adequate means for our own protection and to march with heads erect and bright eyes down the road of our imperial destiny'.[11]

During the evening of the 13 November, Baldwin sent for Birkenhead to come to his room in the House, where he was alone. The Prime Minister began by saying that he did not know whether Birkenhead was aware that 'he had aroused very considerable hostility to himself in some sections of the party, and that in addition his rectorial address had offended ecclesiastical circles'. He then asked him whether it was 'really not possible' for him to fight the election on the official Conservative ticket 'on the understanding that he would join the Government in some suitable but undefined position after the election'.

Birkenhead replied that this was quite out of the question: that he and Austen Chamberlain had stated their views on the subject the previous day, and that that statement was final. Baldwin had got to make his choice, he told him bluntly. If there was any question of resignations, whether the strength he would gain by their accession was greater or less than that which he would lose, this was entirely a question for the Prime Minister and not for them. Finally he advised Baldwin 'to take his own line and act without consultation with anybody: he did not believe that any resignation would follow'.

On this note the difficult interview ended. According to Curzon, who claimed to have had it from the Prime Minister himself, 'moreover, F.E. incensed Baldwin by his cynical insolence, admitting that he had done his damnedest during the last year to injure us in every way, and was proud to have succeeded. What a cad the man is!'[12]

Next day Birkenhead received a letter from Baldwin breaking off the negotiations:

> I have given most careful thought to the subject of our recent conversation and I am convinced that the proposals you and Austen made to me are impossible at the present moment.*
>
> I feel sure however that you will give the Party your full support at the Election in obtaining a complete victory for the policy for which you and I have striven for so long. Above all I feel confident that you will help Derby to keep the flag flying in Lancashire. What is not possible now may be more easily accomplished later and I have every hope that we shall be able to achieve the complete union of the Party.
>
> I ought to thank you for coming to see me and for the frankness with which you expressed yourself to me.

Birkenhead replied briefly thanking Baldwin for his expressions of goodwill. He added: 'I profoundly regret that our common desire to wipe out past differences is defeated by forces which neither of us can control.'

After Baldwin told Neville Chamberlain what had happened, the latter noted in his diary:

> F.E. with great astuteness took his rebuff with the utmost good humour and has gone off hand-in-hand with Derby to fight for the party in Lancashire. Austen, on the other hand, was *froissé* and stiff.[13]

'The negotiations about Austen and F.E. have broken down,' noted Curzon, 'because there were a number of the Party who declined (and with very good reason) to let the latter come back; and as he and Austen stood together, the result has applied to them both.'

---

* He explained why to Austen Chamberlain: 'To have made supernumerary appointments to the Cabinet on the eve of an election would have been open to obvious objections, and, in my view, extremely difficult to justify. The only alternative would have been to replace two of my existing colleagues who have served in the present Cabinet for the past year, and this, as you would be the first to appreciate, is unthinkable. I only write this to make my position perfectly clear.' Baldwin to A. Chamberlain, 15 November 1923. Baldwin Papers 135.

The Cabinet met again on 14 November mainly to discuss foreign affairs, on which Curzon complained that 'obscure members' talked interminably. 'The PM as usual sat there absolutely silent and saying not a word,' Curzon told his wife. 'It is heart-breaking serving under such a man . . . It is all a huge gamble. If we fail, Baldwin will have been guilty of one of the greatest crimes in history, and if it be so he will have sinned from a mixture of innocence, ignorance, honesty and stupidity – fatal gifts in a statesman when wholly dissociated from imagination or vision or *savoir faire*.' [14]

3

On 16 November the Cabinet met for the last time before the election. It was a full meeting, since the cracks revealed by the dissensions of Salisbury and the Free Trade group had been effectively papered over; the rebels had received certain assurances from Baldwin, particularly that there should be no taxes on such essential foodstuffs as wheat, meat, bacon, cheese, butter and eggs, and consequently in Wood's words had 'decided to stay'. These assurances were embodied in the Conservative Party Election Manifesto, which had been drafted by Amery, and was circulated to the Cabinet before being released for general publication in the Sunday newspapers two days later. The manifesto, which was used by Baldwin for his own election address in Bewdley, dwelt on the need for peace in Europe and promised support for the League of Nations, but at the same time indicated that drastic measures were needed to relieve unemployment at home. 'What we propose to do for the assistance of employment in industry, if the nation approves, is to impose duties on imported manufactured goods.' It was also proposed to give a substantial preference to Empire products in a common effort to build greater imperial economic unity. He felt in honour bound, said Baldwin, to ask for release from Bonar Law's pledge. That was the only reason which made the election necessary. [15]

On the face of it the Cabinet and the Government displayed a united front. The threatened split in the Government ranks had been averted and in the event only one junior minister resigned because he felt that he could not support Baldwin's protectionist policy.* Nevertheless there was a great deal of grumbling. Curzon summed up the position in characteristic style:

---

* Colonel Albert Buckley, a Lancashire MP, who was Secretary for Overseas Trade.

Baldwin thinks he is going to maintain his majority and even increase it. But I cannot believe that. Anyhow I do not see how he can get a majority large enough either to carry any big measure of Tariff Reform or to last for any considerable time. Our people are all playing up as best they can. But they secretly, indeed, openly grumble as they hate the commotion, the expense and the risk. Why on earth Baldwin should not have gone tranquilly on for the next three years no sane man can say. His evil geniuses have been the whippersnappers of the Cabinet, Amery, Lloyd-Greame, and I believe N. Chamberlain. They buzz about him night and day, and he is lamentably weak.[16]

Tom Jones, who was much in Baldwin's confidence at this time, helped him with his campaign speeches, although his own political sympathies were with Labour. On 17 November Baldwin confided in Jones that 'whatever else the last few days have done they have revealed to him the tortuous mentality of the Cecils. Lord R. Cecil is to go to the Lords* . . . Much suspicion in the mind of J. C. Davidson that Lloyd George is busy in secret plotting for a Centre Party.'

Baldwin proposed to open his campaign with an attack on Lloyd George, but Jones advised against this course. 'The little man,' said Baldwin, 'has been so surrounded for years with adulation that he thinks he is the only man fit to be Prime Minister. You don't agree?'

'I don't agree,' replied Jones. 'L.G. has far too much humour to suffer from a swelled head. He knows quite well at the time what he's up to.'

'Perhaps "swelled head" is not the word I want,' Baldwin retorted. 'That fits Winston better.'

One observer of the political scene, who longed for the return of Lloyd George as Premier, was the socialist reformer and historian Beatrice Webb. 'He would be most likely to get an agreement with the USA,' she wrote in her diary on 19 November, 'and he knows his Poincaré and his French people. Not poor Mr Baldwin, who is now

---

* 'I am not very keen on having Bob Cecil in the House of Lords,' Curzon wrote on 18 November. 'He asked Baldwin for a peerage as his health will not permit of his fighting a General Election, and of course he could not be refused. He is a terrible nuisance to me in the Cabinet, talking interminably and always wrong about Foreign Affairs. However, in the House of Lords he cannot speak without my consent, and may even at times be useful.' On 30 November Curzon saw the King who told him that 'he had proposed to make Bob Cecil a Baron (on his elevation to the House of Lords), whereupon he had received an indignant letter from Jim Salisbury, who had insisted on his brother being made a Viscount! He [the King] also said that until last week he had never seen or met Bob Cecil in his life and did not know him by sight.' Marchioness Curzon. *Reminiscences*, pp. 193–201. Cecil was created Viscount Cecil of Chelwood.

regarded, alike in his dealings with Poincaré and in his surrender to his Under-Secretaries, as a – politically speaking – "Natural". Today the poor man is perpetually saying that he is stupid, and everyone, whether Conservative, Liberal or Labour, now believes it. I am glad that idol – the honest but stupid man – is discredited.' [17]

Tom Jones spent the first week-end of the campaign with the Baldwins at Astley. The Prime Minister was out addressing various village meetings when Jones arrived, so that he dined *en famille* with Mrs Baldwin and two of the children, Betty and Windham. 'Certainly better bread and meat were never served to a guest than at the Baldwin table,' noted the guest. Unfortunately he was not so comfortably accommodated in the matter of lodging. 'We retired soon after ten – I to a small, cold bedroom at the end of a passage. These rambling old houses should have central heating or at least hot-water bottles.' Before Jones turned in, Baldwin appeared, 'very pleased with his meeting and spoke with much familiarity of old friendly faces he had seen in the several villages'.

Immediately after breakfast next morning the Prime Minister took Jones for 'a walk through the gardens and on to a rest cottage for guests to which the Baldwins invited tired mothers and exhausted typists', marching him through the place and showing him every room up and down and telling him that he hoped some day he would 'come and rest there'. On their way back to the house, they were waylaid by two press photographers, who took a picture of them together with Windham Baldwin and the family dog. Jones would have much preferred not to be photographed, since he had what he called 'a first-rate record for anonymity' during the seven years he had served three Prime Ministers as Deputy Secretary of the Cabinet, and he was much upset when he saw the picture reproduced in one journal above a caption which described him as helping Baldwin in his election campaign.

Afterwards they repaired to the library, where Baldwin proudly exhibited his copy of the *Odyssey* in Greek used by him at Harrow with neat pencilled notes in the margins. He also showed Jones his copy of J. M. Keynes's *Economic Consequences of the Peace* with his own sentence about the hard-faced men who had made money out of the war and been returned to Parliament. Again the subject of Lloyd George came up, and Baldwin remarked that when he was Prime Minister he went too long without a rest and that his judgement was weakened in consequence. Jones agreed and said that he and P. J. Grigg had tried again and again to persuade him to go away for a long holiday and change but he would not. In any case, Jones added, he was not like other men – his vitality was amazing. 'I was never with him alone for five minutes,' said Baldwin.

'I don't really know him – but I was in the Cabinet and as I never said anything there I had leisure to study him under a microscope.' Later, while looking through an album of photographs which Mrs Baldwin produced, Jones came upon a picture of Lloyd George as Chancellor of the Exchequer which had been defaced. 'How they do hate him!' he reflected.

After dinner, Baldwin left Jones in the library, saying that he tried to spend every Sunday evening with his wife. Jones then said good-bye as he was leaving early next morning for London, while Baldwin was going on to Bristol for a large meeting. 'It was an extraordinarily quiet Sunday,' noted Jones. There was only one telephone interruption – from Geoffrey Fry in Bristol asking the Prime Minister to be sure to reassure the local boot industry in the matter of safeguarding. Jones had brought two batches of Foreign Office telegrams with him and had immediately directed the Prime Minister's attention to them, but it was late on Sunday before he looked at them.

> Bonar Law would do as much work in an hour as S.B. in four or five. I am never sure whether the PM is thinking at all or simply wool-gathering. Here in his rural home one feels the old England of the villages is getting a bit of its own back for once in the person of Stanley Baldwin.

On his way to the train next morning in a car decked out with red ribbons, the Conservative Party colours in Worcestershire, Jones noticed the election posters inviting the citizens to 'Vote for Baldwin and No More Food Taxes', which he thought 'pretty misleading for the "Honest" Party'. In London two days later, while accompanying the Prime Minister and his wife to the station to catch a train for Glasgow where he was to address a mass meeting, Jones saw another poster, this time put out by the Labour *Daily Herald*, on the subject of 'Baldwin's Son on Premier's Policy'. After fighting with the Armenian army and being imprisoned by both the Russians and the Turks, Oliver Baldwin had returned to England bitterly disillusioned and discontented with the post-war world. He had recently become a convert to Socialism and in this election was campaigning for the Labour candidate in the London borough of Islington, and attacking his father's policy and personality in platform speeches, much to the chagrin of the family. 'To choose this moment of all moments to repudiate his father's policy,' said Philip Burne-Jones, 'and, in the hour of need, to desert him completely!' Although Baldwin and his wife also saw the poster at the railway station, neither passed any comment upon it: indeed they never mentioned Oliver in Jones's presence. Oliver's conduct was an embarrassing cross which his parents had to bear for the rest of their lives.[18]

As he said good-bye to his chief on the platform, Jones told him not to be unduly discouraged if he found the Glasgow audience not much given to loud and prolonged cheering. 'I too will be dour,' replied Baldwin. As it happened, he was agreeably surprised by the warmth of his reception in Glasgow. There was less enthusiasm in Bradford and Liverpool where he addressed two large demonstrations. The Liverpool meetings were organised by Sir Archibald Salvidge, who invited the local candidates and the principal Tory supporters to meet the Prime Minister at dinner beforehand. Salvidge's description of Baldwin on this occasion is worth quoting.

On his arrival, in answer to his inquiry as to how things were going, I had to confess we were experiencing difficulty in working up enthusiasm. Lack of excitement was, he assured me, a feature of this election everywhere, but he was confident of the result as there would be 'a strong silent vote' in favour of his policy.

His entry into the room to meet the dinner guests was perfect – exactly the right amount of geniality from a Great Man condescending to the faithful. When one realises that little more than a year ago the vast majority of the nation had never even heard of him, he has acquired a marvellous technique. However, at the end of the meal it struck me that he rather hated having to pull out his pipe whilst sitting at the table with ladies present. He only took a few puffs and soon laid it aside, but the popular Press was making such a feature of his pipe that no doubt it had to be produced. It is an attempt to give him a distinguishing mark in the public mind, like Joe Chamberlain's orchid or Winston Churchill's line in head-gear . . .

Mr Baldwin pleased both his big meetings with his fine voice and his direct, unvarnished way of stating his case.[19]

4

Early in the campaign Baldwin asked Jones to read the newspapers as he found them 'so bewildering'. He said that he preferred to read them himself as little as possible because they confused him. There were papers in the house during the week-end that Jones spent at Astley, but he saw no one else reading them. 'He reads the *Morning Post*, I know, and I am pretty sure he reads *The Times* regularly,' noted Jones. 'How much else I know not.'

Few of the newspapers unreservedly supported Baldwin's decision to appeal to the country on the tariff issue – only the ultra-Tory *Morning Post* and the *Yorkshire Post*, which were generally regarded as mouthpieces of the Conservative Central Office. *The Times* and the *Daily Telegraph* gave a more guarded support, while of the popular papers of Conservative complexion, the *Daily Mail* and others controlled by Lord Rothermere were strongly opposed. This was due in large measure to the fact that Rothermere had asked Baldwin for a government post for his son Esmond and been refused. Beaverbrook's *Daily Express* and *Evening Standard*, on the other hand, disliked the dropping of food taxes, feeling that if the tariff issue was to be raised at all, the fight should be conducted on the whole front and that Joseph Chamberlain's policy, which was still the official creed of the Conservative Party, should be revived in its entirety.[20]

Two days before the poll, Jones briefly saw Baldwin in Downing Street and learned from him that the Conservative Party officials estimated an overall Conservative majority of 87. 'Very cheerful at this prospect', Baldwin then went off to speak at some eve-of-the-poll meetings in Worcestershire. Just before leaving to catch his train, he said to Jones: 'I don't want any bands here when I come back!' Nor were there when he appeared in Downing Street three days later. On the day of the poll, the official Conservative forecast had risen to 95. In the event the results showed that the Conservatives were in a *minority* of 97, which showed a swing of 11·8 per cent against the Government. As in 1906, the Tories had been defeated by the cry of 'dear food'.

The Tories lost over ninety seats, eleven in Lancashire alone, mostly to the Liberals who made something of a comeback. The final figures were Conservatives and Unionists 257, Liberals 158, Labour 191. 'It is an overwhelming disaster,' moaned Derby to Salvidge, 'and you and I know whom we have to thank for it. It maddens me to think that the Prime Minister should, within six months of taking office, bring us to this. And how is it ever going to be retrieved? It looks as if the Conservative Party has been smashed up for all time.' To Birkenhead, Derby wrote: 'Our great leader has indeed led us to disaster, and the landslide which I was always a little afraid of but had hoped might be avoided has come.' Curzon was equally scathing. 'You have known for long how poor an opinion I had of Baldwin's fitness to be PM,' he told Lady Curzon, 'and now alas the world knows it too.'[21]

Baldwin and his wife returned to Downing Street in the afternoon following the poll, the Prime Minister having been returned with a majority of 6,000 in Bewdley and not the 10,000 which he had hoped for. He went straight to the Cabinet Room, where Tom Jones was waiting for him. 'There were no ministers about to welcome him,' noted Jones, 'only a couple of private secretaries and the usual messengers. It was all very depressing. He took a pull at his pipe and tried to put a cheerful face on the situation. We ordered tea and I was then left alone with him. We went through the staggering results recorded in the afternoon papers. He scanned eagerly the fate of men personally known to him.' These included his intimate friend John Davidson, who was defeated at Hemel Hempstead, and the Chief Conservative Agent Admiral Sir Reginald Hall, who lost his seat in Liverpool, and on whom much of the blame for the Conservative disaster generally fell.

Jones tried to comfort Baldwin with the thought that he 'had fought an honourable fight, free from exaggeration and abuse'. For Mrs Baldwin it meant a domestic upheaval and she was particularly disappointed at having to move. 'After having just settled in here we must go and live in a small flat,' said Baldwin dolefully. 'Our town house is too expensive for us. I am much poorer than I was before the war.'* Baldwin's talk then took a strangely religious turn. 'Everyone who tries in politics to do the thing he believes in simply and honestly is sure to come a smeller.† The martyrs did. Christ did.' When he left him to make way for his next caller, who was Lord Robert Cecil, shortly to be ennobled as Viscount Cecil of Chelwood, Jones had no doubt that Baldwin's intention was to resign straight away.[22]

The Prime Minister indicated this intention when he met Stamfordham early next morning, which was a Saturday, before going off to Chequers for the week-end where he had invited Neville Chamberlain and Davidson to join him so that they could review the situation together. He asked Stamfordham that the King should postpone seeing him until Monday as he had so far only seen a few of his colleagues. He had asked the country for a mandate for Tariff Reform, he told Stamfordham; this had been refused and the honourable thing would be for him to resign at once. If he were asked about a successor, he went on, he thought that Asquith with his Liberal followers might form a Coalition with the Conservatives. When Stamfordham suggested that someone else such as

---

* He had recently put his Eaton Square house on the market, but it was later withdrawn. He eventually sold it in 1925, after becoming Prime Minister for the second time.
† The word 'smeller' in this context was strange to Jones, who supposed that it was roughly the equivalent of the colloquial 'cropper'.

Austen Chamberlain might head a Coalition Government, 'this did not seem to appeal to him much'.

Next morning the King saw Balfour and told him that if Baldwin wished to resign he (the King) would refuse 'on the grounds that he is still the head of the largest Party in the House of Commons, and for every reason, constitutional and otherwise, it would be right and proper for the Government to meet Parliament and leave it to the representatives of the people to decide whether or no they will support the Government'.

> Lord Balfour said that in his opinion that would be quite a constitutional course for the King to adopt: but raised the question whether, if Mr Baldwin ceased to be the head of the Conservative Party, he could still remain Prime Minister. His Majesty was inclined to think that such a contingency would be merely an expression of the Party and should not affect the Sovereign's choice.
>
> The King asked Lord Balfour if, in the event of Mr Baldwin's resignation, it would be possible for Mr Austen Chamberlain or Sir Robert Horne to form a Government. Lord Balfour was uncertain and rather doubtful about the former, to whom he is personally much attached but who has played his cards badly since the break up of the Coalition. The latter would, in Lord Balfour's estimation, be out of the question, as he is now head of Baldwin and Company* receiving probably a salary of £5,000 a year and he is a poor man.
>
> The King rejoined that sometimes people must put their country's interest before their own.
>
> Lord Balfour went on to suggest Mr Neville Chamberlain as a possible leader.

A week-end's reflection at Chequers convinced Baldwin that his initial impulse to resign was wrong, and this was confirmed by the King at their meeting. The Conservatives would still be the largest party in the new House of Commons, the King observed, and it was Baldwin's duty as Prime Minister to confront that assembly and thus enable the elected representatives of the people to decide whether they wished to keep him in office or not. Baldwin agreed, but at the same time 'expressed himself as absolutely opposed to any Coalition: he had killed one and would never join another'.† He undertook to lay the matter before the

* Balfour seems to have confused Baldwins with the Imperial Smelting Corporation, of which Horne was chairman.

† He was to do so in 1931.

Cabinet next morning, which he did. At this Cabinet the decision to meet Parliament early in the New Year was confirmed, Curzon noting that the Prime Minister 'seemed quite cheerful today and unconscious of the terrible doom he has brought upon our Party'.[23]

In the Party, and even in the Cabinet, there were muttered cries of 'Baldwin must go'. Indeed on the day the Cabinet met, Davidson wrote: 'The intrigue is in full blast, but I doubt whether it will succeed.' That his forecast proved correct was due to the ill-considered agitation fomented by the two leading Press Lords. When Hoare, the Air Minister, went into the Carlton Club, he found the members 'very bitter against Baldwin but at the same time for sentimental reasons they do not like throwing him over and still less were they inclined to do so after Beaverbrook and Rothermere had told the public that they ought to throw him over. This had caused a complete revulsion in his favour.'

To Lord Carson, who had sent him a message of sympathy in his hour of defeat, Baldwin wrote: 'I will never draw down the blinds until I am a political corpse, but if I do become one it will be by an honest blow delivered in open fight and not by a syphilitic dagger from the syndicated press.'[24]*

Baldwin was showing marked signs of strain, but fortunately the Christmas holiday brought a much needed breathing space. On Christmas Eve he wrote from Astley to the Davidsons:

We are in for a green Christmas. We had snow from London to the Cotswolds and then it turned soft. Yesterday was a jewel for beauty. Transparently clear, all the country in deep russet dress, long vividly bright, horizontal sunshine casting long shadows in the morning: a dull midday, and then a divine evening.

I wrote sixty-two letters of thanks yesterday! My Christmas letters this morning comprised an impudent demand for help, a long poem in which a criticism for publication was requested, and a tax demand notice!

. . . the love that binds us three together makes it easier to generate that wider love that alone makes it possible to carry on in public life. Everything else is Dead Sea fruit. The longing to help the bewildered multitude of common folk is the only motive power to make me face the hundred and one things I loathe so much. And the longing to help only comes from love and pity.[25]

* The reference was to Rothermere's brother Northcliffe, whose death in 1922 was believed to be the result of a venereal infection.

The King opened the new Parliament on 15 January 1924 in bitter wintry weather. The customary Debate on the Address terminated shortly after 11 p.m. on 21 January, when a hostile amendment was moved by the Labour member J. R. Clynes and carried by seventy-two votes, all but eleven of the Liberals joining with Labour to defeat the Government. A particularly potent contribution during the final day's debate came from Austen Chamberlain who foretold that Asquith would go down to history as the last Prime Minister of a Liberal administration. 'He has sung the swan song of the Liberal Party,' Chamberlain declared, a prediction which was to prove abundantly true. 'A *delightful* speech,' Baldwin was moved to write to Chamberlain the same night. 'And I don't say that because I agreed with it, but because, dispassionately, it was in my opinion one of the best bits of work as a speech that I have ever heard you make. And that is saying much.'[26]*

Baldwin resigned early next day and the King invited Ramsay Mac-Donald as the leader of the next largest party in the Commons to form an administration, having first sworn him a Privy Councillor. MacDonald agreed and so became the first Labour Prime Minister in English history.

The departure of the Baldwins from 10 Downing Street took place four days later. It was a sad occasion. All the staff and official servants were lined up in the hall as the ex-Prime Minister came down the stairs followed by his wife. In an attempt to lighten the atmosphere, he turned to her and remarked banteringly: 'I'm glad we are leaving these lodgings, Cissy, the beds are damp.'

'But, Stan dear,' she protested, 'they're our *own* beds!'[27]

5

One piece of business which Baldwin had not completed by the time he finally left Downing Street on 26 January was the list of Dissolution Honours which it is customary for an outgoing Prime Minister to recommend to the monarch. He was still thinking over it a week later during a brief visit to Cambridge when he dined at High Table in his old

* In his daily letter to the King, Baldwin described Austen Chamberlain's speech as one of the greatest successes of his parliamentary career. 'It was a fighting speech of a very high order, and in the slashing attack which he delivered on Sir John Simon, Mr Asquith and the policy of the Liberal Party he mingled sarcasm, wit and bitter irony. It was a remarkable speech and will do much to restore Mr Chamberlain to favour with many members of the Conservative Party who have resented some of Mr Chamberlain's public utterances in the past year. His statement that as a result of recent developments coalition is dead helped to produce an excellent effect among members of his own Party.' Baldwin to King George V, 22 January 1924: Baldwin Papers 60.

college. Also dining in Trinity the same night was A. C. Benson, the Master of Magdalene, who afterwards wrote in his diary:

> *2 February 1924* . . . I saw a plain pale little man by the Master, whose face seemed familiar – a lifted eyebrow, a little smile, a perky curl of the lip. I said to Parry [the Master of Trinity], 'Can that be the ex-Prime Minister?' 'Yes,' said Parry, 'it is Baldwin; I found him strolling about and asked him to dinner. He is struggling with a hideous task, his list of honours.' . . .*
>
> Then Parry suddenly said: 'Let us change places.' So I was moved up next the Master, and Baldwin took my hand in a firm grip: 'I have long wished to meet you as Phil's friend.'†
>
> Then he said, in reply to some question of mine, 'Yes, I hope I shall get back to ordinary life again. I used to like reading; but this infernal task of mine – fourteen hours a day having to see people and having to be at your best and guarding every word – is a fearful strain.' I said something about '*semina flammae*', and he said, 'Yes, every smallest word is liable to burst into flame . . .'
>
> He struck me as a very good-natured, sensible, able, tired man, but with plenty of stuff left in him, entirely unembittered and healthily detached.[28]

The 'Baldwin Must Go' movement had been halted largely as the result of the ill-natured attacks mounted by Rothermere and Beaverbrook in their newspapers. Since it might be resumed at any moment, Baldwin realised that if he was to remain as Party leader he must take effective steps to maintain his position. His object now was to reunite the Tories by bringing back the Coalition dissidents to the fold. Consequently, as soon as Neville Chamberlain had returned from a skiing holiday towards the end of January, Baldwin asked him to go for a walk with him in St James's Park. According to Chamberlain, Baldwin appeared very reluctant to come to the point. 'He talked about the pelicans, and the beauty of spring at Astley and I had the utmost difficulty in dragging in politics.' Eventually he came round to the question of future tactics in order to bring about a reunion.

Baldwin said he had not written to Austen as he did not wish to do

---

* The list, published a few days later, followed the conventional pattern. It contained one barony, nine baronetcies, nineteen knighthoods, five privy councillorships and two Dames of the British Empire. The only peer was Sir John Butcher, an Irish diehard lawyer, who became Lord Danesfort. *The Times*, 9 February 1924.

† Philip Burne-Jones.

anything without Neville. In the interests of reunion, he suggested a dinner for the three of them at the Athenaeum Club. 'Better dine with me,' countered Neville, 'then no one will know anything about it.' This Baldwin agreed to do and the dinner was fixed for 5 February at Neville's London house.

'Will you allow me to suggest how you should go about this?' Neville asked before they parted. 'Don't ask Austen any questions and don't suggest that there is any doubt about F.E. or that you have to consult anyone. Say "I have decided to ask you *and your friends* to sit with us on the Front Bench and to invite you to join our councils on just the same footing as if you had been members of the late Cabinet".' Neville emphasised that Baldwin should not show the slightest hesitation. Otherwise Austen might say that Baldwin did not know his own mind and was only playing with him. Again Baldwin agreed, saying he thought Neville's suggestions were on the right lines. Nevertheless Neville remained uncertain how far Baldwin would adopt them.[29]

The dinner took place as arranged, the only other person present being Neville Chamberlain's wife Annie who left them as soon as the meal was over. Austen was rather stiff at first but gradually thawed. By the end of the evening it was 'my dear Stanley' and 'my dear Austen' as if they had never been parted. 'Well,' said Baldwin after Annie Chamberlain had departed, 'I think that in the present circumstances and in the position in which we are now it is time for all of us to get together.' To Neville's considerable relief, Baldwin took exactly the line he had suggested at their meeting, inviting Austen to sit on the Opposition Front Bench and also to come to the first meeting of the Shadow Cabinet which he had summoned for two days hence and to which he had also invited Birkenhead and Balfour.

Austen Chamberlain replied, after a moment's hesitation, that to such a proposal so made he could only give one answer. He accepted, and added that he was in a position to say that Lord Birkenhead would do the same.

They then proceeded to discuss policy at length and they all three agreed that the proper course was to get back to the pre-election attitude on tariff questions. Austen also protested strongly against Baldwin resigning the leadership and submitting himself for re-election like a company auditor. 'Such procedure would be undignified and farcical.' His proper course was to come to the next full Party meeting and to make a clear statement of the policy which he recommended to them. There might be some grumbling, said Austen, but he would certainly get his vote of confidence and very probably by acclamation.

I told him [wrote Austen Chamberlain next day] that F.E. and I
had discussed the situation before I had any reason to think that he
meant to see me: that whilst we felt that we could have easily
organised an opposition which would make his position impossible,
that would not have been in the interest of the Party, for the position
of any successor would have been quite as difficult. We, therefore,
had given no encouragement to any opposition and were confident
that no one would have allowed his name to be put forward in
competition to Baldwin even though the present overture had not
been made and accepted.

He thought it probable that Bob Cecil would refuse to attend if
F.E. were invited, and Salisbury might take the same line. I observed
that neither of them had given any assistance during the election
and that Bob Cecil had not only been, as Asquith phrased it, 'up to
the eyes in negotiations for joining the Liberal Party' before Baldwin
invited him to become a member of the late Cabinet, but according
to my information had been with difficulty restrained by Salisbury
from joining the Labour Government. He in fact had only one idea
at the present time, namely, the League of Nations. He had ceased
to be in any sense of the word a member of our Party sharing its
general aspirations and wishes. If Salisbury took the same line, I
should be surprised and sorry but I presumed that Baldwin had by
this time made up his mind on which side the balance of advantage
lay.[30]

'So reunion has come at last,' noted Neville Chamberlain in his diary,
'thanks, I think I may say, to me.' In the event the meeting of the
Shadow Cabinet, which took place in Baldwin's house in Eaton Square
on 7 February, was attended by all the late Cabinet except Robert Cecil
who refused to come and by all the Conservative supporters of the
Coalition except Horne who was in America. Baldwin tactfully left most
of the talking to Austen Chamberlain, whose proposal that Protection
should be put into cold storage for the time being was generally approved
except by Amery and Bridgeman. 'Baldwin took practically no part
whatever in the discussion,' wrote Derby afterwards, 'and I am bound
to say that if any outsider had been in the room he would have thought
that it was Austen Chamberlain and not Baldwin who was leader of the
Party.' Curzon delivered a schoolmasterly homily to Baldwin on the
theme of his future behaviour, saying that he would be 'forgiven' if the
'unpleasant subject' of tariffs were dropped. 'I think I see what the
general opinion is,' said Baldwin after everyone had spoken. 'I shall

have to do some skilful tightrope walking on Monday for which my figure is not very well suited.'

Monday, 11 February, was the day set for the Party meeting in the Hotel Cecil of Conservative peers, MPs and defeated candidates at the election. The proceedings began with a half-hearted singing of 'For he's a jolly good fellow', when Baldwin appeared on the platform. He looked tired and nervous, but improved as his speech proceeded. 'I do not feel justified in advising the Party again to submit the proposal of a general tariff to the country,' he said, 'except on the clear evidence that on this matter public opinion is disposed to reconsider its judgement of two months ago.' A motion of confidence in Baldwin's leadership was proposed by Balfour and seconded by Austen Chamberlain. As the latter had forecast it was carried with acclamation. 'It was a dull affair,' wrote William Hewins of the Party meeting. 'I shall not be surprised if the Conservatives are quickly back again. The Bonar Law pledge is gone, and the Liberal Party overthrown, "coalitionism", "fusionism", at an end, the Conservative Party restored . . . These are great results and make Stanley Baldwin's tenure of his position very important.'[31] Baldwin's leadership and declared policy were again endorsed at a meeting of the National Union of Conservative and Unionist Associations next day. Although his position could hardly be regarded as secure, in the event several years were to elapse before his leadership was again to be challenged.

The Opposition Front Bench, on which he now took his place, Austen Chamberlain considered inferior to any he had known; in his opinion the only really good speakers were his brother Neville, Hoare, Lloyd-Greame and Wood. Baldwin's opinion of himself as 'not a good Leader of Opposition' Austen Chamberlain endorsed. 'It is too much a one-man show,' he said. At the same time Chamberlain set his face against any attempt by disgruntled Conservatives to dislodge Baldwin from the leadership. To one such Tory backbencher, Warden Chilcott, who had endeavoured to enlist his help in an anti-Baldwin intrigue, he wrote:

I have no obligations to Stanley Baldwin except the ordinary obligation of an honourable man not to work against Baldwin behind his back whilst associated with him as I now am in council. I was quite prepared – and in many ways I should have preferred – to sit upon the back benches and to occupy a position of independence, but for the sake of the Party and of all that it stands for I could not refuse to co-operate with Baldwin when at length after the débâcle he invited me to join *with my friends*.

Before that I had, as I think you know, considered with F.E.

what our course ought to be at the Party meeting on the assumption that we were still independent, and had come to the conclusion with them that whilst it would be easy for us to make Baldwin's position impossible if we took a little trouble to organise people who were like-minded with ourselves, yet we could not secure a measure of unanimity as would be required to render the position of any successor tolerable or even possible.

If we were right – and I think there can be no doubt we were – our only course was to support Baldwin and to make the best of a not very promising situation. I do not pretend to think him a good leader, but I do not think any other leader is possible at the present time. He may gradually develop in power and decision, or he may fail and become convinced that he is unequal to the task. But while he is in the field any movement against him would only strengthen his hold upon his own followers and confirm him in his position.[32]

One Sunday towards the end of February, Baldwin surprised Austen Chamberlain by proposing to drive down to see him at his cottage in Sussex. The object of the visit was to discuss Winston Churchill's parliamentary future and the possibility of Churchill rejoining the Conservative Party. Chamberlain invited Baldwin to lunch, and at the meal he was struck by 'the friendly way he talked of Winston and by the sense which he expressed of the advantage of getting Winston over'. At the two General Elections of 1922 and 1923, Churchill had stood as a Coalition Liberal and been defeated. Baldwin had recently remarked in light-hearted vein to Tom Jones that he wished he 'could say that Winston had left cotton (Manchester) for marmalade (Dundee) and had now gone to ladies' underclothing (Leicester)'.[33] But the electors of West Leicester had rejected Churchill in favour of Mr F. W. Pethick-Lawrence, a Labour Old Etonian and future Chairman of the Labour Party. Ever since the fall of the Coalition, Churchill had been increasingly out of sympathy with the Liberals, and he was convinced like Austen Chamberlain that Asquith's action in putting Labour in office would be fatal to Liberal Party political prospects in the long term. Churchill was now nearing fifty, and if he was to make a political comeback with any chance of holding high office again, he must move quickly.

An opportunity presented itself at a by-election in the Abbey Division of Westminster due to the death of the sitting member. Here Churchill decided to stand as an 'Independent and Anti-Socialist' candidate and he was promised substantial Conservative support in the constituency, which in the event was forthcoming.

Although he shared Baldwin's view as to the desirability of 'getting Winston over', Austen Chamberlain was opposed to Churchill's independent candidature. He explained why in a letter to Birkenhead:

> Briefly the position is this – that it is too early for Winston to come out as a Conservative with credit to himself. On the other hand, the Abbey Conservatives would be unwilling to adopt him as an Independent and Anti-Socialist candidate. I do not know whether Central Office could force him upon them – probably not – but in any case this would involve a split and would not be in Winston's interest. Both the Liberal and the Labour parties, for what they are worth in the Division, would back an out-and-out Conservative against Winston. This being so, no friend of Winston would wish him to stand.
>
> Baldwin proposed to see Winston again and to explain the position to him. We want to get him and his friends over, and though we cannot give him the Abbey seat, Baldwin will undertake to find him a good seat later on (W. can put this plainly to S.B.), when he will have been able to develop naturally his new line and make his entry into our ranks much easier than it would be today.
>
> Our only fear is lest Winston should try and rush the fence. I am sure you will agree with me that this would be a mistake. I want you to send this letter on to Winston, adding your appeal to mine that he should not destroy these happy chances by any rash attempt on the Abbey.[34]

At one moment it looked as if Churchill would indeed be the official nominee of the Abbey Conservatives. However, they eventually selected Captain Otho Nicholson, nephew of the late member. This put Baldwin in an embarrassing position, the more so when Churchill, who was determined to pursue his candidature, appealed to Baldwin to persuade Nicholson to withdraw or at least to secure the non-interference of Conservative Central Office in the fight. 'I am sure you do not wish to be compelled by technicalities to fire upon the reinforcements I am bringing to your aid,' Churchill wrote to Baldwin on 7 March at the outset of his campaign. 'Act now with decision, and we shall be able to work together in the national interest. I have no other thought but to unite and rally the strongest combination of forces against the coming [Socialist] attack.'[35]

Baldwin felt that he could not overrule the local Association, although Churchill complained that there had been 'irregularities' in the selection of Nicholson. There was a further difficulty over ex-ministers who wished to speak in the campaign. Neville Chamberlain, for instance, had promised to support the official candidate, while Austen in his brother's words 'passionately declared that he should speak for Winston'. In the end a speaking truce was imposed on all ex-ministers, but it did not extend to epistolary warfare.

In the middle of the campaign, Balfour sent Baldwin a copy of a letter he was about to despatch to Churchill wishing him well. Baldwin had just come home from a tiring Speaker's dinner in the House of Commons and he immediately went off about midnight to see Balfour whom he persuaded not to send the letter. 'So back to bed feeling more at peace than for several nights', so he described the incident to Mrs Davidson. 'Next morning I opened my *Times* in bed as is my custom and to my horror set eyes on a letter from Amery to Nicholson. I saw in a moment what that meant.' Amery's letter in effect expressed the hope that Conservatives would not vote for Churchill. 'Anti-Socialism, as such, is an uninspiring and sterile creed,' wrote Amery. 'It might conceivably carry its advocates into office for a while. It could give them no real power to shape the life of the nation for good, or to do more than delay for a few years the advance of the dominant political doctrine.'

Baldwin's account continued:

By ten o'clock a letter came round from A.J.B. saying that Amery's letter had altered everything and that it wasn't fair, etc., and his letter ought to go to Winston but he was leaving [for Cannes] at once and left me to do as I thought right.

About eleven o'clock, first communication from Austen: of course he was all over the place and if Balfour's letter was bottled up he would let fly! I found by lunch time that it was common knowledge that Balfour had written the letter and that I had it. I released it, as I was in honour bound to do after Amery's letter, for which I was responsible technically though I never dreamed he would be such a fool. We had succeeded up to that moment in keeping our differences out of the papers, and now the enemy have had a glorious time.

While I write the counting is proceeding and the issue is very open.[36]

In the event the official Conservative defeated Churchill by forty-three votes in a four-cornered contest with Labour in the person of the left-wing Fenner Brockway third and the Liberal candidate forfeiting his deposit at the bottom of the poll.

Although he had succeeded in holding the balance between the two chief contenders at this election, refusing to disown Nicholson and dissociating himself from Churchill, Baldwin found the whole episode most disturbing. 'This incursion of Churchill into Westminster has been a great worry,' he told the Davidsons. 'It is causing trouble in the Party, just as I thought we were pulling together again. Leading the Party is like driving pigs to market!' [37]

6

The electoral disaster of the previous autumn had led to an overhaul of Conservative Central Office. Sir Reginald Hall was replaced as Chief Agent by Mr Herbert Blain, a Liverpool man and a good organiser, who was general manager of London's public transport system and whose appointment was warmly welcomed if it was not actually instigated by Archibald Salvidge. Blain took over from Hall in March 1924, and one of his first moves was to encourage Baldwin to make a series of nationwide speeches expounding a new Conservative creed. Baldwin agreed that this must have something better to offer the electors than Labour's policy: it was not enough merely to slang Labour. 'We are not going to fight the Labour Party by abuse,' he was to say. 'It has to be fought by the only way that will ever win in this country, by substituting something better in the minds of the people. With us, no less than with the Labour Party, there is a desire to help the people of this country, to give them a better life, and opportunities of education and self-betterment.' [38]

Shortly before launching his campaign, Baldwin had a talk with Tom Jones, who recorded what passed between them in his diary:

> After asking how I was getting on, he told me something of the worries of a Party Leader in days when there were no deep political convictions to divide men of good will. He had some troublesome followers who were clamouring for a positive policy without being able to suggest one. The one he had offered had been rejected. There was nothing for it but to await events, and he imagined that was what L[loyd] G[eorge] was doing.
>
> Austen's view was that the Liberal Party was done for, and they made a pitiable spectacle on the Rent Restrictions Bill, when some Liberals voted with the Tories, some voted with Labour, and another group, including Asquith, L.G. and Simon, abstained. S.B. thought Asquith too far gone to be even Master of Balliol . . .

He joked about having to go on making speeches without my help, and said that they had at any rate brought him one vote, but that was the vote of a very distinguished man – Thomas Hardy. This led us to talk about literature, S.B. has to join with Clynes on the 29th [April] in toasting the memory of Byron, with special reference to his European fame. I told him of Mazzini's essay and promised to send it along.[39]*

During May and June 1924 Baldwin delivered ten major speeches on the theme of Tory democracy and its variations, all of which received wide press coverage through the new regime at Central Office. Also noticed was Labour's failure so far to deal adequately with the unemployment problem as well as to maintain imperial and national defence, particularly by postponing the construction of a new naval base at Singapore.

Furthermore Baldwin found time to address more select gatherings such as the Royal Society of St George, where his evocation of the peculiar sights, sounds and 'imperishable scents' of the English countryside remains one of the happiest examples of his prose composition.

The sounds of England, the tinkle of the hammer on the anvil in the country smithy, the corncrake on a dewy morning, the sound of the scythe against the whetstone, and the sight of a plough team coming over the brow of a hill, the sight that has been seen in England since England was a land, and may be seen in England long after the Empire has perished and every works in England has ceased to function, for centuries the one eternal sight of England. The wild anemones in the woods in April, the last load at night of hay being drawn down a lane as the twilight comes on, when you can scarcely distinguish the figures of the horses as they take it home to the farm, and above all, most subtle, most penetrating and most moving, the smell of wood smoke coming up in an autumn evening, or the smell of the scutch fires: that wood smoke that our ancestors, tens of thousands of years ago, must have caught on the air when they were coming home with the result of the day's forage, when they were still nomads, and when they were still roaming the forests and the plains of the continent of Europe. These things strike down into the very

---

* Baldwin's speech at the Byron Centenary Luncheon on 29 April 1924 has been reprinted in his *On England*. 'The side of Byron which impresses me most,' he said on this occasion, 'is that of the great and persistent workman in his high profession of literature. He worked as an artist must work if he is to leave his mark on coming generations.'

depths of our nature, and touch chords that go back to the beginning of time and the human race, but they are chords that with every year of our life sound a deeper note in our innermost being.[40]

The only two Conservative newspapers which came out in support of the official candidate against Winston Churchill during the Abbey by-election were *The Morning Post* and *The People*. Consequently when the editor of *The People* asked Blain at Central Office to arrange for Baldwin to be interviewed by the paper's political correspondent, Mr F. W. Wilson, the proposal was put to Baldwin and he agreed. At this time, *The People* was a right-wing Sunday journal which was owned by Colonel Grant Morden, a Canadian financier: it had been going for more than forty years, having been founded by the late Duke of Northumberland and a group of like-minded Tories with the object of providing, in its own words, 'what was then lacking in the life of the English nation, a weekly democratic Conservative newspaper which would follow the principles laid down by the Earl of Beaconsfield'. The editor was Hannen Swaffer, one of the ablest newspapermen in the business. In the event the interview, for which Swaffer took full responsibility, proved to be the most sensational and at the same time the most embarrassing which Baldwin ever gave a journalist.

The interview took place in Baldwin's study on the first floor of his house in Eaton Square on 16 May and lasted for an hour and a quarter. At the outset Baldwin asked the newspaper correspondent to smoke and he himself lit up a cherrywood pipe, saying that earlier in the day he had visited the British Empire Exhibition at Wembley and had been given 'some Boer tobacco' in the South African pavilion. 'The first time I smoked it I was given some by De Wet,' he added between puffs. 'I rather like it.' [41]

Before getting down to business, they talked about the exhibition which, according to Wilson, the Conservative leader considered the most wonderful show he had ever seen, that it ought to be made permanent or at least kept on for four years. 'Take, for instance, those wonderful panoramas in the Australian exhibit,' remarked Baldwin. 'They give you the whole idea of sheep-farming.' Of course, he added, walking round the exhibition was rather fatiguing. 'I found it so, as I was at top pitch the whole time.'

Turning to politics, Wilson began by asking him what was the real significance of his new programme, as expounded in his recent speeches. 'I have attempted to tell the country what I honestly believe,' Baldwin replied.

You see, every Government in the future, whatever party forms it, must be socialistic in the sense in which our grandfathers used the word. Personally I don't know what Socialism means, but I do know that if the Tory Party is to exist we must have a vital democratic creed, and must be prepared to tackle the evils, social and economic, of our over-populated, over-industrialised country. The cost of living must be reduced, the producer must get more for his article, and it ought to cost the consumer and buyer less. I believe the Tory Party is the only party that can tackle such problems satisfactorily . . . The Socialists fall into class warfare difficulties and the Liberals are too inelastic . . . The Tory Party cannot go on on the old lines. I am certain that if we had not gone to the country and been defeated last year – though that, of course, is not why I went – I believed in something I wanted the country to adopt – we should have died of dry rot in two years, and Labour would have come in with a sweeping majority.

For the next half hour or so Baldwin proceeded to expound his plans for stopping food profiteering, reducing the cost of living index, educating the workers and so on, at times in somewhat vague generalisations. It was only when *The People* correspondent began to question Baldwin about his personal position that the interview assumed something of a sensational character.

'Now, Mr Baldwin, you have apparently got a creed, which we can follow with enthusiasm and preach with conviction. But what is the use of trying to put it over when it is ignored by your hostile Press, laughed at, and when you are attacked and jeered at daily? Quite frankly, many members of your party go about whispering to one another that you are no use, and if one listened to many Tory MPs one would get the impression that you were a kind of effete, moribund old man.'

'Of course, the life of a leader in opposition is always a difficult one,' Baldwin smiled as he replied. 'Every leader in opposition has intrigues. You remember how they treated Campbell-Bannerman. Read his life and see the kind of time he had. Even when he became Prime Minister it continued.* I know I am abused and jeered at and intrigued against. I know it has been going on for a long time. But why?'

Baldwin then proceeded to explain why in what were the most controversial passages in the interview:

* The official biography of the Liberal leader Sir Henry Campbell-Bannerman by J. A. Spender had recently been published.

When I spoke at the Carlton Club meeting I never expected that we [the anti-Coalition Conservatives] would win. I took my political life in my hands and I was prepared to retire from politics. I did not know that Bonar Law would lead us. In fact the night before I spent two hours with him, and he had sealed a letter to the chairman of his Glasgow Association telling him that he would not stand for Parliament again. In that mood I left him.

And then we won. I spoke because I was determined that never again should the sinister and cynical combination of the chief three of the Coalition – Mr Lloyd George, Mr Churchill and Lord Birkenhead – come together again. But today you can see the signs of the times.

But I didn't expect the exiled Conservative ex-Ministers would take things as badly as they did. Before the election last year I welcomed Mr Austen Chamberlain back, and I accepted his friends, though I could easily have stopped their return to our councils.

With Austen came Lord Birkenhead, who had attached himself to the strings of Austen's apron the year before very cleverly. And Austen is one of those loyal men who could not see disloyalty or intrigue even if it was at his elbow. But I am under no illusions as to Lord Birkenhead. If his health does not give way he will be a liability to the Party. But can a leader in opposition shut the door to an ex-Minister?

There was some further talk about Birkenhead, whose health Baldwin had broadly hinted was being undermined by his over-indulgence in alcohol. Wilson pointed out that Birkenhead's speeches in Lancashire during the election could hardly be said to be helpful.

'They were not,' Baldwin agreed. 'They did an unfortunate amount of harm. I think Birkenhead thought that we should come back with a small majority of between thirty and forty, and that he and his Coalition friends would hold the balance.'

'Yes,' interrupted Wilson, 'apparently that was the source of Lord Beaverbrook's estimate. He published the same figure.'

This remark set Baldwin off to talk about the iniquities of the 'Trust Press' and its two principal controllers:

I was attacked all through the election, and I have been attacked since by the Trust Press – by Lord Beaverbrook and Lord Rother-mere. For myself I do not mind. I care not what they think. They are men I would not have in my house. I do not respect them. Who are they? I was attacked, I am told, in the *Evening Standard*, over my arrangement for the budget speakers. I did not read it. Why should I?

The Trust Press is breaking up. The *Daily Mail* is dead; it has no soul. Northcliffe, with all his faults, was a great journalist, with a spark of genius. But this man! I get much correspondence about him. A postcard the other day said: 'If Lord Rothermere wants a halo or a coronet on earth, why don't you get it for him?'

The last time I spoke to Lord Beaverbrook was at Bonar Law's funeral. He had contracted a curious friendship with Bonar and had got his finger into the pie, where it had no business to be. He got hold of much information, which he used in ways in which it was not intended.

When I came in, that stopped. I know I could get his support if I were to send for him and talk things over with him. But I prefer not. That sort of thing does not appeal to me.

As I said, I do not mind attacks on myself. I often wonder if my silent contempt irritates them more than if I were to speak out. I suppose it is my lot to suffer disloyalty. But there are limits.

Take the article in the recent number of *English Life*. That's a pretty dirty bit of work. It is written by 'A Conservative Ex-Minister', and I am pretty certain that if it is not written by Lord Birkenhead, the man I suspect, it was certainly inspired by him.* It was a stab in the back. Now, it attacks my officials – the heads of the Central Office – and that I won't stand. If anybody had attacked a Treasury official when I was at the Treasury, I would have come down to the House and made a very furious speech. And I intend to do so now.

Besides, all this intrigue – this Churchill plotting – is bad for the party, for all the young men who are looking to Toryism for the salvation of the country. What do these intriguers want? Simply to go back to the old dirty kind of politics! Not while I'm leader of the party.

At this point, according to the interviewer: 'Mr Baldwin yawned with disgust and weariness at discussing for so long so unpleasant a subject.'

Finally, Baldwin had something further to say about Churchill. 'I do not think Churchill understands the post-war mind. I think if he got

* The article, entitled 'The Jelly Bulwarks of the Conservative Party', was in fact written by Birkenhead. It referred to Baldwin's leadership as 'impotent'.

[back] into the House he would only annoy Labour and there would be scenes. It is no use just denouncing Socialism as he does. You have got to have an alternative.'

'Yes,' he mused, 'Churchill is a problem!'

On this note the interview ended. At no point – *The People* correspondent was quite positive on this – did Baldwin suggest that anything he said was not to be used for publication – 'off the record', as it is now called. Nor did he mention a proof or ask if he could see one.

'I hope, Mr Baldwin,' said the correspondent, as they walked down the stairs together, 'you will allow me to come and see you again.'

'Whenever I have anything to say to you, I hope you will come,' was the reply, 'or whenever you have anything to tell me.'

'It is, you know,' said Wilson, 'most valuable for anyone writing about politics to get into touch with the main people in them. It is all very well studying the subject from books of anatomy, but it is very necessary to supplement that study with a little dissection.'

According to Wilson, the Conservative leader laughed, shook hands, thanked him for coming and wished him good night. The correspondent returned to his office, where he wrote up the interview and showed it to the editor, who made a few minor changes. These apparently had the effect of slightly toning down a few of Baldwin's harsher observations. The story was then set up in type and it duly appeared two days later under the heading:

BALDWIN TURNS AND RENDS HIS CRITICS
SENSATIONAL DISCLOSURE TO 'THE PEOPLE'

Indeed the newspaper could justly claim, as it did in its next issue, that the interview was 'the greatest political sensation for many years'. Baldwin was spending the week-end with Lord Stanhope at his country house near Sevenoaks in Kent and could not be reached by telephone. Eventually on Sunday evening, Colonel Jackson, the Conservative Party Chairman, despatched one of the Central Office officials by car to Sevenoaks with an urgent request that he should authorise the issue of a denial. This Baldwin apparently gave, since the same night Central Office released a statement repudiating some parts of the interview but admitting the accuracy of others, yet without specifying which were true and which were not.

Next morning *The People* issued a statement to the effect that the interview had been 'specially arranged and was for the express purpose, or was so understood, of enabling Mr Baldwin to give out his policy to the country and also to reply to alleged intrigues'. This produced a further and slightly more specific denial from Central Office. There was no suggestion that the interview should be utilised to reply to alleged intrigues, it was said. Nor were the reflections on well-known public men attributed to Mr Baldwin ever made by him – 'they do not represent views that were ever expressed or held'. Meanwhile extracts from the interview were widely reproduced and commented upon in the national and provincial dailies, the *Morning Post* going so far as to indicate in a leader that 'we are glad these things have been written in public, even if they have not been said'. The *Nottingham Guardian*, to quote another example, claimed that whether or not Baldwin said what he was alleged to have said, 'the sentiments contained in the published interview are shared by 99 per cent of the members of the Conservative Party'.

The following comment was made by the *Glasgow Weekly Herald*:

> The unfortunate thing from Mr Baldwin's point of view is that the personal passages he repudiates are precisely those it would have been most difficult for the interviewer to imagine or invent. On the other hand, it is not without significance that a considerable section of the party is clearly of opinion that the things Mr Baldwin denies having said are precisely those things which so badly required saying.

As might be expected, there was much consternation both in Central Office and in Baldwin's secretariat. Some who were close to Baldwin like Geoffrey Fry greatly feared that Beaverbrook would take libel proceedings in respect of the statement that he had misused information given to him by Bonar Law, but others 'thought it unlikely that Beaverbrook would risk going into the witness box because of his own lurid past'. However, the matter was considered sufficiently serious for the ex-Attorney-General Sir Douglas Hogg to be called in. On his advice Baldwin wrote a letter to everyone who it was felt might have reason to complain of the interview. 'I hope you know me well enough to be certain that I never gave expression to the personal reflections on yourself which are there reported. I am deeply distressed that I should have been so grossly misrepresented.' [42]*

During the days immediately following publication of the interview, Grant Morden was subjected to mounting pressure to repudiate it

---

* Beaverbrook subsequently wrote: 'I met Mr Baldwin afterwards at his request, and accepted completely his repudiation of the words placed in his mouth, with reference to myself. In fact that were, on the face of them, incredible and absurd.' Beaverbrook, *Politicians and the Press* (1926), p. 63.

categorically and publish an unqualified apology. It was even suggested that he should dismiss both the editor and the political correspondent. To his credit, Grant Morden refused, although the pressure came from influential quarters with which he wished to stand well. 'By God, I'll fight 'em,' he told Swaffer. And he did by publishing on the following Sunday a circumstantial account of how the interview came to be written, supplementing the original account with further details of what had passed between Baldwin and Wilson – 'most damaging to S.B. and the Party, if true', noted Tom Jones, adding that 'anyone who knows S.B. intimately cannot but feel that the interview reflects substantially his general attitude to politics and his colleagues'.

On the same day Austen Chamberlain wrote to his sister:

> Baldwin's *People* interview has been the sensation and the scandal of the week. When I first heard of it, I said, like F.E., Baldwin is not the man to speak thus of his colleagues with whom he is acting; and I believe that the reporter had a bad reputation in Downing Street. But Baldwin told me his own story of the interview and it was enough to show that he had been indiscreet in what he said and doubly indiscreet in what he allowed to be said of him.
>
> He **really** is a victim of the *manie des persécutions*. I have talked and written very bluntly to him.[43]

Lloyd George may be allowed to have the last word on the matter. 'Mr Baldwin is an honest man,' he told the National Liberal Federation in Brighton. 'He tells the truth, even in interviews.'

7

The second article in *The People*, which appeared on 25 May, was a further cause of worry to Baldwin's political associates. Baldwin was shown a copy of it by Geoffrey Fry who motored to London the same day from his house in Wiltshire to do so, but he decided to make no public reference to it, and the whole matter was allowed to drop. In the circumstances it is hardly surprising that Baldwin's leadership should have continued to cause uneasiness, particularly with Austen Chamberlain and his friends who had returned to the Conservative fold. 'I find politics very dull,' Chamberlain confided in his sister Ida. 'Baldwin does not interest or attract me. He seems to be stupid and uncommunicative, and his habit of bursting out with some inconceivable folly, like his proposal to buy up and market all Australian corn in the Preference debate without consulting his colleagues or himself knowing what he meant, is both disconcerting and exasperating.'⁴⁴* [44]*

Chamberlain's letters to his sisters were full of complaints about Baldwin's behaviour at this time. On 14 July 1924, for example, he wrote:

> I am kept in a constant state of discomfort by not knowing how much of what he arranges with me is imparted to his colleagues. For instance, he told me last week that he desired that he and I should be the speakers in the debate [on foreign affairs this evening], but I do not see my name mentioned in any of the newspapers, whereas Ronald MacNeill appears as our second speaker. If this means that Ronald MacNeill has prepared a speech under the impression that as ex-Under Secretary for Foreign Affairs he would naturally be called upon, he will be very much annoyed if I take his place; and having accepted his [Baldwin's] invitation to close our quarrel and open a new page, I do not wish to get into fresh difficulties with him.†
>
> Of course, this is only a small personal matter, but the same difficulty arises in regard to bigger things, but even these little personal questions make all the difference to one's comfort and to the amount of friction which one encounters. It is a curious position. No one seems to have much confidence in Baldwin except himself, but he seems to be thoroughly satisfied with what he does. It must at least be admitted that he takes his position seriously and works very hard.⁴⁵ [45]

Unfortunately there were fresh difficulties between the two men and these difficulties appeared in public. The cause of the misunderstanding lay in the manner in which it was agreed that approaches should be made to the Liberals. Any hopes that Asquith may have had of leading a united or virtually united party and turning out Labour at will, so that the King would send for him to form a government, were quickly dissipated through internal differences. 'The Liberal Party is "visibly" bursting up,' observed Austen Chamberlain after Labour had been in office for a

---

* 'His socialistic proposal for the purchase of Imperial food supplies and their distribution as near cost price as possible frightened his own side.' W. A. S. Hewins, *Apologia of an Imperialist*, II, 287.

† Austen Chamberlain was in fact the Opposition's second speaker in the debate, the first being Baldwin.

few weeks. This was clearly a development of which Baldwin and his Shadow Cabinet felt that they should take advantage.[46]

To add to his troubles, Baldwin was faced with an unexpected physical problem in his constituency at this time. All over the country unusually heavy rain fell for mid-summer, followed by floods described as the worst for fifty years. Vast tracts of land were transformed into lakes, many feet deep, owing to rivers like the Severn overflowing their banks. In Worcester the electricity and gas works were flooded, and the city was deprived of light, power and domestic water supply.

Ways and means of attracting the disillusioned Liberals to the Conservative camp were discussed at a dinner given by Sir Samuel Hoare early in July, to which Baldwin and other members of the Shadow Cabinet including Austen Chamberlain were invited for the purpose of meeting Churchill. Baldwin had by now decided, so he told an aspiring young politician named Robert Boothby, who had recently joined his secretariat, that if and when he got back to power there was one man he intended to 'have at his side' and that was Winston Churchill.[47]

'Something may come of that,' Austen Chamberlain remarked after the dinner, 'if Baldwin plays his hand as arranged and as he means to do. He speaks on the 17th [at Lowestoft] and 26th [at Manchester], and Winston and Hoare will appear on the same platform in Edinburgh between the two occasions, and the speeches are intended to respond to one another and to advance co-operation which I and several others think necessary to success . . . Winston was to carry it a step further and Baldwin was to clinch matters at Manchester . . . I undertook to speak on the same lines at Northampton where, through the folly of the Central Office, I was billed for the same day as Baldwin at Lowestoft.'[48]

When he read Baldwin's Lowestoft speech next day in *The Times*, Chamberlain had a shock. As he described it to his sister, it was 'throughout an attack on Liberals *as such* without one word to distinguish between Lloyd George and Winston', and he was moved to ask: 'What is the use of my trying to keep step with him if he behaves in this way, and what pleasure can there be in working with a man so unstable of purpose and so muddled of mind?'

To Baldwin, Chamberlain wrote more in sorrow than in anger:

I am completely puzzled and very disappointed. What is the use of settling a policy if we drop it before it is given a chance? How can I keep in line with you, if, after agreeing a policy, you change your mind without a word of warning to me?

When we met at Sam Hoare's just a fortnight ago, we agreed that at Lowestoft you should recognise the action of those Liberals who are not prepared to join our party but have voted with us in critical divisions, and that you should hold out a hand to them. Almost your last words to me were that you saw your line clearly. I told you that I was speaking the same day and that I would keep step with you.

Why did you change your mind? Lloyd George's speech offered you a splendid opportunity to distinguish between him and the Liberals you had in mind. Yet you lump them all together and repel them all.

Why again did you not tell me that you had changed your mind?

I spoke as agreed with you. Your change of mind makes my speech mark an obvious difference between us. Why, oh, why?*

I am off to the country with a sad heart.[49]

'I cannot see any difference between us,' replied Baldwin, who was 'distressed' to learn of the impression his Lowestoft speech had made on Chamberlain. 'The only papers which pretended to discover a difference are Beaverbrook's. I don't know what his game is, but he is always trying to drive a wedge in between you and me, and so far as I am concerned, he will never succeed.' He added in the same letter:

I followed exactly the line I indicated to Winston after dinner at Sam Hoare's. I purposely put it shortly as I wanted no doubt to exist as to the meaning.

I made our own policy – Imperial Preference and Safeguarding – clear and indicated that that was the dividing line, and those who agreed with us on these important questions could not be happy in their present environment.

For men with such views, our party offered the only home.

And I ended by inviting them on to our platform.

That invitation should now be accepted. Winston, in private, accepts our policy. It is up to him now to address a meeting and say so.[50]

---

* 'All those who feel that they can unconditionally adopt our policy and work loyally with us we will welcome as comrades in arms in the great fight that lies before us, and if any man is prepared to adopt our platform let him come forward on it and say so like a man.' Baldwin at Lowestoft, 17 July 1924.

'Let us welcome in no ungrudging spirit and in no ungenerous manner recruits that may ultimately gain for our own party men who at this moment without joining our party see eye to eye with us in this great issue.' A. Chamberlain at Northampton, 17 July 1924.

As had been arranged, Churchill did what was expected of him at the Edinburgh meeting, which was a representative gathering of Scottish Unionists presided over by Balfour. Shortly afterwards, as Austen Chamberlain had predicted, Churchill was provided with a safe seat by the local Conservatives at Epping. This he was first to contest as a 'Constitutionalist', before formally rejoining the Conservative Party a year later.

Meanwhile Austen Chamberlain and his friends went on grumbling about their leader's conduct. 'Sam Hoare, Horne, etc., feel as I do,' wrote Chamberlain on 26 July, 'that his inability to see the difference between what he said and what he thought he had said is even more difficult to deal with than would be a real change of mind.' [51]

At Manchester, where he addressed a mass meeting on the same day, Baldwin seems to have avoided upsetting Chamberlain again. He was accompanied on the platform by Joynson-Hicks, who had defeated Churchill in a historic by-election in the city sixteen years previously, an occasion in which Baldwin had also participated. This time the speakers had to use microphones, the first time that Baldwin experienced this mechanical aid to oratory, and he disliked it intensely. 'We all hated speaking through the amplifier or whatever its proper name is,' he told Mrs Davidson afterwards. 'I had to ascend a scaffold, surrounded by an immense crowd, possibly 20,000, and I had to stand stock still and speak into a thing like a beehive. You can't look up or down, right or left, and you establish no personal contact with your audience nor do you know if they are gripped . . . It cramped Joynson-Hicks's style more than mine and he was less audible because he didn't stand sufficiently still. But I didn't enjoy it.' [52]

8

During the summer parliamentary recess, Baldwin was much exercised in his mind over the question of Ireland. Under the 'Treaty' settlement and the consequential legislation, the Irish Free State demanded the setting up of a Boundary Commission, as it was entitled to do, in order to regulate the border between the six counties of Northern Ireland and the rest of the country. This Commission was designed to comprise a representative from the south and one from the north together with an independent chairman. But the northern government under Sir James Craig refused to nominate any representative, and the Commission was thus legally invalid. The Labour Cabinet referred the matter to the Judicial Committee of the Privy Council, which reported at the end of

July 1924 that additional legislation would be needed to appoint a third commissioner, if Northern Ireland held to its line. Ramsay MacDonald had kept Baldwin informed throughout the negotiations, and he hoped that the Conservative leader would now agree that Parliament should be recalled at the end of September for the purpose of passing a short measure with all-Party support to provide for the appointment of a third commissioner by the Government.

While he was in Downing Street, MacDonald had not used Tom Jones to anything like the extent that his predecessor had done. However, on this occasion he enlisted Jones's help in an endeavour to persuade Baldwin not to oppose the proposed legislation. MacDonald also hoped that Baldwin would use his good offices with Craig to get him to accept the nomination of a third commissioner, who might be expected to reflect the Ulster point of view.

Jones found Baldwin very awkward to handle when they met at Conservative Headquarters on 29 July. 'Got a diehard reaction,' he noted, 'more so than I ever remember having before from him.' The danger, which both men realised, was that 'if by legislation we override Ulster we'll have the Bill thrown out in the Lords and Ireland will be back again in our politics'. Also, it was clear that any proposal for the transfer of territory would be determined by the chairman's casting vote, since the loser would always be in a minority; consequently the impartiality of the chairman was likely to be severely tested. (The chairman was an Oxford-educated South African judge named Richard Feetham.[53])

Baldwin told Jones that he was 'for going very slow'. Nevertheless he undertook to get into touch with Craig in Belfast with a view to arranging a meeting. 'I don't want to come to you unless it is absolutely necessary,' he wrote to the Ulster Premier, 'as it would be bound to attract attention and cause talk that might do harm.' But Craig pressed him to come to Belfast so that he could also talk over the matter with the other members of his Cabinet, and so he made the journey. He was left in no doubt as to how the Protestant majority felt in the province. As he went on board the steamer to return to England on 18 August, large crowds chanted: 'Not an inch!' – thus echoing Craig's promise that not an inch of northern territory should be surrendered to the south.

The attitude of Craig and his Cabinet was summarised by Baldwin in a letter which he wrote to Edward Wood, shortly after arriving in Aix-les-Bains for his annual holiday:

Craig is willing to accept, 'under duress', as he puts it . . . If the

Commission should give away counties, then of course Ulster couldn't accept it and we should back her. But the Government will nominate a proper representative and we hope that he and Feetham will do what is right . . .

The Lords are the curse. They will never let the Bill through except on the definite assurance that Ulster will accept it. Craig's first idea was to fight the Bill along the line: the Lords to let it through at the last. But I showed him the snag and I told him that he would have to consider at his leisure whether some pronouncement should be made by the 30th [September] so that the Bill could be let through. If the Lords once reject it, we may be in grave difficulties.[54]

As was usual with him, Baldwin felt quite worn out when he reached Aix. 'I am mentally very tired and I find my thoughts wool-gathering on my solitary walks,' he told Joan Davidson. 'My mental debility is indescribable but my qualities of heart are unaffected.' And to his younger son Windham he wrote about the same time: 'Forgive a pencil, but these foreigners never understood pens and they can't write with them themselves . . . I took a six hours tramp on Tuesday, which was a bit long for me, for I'm not in good training yet, but I did enjoy it . . . I have a deadly dose of speeches in the autumn, eight or nine, and the worst of it is one doesn't know yet whether there will be an election or not.' Windham Baldwin had recently begun to earn his own living, which prompted his father to add: 'I wish I could earn a bit now, but it is all the other way.'[55]

It was clear to most political observers that an election was bound to come fairly soon. The question was on what subject Asquith and his Liberal following would join with the Conservatives in the House of Commons division lobby and turn the Government out. Possible pretexts for such an action were certainly not wanting – Ireland, the diplomatic recognition of Soviet Russia, mounting unemployment at home. In the event it was none of these major topics which broke the brittle 'Lib.–Lab.' alliance. The adverse vote that brought down the Government followed on the action of Sir Patrick Hastings, the Attorney-General, in dropping the prosecution of John Campbell, the acting editor of the Communist *Workers' Weekly*, which had published an article appealing to members of the armed services not to fire upon their fellow-workers either in a military war or a class war. The Liberals, who suspected a sinister connection between the withdrawal of the prosecution and the projected Anglo-Soviet treaty, wanted a Select Committee to investigate the matter.

'Do you want to turn the Government out?' Stamfordham asked Baldwin at this time. 'Yes,' replied the Opposition Leader, 'but not on the Campbell issue, but on the Russian Treaties which the country generally condemns.'

Stamfordham, who had come down from Balmoral to London, saw Baldwin at 12.30 p.m. on 7 October. He subsequently reported to the King:

> He [Baldwin] considers the PM instead of smashing the extremists has allowed them to smash him. He likes and trusts the PM and has had from time to time interesting talks with him and always gathered that the PM would adopt a quiet and determined opposition to Communism believing that in five years or so it would die out: but apparently he has not carried out this policy.
>
> As to a Baldwin–Asquith combination the former said this was not now feasible, *whatever it might be after a General Election*. He hears that the Labour Party are not so very sanguine as to electoral results. If the King sent for him he could not form a Government and speaking for himself he did not see how the King could refuse a Dissolution.[56]

Baldwin was agreeable that the Labour Government should remain in office provided they accepted the Liberal suggestion of a Select Committee; but Ramsay MacDonald, whose conduct throughout the affair had been most disingenuous, refused. So the Conservatives and Liberals united shortly after 11 p.m. on 8 October to defeat his Government by 364 votes to 198.*

When he heard the result of the vote, Asquith remarked that in all his parliamentary experience, which went back fifty years, he had never known an instance where the Government of the day 'had so wantonly and unnecessarily committed suicide'. Of course, it is more than likely that MacDonald was afraid that a Select Committee would reveal that he had prevaricated by denying that he had ever authorised the withdrawal of the Campbell prosecution and consequently preferred defeat in the division lobby to exposure in the committee room.

In the event the King reluctantly granted MacDonald a dissolution. Thus the country went to the polls for the third time within two years, the King regretting that 'the appeal to the electorate cannot be made upon a more vital issue' than the Campbell case. Fortunately the Irish

* According to Middlemas and Barnes, Baldwin later asked for the Cabinet records dealing with the matter, which revealed the truth: *Baldwin*, p. 274 note.

Boundary Bill to regularise the Boundary Commission just reached the statute book before the Government fell.[57]

Baldwin had an unopposed return at Bewdley and this left him free to tour the country and in particular to concentrate on the Conservative working man in the Midlands and Lancashire. This was the first election in which the Party leaders were able to broadcast to the nation by radio, or wireless, as it was then popularly called. But whereas MacDonald allowed his speech to be transmitted direct from a mass meeting in Glasgow, thus giving the impression of a blustering demagogue, Baldwin's performance went out from the office of the Director-General of the British Broadcasting Company in Savoy Hill. He spoke quietly and effectively and quickly showed himself to be a master of the new technique. Every individual should take some interest in politics, he said, but he deplored the class warfare preached by some of his more extreme Labour opponents. 'No gospel founded on hate will ever be the gospel of our people.'[58]

The campaign as a whole went off quietly until a few days before Polling Day when there was a sudden 'Red Scare'. The Foreign Office with MacDonald's assent released the text of a letter which had come into its possession and purported to have been written from Moscow by Gregory Zinoviev, Chairman of the Third International, to the British Communist Party; it stated that it was essential to bring into the movement 'the army of unemployed', to create Communist cells among the soldiers, sailors and munition workers of Britain, and to organise risings in Ireland and the colonies. The effect of this notorious letter, which years afterwards was shown to be a forgery, may have been exaggerated, although it doubtless did influence some of the results, particularly in marginal constituencies; it certainly gave a powerful fillip to Conservative propaganda about Communist infiltration of the Labour movement. In fact, the Conservative Party managers paid £5,000 for the letter, and Conservative candidates generally, including the leader himself, thought it genuine, although at this stage Baldwin does not seem to have been aware of its somewhat dubious source and the manner in which the text had reached the Foreign Office. 'There is no doubt that the result of the election was affected by the Zinoviev Letter,' Davidson recalled many years later. 'I have no doubt that we should have got in in 1924, but we would have had a smaller majority.' In fact, the Tory majority over the two other parties combined was more than two hundred.[59]

The Liberals were largely wiped out as a parliamentary party, losing 116 seats, mainly to Conservatives, and over one million votes as compared with 1923. The principal casualty was Asquith, the Party leader, who lost to Labour at Paisley, a result which Baldwin heard 'with real regret'. In a note of sympathy which he wrote from the Travellers' Club, Baldwin assured him: 'I think you would have felt pleased if you could have heard the genuine expressions of regret and sympathy which were uttered spontaneously by typists and lift boys working in the Unionist Central Office . . . It was a simple tribute well worth hearing.' [60] It was also the end of Asquith's political career. Shortly afterwards Baldwin was to console him with a peerage and he retired to the Upper House as Earl of Oxford and Asquith. Meanwhile the once great Liberal Party was reduced to a rump of some forty members in the House of Commons under the uneasy leadership of Lloyd George and Sir John Simon. Labour, on the other hand, suffered what was to prove only a temporary setback, the Party's voting strength in the Commons being reduced from 191 to 151.

Neville Chamberlain, who contrary to the general Conservative swing in the country only managed to hold his Birmingham seat by seventy-seven after four recounts, was quick to appreciate the significance of the new parliamentary picture. 'What alarms me now is the size of our majority, which is most dangerous,' he told his sister. 'Unless we leave our mark as social reformers the country will take it out of us hereafter, but what we do will depend on how the Cabinet is made up. Poor S.B.' [61]

Neville's brother took the same view. On 31 October, after the final results had come in, Austen wrote to Baldwin: 'I am a little dazed, as you will be already thinking gravely of the great responsibilities that face you. So large a majority creates dangers of its own. I have one clear conviction which you will share. Reaction would be fatal.' [62]

Meanwhile Baldwin had gone off with Geoffrey Fry to Oare House, Fry's fine country place near Marlborough, to walk on the Wiltshire Downs and think over the composition of the next Government for which he expected to be responsible.

SEVEN

THE SECOND
TERM

I

The life of the first Labour Government was formally terminated on 4 November 1924 when Ramsay MacDonald went to Buckingham Palace and tendered his resignation as Prime Minister. Later the same day the King sent for Baldwin and entrusted him with the formation of a fresh Government. In doing so, the King urged the new Premier to get to 'really close and powerful grips' with such questions as housing, education, unemployment and the cost of food, and to select for this purpose 'able, efficient and energetic administrators'. According to Lord Stamfordham, 'the King expressed an earnest hope that the Prime Minister would restrain his followers from doing anything in the House of Commons to irritate their opponents, and even to refrain from replying to, or in any way taking notice of, attacks and recriminations which may be initiated by the Opposition'. The King added that he would welcome it personally if Austen Chamberlain were chosen for the post of Foreign Secretary.

Baldwin immediately agreed to Chamberlain's appointment. Indeed, he already had it in mind. At the same time he told the King that he had decided to ask Winston Churchill to join the Government at once. This would have to be done sooner or later, he said, and he thought 'it was better to give him office now rather than run the chance of his having a grievance and being disgruntled at being omitted'.[1]

When Curzon heard, as he quickly did, that the new Prime Minister intended to appoint Austen Chamberlain Foreign Secretary, he reacted strongly. 'I cannot believe,' he wrote to Baldwin, 'that you would put so terrible slur on my administration which was conducted amid extraordinary difficulties but not without success, in the closest and pleasantest co-operation with yourself and your predecessors. It would be too much to expect me to accept such a situation.' Nevertheless he did accept it, after Baldwin had told him that he regarded it 'as of the first importance to have the Foreign Secretary in the Commons'. At the same time Baldwin offered him the non-departmental but prestigious office of Lord President of the Council, which carried with it a seat in the Cabinet, together with the leadership of the House of Lords and the chairmanship of the Committee of Imperial Defence. At first, Curzon was inclined to refuse and retire from politics for good; he only yielded under pressure from his socially ambitious wife. But he did so without enthusiasm, as he knew that the highest place which he coveted had for ever eluded his grasp. On 6 November, he wrote to Lady Curzon: 'There is a Council tomorrow morning at which I shall preside for the first time, as in 1916, as President, and all the new Ministers will be sworn in. How unlike my last experience, when all was new and promising.'[2]

In his Cabinet making, which proceeded with great speed after he had seen the King, Baldwin's taxing problem was how best to accommodate the Coalition Conservatives who had attended the Shadow Cabinet. Austen Chamberlain was glad to take the Foreign Office and flattered that it should be combined with the deputy leadership of the House of Commons. This left Birkenhead, Horne and Worthington-Evans to be provided for. There was also Churchill, now that he had more or less worked his passage back to the Conservative Party haven. Asquith, to whom it will be recalled Baldwin had written commiserating on his defeat at Paisley, sent the Prime Minister a message through a mutual friend. 'Tell him from me that, when it comes to forming a ministry, he must be a butcher.'

The friend, who passed on this message to Baldwin, was Sir William Tyrell, the Deputy Permanent Under-Secretary at the Foreign Office. In the letter in which he did so Tyrell gave Baldwin an interesting account he had received from an anonymous informant of a dinner which had taken place on the morrow of the election at Sir Philip Sassoon's house in Park Lane, when the guests included Birkenhead, Churchill, Beaverbrook, Hoare and Lloyd-Greame.

The conversation ran on the following lines:

F.E. to Winston, 'I suppose you expect to get office?'

Winston replied, 'That will depend very much on what I am offered.'

'No,' said F.E. 'You have been hungering and thirsting for office for two years and you will take anything they offer you.'

On Winston showing resentment, F.E. proceeded to give the

company a sketch of all the tricks and subterfuges he and Winston had resorted to in order to obtain office. Beaverbrook attempted to interrupt him and by that time F.E. was carrying more than was good for him. He thereupon turned on Beaverbrook and said: 'Well, Max, you stepped fairly into the gutter in order to get office: you would have given your eyes at one time for the Board of Trade, but you preferred a peerage.'

After that there was general mudslinging, but my informant was very much struck by the outward deference paid to you and their acceptance of you as the dispenser of patronage.

Beaverbrook showed very plainly his disappointment at the size of the majority which he thinks has robbed him of his power, but he expressed a hope that the lesson you would learn from this election was the power of the Press; and he also expressed the conviction that you would be bound to give office to Winston sooner than see him become the nucleus of dissatisfaction in your own party.

My impression is that you have so many fools in your party wedded to the slogan that anybody as brilliant as Winston must be given office that it would be worth while to silence them.

If, therefore, you decide to include Winston and F.E., I do trust that your offer to them will be on the lines of 'take it or leave it'.[3]

The same day as he saw the King, Baldwin sent for Tom Jones to get his advice on how the Cabinet could best be constituted. 'He was obviously excited,' noted Jones. 'I said the wheel had come full circle much more swiftly than I had expected.'

To this remark Baldwin replied: 'For some time I felt things were shaping themselves towards the disappearance of the Liberal Party, but I did not think it would come so quickly. The next step must be the elimination of the Communists by Labour. Then we shall have two Parties, the Party of the Right and the Party of the Left.'

Baldwin then produced a foolscap list from his pocket, which looked as if it had on it all the possible offices which had to be filled. Since Jones had once been a university professor, Baldwin began: 'What I want from you is a Minister of Education.'

The Prime Minister appeared to favour Sir Cyril Cobb, a former Chairman of the London County Council. But Jones preferred Lord Eustace Percy, who had previously been Parliamentary Secretary to the Board of Education. 'He is really interested in education and has written about it.'

'Now what about Labour? I mean to put Wood in Agriculture.'

'Is Horne available?' Jones asked. 'Wood is certainly interested in Agriculture, but if Horne is not available and if Neville Chamberlain goes to the Treasury, I would put Wood in for the same reason as I would put you Prime Minister. The Labour Members will respect Wood for his character, his frankness in dealing with them, while they will hate his ideas.'

After mentioning various other posts and making a note of Jones's suggestions, Baldwin went on: 'What would you do with Winston?'

'I would certainly have him inside,' replied Jones.

'I thought of putting him in India.'

Jones was horrified by this idea. 'For heaven's sake do not do that,' he said. 'I have seen him lose his head at critical moments in the Irish business, and but for L.G.'s intervention we would have had bloodshed on the Border more than once. If you have to take drastic action in India through Winston, everyone would blame Winston, whereas he might be quite guiltless and his action entirely justified by the action in India. I would put Birkenhead in India. He has a better judgement than Winston, and it will keep him pretty well occupied.'

'But where shall I put Winston?' Baldwin repeated the question.

'Shove him in the Army or Navy; it does not matter much which. Give him the one with most work.'

'That means Derby must go,' the Prime Minister mused aloud. 'I could give "Worthy", say, the War Office, as he will want to be a Secretary of State. I am sending Amery to the Colonial Office. He is a hard worker, keen on the Colonies and on Empire Settlement. I am not sure that the Dominions have forgiven Winston for the Chanak incident, and I do not want him to go to the Colonial Office.' Jones had also suggested the latter office as a possibility for Churchill.

'We could still put Balfour on the C[ommittee of] I[mperial] D[efence],' Baldwin continued; 'and I think of sending Bob Cecil to Geneva under the F[oreign] O[ffice], with Austen as Secretary of State, though I am not very happy about that . . . I think of putting Joynson-Hicks in Health – he knows all about it.'

'Hankey says he would make a first-rate man at the Air Ministry,' countered Jones. 'He once wrote a classic memorandum on the Air.'

'Trenchard* wants Hoare to go there.'

'What are you going to do about the Home Office?'

'I will make no change there,' Baldwin replied. 'I will keep on Willy Bridgeman.'[4]

* Sir Hugh Trenchard, later Viscount Trenchard, was Chief of the Air Staff.

In the event, Austen Chamberlain, Birkenhead, Amery, Cecil, Hoare, Eustace Percy and Worthington-Evans went to the offices which the Prime Minister had earmarked for them in the course of his conversation with Jones. The disposition of the other offices mentioned was largely determined by the actions of Horne and Neville Chamberlain.

Sir Robert Stevenson Horne, later Viscount Horne of Slamannan, was a fifty-three-year-old Scottish lawyer, who had entered politics as a Conservative after a successful career at the Scottish Bar. During the war he had favourably impressed Lloyd George by his work as a temporary civil servant at the Admiralty, with the result that when he came to form his government after the 1918 election Lloyd George appointed him Minister of Labour; hence Horne had the unusual experience of making his maiden speech from the Government Front Bench. A year later he joined the Cabinet as President of the Board of Trade, where he was Baldwin's immediate predecessor, before going to the Treasury as Chancellor in 1921. On the fall of the Coalition he had remained faithful to Lloyd George and had gone into the political wilderness along with Austen Chamberlain and Birkenhead. At the same time he accepted a number of company directorships. Although invited by Baldwin to return to the Treasury in May 1923, he had refused to do so, since Baldwin could not accommodate Austen Chamberlain in the Cabinet at the same time. When Labour was in office, he did agree to be a member of the Conservative Shadow Cabinet, but his attendances were not as frequent as those of his colleagues due to the increasing demands of his business interests. As a bachelor he was much in demand by London hostesses, since he was usually excellent company. Besides this he was a lively *raconteur*; he was also something of a *bon viveur* and like Birkenhead was often to be seen at places like the Embassy Club drinking champagne with good-looking women. Baldwin once remarked when he was staying at Trent Park, Sir Philip Sassoon's place in Hertfordshire: 'I can't help it, but the powder puffs in the bathroom here always remind me of Horne.' His friend Birkenhead's opinion was rather more flattering. 'Sir Robert Horne, in a word, has contributed much to the liveliness, to the charm, and to the good humour of English political life in dark and lowering days when those who could offer these gifts have been rare and shining figures.' [5]

As one of the leading Conservative Coalitionists, whom Baldwin was anxious to include in his new administration, Horne was an obvious choice as Chancellor, since he had previously held the post with some distinction. However, Baldwin wanted Neville Chamberlain back at the Treasury, and so he wrote to Horne offering him the Ministry of Labour, but without saying anything about raising either the status or salary of the office, thus failing to make it clear whether it carried Cabinet rank. 'You have cut an old friend to the quick,' Austen Chamberlain remonstrated with Baldwin afterwards. 'You will remember that the first reason you gave me for not offering Horne the Treasury was that you wanted Neville there. I told you that Horne would accept the Treasury and that I did not think he would take Labour, whilst Neville would gladly go to Health if Horne went to Exchequer. I am afraid my opinion carries no weight with you.' [6]

2

'After our crushing victory,' Davidson wrote in his draft memoirs, 'Baldwin emerged with the necessary strength to take the essential but very bold step of reuniting the Conservative Party. In so doing he alienated several of those who had stood by Bonar and now looked to Baldwin for office, nor did he erase from the minds of the former Coalitionists the memory of their defeat in the Carlton Club. They really did believe that they were indispensable, and were confirmed in that view when Baldwin invited them to join his Government. The atmosphere was not particularly pleasant . . .'

Baldwin had not heard from Horne when Neville Chamberlain called upon the Prime Minister, at the latter's request, at Conservative Headquarters where Baldwin spent most of 5 November putting the finishing touches to his ministry.

'Needless to say, I want you to go back to the Treasury,' the Prime Minister began after Neville had been shown in. Neville made no comment, and Baldwin went on to say that he had offered Horne the Ministry of Labour and was awaiting his reply. At this moment a letter was brought in which turned out to be from Horne. Baldwin read it and said: 'He won't take it.' In his letter Horne carefully chose the phrase 'personal circumstances' to indicate that his refusal was not due to his business commitments. As he told Austen Chamberlain, he 'would not be forced upon a man who did not want him'.

Later in the course of the conversation Churchill's name came up, and Baldwin told Neville that he had decided to take him in at once. 'He would be more under control inside than out,' he remarked, adding that he had thought of making him Minister of Health. According to Neville, Baldwin then asked him what he would like, and Neville replied that he had given the matter full consideration and would like to go back to Health himself, since this included responsibility for housing in which he had a particular interest.

'But who then could be Chancellor?' Baldwin asked.

After Neville had suggested Hoare, and Baldwin had turned this down, what happened was described by Neville in his diary:

> He mentioned Winston but said he supposed there would be a howl from the party. I said I thought there would but that would be so if he came in at all, and I did not know if it would be much louder if he went to the Treasury than to the Admiralty. On the whole I was inclined to say that W[inston Churchill] for the Treasury was worth further consideration.
>
> We then discussed a good many other posts and I suggested Steel-Maitland for Labour and the Duchess of Atholl as Under-Secretary for Education. Both these suggestions seemed to appeal to him. Presently he said he had another visitor.[7]

Baldwin did not say who the next visitor was, but on his way out Neville immediately discovered his identity when he recognised one of Churchill's unmistakable hats in the waiting-room. Apparently Churchill was shown into Baldwin's room by another entrance so that he should not encounter Neville Chamberlain.

The Prime Minister immediately asked Churchill if he would serve as Chancellor. According to Baldwin's official biographer G. M. Young, Churchill thought he was being offered the Chancellorship of the Duchy of Lancaster. When he realised that it was the Exchequer that the Prime Minister had in mind, Churchill was completely taken aback and showed it by his emotion. Tears came into his eyes, as he stammered his acceptance of Baldwin's surprising offer. He thereupon pledged his loyalty, adding: 'You have done more for me than Lloyd George ever did.'[8]

It has been suggested that Baldwin's interviews with Neville Chamberlain and Churchill were part of a deliberately stage-managed drama and that Baldwin intended all along to send Churchill to the Treasury, since he had already been told by Austen Chamberlain that his brother would like to go back to Health and Housing. ('I ought to be a great Minister of Health,' Neville remarked at this time, 'but am not likely to be more than a second-rate Chancellor.') According to Tom Jones, who spent the following week-end at Chequers, Baldwin told him (Jones) that the idea of making Churchill Chancellor originated with Neville Chamberlain. Whatever the truth of the matter may be – and it is not of great importance – the appointment was a clever move on Baldwin's part. It seems to have been made pretty nearly on the spur of the moment.

'No wonder therefore that the Chief Whip whom Churchill came across as he left the Prime Minister's room was overwhelmed when he heard the news which Churchill had assumed could be no news to him,' wrote C. P. Scott of the *Manchester Guardian*, who claimed to have got the story from Mrs Churchill. 'Horne was the obvious man or, failing him, Neville Chamberlain. But Baldwin was angry with Horne, according to Mrs Churchill, for refusing to take the Chancellorship when he was in difficulties in forming his first Government and had been further annoyed by a memorial from a number of Tory members protesting against Churchill's appointment to any office at all. No one was more surprised than Churchill himself.'[9]

Baldwin afterwards justified Churchill's appointment to Tom Jones in these terms:

> My feeling was that the Treasury officials in the old days used to tell me that they believed Winston would make a good Chancellor. Then it would be a good thing to keep him fully occupied with finance, which should not bring him very much into direct contact with Labour. Had he been at Housing he would constantly be in danger of getting at loggerheads with them. Lastly, having decided to bring him into the Cabinet, to give him the Chancellorship would be bound to remove every possible personal grievance. It would be up to him to be loyal if he is capable of loyalty.[10]

'I am alarmed at the news that you have made Winston Chancellor,' Austen Chamberlain wrote to the Prime Minister, 'not because I do not wish Winston well but because I fear that this particular appointment will be a great shock to the Party.' However, younger Conservatives like John Davidson welcomed it. 'Winston's appointment is genius,' he wrote to Baldwin. 'You have hamstrung him, so that his hairy heels are paralysed. He will do all right.' As has been seen, the appointment surprised Churchill himself as much as anyone, and it took him some days to get accustomed to it. 'I have been reflecting deeply upon the very great duties you have entrusted to me,' he told the Prime Minister.[11]

Then there was Birkenhead. 'I should not, of course, refuse the Woolsack if it were offered to me,' he remarked at this time; 'but I have made it plain that I am not desirous of exposing Baldwin to the embarrassment of dismissing Cave.'[12] In the event, according to the Prime Minister, he was 'very pleased' to go to the India Office. 'He said he had a sharp tongue and had said bitter things about me. He hoped that was past. He would help all he could, and if any action of his hurt me in future he hoped I would tell him so, have it out, and be done with it.'

The appointment which probably attracted most adverse criticism was that of the donnish Sir Arthur Steel-Maitland as Minister of Labour. 'Yes, I know,' Baldwin told Jones. 'I have been thinking of that post for eighteen months. At the end I had about ten minutes in which to decide, as Horne had refused. Neville recommended Steel-Maitland. He is able enough – got all those Firsts at Oxford – but is he human enough? He would have done better at the Board of Trade. He will do well in administering the Office, but I am frankly afraid of him in the House.' 13 *

Austen Chamberlain did not share his brother's opinion of Steel-Maitland's capabilities as appears from what he wrote to his sister Hilda after the Cabinet appointments had been announced:

Twitt's Ghyll. 9 November 1924. Setting aside the exclusion of Horne, which is not only a great grief but a great loss to me, and with the exception of Labour I think all the Ministries adequate and some of them exceptionally well filled. Health [Neville Chamberlain], India [Birkenhead], Exchequer [Churchill], and Agriculture [Wood] are the ones I class as exceptionally well filled. Hoare very good at Air, Bridgeman and Worthy [Worthington-Evans] adequate at Admiralty and War Office (tho' the latter appointment will not be liked in the Office for he was born a bit of a bounder and will always remain so). Jack Gilmour obviously the right man for the Scottish Office and Jicks [Joynson-Hicks] probably equal to the Home Office, though Hogg would have been a much stronger appointment.

Only Labour is a thoroughly bad appointment. I wish S.B. had asked some wise Civil Servant whether the service thought him a good administrator or the kind of man who would make a good chief in a critically important office! The odds are that either S.B. will out S[teel]-Maitland or S.-M. will out us all before long.

Besides four Cabinet Ministers from Birmingham and no one from Lancashire! That is asking for trouble, and S.B. hadn't enough

---

* Steel-Maitland, who was MP for East Birmingham, got a Triple First at Oxford (Mods, Greats and Law) and was elected a Fellow of All Souls; he also rowed for the university against Cambridge and was President of the Union. He held junior office between 1915 and 1919 but was not included by Lloyd George in his second Government, whereupon he joined the Board of the Rio Tinto Company, eventually becoming Managing Director and resigning to become Minister of Labour in 1924. As Baldwin had anticipated, he was not a success in the House of Commons, being too academic for the general liking.

places to go round and S.-M. was so comfortably on the shelf whence no one else would have thought of taking him down. And S.B.'s way of doing things, as apart from the things done, has bitterly wounded Horne who was a real friend of his as well as of mine, and in a lesser but sensible degree hurt Derby.*

I have not had the smallest influence on any of his appointments except the inclusion of Fred [Birkenhead] and have been left entirely in the dark about them till I heard Club gossip or read them in the press.

Although the King gave his formal approval to the Cabinet appointments, as he was constitutionally obliged to do, he complained that he had not been consulted by Baldwin in advance, particularly about those of Churchill and Steel-Maitland which he told Baldwin through his Private Secretary he had been 'astonished' to read of in an evening newspaper. His Majesty also shared Austen Chamberlain's feelings for Hogg in preference to Joynson-Hicks, and he instructed Stamfordham to write to the Prime Minister in this sense, which he did.

The King wishes that time could have permitted him and you to discuss your various selections before the offers had been made for their respective posts. His Majesty is sorry that you have not been able to appoint Sir Douglas Hogg to the Home Office, where in these times the not only possible but probable difficulties in the internal government of the country necessitate an exceptionally able and strong administrator and one who has held a pre-eminent position at the Bar. The fact also that the Home Secretary is the King's Principal Secretary of State and in fact constitutionally His Majesty's Private Secretary is a reason, though a minor one, for the King's special interest in the appointment.[14]

The week-end during which Austen Chamberlain wrote from his Sussex cottage, Baldwin was at Chequers with his wife and daughter

* 'I have received quite a nice letter from Baldwin explaining why he did not offer me any post,' Derby wrote to Austen Chamberlain on 8 November 1924. 'About that I have absolutely no feeling . . . But I do think Baldwin might have written to me sooner. The papers are still saying that I was offered a post and refused it. I have had to contradict that and this would not have been necessary if he had only just written me the letter he has now written me before he announced his Government instead of after, and I cannot help feeling that he treated me somewhat discourteously.' Chamberlain Papers AC 35/5/6. Baldwin's letter, saying he was making Derby's brother George a junior minister and his son Edward an Assistant Whip is printed in Churchill, *Lord Derby*, p. 576. Derby's reaction was to express disappointment 'that my brother should have been preferred to my son'.

Betty, the first time since his resignation the previous January. The only outside guest was Tom Jones, who came down primarily to discuss the agenda for the first Cabinet which had been fixed for 12 November. On this occasion, Baldwin told Jones that he had very much on his mind the question of himself introducing a short Bill in Parliament to provide Prime Ministers with pensions when they went out of office. 'He would, of course, exclude himself from the operation of the Bill,' Jones noted, 'but he was very anxious to prevent in future what had happened to Asquith, L.G., and MacDonald – Mrs Asquith having to go on a lecturing tour to the States, L.G. writing for the Hearst Press, and MacDonald taking £30,000 from Sir Alexander Grant.'

Baldwin was delighted to be back at Chequers. 'The spell of the wonderful house is more potent than ever,' he wrote to Lord Lee, 'and I give thanks for the spirit that made you both make that glorious offering. More and more do I respect those who can give things that do cost them something in their lifetime. It is not common.' Looking through the Visitors' Book, Baldwin saw that Ramsay MacDonald had recorded: 'Farewell to this house of comforting and regenerating rest,' when he left on the previous week-end. 'I am sure Ramsay is very sore at having to give up Chequers, I must write to him,' Baldwin remarked to Jones. 'I was very curious to find out what parties had been down with him here, and it is very interesting to find from the Visitors' Book that he has not had a single colleague here.'[15]

Baldwin can hardly have failed to notice that apart from the MacDonald family circle the first visitor whose name appeared in the book, after the Labour Prime Minister had taken possession of Chequers, was not a member of his own Party but the aristocratic and wealthy Conservative Marquess of Londonderry who had been invited there with his wife in February. It must have appeared odd to Baldwin, as it did to Beatrice Webb, that his Socialist predecessor, who might have been expected to be opposed to everything socially and politically that the Londonderrys represented, should have chosen to entertain them in this way. Beatrice Webb complained that MacDonald 'did not ask any of his most important Cabinet colleagues to stay at Chequers but did invite society *"grandes dames"* including Lady Londonderry'. Mrs Webb's husband Sidney who had been created Lord Passfield so as to enable him to be a Labour spokesman in the Upper House – she refused to use the title – was one of the Cabinet colleagues thus ignored. Indeed Mrs Webb thought that Lord Lee would have done better to give Chequers to the nation as a home for children or for scholars and impecunious teachers. 'Ought there to be such places as Chequers?' she asked. 'These places would not have arisen unless there had been a class of persons with the wealth and the leisure to create them.'

Lord Haldane, who had been Leader of the House of Lords in the MacDonald Government, resented it even more than his colleague Passfield that he had never been invited to Chequers. Afterwards he was to write in his autobiography with both Baldwin and MacDonald in mind:

When this generous gift [Chequers] was announced in the House of Lords, I rose and shook my head and prophesied that it would prove a dangerous temptation. Prime Ministers who had sprung from the middle classes and are attracted by the pleasures of a country house life to which they are not accustomed are apt to be unduly drawn there. The result is that they lose two days, in each week, in which they ought to be seeing their colleagues and having at least a few of them for a talk on the Saturday and Sunday evenings. It is consequently very difficult for a colleague to see his Chief at the only times when the latter is readily available. This difficulty has not been confined to the case of Ramsay MacDonald. But with him it proved a damaging obstacle.[16]

It is uncertain whether Mrs Webb, or Baldwin for that matter, was aware of the reason for the invitation to the Londonderrys. A short time before, the King and Queen had given a dinner at Buckingham Palace to which MacDonald and most of the members of the Government were asked together with a number of other guests who included Lord and Lady Londonderry. At dinner the Labour Premier was placed between Queen Mary and Lady Londonderry, MacDonald being on the Queen's left and Haldane on her right. On this occasion Ramsay MacDonald and Lady Londonderry took to each other at once, finding a common bond in the Scottish Highlands and Celtic folk lore to which they were both devoted. The invitation to Chequers naturally followed from this meeting, and as will be seen a close and even intimate friendship was to develop between MacDonald and Lady Londonderry with unfortunate results for both in the long term, as well as for Londonderry himself.

At this time, the forty-six-year-old Marquess was Minister of Education in the Government of Northern Ireland, but his coal-mining interests in County Durham frequently brought him to England as well as his wife's activities as a leading London hostess. Lady Londonderry, who was ambitious for her husband, hoped that he might eventually become an English Cabinet minister, and she worked hard to this end. No doubt she encouraged him to write to Baldwin as he did on the morrow of the Conservative victory at the polls in the autumn of 1924:

> We have a desperate struggle before us in the next few years and I am proposing to devote a great deal of my time to defeating the Socialist menace in one of the reddest portions of the kingdom [Co. Durham].
>
> I am glad we did so well over the country. It was a great Conservative victory in which your attitude and speeches played the leading part assisted only in a small degree by the follies and ineptitude of our opponents.
>
> The country from every point of view wants a Conservative administration and we have a great opportunity.[17]

All twenty-one members were present at the first meeting of the new Cabinet with Baldwin in his place in the middle of the table below the portrait of Sir Robert Walpole. Besides confirming the procedure for keeping the minutes and recording the 'conclusions', which had been initiated by Bonar Law, the principal decision was the appointment of a small Cabinet committee to examine the authenticity or otherwise of the Zinoviev letter, under the chairmanship of Austen Chamberlain, with Curzon, Birkenhead and Cecil as the other members. Generally the Prime Minister followed the pattern which had emerged in his first ministry. In the words of a newcomer, Lord Eustace Percy, 'he was content to act as an indulgent chairman, letting its members have their head but rarely giving them a lead. The odd thing is that, nevertheless, it was, from first to last, unmistakably a Baldwin Cabinet.'[18]*

'It is of course a tragedy that so great an army should have so uninspiring a Commander-in-Chief,' Birkenhead confessed to a friend at the outset of Baldwin's second administration. 'But this cannot be helped; and I think he will be well under control. The temper of the new elements in the House of Commons is by no means diehard.'[19]† Within

---

* Initially it consisted of Curzon (Lord President), Cave (Lord Chancellor), Salisbury (Lord Privy Seal), Churchill (Exchequer), Austen Chamberlain (Foreign Office), Joynson-Hicks (Home Office), Bridgeman (Admiralty), Worthington-Evans (War Office), Amery (Colonies), Hoare (Air), Wood (Agriculture), Percy (Education), Birkenhead (India), Neville Chamberlain (Health), Steel-Maitland (Labour), Cecil (Duchy of Lancaster), Gilmour (Scottish Office), Lloyd-Greame (Trade), Peel (Works) and Hogg (Attorney-General). In 1925 Balfour and W. Guinness succeeded Curzon and Wood respectively; in 1927, McNeill (Cushendun) succeeded Cecil; and in 1928, Hogg (Hailsham), Peel and Londonderry succeeded Cave, Birkenhead and Peel respectively.

† The recipient of Birkenhead's letter showed it to the eccentric millionairess philanthropist Lady Houston, who made a copy of it which she sent to the Prime Minister. 'Birkenhead's

a few months, such was Baldwin's skill as a political catalyst, Birkenhead was almost eating out of his hand; and when he eventually left politics for the City, he admitted that the moment of parting was sad. 'Your own personality,' he wrote to Baldwin, 'has converted a Cabinet, which assembled upon the crater of some bitter and recent memories, into a band of brothers. I leave them and you with emotion, and if I may be allowed to say so, with affection.' [20]

In his sensitive and thoughtful autobiography, Eustace Percy, who at thirty-seven was the youngest member of the Cabinet, has accurately described the task which Baldwin set himself at the outset of his second term, both at home and abroad, as stabilisation and settlement, or in Baldwin's own words written long afterwards as 'the healing of the nation'.

> To that end Baldwin had succeeded in reuniting his party in a Cabinet some of whose most experienced members had bitterly resented, and indeed despised, the part he had played in the previous two years. The achievement should not be underrated; Birkenhead, who had perhaps felt more resentment and contempt than the others, paid a touching tribute to it in his brief farewell to the Cabinet at the end of 1928. And if no one but Baldwin could have achieved the initial reconciliation, he alone, I think, could have held this mixed company together in such good-feeling for nearly five years, by his curious gift of unobtrusive moral authority.
>
> This reunion gave him, on the whole, an effective administrative team, including, in the two Chamberlains, at least two colleagues on whom he could rely for the initiation and execution of large, if cautious, policies, abroad and at home. He supported both, loyally and, on the whole, understandingly; and his support contributed more, probably, to their very solid achievements than any attempt he could have made to alloy their policies with bright ideas of his own, in the Lloyd George manner. [21]

Among the hundreds of letters of congratulation which Baldwin received on his return to Downing Street in November 1924 was one from a ten-year-old boy in Canada, who was also called Stanley Baldwin. 'Dear Namesake,' the Prime Minister personally replied to him, 'I am glad you wrote to me and don't ever forget that you have got a name worth taking care of when you grow up. I will try and not let it down

---

ambition is to oust you and become PM himself,' she wrote in a covering letter. 'Of course the country would never have him.' Baldwin Papers 159 f. 221.

so long as I bear it and you do the same after my work is finished. Good luck to you.' [22]

A few weeks later Baldwin returned to his native Worcestershire to receive a silver casket containing a congratulatory address from the townspeople of Stourport and Wilden. He chose the occasion of the ceremony at Stourport to make a simple declaration of his political faith. He remarked that for twenty years he had worked with all classes of people and enjoyed the goodwill which he had inherited from previous generations of his family who had 'left behind a name for honesty, fair play, right judgement, and kindliness to those with whom they worked'.

> There is only one thing which I feel is worth giving one's whole strength to, and that is the binding together of all classes of our people in an effort to make life in this country better in every sense of the word. That is the main end and object of my life in politics.

3

Baldwin's return to Downing Street was marked by the resumption of his former intimate relations with Tom Jones, the Deputy Secretary of the Cabinet, particularly in the role of speech writer. On the first occasion that he sent for him the Prime Minister asked him for material for a speech he had to make to the London School Teachers. 'So many of the teachers are tinged with Bolshevism – so many cranks about,' he observed; 'perhaps you could say something about that, and I will talk about my old school days.' That was the sum total of his instructions, Jones noted at the time; nevertheless he was able to produce a suitable oration as he was to do on numerous other occasions. Jones took the opportunity of expressing his satisfaction that the Prime Minister was 'showing so much more confidence in himself', as evidenced by the first two Cabinet meetings over which he had presided. Baldwin thereupon read out a letter which he had received from a banker, presumably Montagu Norman, 'congratulating S.B. on putting Winston in the Treasury and denouncing Horne for allowing personal interests to come between him and service of the State'. At their next meeting, a few days later, Baldwin spoke of Beaverbrook, 'whose spectre is never far from S.B.'s mind', in the context of the premature death of Edwin Montagu which had just occurred at the age of forty-five; it will be recalled that Baldwin had been considered as his successor at the India Office after Montagu had been dismissed by Lloyd George in 1921. 'Beaverbrook

had just come back from Edwin Montagu's funeral in the same coach as
Winston. Winston was much moved at the loss of an old friend and
colleague, but Beaverbrook was utterly callous and could only retail
sordid gossip of old intrigues.' [23]

The influence of the Coalition Conservatives in the Cabinet, particularly Churchill and Birkenhead, became apparent on the occasion of the
first political crisis which occurred during the period of the second
Baldwin Government. This was over Egypt. Since 1922, Egypt had
ceased to be a British protectorate and had become a sovereign state
under King Fuad, the former Sultan, although the Egyptian army continued to be commanded by a British general. At this time the Sirdar, as
the commander-in-chief was called, was Sir Lee Stack, who also acted
as Governor-General of the Sudan. On 15 November 1924, Stack was
murdered in a Cairo street by an Arab nationalist. Without waiting for
instructions from London, Field-Marshal Lord Allenby, the High
Commissioner, immediately handed the Egyptian Government an ultimatum demanding an apology, an indemnity of half a million pounds
and unlimited extension of irrigation for the benefit of the Sudan. These
demands were presented by Allenby in person, who appeared in a
lounge suit to the accompaniment of an impressive escort of cavalry.

The news of this *démarche* reached London on the following Saturday
afternoon while Baldwin was at Chequers and most of the Cabinet had
likewise departed for the week-end. Tom Jones was on the point of
leaving the Cabinet offices to go home shortly before five, when he was
rung up by the Foreign Office and asked to summon an immediate
Cabinet to discuss Allenby's action. 'We telephoned furiously all over
the town,' noted Jones, and as a result six ministers arrived an hour
later at the Foreign Office where the meeting was held in Austen
Chamberlain's room; besides Chamberlain they comprised Birkenhead,
Churchill, Amery, Steel-Maitland, Lloyd-Greame and Hogg. (Amery was
actually fetched out of a Turkish bath.) By the time they had assembled
the Foreign Secretary had drafted a telegram which he read out in terms
severely reprimanding Allenby, whose behaviour he described as 'very
like the action of the little boy who puts his thumb to his nose and extends
four fingers in a vulgar expression of defiance or contempt'.

The outcome of the meeting was recorded by Jones in his diary later
the same evening:

The telegram would not only castigate Allenby but would request
that he should substitute a fresh series of demands in place of those
which he had submitted to the Egyptian Government. Birkenhead

at once pointed out the gravity of this procedure. Allenby would be certain to resign, which would be very awkward in the midst of the crisis, and, though we might ask him to stay on, it would become known and would greatly weaken our prestige with the natives.

Amery took the opposite view and was all for strong action, whatever the consequences. The others were hesitant until Winston arrived. He put Birkenhead's points with great eloquence, and swung everybody round to support the man on the spot – except Amery. Austen himself confessed that he had been persuaded, and he got on the telephone to the PM at Chequers and put the position reached by the meeting. The PM, of course agreed, and I think we have turned a very nasty corner.[24]*

Baldwin was always more interested in the domestic than the foreign front and he was content to leave the latter largely in the hands of the Foreign Secretary so that he himself could concentrate on what he called the need for a stable united front at home. When he became Prime Minister for the second time, there were still over a million unemployed and exports were continuing to fall. More than half the total population were town-dwellers. As a countryman, Baldwin was concerned at the manner in which the agricultural community was steadily decreasing. As he pointed out to Tom Jones in discussing one of his speeches, there were far fewer people living in the country all the year round, since many former landowners had been squeezed out by the death duties imposed by successive Liberal governments whose Free Trade elements had always been opposed to the landed interest. Baldwin accepted the change and far from seeking to put back the clock he encouraged Neville Chamberlain in the massive programme of social reforms of the type which the Conservatives had bitterly opposed barely two decades before. These reforms in health, housing and local government, subsequently embodied in legislation and providing for such needs as widows' and old age pensions and increased national insurance, were the hallmarks of the new Conservatism which the Prime Minister warmly endorsed.[25]

His own particular interest, as might be expected from his background, lay in the sphere of industrial relations. During the early months of his ministry he persuaded the Cabinet – the only occasion on which

* 'I believe we should have followed Joseph Chamberlain's action over the Jameson Raid,' Amery afterwards wrote, 'and disavowed Allenby rather than create grounds for any suspicion that we were eager to seize an opportunity for inflicting permanent injury on Egypt. As it was the correspondence that followed, aggravated by the appointment of Neville Henderson as Minister attached to Allenby, bitterly offended Allenby and led to his eventual resignation . . .' L. S. Amery, *My Political Life*, II, p. 305.

he used his influence in this manner – to withhold support from a Conservative Private Member's Bill which was designed to alter the basis of the trade union political levy. Since 1913, trade unions had been allowed to raise a levy from their members for political purposes such as the support of the Labour Party. Members could contract out, if they wished, but in practice this meant that many trade unionists who were not particularly enamoured of the Labour Party paid up rather than draw attention to themselves by contracting out. The bill, which was introduced by a Scottish Conservative backbench lawyer, Frederick Macquisten, who had previously attempted without success to make female homosexual practices criminal, proposed to reverse the procedure by obliging all trade unionists desiring to pay the political levy henceforth to contract in.

He would intervene at an early stage in the debate on the second reading, the Prime Minister told the Cabinet on the previous evening, when he summoned a meeting in his room in the House of Commons. He would impress on the House, he said,

> that one of the main principles of the Government's policy is to do everything possible to promote peace in the industrial world. While making clear that the Government believed the present system of levying contributions from Trade Unions for political purposes was unjust and wrong, they were not prepared at the present time to bring their great majority to bear in support of a measure which must inevitably have the effect of arousing acute controversy and embittering relations among those who alone were in a position to bring about the desired pacification.

According to Edward Wood, who was present, no one said anything for some moments. The silence was finally broken by Birkenhead who observed that 'if the Prime Minister could say to the House tomorrow what he had now said to the Cabinet, he thought that the speech would be made with the unanimous support of the Cabinet, and would carry conviction to the House'. At the same time, Birkenhead picked up a House of Commons envelope which was lying on the table in front of him and wrote a few words on it which he passed across to the Prime Minister:

> I think your action shows enormous courage and for that reason will succeed.[26]

Birkenhead's prediction was abundantly fulfilled next evening (6

March 1925), when the Prime Minister moved an amendment to Macquisten's Bill to the effect that 'a measure of such far-reaching importance should not be introduced as a Private Member's Bill'. His speech on the theme of peace in industry, which he concluded by quoting a well-known prayer from the Anglican liturgy, was generally hailed as a masterpiece of parliamentary eloquence, even forming the subject of a laudatory article in the *New York Times*. In his old age, Baldwin would look back upon it with more satisfaction than any other speech he had made anywhere. 'I remember the occasion so well,' the Clydeside Labour MP David Kirkwood long afterwards reminded him, 'because we on our side of the House were on the edge of our nerves and mighty gritty when you began. Yet in a few minutes you were speaking to a House quiet through interest and appreciation. It is one of the few occasions in my experience in which the word has become flesh . . . that the antagonism, the bitterness, the class rivalry were unworthy, and that understanding and amity were possible.'

Some of the earlier passages in the speech, in which he described his own experiences as an employer of labour in his family ironworks, where strikes and lock-outs were unknown, have already been quoted. He went on to appeal for a close partnership between both sides of industry, 'learning to understand each other and not to fight each other'. He concluded on a personal note:

> For two years past, in the face of great difficulties . . . I have striven to consolidate and to breathe a living force into my great Party . . . I want my Party today to make a gesture to the country [of peace] and to say to them: 'We have our majority; we believe in the justice of the Bill which has been brought in today, but we are going to withdraw our hand, and we are not going to push our political advantage home at a time like this. Suspicion which has prevented stability in Europe is the one poison which is preventing stability at home, and we offer the country today this. We, at any rate, are not going to fire the first shot. We stand for peace. We stand for the removal of suspicion in the country. We want to create an atmosphere, a new atmosphere in a new Parliament for a new age, in which the people can come together . . .'
>
> I know – I am as confident as I can be of anything – that that will be the feeling of all those who sit behind me, and that they will accept the Amendment which I have put down in the spirit in which I have moved it. And I have equal confidence in my fellow-countrymen throughout the whole of Great Britain.

Although I know that there are those who work for different ends from most of us in this House, yet there are many in all ranks and all parties who will re-echo my prayer.

'*Give peace in our time, O Lord.*' [27]

'He has won the leadership for years to come,' was the opinion of a shrewd parliamentary lobby observer. Looking back in old age, Davidson considered the peroration one of the most moving he had ever listened to.

Among the letters which Baldwin received on this occasion was one from Curzon written in bed on the eve of a major operation. 'Let me congratulate you on your wonderful speech,' wrote the ailing Lord President. 'It was a sure instinct that persuaded you to make it: and the reception it met with must be as welcome to you as it was delightful to your colleagues.' It was Curzon's last letter to the Prime Minister. Less than a fortnight later he was dead.

The last Cabinet which Curzon attended was on 4 March when he spoke out strongly against the German proposal which Austen Chamberlain favoured that Germany's western frontier with France should be guaranteed by a Four-Power Pact, since the military commitment involved would not be in the British interest, although he was agreeable to a non-aggression pact. Curzon's line was backed by Churchill, Birkenhead and Amery and nearly led to Chamberlain's resignation, only averted by a soothing letter from Baldwin to the Foreign Secretary in Geneva. ('It is a terribly trying time for you . . . We have immense difficulties ahead: I only state this as a fact – we must recognise them. But we will win through.') Opposition to the proposed pact subsided with Curzon's death. Chamberlain remained at the Foreign Office, and as will be seen the idea of the guarantee with some modifications was eventually embodied in the Treaty of Locarno. [28]

The customary tributes were paid by the Party leaders in Parliament to the departed statesman. Baldwin concluded his with these words:

A Prime Minister sees human nature bared to the bone, and it was my chance to see him twice when he suffered great disappointment – the time when I was preferred to him as Prime Minister, and the time when I had to tell him that he could render greater service to the country as Chairman of the Committee of Imperial Defence than in the Foreign Office. Each of those occasions was a profound and bitter disappointment to him, but never for one moment when he had faced the facts did he show by word, look or innuendo, or by any reference to the subject afterwards, that he was dissatisfied. He bore no grudge, and he pursued no other course than the one I expected of him, of doing his duty where it was decided that he could best render service.

I felt on both those occasions that I had seen in him, in that strange alloy which we call human nature, a vein of the purest gold. He died as he would have desired, and as we should all desire to die, in harness, a harness put on himself in youth and worn triumphantly through a long life, a harness which he never cast off until his feet had entered the river. It may well be when we look back on that life of devoted service to his country, and of a perpetual triumph of the spirit over the flesh, that in some places on this earth, early on that Friday morning, may have been heard the faint echoes of the trumpets that sounded for him on the other side.[29]

4

A few weeks later, the trumpets sounded again, this time for one whose loss Baldwin mourned most deeply, who died at Wilden on 16 May 1925 just short of eighty. Early in the year his mother had influenza and thereafter she seldom left her bed. Hurrying to Wilden the day before his great political levy speech, Baldwin thought he had seen her for the last time. 'They expect complete unconsciousness before long, and a painless end when the heart will just cease to beat.' And this was how it happened. Yet right up to her last illness she had been wonderfully well, still writing verses as busily as ever, one of them, on the subject of 'Our Happy Dead', having been printed in the *Morning Post* on Armistice Day. In her old age she was sustained by an extraordinary sense of inner happiness. Rudyard Kipling who saw her at Christmas reported that 'Louie is about as utterly happy as any woman can be; and, I believe, felicity is an antiseptic against all decays. Certainly no part or fraction of her mind has felt time in the least. She is as quick – as the girl that she really is!'

Her son never failed to write to her regularly, particularly on anniversaries, and she would respond in kind. 'You have been a joy and comfort to me all your life, as you were to your dear father for forty years, and we love you and thank you for it,' she wrote to him on his fifty-seventh birthday in 1924. 'And you have inflated your mother with pride of many kinds on your account, all of which I hope and believe your father knows about as well as myself . . . I have seen you both in immense prosperity of all kinds, and in comparative adversity *pro tem*, and God has been with you in both and is with you now, and that surely is the only thing that really matters . . .'[30]

At Baldwin's suggestion, the poet and literary critic J. W. Mackail, who had married the Premier's cousin Margaret Burne-Jones, wrote a sensitive obituary appreciation which appeared anonymously in *The Times*. The day before the funeral, for which he went down to Wilden, Baldwin had an engagement to unveil the memorial known as 'Rima' by the sculptor Jacob Epstein to the writer and field naturalist W. H. Hudson in Hyde Park. Rather than disappoint the committee headed by Hudson's friend and fellow-writer R. B. Cunninghame Graham, who had commissioned the work, by excusing himself when he might well have done, the Prime Minister chose to go through with the ceremony on that May morning, an action described by Cunninghame Graham as 'a heroic thing', seeing that his mother had just died and was still unburied.

One generally unknown fact about Hudson, to which Baldwin was able to refer in his speech, thanks to Tom Jones's researches, was that at the turn of the century when Hudson was still extremely poor he had been granted a small Civil List pension of £150 by Balfour at the suggestion of Lord Grey. Then, some years later, as Baldwin put it, 'when his wife died and his meagre income was minutely supplemented, he surrendered that pension at his own desire and in spite of the protests of those administering it, because he felt he could do without it and that, infinitesimal as the relief would be, he did not wish to let another grain of sand add to the weight of the already overburdened taxpayers of the country'.

'He it was who made familiar to thousands the hidden beauties of our southern counties,' Baldwin went on. 'He taught Londoners who had never heard of them the names of places like Whitesheet Hill, Chilmark, Swallowcliffe and Fonthill Bishop – names of beauty and romance which always fill me with profound gratitude that the names of flowers, of villages, of stars and birds, were given in those dark centuries, long before our people were educated and had the advantage of cheap literature and a popular Press.' Finally, he said:

There are three classes which need sanctuary more than others: birds, wild flowers and Prime Ministers. Prime Ministers want some place where they will not be snapshotted, where they can be private, and where they can perch for a moment on a fence and look at the landscape without being 'shooed' off. Thanks to Lord Lee, I have my sanctuary at Chequers, and therefore I feel it incumbent upon me to be here today to open this sanctuary for my fellow-sufferers who find London at times a little crowded and a little lacking in that privacy they require for their best development.

There is another reason why we are beginning to feel the necessity of something of this kind. Those of us who love the country and country things feel in our bones the urbanisation of our land and the need that something should be done to preserve our birds and our flowers. It behoves us all to act because of that love which exists in English people wherever they may be found, the love and craving for beauty which they can rarely see, rarely know, and rarely realise in their own lives. We ought to do everything we can to foster that spirit, and it is in belief that this day we are helping to draw people's attention to bird life that I rejoice to be allowed to unveil this memorial.

It is customary for the unveiler of a memorial or other work of art, when he or she has pulled the cord exposing it to view, to look briefly at the work and then bow to the artist who is usually present, as Epstein was on this occasion. However, according to various eyewitnesses, the Prime Minister was so staggered at what he saw when he pulled the cord that his jaw fell and he forgot the artist entirely. In fact, what he had revealed was a panel depicting the nude figure of Rima, the Genius of the Forest in Hudson's *Green Mansions*, in the midst of a flight of birds of such monstrous appearance, so it seemed to some of the spectators, that they were unknown to the ornithologist. Today it causes few eyebrows to be raised. But in 1925 'Rima' was as unconventional in design as the artist's other works, such as his memorial to Oscar Wilde in the Père Lachaise cemetery in Paris; and there was a widespread demand that it should be removed from Hyde Park, a demand backed up by frequent daubings of black paint and other Philistine attempts at disfigurement. Nevertheless 'Rima' was to withstand every attack in print and otherwise and it still stands on its original site, indeed almost on the exact spot where Hudson often slept when he first came to England from South America, lonely and penniless.[31]

Next morning, according to his son Windham, the Prime Minister 'sped down for a day to ghostly Wilden. The funeral, with its pomp and symbolism; the recognition of long-lost faces in a black mass of muted relatives; the sherry and the cold collation that, he muttered, put him in mind of a hunt breakfast – so closely mixed in the minds of some are comedy and grief; and Edith, the last of the Macdonald sisters, left in the old house to close the long chapter in her own good time.* These things made up one spring day in the country, one strange holiday from the House of Commons.'[32]

Until the House rose for the summer recess in August, parliamentary business was mainly devoted to the comprehensive programme of legislation in the field of local government, pensions and national insurance introduced by Neville Chamberlain, also the various stages of the Finance Bill embodying Winston Churchill's first Budget. These were all described by Baldwin in the Prime Minister's customary but unofficial daily letter to the King. Indeed, one such despatch earned Baldwin a royal rebuke for the light-hearted manner in which he described the appearance of the Commons chamber during an all-night sitting. The occasion was the Committee Stage of the Widows', Orphans' and Old Age Pensions Bill, which was taken on the floor of the House. Progress was considerably impeded by the deliberate but quite legitimate tactics of obstruction employed by the Labour Opposition, who kept the House sitting late for two consecutive nights.

> After midnight a change gradually came over the proceedings. In the early hours of the morning the House bore many resemblances to St James's Park at midday. Members were lying about the benches in recumbent positions, some being overcome with sleep oblivious of their surroundings, while others occasionally feigned an interest in the proceedings by making interruptions from a sleepy and recumbent posture. The Labour Party's attempts at obstruction became intensified, and there was a tendency for the weariness of the flesh to be exhibited by signs of temper and irritation. Mr Wheatley especially showed himself to be an expert in obstructive tactics. On one amendment he actually spoke for an hour and a quarter without transgressing the rules of order – a very striking and masterly performance but one with which Members at that stage of the night would willingly have dispensed.[33]

When he had read this account, the King instructed Lord Stamfordham to write to the Prime Minister stating that such unseemly behaviour ought not to be treated with levity. 'Members of Parliament now include ladies,' wrote Stamfordham, 'and such a state of things as you describe seems to His Majesty hardly *decorous*, or worthy of the tradition of the Mother of Parliaments.' He then went on to suggest that his letter should

---

* Edith, the youngest unmarried Macdonald sister, died in 1937, aged eighty-eight, and was buried beside Alfred and Louisa Baldwin in Wilden churchyard.

be shown to the Speaker. This suggestion drew a strong protest from Baldwin, who pointed out, no doubt on the advice of the learned clerks of the House, that such a suggestion if acted upon would be a breach of the sacred Bill of Rights. Baldwin thereupon despatched his own Private Secretary Ronald Waterhouse to Buckingham Palace with a demand that Stamfordham's letter should be withdrawn, reminding the King that 'one of the earliest historical objects of the House of Commons was to exclude the Crown from interfering in its proceedings', and quoting Erskine May, the leading authority on parliamentary practice, as laying down that 'the King cannot take notice of anything said or done in the House, but by the report of the House itself'.

Although the Prime Minister's reports of parliamentary proceedings to the sovereign originated as far back as the reign of George III, Waterhouse stressed that, while the King might allude to their contents in private conversation, any written representations based upon them might well be regarded as a trespass upon the privileges of the House. Accordingly, after consulting the King, Stamfordham wrote to Waterhouse withdrawing his letter, but adding that His Majesty could not help thinking that 'his subjects generally would not be surprised were they to know that the information conveyed to him, be it unofficial or not, had been commented on in such terms as those of my letter'.[34]

The King was constitutionally on stronger ground when he again wrote to Baldwin, as he did about this time, expressing grave doubts whether it was a good thing that Cabinet Ministers should write articles for the press, 'receiving payment for the same'. The allusion was to Birkenhead, who since he had become Secretary of State for India had been contributing regularly to newspapers and magazines in defiance of a Cabinet resolution passed in Bonar Law's time to the effect that Ministers should refrain from writing signed articles on current topics to the press during their tenure of office. After the matter had been raised in the House of Commons with specific reference to Birkenhead, the Cabinet repeated its earlier decision that the practice should cease.*

According to his son, Birkenhead yielded with an ill grace and nourished an abiding grievance, since he had given up a great practice at the Bar

---

* On 9 June 1925, Captain Wedgwood Benn, MP, asked the Prime Minister in the Commons, whether 'in view of the fact that there is a Bill before this House to abolish capital punishment, does the Right Hon. Gentleman consider that a member of the Government should express his views on the subject of capital punishment in articles?' Baldwin replied: 'I think we had better wait and see.' Whereupon another Member (Mr Stephen) asked: 'Will the Prime Minister read these articles by Lord Birkenhead?' To which the reply was: 'I have a good many things to read.' A copy of these exchanges was sent to the King, who commented: 'I don't think much of the PM's replies.' RA K 2003/2–3.

for public work and he saw no reason why he should not continue to supplement his salary by journalism which he had done as Lord Chancellor in the Coalition Government without apparent objection. Had he not taken office under Baldwin, he would as an ex-Lord Chancellor have been entitled to a pension of £5,000, and it was to compensate him for having forgone this together with having to cancel most of his contracts for the supply of articles to the British and overseas press and incidentally to forestall his possible resignation that Baldwin went to F. S. Jackson, the Conservative Party Chairman, and persuaded him to make Birkenhead two substantial *ex gratia* payments from Party funds, amounting in all to £10,000.

However aggrieved he may have felt at the time, Birkenhead accepted the money without demur and wrote to Baldwin: 'I recognise so completely the loyalty and kindness you have shown me in the matter of my articles that I am prepared to do anything to diminish your difficulties.'[35]

5

On the advice of his principal Treasury officials and the leading City financiers and bankers led by Montagu Norman, Winston Churchill had with Baldwin's assent made the momentous but, as Maynard Keynes accurately predicted at the time, disastrous decision in the spring of 1925 to return to the gold standard at the pre-war parity, thus fatally overvaluing the pound in terms of foreign currencies, with the result that exports were penalised and imports encouraged to the detriment of the balance of trade.* It was this decision that dominated his Budget, in itself a strictly orthodox presentation, which in Baldwin's view followed 'the soundest lines of prudence and Conservative finance', reducing income tax by sixpence, giving some relief to surtax payers and, somewhat surprisingly for a whole-hearted Free Trader, imposing duties on artificial silk and lace. (The object of these duties was to meet the cost of the new contributory old age pensions scheme rather than by increasing direct taxation.) 'Winston is really gambling on the chance of a steady revival of trade in the next twelve months,' Tom Jones noted at this time, 'and he is the only one in the Cabinet who seems to have, what L.G. had, a sense of the dramatic in making proposals to the nation.'

The Chancellor's drastic proposals for tightening up the administration of unemployment relief came as a shock to Steel-Maitland, the Minister

---

* Afterwards Churchill used to say that 'the biggest blunder of his life had been the return to the gold standard'. See Lord Moran, *Winston Churchill: The Struggle for Survival* (1966), p. 303.

of Labour. Jones has described Baldwin's characteristic part in preventing a head-on clash between the two ministers:

17 May 1925 . . . At 4.15 the PM presided over the Unemployment Committee, and did it in such good-tempered fashion that the conflict between the Chancellor and the Minister of Labour never emerged. For the first five or ten minutes the PM did nothing but work away at his pipe; scouring it out and filling it, lighting it and re-lighting it, meanwhile telling some quite amusing stories. We also had tea served, and by the time we came to business we were all in the friendliest mood. The upshot was to agree to a draft Bill being prepared, which Bill will go about half-way Winston wants to go.[36]

Churchill's most persistent antagonist in the Cabinet was Leo Amery, the leading Protectionist and Secretary for the Dominions and Colonies. In his autobiography, Amery wrote of the Chancellor and Prime Minister at this period:

He [Churchill] was, if I may coin the phrase, a great Englander, one whose patriotism was essentially dedicated to England; a great England, but still England. He could be proud of the British Empire as a manifestation of the British race's adventurous and colonising spirit, as a scheme of beneficent rule over backward peoples, and as an element in England's influence in world affairs. But the conception of wider patriotism for a Commonwealth of equal partners, including but transcending our several national patriotisms, had not then begun to interest him or affect his attitude to political or economic problems.

That we should find ourselves at friendly variance over the main issues of policy was inevitable. My diary is an almost continuous story of our day-to-day differences in Cabinet and in the conduct of inter-departmental business. Baldwin once jestingly said that more than half the time of the Cabinet was taken up by Churchill's speeches and my rejoinders. To which I could only reply that mine was not the lion's share in the argumentative feast. In all these encounters I enjoyed the sympathy, but not the effective support of the majority of my colleagues. The advantage of the position rested with the Chancellor of the Exchequer who defended the economic *status quo*, who held the purse strings, and with whom his colleagues, and more particularly the Prime Minister, were naturally anxious not to differ unnecessarily.

The real blame for frustrating the [economic] policy in which he sincerely, though somewhat vaguely believed, and for failing to fulfil his own election pledges, lay with Baldwin himself. He had given Churchill the strongest position in the Cabinet as a tactical move in his policy of keeping Lloyd George isolated. His own laziness and love of peace, coupled with the growing conviction that policies cannot be made, but must be allowed to grow of themselves, and that the supreme duty of a government is to stay in office, did the rest.[37]

Amery was writing nearly thirty years later with the advantage or disadvantage of hindsight. An instructive contrast is provided by the close-up view of both Churchill and Baldwin which is reflected in a letter which Neville Chamberlain wrote to Baldwin at the time:

30 August 1925. Looking back over our first session I think our Chancellor has done very well, all the better because he hasn't been what he was expected to be. He hasn't dominated the Cabinet, though undoubtedly he has influenced it: he hasn't tied us up to pedantic Free Trade, though he is a bit sticky about the safeguarding of industries. He hasn't intrigued for the leadership, but he has been a tower of debating strength in the House of Commons. And taking him all round, I don't think there can be any dispute but that he has been a source of influence and prestige to the Government as a whole . . .

There is no doubt that you made us both happy, and I for one have never for a moment regretted the decision I made then or envied Winston his pre-eminence. What a brilliant creature he is! But there is somehow a gulf fixed between him and me which I didn't think I should ever cross. I liked him. I liked his humour and his vitality. I liked the way he took that-to-me very unexpected line over the coal crisis in Cabinet. But not for all the joys of Paradise would I be a member of his staff! Mercurial! a much abused word, but it is the literal description of his temperament.

But really the outstanding feature of the session is the development and growth of your own position. I do wish I knew who wrote that astonishingly shrewd, subtle and penetrating study in *The Times*. He knows you well, it is clear. His comparison of you to Lincoln in your 'essential loneliness of spirit' shows that he has got below the surface . . .*

* In the article, which was signed 'Back Bencher', the author wrote: 'In his shrewd and deep simplicity of character, his patience, his passion for the community and its welfare, his refusal to

Lincoln had at all costs to preserve the unity of the North. You have got to preserve the unity of the country. Lincoln was inexperienced and full of oddities which at first sight did not impress. He used to hesitate long before deciding, he was accused of weakness and vacillation, many thought him a fool. But he did decide on momentous occasions, often against the advice of his friends, and his Cabinet, and he generally turned out to be right because he had an extraordinary faculty for understanding the view of the ordinary man.

Well, that's your strength and it is gradually becoming apparent to a wider and wider circle. I rejoice at the growth of your influence because I believe it is wholly good for the party and the country that they should prefer to trust a man of your character before the superficial brilliance of an essentially inferior nature like Lloyd George.[38]

Churchill himself expressed a more cautious feeling of optimism. 'I have been very happy under your leadership,' he told Baldwin at the end of his first year at the Treasury. 'I am sure that you have a winning hand to play if only you have the firmness and patience to play it regularly through. Gradually but surely the nation will revive its strength and be conscious of an increased well-being . . . As long as we stick to the platform of the General Election all will be well and we shall wear down our foes, and what is more important do our duty in securing the country its promised breathing space.'

Throughout his second term, Baldwin's relations with Churchill were easy and even affectionate. Each would remember the other's birthday and send an appropriate message. 'A brief reference to *Dod* shows me that you are still a child,' the Prime Minister wrote to the Chancellor on 30 November 1928 – in fact Churchill was fifty-three at this date, less than seven years Baldwin's junior – 'so I may say "Many Happy Returns" and a happy birthday to you today.' Baldwin also showed concern for Churchill's health and would counsel him not to overwork. 'Do remember what I said about resting from current problems. Paint, write, play with your dams.'[39]

The crisis in the coal industry, mentioned by Neville Chamberlain in his letter to Baldwin quoted above, blew up in July 1925. While the

treat his fellow-countrymen as enemies, perhaps too in an occasional gaucheness, and in an essential loneliness of spirit, it is Abraham Lincoln whom Mr Baldwin recalls. Like Lincoln he has that rarest and finest quality of a leader, the power of liberating and calling in aid the deeper moral motives in the hearts of men.'

French were in occupation of the Ruhr, the German miners were idle, the British industry did well in comparison with its European competitors and miners' wages rose. But with the French withdrawal from the Ruhr and the return of German and Polish production to full capacity, coupled with the over-valuing of the pound, exports of coal from Britain declined almost to nothing. The mine-owners demanded longer working hours in the pits and lower wages; the miners' leaders bluntly refused. Neither side showed particular intelligence. 'I should have thought that the miners' leaders were the stupidest men in the kingdom,' Birkenhead remarked, 'if I had not met the owners.'[40] On the owners threatening a lock-out, the General Council of the TUC intervened to support the miners' case with the Government. This move resulted in the setting up of a Court of Inquiry under the chairmanship of Hugh Macmillan, a distinguished jurist, later Lord Macmillan. The Court reported at the end of July largely in the miners' favour. At the same time, the economist Sir Josiah Stamp, who was a member of the Court, argued with some truth in a separate memorandum that the difficulties in the industry were due to 'the immediate and necessary effects of the return to gold'.

The TUC General Council reacted by ordering a nationwide embargo on the movement of coal. This forced the Government's hand, since it was not then prepared for a coal strike, let alone a general strike, which was what the embargo would almost certainly have brought about had it been implemented. Baldwin proposed the payment of a subsidy to be spread over nine months during which a Royal Commission would investigate the industry, and which was designed to fill such gap as would remain between the terms offered by the owners and the terms which the men were willing to accept. Although realising that the subsidy meant a surrender to the unions, Churchill strongly supported it in the Cabinet. It was agreed to on 'Red Friday', as the date became known in the trade union calendar. The amount of the subsidy was calculated at £10 million – actually it worked out at £23 million. It was a high price to pay for the postponement of the day of reckoning, but Baldwin justified it on the ground that the machinery for the organisation of essential supplies and services had lapsed under the Labour Government and needed the nine months to revive. The respite, he told Tom Jones, would give the country time to realise the attitude taken by the Labour leaders and to make up their minds what to do should the time again come when the TUC took the step of challenging the Government. 'The present agreement affords one more chance to secure industrial peace; if the community is driven to arrange for the supply of its own needs it will do so with a thoroughness which will astonish the Communists.'

Nevertheless the subsidy and the apparently easy victory of the TUC caused a distinct feeling of unease among the Conservative Party stalwarts like Salisbury, the Lord Privy Seal. 'I shall be only too glad if my confidence can be restored,' he told the Prime Minister, 'but the moral basis of the Government seems to me to have dropped out.' Upon which Baldwin could only ask pathetically: 'That is not very helpful is it, after we have all been working like beavers?' [41]

It was a relief to Baldwin and his wife to get away with the Davidsons to Aix and to be free for a few weeks from engagements, 'including those wretched miners whom I had hoped never to see again'. When Jones saw the Prime Minister on his return, he was in excellent form. 'I know now what [Theodore] Roosevelt meant when, after a holiday, he felt like a "bull moose". This is the best holiday I have had since the war. I have read no papers beyond glancing at the headlines in the middle page of *The Times*. What is Labour like? Are they quarrelling amongst themselves at all?' After Jones had summed up the position, Baldwin continued to talk about his holiday like a schoolboy, producing from a piece of blotting paper in his pocket 'a lovely little blue Gentian flower which he had picked'. According to Jones, he ranked among the most memorable incidents of his holiday a handsome youth coming down the mountainside followed by a herd of cattle and goats with tinkling bells. 'If only he could keep his physical vigour right through the Session,' noted Jones, 'he might get something done.' [42]

On his return from holiday, Baldwin paid a visit to Glasgow, where he explored the slums in company with Dr Chalmers, who had been the city's medical officer of health. It was the second time he had been shown slum property, the first being at Dundee which he had visited earlier in the year. 'Oddly enough I have never been in real slum houses,' he wrote to Davidson on this occasion, 'and I as near as two pins sat down and howled: the whole thing came to me with such force. Five and six in one room. Think of the children!' After the Glasgow visit, he wrote to Stamfordham, who showed his letter to the King.

They [the slums] are terrible and gave me the opportunity of saying something in public and more in private to stimulate the people of the city to fight the difficult problem with unusual energy.

But the curious thing was that, contrary to expectation, I had an amazingly popular welcome throughout the town. The reception we had in the poorer quarters was remarkable. The booing was completely drowned by the cheering and the red flags numbered under a dozen, compared with the hundreds of Union Jacks.

And nowhere was the enthusiasm more marked than among the women and children. I don't lay too much stress on this but I feel that the visit did good and was certainly a stimulus to the decent elements.[43]

Throughout the summer and autumn of 1925, Austen Chamberlain worked assiduously to bring about the European Pact of Mutual Guarantee on which he had set his heart. At Geneva in September, where he attended the League of Nations Council, he was able to settle the arrangements for the Five-Power Conference which to suit Mussolini's convenience was to be held in the Palace of Justice in the Swiss town of Locarno near the Italian border. Baldwin and the French Premier Paul Painlevé, who was also War Minister in the French Government, had already given their blessing to the projected conference, when Baldwin broke his homeward journey from Aix to Paris. 'I am in the lap of cosmopolitan luxury,' he wrote to the Davidsons from the Ritz Hotel on 14 September, 'filled with food and wine and just returned from lunching at the War Office with Painlevé, Briand [Foreign Minister] and Caillaux [Finance Minister]. What a kaleidoscopic life!'

The Locarno conference was due to open on 5 October, but this was nearly wrecked by the Germans who suddenly announced that the question of war guilt must first be settled. Chamberlain told Baldwin that he was quite willing for another Cabinet minister to be included in the British delegation to strengthen his hand in the final negotiations, but Baldwin would not hear of it. 'I would not dream of suggesting you should take another Minister with you,' he wrote to the Foreign Secretary on 27 September from Balmoral where he was on a brief visit to the King. 'We have all perfect confidence in you and I know you will do everything that can be done to make further progress in the direction we have all been working for so long. I saw that amazing gaffe of the Germans and groaned over it.'[44] Fortunately Chamberlain refused to be blackmailed. ('The German Government, like a nagging woman, must have the last word.') In the face of his resistance, the Germans gave way and the conference opened as planned. Ten days later, on 16 October, which by a happy coincidence was Chamberlain's birthday, the Treaty of Locarno was agreed and initialled by the Foreign Ministers of the five countries involved – the United Kingdom, France, Belgium, Italy and Germany – who thereby undertook to guarantee the peace in western Europe.

Under the Locarno Treaty the five signatories guaranteed the inviolability of the German–Belgian and the German–French frontiers as fixed by the Treaty of Versailles; thus Britain and Italy were committed to declare war on Germany if Germany attacked France, and to declare war on France if France attacked Germany. The two main objects of the treaty and accompanying agreements to which Britain was not a party, both immediately realised, were the evacuation of the occupied Rhineland by France and the entry of Germany into the League of Nations.

'I have lived such days and celebrated such a birthday as it is given to no man to experience twice,' wrote the British Foreign Secretary after his whole staff had given him a real birthday cake with candles. 'I felt myself a little child again in spirit.' At the same time his brother Neville wrote in his diary: 'A great moment for him, the greatest in his life up till now, perhaps in the future. How long it will last depends on the actual results of the Pact. But if they are such as to ensure peace, as everyone believes today, then Locarno will be famous in history.' Austen Chamberlain's contribution to the settlement, in which for the first time in history the great powers had renounced the absolute right of war, was marked by his being created a Knight of the Garter by the King, an honour warmly endorsed by Baldwin.

The actual signing of the treaty took place in the Golden Room of the Foreign Office in London on the morning of 1 December 1925. Baldwin and Austen Chamberlain signed for Great Britain. On the previous night, the Foreign Secretary, happening to look round the Golden Room, had noticed a blank space on the wall. He was told that it was normally occupied by a portrait of King James II which had been temporarily removed for cleaning. He felt that the Stuart monarch was not perhaps the most suitable person to commemorate the occasion. He accordingly got into touch with Lord Londonderry and asked if he could borrow a portrait of his celebrated ancestor Lord Castlereagh to fill the vacant place. Londonderry obliged with the well-known portrait by Sir Thomas Lawrence, and so it came about that the moving spirit of the Treaty of Vienna looked down upon the signing of the Treaty of Locarno.

'This morning the Locarno Pact was signed at the Foreign Office,' wrote the King in his diary. 'I pray this may mean peace for many years. Why not for ever?' [45]

6

Two days after the signing of the Treaty of Locarno, another document of considerable historical importance was signed, this time in Baldwin's room in the House of Commons. This amended and supplemented the

Anglo-Irish treaty of 1921 and settled the thorny question of the border between the North and South of Ireland.

When Baldwin returned from his holiday at Aix, the three-man Irish Boundary Commission had been deliberating for nearly a year and was expected to publish its Report very shortly. There was a strong likelihood that the side which stood to lose the greater amount of territory by any proposed changes, in all probability the North, would react violently. Tom Jones consequently suggested to Baldwin that Craig, the Ulster Premier, would be prepared to accept the Report if it were imposed on him by the British Government. ('He could shift the onus on to you and you can carry it much more easily than he can.') On the other hand, the imperialists in the British Cabinet, Amery, Joynson-Hicks and Salisbury, were for the Prime Minister consulting with Craig in advance. But Jones pointed out the dangers inherent in such action. 'Once you begin to discuss and negotiate and adjust, you are in the Irish bog again. It is once more a crucial case for your own personal courage.'

'I could not do right off what you wanted about Ireland,' Baldwin told Jones next day. 'The moment the subject was mentioned in the Cabinet they all got excited; Salisbury and Jix were bursting their buttons with eagerness to talk so I am going to see Feetham [the Chairman of the Commission]. I think I will see him at the Travellers' [Club] and I will tell him that, while I do not want to know the details of the Boundary Report, what I want is his opinion on the chances of bloodshed on the border when the Report comes out. If I can be assured on that, then I can come back to the Cabinet and tell them that I think the Report ought to go through automatically, after any proper precautions have been taken.'

The three Commissioners agreed the first draft of the Report on 5 November. Unfortunately two days later, before Baldwin could see Feetham, the ultra-Tory *Morning Post* published a map giving a partially accurate picture of the proposed boundary changes, the particulars having been 'leaked' probably by the Northern Irish member of the Commission, J. R. Fisher. Public confidence in the Commission was badly shaken by this premature publication, although Craig was relieved at the relatively small transfers proposed and seemed disposed to accept them. In the South, however, there was marked disappointment, amounting to feelings of betrayal, notwithstanding that the South stood to gain on balance both in territory and Catholic population if the transfers went through. In fact, the Southern Irish Commissioner Eoin MacNeill had assented to the award, but pressure mounted for him to resign and he did so a fortnight later, ostensibly to avoid having publicly to endorse findings which were unacceptable to the majority of his fellow countrymen.[46]

Meanwhile Baldwin invited William Cosgrave, the Premier, and his principal colleagues in the Irish Free State Government to come to London.* At the same time he tactfully asked Amery, Joynson-Hicks and Salisbury, as well as Birkenhead and Churchill, to join him in various stages of the negotiations, to which Sir James Craig was also to be brought in. After a couple of days Cosgrave had to return to Dublin, but he left three of his ministers – Kevin O'Higgins (External Affairs), Patrick McGilligan (Labour) and John O'Byrne (Attorney-General) – to continue the talks during the week-end of 28–29 November at Chequers with Baldwin and Sir John Anderson, the Permanent Under-Secretary at the Home Office. Tom Jones and Patrick Duff, one of the Prime Minister's private secretaries, were also present.

From the first day's discussion, which took place in the Long Gallery, there emerged two possibilities, 'each honourable', as Baldwin described them. One was to accept the existing boundary. That, in the view of the Free State representatives, would be only possible for them in the event of their getting concessions from the North. In the event of their failing to obtain any such concessions, the alternative was to impose the line prescribed by the Boundary Commission. 'If that is agreed to,' Baldwin told the Irishmen, 'then we shall have to consider how to put it through with the least possible disturbance.' Meanwhile the Prime Minister undertook to consult Craig. 'As signatory of the Treaty,' he added, 'England wants to do her best to get Ireland over her difficulties.'

The Irish ministers were invited to stay the night at Chequers, but they preferred to go back to their Embassy in London and return next morning to continue the talks. Before leaving Chequers, they were given a quarter-inch map showing the exact demarcation line proposed together with some explanatory extracts from the Commission's draft Report. This was handed to them by Mr F. B. Bourdillon, the Foreign Office official who had acted as secretary of the Commission. From this it was quite clear, as Baldwin told the three Irishmen when they met again the

---

* Some months previously Baldwin had an embarrassing correspondence with Cosgrave arising out of a speech on the boundary issue by Ronald McNeill, the Under-Secretary for Foreign Affairs, and a diehard Ulster Unionist, which had drawn a strong protest from Cosgrave. 'I can only suppose that in the free and easy atmosphere of a village garden party the old fighting instincts reasserted themselves,' wrote Baldwin to Cosgrave, 'and for the moment he forgot that the Government, of which by the way, he is not a Cabinet Minister but an Under-Secretary, is pledged to support the Treaty . . . England and Ireland are so near each other that in the early stages of a marked change in their constitutional relations we are both likely to be placed in positions of difficulty by the utterances of some of our own followers. I hope therefore that whenever such difficulties or misunderstandings arise we may try to surmount them by writing freely and frankly to each other as you have done to me in this instance.' Baldwin to Cosgrave 2 July 1925: Baldwin Papers 99 f. 8.

following morning, that the proposed line was very much more favourable to the Free State than appeared from the map published in the *Morning Post*.

'I do not suggest that the new line is all you want or what your people have been led to expect during the agitation that followed the Treaty,' Baldwin went on. 'I have said over and over again that every conceivable award will leave a legacy of irritation at certain points. You must have faced that when you demanded the redrawing of the line. But it does seem to me that if you turn down an award which is going to transfer to the Free State so many of your co-religionists you are undertaking a grave responsibility.'*

O'Higgins objected to the predominantly Catholic town of Newry remaining in Northern Ireland. An award which left Newry and its hinterland within the jurisdiction of the North, he argued, could not be based on the Free State's interpretation of the Treaty or the evidence. 'Newry is the acid test,' he said.

'You have to contemplate the award becoming law,' observed Baldwin. 'Do you feel it would be better for you not to have seen it?'

'The less contact we have with the Report the better,' O'Higgins replied. He added that he had no objection to Baldwin stating the figures which the Prime Minister then proceeded to do.

At this point James Craig, whom Baldwin had summoned from London by telephone, was announced. He was accompanied by Charles Blackmore, the Secretary of the Northern Irish Cabinet, but somewhat surprisingly not by any ministerial colleagues, although Londonderry, who held the portfolio of education in the Ulster Government and was in London at this time, would have been the obvious choice, since he had been a member of the abortive Irish Convention in 1917.†

Baldwin then summarised for Craig's information the proposed territorial and population transfers, after which O'Higgins delivered an eloquent statement of the Free State case, not forgetting to mention that Craig had been opposed to the Boundary Commission from the start. 'If we could point to substantial improvement in the position of the National-

---

* The proposed transfer by Northern Ireland to the Free State included nearly 28,000 Roman Catholics and over 183,000 acres as against a transfer by the Free State to Northern Ireland of less than 3,000 Catholics and 50,000 acres. The latter were largely confined to East Donegal where there was a substantial Protestant population. These and other details are contained in the summaries of statements made at the Chequers meeting, 28 and 29 November 1925, in the Baldwin Papers 99 ff. 164–83.

† Londonderry was deeply offended by what he considered a deliberate slight, and he resigned from Craig's Government shortly afterwards on the ostensible pretext of the increasing demands of his coal-mining interests.

ists in Ulster, an emancipation of the minority,' O'Higgins concluded, 'we might survive on the *status quo*. What are the disabilities? Special police, the coercion which would be necessary to hold Tyrone and Fermanagh, 45,000 special constables in a statelet of six counties; abolition of proportional representation, changing the Constitution in order to deprive Nationalists of their due place in Parliament and local administration. It was not just rhetoric to say that the Catholic Nationalists are living in conditions of Catholics prior to Catholic Emancipation.'

The only comment which Craig made on this tirade was that he thought O'Higgins would exonerate him and his colleagues in regard to the Commission. 'We said Sinn Fein were living in a fool's paradise as to what would happen.'

'Your attitude was one of complete hostility,' said O'Higgins. 'That confirmed us in our view.'

'I have told all Prime Ministers,' rejoined Craig, 'that in my opinion a great deal of harm has been done already in Southern Ireland by bringing up people to expect too much from a Boundary Commission.' Here Craig was right, since the core of the problem lay in the differing interpretations of Article 12 in the Treaty of 1921 which provided for the setting up of the Boundary Commission. The Free State ministers believed that large transfers would be made, while Craig and his colleagues held the view that only minor rectifications of the border were implied by Article 12.

At this point the conference adjourned for lunch. Mrs Baldwin was waiting in the hall and had a brief talk with Craig, who with characteristic courtesy suggested that she should take O'Higgins into the dining-room. 'You are my old friend, and you come first,' was the reply. Then, turning to the Free State leader, she said, 'I am sure, Mr O'Higgins, you will understand why I am taking in Sir James, but I want you to sit on the other side of me.' Then, in a gallant attempt to put them at their ease as they took their places at the luncheon table, she remarked that she was 'the boundary line attached to both of them', but was 'far too well-covered to be a bone of contention – which mild joke they were pleased to approve of'.

Lucy Baldwin has described what subsequently happened that day as she saw it. Her account is not without a certain element of comedy.

I do not think I ever sat through such a luncheon; one could feel the tension in the air; I don't know what I talked about, but I never ceased talking, and I was ably seconded by Mr Jones and Mr Duff. During luncheon I mentioned to Sir James, and in the hearing of

Mr O'Higgins, how proud I should be if I were able to have both their signatures in my [visitors'] book as a token of what had happened or would happen that day.

After luncheon they dispersed to the Long Gallery, and then there began excursions and alarms. One heard hurried steps; one saw hurrying forms in twos and threes. I wandered aimlessly about the great hall, sometimes catching sight of two or three in earnest consultation on the south terrace, and after a time there came a sort of feeling as if all the doors in the house were open, and whispering were going on in every direction, and I was finding the hall a very draughty place. Every now and then Stanley's face would appear above the gallery, to give me a smile and a wave of an encouraging hand, only to disappear immediately afterwards.

When the hall became too draughty to be pleasant, I decided to go into the little white parlour which was the room which had always been assigned to me, and was my personal sitting-room. I opened the door and was – I don't mind saying so – horror-struck to see the back of a strange man who was gazing into the rose garden, a man whom I had never seen before. I felt now the moment had indeed come, and this must be the assassin and the end of it all. I was terrified to leave him absolutely alone, and so I made a sort of sentry go up and down the outside of my room, determined that he should not get out without my knowing it. Mr Duff hurried through the hall, and I was able to attract his attention and to break the news of the mysterious being hidden in my sitting-room.

Her husband's secretary, who did not seem in the least perturbed, told her that it was only Mr Bourdillon, the Secretary of the Boundary Commission. 'Both sides have declined to see him,' added Duff, 'and wish to pretend that they do not know he is here!' The upshot was that after he had been given a cup of tea the unfortunate Bourdillon was surreptitiously hurried into a car and sent back to London.

It was now getting dark, and it was tea time when the company came down from their discussion in the Long Gallery. I could not learn anything from their faces, except from a smile which Stanley gave me, but as I was giving Mr O'Higgins his tea, he said: 'Did you say you had a book you wished me to write in?' I replied: 'Yes, will you be able to do so?' and he said: 'I think it will be all right.'

The same remark was made to me by Sir James Craig when I gave him his tea, and he, too, in a whisper, said: 'I think it will be all right!' So when tea was finished I got out my book, and I said to the company: 'Now, gentlemen, are you going to make me the happiest woman in England at this moment? Will you come and sign?'

And in turn, Sir James Craig, C. H. Blackmore, Kevin O'Higgins, P. McGilligan, J. O'Byrne and John Anderson signed the book. And, greatest triumph of all, Stanley sent them back to London in the same car; truly an historic event and a great tribute to his tact and diplomacy.[47]

After they had gone, Baldwin pencilled two words in Latin ('*Pax pacem*') underneath their signatures in the Visitors' Book to show that peace had indeed been concluded between the two opposing sides.

On the way back to London, the car had a puncture, and while the tyre was being changed Craig and the three Free State ministers walked up and down the road conversing in the most friendly terms. The truth was that in spite of their political differences they had much more in common under the skin than either had with Baldwin and his English colleagues. 'You, know, boys, my position,' Craig had already told the southerners before they left Chequers with a glance in Baldwin's direction. 'I am pledged not to surrender an inch of Northern territory. Subject to that, I want to help you all I can to get as much as you can out of these fellows.' This squared with what Baldwin had already said to Craig about the Southern Irish delegation before the conference broke up: 'They want to bury the Boundary Commission. If they agree with you, then we'll have a Cabinet tomorrow to see how much we can give.'

The next few days were spent in settling the details of the tripartite agreement. Birkenhead, who led the discussions on the British side, had always shared Craig's view of how the controversial Article 12 of the Treaty should be interpreted. He summed up the position in a private letter which he wrote to Lord Reading the Viceroy of India, on the day the agreement was signed:

You know I always contended and advised my colleagues that Article 12 of the Treaty meant, and could only mean, a rectification of frontier and not a reallocation of great areas and towns. Sumner and Cave, then briskly competing for the Woolsack which they rightly thought would soon be vacant, took, or purposed to take, the opposite opinion; and so advised the House of Lords. It is satisfactory to me that the Commission's finding has so completely confirmed my own view and discharged me of the responsibility which individually I incurred in relation to my former colleagues.

But the finding involved other grave consequences. It threatened to submerge the pro-Treaty Free State Ministers, with the result that the Government of the country must have passed into the hands of republican, perhaps even of revolutionary elements. In these circumstances, and after great argument and disputation in the Cabinet and out of it, we have practically agreed to waive Article 5, in other words to relieve Ireland from her share of war indebtedness. She has, however, undertaken a liability amounting roughly to some eight million pounds, and hitherto discharged by us to compensate the Loyalists who suffered in the Civil War.

The discussions were conducted by Churchill, Salisbury and myself on behalf of the Government with three Irish Ministers. Incidentally they have resulted in the establishment of a greater degree of cordiality between Southern and Northern Ireland than has ever existed. They both developed a friendly and competitive enthusiasm in the task of plundering us.[48]

In the result, the 'Amending Agreement supplementing the Articles of the Treaty' revoked Article 12 and preserved for Northern Ireland the entire six counties as defined by the Government of Ireland Act. It also waived the Free State share of the British National Debt amounting to £155 million. The preamble described the Government of the Irish Free State as 'being united in amity in this undertaking with the Government of Northern Ireland' and the two Governments as 'being resolved mutually to aid one another in a spirit of neighbourly comradeship'. It was further agreed that they should 'meet together as and when necessary for the purpose of considering matters of common interest'.

The actual signing took place quite informally in Baldwin's room in the House of Commons on 3 December 1925. One of the Free State signatories was Ernest Blythe, then Minister of Finance, whose internment as a suspected enemy sympathiser during the war had been confirmed by Baldwin when he was a member of the Aliens Committee. Salisbury was the last to arrive; as Blythe has recalled, he was handed the document and proceeded to read it. For some reason Salisbury had second thoughts about signing it, for he looked at his watch, got up and said: 'Excuse me, I have an appointment.' Noting this, Craig whispered to Blythe who was sitting beside him: 'This fellow can't take his fences!' Baldwin looked slightly taken aback at Salisbury's withdrawal, but Birkenhead pushed the document in front of him, saying: 'Go ahead!' The Prime Minister thereupon inscribed his signature, followed by Churchill, Joynson-Hicks, Birkenhead and Amery for the British

Government; Cosgrave, O'Higgins and Blythe for the Irish Free State; and Craig and Blackmore for Northern Ireland. Immediately afterwards Baldwin gave a dinner party at which Cosgrave and Craig were the principal guests.[49]

'You have done the right thing in a big way,' Craig told Churchill, while Baldwin wrote to Cosgrave: 'I am sure that history will attach high value to the contributions which you and Sir James Craig brought to the negotiations. The patience and determination with which you sought peace in circumstances of grave difficulty are the surest promise of the future welfare of Ireland.'

'The best day's work I ever did, and the best for Ireland,' Kevin O'Higgins afterwards remarked to Mrs Baldwin, referring to the historic Sunday at Chequers when the basis of the agreement had been laid.[50] Unfortunately its long-term objects of healing the wounds of a divided Ireland in a spirit of neighbourly comradeship failed to be realised. O'Higgins was assassinated two years later by a republican gunman, and more than forty years were to pass before the next meeting between the Northern and Southern Premiers took place. By the latter date everyone who had signed the 1925 Agreement with the sole exception of Ernest Blythe was dead.*

7

From the moment he became Prime Minister for the second time, Baldwin had been convinced that sooner or later the Trades Union Congress would have recourse to a General Strike. The coal-mining subsidy to which the Cabinet agreed on 'Red Friday' he regarded as a breathing space before the final test of strength between the colliery owners and the miners. Meanwhile a Royal Commission had been set up under the chairmanship of the Liberal ex-Minister Sir Herbert Samuel to report on the industry, and while it was deliberating the emergency organisation for the maintenance of essential supplies and transport, which Parliament had provided for in 1920 but which it had hitherto never been found necessary to put into effect, was quietly perfected. The country was divided into ten areas, each under a civil commissioner, who was a junior member of the Government and who could in the

---

* O'Higgins was killed near Dublin on 10 July 1927, while on his way to attend Mass, allegedly for having ordered the execution of the republican Erskine Childers. On 14 January 1965 Mr Sean Lamass, the Southern Irish Premier, crossed the border, and met Captain Terence O'Neill, the Ulster Premier at Stormont.

event of violence exercise full governmental powers without reference to Whitehall. The central direction was in the hands of a Supply and Transport Committee under the Home Secretary Joynson-Hicks, who had the help of the Postmaster-General Sir William Mitchell-Thomson, who was Chief Civil Commissioner, with Baldwin's friend Davidson as Deputy Chief.[51]

Some news of these plans leaked out, but they seem to have been generally ignored, since the Labour leaders had no idea of the extent and thoroughness of the preparations which had been made to cope with an industrial stoppage on a national scale. The Government also had the advantage of the recent rapid development of road transport for the maintenance of food supplies. Previously a rail strike could have paralysed the life of the community within a few days.

The Samuel Commission reported on 11 March 1926. It recommended a drastic reorganisation of the industry including the nationalisation of royalties and the amalgamation of smaller pits, also an immediate reduction of wages. In the knowledge that the subsidy was due to end on 30 April, the Government accepted the report and left owners and miners to settle the details between them. But they failed to reach any agreement. The owners demanded not only lower wages but increased productivity, which meant longer hours. The miners' reaction was summed up by A. J. Cook, the left-wing Secretary of the Miners' Federation: 'Not a penny off the pay, not a minute on the day', while Herbert Smith, the President, when asked what the miners could do to help the industry, answered: 'Nowt. We've nowt to offer.' In vain both Baldwin and the TUC General Council tried to persuade the miners to accept some wage reduction, hoping that in this event the owners would make some concessions, but the miners' leaders would not budge.

Londonderry, who was a prominent owner though not a participant in the negotiations, wrote sympathising with Baldwin as time was fast running out:

13 April 1926. I am very sorry to see that notwithstanding all the efforts which have been put forward by so many in different capacities the whole weight of the controversy has been thrown on your shoulders. As you know I am, and have purposely remained, on the outside, but I am pleased to see that the owners have done everything they could in these later stages to come to an agreement with the miners. Cook and Smith dare not take up any other attitude, because neither has any real personality, and they are simply trying to obtain a continuance of the subsidy, and so discharge what they consider to be the duties of their positions. They know there are many others ready and willing to take their places if they appear to falter . . .

If it is true that only a limited production is required, then all theories of increased output fall to the ground. I put this to you with all respect and humility because we collectively, owners and men, have failed to do what I earnestly hoped and prayed we could do, which was to join together and work out a solution to the problem. If our failure is due to deeper reasons than those which appear on the surface, it is for those outside the industry to diagnose the causes which are nullifying the best elements in the representatives of each side.[52]

The ending of the subsidy was immediately followed by a lock-out, which began on 1 May. The miners thereupon delegated their authority as a negotiating body to the TUC General Council, which called a General Strike to start two days later. Both Government and the Council negotiated rather hesitantly throughout 2 May, neither side showing any disposition to yield before the other. The so-called Cabinet 'Big Three' were Baldwin, Birkenhead and Steel-Maitland, while the Council was represented by Arthur Pugh, the chairman, A. B. Swales, the vice-chairman, Walter Citrine, the general secretary, and J. H. Thomas, the boss of the railwaymen's union and former Labour minister. At one point, as Tom Jones noted, Birkenhead referred to Thomas as 'Jimmy', whereupon Thomas retorted with 'Frederick'. Thomas also brought up the question of the reduction of hours as a proposal which had once received Lloyd George's blessing.

'I was not in his confidence,' replied Baldwin.

'You were his colleague,' said Thomas.

'Not in his confidence,' the Prime Minister repeated.

'But in anticipating the succession with Davidson's help,' rejoined Thomas, unable to resist the chance of getting in a barb.

The Cabinet, which was in frequent session during this week-end of crisis, was still deliberating shortly after midnight on 2/3 May when a message was delivered to the Home Secretary that the strike had in effect already started with the refusal of the printers in the *Daily Mail* offices to print an editorial. 'The *Daily Mail* has ceased to function,' announced Joynson-Hicks. 'Hear, hear!' said Birkenhead, who was promptly rebuked by another minister: 'Not a time for flippancy.' Thomas Marlowe, the editor of the *Daily Mail*, was already in bad odour with the Labour movement for having originally published the Zinoviev letter, and when he wrote a leader endorsing an advertisement put out by the Government calling for volunteers to mitigate the effects of the strike should it take place, the compositors immediately stopped work and Marlowe gave the news over the telephone to one of Baldwin's secretaries. Feeling that the King should be informed of this development, the Prime Minister told Waterhouse to get in touch with one of the King's private secretaries at Windsor Castle. Eventually Clive Wigram, the assistant secretary, was roused from sleep and told what had happened. 'Don't be alarmed in the morning,' said Waterhouse. 'Tell His Majesty that he should not go off the deep end.' To which Wigram replied: 'That's all right, my dear fellow. We don't take the *Daily Mail* – or the *Daily Express*.'[53]

At 12.45 a.m. on 3 May, the following note, signed by Waterhouse, was handed by the Prime Minister to Pugh, Swales and Thomas to take to the miners' representatives who were waiting in the Treasury Board Room.

It has come to the knowledge of the Government not only that specific instructions have been sent under the authority of the executive of the Trade Unions represented at the conference convened by the authority of the General Council of the TUC directing their members in several of the most vital industries and services of the country to carry out a General Strike on Sunday next, but also that overt acts have already taken place including gross interference with the freedom of the press.

The Government must therefore require from the TUC both a repudiation of the actions referred to that have already taken place and an unconditional withdrawal of this threat before it can continue negotiations.

At 1.30 a.m. two of the delegates returned to 10 Downing Street apparently intending to tell the Prime Minister that they and their colleagues repudiated the 'overt act' and were ready to continue the negotiations. But it was too late. Baldwin, who was worn out by three days of almost continuous discussion, had gone to bed. The delegates declined to talk to the private secretaries, who were still on duty, and said they would send a letter instead. By now the machinery of the strike was gathering momentum.

A friend afterwards asked Baldwin, 'Is it true that you went to bed to avoid receiving their surrender?'

'No,' Baldwin replied. 'I had done all I could and there was nowhere else to go.'[54]

When the Prime Minister woke up on the first day of the strike, his mind was made up on the line he would take. In the afternoon the situation was debated in the House of Commons. Baldwin defined the issue as a challenge to constitutional government. At the same time he was determined to leave the door open for a speedy retreat by the TUC. 'The issue is really quite simple,' he remarked to Davidson as they walked across Green Park. 'This is an attempt to take over the function of the Government by a body that has not been elected. If they succeed it will be the end of parliamentary democracy which we have taken centuries to build. There can be no negotiations. It can only end in a complete surrender.'

Davidson subsequently recorded his impression of the Prime Minister at this time:

> It has got to be made absolutely clear, in everything which is written about Baldwin and the General Strike, that his vision and his judgement were clear and decisive, and that he didn't waffle. The idea was always put about that he was under pressure. But there was no question of pressure; he saw the thing as clear as crystal. The decision he took was that there should be no parley . . . the Constitution would not be safe until we had won the victory, and the victory depended on the surrender of the TUC.[55]

On the morning of 4 May, Jones found the Prime Minister alone in the Cabinet room, obviously rested and happier in mind than he had been for some days. They talked of the previous night's debate in the Commons, when he had said: 'Everything that I care for most is being smashed to bits.' Jones had listened to the debate. 'Wasn't the Goat bad?' To which Jones replied: 'Yes, and Ramsay was worse.' Baldwin said he thought that MacDonald was feeling the position acutely, since he and the other Labour Party leaders were entirely opposed to a strike against the State but were not strong enough to tell their followers the truth, pretending that what was happening was an industrial dispute. Churchill, who came in at this point, put the matter with characteristic clarity. 'There are two disputes on: there is the General Strike which is a challenge to the Government and with which we cannot compromise. Strike notices must be withdrawn unconditionally. There is also a trade dispute in the coal industry: on that we are prepared to take the utmost pains to reach a settlement in the most conciliatory spirit.'

At the same time, Churchill announced that he had commandeered the offices and machinery of the *Morning Post* with a view to bringing out some sort of Government news sheet or newspaper, as he preferred to see it. This was the origin of the *British Gazette*, a four-page production which was run off on the *Morning Post*'s machines and appeared daily throughout the strike under Churchill's general editorship. But it was Davidson who as Deputy Chief Civil Commissioner had really taken over the *Morning Post*, although he agreed with Baldwin's suggestion that Churchill should be entrusted with the day-to-day running of the *British Gazette*. 'Well,' Baldwin said to Davidson in discussing this novel appointment, 'it will keep him busy, stop him doing worse things.' After Davidson had assented, Baldwin added: 'I'm terrified of what Winston is going to be like.' [56]

However, on the whole the experiment was successful, in spite of Churchill's restless energy and constant interference in the technical details of production, which caused more than one entreaty from the *Morning Post* office that Churchill should be kept away while the *British Gazette* was going to press. ('He butts in at the busiest hours and insists on changing commas and full stops until the staff is furious.') 'Don't forget the cleverest thing I ever did,' Baldwin said to his official biographer G. M. Young. 'I put Winston in a corner and told him to edit the *British Gazette*.' [57] Certainly it is not difficult to imagine the bitter class feeling which would have resulted had Churchill been in overall charge as Prime Minister instead of merely editing the official Government newspaper. As it was, he denounced the strikers as 'the enemy' in the columns of the *British Gazette* and demanded their 'unconditional surrender'.*

Certainly the strike displayed all the overtones of a class war as between 'We' and 'They'. Yet there was surprisingly little violence except at the London docks, which had always been a danger spot and where the troops were called in. There was no shortage of volunteers to drive lorries, buses, milk trains and the underground railway in London and also to act as special constables. The latter included Admiral of the Fleet Lord Jellicoe. Baldwin was amused by the story which G. M. Young told him of Jellicoe's interview presumably at police headquarters when he went to offer his services. [58]

Name?

Jellicoe.

---

* The *British Gazette* under Churchill's editorship ran for eight issues from 5 May to 13 May, excluding Sunday, 9 May, and was printed by a volunteer staff. Its circulation figures were probably a record for any newspaper, starting with 232,000 on the first day and rising to well in excess of 2,000,000 on the eighth. 'The *British Gazette* may have had a short life; but it has fulfilled the purpose of living,' wrote Churchill in an unsigned article in the final issue. 'It becomes a memory; but it remains a monument.'

Ever done anything?

I commanded the Grand Fleet.

Fleet of what?

A rousing message from Baldwin to the British people was hurriedly drafted by Jones for publication in the *British Gazette* and 'improved' by the Prime Minister when Jones called with the draft for Baldwin's approval shortly before lunch on 5 May. Jones found the Prime Minister sitting with Mrs Baldwin in the drawing-room of No. 10. The room was dark, as there was a fog outside, but they were avoiding the use of electric light in order to save power. The message as amended was published next day over the Prime Minister's signature.

> Constitutional Government is being attacked. Let all good citizens whose livelihood and labour have thus been put in peril bear with fortitude and patience the hardship with which they have been suddenly confronted. Stand behind the Government who are doing their part, confident that you will co-operate in the measures they have undertaken to preserve the liberties and privileges of the people of these islands. The laws of England are the people's birthright. The laws are in your keeping. You have made Parliament their guardian. The General Strike is a challenge to Parliament and is the road to anarchy and ruin.[59]

At the same time, it was announced that Mrs Baldwin was organising a special convoy of motor cars to assist business women and girls living in the suburbs of London to reach their places of work, and to convey them back to their homes. Car owners were asked to communicate immediately with Mrs Baldwin in writing or by telephone to 10 Downing Street, whose number unlike today appeared in the London telephone directory. The response was considerable, owner-drivers willingly putting their vehicles at Mrs Baldwin's disposal as a patriotic duty.[60]

On the evening of 8 May, when the strike had been going on for nearly a week, Baldwin broadcast to the nation, 'with great vigour and determination', Jones thought as he listened to him, although his voice coming through a loudspeaker seemed nothing like as pleasant as Jones had previously heard it. 'I am a man of peace,' said the Prime Minister. 'I am longing and working and praying for peace, but I will not surrender the safety and the security of the British Constitution. You placed me in power eighteen months ago by the largest majority accorded to any Party for many, many years. Have I done anything to forfeit that confidence? Cannot you trust me to ensure a square deal to secure even justice between man and man?'[61]

Next morning, which was a Sunday, Baldwin felt the need of some fresh air and exercise. Accordingly he drove out to Hampstead Heath with his younger son Windham and Tom Jones. In the car he showed Jones 'an almost affectionate letter which the Prince of Wales had sent him last night about a quarter of an hour after listening to the PM broadcasting. The PM was obviously much moved at receiving so promptly so cordial a message from the Prince.'[62]

> St James's Palace,
> Saturday night

My dear Prime Minister,

I've just listened to your broadcasting speech. It's *wonderful* and will help a lot I'm sure – I can't say more.

It's a very trying time for me as you know the way I feel and seeing you when you have a spare moment just makes all the difference to this terrible period of inactivity for me. But I don't want to add to 'your engagements at this time' – I'm thinking of you *all* the time.

> Yours,
> EDWARD P

The General Strike entered its second week with every indication that the Government's attitude was hardening, while public opinion outside the trade union movement continued to be unfavourable to the strikers, with the exception of the miners. Furthermore the Government was much encouraged by a speech in the House of Commons from Sir John Simon, in which the Liberal lawyer declared that the General Strike was illegal, that the Trade Disputes Act of 1906 did not cover it and that all the trade union leaders concerned were personally liable for damages 'to the uttermost farthing' of their possessions. This opinion, which has been challenged by some legal experts, was confirmed a few days later by a High Court judge (Mr Justice Astbury) in the Chancery Division on the ground that no trade dispute had been shown to exist in any of the unions affected except the Miners'. Then, on 12 May, after Sir Herbert Samuel had proposed a National Wages Board in the coal industry which might impose some reductions in wages, but only when the recommendations made by the Royal Commission had been 'effectively adopted', the TUC General Council decided to throw over the miners and to call off the General Strike unconditionally. Baldwin, for his part, promised that the Government would do all it could to bring miners and owners together for a lasting settlement. 'We trust your word as Prime Minister,' J. H. Thomas told him on behalf of the TUC. 'We ask you to assist us in the way only you can assist us – by asking employers and all others to make the position as easy and smooth as possible.' Baldwin replied that he would. Ernest Bevin, the general secretary of the powerful Transport and General Workers' Union, who accompanied Thomas and Pugh to the final meeting in Downing Street, demanded some positive assurance on the reinstatement of strikers and the resumption of negotiations with the miners; he also wished to know when they would have a further meeting. But Baldwin refused to be bounced. 'You know my record,' he said. 'I think it may be that whatever decision I come to the House of Commons may be the best place in which to say it.' [63] After which everyone went back to work except the miners.

The strike collapsed because the Government had been prepared for it, while the unions had not. As Tom Jones wrote at the time,

the General Strike could not succeed because some of those who led it did not wholly believe in it and because few, if any, were prepared to go through with it to its logical conclusion – violence and revolution . . . The chief asset in keeping the country steadfast during the negotiations was the Prime Minister's reputation for fair dealing enhanced later by his sincere plea against malice and vindictiveness. His seeming weakness had been his strength. Had he yielded to the Diehard influences he would have prolonged the strike by rallying the whole of Labour in defence of Trade Unionism. He was wise to give them the chance and he was enthusiastically supported in his course by the majority of the House of Commons. [64]

8

On the same day as the General Strike was called off, Baldwin again broadcast to the nation. 'Our business is not to triumph over those who have failed in a mistaken attempt,' he said, and he went on to assure his large audience that he would lose no time in resuming negotiations with the miners and owners. He offered to operate the Samuel report, including a short-term subsidy, if the two sides of the industry would accept it first. However, the miners refused and the stoppage dragged on unhappily for the remainder of the year; the miners were eventually driven back to the pits by cold and starvation, being forced to accept both longer hours and lower wages as well as district agreements. By this time the seven-hour day in the mines had been replaced by an Eight Hours Act, the debates on this measure being marked by stormy scenes in the Commons, during which the Prime Minister was subjected to a bitter personal attack, the first of its kind he had suffered since he had entered Parliament.

The attack was sparked off by a statement in a Labour weekly edited by George Lansbury, MP, a left-wing teetotaller and non-smoker, to the effect that a quarter of a million pounds of the capital in the Baldwin family business belonged to the Prime Minister. Baldwin quietly admitted that he owned the shares, that they were the bulk of his fortune, and that if he had sold them in the war he would now be a rich man. As it was, they had not paid a dividend since 1922, the price of the £1 ordinary shares having tumbled from 61s. to 10s. 6d. – indeed they were soon to be written down to 4s. – and he made it clear that he expected to receive no income from them for years to come. (His prediction was correct, since the dividends on Baldwin's continued to be passed until 1934, when the shares paid 2½ per cent.) The storm blew up again during the third reading of the Eight Hours Bill when one member was suspended for calling the Prime Minister a murderer and another described him as 'the greatest enemy of the working class in the present generation'.[65]

'The Labour Party is not a comfortable household,' Baldwin remarked in one of his daily reports to the King. 'There are so many occasions when the peace of the home is rudely shattered by some of the boisterous and ecstatic children bursting into shrieks or falling into paroxysms, which are as offensive to the ears of their parents and their more sedate brothers as they are to their neighbours in the surrounding tenements.' The parliamentary Labour Party as a whole he felt was not so much embittered as dispirited and, as he told the King, 'they do not seem to appreciate to the full the joys and functions of opposition'. He contrasted their behaviour with the youth and activity of his own backbenchers, quite different from the hard-faced men who had been such a conspicuous feature of the first post-war House of Commons. 'It is a source of satisfaction to all that this element has been largely diminished and that in its place has appeared a band of keen and ardent young Conservatives with a genuine desire to serve the public interest, rather than that of any particular class or faction of their own particular selfish interests.'[66] These were men of the stamp of Oliver Stanley, Harold Macmillan, Robert Boothby and John Loder (later Lord Wakehurst), who were expounding a new and up-to-date version of Disraeli's Tory democracy, pleading for the recognition of the importance of the trade unions and for the development of a sense of partnership between management and workers in industry. It was said that these views found some sympathy in the Cabinet. According to the *New Statesman*, 'Mr Baldwin's mind is supposed to be in the balance.'

Unfortunately, in spite of Baldwin's optimistic report to the King, the old diehard element was still strongly entrenched on the Tory back benches, where the majority was out to reap the fruits of the Government's victory over the unions, and indeed this feeling was reflected generally in the Conservative constituency parties, that is at grass roots level. As a leading exponent of peace in industry, Baldwin was all for letting bygones be bygones and trusting the unions, but in his position as Conservative Party leader he could not be impervious to pressures from the right which insisted on clipping the unions' wings.

Some party political reaction to the General Strike was inevitable in the nature of things and it found expression in the Government's Trade Disputes and Trade Union Act of 1927, which declared illegal any sympathetic strike or any strike 'designed or calculated to coerce the Government by inflicting hardship on the community'. In future union members paying a political levy had to contract in instead of contracting out, thus implementing the terms of the Macquisten Bill for which Baldwin had said the country was not ready in 1925 and which he had persuaded the Cabinet to reject at that time. Even the young Conservatives led by Harold Macmillan accepted the measure in principle, while attempting without much success to improve it in committee, for example by supporting an amendment moved by Sir Leslie Scott and backed by the Liberal Sir Alfred Mond providing for a period of delay and conciliation before strikes in the essential public service industries could take place. In the event the Trade Disputes Act, carried by means of the 'guillotine' closure procedure which had not been used since 1921, aroused great bitterness in the Labour movement; and Baldwin, whose reputation for moderation slumped by reason of his acquiescence in this measure, was to live to see its eventual repeal which took place shortly after Labour's sweeping victory in 1945.

Neville Chamberlain had wished to include a constructive clause in the Trade Disputes Act providing for a sixty-day 'cooling-off' period in any industrial dispute together with some form of compulsory arbitration similar to what was later put forward in the Scott–Mond amendment. He discussed this with Cunliffe-Lister (as Lloyd-Greame was now called), while the Bill was being drafted and he was staying at Swinton, Cunliffe-

Lister's place in Yorkshire. As he was going on to spend a few days with Baldwin at Astley, he promised to press the proposal strongly with the Prime Minister. What happened then throws a curious light on Baldwin's character when, in Chamberlain's phrase, he would suddenly go out of gear. Later, when they had all returned to London, and Cunliffe-Lister brought up the matter, Baldwin denied all recollection of it.

'Well, I can't make head or tail of this,' said Chamberlain when he heard of it. 'I started on him when I got there before dinner and argued it with him and put it very strongly to him, and then we went at it again after dinner and I went on pressing it and his reaction seemed favourable – until I saw he'd gone out of gear. He started sniffing blotting paper. He had a way of sniffing blotting paper when he wasn't paying attention, and so I just don't know what he means.'

Cunliffe-Lister agreed. 'I'm sure Baldwin wasn't lying to me,' he said afterwards. 'I don't think Baldwin ever told a lie consciously. But it just was that he must have gone completely out of gear.' [67]

Chamberlain circulated his proposal to the Cabinet who referred it to a small Cabinet committee, where it was narrowly defeated owing to the absence of Lord Cave from the chair and the opposition of Birkenhead, Joynson-Hicks and Steel-Maitland. After the Scott–Mond amendment had been likewise rejected, Chamberlain commented in his diary: 'The debate showed how much we have lost by not adopting my proposal.' *

Certainly Baldwin appeared to be seized with a kind of mental inertia after the General Strike. 'Sick in body, far more sick in mind' was the verdict of one parliamentary lobby correspondent, while another critical observer doubted whether the Prime Minister would ever be able to return to the moral level on which he stood in 1926. 'He might have done anything. He did nothing. And ever after he seemed to be trading on an accumulated fund of confidence which was never replenished.' In *Winds of Change*, the first volume of his memoirs, Harold Macmillan depicted the parliamentary scene at this period:

> Baldwin seemed to be losing his grip on the situation, and the party was distracted by all kinds of minor or at least irrelevant issues. The die-hards were putting up resistance to many of Neville Chamberlain's reforming plans, and much of our time was spent on

---

* 'The Chamberlain clause, if adopted, could have made the establishment of the Industrial Disputes Tribunal [in 1940] unnecessary, and might have survived the Socialist repeal in 1946 of the 1927 Act; for the prohibition of a strike, if reference to the Tribunal had been made by either side, lasted until 1959.' Iain Macleod, *Neville Chamberlain* (1961), p. 121.

abortive proposals for the reform of the House of Lords, on which the party was more or less equally divided – for and against. The betting tax and the Prayer Book controversy occupied the minds of many Members, while the great economic problems of the nation remained unsolved. This was all the more galling because during these years Europe and the world in general were making marked progress towards recovery.[68]

However there was one important matter in which the Prime Minister was able to give a decision at this time and which deserves to be briefly mentioned here. This concerned the future of the RAF as an independent force. It might have been thought that the recommendation of the Balfour committee which had reported during Baldwin's first premiership in 1923 would have settled the matter for good.* Unfortunately it was reopened as the result of a Treasury minute which set up a 'Fighting Services Economy Committee' under the chairmanship of Lord Colwyn in 1925 to scrutinise the whole field of expenditure by the defence departments and recommend cuts. Colwyn was a successful businessman who had served on similar bodies in the past, and on this occasion he and his committee moved quickly, hearing witnesses and presenting their report within four months. They examined charges of incompetence and extravagance brought against the Air Ministry by the two older service departments and found them not proven. They rejected any proposal to abolish or dismember the Air Ministry and RAF and distribute its units among the other two services just as the Balfour committee had done. Nor did they look with favour on the proposal also advocated by some witnesses, to create a separate Ministry of Defence in order to exercise 'collective control' over the Chiefs of Staff. Finally they recommended the strengthening of the Air Ministry's control over the Fleet Air Arm.

Trenchard, the Chief of the Air Staff, correctly anticipated that the Admiralty and War Office chiefs would not accept these recommendations without a challenge, and he appealed to Baldwin to be firm. After seeing the Prime Minister, he wrote to him on 4 February 1926:

I am convinced – and all the experience of the last few years bears me out – that until the Admiralty and the War Office are told once and for all, in no uncertain voice, that the Royal Air Force is now as firmly established as the Navy and the Army, and that the issue of its independence is finally closed, we shall never have peace.

The Colwyn Committee have stated what should be the Air Force

* See above, p. 161.

charter. 'We affirm,' they have written, '*the necessity for an inde-pendent Air Ministry to administer a single unified air service, which should carry out all air work, whether for the Navy, Army or central Air Force.*' (Trenchard's italics)

For the next few months a vigorous wordy warfare proceeded, mostly between Bridgeman, the First Lord of the Admiralty, and Admiral Earl Beatty, the First Sea Lord, on the one hand, and Hoare, the Air Minister, and Trenchard, the CAS, on the other, with the War Office occasionally chipping in. There was a short pause during the period of the General Strike, when all three services were engaged in keeping essential supplies flowing and helping to preserve law and order. The struggle was resumed after the strike had ended. Finally, about six weeks later, Baldwin gave his decision which did not satisfy all sides completely but which each in the circumstances felt bound to accept.

First of all, the Prime Minister made it clear that he saw no reason to modify in any way the conclusions reached by the Balfour committee three years previously. Thus the Air Ministry should continue to be responsible for the raising, training and maintenance of the Fleet Air Arm, which should however when serving on board aircraft carriers at sea come under the operational and disciplinary control of the Admiralty. Shore-based aircraft for purposes of coastal reconnaissance – in other words, RAF Coastal Command – should come under the Air Ministry and Baldwin rejected outright the Admiralty's claim to direct and control them. Finally he rapped both departments over the knuckles for failing to maintain a sufficiently close liaison with each other in the past and adjured the two service ministries particularly concerned to show more mutual goodwill and better co-operation in future.

The navy must utilise to the full the experience in regard to aerial matters accumulated by the air force as the result of research, experiment and flying in all parts of the world. The air force must regard it as an obligation of honour to give the navy a Fleet Air Arm of the highest attainable efficiency. I do not feel satisfied that this has been the case during the last two years . . .

It is impossible to achieve progress if decisions of the Government are to be put in question at every opportunity.

In spite of his fatigue and tendency to inertia which was becoming increasingly evident at this time, this decision reflected Baldwin's skill as an arbitrator between two ministerial colleagues and their staffs in a dispute, which, had it been allowed to drag on, might have seriously impaired relations between the armed services and weakened their efficiency. Furthermore, by his decision Baldwin finally established the independence of the RAF under its own service ministry.[69]

No doubt increasing malaise – he was also suffering from acute attacks of lumbago – had much to do with Baldwin's mental condition at this time. 'I am anxious to get him away,' noted Tom Jones after Baldwin insisted on working on during August, 'because I feel that his tiredness has made him irritable and warped his judgement.' Lucy Baldwin co-operated with the secretaries, as Jones relates in his diary:

> *23 August 1926.* The PM went off on Sunday with Mrs Baldwin after all, and I was told the tale today. On Mrs Baldwin's return [from Worcestershire] between 4.0 and 5.0 p.m. on Saturday, Waterhouse told her that the only way of getting him off was by doctor's orders. She persuaded the PM to be willing to have a doctor called in, and Waterhouse proceeded to telephone round to no less than fourteen distinguished physicians, all of whom were away. Finally he got hold of one, and on his arrival at No. 10 briefed him fully as to the PM's symptoms, and as to what we Secretaries wished should be done.
>
> S.B. himself had no idea who or what sort of specialist the doctor was. The doctor played up splendidly, and warned the PM that unless he went away at once he was within measurable sight of a complete breakdown. This was duly telephoned to Wigram in the North, and at 10.20 on Saturday night the King's consent came through.

Fortunately Baldwin possessed remarkable powers of resilience. He returned from one holiday at Aix-les-Bains by way of Avignon, whence he wrote to Jones:

> I had a wonderful month at Aix. I must have been more tired mentally than I realised: I have done no work and couldn't. As I always tell you, I am a lazy devil by nature. But I feel extraordinarily well now and am looking forward to seeing you again with eagerness.
>
> How Rome dwarfs everything where her hand has been! What a people! Half the troubles of the Irish come from the fact that they never knew the Roman.

On reaching the Hotel Bernascon in August 1926, he immediately wrote thanking the King for granting him permission to leave England in view of the continued coal strike. He added:

I had a sudden and acute attack of lumbago on Saturday and although I am exceedingly strong and quite sound, I had got to the point where I needed a complete rest for a short time, before facing the work of the autumn and winter.

Your Majesty will be amused to hear that I crossed yesterday with a number of members of the Council of the TUC. We had a most friendly conversation and parted with mutual protestation of affection, and on their side I hope respect as well.

In the spring of 1927, Baldwin was suddenly taken ill as he was leaving a dinner at the Royal College of Surgeons on the occasion of the Lister Centenary Celebration. Sir Berkeley Moynihan, the President, and Lord Dawson of Penn, the King's doctor, who was also a guest, managed to keep him in a separate room, so that the other departing guests did not notice anything untoward. The Prime Minister was then taken back to Downing Street and put to bed, where Dawson saw him briefly and promised to return next morning for a more thorough examination. Ronald Waterhouse, who was also in attendance, wrote to Stamfordham, the King's Private Secretary:

8 April 1927 . . . This morning Lord Dawson overhauled the PM thoroughly, and told me as follows: If he were a non-public man, it would be a case of going to bed for a week, and abroad for a month. This being impossible, a middle course must be adopted. The PM must go to Chequers and rest in bed. There was no cause for anxiety, however, as, organically, all was well. It was merely a case of the heart of a very tired man going on strike, and therefore every available moment must be put to advantage, in order to have him back here on Monday for the Budget without arousing rumours. To this end I was to communicate at once with you, and, using Lord Dawson's name, ask His Majesty to excuse the PM's arrival at Windsor this afternoon. Lord Dawson will be at Chequers tomorrow, and will then report further . . .

So far there has been no leakage whatever, because the knowledge has been confined to so few people . . . Most fortunate it was, firstly that we were in that particular company, and secondly, that today being Friday, he can be got away without attracting attention, and with a free week-end ahead. We are taking every precaution to keep the whole story unknown.

The secret was well kept and Baldwin was back in his accustomed place on the Treasury Bench as arranged with few people being any the wiser. 'I have never been laid up in this way before,' he wrote to Stamfordham from the House, 'and I hope I shan't again.' However, his secretaries did some pruning of his engagement book, so as to keep him as fit as possible for the tour of Canada which the Prince of Wales and his younger brother Prince George were to undertake in the summer and on which he had accepted an invitation to accompany the royal princes.[70]

One engagement which he made for himself at this time was to invite his young friend and fellow Old Harrovian Neville Ford, then an Oxford undergraduate, to lunch at Chequers. Ford, the son of the Harrow headmaster Lionel Ford, had been head boy and had also distinguished himself at cricket and squash, in which sports he was later to gain a Double Blue at Oxford. There had been a change of headmasters at the school when Neville Ford was head boy and Baldwin, who had recently become Prime Minister for the second time, offered to come down and lend Ford his moral support. 'You may have time to test your statesmanship,' he had written to the boy about the change. 'It is rather like an XVIIIth-century Prime Minister changing his King . . . If an occasional visit of an informal nature to the school in the early days of the new regime would be of any use, then again command me.'

The following letter he wrote in his own hand as he did with so much of his correspondence:

> 10 Downing Street,
> Whitehall.
>
> 15.V.27
>
> Dear Neville,
>
> If you have nothing better to do and can beg, borrow or steal a car, come over to Chequers to lunch next Sunday.
>
> It is only a little over twenty miles, and it would be a real pleasure to see you again and hear what impression Oxford is making on you, and equally you on Oxford.
>
> There will only be a very agreeable married couple and ourselves.
>
> If you would feel happier with a companion, bring Crawley* with you, if it would be agreeable to both of you.
>
> But alone or accompanied you will be welcome.
>
> Yours sincerely,
>
> STANLEY BALDWIN

* Aidan Crawley, a friend of Ford's at Harrow and Oxford, afterwards Under-Secretary for Air in the 1950-1 Labour Government, later Conservative MP.

Meanwhile an embarrassing decision in the sphere of Anglo-Russian relations was taken by the Cabinet, with which Baldwin agreed and which he was obliged to defend in the House of Commons. On 12 May 1927, the Metropolitan Police, on the orders of the Home Secretary Sir William Joynson-Hicks, raided the premises at 49 Moorgate in the City of London which were shared by the Soviet Trade Delegation and Arcos Limited, a British-registered trading company which worked closely with the Soviet mission. Acting on a tip-off, almost certainly from a double agent, the police had reason to believe they would find a stolen War Office manual in the offices of what was supposed to be a purely commercial organisation. The manual was not found, but the search, which was carried out by a large force of plain-clothes and uniformed policemen amounting to some 200, did result in the seizure of some other apparently compromising material, which indicated that the Soviets were carrying on espionage and provocative activities under cover of the diplomatic immunity enjoyed by the Trade Delegation. The Russians protested vigorously, and after an angry exchange of notes between the two Governments Baldwin announced that, unless Parliament decided otherwise, diplomatic relations would be broken off.

The unfortunate Arcos raid incidentally revealed something of the activities of the British Secret Intelligence Service, to the evident discomfiture of the Prime Minister and his colleagues, particularly Joynson-Hicks and Austen Chamberlain who as Foreign Secretary disliked the prospect of a breach of relations. In a statement which he made to the House of Commons ten days after the raid, Baldwin indicated that part of the Government's case against the Soviets consisted of intercepted telegrams between London and Moscow, and Moscow and Peking, proving that the Soviet Union was carrying on propaganda against British interests in China. The Soviet Chargé d'Affaires in London thereupon pointed out that no telegraphic correspondence *en clair* had passed between him and the Foreign Affairs Commissariat in Moscow and that 'Mr Baldwin must have been referring to some alleged cypher telegrams decoded by a department of the British Government'.

An official Labour Opposition motion deploring the severance of Anglo-Russian diplomatic relations was debated in the House of Commons on 26 May. In a powerful speech supporting the motion, Lloyd George made Baldwin feel distinctly uncomfortable. The Prime Minister had charged the Soviet Government with espionage for the purpose of obtaining information about Britain's army and navy. 'Are we not doing that?' asked the former Premier. 'If the War Office and the Admiralty and the Air Force are not obtaining by every means every information about what is being done in other countries, they are neglecting the security of this country . . . it is the business of Governments to find out exactly what is being done about armaments in every part of the world . . . If the Soviet Government are doing it they are offending in common with every Government in friendly relations with us in the world.' Lloyd George spoke from considerable experience, as the Government knew. Nevertheless the motion was lost by 367 votes to 118, and the respective diplomatic missions in London and Moscow were closed down, not to be reopened until Labour returned to office in 1929.

One member of the Cabinet had no reservations about the decision. 'At last we have got rid of the Bolsheviks,' Birkenhead wrote on the same day as the debate. 'Personally I am delighted, though I think we ought to have done so the moment the General Election was over; and I have been trying to procure such a decision ever since . . . We have got rid of the hypocrisy of pretending to have friendly relations with this gang of murderers, revolutionaries and thieves. I breathe quite differently now we have purged our capital of the unclean and treacherous elements.' [71]

It was a relief to Baldwin to get away to Canada. The 'nineteen wonderful days in Canada', as Baldwin described his overseas tour to the King, during which he delivered twenty-six speeches, included an impressive ceremony in the middle of the International Peace Bridge spanning the Niagara river, when the Prince of Wales was met on the American side by Vice-President Dawes with whom he shook hands across a wide silken cord which the Prince then proceeded to cut.

On this occasion Baldwin spoke with his customary felicity of phrase. 'All bridges are proofs of friendship,' he said; 'across them men of good will may go on their lawful occasions, whether of commerce or of culture. But this bridge is no ordinary bridge: it stands as a sign and symbol of more than a century of peace between the United States of America on the one hand, and on the other Canada, with all the nations of the British Empire. I wish that the path to international peace was as smooth as this great highway.' [72]

In a letter which he addressed to the King on his homeward voyage, the Prime Minister wrote enthusiastically of 'the complete success of the Prince of Wales's visit and of the admirable way in which he has played his difficult part'.

S.S. Empress of Scotland, 24 August 1927 . . . I believe this visit has done good. I had the honour of travelling with the Prince of Wales as far as Calgary: the warmth of his welcome everywhere was a revelation to me. Popular enthusiasm was extraordinary, and I think that Prince George's appearance in an official capacity gave immense pleasure. He was naturally rather shy at first but I think the spontaneity of the welcome he got pleased and encouraged him and he did his part well.

The Prince of Wales was at his best and it was a real pleasure as well as an honour to be with him.*

The work has been hard. In the last six days I travelled nearly 3,000 miles and spoke at Calgary, Regina, Winnipeg, St John's, Monckton, Charlotte Town, Halifax and North Sydney.

I am particularly anxious to counteract the effect of much loose talking in and out of England, and of the stuff that Mr Lloyd George puts into the yellow Yankee press. There has been too long an idea uncontradicted that we are played out, idle, hopeless and so on, and I went for that with all the energy I could command. The reception I got in consequence was amazing. I broadcast all over the North and West and at Winnipeg there must have been 1,500 present. There can be no question of the strength and depth of the feeling of the unity of the race wherever it may be and of its unity under the Crown.

It was a wonderful experience which I hope will be of the greatest service in my work . . . [and] . . . will be of service to the Empire.

At the same time, the Prince's equerry, Captain Lionel Halsey, also wrote to the King:

I feel sure the combination of the Prince and the Prime Minister has been an unqualified success. There has never been any clash of any sort, and there is no doubt that the Canadians were genuinely pleased at such a visit taking place in the diamond jubilee year of their Federation . . .

Mr Baldwin has been a tremendous success wherever he has been,

* The Prime Minister's high opinion of the Prince was not fully reciprocated. Recalling their tour many years later, the Duke of Windsor (as he then was) wrote: 'We continued westward to Alberta; I to stop at my ranch, Mr and Mrs Baldwin to do some sightseeing in the Rockies. I saw a good deal of them on the train. The Prime Minister was a fluent conversationalist. Listening to him expounding on such varied topics as the apple husbandry of Worcestershire, cricket, and the revision of the Prayer Book – then a subject of violent controversy in Parliament – I was impressed by his erudition even more than by his reputation for political sagacity. However, as I studied Mr Baldwin, I thought I detected traces of the arrogance that some Englishmen display when travelling abroad. The deeper we penetrated the North American continent, the more he became the embodiment of old John Bull himself. In my house of Sovereignty I was to discover that side of him.' *A King's Story* (1951), p. 220.

and his speeches have appealed in a very wonderful way to the Canadians – but it has been a very hard task for him and far from a holiday.[73]

When he got home, the Prime Minister spoke of what he had seen with poetic imagery and fresh hope in his heart. 'I see again the cliffs of Quebec rising above that majestic river,' he recalled in the preface to *Our Inheritance*, a volume of his speeches, which included a dozen he had made in the course of his Canadian trip, 'the great train carrying us onwards through boundless cornfields in the Middle West, great cities standing where the pioneer's axe once hardly made its way, limitless forests whose fringes still recede further to make way for the industry of man . . . One who visits Canada and sees her in the radiance and glory of her morning learns a new hope, a new security.'[74]

9

Baldwin used to speak of his sense of isolation in the highest political office. 'I don't think that anyone who has not been Prime Minister can realise the essential and ultimate loneliness of that position,' he confessed to Lord Oxford at the end of the second year of his second term: 'there is no veil between him and the human heart (or rather no veil through which he cannot see) and in his less happy moments he may feel himself to be the repository of the sins and follies of the world.' He returned to the subject a few weeks later in a speech at Worcester:

> It is the loneliest job in the world, and for this reason a Prime Minister cannot share his ultimate responsibilities. He is in the position of the captain on the bridge of a ship: he must try to look far ahead, with much knowledge that is hidden from most of the people in this country . . . Above all things, he must possess his soul in patience, and must harden himself to be indifferent to daily criticism.

He was particularly conscious – and the feeling preyed on his mind – that a decision for which he was praised at the time might well turn out to be the wrong one, just as an unpopular action on his part might equally prove to be justified by subsequent events. 'The PM's job is not so good as it used to be,' he remarked towards the end of his second term. 'I have been reading about Melbourne for the last few hours. He led an easy life.'[75]

Certainly the loneliness of which he complained did not extend to his private life. His wife was never far away from his side to comfort and cheer him; he was well served by two devoted private secretaries in Ronald Waterhouse and Geoffrey Fry; Tom Jones was a sympathetic confidant besides being an admirable speech writer with a remarkable aptitude for research; and there were the faithful Davidsons with whom he could relax and unburden himself of his worries. Also, there was always Chequers for the week-ends with clock golf on the lawn, strolls across the meadows, where the friendly lambs would come up to the Prime Minister, who on occasion would be photographed with them, and finally patience in the Long Gallery.

Tom Jones has preserved in his diaries the atmosphere of the table talk at Chequers in which Mrs Baldwin took an animated part. 'The worst of country life,' she once remarked to Jones, 'is that the men take to drink, and the women go off their heads.' When Jones pretended to be startled at this generalisation, she added in all seriousness 'But I can give you lots of names.' Lloyd George, as ever, provided a staple diet of conversation at meal times. 'I am sorry for Dame Margaret,' said Mrs Baldwin. 'I should not like to be his wife.' 'He is a dynamic force,' her husband broke in, 'I have always said that.' 'Would you have liked to be Napoleon's wife?' Jones asked his hostess. This suggestion horrified her, whereupon Jones observed that Lloyd George 'belonged to that order of mankind'.

Mrs Baldwin also told Tom Jones during the same visit that she had recently sat next to Bernard Shaw at dinner and thought he was nothing but a *poseur*. 'He is a bad influence; he scoffs at all the things that matter.' Jones put up a vigorous defence of the controversial G.B.S., pointing out that at any rate he disciplined himself and at least believed in a Life Force. 'But he will never say, God,' retorted Mrs Baldwin. Jones could convey no impression at all of what Shaw stood for and had done. 'I am not clever,' was Lucy Baldwin's parting shot on this topic.

Changing the subject she went on to tell Jones of the extraordinary letters which she said reached Prime Ministers' wives. 'I have just had one complaint that I give garden parties in Lent. What I do is to have quite simple "At Homes" on Thursday at No. 10.' This correspondent also reminded her that Charles II in Lent had gone daily to church in state. 'But,' queried the Prime Minister with a humorous twinkle, 'did he spend his nights at home?'[76]

In his early days at Chequers during his first Premiership Baldwin used to make the journey by road, but after the car skidded dangerously he henceforth went by train to and from Wendover, only motoring the few miles between there and Chequers. Jones noticed that he always bought his own tickets for himself and his wife. Lloyd George would have left such a detail to a secretary, noted Jones, but Baldwin liked to write his own cheques and address his own envelopes. Returning after one week-end with the Baldwins to London, Jones noticed that at Wendover railway station the Prime Minister bought *The Times* and the *Morning Post* and a picture paper for his wife. They had a reserved compartment. According to Jones, Baldwin read the leading articles in less than five minutes, noticed the news of a friend's death, and then settled down to solve the crossword puzzle in the *Daily Telegraph*, which he finished just as the train steamed into Baker Street.

As in Baldwin's earlier tenure of Chequers, there were visitors at most week-ends, but they included few political colleagues apart from the Davidsons and the Bridgemans and occasionally Neville Chamberlain, Eustace Percy, Ormsby-Gore and Anthony Eden, then a rising young MP whom the Foreign Secretary Austen Chamberlain had appointed his PPS. Montagu Norman, the banker, appeared regularly, and there were various literary guests including Rudyard Kipling, J. M. Barrie, Angela Thirkell and the Mackails. The ex-Premier Lord Oxford and Asquith came with his wife in February 1925, the Prince of Wales in October 1926 and the King and Queen in April 1927. Shortly before the latter royal visit, Queen Mary had sent the Prime Minister a drawing of the Long Gallery by the Victorian travel writer and autobiographer Augustus Hare. 'The gift will be greatly treasured in time to come by other occupants of that beautiful house,' wrote Baldwin in thanking the Queen, 'but by none more than myself, for it represents the particular and favourite spot in the whole house which my family and I invariably use.' Lord and Lady Lee also kept in touch, and in 1925 Lee presented a three-quarter-length contemporary portrait of Sir Walter Raleigh, dated 1598, 'so that Prime Ministers may enjoy the company, and the memory, of another great Englishman'.

For every week-end that the Prime Minister spent at Chequers, he was entitled to draw the sum of £15 from the Trustees. In Baldwin's time no charge fell upon public funds and indeed did not do so until 1932 when dry rot was discovered in the ancient timbers and an expenditure of over £4,000 was required to put it right. Early in 1927, the Prime Minister's personal accounts became mixed with the accounts for official entertaining, so that Baldwin had to get an old friend, Sir John Withers, the Member for Cambridge University who was also a solicitor, 'to look into it and clear up the mess'. This may have been partly the fault of the curator-housekeeper, since the Trustees appointed a new one named Mrs Sinclair at this time. In doing so, the Secretary to the Trustees defined her duty which has remained the practice ever since:

> It should be your endeavour to make the Prime Minister feel that when he is at Chequers the house is his home and everything should be done to promote his convenience and comfort and his enjoyment of the house.[77]

Distasteful as many of them were to him, Baldwin had to cope with the personal questions inseparable from the Prime Minister's private office. Most of these were concerned with political honours, appointments and promotions, or money in one form or another. When Thomas Hardy died in 1928, Baldwin, Kipling and Shaw were among the pall-bearers who deposited the writer's ashes in Poets' Corner in Westminster Abbey. The occasion left a vacancy in the ranks of the Order of Merit. Kipling had refused the OM years before. Shaw had never been offered it. Now in his seventy-second year, he seemed the obvious choice. But Baldwin shied away from the prospect of Bernard Shaw, OM. According to Jones, Baldwin was afraid that he might accept it, and then ridicule it publicly. In the event, the honour went to a safer and more conventional Irishman, Sir George Grierson, an authority on the languages of India.

Incidentally, Shaw had an interesting correspondence with the Prime Minister on the subject of T. E. Lawrence ('Lawrence of Arabia') at this time. Lawrence, who had changed his name to Ross and later to Shaw so as to avoid publicity, was most anxious to rejoin the Royal Air Force in the ranks from which he had been discharged after a few months' service in 1922 because his identity was revealed in the press. He had joined the Tank Corps, but never ceased to pull strings to get back to the RAF, appealing to Trenchard, the Chief of the Air Staff, and other influential friends. After Trenchard had withdrawn his objections the application was referred to Hoare, the Air Minister, who turned it down. Lawrence was so upset that he told his friend Edward Garnett that he intended to take his own life since he was convinced, as he told Garnett, that he was 'no bloody good on earth'. Alarmed by the threat of suicide, Garnett immediately wrote to Bernard Shaw, who passed his letter to Baldwin, adding that 'some decision should be made since there is a possibility of an appalling scandal, especially after Lowell Thomas's book'.* In the result, the Prime Minister intervened and Lawrence in

---

* Lowell Thomas, an American journalist whose book *With Lawrence in Arabia*, published in 1924, was a hero-worshipping account of Lawrence's desert campaign against the Turks in the First World War.

the guise of Aircraftman Shaw was reinstated in the RAF to his intense delight. Incidentally Baldwin's action enabled Lawrence to write *The Mint*.

Some years later, Lawrence wrote to Bernard Shaw expressing his gratitude for what he and Baldwin had done for him:

> If you meet Baldwin in the near future, will you please tell him that the return to the Air Force secured me by him (on your initiative) has given me the only really contented years of my life? Please say that I've worked (and played) all the time like a trooper: that my spell of service has been spent in doing my best to raise the pride and respect of the ranks and to make them pleased with their duties . . .
>
> I tell you all this, not to boast of it, but to show that you and Baldwin, in gratifying what may have seemed to you my indulgence, have not harmed the public service. I have done all I could, always: and could have done more if they had given me more rope. The Air Force is pretty good, down below. I think it deserves more imaginative handling than it gets.[78]

The scrutiny of recommendations for political honours, particularly those who had subscribed liberally to Conservative Party funds, Baldwin was content to leave to Davidson, who succeeded Jackson as the Party Chairman, in 1926.* (One aspirant who had put up £100,000 in expectation of a peerage threatened to sue Davidson for the return of his money, and Davidson was eventually authorised by Baldwin to repay this sum which was done.) Then there were some embarrassing payments out which had to be made after the Leader had approved them, such as Birkenhead's £10,000 as compensation for ceasing to write for the press. A certain Mr Donald Im Thurn was given £5,000 for his services in connection with the Zinoviev Letter, which he bought from a Russian *émigré* source and which long afterwards was shown to be a forgery, though neither Baldwin or any of the other leading Conservatives had any notion of this at the time. Finally, there was the awkward case of Mr Reginald Clarry, MP, whose defeat of the Coalition candidate at the Newport by-election on the eve of the Carlton Club meeting had augured the downfall of the Coalition: he had to have £1,000 and a guarantee of his bank overdraft to stave off bankruptcy proceedings, thus averting another by-election, which would have been inconvenient for the Government at this time.[79]

* Forty new peerages were created on Baldwin's recommendation during the period 1925–9, only ten less than in the period of the Lloyd George Coalition 1918–22.

In January 1929 Baldwin had an extraordinary meeting with his old political enemy Beaverbrook, who had offered the Prime Minister £25,000 to be distributed for any charitable purpose that Baldwin might see fit. Beaverbrook and several of his associates had been involved in a bad motor accident at Surbiton and he had been seriously ill for some weeks. At one point, he thought he would not recover and, as he had a fear of dying with an uneasy conscience, he made the gesture to Baldwin 'in gratitude for my good fortune'. Baldwin wrote to Beaverbrook saying he would certainly undertake the task of distributing the money but would like to have a talk with him first about how it should be done. Consequently he went to see Beaverbrook at his London house, since Beaverbrook was not well enough to come to Downing Street.

Next day Baldwin told Tom Jones of the outcome. 'He is an extraordinary mixture,' said Baldwin, 'and I think that since the death of his wife the better elements of him have been coming to the surface.* He had a really narrow escape from death the other day and I found him very earnest about things.'

'One always knew from his friendship with Bonar,' Jones broke in, 'that there must be a good side to the man despite all stories to the contrary.'

'Well,' Baldwin went on, 'yesterday he told me that after Bonar's death he had played a low mean game and that he was sorry. Whereupon I said I wished to bear no malice towards any man, and I shook hands with him.'

This admission greatly amused Jones, whom Baldwin thereupon asked: 'Why do you laugh, you old cynic?'

Jones replied: 'I think your having said you would not see Beaverbrook in your house and then going to Beaverbrook's house and shaking hands with him is a subject for mirth. I think he has been so clever in landing you with this job of spending £25,000 to celebrate the sparing of his life.'

'Well,' Baldwin concluded his account, 'we got to business on that, and I asked him did he want to endow a Professorship or to help one or two big objects, like cancer research, or was I to give it away in packets? He replied, "Packets," adding that he had in train a scheme for some foundation for endowment later on. So that's that.'†

It was early in his second term as Prime Minister that Baldwin dis-

---

* The first Lady Beaverbrook died in 1927.

† The money was distributed, largely on the advice of Lord Dawson of Penn, to various hospitals and the university medical faculties of London, Oxford, Bristol, Manchester, Sheffield and Glasgow.

covered his gift for the microphone which he was to develop with striking effect, particularly during the General Strike, and which was to make him the most successful radio speaker of the time. His slow, conversational fireside manner, suggesting that he was thinking aloud, went down extremely well in the country at large. He prepared his speeches carefully, whether for delivery on the platform or in the House of Commons, or at lunches and dinners, and although he had considerable help from Tom Jones in their composition they all bear the unmistakable stamp of his personality. The earliest collection of his speeches, which he published in 1926 under the title *On England*, proved so successful – it sold 30,000 copies – that he was to be encouraged over the years to bring out four more such volumes. His own manner of delivery he was at pains to cultivate, and he would also sometimes comment on the speeches of others, both Cabinet colleagues and backbenchers, actual or potential.

Ministers who speak to a departmental brief in the House are obliged to read their speeches in case there should be any doubt as to what they actually said, and these recitations are apt to be boring. To one such effort which was delivered by Sir Samuel Hoare, the Air Minister, Baldwin reacted by sending the speaker a note as soon as he had sat down:

> I give you first prize for reading. Just the right pace to follow, with proper pauses for digestion.
> Nearly everyone goes too fast.
> You also avoided the almost inevitable spurt which most of us put on when getting into the straight.

Again, having heard A. P. Herbert, the future Independent MP for Oxford University, then on the staff of *Punch*, speak at several dinners, including the Worcestershire Society, to which he had invited him, Baldwin sent Herbert the following letter which he wrote in his own hand:

> 10 Downing Street
> Whitehall
> 31.X.1928
>
> My dear A.P.H.,
> I am going to risk being cut by you next time we meet and losing the Freedom of Hammersmith. But you are young and I am old and I am thinking of the future.

I want you to take heed to the delivery of your speeches. It is at present without form and void.

It is like an intermittent machine-gun fire, rapid, but dropping at the end almost into inaudibility. Ordinarily this wouldn't matter, but your stuff is A1.

When you can put it over you will be in the top flight of after dinner speakers. Study method. To my mind, at his best, Gordon Hewart* is a model; every word and phrase tells. And so might your stuff: it is good enough but it doesn't get across properly.

You may say, What business is it of yours? or Mind your own speeches. True, but you can be a first-class coach without being a first-class oar (Rudie Lehmann)† and I can judge a speech.

You have it in you to be so good and that is why I have butted in. That's all.

S.B.

'What a wonderful thing,' commented Herbert, 'that a Prime Minister should take the trouble to write so beneficent a letter to a young man he hardly knew! I glowed with gratitude, obeyed the advice, and, I believe, improved.' Indeed, as a result of the advice, Alan Herbert became one of the best and most popular after-dinner speakers in the country. For this he was never to forget what he owed to Baldwin.[80]

10

Unlike some Prime Ministers, Baldwin did not indulge in periodic government reshuffles. The only Cabinet changes which he made during his second term were caused by one death (Curzon) and four resignations (Wood, Cecil, Cave and Birkenhead).

When he succeeded Curzon as Lord President in 1925, Balfour was in his seventy-seventh year, but until his health failed three years later he regularly attended the meetings of the Privy Council, Cabinet and Committee of Imperial Defence. He also acted as Chairman of the Inter-Imperial Relations Committee; under his guidance and inspection this Committee issued a report which paved the way for the Statute of Westminster in 1931 by recognising the equal status, both in domestic and foreign affairs, of the dominions and colonies with the mother country. His valediction to public life occurred on the morrow of his

---

* Lord Hewart, Lord Chief Justice of England from 1922 to 1940.
† Rudolph Lehmann, journalist, Liberal MP and Captain of the Leander Rowing Club.

eightieth birthday, an occasion described by Baldwin in a letter to the King, although Balfour continued to hold his office for the remainder of Baldwin's second term.

26 July 1928. An interesting little ceremony took place in the Speaker's Court this afternoon. Friends of the Earl of Balfour, numbering over 160 in the Upper House and over 150 in the Lower House, had united to give him some memento on the occasion of his eightieth birthday. Their choice had fallen on a Rolls-Royce motor car, which was standing in the centre of the Court, surrounded by a large company in happy disorder and deaf to the summons of the division bell. It was entrusted to the Prime Minister, Mr Lloyd George and Mr Clynes* to express the message of good-will. Lord Balfour made a most happy reply, his words being emphasised by those same gestures which were so familiar to past generations of politicians. Then he was driven away to the old-time accompaniment of three good cheers.[81]

In November 1925, Edward Wood was appointed Viceroy of India in succession to Lord Reading, at the same time being raised to the peerage as Lord Irwin, while his place in the Cabinet and at the ministry of agriculture was taken by Colonel Walter Guinness, later Lord Moyne. At first Baldwin was unwilling to spare Irwin, whose appointment was originally suggested by Birkenhead with the King's warm approval, but he was eventually convinced that Irwin would be an ideal Viceroy to launch India on the road to Dominion status. The actual instrument of reform was an all-Party constitutional commission led by the Liberal Sir John Simon, whose appointment Baldwin announced towards the end of 1927.

As Chancellor of the Duchy of Lancaster, Lord Cecil of Chelwood was responsible for League of Nations affairs under Austen Chamberlain, with whom he did not get along at all well. In the summer of 1927 Cecil found himself at odds with the Cabinet on the subject of naval disarmament, and this difference with Baldwin and his other colleagues precipitated his resignation. He was succeeded at Geneva by the diehard Tory Ronald McNeill, who also took Cecil's place on the Government Front Bench in the Upper House as Lord Cushendun. Thus, in demanding a greater naval strength than the United States, who wished for a ratio of 5 : 5 : 3 for Britain, the USA and Japan, Baldwin and his Cabinet strength-

---

* J. R. Clynes, Labour MP and former leader of the Parliamentary Labour Party. He was narrowly defeated for the leadership by Ramsay MacDonald in 1922, later becoming deputy-leader.

ened the isolationists in the United States and the militarists in Japan, besides wrecking the Naval Disarmament Conference at Geneva and incidentally making an enemy of the influential League of Nations Union at home, as Baldwin was later to realise to his cost.[82]*

Cave's resignation, which occurred just before his death, early in 1928, created a vacancy on the Woolsack. Baldwin's immediate reaction was to offer it to Birkenhead, but Birkenhead declined as he had already made up his mind to retire from the Government later in the year and go into the City. Baldwin then offered it to the Attorney-General Sir Douglas Hogg, who was probably the ablest minister on the Treasury Bench, being widely tipped as Baldwin's successor in the Conservative leadership. Neville Chamberlain remarked at the time that 'it was all rushed through in a very unfortunate way', since Hogg had always told Chamberlain that he would like to have his advice before deciding in the event of being offered the Woolsack on Cave's retirement.

. . . though he didn't think he had quite committed himself, he admitted when he came to see me on Tuesday [27 March] that he had not been very definite in saying no [when he saw Baldwin on the previous Friday]. I strongly urged him to delay and said I would ask the PM to press F.E. again, but on Wednesday morning I found it was too late as S.B. had already given the Attorney-Generalship to Inskip and made Merriman Solicitor.

Poor Douglas was very unhappy for he had realised that when it came to the point he wanted to continue his political career and of course the tragedy is that he is now barred from the chance of becoming PM when S.B. retires. To my mind this is a great misfortune for I believe he would have had a good chance and I am sure he is the best man we have for such a position.

Thus it was that Sir Douglas Hogg became Lord Chancellor as Lord Hailsham. 'The appointment of Sir Douglas Hogg is the only possible one,' Baldwin told the King in asking for his approval, 'as there is no other suitable candidate.'[83]

Six months later, Birkenhead left politics for ever, bidding an almost tearful farewell to the Prime Minister and the Cabinet which was reflected in the private letters he exchanged with Baldwin. 'You will

* 'It is at least possible,' wrote Cecil later, 'that if we had settled the cruiser question, *as Japan was most anxious to do*, we should have helped to strengthen the peace-party in that country and the invasion of Manchuria might never have taken place.' John Raymond (ed.), *The Baldwin Age*, p. 97.

not misunderstand me,' wrote the latter in accepting Birkenhead's resignation, 'when I tell you that we shall part on my side at least with a feeling of personal regret that I could not have believed possible four years ago!' To which Birkenhead replied: 'I regret greatly leaving an office where I have spent the happiest and most interesting years of my life.' 'All good to you, my dear F.E.,' rejoined Baldwin.[84]

Birkenhead's place at the India Office was taken by Lord Peel, the Minister of Works, who had held the office before. To replace Peel at the Office of Works, with a seat in the Cabinet, Baldwin did not promote one of the non-Cabinet or junior ministers, as might have been expected. Instead he appointed the Marquess of Londonderry, who had recently resigned his post as Minister of Education in Northern Ireland and whose wife now achieved her ambition of seeing him in the English Cabinet. 'It was not altogether a popular choice, and I was largely influenced by Winston,' Baldwin told Londonderry's son some years later.* 'In offering him the job I paid him a little compliment, which I hoped would show that I was seeking his friendship as well as his services. Instead of writing him a note or summoning him to Downing Street, I paid him a visit at his house and asked him to join my Cabinet. After all, I had done four years in my second term as Prime Minister, and he had never been in the Cabinet before; it was, too, the junior post of all.† However, he seemed not to notice my gesture. I always had the impression that your mother looked down on my wife and myself.'

> Your parents started off to play politics in the old style. They proceeded to entertain politically on a vast scale, with, of course, the set purpose of political advancement. F.E., with that caustic wit of his, used to describe your father as 'catering his way to the Cabinet'. It was very magnificent and beautifully done, but to me it was out-of-date and at times in dubious taste. It did not fit in with my idea of true Tory democracy. Central Office, of course, loved it. These methods were not calculated to make your father popular with his colleagues.

* Londonderry and Churchill were second cousins, being related through the third Marquess's daughter Lady Frances Anne Vane-Tempest, who married the seventh Duke of Marlborough and was the mother of Lord Randolph Churchill.

† According to the Cabinet minutes for 29 October 1928, Baldwin in welcoming their new colleague Lord Londonderry pointed out that 'he was only the second new member of the Cabinet since the Government had come into office' (Cab. 23/59/44). This was a curious lapse of memory on Baldwin's part, since Londonderry was in fact the fourth, the others being Balfour, Guinness and Cushendun.

A few months later Londonderry had a difference of opinion with Baldwin which was to rankle for some time. It arose out of an invitation which the Prince of Wales had accepted to visit the coalfields in Northumberland and Durham, which were among the hardest hit in the prevailing economic depression. The invitation came from Sir Alexander Leith, a former High Sheriff for Northumberland and a leading Conservative in the north-east of England, who felt that the Prince's appearance 'might put some heart back into the miners and show them that they were not entirely forgotten', since, as Sir Alexander told the Prince, 'the Government doesn't seem to understand how serious the situation is up there'.

Hearing of the proposed visit (probably from Lord Londonderry) and fearing that it might have 'political repercussions' but not knowing who was behind it, Baldwin sent an urgent message to the Prince of Wales to come and see him in his room in the House of Commons before he set off for the north-east. When the Prince arrived one bitterly cold afternoon towards the end of January 1929, he found a worried-looking Prime Minister, who seems to have thought that the visit had been arranged by one of the Labour leaders, such as Ramsay MacDonald himself who was MP for Seaham Harbour, the mining constituency in Durham where Londonderry had his principal collieries. Anyhow he remarked to the Prince that with the prospect of a general election in the fairly near future unemployment might well be used as a stick with which to beat the Conservatives.

'You know I stand outside politics,' said the Prince. According to the Prince, Baldwin continued to look uneasy and it was not until the Prince told him that it was Alexander Leith ('a member of your own Party') who had suggested the visit and was in charge of the arrangements, that the Prime Minister gave a sigh of relief. 'Wonderful man, great friend of mine,' he said. Indeed they had been at Harrow together and of course that put quite a different complexion on the matter. 'I'm delighted,' Baldwin went on, as he showed the Prince out. 'I hope you have a successful trip, and don't find the cold too trying.' As he left the House of Commons, the Prince wrote afterwards recalling the incident, 'I was somewhat puzzled as to the precise difference between Conservative and Socialist humanitarianism.'

After the Prince got back from his three-day tour, Londonderry, who felt that he had not been sufficiently consulted as one of the leading coalowners in the north-east, wrote to Baldwin that he was 'rather aggrieved' and that the visit was 'really unfortunate from my point of view'. And well it may have been. But there was nothing that Baldwin could do about it except sympathise.

Londonderry House. 1 February 1929 . . . In the first place it was in no sense a private visit. The Prince's advent to the colliery villages was advertised in every possible way, with bands of photographers and press men and all concomitants of publicity. The Prince of Wales's dicta as to 'appalling conditions', 'perfectly damnable', 'ghastly', etc., are now being broadcast throughout the world and the County of Durham and the coal trade is pilloried in a most unfair and unfortunate way.

I can tell you one characteristic instance and that is that a row of houses which the owners had condemned, and also erected other houses to take their place, was inspected by the Prince of Wales who indulged in condemnatory remarks.

I am bound to say that I resent the whole of this tour and I think it has been carried out under most unfortunate auspices. I do most sincerely hope that the Prince of Wales will not be allowed to enlarge upon the thoroughly stage-managed point of view which no doubt exists in his mind.

The Public seem to be quite unaware that most of the miners in Durham live rent free or receive a rent allowance; that they also receive free coals and, if they are off work three days a week, they receive the dole!

There was one typical instance which was brought to my notice of how the Prince of Wales was shown a pay bill of nine shillings which, of course, was supplemented by the dole. This latter information was not given to him and his remark was: 'Is that due to bad management?' to which he received the reply from the miner: 'No, to hard management.'[85]

The 1924 Parliament was now nearing the end of its life. Since no Government runs a full five years to the day, Baldwin and his Party managers decided that the spring of 1929 would be the latest date on which they could conveniently go to the country. 'A big year will soon begin,' Baldwin had written to Churchill in the previous summer, 'and much depends on our keeping fit. You will have a great deal to do as Chancellor and you need to be at your best, and our combined judgement will have many a test. I am sure if we keep together and go forward boldly into the New Year we can win a great victory.'

The Prime Minister even considered reconstructing the Cabinet and announcing its new composition on the eve of the Election as a kind of caretaker Government. He discussed the appointments he had in mind with Tom Jones. What did he think of Churchill for the India Office?

Reversing his earlier opinion, Jones said he was 'all for it, that he [Churchill] would rise to the height of a great opportunity, that there was nothing petty about him, that we officials might quarrel and denounce him to his face, but he was not vindictive'. Neville Chamberlain had expressed a preference for the Colonial Office ('That is just filial piety,' observed Jones), although Baldwin wanted him to be Chancellor of the Exchequer. 'It would be an extraordinarily popular appointment in the party,' he told Neville. 'For one thing they liked to have the next man to the PM in that office.' But, as he said to Jones, 'if Neville won't go to the Treasury, we might send Worthy [Worthington-Evans] or Philip [Cunliffe-Lister] there. What about Walter Elliot for Labour?' Besides Londonderry for the Air Ministry, he also thought of Walter Guinness for the War Office, Ormsby-Gore for the Office of Works ('He is interested in the art side of things') and Sam Hoare as Health Minister, 'because he had shown some interest in such problems and in the slums'. On the other hand, 'Sam Hoare knows all these foreign languages, and I could put him in the Duchy and use him at Geneva for a couple of years.'

'I think we must keep Horne out, don't you?' Baldwin went on. 'And then I thought of keeping out all who are older than myself. That is the sort of rule I could apply. This would then exclude Balfour, Cushendun, Salisbury, Bridgeman and Jix. Austen I should have to keep at the Foreign Office as he is irreplaceable . . . I shall be sorry to lose Willy Bridgeman. I must think out the whole business in Easter week. Would it be wise to announce the composition of the Cabinet just before the Election?'

Jones expressed strong doubts about the wisdom of this course, pointing out that while each appointment would conciliate some section, it would alienate others. 'Well, think it over,' said Baldwin, 'and we will discuss it again.'

Baldwin returned to the subject some weeks later when Jones was spending the week-end at Chequers. 'Amery has sent me a melancholy grouse about some squabble with Winston – a comforting sort of epistle to receive just now,' he told Jones. 'He has been wanting me for weeks to announce a reconstruction of the Cabinet. He fancies himself for the Treasury, and would send Winston to be Lord President of the Council.* Amery does not add a gram to the influence of the Government.'[86] Baldwin refused to consider Amery for a moment as Chancellor of the Exchequer, since Amery was a full-blooded Protectionist and Baldwin had no wish to repeat the experience of the 1923 election.

---

* In charge of defence matters, replacing Balfour whose ill-health now prevented him from coming to Cabinet meetings.

Amery's opinion of Baldwin, written some years later, supplies an interesting contrast with his leader's view of him:

> Baldwin's personality is likely to remain a puzzle to future historians, as it was to his contemporaries. It was in some respects a disconnectedly divided personality. Outwardly he was the typical Saxon, bluff and phlegmatic, tolerant and always ready to see the other man's point of view, a lover of the countryside and of the kindly English virtues. All this was a very real side of him, even if he was actor enough to make the most of it in order to create the Baldwin he wished to be, and wished the public to trust. But underneath, cropping up unexpectedly at intervals, there was the strong Celtic Macdonald strain – emotional, impulsive, secretive, and intensely personal in its likes, dislikes and moral judgements.
>
> Intellectually a similar lack of cohesion often showed itself between his political beliefs and his actions. He was, in any case, profoundly illogical and intuitive, browsing over a problem until the vague cloud of his thoughts condensed into some conclusion which might, as often as not disperse again into nebulous inactivity, but might also lead to some sudden decision. He could be unexpectedly and even incomprehensibly impulsive . . . His motives were more often personal than based on policy, oscillating between purely moral judgements of men's characters and shrewd political manoeuvre. In Cabinet he would suck his pencil, or screw his mouth round in a circle, studying the personality of his colleague rather than attending to their arguments, quite content, as a rule to accept the views of the majority and only very rarely – but then effectively – intervening to get his own way. By nature indolent his inertia was fortified by a profound scepticism as to the results of any particular legislative or administrative action.[87]

In April 1929 Geoffrey Dawson, *The Times* editor, spent a Saturday afternoon alone with Baldwin at Chequers, in the course of which they discussed a wide range of topics including Baldwin's contemplated reconstruction of his Cabinet. This inspired a not particularly friendly leader in *The Times* entitled 'Reconstruction', which was certainly approved by Dawson, if not actually written by him. This commented on the Prime Minister's alleged mistakes and missed opportunities and explained why a ministerial reconstruction would not then be desirable.

There are many occasions, notably when the Prime Minister went to Canada the year before last, which gave him the chance of reviewing the condition of his team from a distance and reforming it on his return. These chances were missed, and the consequences of this failure are not yet expended.

All that Baldwin could decently or possibly do at this stage, the article concluded, was that he 'should make it absolutely clear to the country that, if and when he returned to power, he does mean to reshape his Government drastically for another spell of work'.[88] In the result, Baldwin decided to postpone the announcement of any reconstruction.

A few days after his talk with Tom Jones, Baldwin attended an election fund-raising dinner given by Londonderry in the banqueting hall at Londonderry House. According to Lord Astor, one of about sixty guests, who listened to an off-the-record speech by Baldwin over the cigars and brandy, 'the PM drew a lurid picture of what would happen if Labour came back – civil war in Egypt, India in confusion, super-tax mounting, etc., etc.'.

When Jones, who got his account of the dinner from Astor, mildly censured the Prime Minister for what he was reported to have said, Baldwin retorted: 'I know on which corns to tread, but I confess I was glad to blow it all away on the river the morning after. There was not one of the diners with whom I would change places for all their wealth. It was an infinitely pleasanter sight watching the Cambridge crew [practising for the Boat Race]. Not one of them wanting even an OBE.' In fact, Baldwin had cancelled a meeting of the Committee of Imperial Defence, on which he was to have presided, and thus 'upset twenty or thirty potentates, in order to see the crew practice'.[89]

In spite of the loss of four out of six by-elections and the inevitable swing away from it which any Government must expect after four years of office, Baldwin fully expected to win the forthcoming General Election. Although unemployment continued at a high level, there were 600,000 more men at work than in 1924, and Baldwin could point with pride to a succession of achievements to the Government's credit, such as nearly a million houses, considerable slum clearance, hundreds of new schools, cheap electricity, improved pensions, untaxed tea, a complete reform of local government and the so-called 'flapper vote' by which the franchise was enlarged to include all women between the ages of twenty-one and thirty. And then there was Locarno, a great milestone along the road of world peace, as well as the constitutional reforms being planned in India and other parts of the Empire with the object of eventual self-rule. Of course, in the final reckoning there was a possibility of stalemate between the Conservatives and Labour with the Liberals led by Lloyd George holding the balance. 'S.B. said the King's Government must be carried on, but that he personally would not serve with L.G.,' noted Neville Chamberlain in his diary after he had discussed this possibility with Baldwin in March. Chamberlain remarked that he was in the same position, and 'S.B. said in that case he supposed the leadership would go to Winston'.[90]

A few days previously, Baldwin had seen Ramsay MacDonald and told him that, just in case he (MacDonald) should become Prime Minister again, he ought to know something of what the Conservative Cabinet had in mind over a number of pending projects such as the Report of the Simon Commission on India. Somewhat surprisingly, MacDonald 'said quite definitely that he hoped he would not be PM', to which Baldwin replied: 'Be that as it may, there are one or two things, if you do come back, on which I should like you to keep your eyes skinned. The American money power is trying to get control of some of the natural resources of the Empire. They are working like beavers.' He instanced Northern Rhodesia, where he thought there were considerable copper deposits, of which the Americans were trying to gain control.[91]

Parliament was dissolved on 11 May 1929, and on the same day Baldwin wrote to the King, who was recovering from a prolonged attack of pneumonia to which he had nearly succumbed:

> The Prime Minister is glad to be able to pay a tribute to the un-failing loyalty of his Cabinet. Individually they have worked in their own spheres with ability and resource, while collectively they have contributed real knowledge to the Cabinet discussions that have taken place. The Prime Minister also feels that he must make some reference to the Whips under the command of Commander Eyres-Monsell. By their cheerfulness and tact they have materially assisted in keeping together so large a party without dissatisfaction or disintegration.
>
> The final months of the present Parliament have been over-shadowed by Your Majesty's illness, and the deep anxiety with which Parliament and the Nation, and indeed the whole world, watched your Majesty's progress, is significant proof of the affection and admiration in which Your Majesty's Person and the British Throne are held.
>
> Having written this last letter of the present Parliament, the Prime Minister awaits the verdict of the Polls.[92]

EIGHT

THE PARTY REVOLT

I

'I am trusting to the decency of the British public,' Baldwin remarked to Tom Jones on the eve of the poll in May 1929. 'I believe they will recognise the good work we have done and will not be deluded by Lloyd George.' Baldwin's belief had been strengthened by the reception he and his wife had during his national campaign, particularly in Lancashire. He wrote to Mimi Davidson from Knowsley on 20 May:

> Enthusiasm delightful to see . . . It was like a royal procession, the occasional 'boo' drowned by cheers, and near the theatre [in Blackpool] the crowd was kept behind barricades. The theatre was packed to suffocation with about 5,000. Then we walked through the barricaded crowd to a point overlooking the beach. You never saw such a sight. The police estimated the crowds on the front and down below on the beach at 200,000. I couldn't hazard a guess: I had never seen anything like it. I said a few wise and cunning words which met with warm approval, and, mark you, all these crowds had heard me relayed from the theatre.[1]

He was further encouraged by the optimistic reports from Party Headquarters, which forecast the Conservative majority at around fifty over the combined strength of the other two parties. Unfortunately the enthusiasm shown by his supporters in Lancashire did not reflect the over-all popular feeling throughout the country, which indicated through the ballot boxes that great numbers of voters were tired of the Tories – 'torpid, sleepy, barren,' Lloyd George called them – and wanted a change. In particular, Baldwin's statement, widely reported in the national press, that if he and his Party were returned to power, he would continue Austen Chamberlain at the Foreign Office went down badly with many people, who considered that Chamberlain was too friendly towards the French – 'I love France like a woman,' he once said – at the expense of the Americans, with whom he had allowed relations to deteriorate almost to the point of hostility.

The Prime Minister was also criticised, somewhat unfairly, for the choice of 'Safety First' as the slogan on which he based his appeal to the country, coupled with a portrait of himself which bore the caption: 'The Man You Can Trust.' In fact, it was suggested by an advertising agency employed by Conservative Central Office and the responsibility for it rested with Davidson and the Party managers; although it was approved by Baldwin, according to his son Windham, he never considered it an inspiring one. Its adoption should be regarded in the light of the current national campaign to reduce accidents on the roads, and the public was already familiar with 'Safety First' posters which adorned public buildings and hoardings up and down the country. 'It wasn't I think really fair to criticise the slogan as being too negative,' wrote Davidson afterwards; 'it wasn't negative, it was deliberately intended to try and prevent the adoption of Socialist programmes for the country.' No doubt the popular mood of 1929 needed something more exciting. If anything, it was in advance of its time, since two years later it was to be repeated with resounding success by the candidates standing under the banner of Ramsay MacDonald's 'National' Government.[2]

Baldwin and his wife sat up with Tom Jones and the rest of the secretariat and party chiefs to hear the results. By the time they went to bed about 3 a.m. it was clear that it was 1923 all over again and the Tories were out. Jones noted that the Prime Minister found it hard to reconcile the results with his reception on tour, as well he might. As in 1923, the Liberals held the balance with 59 seats as between Labour's 287 and the Conservatives' 261, although owing to the eccentricities of the British electoral system slightly more people voted Tory than Labour.

'Mr Baldwin regrets the loss of some of his best young Members of the House of Commons,' noted Stamfordham in a memorandum to the King; 'but it is the result of the action of the Liberal Party, who have put up representatives to contest almost every constituency with no chance of winning but taking away the votes which would have been given to the Conservatives: and all this done with money which was subscribed to the Liberal Party with the specific object of keeping the Socialists out of power.'[3]

Jones saw Baldwin briefly next morning before he left with his wife and his private secretary Patrick Duff for Chequers where he planned to think over whether he should resign immediately or face Parliament as he had done after the 1923 election. 'I must lead the Opposition,' he admitted in a moment of confidence, 'but I am a poor man, and I cannot afford to run a house in London and keep on the old home in Worcestershire.' It would have been unthinkable for him to accept a bunch of company directorships like Horne or write lucrative articles for the newspapers like Lloyd George, both of whom he had frequently denounced to Jones, and Jones dared not suggest that he do so. But although he himself voted Labour, Jones had a deep affection for Baldwin and he persuaded his friend Lady Astor to offer the defeated Premier a part of her large house in St James's Square. Sir Philip Sassoon also offered him the use of Trent Park to compensate for the loss of Chequers. But Baldwin would not think of accepting either generous offer. He preferred to sell his house in Eaton Square and take a smaller one at 11 Upper Brook Street which he and his wife found after a considerable search through the Duke of Westminster's agent.[4]

'This reverse has come as a great shock,' Duff wrote to Windham Baldwin when they reached Chequers. 'Still this isn't the end of everything. As the PM says, no one has ever done anything big and good if he has always had success and hasn't had some thumping clouts on the head on the way. And this may be just the recoil for a bigger jump, like 1923 was.'[5] Among the Labour victors in the constituencies was Baldwin's elder son Oliver, who won Dudley (for Labour) in his native Worcestershire, and was now to view his father across the floor of the House of Commons, a spectacle which his mother could never brace herself to face from the gallery. He had latterly composed his private differences with his father, and at this time he wrote him a touching letter of sympathy in his hour of disappointment:

Now that the agony is over, and you can get a little rest before the House meets, I thought I would tell you what I have meant to for some time past: but now, it seems, a more opportune moment and I hope it will soothe the mosquito bite of defeat. Wherever I have gone on my political rounds during the past six years I have never heard any of our supporters speak other than in a kindly way of your personal self. Our only regret is that you have not been able to put what you have said into practice. That is all.

To you who have generally been victorious, the results may disappoint you, but take it from one who, until the other day, has always been on the losing side, always in the minority and generally

alone, that victory or defeat are both flatterers and as such are of no
serious consequence. You may be judged by History for your political
actions, but you will be judged by God for the spirit that is in your
heart.[6]

This opinion was endorsed by another Labour supporter. 'His personal
prestige in the country is not impaired,' wrote Tom Jones on the morrow
of the election, 'and he set a tone throughout the fight which commanded
universal respect.'

Jones spent much of Sunday, 2 June, closeted with Baldwin in his
study at Chequers. Afterwards he noted in his diary:

I found him in a state of great nervous tension, the L.G. obsession
weighing heavily upon his mind. Austen was in favour of meeting
Parliament; so was Winston. I said very little, but he spoke with
great rapidity – most unusual with him, and only possible when
roused by L.G. It was L.G. who had put the Socialists into office,
and it was L.G. who throughout the day dominated our discussion.
What would he do? As the day wore on I moved round to the view
that the PM ought to resign straight away. Duff strongly held this
opinion. What we all feared was that L.G. might keep S.B. in office
for a week or a month, and humiliate him and his party in every
conceivable way.[7]

During the afternoon Stamfordham motored over from Windsor to
find out whether Baldwin's intention was to stay in office and meet
Parliament or to resign. Baldwin began by saying that 'never in his life
had he been placed in such a difficult position'. Stamfordham gathered
that on the whole he favoured resignation, and he summarised his views
to the King:

In all his addresses during the past few weeks he has appealed to the
Democracy to trust him as they did in 1924 and these were the final
words in his broadcast message on the eve of the General Election.
The votes of the people, enormously increased by he himself having
given the Women's Franchise, shows that the country has refused
again to place its confidence in him and that the new electorate does
not want him. He has been beaten and in the true English spirit he
accepts his defeat and, if he resigns, the Democracy in an equally
British spirit will take off their hats to him as a good sportsman, who
has had his run, been beaten and takes his beating like a man. And,

what is more important, this will count in his favour whenever the next General Election takes place.

If on the contrary the Prime Minister holds on and says he will meet Parliament, the voice of Democracy will say: 'Here is this man clinging to office, he won't take his defeat, he is trying to prevent the Labour Party from enjoying their victory.' There will also be an idea that he is trying to make terms with the Liberal Party to keep him in office and, moreover, if he should hold on and meet Parliament the Government will be bound to be defeated very shortly.[8]

Jones went on to Cliveden where he spent the night with the Astors. While he was there the Labour leader J. H. Thomas rang up Lord Astor and told him that unless Baldwin resigned at once 'there would be a most awful howl from Labour'. When Jones reported this to the Prime Minister next morning in Downing Street he found him a changed man – 'his nervousness gone because his mind was made up'. He had decided to resign and he informed his Cabinet colleagues accordingly at an informal meeting in the Cabinet room the same afternoon. Since the King had not recovered sufficiently from his illness to come to London to receive his resignation, Baldwin went down to Windsor where the King received him in his bedroom. He told His Majesty that the public might regard it as 'unsporting' of him if he did not resign immediately and might suspect that he was contemplating some deal with the Liberals to keep Labour out. The King assented and immediately sent for Ramsay MacDonald who agreed to form a Government.

On 8 June 1929 the new administration headed by MacDonald went to Windsor to receive their seals of office. On the same day, Neville Chamberlain, who cherished as little love for Lloyd George as Baldwin did, wrote in his diary:

The election has come and gone in disaster. We are out and R. MacDonald has formed his second Cabinet. After all, S.B. dallied so long with reconstruction that it never came . . . I thought perhaps the general respect and affection with which he is regarded would have overborne everything else, but it was not so . . . L.G. finished up with less than sixty seats. His effort to revive his party has failed, thank Heaven, and we may hope that the process of disintegration will now continue until it is absorbed by others . . . There is no conversion to Socialism. It is merely the present discontents showing themselves in a desire for change.

As he doubtless told his leader, Neville Chamberlain thought that after two years MacDonald might successfully appeal to the country after a 'millennium' budget 'at the expense of the rich', and come back with a working majority for another five years. 'On the other hand,' Chamberlain added with some prophetic insight, 'the new government may make such blunders that, before two years are up, the country will be glad to be rid of them.' 9

2

Immediately after his resignation, Baldwin and his wife accepted an invitation from Sir Philip Sassoon to stay at Trent Park, Sassoon's magnificent place in Hertfordshire with its superb gardens and private golf course, so as to recover from the fatigues and disappointments of the previous weeks. Tom Jones joined the house party, bringing with him a bundle of letters for Baldwin's signature. The letters were addressed to the recipients of the Dissolution Honours, a list which, according to Jones, had spoiled the Chief's last few days in office but had hardly spoiled the Ascot race meeting where Baldwin and Lucy watched the racing from the Royal Enclosure, because, as he told Jones, 'I saw there so many faces of those who would be disappointed when they read the list.' The list which the King approved on Baldwin's recommendation comprised five new peers, six baronets, seven privy councillors and eleven knights. The peers included Joynson-Hicks, who became Lord Brentford, and Hamar Greenwood, whom *The Times* aptly described when the list was published as 'a curious relic of the Coalition'. Baldwin's host at Trent Park was one of the new privy councillors. Among the others who had served Baldwin in various ways was his private secretary Geoffrey Fry who was rewarded with a baronetcy, and Tom Jones, who had previously refused a knighthood but now agreed to become a Companion of Honour, a mark of distinction which few would deny that he had earned by faithful devotion to duty. One parliamentary lobby correspondent, in commenting on the list, described it as more remarkable for what it omitted than for what it contained. 'It seems more and more difficult,' wrote *The Times* in a leading article, 'to resist the conclusion that "Honours" seldom fall to politicians who do not pursue them.' 10

For the second time in less than six years Baldwin had led his Party to electoral defeat. It is hardly surprising that some of his followers should have begun to murmur and as the months passed to talk of the need for a change in the leadership. The movement was to escalate, more perhaps to Neville Chamberlain's embarrassment than Baldwin's, since Chamberlain, though widely acknowledged in the Party as the heir-apparent, was too loyal to Baldwin to entertain any designs to supplant him. The two men met after the summer recess and Chamberlain noted in his diary at the time:

> I told him of criticisms that were reaching me from all quarters about his want of leadership and told him that he must give a lead and be a bit more aggressive if the Party was to be held together . . .
>
> It is all very depressing and particularly embarrassing for me because everyone I meet tells me of S.B.'s failings and many suggest that I should do better in his place. Heaven knows I don't want the job. It is a thankless one at any time and never so more than now when the Party is all to pieces. Moreover S.B. is my friend as well as my leader and I would not on any account play L.G. to his Asquith.[11]

The position was complicated by Beaverbrook's crusade for Empire Free Trade in his newspapers and his declared intention of running 'Crusaders' at by-elections. As an old protectionist Baldwin had some sympathy with Beaverbrook so long as his objects were confined to imperial preference and did not involve the imposition of domestic food taxes. Baldwin invited Beaverbrook to meet him and Neville Chamberlain at his house on 12 November. ('It seems not inappropriate that this letter should be written on Armistice Day,' to which Beaverbrook replied: 'I will be there at ten a.m. and bareheaded.') This meeting, like others which followed during the succeeding months, was friendly but inconclusive. Although he was given to intriguing against him and even trying to depose him from the Party leadership, Beaverbrook had to admit that at their meetings he fell under the spell of Baldwin's personality. 'I went to see Stanley Baldwin,' he wrote to the editor of the *Morning Post* on 19 February 1930. 'You know I like him. Further, I come under the influence of his charm every time I talk to him.' However, the overtures eventually came to nothing, and the old vendetta was resumed by Beaverbrook, who could now count on the support of Rothermere and the *Daily Mail*. 'I will make no progress in co-operation with Stanley Baldwin,' Beaverbrook wrote to an American political correspondent on 14 May. 'He is a useless fellow and I hope he will have to walk the plank, or get the black spot, or anything else you like to call it.'[12]

Baldwin counter-attacked with unexpected vigour, particularly when

Rothermere foolishly overplayed his hand to the extent of demanding that he would not support Baldwin unless he was acquainted in advance 'with the names of at least eight or ten of his most prominent colleagues in the next Ministry'. At a Party meeting in Caxton Hall on 24 June 1930 Baldwin read out Rothermere's letter, on which he commented: 'A more preposterous and insolent demand was never made on the leader of any political party. I repudiate it with contempt and I will fight that attempt at domination to the end.' On this occasion he received an overwhelming vote of confidence, and next day when he walked into the Commons chamber he was loudly cheered, more so indeed by the Labour benches than the Conservative.

However, Austen Chamberlain for one considered that Baldwin had made a mistake by trying to put Beaverbrook in the same class as Rothermere. He wrote to his sister Hilda:

> The difference between the two men is illustrated by their replies this morning to his Saturday's speech. Beaverbrook is dignified, avoids personalities and goes to the root of the matter. Rothermere scolds like an angry fishwife. Another man than Baldwin would, I think, have kept Beaverbrook and might yet get him on our side.[13]

For the moment Tory discontent was diverted on the head of the Party chairman John Davidson, stimulated by broadsides from the Beaverbrook–Rothermere press which bitterly attacked his management and called for his resignation. In the event Davidson yielded the chair at Central Office to Neville Chamberlain who had offered to take on the job. 'It was the only time when I ever felt rather tried by Baldwin,' Davidson admitted looking back long afterwards, since it was plain that Baldwin was quite willing to let him leave Palace Chambers. And so Davidson went quietly. 'I did not want to make it difficult for S.B.,' he remarked, 'but I did think that when he announced my resignation he might have said something in public of appreciation of the work I had done.' It says much for Davidson's forbearance that the incident made no difference to their personal friendship.[14] 'The tide is flowing our way strongly but shall we escape fresh blunders?' wrote Austen a week or two after his brother had taken over from Davidson. 'Both Neville and I are driven nearly to despair by S.B.'s ways, but between us we are getting some order into our affairs by degrees, greatly to the satisfaction of our colleagues. Neville does the heavy work and I do the trimmings.'[15]

Incidentally Austen Chamberlain was annoyed that his brother had been saddled with the Party Chairmanship, and wrote to his sister Ida:

I am more than ever vexed that S.B. should have prevailed upon him to take the Central Office. It requires too much time and what is worse it involves him in difficulties and enmities which ought not to be his affair. So much do I feel this that I even sounded him as to my undertaking to bell the cat and gently indicating to S.B. that it was time for him to go but Neville thought I should do more harm than good and asked me not to try it. So there we are – none of us happy except S.B. and his cronies and Neville's future chances being seriously jeopardised by his new office and his old leader.[16]

A few days after the Caxton Hall meeting, Beaverbrook and Rother-mere returned to the attack. In fact, Rothermere made it known to Neville Chamberlain that both he and his fellow press baron would give the Conservative Party '100 per cent' support provided Chamberlain was substituted for Baldwin as leader. Neville Chamberlain's reaction to Rothermere's 'straight tip' was characteristic:

The commonest loyalty makes it impossible to listen to such a suggestion, and yet the tragedy is that – most reluctantly – I have come to the conclusion that if S.B. would go the whole party would heave a sigh of relief. Everywhere I hear that there is no confidence in his leadership or belief in his determination to carry any policy through. Yet it looks as if I might have to go down fighting for S.B. when my own desire is, as it always has been, to go for the free hand.[17]

The 'free hand' which Chamberlain had in mind was freedom to negotiate preferential trade treaties with the Dominions subject to parliamentary ratification. This policy was to be put to another Party meeting which had been convened for the end of October, also at Caxton Hall, to challenge Baldwin's leadership.

At the beginning of October, after he had returned from his annual holiday at Aix-les-Bains, Baldwin spent a couple of days with his old political friend Willy Bridgeman (who had become Lord Bridgeman) at the latter's home in Shropshire. After Baldwin had left, Bridgeman wrote with some misgivings to Neville Chamberlain:

S.B. came to me at Leigh for two nights, and for a short period we managed to get him to talk about politics, and it seemed that he was prepared to go on the lines sketched out by you when we last met. We did our best to open his eyes to the requirements of the situation and the necessity of some vigorous pronouncement. I am sure he cannot retire now without doing harm – irreparable to himself – but also unsettling for the party who would not recover from it in time for an early election.

All the same I felt that, though he was convinced he ought to stay on and put up a strong case, his heart did not seem to be in the business. That may only have been the result of a long holiday and distaste for the resumption of work, and the fact that amongst friends there was no need for him to conceal his inmost feelings. But he must avoid the appearance of apathy, as that is one of the principal charges brought against him. He must not cultivate the attitude of being in a transcendental plane above the sordid turmoil of political strife, but try and enjoy a bit of hard fighting and hard work.

All the way up in the train he would do the *Times* cross-word instead of reading the speeches and news. Nobody saw him fortunately. If they had they would have wondered if he really was a keen party leader. I hope when he gets to work he will throw off this detached appearance.[18]

Bridgeman's words were strongly echoed by Austen Chamberlain who wrote to his brother a few days later:

I am very unhappy about the situation. In the first place I cannot conceal from myself that the retirement of Baldwin at this moment would be hailed as a triumph for themselves by Rothermere and Beaverbrook and would be thought by many people to be so. This is in itself sufficiently revolting and it is besides a real danger for the future.

On the other hand, I doubt whether Baldwin can recover his position. For one thing, he seems to me to be living in a fool's paradise and to deceive himself completely about the state of things. For another, he is, I fear, incapable of giving that active fighting lead which is so essential.[19]

However, Austen's brother Neville was more cautious. 'If any move is made,' he told Austen, 'it should really come from the House of Commons which makes, and can presumably unmake, leaders.'[20]

The week-end before the second Caxton Hall meeting, the Astors had a house party at Cliveden which included Ormsby-Gore, Walter Elliot, Robert Boothby, Harold Macmillan, Brendan Bracken and Terence O'Connor, 'all young disgruntled Tories, all angry with S.B.', in the words of another guest, Tom Jones. 'The tide has turned very much in favour of L.G. because of his incomparable executive power,' noted Jones, 'and I think most of this group would follow if he could be got into the saddle again. Everybody cursing S.B. for running after Beaverbrook . . .'21 These young Tories looked to Winston Churchill for a lead, since he was known to favour an arrangement with Lloyd George and his Liberal followers to turn the Labour Government out and revive the old Conservative–Liberal Coalition, a prospect which was most distasteful to Baldwin and Chamberlain.

Two or three days before the meeting, Baldwin met Derby and they had a long talk. 'Tell me as an old friend,' Baldwin asked the 'King of Lancashire', 'do you think I ought to resign?'

'Well, old man,' replied Derby, 'I hate to say it but I think you ought.' According to Baldwin, Derby 'repeated all the old stuff about apathy and the impossibility of my keeping a united party'. Although he told Baldwin that he was not going to the meeting and was never going to take any further part in politics, in fact Derby turned up and subsequently told Salisbury that 'the meeting had completely changed his view' and that he would do all he could to support Baldwin and the Party.22

Fortunately for him, Baldwin struck the right note at Caxton Hall, although he was apprehensive before the meeting began. 'Photograph me now, gentlemen,' he told the press photographers who crowded round him at the entrance. 'It may be the last time you will see me.' However, as Geoffrey Fry told Tom Jones, he 'had a marvellous reception, made a very good speech, very dignified . . . said there was no question of his resigning. All the niceness of the man came out.' The 'free hand' on fiscal policy, for which Baldwin asked, was endorsed with only one dissentient – Beaverbrook; and the meeting went on to pass a vote of confidence in the Leader by 462 votes to 116. 'I was not surprised at the size of the minority,' Bridgeman wrote to Neville Chamberlain a few days later. 'If only people knew who were there, they would realise that if we were 4 to 1 in numbers we were 20 to 1 in intelligence. I have already hinted to S.B. that he must keep on fighting as a party leader, and you are right in thinking that he should see and talk to as many people as possible.' 23

When Jones called on Baldwin at his room in the House of Commons the following afternoon, he found him looking tired but 'fairly satisfied' with the result of his speech despite the news which had just come in of the victory of Beaverbrook's 'Crusader' candidate over the official Conservative candidate at a by-election in Paddington. Rudyard Kipling had been to see Baldwin the same morning. 'Kipling says I must not be seen so much with philosophers and poets,' he told Jones, 'so you and he must keep away. I suppose it means that for the next twelve months I ought to stick to politics and politicians, and never read a book. It is a grim prospect. I suppose I must see the party through the next election, change the country over to a protectionist basis, and then clear out.'

Jones told Baldwin about the gathering at Cliveden and begged him to make a point of seeing 'a great deal' of the younger Tories. 'Well, I put Oliver Stanley on the Indian Conference,' replied Baldwin. He then asked: 'Do you think Walter Elliot will make a Leader of the Party?' Jones said that he had many qualities, a keen intelligence, wit, earnestness, honesty, but he was not sure about his courage.

> I begged him to make no public reference to Beaverbrook and Rothermere, to ignore them completely. They could not go on screaming the same thing day after day without boring their readers and lowering their circulation. I told him that the last approach to Beaverbrook was a mistake in the eyes of the man in the street, but had probably been dictated by the Central Office. I gathered it was Neville's advice.
>
> We then talked about Girton and Women's Colleges, as he has to speak at a Girton Dinner tonight. I had lent him Virginia Woolf's *A Room of One's Own*, and I tried to persuade him to read aloud at Hyde Park Hotel V.W.'s description of the lunch at the Men's College and the dinner at the Women's College.[24]

Baldwin, it may be remarked here, was given to reading novels, as indeed other English Prime Ministers have been. One which he greatly enthused over was *Precious Bane* by Mary Webb, a tale set in north Shropshire, copies of which he sent to many of his friends. The well-publicised pleasure which this novel gave him greatly contributed to its success, besides inspiring Baldwin to write an introduction to a new edition, which came out towards the end of his second ministry, although by this time Mary Webb was dead. 'I was glad to think,' wrote Baldwin, 'that I was in time to send her a few words of appreciation.'* She thanked him, sent him a bunch of violets, and asked if she might dedicate her

---

* In this Introduction Baldwin wrote: 'The strength of the book is not in its insight into human character, though that is not lacking. Nor does it lie in the inevitability with which the drama is unfolded and the sin of an all-absorbing and selfish ambition punished. It lies in the fusion of the elements of nature and man, as observed in this remote countryside by a woman even more alive to the changing moods of nature than of man. Almost any page at random will furnish an illustration of the blending of human passion with the fields and skies.'

next book to him. A copy of *Precious Bane* had originally been given to
Baldwin by Tom Jones at the instigation of the publisher Hamish Hamilton, to whom the Prime Minister subsequently expressed his gratitude.
Baldwin spoke of the book with such effect at a Royal Literary Fund
Dinner in April 1928, that a hitherto neglected masterpiece suddenly
became a bestseller. Another work which strongly appealed to Baldwin
was F. S. Oliver's *The Endless Adventure*, a study of the career of Sir Robert
Walpole whose political philosophy was much akin to his own, and a
book which was to have a considerable influence on Conservative thinking.[25]

Being Opposition leader also gave Baldwin more time for academic
interests: he was such as Rector of Glasgow University and Chancellor of
St Andrews. Then, following Balfour's death in March 1930, he was
invited to succeed him as Chancellor of Cambridge and accepted gladly,
as indeed became one who had only secured a Third in the History
Tripos. His installation and the accompanying ceremonies were attended
among others by General Dawes, who had recently been appointed
American Ambassador. Baldwin described the occasion to the Davidsons:

> It was a heavy day: the installation at noon, the lunch in Caius Hall,
> the degree ceremony, a garden party at Magdalene, a dinner at Trinity
> and a reception at the Lodge. I had the perfect page in attendance
> all day. He was in court dress and acted as to the manner born. Two
> funny things happened. Of course a Trinity dinner is always a family
> party, no reporters, absolutely private. Dawes sent his speech to
> the Press Association and so it was published. But funnier still, an
> American movie man turned up. Would we stop the procession on
> its way to the Senate House from Trinity for the American Am-
> bassador to make a speech? On explaining to him that this wasn't
> done, he replied: 'But the American Ambassador has given his con-
> sent.'[26]

'I would far rather be Chancellor of Oxford than Prime Minister and
the task would certainly be a lighter one,' wrote Birkenhead to Baldwin
when he heard the news of his appointment to Cambridge. Birkenhead
had been seriously ill from the effects of a broken blood vessel whilst
holidaying at Biarritz, and Baldwin had made sympathetic inquiries to
which Birkenhead replied: 'The Doctors, both French and English,
give me great encouragement to believe that, unless I am unlucky, in
three or four months I shall be completely restored to normal health.'
They had kept in touch since Birkenhead had left politics for the City,

their old differences had long since been forgotten, and it is noteworthy that when Birkenhead's only son and heir came of age 'F.E.' should have asked Baldwin to propose the toast of his health at the birthday dinner in Gray's Inn Hall, 'a night never to be forgotten, when this great gathering of his father's friends met to launch him out on the great sea of life'. Unfortunately soon afterwards Birkenhead went down with bronchial pneumonia, which proved fatal. As his friend Winston Churchill put it at the time, 'he burned all his candles at both ends. His physique and constitution seemed to be capable of supporting indefinitely every form of mental and physical exertion. When they broke the end was swift. Between the setting of the sun and night there was only the briefest twilight. It was better so.' Birkenhead died on 30 September 1930, barely two months after his fifty-eighth birthday. Baldwin recalled what he had written to Birkenhead when he resigned from his Government: 'For four years your counsel in Cabinet has been invaluable: in dark days you were a tower of strength, and you have been a generous colleague and a loyal friend.' [27]

As Chairman of the Rhodes Trust at this time, Baldwin was largely instrumental in reviving the scholarships tenable by Germans at Oxford under the will of Cecil Rhodes, which had lapsed on the outbreak of war in 1914 in the interests of what he called 'the removal of misunderstandings and the promotion of friendship between German and English-speaking peoples by educational means'.

Another outside interest which Baldwin took up was the Pilgrim Trust, founded in 1930 by the American philanthropist Edward S. Harkness, who endowed it with £2 million for such purposes as the repair of ancient buildings, the purchase of works of art and the promotion of social welfare schemes in Britain. Baldwin agreed to become the first chairman of the Trustees, who included the jurist Lord Macmillan, and the author John Buchan, later Lord Tweedsmuir and Governor General of Canada. Tom Jones retired from his post as Deputy Secretary of the Cabinet to become first Secretary of the Trust. (He eventually became Chairman.) Offices were taken in a pleasing house at 10 York Buildings, Adelphi, later destroyed by enemy action in 1940. 'Sort of house one could settle in with one's wife,' Baldwin remarked after the first Trustees' meeting. [28]

Shortly before the new parliamentary session, Baldwin sent Londonderry, then on holiday in Scotland, a telegram asking whether he and his wife would give the customary Conservative reception in Londonderry House on the eve of the State Opening of Parliament by the King. In view of Baldwin's remarks to Londonderry's son Castlereagh on the subject of these parties, quoted above, Londonderry's reply to Baldwin is of some interest:

Loch Choire Lodge, Kinbrace, Sutherland. 11 October 1930

I am always glad to give the party, as you know, if it is necessary, and this was my understanding with Neville. He very kindly tried others but I expect they all declined. My difficulty is that I have to plead poverty for so many urgent calls, when the newspapers write us up as the perpetrators of Bacchanalian orgies. I hope Neville is right when he thinks these parties do a great deal of good. We get the smug-faced citizens of London with their wives and daughters who vote Conservative anyway. I always wish that we could touch other strata where the bulk of the votes lie: but please rest assured that we are always delighted to do anything that gives *you* the smallest assistance . . .

We are having a small reception for the Imperial Conference on the 20th [October]. I set great store by this because I want to do the best I can for the Dominion Ministers, and I do hope that you and Mrs Baldwin will be good enough to come.

Ramsay MacDonald was here for a couple of days. I liked him very much but he is not the man for his job, and he is obviously pressed along in directions in which he has no desire to go.[29]*

MacDonald was showing clear signs of mental strain and fatigue at this time which Baldwin did not fail to notice. When he heard the news of the disaster to the airship R101, which crashed on a hilltop in northern France in the early hours of 5 October 1930, killing forty-eight people including the Air Minister Lord Thomson, Baldwin immediately called on the Prime Minister to offer his sympathy. According to Harold Nicolson, who lunched with the Prime Minister at Chequers later the same day, Baldwin and MacDonald were 'agreed that no man's health could stand being Prime Minister'. MacDonald complained that he could

---

* MacDonald also stayed with the Duke of Sutherland at Dunrobin Castle, as well as with the King at Balmoral. When Beatrice Webb read of the Prime Minister's peregrinations in *The Times* she was moved to the following caustic comment: 'Alas! Alas! Balmoral is inevitable; but why the castles of the wealthiest, most aristocratic, most reactionary and by no means the most intellectual of the Conservative Party? "Because," J.R.M. would answer if he laid bare his heart, "I am more at home with them than I should be with you or any other member of the Labour Party." Considering that he represents Seaham his friendship with the Londonderrys almost amounts to a public scandal. This silly little episode will do the PM untold damage with the non-commissioned officers of the Labour Movement. He *ought* not to be more at home in the castles of the great than in the homes of his followers. It argues a perverted taste and a vanishing faith.' *Beatrice Webb's Diaries 1924–1932*, p. 249.

only sleep for two hours a night and could do no work. ('The moment I disentangle my foot from one strand of barbed wire it becomes entangled in another.') Nicolson also recalled that when MacDonald began to introduce Richard Bennett, the Canadian Premier, who was also a luncheon guest, to Mrs Nicolson, he forgot the Canadian's name, making a hopeless gesture, his hand on his white hair, and repeating pathetically, 'My brain is going, my brain is going.'[30]

3

Baldwin's tendentially unpredictable behaviour at this time proved a sore trial to Neville Chamberlain, who was trying hard to keep the Party together in the face of mounting dissensions. The Tory leader would suddenly cancel meetings without letting any of his colleagues know, and once, when he cried off making a short appearance in a film about Disraeli on the pretext that he had strained a ligament in his foot during his sleep, Chamberlain commented sardonically: 'Any ordinary mortal would have telephoned to save me going round to his house, but the poetic temperament does not work that way.' Then after a Party luncheon in November 1930 to the Australian delegation at the Imperial Conference, Chamberlain complained: 'S.B. would only make jokes about his leg and couldn't be got into general conversation.' A few weeks later, he noted in his diary that the leadership question was again growing acute. 'I am getting letters and communications from all over the country . . . Sam Hoare . . . reports that the feeling in the House could not be worse. I cannot see any way out. I am the one person who might bring about S.B.'s retirement but I cannot act when my action might put me in his place.'[31]

Matters came to a head towards the end of February 1931. Particularly hostile criticism came from Derby who wrote to Neville Chamberlain on 25 February:

I have only been back in England for ten days or so, but even in that time I am aghast at the feeling that there is with regard to Baldwin and his leadership. There was always a certain amount of feeling last summer but it is nothing compared to what it is now and largely I think due to the very inept speech he made with regard to India, as naturally India looms large in the eyes of Lancashire owing to the cotton trade. If I have heard the view expressed once I heard it expressed twenty times that we shall never win the Election under his leadership. He can make extraordinarily good speeches and everyone likes him but he has got absolutely no drive and moreover is supposed to be hand-in-glove with Ramsay MacDonald.[32]

After suggesting that Hailsham might be acceptable in place of Baldwin 'with some energetic person like yourself as leader in the House of Commons', Derby returned to the attack in another letter to Chamberlain a few days later:

The worst of Baldwin is his leadership. His policy is good: he makes, as a rule, very excellent speeches, but after that he fails as a leader. He has no hold on his party; he doesn't seem to want to keep in touch with them. He listens to all the agreeable things that are said, and not to any of the disagreeable ones, and he never seems to want to cultivate the good opinion of the younger members of his party.

Between ourselves, I think Mrs Baldwin has done him incalculable harm. She may be quite right to spare him as a general rule, but surely she ought to let him know some of the criticisms which I know she hears herself but which she keeps from him. The worst thing for a man like that is to be allowed to live in a fool's paradise.[33]

Sir Robert Topping, the General Director of Conservative Central Office, now deposited a disquieting memorandum on Chamberlain's desk in which he analysed the 'gradual drift away' from Baldwin which had taken place since the Caxton Hall meeting in the previous October.

There has, of course, been dissatisfaction with the leadership of the Party ever since the Beaverbrook and Rothermere campaign started, but for a long time it was confined to a comparatively small section. Today, however, the feeling that he is not a strong Leader is widely felt and, in my opinion, cannot be ignored . . .

The position appears to me to be so serious that I feel compelled to place my impression of it before you, and while I would not at all relish the task, if it is considered my duty to place these impressions before the Leader himself, I am prepared to do so.[34]

Topping also pointed out that many Conservatives were worried about India, which had been given a pledge of eventual Dominion status by the Viceroy Lord Irwin, a policy with which Baldwin was in complete sympathy. Anxious to expedite it, Ramsay MacDonald had convened a Round Table Conference in London in the previous November and the Indian delegates took the opportunity to demand its rapid implementation. At the same time, Winston Churchill publicly dismissed the Indian claims as 'absurd and dangerous pretensions', a view which gained considerable support among the Party diehards in preference to the Irwin policy in New Delhi which had Baldwin's backing. Churchill signalised his break with Baldwin on the Indian issue by resigning from the Shadow Cabinet.

When he had read Topping's memorandum, Neville Chamberlain consulted several of his senior colleagues, notably his brother Austen, Cunliffe-Lister, Hoare, Hailsham, Bridgeman and Eyres-Monsell, the Chief Whip. Everyone except Bridgeman agreed that Baldwin must go and that he should be shown the memorandum. The question was, when? Hailsham suggested a short delay, as Baldwin was due to make a major speech the following week at Newton Abbot and it would be rough on him to administer such a shock when he was preparing for a great effort. Austen Chamberlain, on the other hand, felt that he should be told as soon as possible. The matter was eventually left in Neville's hands. The latter's decision to delay no longer was due to what he read in the papers on 28 February about a by-election pending in the St George's division of Westminster caused by the sudden death of the sitting member Sir Laming Worthington-Evans. It was announced that Sir Ernest Petter, an industrialist with no particular knowledge of politics, would contest the seat as an independent anti-Baldwin candidate with the support of Beaverbrook and Rothermere; also that Colonel J. T. C. Moore-Brabazon (later Lord Brabazon of Tara), the pioneer motorist and aviator, who had served as a junior minister under Baldwin and had been the official Conservative candidate, had withdrawn since he felt unable to support his leader.

On the same day that Sir Ernest Petter's candidature was announced, Austen Chamberlain wrote frankly to his sister Ida about Baldwin:

S.B.'s leadership was always the 'accident of an accident'. Considering his total lack of any of the qualities which are ordinarily needed to bring a man even into the front rank, the largeness of his following in independent quarters and the considerable success which for a time he achieved were remarkable; but even more remarkable is the total slump which has followed. No one so poor as to do him reverence! Men who have most loyally supported him through thick and thin now declare him impossible. Agents say that his name has ceased to be an asset and become a drawback. Lancashire has left him; Scotland no longer trusts him; in London his name stinks. Old contributors to Party funds refuse to subscribe; officials are in despair. He has got to be told squarely what the position is and invited to consider it and poor Neville has to do the job.

Never has any party been more patient with incapacity; never has any man been given so many chances and pulled out of the water so many times; but I think that at last the end has come and that the Party will be forced to get rid of its old man of the sea if it is not prepared to be drowned by him . . .

I have urged Neville to act at once. St George's is one degree worse than East Islington, for the candidate comes out directly on the question of leadership and I believe it to be not unlikely that he will be successful. How sick it all makes me! And I am the more sick because I fear that Neville's immolation of himself on the Party altar has diminished his chances of the succession by withdrawing him from our debates and by identifying him with S.B. so much as to obscure his own personality.[35]

On 1 March, the Topping memorandum, from which a number of the more wounding phrases had been omitted, was sent round by hand to Baldwin's house in Upper Brook Street. Baldwin was a little stunned, but his wife's immediate reaction was rather one of relief. 'At long last,' she remarked, 'we will be able to spend some time with our own people.' Neville Chamberlain arrived after lunch, fully expecting that Baldwin would at the least defer his resignation, digging in and rallying his followers against the press lords' intervention in St George's. But when he learned from Chamberlain that he and his principal colleagues thought that there should be a change of leader, he said: 'Very well, the sooner the better. Let's have a meeting of my colleagues tomorrow morning when I can say Goodbye.' Whereupon Chamberlain returned to Central Office and the news that Baldwin had decided to go spread rapidly, so that the editor of *The Times* had a leading article set up in Printing House Square entitled 'Mr Baldwin Withdraws'. Whilst this was being done, Davidson and Bridgeman walked over after dinner to Upper Brook Street where they found the Baldwins 'quite convinced that they were about to retire from politics altogether and retreat to their home in Worcestershire where they looked forward to a period of complete leisure'. They also spoke of cutting down their living expenses and even of selling the Astley estate. ('The financial cloud depressed me beyond words,' Mrs Baldwin noted in her diary.)

'Well,' Lucy Baldwin greeted the visitors, 'we four were together at the beginning of Stanley's leadership and now we're together for the farewell.'

'Farewell, be damned,' said Bridgeman, who, said Baldwin afterwards, had 'rolled in like an old Admiral and protested against my going out in so ignominious a fashion. Could I not make some stand, and go out on some first-class issue?' Bridgeman went on to suggest that Baldwin should come out and fight St George's himself, so as 'to challenge the right of the Press millionaires to dictate procedure to the Party'. The idea appealed to Baldwin and he immediately wrote a note to Neville Chamberlain asking him to come and see him next morning on the way to the office.

Chamberlain arrived punctually and asked Baldwin what he wished to see him about. 'I have decided to go down fighting,' Baldwin replied, 'and I propose to be adopted as the official candidate for St George's.'

'S.B., you can't do that,' said Chamberlain with a look of surprise.

'Why not?'

'Think of the effect on your successor.'

Baldwin suspected that Chamberlain's reply was not wholly disinterested. In fact, Chamberlain had been talking over the matter with Hailsham and each had agreed he would be willing to serve under the other, leading the Lords and Commons respectively. The claims of Churchill and Horne were also being actively canvassed, although Chamberlain had gathered from a reliable informant that the Hailsham–Chamberlain combination was 'what the City would like, and that if it were known that we would act together no other alternative would have a chance'.

Baldwin's interview with Chamberlain ended curtly. 'I don't give a damn about my successor, Neville,' he said.[36]

A few days later, Chamberlain learned from Joseph Ball, the Director of the newly established Conservative Research Department, who had got it from Davidson, that Baldwin 'had now definitely made up his mind not to go unless he was kicked out'.* Furthermore, he was 'very

---

* Ball was something of a mystery man, who had been recruited for Conservative Central Office by Davidson when the latter was Party Chairman. He had connections with secret intelligence sources and played a leading part in the negotiations which led to the purchase of the notorious Zinoviev letter on behalf of Central Office. Davidson has admitted that he and Ball 'ran a little intelligence service of our own, quite separate from the Party organisation'. Its purpose was to penetrate the Labour Party which it successfully did, since according to Davidson 'we had agents in certain key centres and we also had agents in the Labour Party Headquarters'. By this means the Conservative Research Department was able to obtain advance information of Labour's policy plans and copies of their literature, which it was consequently in a position to study and answer almost simultaneously with their publication by Transport House: Robert Rhodes James, *Memoirs of a Conservative*, p. 272. It is unlikely that Baldwin knew anything of these activities or that he would have approved of them even if he had known. Ball was knighted in 1936 and died in 1961, aged 72.

angry with some of his colleagues', particularly Hailsham, whom he was convinced had been plotting against him, and also Chamberlain for not supporting him more vigorously as Party Chairman. 'Personally I do not believe anything but a very early General Election can save him,' Chamberlain wrote to his sister Ida at this time, 'and evidently other people think so too as my friends tell me that there is any amount of lobbying going on for Winston and Horne as successors.'[37]

4

'Things are getting difficult,' noted Lucy Baldwin in her diary: 'I wonder how much more one can bear.' On 3 March 1931, Sir Clive (later Lord) Wigram, who had succeeded Lord Stamfordham as Private Secretary to the King, saw Baldwin and asked him what he thought of the political situation.* 'He said he thought it was distinctly rocky,' according to Wigram, 'and, with a wink, added that his own situation was not too bright.'

Wigram asked him if, supposing Ramsay MacDonald resigned and the King sent for Baldwin, would he be able to form a Government? 'No, certainly not,' he answered without hesitation. 'Lloyd George would have me out in a week on a vote of confidence on tariffs. If the King sent for me, I could only recommend a dissolution.'[38]

At this crucial moment in Baldwin's political fortunes, two fortuitous happenings contributed to postponement of the demand for his resignation. One was the courageous action of Mr Duff Cooper in giving up the safe Conservative seat which he had been nursing at Winchester and offering himself to the constituency association at St George's as its official standard bearer in the by-election. Alfred Duff Cooper, just turned fifty, was a politician with literary leanings who had begun his career in the Foreign Office before marrying a duke's daughter, the

* Stamfordham died in the same month aged eighty-one. As Arthur Bigge he had been in the sovereign's service since 1895, being created Lord Stamfordham in 1911 and becoming Principal Private Secretary in 1913, which post he retained until his death. 'I learned to appreciate his judgement,' wrote Baldwin to the King at this time, 'to admire his character, and to value his friendship more and more as the years went by. And since I had the honour of serving your Majesty, I have realised what the personal relationship meant to his Sovereign, the service and friendship of a man wise and loyal and true to the very fibre of his being. No one can wholly fill the place left by one associated with the early years of life: his departure opens the floodgates of memory and the broken link can never be reforged.' Baldwin to King George V, 2 April 1931: RA AA.49/131.

beautiful and vivacious Lady Diana Manners, and entering politics as Tory MP for Churchill's old seat at Oldham. He had held junior office in the second Baldwin government and had lost Oldham to Labour in the 1929 General Election. He was keen to get back to the House and with the aid of a handsome military bearing, a good speaking voice and a brilliant wife, he was the ideal official candidate for this largely upper-class constituency where the Press Lords had threatened to split the Conservative vote.

Baldwin's second stroke of luck arose over India, by reason of the announcement that Lord Irwin, the Viceroy, had been able to reach an understanding with the Congress Party leader Mahatma Gandhi, which had resulted in Gandhi's calling off his campaign of civil disobedience. It gave Baldwin an opportunity of publicly complimenting Irwin on his success and at the same time of restating British policy towards India in a speech in the House of Commons on 12 March 1931, which Tom Jones for one regarded as the best he had ever made.

> The unchanging East has changed, is changing with alarming rapidity, and there are many people who are blind not to see it . . . The ultimate result depends, not on force, but on good will, sympathy and understanding . . . The great work of Lord Irwin is that he has bridged the gulf by ability and by character, and when the history of the time comes to be written, his name will stand out as one of the greatest Viceroys, and as a Viceroy I had the honour myself of sending to India.

'This for the moment has confirmed him in the Leadership,' wrote Jones a few days later, 'but the Party is honeycombed with faction and disloyalty and how long he can hold his position no one can tell. Much will depend on the way the St George's election goes. There are, I need hardly say, many aspirants for the leadership . . . [but] there is no general agreement on anybody. Winston, at the moment, is the darling of the diehards.'

At a meeting of the Conservative Shadow Cabinet at this time, Austen Chamberlain, without consulting his brother, bluntly asked Baldwin when he was going to release Neville from the Party chairmanship. 'He put it mostly on the ground that the Front Bench debating strength had been reduced unduly by Winston's defection and Worthy's death,' Neville noted in his diary, 'but it was pretty plain what he had in mind.' Baldwin replied that he had not thought about it and Austen Chamberlain retorted that he ought to have done, upon which Baldwin said that he

and Neville must discuss it.[39] Of course, what Austen had in mind was
the need for a change in the leadership, and it immediately determined
his brother to ask to be relieved of his job at Central Office, although he
assured Baldwin that Austen's question took him entirely by surprise.
('He had not said anything of his intentions to me beforehand; in fact
we had not even discussed the question.')

On 13 March, Neville Chamberlain accordingly wrote to Baldwin,
enclosing his letter of resignation:

There is however another consideration which makes me desire a
change. When Topping handed me his memorandum on the state of
feeling in the party about the leadership, I found myself in a singularly
painful and embarrassing position. It was not only that I had to decide
on either keeping from you information which might vitally affect
your own actions or taking whatever risks there might be to our
own relations by conveying it to you. There was always the con-
sciousness that my name is one of several who might succeed you if
you decided to retire and although I do not think that I have been
ever influenced by any such considerations it is intensely disagreeable
to think that interested motives might be attributed to me by others.

You have always said that you have never doubted my single-
mindedness or my loyalty to you and I have never doubted the
sincerity of your words. But in this last week I have been conscious
of a difference in our relations and that makes me anxious to escape
from a position which has made any shadowing of our friendship
even possible.[40]

Some uncomfortable meetings followed with Baldwin, who eventually
agreed to accept Neville Chamberlain's resignation as Party Chairman.
His successor at Central Office was Baldwin's old friend Lord Stonehaven,
formerly John Baird, who had recently been Governor-General of
Australia and whose name had first been suggested by Bridgeman. 'He
is a little diffident but liked being asked,' Baldwin told Chamberlain.
But Chamberlain retained control of the Conservative Research Department which he had founded, which was to be an important instrument
in the formulation of future policy.

Relations between Baldwin and Neville Chamberlain had been subjected to increasing strain with the publication of a letter from Baldwin
to Duff Cooper in *The Times* on 24 March indicating that the by-election
campaign was being mapped out without reference to Chamberlain, who
asked Baldwin whether his plans had been intentionally kept from him.

'If there has been no such intention,' he added, 'then I can only say that it seems inexcusable that public references should be made to plans which require the co-operation of the Central Office without communicating them to the Chairman of the Party.'

Baldwin immediately replied:

> 10 Upper Brook Street W1
> 24 March 1931
>
> My dear Neville,
>
> I am distressed that you should think for a moment that I should intentionally keep anything from you, such is not the case, nor could be the case.
>
> I felt that after St George's it was essential that I should get out into the country and that a preliminary intimation should be given at once and I embodied that in my message to Duff Cooper.
>
> I was very occupied most of yesterday and hoped to talk to you today or tomorrow.
>
> Of course I could not make any plans (nor have I yet begun to) until I had talked it over with the Chairman.
>
> Do let me assure you that *nothing* that has occurred during these trying weeks has affected in any way my affection in regard for *you*. It has not been an easy time for either of us.
>
> Very few things in politics have the power to hurt me: it would hurt me if I felt a shadow of misunderstanding between us.
>
> If my manner has shown you that I have been worried, well, worried I have been: and God only knows whether history will write me down as a limpet or a patriot!
>
> > Yours ever,
> > S.B.
>
> If you can give me an hour this afternoon or evening, I should be grateful: perhaps I have been chary of asking you often when I know so well what the calls of the office are.[41]

It was a straight fight in St George's between the official Conservative pro-Baldwin candidate who had the support of Central Office and the independent Conservative anti-Baldwin candidate who was backed by the Beaverbrook–Rothermere newspapers. From Baldwin's point of view, everything turned on the result, since if Sir Ernest Petter defeated Duff Cooper, Baldwin's resignation as Party leader was inevitable. The constituency, which no longer exists, was largely Tory in sympathy, comprising as it did the whole of fashionable Mayfair and Belgravia and taking in Pimlico and parts of Chelsea. However, it did contain some Liberals whose votes were by no means negligible; there being no Liberal candidate, these in the event were to go to Duff Cooper, since the politically ingenuous Petter made an initial error when, asked for a statement by the local branch of the League of Nations Union, he said that he was too busy to attend to such matters as the League of Nations.

No campaign like it had been seen since the famous Westminster Election of 1784 when the beautiful Georgiana Duchess of Devonshire traded kisses for votes in the course of her canvass for the Whig candidate Charles James Fox. In St George's in 1931 leading Tory hostesses like Lady Londonderry, Lady Cunard, Lady Stanley and Lady Juliet Duff, kept open house for the official candidate and his principal supporters, so that they did not lack either refreshment or moral encouragement day and night. Duff Cooper's mother-in-law, the Duchess of Rutland, and Lady Cunard bravely attended Petter's meetings, at one of which the Duchess had to take refuge under a table when chairs were hurled around and broken. Lady Cunard would sit ostentatiously in the front row at these meetings reading the *Daily Telegraph* or *The Star* which were both pro-Baldwin, and whenever Lord Beaverbrook's or Lord Rothermere's name was mentioned from the platform she would look up and mutter loudly: 'Degenerates: they're both degenerates!' [42]

Party political leaders do not normally take part in by-election campaigns; but, as he explained at a mass meeting in the Queen's Hall two days before the poll, Baldwin chose to ignore the convention 'because of the exceptional circumstances of this election'. As he was speaking, sandwichmen paraded up and down outside the hall displaying boards with the legend, 'A Vote for Duff Cooper is a Vote for Gandhi', while Rothermere's *Evening News* carried the banner headline, 'Gandhi is Watching St George's'.

The papers conducted by Lord Rothermere and Lord Beaverbrook [said Baldwin] are not newspapers in the ordinary acceptance of the term. They are engines of propaganda for the constantly changing policies, desires, personal wishes, personal likes and dislikes of two men. What are their methods? Their methods are direct falsehood, misrepresentation, half-truths, the alteration of the speaker's meaning by publishing a sentence apart from the context such as you see in these leaflets handed out outside the doors of this hall; suppression and editorial criticism of speeches which are not reported in the paper. These are methods hated alike by the public, by the whole of the rest of the press.

Baldwin went on to quote several examples. One was the refusal of these papers alone to publish his wife's appeal for the provision of anaesthesia for mothers in childbirth. Another was the reaction of the *Daily Mail* to the expression 'insolent plutocracy', which that paper remarked came ill from Mr Baldwin 'whose father left him an immense fortune which, so far as may be learnt from his own speeches, has almost disappeared', adding that 'it is difficult to see how the Leader of a party who has lost his own fortune can hope to restore that of anyone else, or of his country'.

The article in which these remarks appeared was signed simply 'Editor'. Baldwin now proceeded to castigate the writer in terms which no modern Prime Minister has ever used of a journalist and his employer.

> I have no idea of the name of that gentleman. I would only observe that he is well qualified for the post which he holds. The first part of that statement is a lie and the second part of the statement by its implication, is untrue. The paragraph could only have been written by a cad. I have consulted a very high legal authority and I am advised that an action for libel would lie.

As he paused for a moment, a voice from the body of the hall shouted, 'Take it!' To this interruption Baldwin responded with a devastating phrase which had been suggested by his cousin Rudyard Kipling:

> I shall not move in the matter, and for this reason – I should get an apology and heavy damages. The first is of no value, and the second I would not touch with a barge pole. What the proprietorship of these papers is aiming at is power, and *power without responsibility – the prerogative of the harlot throughout the ages.*

The candidate's wife has recorded how she saw 'the blasé reporters, scribbling semi-consciously, jump out of their skins to a man', when they heard Baldwin's scathing words unfalteringly uttered. Their impact, long remembered, sealed Baldwin's triumph as well as that of Duff Cooper, who defeated his anti-Baldwin opponent by over 5,000 votes. The press lords' wings were effectively clipped and Empire Free Trade became a lost cause.

Baldwin's leadership was never again to be challenged by members of his own political party. Neville Chamberlain, who might have grasped the palm, resigned himself to the prospect of waiting for it. He had a touching reconciliation with Baldwin ('We parted shaking hands, and with the clouds removed'), but at the same time he frankly told his leader that 'the situation with his colleagues was most serious', and that he must adopt a more aggressive attitude towards Labour. 'If he would henceforth attack the Government as he attacked the two lords he might yet regain his position,' Austen Chamberlain wrote to his brother, 'but I don't believe he is capable of doing it.' Before handing over the Party chairmanship to Stonehaven, Neville Chamberlain also reached an accommodation with Beaverbrook who conceded that 'the cause is infinitely greater than the quarrel' and consequently undertook to support the official Party line at the next General Election. For this achievement Chamberlain was congratulated from many quarters (as he noted in his diary), 'except S.B. who can't bear the thought of making it up with the press lords and doesn't see how it has helped his own position'.[43]

Baldwin's friend John Davidson rightly attributed the narrow margin by which his leadership survived to his failure in opposition as had been the case in 1924:

> He was not a good Leader of the Opposition and he did not enjoy the position. To be an effective leader one must be constantly attacking the Government and S.B. disliked doing this. He could be harsh when really roused, but he couldn't bring himself to talk to the men opposite him in the House of Commons in the way that Disraeli, Joe Chamberlain, even Balfour occasionally, and Bonar [Law] did; he couldn't inject any bitterness into his assaults, and they wholly lacked force and venom. He always saw the other side's point of view, and appreciated when its case was a strong one. In that sense he wasn't a good debater, and had no use for smart answers and making minor debating points against his opponents. When he was speaking on a matter of principle, that was a different thing.[44]

When Duff Cooper took his seat in the House of Commons, Baldwin acted as one of his sponsors, walking on his right – 'a rare honour to be accorded by the leader of the party', the new member later described it. But then, as Duff Cooper added, 'he knew how important the result of the election had been to him'.[45]

5

'I thoroughly enjoyed hitting those two rascals and it has done a lot of good,' Baldwin wrote to his old Aunt Edith at Wilden after the Queen's

Hall speech. 'It has been a very difficult and trying time these last two or three months, and I have a heavy programme ahead throughout the summer. However, *if* there isn't an election, one hopes for a good holiday in August. I don't think the Government can last beyond October . . .' In the event Baldwin's prediction was realised through the economic crisis which convulsed the country and led to the break-up of the Labour Government in the holiday month of August.

The history of the crisis with its political overtones has frequently been related, and it is only necessary to describe it briefly here in the context of Baldwin's role in it. As the result of a Liberal amendment to a Conservative motion in the Commons calling for the appointment of an independent Committee to make recommendations for 'effecting forthwith all practicable and legitimate reductions in the national expenditure', the Government set up such a body under the chairmanship of Sir George May, who had been secretary of the Prudential Assurance Company and was one of the leading actuaries in the country. By this date (March 1931) unemployment figures had risen to 2½ millions, and Philip Snowden, the financially orthodox Labour Chancellor of the Exchequer, hoped that the economies recommended by the May Committee coupled with proposals for increased taxation would balance the drastic Budget, which he planned to introduce in the autumn, following on a stop-gap Budget in the spring. Meanwhile the collapse of the American stock market was followed by a similar collapse in Austria and Germany, where the banks were obliged to repudiate their international liabilities by declaring a moratorium. This was bound to affect the Bank of England and hit sterling, which in fact happened in mid-July when £33 million in gold and a further £33 million in its foreign currency holdings were withdrawn.

Meanwhile, Ramsay MacDonald began to think more and more of an all-Party coalition as the only way to surmount the impending crisis. Early in July, Lord Stonehaven, the new Conservative Party chairman, reported to Neville Chamberlain that the Labour Premier had sounded him out in this sense. 'He thought a national government should be formed', since 'they did not wish to be forced to vote against the two things they thought necessary, viz. reform of unemployment insurance and a tariff'. Chamberlain passed on this news to Baldwin and, as he noted in his diary on 6 July, 'we agreed that our party would not stand it for a moment'. Speaking at Hull eleven days later, Baldwin publicly rejected 'the idea that a national government such as existed during the war should be set up in the present difficulties'. He had brought down one coalition government and he had no wish to join in the establishment of another. That would be all very well where it was a question of helping Germany out of her financial troubles, Chamberlain pointed out when they met again on 24 July, but MacDonald would not ask him to coalesce for that. As the pressure on sterling mounted, the possibility that Chamberlain foresaw was 'a panic in the City, a hundred million deficit in the Budget, a flight from the pound, and industry going smash'. It was then that MacDonald would come to him, Chamberlain argued, 'because he would not be able to count on his own people to support him'. However, Baldwin remained unconvinced that there was any immediate need for a coalition of the kind Chamberlain as well as Mac-Donald had now come to envisage. As Baldwin walked across Palace Yard on the last day of Parliament, he said to Maurice Hankey: 'I will do everything I can to help the Government in making economies, but I will not enter a Coalition Government.'[46]

When Chamberlain spoke to Baldwin, he had been informed in advance of the main recommendations of the May Committee, whose Report was published on 31 July, the day after Parliament rose for the summer recess. Baldwin took a copy with him to Astley to ponder over before setting out with his wife on 8 August for their annual holiday at Aix-les-Bains. Before leaving London, he had seen Snowden and agreed to let him have his impressions and those of his friends within the next two or three weeks. At the same time, Snowden wrote to Samuel, the Liberal leader, asking for his views before deciding whether to set up a three-Party committee to consider the next steps to resolve the crisis. 'There is no great urgency,' Snowden added, 'as the Government will not have completed their consideration of the Report and reached tentative decisions before September.'

Snowden badly misjudged the effect of this sensational 300-page Report on public opinion, particularly abroad, 'the most foolish document', observed the economist Maynard Keynes, 'I ever had the misfortune to read'. To meet an expected deficit of £120 million, or £170 million in a full year, the Committee by a majority, with the two Labour members dissenting, recommended that only £24 million of this deficit should be met by increased taxation as against £96 million by economies, of which two-thirds should be at the expense of Unemployment Relief. This meant cutting the relief by 20 per cent. It was orthodox finance on the Gladstonian model with a vengeance and not surprisingly raised a howl from Labour. At the same time the gloomy picture presented of the parlous state of Britain's economy accelerated the course of withdrawals by foreign depositors in London. In Neville Chamberlain's words, 'the May Report confirmed the most pessimistic views circulating abroad as to the insolvency of the Budget . . . The credits had to be encroached upon, and they began to melt away at such a pace that it was only a matter of days before they disappeared completely. Enquiries in Paris and New York showed that there was no chance of a loan in either quarter.' In these circumstances the London bankers bluntly told Ramsay MacDonald that 'the cause of the trouble was not financial but political, and lay in the complete want of confidence in His Majesty's Government existing among foreigners', and that 'the remedy was in the hands of the Government alone'. Consequently the Cabinet Committee appointed to consider the implications of the May Report decided that the Budget must be balanced at all costs, but 'there must be equality of sacrifice'. It was a grim prospect.

Baldwin and his wife had planned to motor the whole way to Aix, for their usual holiday; but they only got as far as Angers in Normandy when he received a telephone call from Davidson on the evening of 11 August urging him to return to London immediately as 'the Government was breaking up'. Baldwin hesitated, since he was always reluctant to alter his plans, but an immediately following telegram from Geoffrey Fry decided him to return at once; this he did next day, motoring the 200 miles to Le Havre to catch the night boat, which got him to London early in the morning of 13 August. Warned by Davidson that the idea of a 'Government of All the Talents to rescue the Labour Party from its dilemma' was being widely mooted, his reaction was quite definite. 'Well, they've got into this mess. Let them get out of it. As the situation develops I may or may not have to take some part in it, but that time hasn't arrived.' [47]

This seems to have been his attitude when he and Chamberlain went to Downing Street the same afternoon to see the Prime Minister and Snowden, who said they had decided that the Budget must be balanced and that economies must be made to the extent, though not necessarily in the precise ways, recommended by the May Committee. 'If they could be assured of our general support,' wrote Chamberlain to his sister Hilda at this time, 'they propose to summon Parliament in the first fortnight in September to pass a supplementary Budget and an Economy Bill.' He continued:

> To secure such a measure of relief and to do it through a Socialist Government seems to me so important in the national interest that we must give it our support provided the proposals for 'equal sacrifice' do not imperil British credit or too brazenly affront ordinary rules of justice and fair play. And I don't think they will do either . . .

Anyway the decisions are left to me as S.B. is not coming back. I think he would agree that crises of this kind are not his forte. He had apparently given no thought to the situation, asked no intelligent question, made no helpful suggestion and indeed was chiefly anxious to be gone before he was 'drawn into something'. He left a final message for me that he was most grateful to me for sparing him the necessity of returning and he would 'back me to the end!'[48]

Baldwin returned to France the same evening, picked up his wife at Angers and together they motored on to Aix. From a letter which he sent Chamberlain on 15 August, it is clear that what he envisaged eventually was not a coalition but a fresh Conservative Government.

I think in the long view it is all to the good that the Government have to look after their own chickens before they come home to roost, and get a lot of the dirt cleared up before we come in. To have the consequences of their finance exposed – and acknowledged to the world – within four months of their Budget will be a wonderful lesson.[49]

A day or two later the Baldwins had lunch with Duff Cooper and his wife at Talloires on the Lake of Annecy, where the Duff Coopers were staying. Lady Diana, mindful of her husband's political future, put on the best meal that money could buy. Her attire was somewhat unconventional for those days, trousers, a fisherman's shirt and a large straw hat, which her husband reluctantly allowed her to wear on condition that she said nothing embarrassing during lunch. However, they had all barely sat down under the chestnut trees by the lake, when Lady Diana turned to Baldwin and said: 'Come on now, tell us every word Ramsay said, for Duff tells me nothing.' There was a smiling grunt for an answer, while her husband coloured with embarrassment feeling as he afterwards admitted that his political future was at the bottom of the lake. Meanwhile Mrs Baldwin looked horrified and exclaimed disapprovingly: 'My husband tells me nothing either, but then I would *never* ask him!' There was an uneasy silence after which the conversation was confined to such uncontroversial topics as the swans on the lake. Fortunately the host's political future was not adversely affected, and Baldwin, who owed a lot to Duff Cooper's recent electoral victory, did not forget him when the time came for official preferment.

An urgent telephone call from Chamberlain on the evening of 20 August summoned Baldwin back to London, this time for good. He broke his journey for a night in Paris, where he was joined by Davidson who came over from London to bring him up to date on the latest news. 'In short, the Government are rattled and divided,' Baldwin wrote to his wife next morning (22 August) which was a Saturday, incidentally contradicting Lucy Baldwin's recent remark to Lady Diana Duff Cooper. 'J.R.M[acDonald] was for resigning at once, yesterday afternoon, and for ''making a statement'' for the week-end after he had dined! . . . By Monday I may be in a position to write with more certainty. I might be summoned to form a Government at any moment: again I might not! So there it is. When I feel inclined to fret and grumble, I think of soldiers. One ought to be proud that some people think one can be of some use to the country.'

Judging by the size of the crowd which turned up at Victoria Station to greet Baldwin when he arrived the same evening, between three and four hundred people thought so, their feelings expressed by one beery gentleman who shouted, 'You'll save the country!' Since Baldwin's house was closed, Davidson put his own house in Great College Street at his leader's disposal, and after dining there with Davidson Baldwin went to the Conservative Research Department in Old Queen Street for a meeting with Neville Chamberlain, Hoare and such other members of the Shadow Cabinet as Chamberlain had been able to reach in the holiday season. There Chamberlain confirmed what Baldwin had already heard from Davidson, namely that MacDonald had decided to resign and to advise the King to send for the leaders of the other two parties for consultation as to the next step with a view to forming some kind of three-Party government.

Hoare's impression of Baldwin on this occasion was that 'the last thing in the world that he wished for was either a return to office or the end of his holiday'. Having destroyed one coalition, he kept repeating, he did not wish to form another. 'Only if a National Government was really inevitable,' Hoare later recalled, 'was he ready to take his part in it. Chamberlain and I were inclined to be impatient when we saw him so reluctant to take the only course that seemed to us possible. Our impatience became irritation when the King, on MacDonald's advice, sent for him the next morning and he could not be found.'[50]

What happened on the Sunday morning was that after breakfast Baldwin telephoned Geoffrey Dawson, the editor of *The Times*, and asked if he could come and see him at his house in Lowndes Street. He arrived about the middle of the morning and stayed talking until lunch-time when they drove to the Travellers' Club together. Dawson said that he had been in touch with the King's Private Secretary, Sir Clive Wigram, and had told him that he thought 'it was everything to get a plan of national economy put out in public by a Labour Government [before it broke up], since it was the only course that would have a permanent effect in reversing a policy of extravagance'. According to Dawson, Baldwin agreed entirely with this view and was 'in hopes that the crisis would be temporarily settled on these lines by tomorrow . . . He then fell to discussing what should be the personnel of a new Government if by any misfortune he was to be called upon to form one at once, saying that it was easier to talk these matters over with me than with any of his political colleagues.'[51]

When Baldwin reached the Travellers' Club, where he was to lunch with Hoare, there was a message waiting for him to the effect that the King wished to see him at three o'clock. He had just time to dash off a note to his wife at Aix with this news. 'The crisis will not be a short one,' he added. 'We shall know tomorrow whether the PM will carry on to meet the House. If he can, I shall probably be able to come out in two or three days. If he throws his hand in, I don't know what will happen.' Nevertheless he seems to have thought that in the event of MacDonald's resignation the King would send for him to form a government.

There is a possibility that this might have happened had the King seen Baldwin that morning instead of Samuel. As events turned out, when Wigram telephoned Davidson's house to ask Baldwin to come to Buckingham Palace at 12.30, Baldwin had already left apparently without saying where he was going except that he would be lunching at his club. Hence Samuel was summoned to the Palace first. His advice to the King proved decisive. He told the King that, 'in view of the fact that necessary economies would prove most unpalatable to the working class', it would be to the general interest if they could be imposed by a Labour Government. But if Ramsay MacDonald failed to secure sufficient support from his Cabinet, then the best alternative would be 'a broad-based Government' composed of members of the three parties with MacDonald continuing as Premier, and 'with the single purpose of overcoming the financial crisis'.[52]

At the afternoon audience, the King asked Baldwin whether he would be prepared to serve in a National Government under MacDonald. Baldwin replied that he would. To the further question whether he would be ready to carry on the Government himself in the event of MacDonald declining, Baldwin agreed provided he could be assured of Liberal support in putting through the economy programme. After the Tory Leader had left the Palace, Wigram noted that 'the King was greatly pleased with Mr Baldwin's readiness to meet the crisis which had arisen, and to sink Party interests for the sake of the Country'.

Shortly after ten o'clock that night Ramsay MacDonald went to the Palace looking 'scared and unbalanced', according to Wigram. He informed the King that at the Cabinet which he had just left eleven members had voted in favour of the economies, including a 10 per cent cut in the dole, and eight against. In view of this irrevocable split, MacDonald felt that he had no alternative but to tender his resignation. On the King assuring him that 'he was the only man to lead the country through the crisis' and hoping he would reconsider his decision, since 'the Conservatives and Liberals would support him in restoring the confidence of foreigners in the financial stability of the country', MacDonald asked whether the King would confer with Baldwin, Samuel and himself in the morning. (The Cabinet had already agreed to this proposal.) The King replied that he would gladly do so, and MacDonald returned to Downing Street where Samuel was waiting for him. Shortly afterwards, in response to urgent telephone messages, they were joined by Baldwin, Neville Chamberlain and several financial experts from the Bank of England.

After the bankers had outlined the minimum economy measures necessary, they left, and the politicians got down to business. What happened then was recorded by Chamberlain in his diary, from which it is clear that the Prime Minister was still intent on resignation. 'For himself, he would help us to get these proposals through, though it means his death warrant, but it would be no use for him to join a Government. He would be a ridiculous figure unable to command support and would bring odium on us as well as himself.'

Chamberlain then intervened. Had the Prime Minister considered, he asked him, that while he might not command many votes in the House of Commons he might command much support in the country? And would not a Government including members of all Parties hold a much stronger position than a two-Party combination? To this MacDonald replied that his mind was not fully made up but his present mood was for resignation. The account given by Chamberlain in his diary continues:

I then suggested that many people would not understand why, if he supported the new Government, he refused to enter it and would criticise him on that ground. He replied that was a worrying point, but people would say he had stuck to his office for the sake of the salary, to which I replied that if several of his colleagues accompanied him the odium would at least be spread.

Finally I asked him if he had considered the effect on foreign opinion which was all important . . . This argument took him in a weak place. He said without egotism he thought his name did carry weight in America . . .

Samuel supported me strongly though S.B. maintained silence and we did not pursue the matter further then.[53]

When Baldwin left this meeting, he shared Chamberlain's impression that MacDonald still intended to resign and that he would not serve under a Tory Premier. 'Last night it looked as if I should have to form a Government,' Baldwin wrote to his wife next day (24 August). 'The PM said he couldn't join me.' The impression persisted as he walked with Davidson to Buckingham Palace for his meeting with the King. 'Nor did he think this a bad thing,' remarked Davidson later, 'since he had little love for Coalitions.'[54]

During the next two hours the situation changed dramatically. 'This morning the King, Samuel and I met,' Baldwin told his wife afterwards; 'and Ramsay, with real courage, deserted by some of his leading colleagues and by his Party, offered to form an *ad hoc* Government to put through the financial legislation necessary and then dissolve for a general election which will come probably in October.' The offer, endorsed by Samuel and Baldwin, was warmly welcomed by the King. Later the same day, Ramsay MacDonald returned to the Palace and kissed hands on his appointment as Prime Minister of a new 'National' Government.

NINE

THE NATIONAL GOVERNMENT

I

It was agreed at the Buckingham Palace conference on 24 August 1931 that the new administration would not be 'a Coalition in the ordinary sense of the term, but co-operation of individuals', and that the Cabinet should be 'reduced to a minimum'; also that the elections which would follow in due course would not be 'fought by the Government but by the Parties'. Sir Maurice Hankey's first task as Cabinet Secretary was to draft a 'manifesto' embodying these points for publication in the newspapers next morning. This he did in the following form after receiving the new Prime Minister's 'general instructions', and 'written contributions' from Baldwin and Samuel:

> The Prime Minister, since kissing hands on appointment by His Majesty this afternoon, has been in consultation with Mr Baldwin, Sir Herbert Samuel and Mr Snowden as to the names to be submitted to the King for inclusion as Ministers in the new Government. Considerable progress has been made.
>
> The specific object for which the new Government is being formed is to deal with the national emergency that now exists. It will not be a Coalition Government in the accepted sense of the term, but a Government of co-operation for this one purpose. When that purpose is achieved the political Parties will resume their respective positions.[1]

When Baldwin told the Conservative Shadow Cabinet what he had accepted in their name, not a single voice was raised against him. 'They were thinking of their offices,' he commented afterwards. This opinion was endorsed by Davidson, who wrote in his draft memoirs:

Chamberlain, I am sure, had his eye on the Chancellorship of the Exchequer, and Sam Hoare also was a man of unlimited personal ambition. Although they put the national interest first, they – and some other leading Conservatives – had thought a good deal about what positions they would have in a National Government.[2]

MacDonald limited his Cabinet to ten members; and, although as Prime Minister he knew he could not count on the support of more than a handful of his own Party followers, he insisted on Labour having four places, the same number as he allotted to the Conservatives, leaving the balance of two to the Liberals. He also insisted that Snowden should continue at the Treasury and he vetoed the suggested inclusion of Hailsham whom he described as 'particularly obnoxious to the Labour Party', no doubt on account of the part he had played in getting the Trade Disputes Act through Parliament. Besides MacDonald and Snowden, Labour was represented in the Cabinet by Sankey who remained Lord Chancellor and J. H. Thomas who combined the portfolios of Dominions and Colonies. 'I am going to be Lord President of the Council,' Baldwin wrote to his wife. 'Politically I think it is the best thing for me.' It also gave him agreeable quarters in the Privy Council offices. ('I have just seen my room. It is a beauty, looking over the [Horse Guards] Parade, and getting all the afternoon sun.') The other Conservatives in the Cabinet were Neville Chamberlain and Cunliffe-Lister, who returned respectively to the Ministry of Health and the Board of Trade, and Hoare who got the India Office. The two Liberals were Samuel and Reading, who took the key posts of Home Secretary and Foreign Secretary. Incidentally Neville Chamberlain's brother Austen was bitterly disappointed at not being given the Foreign Office; but he agreed instead to become First Lord of the Admiralty without a seat in the Cabinet, feeling that he appeared (as he put it) 'not as someone who gives all he can to help in a crisis but as an old party hack who might be dangerous outside and so must have his mouth stopped with office'. In short, he said, he had allowed himself to be 'deeply humiliated' and 'with no advantage to the Government or the country'. And, as he wrote to his sister Hilda, 'you can imagine that I have found my position almost intolerable. For thirty years or more I have been at the very centre of events. After such an experience it is not easy to adjust oneself to the position of the fly on the wheel.'[3]

'It is a Cabinet of Ten with a lot of outside Ministers, and has to be run like the War Cabinet,' Hankey noted in his diary at the time, 'but

I am allowed to send the Minutes to most of the outsiders.* It is an awkward machine with its three parties, all rather jealous of their own position. As the only neutral person all sorts of difficulties arise for me.'

The Cabinet met for the first time on 26 August and appointed small committees to deal with finance, taxation and economics. This was preceded by a meeting of the full senior ministerial team of seventeen, at which Samuel paid tributes to Baldwin for 'serving with a Prime Minister whose views had been different from his own in many matters' and also Austen Chamberlain and other Conservative Ministers, 'who had put all other considerations aside in the interests of public security'. Upon which Baldwin remarked that he and his colleagues 'would do their best'.[4] One difficulty which MacDonald asked Hankey to resolve was the question of precedence at Cabinet meetings in the event of his absence. Hankey suggested that the order of precedence should be as follows: the Prime Minister, Baldwin, Snowden, Samuel, Reading and Sankey. However, MacDonald insisted on Sankey, the Lord Chancellor, coming fourth. Then Chamberlain objected to Reading being added to the Cabinet finance committee, which consisted of Snowden, Samuel and himself, on the ground that the balance of parties would be upset. He also objected to Lord Cecil of Chelwood continuing to represent the Government at Geneva and leading the British delegation to the League of Nations Assembly. These were the kind of differences which Baldwin's tact added to Hankey's were required to smooth out with the Prime Minister during this critical period.

Meanwhile the King had gone back to Balmoral. 'I wish you and your colleagues every success in the difficult task imposed upon you,' he wrote to Ramsay MacDonald on 27 August. 'I am happy to feel that I have been able to return to my Highland home without changing my Prime Minister, in whom I have full confidence.' This confidence, it may be added, was not shared by the Chamberlain brothers. 'It really is hard lines,' wrote Austen at this time, 'after being led for these last two years by a man so unhelpful and inert as S.B., Neville should now be driven to exclaim to me that Ramsay is "infinitely worse".'[5]

The House of Commons met on 7 September to pass the emergency

---

* The principal ministers outside the Cabinet were Lord Peel (Privy Seal), Lord Crewe (War), Lord Amulree (Air), Sir Austen Chamberlain (Admiralty), Sir Archibald Sinclair (Scotland), Sir Donald Maclean (Education), Sir Henry Betterton (Labour), Lord Londonderry (Works), William Ormsby-Gore (Paymaster-General), G. C. Tryon (Pensions), P. J. Pybus (Transport) and Sir William Jowitt (Attorney-General). Crewe, Sinclair, Maclean and Pybus were Liberals; Amulree and Jowitt were Labour; the remaining six were Conservatives. The junior ministers included Sir Philip Sassoon (Air), Malcolm MacDonald (Dominions), Anthony Eden (Foreign Affairs), Oliver Stanley (Home Affairs), Walter Elliot (Treasury) and Duff Cooper (War).

Budget and Economy Bill. There was little opposition to Snowden's proposals for meeting the anticipated deficit of £170 million, which he did by raising £76 million in increased taxes including income tax at 5s., and the balance by suspending national debt redemption and imposing cuts in state salaries and benefits including the unemployment 'dole' by 10 per cent. Both the King and the Prince of Wales voluntarily surrendered £50,000 each from their income as a contribution to the emergency. These measures had the effect of temporarily staying the drain on gold from London. Unfortunately some naval ratings of the Atlantic Fleet at Invergordon refused to obey orders as a protest at the cuts, some of which by a misunderstanding exceeded 10 per cent. This incident assumed the proportions of a naval mutiny in foreign eyes, and investors thinking that it was the prelude to a revolution in Britain began to withdraw more gold from the vaults of the Bank of England.

Under pressure from the Bank, the Government immediately rushed a Bill through Parliament in a single day suspending the Gold Standard, which had the effect of relieving the Bank of its statutory obligation to sell gold on the international money market. The pound fell by a quarter in terms of dollar and other foreign currencies, although the man-in-the-street who had no occasion to buy foreign exchange noticed little or no difference since he had been using paper money since 1914 when gold sovereigns had disappeared from circulation. 'The parties very good – no panic so far,' noted Lucy Baldwin in her diary, 'but humiliation of course for us as a nation.'

Meanwhile *The Times* had come out with a powerful leading article from the editor's pen urging that a General Election should take place as soon as possible. 'Is there any reason,' asked Geoffrey Dawson, 'why the appeal to the country, whenever it may come, should not be made – on a broad programme of reconstruction which will include a tariff – by the National Government as such?' This view was echoed by the evening papers, and many Conservatives declared their support for it, including the powerful 1922 Committee of Conservative backbenchers in the House of Commons. Neville Chamberlain was strongly in favour of a tariff as the only practical means of reversing the adverse trade balance and this was endorsed by the Conservative Business Committee which included Baldwin. Chamberlain noted in his diary on 24 September:

All were in favour of the national appeal by a national government under MacDonald, provided the programme embodied the full tariff. All agreed that the elections should be held at the earliest moment. All agreed that, if we went to election with R[amsay]

M[acDonald] as PM, we must accept him as PM when we come back, though we might well have an understanding as to the filling of the posts in the new Government.[6]

MacDonald and Thomas in the Cabinet were disposed to go along with the Conservatives, but Samuel and Reading, the two Liberals, being convinced Free Traders, were not, while Snowden and Sankey hesitated to commit themselves. This seeming deadlock greatly worried the King, who was afraid that if the Liberals resigned MacDonald would follow suit and that would be the end of the National Government.

On 28 September Wigram reported to the King, who was still at Balmoral, that while the Prime Minister did not actually turn down a General Election he had no heart for it. 'Without doubt he is sentimental and an idealist. He does not like the idea of smashing up the Labour Party at the head of a Conservative organisation. He does not know how to run with the hare and hunt with the hounds.'

In view of these developments the King returned to London. When MacDonald saw the King on 3 October, he told him that 'he was beginning to feel that he had failed and had better clear out'. The King's immediate reaction was to say that in this event he would not accept his Prime Minister's resignation and that it was his positive duty to find a solution. He spoke quite bluntly to MacDonald who, he said, 'must be more patient and brace himself up to realise that he was the only person to tackle the present chaotic state of affairs'.[7]

MacDonald went back to the Cabinet. At last, shortly before midnight two days later, a formula was reached to which all ten members of the Cabinet agreed. The National Government would go to the country and ask for a 'doctor's mandate' to apply every remedy they could agree on to cure the country's ills, each Party issuing its own manifesto with a general pronouncement from the Prime Minister signed by him alone. This was to lay its emphasis on Party co-operation as long as the crisis lasted. ('The Government must therefore be free to consider every proposal likely to help, such as tariffs . . .') Parliament was immediately dissolved and polling in the General Election fixed for 27 October. The King declared himself to be 'very pleased' and congratulated the Prime Minister when he came to the Palace to ask for a dissolution.

'I hope we may win the victory which we anticipate,' Neville Chamberlain had written at the outset of the election campaign, 'but if we do I foresee a pack of troubles as soon as the election is over, first in the formation of the Government and then in the formulation of policy.'[8]

The resultant Tory gains – 200 at the expense of Labour – were far greater than either Chamberlain or Baldwin anticipated. The Conservatives won 473 seats, which together with their National Labour and National Liberal allies, led respectively by Ramsay MacDonald and Sir John Simon, enabled them to count on a total strength of 521 in the new House of Commons. Labour came back with a mere 52, the whole of their former Front Bench having been defeated with the exception of George Lansbury. In the aggregate returns the Liberals were split three ways – the 'pure' Liberals or Liberal Nationals led by Samuel, who gained 33 seats, the Simonite or National Liberals, who gained 35 seats, and the Lloyd George family, consisting of Lloyd George, his son, his daughter and his son-in-law, who preferred to sit as an independent group. MacDonald and his National Labour following only captured 13 seats, but these included the Prime Minister's at Seaham.

For the first time Tom Jones and his wife voted Conservative. 'We had to do it,' said Jones afterwards. ' "Labour" had to be thrashed, but it cannot be destroyed. We could not trust them with the Bank of England – just yet. But that too will come. Meanwhile here is a Parliamentary Dictatorship and the Tory wolves will howl for high tariffs and will give S.B. hell.' [9]

Baldwin took the results of the election calmly. 'The workers throughout the country have put their trust in the National Government: we must not fail them,' he remarked when he heard the final figures. 'The magnitude of the [Labour] defeat makes it all the more imperative that we should be faithful to our trust.'

Shortly afterwards Baldwin and his wife were invited to dine and sleep at Windsor Castle. Taking Mrs Baldwin aside during this visit, the King said to her: 'I want to tell you, Mrs Baldwin, that your husband has done what only one man in thousands would have done. He could have been Prime Minister but he stood down to serve under another for what he thought was the best for his country.'

'Thank you, sir,' replied Lucy Baldwin humbly. 'I am content.' [10]

2

At a hurriedly summoned meeting of the Cabinet on 29 October 1931, Ramsay MacDonald announced that he proposed to reconstruct the Government and he asked that the offices of all ministers might be put at his disposal 'in order to give him a free hand in the reconstruction', in which he would invite the co-operation of the other party political leaders. He also proposed to enlarge the Cabinet to its normal size, since it would be necessary to refer a number of 'complicated and technical questions' to Cabinet Committees.[11]

The troubles foreseen by Neville Chamberlain in the reconstruction were soon embarrassingly apparent. 'Stan very worried by office seekers,' noted Lucy Baldwin as soon as the election results were known. 'He does so hate saying no to his friends.' On 2 November, Baldwin saw the King and began by saying that he was 'very tired'. He then remarked that the Prime Minister was 'inclined to be wobbly and unable to make up his mind over the new Cabinet and had not advanced very far in its composition. Every newcomer was inclined to sway him.' Upon which, according to Wigram's account of the audience, 'the King told Mr Baldwin that he thought the Old Gang should be cleared out – Amulree [Air Minister], who did not fly, Austen Chamberlain (who Mr Baldwin said, had written that he was quite prepared not to be offered office), Reading, Crewe and Peel'.

Baldwin went on to say that he was afraid that 'his Party might kick if they did not have some of the key positions – such as the Exchequer, Home Office, Foreign Office and Dominions Office'. The King said that he thought that Baldwin should go to the Treasury in preference to Neville Chamberlain who was 'so good as Minister of Health' and 'would be suspected of ultra-protectionist views' if he became Chancellor of the Exchequer. Baldwin replied that he had asked for no portfolio for himself and added that 'there would be plenty for him to do, as the Prime Minister knew nothing of his new Party, especially the Conservatives – many of them young, impetuous and ambitious men – who had no chance of making reputations with no Opposition to speak against'. Finally Baldwin advocated Neville Chamberlain as Foreign Secretary rather than his brother Austen, who was in failing health and in any event had renounced any claim he might have to office so as to make way for some younger man. ('I admire the spirit of it,' said Baldwin of Austen's gesture, 'and I hope the same spirit may be mine in due time.') Failing Neville Chamberlain, Baldwin suggested Cunliffe-Lister, but the King objected that his caustic wit would not go down with the foreign ambassadors. He also told the King that MacDonald had offered him 11 Downing Street, for which he 'was very grateful, as he was very badly-off now and a house with no rent and taxes would be a god-send'.[12]

Although several other veterans in the original National Government, like Lords Reading, Amulree and Crewe, also retired on the ground of age at this time, Baldwin realised, as Austen Chamberlain put it to him, that while it was necessary for all the Parties which supported the

Government to be represented in it, nevertheless 'the number of places available for the recognition of the many claims of your own supporters will bear no proportion to their numbers in the new House of Commons'. This fact greatly complicated Baldwin's dealing with MacDonald. When Geoffrey Dawson called on the Lord President at the Privy Council office on 4 November, Baldwin remarked that 'he'd had the most unpleasant week of his life' and that Cabinet-making was still going on with the Prime Minister who had retreated to his Scottish home at Lossiemouth. For his part MacDonald complained that 'no sooner had he made a list than Baldwin came in and said it would not do'; indeed it was reported that the Prime Minister had been 'rather high and mighty with Baldwin'. Eventually, after considerable wrangling between the two men, the list of Cabinet appointments was completed on 6 November. It was immediately sent to the King who happened to be walking in the garden at Buckingham Palace at the time, and it was approved by him there.[13]

The Cabinet, which now reverted to its old size, hardly reflected the strength of the Parties in the House of Commons. However, the Conservatives were in the majority, since they were allocated eleven out of the twenty places available, while the Simonite and the Samuelite Liberals together got five places and National Labour (MacDonaldites) four. Baldwin was content to continue as Lord President of the Council, but his salary was only £2,000 compared with £5,000 attached to the other senior offices, so that, as has been seen, he was given as compensation the use of the Chancellor of the Exchequer's official residence at 11 Downing Street. 'It was very comfortable,' he remarked, 'and I could always keep my eye on my Prime Minister.'[14]

Neville Chamberlain got the Exchequer minus the official residence, which he does not seem to have minded as much as his brother Austen did when as Chancellor he had to yield it to Bonar Law in 1918. Otherwise the Tories secured most of the plums except the Foreign Office and the Home Office, which went to Simon and Samuel respectively, and the Woolsack which Sankey continued to occupy. The three service ministries all went to Conservatives – War (Hailsham), Admiralty (Eyres-Monsell) and Air (Londonderry), although Londonderry really owed his appointment more to MacDonald than to Baldwin. Chamberlain was anxious that Cunliffe-Lister should continue at the Board of Trade, but Snowden, who went to the Lords as Privy Seal, and the Prime Minister could not stomach the idea of an ardent Protectionist at Trade as well as the Treasury, and consequently the office went to the Liberal Walter Runciman, while Cunliffe-Lister got the Colonial Office instead, which was separated from the Dominions. Hoare carried on at the India Office.* Outside the Cabinet Davidson returned to his old job of Chancellor of the Duchy of Lancaster. Among the younger Tories, again installed as junior ministers on Baldwin's recommendation, were Walter Elliot, Anthony Eden, Oliver Stanley and Duff Cooper, while a newcomer Kingsley Wood succeeded Londonderry as First Commissioner of Works. Ramsay MacDonald's thirty-year-old son Malcolm continued as Under-Secretary for the Dominions under J. H. Thomas.

There were several conspicuous omissions. Lloyd George's exclusion was inevitable, since he had broken with both Samuel and Simon, and Baldwin would not have him at any price. So also was Churchill's on account of his stand over India. Nor for various reasons could places be found for Amery, Percy and Steel-Maitland who had all been members of Baldwin's Cabinet from 1924 to 1929, although Baldwin tried hard to overcome MacDonald's objections to Amery on the ground that he lacked a sufficient 'national outlook'.

Ramsay MacDonald, although he showed himself at first to be a conciliatory and resourceful chairman of the Cabinet, could seldom afford to take a strong line, since he had such a small personal following in Parliament, and in effect he became the prisoner of the Conservatives. His jailers were Baldwin and Chamberlain, of whom the Liberal leader Herbert Samuel has left a vivid pen picture at this time:

> The attractive personality of Stanley Baldwin contributed to the smooth handling of affairs. The real power lay with him, but he was careful not to let the fact appear. Reticent in Cabinet, one might almost say taciturn, Baldwin rarely, if ever, initiated a proposal; but often, when a discussion was taking an awkward turn, he would intervene at the end with some brief observation, full of common sense, that helped us to an agreement.
>
> Neville Chamberlain, on the other hand, was always ready to take the lead, particularly on economic questions which then held the field and which had always been his special province. His ideas were positive and clear-cut; he was tenacious in pursuit of them, whether

---

* The Cabinet consisted of MacDonald (Prime Minister), Baldwin (Lord President), Sankey (Lord Chancellor), Snowden (Privy Seal), Neville Chamberlain (Exchequer), Samuel (Home), Simon (Foreign), Cunliffe-Lister (Colonies), Thomas (Dominions), Hailsham (War), Hoare (India), Londonderry (Air), Sinclair (Scotland), Runciman (Trade), Maclean (Education), Eyres-Monsell (Admiralty), Hilton Young (Health), Gilmour (Agriculture), Betterton (Labour) and Ormsby-Gore (Works). In 1932 Sir John Gilmour took Samuel's place as Home Secretary, Walter Elliot became Minister of Agriculture and Sir Godfrey Collins Secretary for Scotland. Baldwin also held the Lord Privy Seal for a time after Snowden's resignation.

in the Cabinet itself, or its Committees, or in the conversations that, as in all governments, were continually proceeding among its members. Courteous and agreeable in manner, Chamberlain was always willing to listen to arguments with a friendly spirit – but a closed mind.

One significant result of the 1931 General Election was the disappearance of the Socialist bogey which Winston Churchill had described during the campaign as its 'appeal to class-hatred and revolutionary promptings'. A few weeks afterwards, Churchill admitted to a newly-elected member in the Smoking Room of the House of Commons: 'As you know, I was against the National Government. I may have been wrong. It may have been that that great mass of cotton wool [Baldwin] was the best defence against the Socialist battering ram.' Churchill had returned from a painting holiday in the south of France to fight the election, at which incidentally Samuel had urged the Epping electors without success to reject him. This may have prompted Churchill to add, after a momentary pause for reflection: 'If Baldwin's career was to be painted, it would need a very large canvas, very large.'[15]

The question of overriding urgency, if Britain was to be set on the road to economic recovery, was the extent to which a protectionist policy should be adopted by the National Government. With this Baldwin was particularly concerned, although he was content to leave the details to be worked out by Chamberlain and Runciman. The Conservative Party as a whole wanted Protection, and the rumour which spread abroad that tariffs were to be imposed began to flood the country with foreign goods. To stem this flow and halt further unemployment, the Government immediately introduced an Abnormal Importation Bill imposing a 100 per cent duty on 'excessive imports'. This was passed by Parliament without opposition from Samuel and his Liberal National followers. A Cabinet committee was thereupon set up with Neville Chamberlain in the chair to examine the whole question of the balance of trade, and since the committee had a protectionist majority its recommendations were bound to lead to a clash with the Samuelites.

The Government's next important measure was the Statute of Westminster, designed to confer full self-government on the Dominions. The result of the deliberations of the Inter-Imperial Relations Committee, which Baldwin had appointed in 1926 under the Chairmanship of Lord Balfour, it symbolised Britain's impending renunciation of her former imperial mission. The second reading, moved by J. H. Thomas on 12 November, was vigorously opposed by Winston Churchill who objected

to the replacement of the historic term Empire by the novel conception
of a Commonwealth, and in particular he attacked its implications in
respect of India and Ireland. In his speech, delivered from the back
benches and described by his fellow-backbencher Leo Amery as
'thoroughly mischievous and wrong-headed but most effective', Churchill
pointed out that its provisions for unfettered Dominion sovereignty
would enable the Irish Free State to repudiate the Treaty of 1921 unless
a clause were written into the measure expressly to prevent her doing so.
He went on to declare that he would support an amendment to this effect.
Although Cosgrave in Dublin gave an assurance of good faith, the amendment was moved by the diehard Tory backbencher Colonel Gretton
during the committee stage, which was taken on the floor of the House,
and warmly endorsed by Churchill.

Baldwin replied for the Government in a speech in which he pointed
out what the likely consequences would be if Gretton's amendment were
passed:

> The Dominions are rightly and properly jealous of their status and
> they are jealous of each other's status as regards the Mother Country,
> and if you think that you can do something which offends Ireland,
> and is only going to offend Ireland, you are making the mistake of
> your lives. You are going to offend, not only the Irish Free State,
> but you are going to offend every Irishman in Australia, in Canada
> and in the United States of America. You will offend every Dominion,
> even the most British of them, and none will feel it more than
> Canada, which is often held up to us as an example.
>
> I can think of nothing more fatal for this House to do, a Tory
> House of Commons, full of Tories, than to think, with Dominions
> that enjoy a state of economic equality based on Treaties . . . that by
> inserting these words against the will of the Dominions . . . they
> are helping that cause for which many of us have fought for a whole
> generation. Not a bit! They will set it back for years. It is . . .
> because it may go out to the world that, for all our talk, we do not
> trust the Dominions, and that Dominion status means nothing to us,
> that I oppose this new Clause.[16]

Baldwin went on to say that he was aware that several of his very old
friends were supporting it, as they had a perfect right to do. At the same
time, he asked those for whom he said 'this is not a matter of conscience
but largely of old-time association, to try to judge the matter from the
larger point of view, and from the point of view of the whole Empire,

to see that this new Clause is defeated by a large majority'. In fact, the majority was large – over 300, the actual figures being 50 for and 360 against. The minority included most of the Ulster Unionists and the other diehard elements in the Tory Party. Meanwhile in the Lords, Baldwin's old friend Carson failed to secure support for a similar amendment from Hailsham and Salisbury.*

The long honeymoon period in Anglo-Irish relations, which had lasted since 1921, was now nearing its end. In February 1932 the Cosgrave administration was voted out of office in Dublin, and Mr Eamonn de Valera became President of the Executive Council of the Irish Free State, the state which he had so bitterly opposed during the unhappy civil war and which he had been so reluctant to acknowledge. On assuming office, Mr de Valera announced that he intended to abolish the oath of allegiance which members of the legislature were required to take. He also made it clear that he would diminish the position of the Governor-General, and he further proceeded to withhold payment of the land annuities on the pretext that the agreement providing for their regular payment to the British National Debt Commissioners had never been approved by the Dail. In view of these developments Ramsay MacDonald appointed a Cabinet committee, which included Baldwin, Hailsham and Thomas and was known as the Irish Situation Committee; it was charged with the formidable task of trying to come to terms with the de Valera government on all outstanding issues of difference between them, 'constitutional, financial, defence and economic'. Meanwhile, de Valera's action over the land annuities led to an unfortunate 'economic war' between the two countries, which was not to be called off until Baldwin became Prime Minister again, and put in train the steps for a settlement of the dispute.

As Lord President, Baldwin was in practice the Prime Minister's deputy and had to take his place when MacDonald was abroad or ill, as happened on a number of occasions, which began towards the end of 1931 when MacDonald was obliged to spend three weeks in a nursing home as the result of prolonged fatigue. The Prime Minister was also having trouble with his eyes which necessitated an operation. ('I do wish that you would

* 'I cannot pretend that I am happy about the discussions on the Statute of Westminster Bill,' wrote Salisbury at this time. 'Of course, the situation was profoundly modified by the upshot of the debate in the House of Commons. We had on the one side the overwhelming view of our friends in that House against any amendment in this respect; and on the other side we had the commitments of Cosgrave and Baldwin. These latter are of course not the same thing as an actual provision inserted in the Statute, but I feel quite certain that in the face of the vast majority of our friends in the Commons accepting these commitments there would not be the slightest hope of an amendment in the Lords being ultimately successful and I am sure you will agree with me in this.' Salisbury to Carson 28 November 1931: Carson Papers (Public Record Office of Northern Ireland).

persuade Mr MacDonald not to ruin his eyesight reading papers,' a member of the staff at Chequers is said to have remarked to a visitor, 'Mr Baldwin never did.') 'Ramsay is feeling very tired,' Baldwin remarked to Tom Jones at this time.

> He has told me he would never fight another election. He will retire with the close of the present Parliament. I feel very much the same. I must carry on for this Parliament and use what prestige I have got to keep our fellows together. We shall put the tariff through and if it does well it will drop out of party politics very much like Free Trade did. Then leave suitable time to change the title of our Party to National, as there will be little which really divides us from the great bulk of the Liberals. Then too will be the time for the new men to take over.

Meanwhile, the Cabinet trade committee under Chamberlain had recommended that a general 10 per cent tariff should be imposed on all imported goods with a number of specified exceptions, including all imports from the Dominions, which were to enjoy preferential treatment, the details to be worked out at a conference later the same year in Ottawa. When the committee's report came before the Cabinet on 21 January 1932, the Liberals and Snowden threatened to resign, since they regarded the committee's recommendations as amounting to full Protection. The same night MacDonald telephoned Sandringham and told the King's Private Secretary that in view of what had happened he might have to tender his own resignation and that of the whole administration. However, this possibility was averted when the Cabinet met again next morning and the Free Traders accepted a suggestion from Hailsham that to prevent the National Government from breaking up so early in its life it would be better to sacrifice the rule of collective responsibility and to accept a majority decision in the Cabinet. Snowden urged that the dissentients might be allowed to speak and vote against the committee's recommendations in Parliament, and this was duly agreed.

Discussing the matter shortly afterwards with Tom Jones, Baldwin remarked: 'Snowden's view is that once the four Ministers have made their protest and cast their vote the subject will then drop.' Upon which Jones commented: 'What the Ministers have done is really to carry the expression of their dissent a step further than the practice of placing it on record in the Cabinet Minutes. And just as you drop your dissent once you record it, so they should drop it after stating it to the House.'

'Quite so,' Baldwin agreed.[17]

The 'agreement to differ', as this arrangement was called, could only be a temporary expedient for preserving the coalition intact, and in the event it failed to survive the Ottawa Conference in the summer with its prospect of Imperial Preference. J. H. Thomas, the Dominions Secretary, considered that his office entitled him to lead the British delegation, but his tactlessness allied with a characteristic habit of telling Rabelaisian stories in the presence of ladies, especially when he had been drinking, hardly rendered him a suitable leader, and at Neville Chamberlain's prompting Baldwin claimed the right as an ex-Prime Minister since MacDonald was not going. 'My idea is to go for a few big things in the way of freer trade within the Empire,' Baldwin told Jones as he was about to embark with the rest of the delegation on the *Empress of Britain*, 'and leave the rest for subsequent detailed discussion by committees and another conference next spring.'

'Neville is perhaps carrying the burden and very well he does it,' Baldwin wrote to Mimi Davidson on 15 August. 'It is a sacred trust to him and I am sure he feels he is labouring in his father's presence.' And in a broadcast which he made on his return home a fortnight later, he said: 'The great fact that stands out is that the Conference has succeeded in agreeing on a revised trade policy which brings into effect a genuine reciprocity over an enormous area.' Baldwin's objective was thus largely achieved, although paradoxically enough tariffs had the effect in the long term of reducing British exports over-all more than they reduced imports, since the bulk of the latter consisted of food and raw materials and in any event they could be reduced little; also the Dominions were to benefit more than the mother country.

At all events the Ottawa decisions were more than the Samuelite Liberals could stand and they now decided to withdraw *en bloc* from the National Government, although continuing to give it 'general support'. 'The dirty dogs,' Baldwin exclaimed when he heard the news in the middle of September. 'They always behave like this when rough weather approaches.' To MacDonald he wrote at the same time from Aix:

First, my sympathy is with you. I will not express my feelings in a letter, but I shall have plenty to say. First, don't worry. You are bound to carry on. The many questions arising can be discussed during the autumn, but your duty is straight and clear. You must stick to the ship till we are in calmer waters.

Secondly, something is due to your loyal supporters. You must hold up the decisions for a fortnight. I have never bothered you about the House, but it doesn't run itself and you need plenty of vitality to face it day in and day out. I have had ten days here, my first clear holiday for two years, and if you can't give me till the end of next week, I can't guarantee the necessary steam for the job nor the calmer judgement that only comes with an untired mind. Neville, on whom the brunt of the Ottawa debates must fall, was done in when we returned: and if he can't have a decent rest you will only have him laid up with gout at some critical moment. Half the mistakes from 1918 on have been the work of tired men. Run no risks for the sake of a few days . . .

I see *all* the difficulties, but though the boat may rock when our allies jump off, it may well sail henceforward on a more even keel.[18]

The Prime Minister did as he was asked and the Liberals obliged by deferring their action until after Ottawa had been discussed in the Cabinet on 28 September. Next day their decision was published in the newspapers in the form of a letter. Snowden followed suit with a similar letter and Baldwin temporarily assumed Snowden's office of Lord Privy Seal in addition to that of Lord President.

Tom Jones, who was likewise spending a holiday at Aix, has recalled how Baldwin discussed his letter on the terrace of the Hotel Bernascon. ('The terrace commands a view of the lake and the mountains beyond and our talk was often interrupted by S.B.'s ecstatic comments on the scenery.') Baldwin also alluded to the possibility of his followers pressing for his becoming Prime Minister in MacDonald's place if the Liberals went. 'I told Ramsay when the National Government was formed,' he added, 'that if they tried to hound him out unfairly, I would go out with him. They could boot me out too.'[19]

MacDonald was greatly depressed by these defections, whose purport he saw only too clearly. 'The country will have a shock; the Opposition Parties a score; and the outside world will see cracks in the national unity,' he told the King. 'The new Government will also be, to all intents and purposes, a single-party administration, and I think Your Majesty will find that a Prime Minister who does not belong to the Party in power will become more and more an anomaly, and, as policy develops, his position will become more and more degrading.'[20]

Time was indeed to prove him right.

3

Throughout 1932 and 1933 there was a concerted campaign led by Churchill to reverse the official Government policy over India which was to be embodied in the Government of India Act. In February 1933, a hostile motion was narrowly defeated at the National Union of Conservative Associations; but Baldwin refused to be discouraged, although Churchill's action caused a marked coolness between them. Henry ('Chips') Channon, who was a Conservative MP at this time, used to relate a story he heard from Churchill. There is a small lavatory off the long corridor near the Members' Lobby with only enough room for two men to relieve themselves at the same time. On one occasion when Churchill entered he saw to his embarrassment that one of the 'pissoirs' was occupied by Baldwin.

> It was too late to retreat as he had been seen so in he went. Baldwin was silent, but as he did up his trousers he turned to Churchill and remarked, 'I am glad that there is still one common platform upon which we can still meet,' and walked away. Winston tells the story with a wealth of gesture.[21]

Baldwin's official biographer G. M. Young once said to his subject: 'It must have been clear to you and MacDonald and Neville Chamberlain that Churchill at all events was *safer* inside the Cabinet than outside. What kept him out?' To which Baldwin replied: 'India. He had gone about threatening to smash the Tory party on India, and I did not mean to be smashed.' Baldwin was determined that India should not become a shuttlecock of party politics as had happened with Ireland so that accommodation became impossible. 'You had an alternative policy according to the Government which ruled the country,' he told the Conservative Party Central Council in December 1934, 'with the inevitable result that the end was chaos, and the settlement was one that neither party would have looked on, ten or fifteen years before, as even possible or desirable.' He spoke in similar terms at this time to W. P. Crozier, the editor of the *Manchester Guardian*,* when he declared that 'it had been a great misfortune' that the Irish question

---

* W. P. Crozier (1879–1944), the son of a Wesleyan Methodist minister in Durham, was a brilliant journalist who took a Double First at Oxford. He joined the *Manchester Guardian* in 1903 and edited it from 1932 until his death.

had become a purely party question so that each side was absolutely rigid, and the result in Ireland ultimately was revolt and civil war. He had all that in mind with regard to India and it had been his object throughout to put the India question on a non-party national plane. It had been a disappointment to him that Labour split over the National Government so that now he had on one side of the National Government 'only about half a dozen of these fellows'.[22]

On the eve of the second reading of the Government of India Bill, Baldwin explained his attitude in a broadcast:

We are pledged to the development of self-government in India since 1919. We should have failed in one of our main imperial understandings if we were not able to extend the field of self-government in India. And we who invented this system of government, and pride ourselves on understanding it, will be there to watch over and preside over its further development. The British Raj is not cravenly withdrawing from India. It will remain there until its work is complete and its presence no longer necessary.

No legislative measure had produced a greater wordage, spoken and printed, since the Irish Home Rule Bills. In addition to a substantial output of Reports, White Papers and Blue Books on the subject of Indian autonomy, the parliamentary debates provided nearly 2,000 speeches containing over 15 million words and filling over 4,000 pages of the official record, to much of which Baldwin was condemned to listen from his place on the Government Front Bench. Yet the end product was relatively mild and its content hardly justified Churchill's terrific stand against the measure both inside and outside Parliament. While it established an all-India federation and greater autonomy in the provinces, the reality of power still lay with the British Government at the centre.

Perhaps Churchill himself sensed this in some degree when he sent Baldwin a note with his New Year greetings for 1934:

India apart, you have my constant good wishes . . . After all it is the European quarrel that will shape our lives. There indeed you must feel the burden press.[23]

What Churchill called the 'European quarrel' had been posed by the emergence of the Nazi leader Adolf Hitler as German Chancellor and the fact that Germany was secretly rearming contrary to the Versailles Treaty.

Germany thus threatened to upset the balance of power in Europe, as Japan had already done in the Far East, when she invaded the Chinese territory of Manchuria, bombarded Shanghai, where Britain had many commercial interests, and finally established the Japanese puppet state of Manchukuo. In the case of Japan, pious resolutions passed by the League of Nations had little effect, while in Europe Hitler prepared to withdraw his country from the League altogether. Meanwhile the Disarmament Conference was meeting at Geneva, and Baldwin hoped that its deliberations would result on his initiative in the abolition of the bombing aeroplane, so shocked had he been by the Japanese bombing of Shanghai ('Shanghai is a nightmare') and the evidence he heard in the early months of 1932 when he presided at meetings of the Committee of Imperial Defence. Baldwin's line found favour with most of the Cabinet, although Londonderry, the Air Minister, who was also Britain's representative at the Disarmament Conference, not unnaturally protested against the marking down of his service for virtual elimination.

Unfortunately the participants at Geneva failed to reach general agreement. During his summer holiday that year in Aix Baldwin continued to brood on the perils of unrestricted aerial warfare following on the conference deadlock. His ideas finally crystallised in the form of a speech which he made in the House of Commons on 10 November 1932 and which was designed to shock public opinion. Fear was what the world was suffering from, he said, and there was no greater cause of that fear than fear of the air. He went on:

> I think it is well also for the man in the street to realise that there is no power on earth that can protect him from being bombed. Whatever people may tell him, *the bomber will always get through*. The only defence is offence, which means that you have to kill more women and children more quickly than the enemy if you want to save yourselves.

Although he did not mention them by name, Baldwin inclined to the school of thought represented by Lord Trenchard, the former Chief of the Air Staff, and the late Lord Thomson, the Labour Air Minister who had lost his life in the R 101 disaster, that in any future war the way to win would be by the systematic bombing of great industrial localities, leaving both victors and vanquished with ruined cities and suffering civilians. The conventional air ministry view was that the only defence against the bombing aeroplane was the threat of retaliation in kind, and Baldwin spoke as he did with the approval of the ministry experts. As for such expedients as the reduction in the size of aircraft, as had been suggested at Geneva, that was quite unrealistic, he observed. ('Immediately every scientific man in the country will turn to making a high-explosive bomb about the size of a walnut and as powerful as a bomb of big dimensions.') Likewise the prohibition of bombing, which no combatant in war would observe, and no one could stop flying, while it was impracticable to prohibit bombing without controlling civil aviation as well, since civil aircraft were readily adaptable as bombers.

He ended on a despairing note:

If the conscience of the young men should ever come to feel with regard to this one instrument that it is evil and should go, the thing will be done; but if they do not feel like that – well, as I say, the future is in their hands. But when the next war comes and European civilisation is wiped out, as it will be, and by no force more than by that force, then do not let them lay the blame upon the old men. Let them remember that they, they principally and they alone, are responsible for the terrors that have fallen upon the earth.

To what conclusion did Baldwin's speech lead? asked Churchill pointedly. 'It created anxiety, it created also perplexity. There was a sense of – what shall I say? – of fatalism and helplessness about it.' It certainly reflected Baldwin's mood at a time when a wave of pacifist feeling swept the country. This was expressed in the notorious motion carried by a substantial majority of the undergraduate members of the Oxford Union debating society in February 1933 that 'this House will not fight for King and Country'.

In the same month Austen Chamberlain invited Baldwin to address a meeting of the League of Nations Union in Birmingham. Baldwin declined the invitation in a characteristic note to Chamberlain:

11 Downing Street, Whitehall, SW 17 February 1933 . . . I should be reluctant to add to my work by an extra speech on a Saturday night: but further than that, I have always avoided these meetings of the League, except one which I addressed in the Albert Hall – or maybe two. There is so much I dislike in the Union propaganda and I should have to steer between the Scylla of cursing them and the Charybdis of mush and poppycock, and I might be wrecked on either!

So I will beg you to say how I recognise the honour done to me in asking but in view of heavy commitments – Thank you.[24]

Nine months later, John Wilmot, a left-wing Labour candidate, won the Tory stronghold of East Fulham in a by-election, turning a 14,000 Conservative majority into a minority of 5,000. Coming a fortnight after Germany had walked out of the Disarmament Conference and left the League, the result was hailed by the newly elected MP 'as a message of hope to all who are working for peace in every country'. The British people demanded, he said after the poll, that 'the British Government shall give a lead to the whole world by initiating immediately a policy of general disarmament', since the Government had brought the Disarmament Conference to the point of failure and Britain was 'nearer to war than we have been since 1918'. At the same time George Lansbury, the Labour Party leader in the House of Commons, came out in favour of a policy of general disarmament. 'I would close every recruiting station, disband the Army and disarm the Air Force,' he said. 'I would abolish the whole dreadful equipment of war and say to the world: "Do your worst." ' [25]

Baldwin was greatly shaken by the result and he asked for a special report on the by-election from Central Office. The task of preparing it was entrusted to Arthur Baker, *The Times* parliamentary lobby correspondent, who had covered the election campaign for his paper. According to John Davidson, he reported that 'East Fulham had been lost purely on the pacifist issue'. This was an exaggeration, as housing and the hated means test for unemployment relief were also contributory factors. But peace propaganda did have an effect, and Baldwin, who was himself something of a pacifist at heart, found Baker's report very disturbing.

As an example of which way the wind was blowing in London at this time, Mrs Baldwin was approached by a woman who said to her: 'You won't let them have a war, will you?' 'What do you mean?' she asked, somewhat startled by the question. The woman replied: 'They're talking about you and your husband starting a war.'

Baldwin's official biographer G. M. Young, who had many talks with his subject on this among other topics, was convinced that he never quite recovered from the shock of East Fulham. 'He was afraid of the pacifists: he could not bring himself quite to say, perhaps not quite to think: "Germany is arming, and we must arm too." ' [26]

When Sir Robert Vansittart, the permanent head of the Foreign Office, came to see Baldwin shortly after East Fulham to urge the case for speedy rearmament, Baldwin told him that he could not afford to take risks. 'I cannot go to the country on rearmament,' he said bluntly. While it was a subject which ministers did not neglect, he went on, it had to be handled gingerly. The British public would have to be educated to accept that it was necessary. To press on with it at the moment, he thought, would be fatal. 'It would alienate support from the National Government and cause it to lose the next election.' He knew, he said, that the Socialist Government that would replace it would not rearm at all, and he was 'not prepared to gamble with the security of the country'.

Shortly after East Fulham, Davidson arranged a private meeting between Baldwin and Hitler's roving Ambassador, Joachim von Ribbentrop, at the instance of Ernest Tennant, a London merchant banker who had good contacts with the new regime in Germany. The meeting took place at a luncheon party at Davidson's house in Westminster and, according to Davidson, was a success, 'although S.B., never at his best with foreigners, did not really take to Ribbentrop', who 'was not at this time, however, the unpleasant creature that he afterwards became'. In the result, Baldwin was less favourably impressed than Davidson with Ribbentrop's repeated protestations of his master's pacific intentions and the vague hints thrown out by Ribbentrop about the possible return of the former German colonies and expansion eastwards at the expense of the Soviet Union. But he did invite Ribbentrop to tea in Downing Street and at this second meeting he introduced him to Ramsay Mac-Donald. There was some talk about Baldwin paying a visit to Berlin early in 1934, but nothing came of the idea, since Baldwin held to the view that visits to foreign capitals were the province of the Foreign Secretary and he did not wish to poach on Simon's territory. 'Baldwin wanted peace, but he was not prepared to have peace at any price,' noted Davidson afterwards. 'It was my view then, and it was emphatically Baldwin's view, that we could not make sacrifices to Germany to have peace . . . I don't think that at any time he believed in Hitler as an honest man . . . With regard to Germany, S.B.'s attitude was one of retaining our strength, but he also had a really profound hope of peace; furthermore, he did not have much faith in the French, either in their methods of keeping the peace or their likely strength in the struggle if it came.'[27]

At the end of February 1934, Londonderry told the Cabinet that the British air force front-line strength was only half that of France and Russia. His warning was reinforced a week later on 8 March by Churchill when the House of Commons debated the Air Estimates providing for four new squadrons, and Churchill invited Baldwin to declare, with the authority of the Cabinet, what the Government policy was. 'Germany is arming fast and no one is going to stop her,' Churchill thundered from the back benches. 'No one proposes a preventive war to stop Germany breaking the Treaty of Versailles. She is going to arm; she is doing it; she has been doing it . . . The spirit of aggressive nationalism was never more rife in Europe and in the world. Far away are the days of Locarno, when we nourished bright hopes of the reunion of the European family.'

Replying to this challenge, Baldwin said that he would try to be a realist. He still hoped that the Disarmament Conference would succeed, but 'if all our efforts are futile', then 'we must immediately spend large sums of money' in order to achieve parity with the principal European air forces. His words took the form of a definite pledge repeating in stronger language what he and the CID had advocated when he was Prime Minister eleven years previously:*

> If our efforts for an agreement fail, and if it is not possible to obtain this equality in such matters as I have indicated, then any Government of this country – a National Government more than any, and *this* Government – will see to it that *in air strength and air power this country shall no longer be in a position inferior to any country within striking distance of our shores.*[28]

Shortly afterwards Baldwin was asked a pertinent question by W. P. Crozier, according to the latter's account:

> Was no sort of air convention now practicable and was there no chance of this country agreeing to a scheme of either internationalisation or international control of civilian aircraft as being the only thing that would make the abolition of air forces possible?

He said that so far as he knew no scheme of controlling civilian aircraft was practicable, and no country so far as he knew had put forward any practicable scheme. He mentioned that it was he personally who had introduced into the Cabinet the question of disarmament in the air, but he was obviously disappointed about the prospects. *He said the upshot was that we could simply not avoid increasing our air force.* It ought to be realised that the whole situation had been altered for the worse by the rise of the new Germany. 'No one,' he said and repeated more than once, 'knows what the new Germany means – whether she means peace or war.'

He said that he himself was no alarmist. He did not believe in war in the near future and he did not think about it, though he was bound to say that most of the people who talked to him on the subject took a gloomy view about Germany's ultimate intentions. At all events he held that the Government could not take risks. It was the trustee for the people of the country and it had got to have adequate means of defence so far as those could be provided.

* See above, p. 167.

The Solicitor-General, Sir Donald Somervell, later Lord Somervell of Harrow, who was sitting on the Treasury Bench during the air debate on 8 March 1934, thought that Baldwin made 'a first-rate speech' which 'got a very good reception'. Somervell, who had become Solicitor-General at the age of forty-four barely two years after his first election to the House of Commons in 1931, was an exceptionally versatile lawyer with a brilliant academic career, having been the first Oxford graduate with first-class honours in chemistry to be elected to a fellowship at All Souls. He had a great respect for Baldwin and it was this which determined him to enter politics as a Conservative rather than a Liberal where his sympathies originally were. He also kept an interesting political diary, in which he wrote at this time:

> My analysis of Baldwin has been for some time complete single-mindedness in the main policy and line. He is completely devoid of self-seeking, and incapable of any ulterior motive. Once his main line is laid down he is a very astute advocate. He knows how to appeal to – if you like – the limitations of his audience, if he is convinced of his cause. Winston is supposed to have said: 'They talk of the honest, stupid Baldwin; believe me, he is the most ruthless and astute politician of our day.' But however badly Winston treated him, Baldwin would never hit back out of personal animus, but only to deflate Winston in what he believed was a mischievous course. And that he can do in a way to earn Winston's admiration.
>
> I have the happiest memories of my relations and talks with S.B. I was fond of him and he of me and he talked freely to me, not that I saw a great deal of him. I remember saying to him once that one heard a lot about intrigue in politics, but I thought it was exaggerated. He looked at me with a friendly smile and said: 'You know if I was minded to go in for an intrigue, I wouldn't ask you to come and help. I don't think it's your line.' [29]

Somebody once said of Baldwin that he always hit the nail on the head but it never seemed to go any further. In this instance at least there was some truth in the remark. After four months had gone by and the Government had given no outward sign that it intended to redeem Baldwin's pledge of air parity, Churchill reminded him of it in a speech which he delivered to his constituency on 7 July 1934 after MacDonald had gone off to North America on a health voyage leaving Baldwin in charge at home:

All the power now that the Prime Minister is on holiday lies in the hands of Mr Baldwin, and where the power lies, there also lies the responsibility. You cannot have decisive power without responsibility.

Mr Baldwin promised in the House of Commons in March that if the Disarmament Conference failed we should have an Air Force which would be equal to that of any Power which could get at us.

Lord Londonderry, the Air Minister, and Mr Eden, the able but much too pliable Under-Secretary for Foreign Affairs, told us in unmistakable terms that the Disarmament Conference has failed. How could it help failing when the Germans are arming day and night? Why, then, is the promise not fulfilled? Why is the necessary action not taken? Why stand we in jeopardy every hour?[30]

The delay in making a public announcement on future air policy was due to a prolonged wrangle in the Cabinet as to the amount of money which should be allocated to defence requirements and to Chamberlain's proposed scaling down of expenditure for the next five years from £76 million, which the Cabinet Disarmament Committee had advocated, to £50 million 'in the light of politics and finance'. Largely on Baldwin's initiative, this proposed cut was restored, and on 19 July 1934 the Lord President of the Council was able to inform the House of Commons that the Government had decided to increase the strength of the RAF by 41½ squadrons or about 820 aircraft over the next five years. Londonderry made a similar statement in the House of Lords, taking the line that, although all hope of 'something materialising at Geneva' ought not to be abandoned, the idea of parity in the air with any Power within striking distance must now be a cardinal principle of British air policy. If this new policy was effectively carried out, he argued, 'it would strengthen Britain's influence for peace, and, far from inaugurating a new race in armaments, might effectively stop one'.[31]

These statements provoked an outcry from the Opposition and a Labour motion of censure on the Government was put down with Liberal support. 'We deny the need for increased air armaments,' said Mr Clement Attlee, MP, speaking on behalf of the Parliamentary Labour Party. 'We deny the proposition that an increased British Air Force will make for the peace of the world, and we reject altogether the claim to parity.'

The censure debate took place on 30 July and it provided Baldwin with the occasion of what perhaps was his most striking utterance on the subject of defence, to which he hoped that the Germans as well as the British people would pay heed:

Since the day of the air the old frontiers are gone. When you think of the defence of England you no longer think of the chalk cliffs of Dover; you think of the Rhine. That is where our frontier lies.

Next day Neville Chamberlain noted in his diary: 'The session ends with the party in good heart, and the Government stronger than ever. But there are some ominous signs – the murder of Dollfuss, the imminent death of Hindenburg, the slowing down of trade recovery, and the internal conditions in USA, France and Germany.' In particular, the killing of the Austrian Chancellor Engelbert Dollfuss in Vienna by Austrian Nazis, following on the heels of 'the night of the long knives' in Germany when Ernst Roehm and about two hundred others including the Defence Minister General von Schleicher and his wife were shot out of hand on Hitler's orders on suspicion of intriguing to supplant him, showed the world the lengths to which Nazi terrorist methods could go both at home and abroad.* A few days later, the last constitutional restraint on Hitler's absolute power in the German Reich was removed by the death of President Hindenburg.[32]

4

Although Ramsay MacDonald was titular Leader of the House of Commons as well as Prime Minister of the National Government, Baldwin frequently deputised for him in the management of parliamentary business, so much so that Attlee and Simon came to regard him in effect as Leader of the House. 'Of all the offices I have held,' he was to say when he eventually gave it up, 'I have never had more work to do and had less pay than I have had as Lord President of the Council. It is one of the hardest posts that I have ever occupied.'

Since Sir Philip Sassoon, the Under-Secretary for Air, was not a member of the Cabinet, and Londonderry, the Air Minister, was in the Lords, Baldwin came more and more to answer for air policy in the Commons. This arrangement would have worked out all right, if Baldwin's relations with Londonderry had been easy and intimate. Un-

---

* Roehm, a homosexual, was summarily executed after being surprised with a youth in his quarters. Sir Donald Somervell, then Solicitor-General, wrote in his diary on 7 July 1934: 'I suggested to S.B. that a fair parallel would be if he went and offered Sir Oswald Mosley in bed the choice of committing suicide or being shot. S.B. replied at once, "No, not me, the Prime Minister and Ralph Glyn."' Sir Oswald Mosley had recently founded the British Union of Fascists. Sir Ralph (later Lord) Glyn, a Tory MP, was Parliamentary Private Secretary to Ramsay MacDonald at this date.

fortunately they were neither and the consequent failure in communication led to some unfortunate misunderstandings. There was no bond of sympathy between them. As Baldwin afterwards told Londonderry's son Castlereagh, 'I always tried to be friendly with your father, but he was aloof and standoffish,' although Baldwin was careful to add that he could always count on his complete loyalty as a colleague. ('Loyalty is the rarest virtue in politics.')[33] For his part, Londonderry was sorry to think that he was never able to gain Baldwin's confidence. 'I often tried to get closer to you but I did not succeed. I think, as a matter of fact, that I was a little too outspoken and that you resented once or twice the opinions which I expressed, whilst others, who may be said to be more far-seeing in their own interests, have taken good care not to cross you in any way.' Londonderry also complained to Baldwin, looking back some years later, that, 'although you were responsible for the more important Air matters in the House of Commons, you never consulted me once, but were in the habit of sending for little Bullock, who always informed me, of course, but who never seemed to convey to you the real points we wished to be emphasised, as there were always misunderstandings after all your speeches relating to Air matters in the House of Commons'.[34]*

One example of such a misunderstanding must suffice here. At the opening of the new parliamentary session in November 1933, defence with particular reference to the air was debated in both Houses with Londonderry answering for the Government in the Upper House and Baldwin in the Commons. Whether Londonderry mistook his brief or whether (as he subsequently asserted) a sentence was taken out of its context, at all events his figures were challenged by Lansbury and other members in the Commons who had heard Londonderry's speech. Lansbury was rightly ruled out of order by the Speaker. But surely it was a Government statement? Lansbury persisted. Baldwin answered, in accordance with parliamentary custom, that he had no knowledge of what had been said 'in another place'. No doubt the incident was relatively small in itself. Nevertheless it enabled Lansbury to score off the Government and it did underline a certain lack of co-ordination between the two ministerial statements. In the result Baldwin now began to look more and more to Cunliffe-Lister for help on air defence matters rather than the departmental minister.

Baldwin's friend John Davidson later wrote somewhat unsympathetically of Londonderry:

* Sir Christopher Bullock (1891–1972), Permanent Secretary of the Air Ministry. He was dismissed in 1936 following the findings of a board of inquiry. See below, p. 441.

Although it was clear that the Air Ministry was absolutely right in refusing to equip the RAF with obsolescent aircraft, there seemed to be a certain lack of drive in their programme. I know that S.B. attributed the responsibility to Londonderry personally . . .

Londonderry had the reputation of being a rather soft, Regency-beau type of man. Although he had a certain amount of cunning and capacity, he was not really equipped for thinking. As a mine owner in Durham he had quite a good reputation, but the people who were his agents were regarded as a pretty hard lot. He was never really fit for Cabinet rank, and his association with the Air Force was, although keen, rather on the social than the technical side. Amongst the politicians of the Party – people like Bridgeman and Wood and Sam Hoare – he was regarded as a lightweight and only fit for an under-secretaryship. Philip Sassoon was rather of the same stamp . . .

He hadn't got the capacity to deal with his Air Council or to give them a positive lead, and their intelligence department was always regarded by the two other fighting departments and by the Foreign Office as extremely weak. But Londonderry took himself very seriously and that was in a sense a tragedy, because others didn't take him at all seriously . . . He owed his preferment really to the fact that Ramsay MacDonald greatly enjoyed standing at the top of the grand staircase in Londonderry House as the first Minister of the Crown in full evening dress.[35]

W. P. Crozier, the editor of the *Manchester Guardian*, who called on Baldwin in the House of Commons when the Cabinet discussions on the first substantial increase in British air strength were at their height in June 1934, wrote a vivid account of their meeting, hitherto unpublished, from which the following is an extract:

Baldwin was in his private room. It communicates with Palace Yard by a narrow little back staircase and a side door, so that it is rather like something out of Dumas. Baldwin's face, seen close to, was most interesting. I had never seen him before, and in his photographs his face had always seemed to be chiefly amiable and a little whimsical, just as his speeches sound simple, honest and ingenuous. Actually he is not like that at all.

His face is rugged and nobbly; his right eye is either going wrong or has some sort of a cast in it and mostly half shut. But the characteristic of his face is its determination and shrewdness – or rather, because it is much more than shrewdness, a sort of deep rustic craftiness. More than any other politician he reminded me of Lloyd George in this, but while L.G. is gleefully and maliciously cunning, Baldwin seemed to me to look shrewd and crafty in a rather grim and hard way. I got quite a new idea of him and for the first time understood how he had come to be leader of the Tory party and Prime Minister. The good-natured mellow look of the photographs was only there when he greeted me and said good-bye, saying that I was to come again whenever I would like a talk. During most of the conversation he tried vainly to light his pipe.[36]

As secretary of the Pilgrim Trust, Tom Jones continued to see a good deal of Baldwin and he has preserved the flavour of his table talk. He noted that Baldwin suffered from a certain deafness at this time which he thought affected his political judgement. 'He often does not hear me despite my loud voice and clear speech,' wrote Jones in November 1932. 'It is only in the last twelve months I have noticed this. His continued silence and passivity greatly weaken his influence and it is very difficult to bring him to the point of positive action.'

20 October 1932. Had lunch alone at No. 11 with S.B. yesterday, taking what he called 'pot-luck', which included two eggs apiece cooked in those little dishes with handles, whose name I forget, and delicious cold ham 'cured by my own cowman' at Astley, Cheddar cheese and salad and coffee and lots of talk. He has been reading Brett Young's *House under the Water* and Stephen Gwynne's *Life of Mary Kingsley* – 'great stuff, those Victorian women', says he; 'don't see their likes nowadays'. He was delighted with a story I gave him for the speech the night before at the dinner of the Royal College of Physicians in memory of Harvey . . .

19 February 1933 . . . On Thursday morning I had an hour at No. 11 with S.B. He was in fine form. This being second and not first suits him perfectly and frees him from final decisions and therefore from worry. He talked fast about politics, Cambridge, books . . . 'Cambridge is still alive. I went to hear them bombard the electrons and I dined with a club called "The Family" – Housman, poet, there, most unclubbable man. I could get nothing out of him. Was told after I could have drawn him with obscene stories, but I gave them up when I left Harrow.'

Somehow at this meeting the name of Helen Waddell came up.

Baldwin had been much impressed by her books, particularly *The Wandering Scholars* and *Medieval Latin Lyrics*, and he invited Jones to meet her one Saturday morning at breakfast when he could get hold of the accomplished and sensitive Irish writer who now shared with the late Mary Webb the leading place in his literary affections.* When Parliament was sitting, Baldwin usually spent the week-end at 11 Downing Street and like Lloyd George would often ask friends to breakfast with him.

12 March 1933 . . . On Saturday a week ago – March 4 – I breakfasted at No. 11 with S.B. and Helen Waddell whom I had not met before. Just three of us and S.B. invited us to start with a Pork Pie. I expressed my horror but this was specially made for him. The two guests quailed and refused.

He began: 'I have time till 10.30 and then I'll turn you out as I've got a scoundrel coming to see me who says he was promised a KCVO in return for £10,000 to a hospital. He is a member of my Party so I cannot refuse to see him. I shall tell him he is liable to be prosecuted for trafficking in Honours.'

We switched quickly from this unsavoury topic and left politics severely alone and got H.W. to talk of the Mediaeval Chroniclers, of translating, of concentrated phrases, of tales in Plutarch, of John of Salisbury, of St David and his Cathedral . . .

I can't recall her examples of fine phrases. One, I think, from Tacitus was '*quies tardior*'. S.B. said he was moved once in the House of Commons by an Irish member Flavin who said: 'As brave a heart beats under the tunic of a Dublin Fusilier as under the kilt of a Scots Highlander.'[37]

Helen Waddell recalled afterwards that as Baldwin helped her into her coat, when she was leaving, he said: 'You'll come and do this often? It's done me a world of good.' According to her, he said this twice.

Early in 1934, when the subject of defence was beginning to be

---

* Helen Waddell (1889–1965) had recently been introduced to Baldwin at a luncheon party expressly given for the purpose at Baldwin's request by the economist Sir Basil Blackett, whose sister Monica was her close friend. 'I just fell for Baldwin,' Miss Waddell wrote after this meeting. 'Not a bit like the stockbroker's photographs, but rather like a classical scholar turned farmer, with a kind of innocence about him. I was beside him at lunch and we talked hard, but most of all about the Wiltshire downs. He made his last cabinet at a funny little village called Oare . . . He was extravagant in praise of *The Scholars*, said I'd forever put him in my debt; the *Lyrics* likewise.' Monica Blackett, *The Mark of the Maker: A Portrait of Helen Waddell* (1973), p. 96.

publicly discussed, Baldwin and Jones had a revealing talk about Lloyd George, for whom Jones retained a great affection and who he suggested should be made Foreign Secretary in place of John Simon.

T.J. Have you thought lately of taking L.G. into the Government?

S.B. I have thought of everything.

T.J. Your talk on Saturday made me very solemn. We are heading for a grave situation when it will be important to have a genuine National Government. If we are to re-arm and to avoid trouble in India it might be worth bringing L.G. in.

S.B. Do you really think he would work under anybody?

T.J. He is over seventy; he has mellowed; Dawson tells me he has still lots of vitality. He wakes at 5 a.m. and works at his *Memoirs*. He likes you and will work under you; he won't work with Ramsay. Why not send L.G. to the FO? It is essential that if he came into the Cabinet he should be fully occupied and the FO or Agriculture would satisfy that condition.

S.B. It would certainly never do for him to be like me, without an office.

T.J. Elliot's policy is bound to lead to all kinds of difficulties presently, especially with the consumers, and if he is wise he will move from Agriculture. L.G. has long fancied himself as fitted for that office. But there is much to be said for putting him in the FO to deal with the scoundrels of Europe. You either want that type at the FO or the more saintly type like Grey or Edward Wood.

S.B. Someone said that the ideal Foreign Minister is the simple English gentleman, so long as you have got a Tyrell behind him. Now L.G. is neither simple nor a gentleman.

T.J. Well, I think the opposite ought to be tried at the FO. You are now in a different position *vis-à-vis* L.G. from twenty years ago; you are on top and the fires of his ambition have died down; as he is always saying: 'I have had my day.'

S.B. Yes, it is an extraordinary situation. In those days I had developed a protective barrage of innocence in the midst of wickedness. I gradually covered myself with stripes in the jungle until I got into a position where I could hurl my pebble and bring him down. Has he any following in the country?

T.J. I think not, and he would be very unpopular with many in the House.

S.B. And Labour still distrusts him. I should like to see in

> any reconstructed Government a strong Labour leader like Bevin.*
>
> T.J. I think bringing in L.G. and Bevin would impress the country with the gravity of the situation and make them realise that we seem to be shaping for another war.
>
> S.B. I would not put it that way. I would say that we are the only defenders left of liberty in a world of Fascists.[38]

Jones did his best over Lloyd George, but the odds were against him. Both Ramsay MacDonald and Neville Chamberlain were opposed to the idea of bringing him into the Government. At the end of the year Jones noted that 'Ramsay sits in the saddle despite various efforts to dislodge him. But even if he fell, S.B. would find it impossible to take L.G. on without splitting his Cabinet in two. I don't think he will face that though his attitude to L.G. is much friendlier than of yore.'[39]

On 17 January 1935 Lloyd George celebrated his seventy-second birthday in Wales by launching, amidst a blaze of press publicity, a programme for a 'New Deal' to help the unemployed and revive the country's economy. He followed this up with a nation-wide campaign to propagate his views. Jones wrote to an American friend:

> S.B.'s position is, of course, one of great difficulty. There is his loyalty to Ramsay, for whom L.G. has no use; to Neville as his Chancellor, for whose policy [of cheap money and tariffs] L.G. has no sympathy; and to the Tory party, which would split if L.G. were brought into the Cabinet. The young Tories would welcome L.G. but the majority would be hostile. On the other hand L.G.'s campaign in the country is much more effective than that of the Government because they have no comparable showman who focuses interest upon himself and his speeches as he does. L.G. wants a small Cabinet on War lines. The corridors are humming with rumours.[40]

The upshot was that Lloyd George was invited to attend a Committee of the Cabinet which cross-examined him on his proposals through ten sittings. 'Our meetings were studiously pleasant,' said Lloyd George afterwards, 'but they knew in their hearts that they were going to knife me. What they didn't know was that I had a dagger in my sheath for them, too!'[41]

---

* Ernest Bevin (1881–1951), later Minister of Labour and Foreign Secretary, was at this time Secretary of the Transport and General Workers' Union and a leading member of the TUC General Council.

Frances Stevenson, Lloyd George's devoted secretary and future wife, was less charitably disposed towards Baldwin at this time. 'Personally I think he is as crafty as the craftiest politician, and hopes that the situation "*solvebitur cunctando*",' she wrote in her diary. 'He is not going out of his way to bring in one who would in all likelihood challenge his sovereignty, usurp his position, and in any case make things damned uncomfortable for him. Meanwhile . . . the political haunts are buzzing with excitement and speculation. There is no doubt that D [Lloyd George]'s proposals have caught on in the country. We are overwhelmed with approval from every quarter, and of every political complexion.' [42]

Nothing came of the idea of bringing Lloyd George into the Cabinet. And very little of his firework dagger which turned out to be a damp squib. This was the so-called 'Council of Action for Peace and Reconstruction', which was designed to attract men and women of all parties and no party and run election candidates. It failed to do so, although Lloyd George spent £400,000 on it from his political fund. After a brief interval Lloyd George returned to his farm in Surrey to experiment with stock, poultry and fruit and to the task of completing his war memoirs. His political career was over. On reflection, Baldwin came to the conclusion that the Government was right not to have Lloyd George as a ministerial colleague. 'I've often told you that L.G. has never really led a Party,' he said to Tom Jones. 'He is not a cohesive but a disintegrating force.' [43]

5

Meanwhile the subject of air rearmament continued to excite controversy among the politicians and the public, as suspicions mounted that the Germans were secretly equipping themselves with military aircraft capable of striking at the heart of Britain. On 7 July 1934 Churchill in a speech to his constituents, clearly designed to reach a much wider public, called for a large vote of credit to double the strength of the RAF immediately, and for a larger vote as soon as possible to redouble it. A month later, Professor F. A. Lindemann, Churchill's friend and adviser on scientific matters, wrote a letter to *The Times* in which he warned that 'bomber aeroplanes in the hands of gangster governments might jeopardise the whole future of our Western civilisation' and called for a concerted scientific effort in the field of air defence research. In September, Churchill and Lindemann, who were on holiday together in Cannes, journeyed to Aix-les-Bains where they interrupted Baldwin's repose to urge upon him new methods of defence, such as the construction of aerial mines to be incorporated in kite-balloon barrages. According to Churchill, Baldwin 'appeared deeply interested' and advised them to get in touch with the air ministry, where a departmental committee, nominally functioning as a sub-committee of the CID, had recently been set up under the chairmanship of Air Marshal Sir Robert Brooke-Popham to formulate future air defence plans.[44]

Shortly after his return to London, Lindemann did attend a meeting of the Brooke-Popham committee, but he was not reassured by its proceedings. He thereupon wrote to Baldwin advocating the appointment of an independent committee under the chairmanship of a man of the type of the industrialist Lord Weir, who had been a successful war-time air minister. The committee should include both service representatives and scientists, he urged, 'whose definite instructions would be to find some method of defence against air bombing other than counter-attack and reprisals'.

Presumably Baldwin passed this letter to Londonderry, to whom Lindemann also wrote controverting the view previously put forward by Baldwin with Air Ministry approval that 'the bomber will always get through'.

> I do not know on what evidence this conclusion was founded; why for ten years the possibilities of the kite-balloon barrage were neglected, nor how much energy had been devoted to research into methods of this sort. Whatever the reason, I gather that until recently, at any rate, it was definitely the opinion of the Air Ministry that no defence could ever be discovered.
>
> This view appears to me profoundly improbable. An antidote has always been found hitherto for every offensive weapon and I see no reason to suppose that aircraft are the only exception; in fact, many arguments would tend to prove the contrary. But once a Department has adopted such a defeatist line, it is clearly going to be very difficult to persuade those concerned to make very great efforts to prove that they have been in error. For this reason and because some of the methods that ought to be considered lie in intermediate regions between those covered by the various defence ministries, it seems unlikely that a purely Air Ministry Committee would attain the desired end.[45]

Throughout the summer and autumn of 1934 the Air Ministry's estimates of German air strength grew steadily, so that when Parliament opened in November the existing level was reckoned to be 1,000 military aircraft, of which 300 were first-line, which latter were expected to increase to over 500 with an equal number of reserves by the end of 1936, so that within two more years Germany might well have 1,800 or even 2,000 first-line aircraft. Clearly, if the principle of air parity was to be maintained, a further expansion of the RAF was inevitable.

When the Cabinet met on 28 November, it was confirmed that Baldwin should intervene during the opening debate on the Address in the House of Commons later that day when the question of the relative British and German air strengths was expected to be raised by Churchill. At this Cabinet several alternative estimates of current German strength were before the ministers including a Foreign Office source which put the figure at 600 and a French source which put it at 1,100. However, Londonderry stated that the total of 1,000 German military aircraft had been carefully checked. At the same time he observed that 'it would be most unwise to state any figure in the House of Commons which could be successfully challenged by Germany', and this was generally agreed.[46] Since the British first-line strength at this time was 500 machines comprised in 43 squadrons, it will be seen that what Baldwin stated in the House was true enough. His statement was designed, as he had earlier told his Cabinet colleagues, to let Germany know in 'clear but friendly' terms that Britain was aware of and was not indifferent to what was taking place there in the matter of air rearmament.

It is not the case that Germany is rapidly approaching equality with us . . . even if we confine the comparison to the German air strength and the strength of the Royal Air Force immediately available in Europe. Germany is actively engaged in the production of service aircraft, but her real strength is not 50 per cent of our strength in Europe today. As for the position this time next year, *if she continues to execute her air programme without acceleration* and if we continue to carry out at the present approved rate of expansion announced in Parliament in July . . . so far from the German military air force being at least as strong and probably stronger than our own, we estimate that we shall have in Europe a margin – in Europe alone – of nearly 50 per cent.

Churchill, who had his own intelligence sources, claimed that the Germans would attain parity with the RAF within the next twelve months and would have double Britain's air strength by the end of 1936. Baldwin challenged these figures as being 'considerably exaggerated', but he did not predict, as was later suggested by his opponents, that Britain would have a safe margin of superiority by the latter date. What he actually said in the debate, to quote his own words, was that 'it is impossible to give any accurate estimate for longer than two years, but that we were able to maintain a position not inferior, whatever happened'.[47]

Meanwhile Londonderry had deferred replying to Lindemann's letter until he was in a position to tell 'the Prof' that he had appointed a departmental committee of the Air Ministry under Mr (later Sir) Henry Tizard, who was an expert in aeronautical research as well as a practical airman, 'to consider', in the words of the committee's terms of reference, 'how far recent advances in technical knowledge can be used to strengthen the present methods of defence against hostile aircraft'. The idea of the Committee for the Scientific Survey of Air Defence, as it was known officially, did not originate with Londonderry, although he deserves some credit for sponsoring it. In fact, it was the brain child of Mr H. E. Wimperis, the inventor of the course-setting bombsight and at this time director of scientific research at the Air Ministry. He persuaded his political chief to set up the Tizard Committee, on which he himself served, besides two other 'independent' scientists, Professor A. V. Hill and Professor P. M. S. Blackett, in addition to the chairman.

In writing to Lindemann, which he did on 20 December, Londonderry told him about the new committee. It would be useful, he added, if Professor Lindemann would communicate with Tizard and make suggestions for consideration by the committee. Lindemann's reaction was hostile. He immediately regarded the committee, in spite of its composition, as really a departmental committee, a type which he had always distrusted. What was more, he saw it as a plot by the Air Ministry and Tizard to circumvent his own proposal. 'I can scarcely believe that the somewhat unimportant Tizard Committee can have the authority or power that is required,' he told Austen Chamberlain at this time, 'more especially if it is a question of getting work done by the War Office or some other Department.' Eventually Lindemann agreed, with much reluctance, to join the committee, after he had learned that it was to work closely with the CID.[48]

At its first meeting, which was held on 28 January 1935, the Tizard Committee heard through Wimperis that Ronald Watson-Watt, a member of the ministry's meteorological staff, believed that it might be possible to detect the presence of aircraft by a radio beam. Shortly afterwards a successful experiment to this effect was carried out at Daventry with an aircraft in flight. This was the origin of the radio defence technique, generally known as radar, which was to be developed so rapidly that England was to be equipped with an effective warning system when the time came for its use against the German enemy in 1939.[49]

Lindemann, who was unaware at this time of the important discovery which had been made of radar, continued to pour cold water on the Tizard Committee and he encouraged Austen Chamberlain to press his criticisms on Baldwin. On 14 March 1935 Londonderry wrote privately and confidentially to Baldwin in response to the latter's request for his comments on these criticisms, that 'Tizard's committee is working in full co-operation with the representatives of all the three Services and that, far from being a delay, which Lindemann seemed to expect, there has been the utmost despatch in getting down to work and making progress'.

> While I have, from the first, emphasised the necessity for full liaison with the other Services, I remain of the opinion that we shall get much quicker results if the Committee is in direct and working touch with the Air Ministry, than by any other means.
>
> I may tell you that the very promising suggestion which has already been made by this Committee was tested practically in the air *within a week* of its inception, and financial authority has been received to proceed with the development and full scale trials of this new method, and *without any restriction on the staff or funds* which we had considered to be necessary for the purpose.
>
> I cannot imagine any such results being obtained from the action of an independent Committee or a Committee working directly with the CID. This seems also to dispose of the criticism with regard to funds . . .
>
> It is not too much to say that in view of my advisers and myself, our potential capacity to defend the country against air attack has been materially increased by the work of the last fortnight and, provided that we are careful, not only to keep the other Services in touch with what is going on, but also to allow full weight to their opinions in the counsels of the Committee, I think the system which we have initiated would be hard to improve; that is to say a small and active Committee working in close harmony with a sympathetic department.[50]

The subject of national defence had just been pinpointed by a Government White Paper which was jointly drafted by MacDonald, Baldwin, Chamberlain and Hankey and appeared at the beginning of March over the Prime Minister's initials. It emphasised the extent of German rearmament and indicated that if unchecked it would lead to war. Baldwin described the White Paper when it was debated in the House of Commons as a document 'in which a democratic government tells what it believes to be the truth to democracy' and as being a declaration that British defence should be strong enough 'to repel an aggressor or to fulfil obligations'. His words were underlined by General Goering's announcement on the eve of the debate that Germany possessed an air force in defiance of the Versailles Treaty and Hitler's statement a few days later that the German army was to be raised to thirty-six divisions (half a million men) and compulsory military service introduced.

Later the same month, Sir John Simon, the Foreign Secretary, accompanied by Anthony Eden, his Under-Secretary, visited Paris and Berlin to discuss the possibility of concluding a multi-lateral Western Air Pact and an Eastern Pact of Mutual Assistance. Nothing came of the idea, since Hitler refused to contemplate the prospect of fighting on the same side as Soviet Russia against Poland with whom he had just concluded a ten-year non-aggression pact. However, he did agree to the conclusion of an Anglo-German naval agreement. At the same time, in his conversations with Simon and Eden, he declared that the *Luftwaffe* had already reached equality in numbers with the RAF and that it aimed to attain parity with France including her air force in North Africa. Further inquiries in Berlin revealed that the Germans placed Britain's first-line strength, accurately enough, at between 800 and 850 aircraft and that they reckoned the French equivalent force at about 2,000.[51]*

Hitler's claim to parity alarmed both the British Cabinet and the British public and received considerable publicity particularly from the Rothermere press, whose proprietor was also received by Hitler at this time and had learned from the Fuehrer's own lips that the German air force now numbered not less than 1,100. Meanwhile, on 9 April, a high official in the German Air Ministry informed Group Captain Don, the British Air Attaché in Berlin, by way of clarification, that Germany's first-line strength amounted to some 910 machines, the equivalent of the total British first-line strength, both at home and overseas, including the fleet air arm. This information was immediately passed to the Foreign Office in London, and on 10 April Simon wrote to the Prime Minister, sending copies of his letter to Londonderry, Baldwin and Neville Chamberlain.[52]

After pointing out that there were only 583 first-line aircraft stationed in United Kingdom aerodromes under Air Ministry control, which

* Actually the French first-line strength was 1,400 at this time.

seemed to give the Germans a 30 per cent superiority, Simon added that he could see 'no likely motive for the German Air Ministry deliberately to exaggerate to our Air Attaché the figures of their present air armaments'. He continued:

I understand that the Air Ministry now believe there to be 1,375 machines of military type in Germany; and our secret reports give a total of 3,000 machines of every type now in existence. In fact therefore the front line has already considerable reserves.

Still more disturbing than the *numbers* of first-line military aeroplanes in Germany is the information we have from secret sources as to *the speed at which these aeroplanes are being manufactured*. The same German Air Ministry official recently told Group Captain Don that Germany was aiming at a factory output sufficient to double her first-line strength in two months; and we have very good reason to believe that the present rate of production of aeroplanes is at least 200 per month and very probably more. The number of men employed in the German aircraft industry doubled between the autumn of 1933 and the autumn of 1934, and has increased by a further 83 per cent since last October. I very much doubt if our own factory production can equal these figures; and I understand that the true measure of a country's strength in the air is just this factor of the relative power of output and rapid expansion of production.

Two very pointed questions were asked in the House of Commons this afternoon on this subject and the Under-Secretary for Air admitted that the matter was one of grave concern.

I cannot think that you will not share my grave apprehensions on this question, and I would like to suggest that this matter should be submitted to a Committee of Imperial Defence committee for an immediate report with definite conclusions, not only on German military and civil air strength and on her manufacturing capacity, but also on the actual air policy which she is following and its likely repercussions on the whole defence position of this country. The danger which it reveals is growing every day and one may have considerable doubts whether once left behind by Germany in the air, we shall ever be able to attain a level of parity with her again.

The conclusion which might have to be drawn from the above figures, if they are correct, is that this country is seriously open to the threat of sudden attack by a Continental Power in a degree to which it has not been exposed for hundreds of years.

Londonderry responded the same day by assuring the Prime Minister that he already had in hand the preparation of a memorandum by the Chief of Air Staff Sir Edward Ellington for circulation to him and the rest of the Cabinet urging the advisability of the further expansion of the RAF, not only in view of the air force which Germany already possessed, 'of whose precise strength we are at present uncertain', but particularly in view of Hitler's parity claim. The consequent 'Memorandum of the German Air Programme and its bearing on British Air Strength', based on Ellington's assessment, appeared on 15 April.[53]

Neither the Air Minister nor his CAS in this document accepted Hitler's claim at its face value. They regarded it as 'a serious overstatement', if it was intended to imply that Germany already possessed an air force equal in size to the RAF and made up of 'fully-organised, trained and equipped first-line squadrons'. Including reserves and training machines, Germany might now have 1,300 aircraft of military types and 1,000 pilots available for the formation of squadrons; and by allowing very low reserves it might be possible to classify 800 or 850 of these as first-line. 'But, even if it is assumed that the claim is substantially correct only as regards numbers of aircraft as opposed to organised units, it postulates a considerable degree of acceleration of her previous programme.' In short, the RAF was substantially stronger 'if all relevant factors are taken into account'. There were, therefore, 'no grounds whatsoever for anything in the nature of panic'.

Nevertheless there was 'grave reason for anxiety as to the future'. Strength in the air was not merely a matter of numbers: it depended also upon efficiency, reserves, industrial organisation and the study of strategy and tactics. 'We are at present, and for the next three years at least, far ahead of the German Air Force in efficiency,' the CAS believed. 'The position as to reserves, however, is less satisfactory and there is reason to believe that the organisation of the aircraft industry for war purposes in Germany is already in advance of that in this country.' Londonderry concluded the memorandum:

> Herr Hitler has himself declared that he does not care how many aircraft we possess and has actually invited us to attain parity with France. I do not doubt, therefore, that the immediate announcement of a decision further to expand the Royal Air Force would have a beneficial effect.

Both Londonderry and Ellington were opposed to a large and rapid expansion of the RAF, so as to prevent the accumulation of obsolescent machines. Hence Londonderry cautiously advocated a gradual expansion to 1,500 first-line aircraft by 1940. The difficulties already encountered in the design and development of new types of aircraft, and the limited number of aircraft manufacturers and designers, were further reasons for avoiding unnecessary haste. In training, too, further expansion would mean at least a temporary lowering of standards. In all this, Londonderry shared Ellington's belief that the quality of an air force was more important than its quantity. The trouble was that there was a growing popular obsession with figures; as Londonderry put it, 'the public, the Press and several members of the Government wanted quantity and did not give a dam for quality, to use Sir Edward's own phraseology'.[54]*

6

To Londonderry's disappointment, his memorandum failed to satisfy the Cabinet, which was already under considerable outside pressure for a more rapid expansion of the RAF than the minister proposed. In the result, on 30 April, it appointed a small Cabinet committee known as the Air Parity Sub-Committee to recommend, in consultation with the Air Ministry, what should be done to implement Baldwin's pledge of 'air parity with our nearest neighbour within striking distance' as rapidly as practicable. The chairman was Sir Philip Cunliffe-Lister and the other two members were Walter Runciman and William Ormsby-Gore, later Lord Harlech. Together they were to undermine Londonderry's ministerial position with fatal consequences for its holder.

Cunliffe-Lister and his two colleagues got down to work straight away and produced a report in under ten days. 'Parity', they wrote, must be interpreted to mean 'numerical equality with the total German air force', reckoned in first-line aircraft, that is in squadrons with machines and pilots properly organised and located at their stations. Further, Hitler's claim to possess from 850 to 900 first-line aircraft must be taken to be true. The sub-committee accepted the British Air Staff's estimate that Hitler aimed to expand these to 1,500 by April 1937 and concluded that Great Britain must reach the same figure at the same time, thus accelerating Londonderry's proposal by three years. Allowing for reserves, this meant producing 3,800 machines during the next two years, and the sub-committee was confident that the British aircraft industry could do it.

* Ellington always used the expression in the sense of the Duke of Wellington when he referred to a 'dam' as a small Indian coin, equivalent to one-twelfth of a penny.

The Cabinet accepted the report so far as it referred to fighters and light bombers, but being impressed by the serious delay involved in the production of medium and heavy bombers, they asked the sub-committee to see what they could do to speed matters up. The result was another report, dated 17 May, which attempted to work out the proportion of the various types of aircraft that would be needed to achieve the target of 1,500 first-line aircraft by the spring of 1937. The only way to get the requisite number of medium and heavy bombers was to take a chance and order them in bulk before the prototypes had been tested. Cunliffe-Lister considered that the circumstances were sufficiently urgent to justify such a gamble and the sub-committee recommended accordingly. Four days later the second report came before the Cabinet and it was agreed that it should be done.

Meanwhile the Londonderry–Ellington memorandum had been sent by the Cabinet to Lord Weir and two other experts on industrial mobilisation with a request for their advice and help. On 18 May Weir had gone to Londonderry House where he met the Air Minister and other members of the Air Council including the CAS and Sir Cyril Newall, who was responsible for supply and organisation. The question at issue was how a total of 3,800 new machines, comprising first-line and reserves, could be supplied by April 1937. It was generally agreed that air-frames rather than engines were the main difficulty. After the meeting Weir made some notes of what had passed and the questions he had put; these he sent to Baldwin.

Generally, what is happening is what I have always feared, and what I have expressed to the CID. Our technical structure behind our production facilities has been allowed to become too weak to carry an emergency load such as is now contemplated . . .

I asked Ellington if he was organising on the lines of the big blow or of the old sustained effort. He said the latter. I asked if North France was contemplated as a base. He said yes. I asked about metal construction and timber. He said all metal, but Newall thought they might be able to deal with some timber squadrons. I asked if De Havilland had been consulted, but they were not sure. Ellington and Newall agreed with me as to the supreme danger of low-flying daylight squadrons.[55]

On 22 May 1935 Baldwin announced the accelerated programme to a packed House of Commons. During the debate Churchill claimed that 'there is no doubt that the Germans are superior to us in the air at the present time, and it is my belief that by the end of the year, unless their rate of construction is arrested by some agreement, they will be possibly three or even four times our strength'. This was a considerable exaggeration, but Baldwin did not contradict it. In fact, he seemed to concede the justice of Churchill's claim since he admitted that he had been misled as to the rate at which German rearmament in the air had been proceeding during the previous six months. With regard to the figure of 50 per cent numerical superiority of the RAF over the *Luftwaffe* he had given then, nothing had come to his knowledge since that date to make him think that the figure was wrong. He went on:

I believed I was right. Where I was wrong was in my estimate of the future. There I was completely wrong. I tell the House so, frankly, because neither I nor my advisers, from whom we could get no accurate information, had any idea of the exact rate at which production could be, and actually was being, speeded up in Germany in the six months between November and now. *We were completely misled on that subject.* I will not say we had no rumours. There was a great deal of hearsay, but we could get no facts, and the only facts at this moment that I could put before the House are those which I have from Herr Hitler himself, and until I have reason to doubt them, which I have not at present, I put those figures before the House.

On these figures – 800 to 850 first-line aircraft – the Government would go ahead with the new programme of expansion, reserves and training. At the same time he emphasised, as Ellington had done in his assessment of the situation, that there was no occasion for panic.

But I will say this deliberately, with all the knowledge I have of the situation, that I would not remain for one moment in any Government which took less determined steps than we are taking today.

Finally, on the question of responsibility for what had happened, he had this to say:

There has been a great deal of criticism, both in the Press and verbally, about the Air Ministry as though they were responsible for possibly an inadequate programme, for not having gone ahead faster, and for many other things. I only want to repeat that whatever responsibility there may be – and we are perfectly ready to meet criticism – *that responsibility is not that of any single Minister; it is the responsibility of the Government as a whole, and we are all responsible, and we are all to blame.*

Baldwin was loudly cheered by the Conservative majority as he sat down at the end of his speech. The House of Commons usually warms to a man who confesses that he has been at fault, and in this instance, as Churchill observed, 'there was even a strange wave of enthusiasm' for him. 'Indeed,' Churchill added in the account of the debate which he subsequently wrote in *The Gathering Storm*, 'many Conservative Members seemed angry with me for having brought their trusted leader to a plight from which only his native manliness and honesty had extricated him; but not, alas, his country.' [56]

So far as the unfortunate Londonderry and his advisers were concerned, Churchill wrote in the same work:

> The Air Ministry now led its chief into an elaborate vindication of their own past conduct, and in consequence was entirely out of harmony with the new mood of a genuinely alarmed Government and public. The experts and officials at the Air Ministry had given Mr Baldwin the figures and forecasts with which he had answered me in November. They wished him to go into action in defence of these statements; but this was no longer practical politics. There seems no doubt that these experts and officials of the Air Ministry at this time were themselves misled and misled their chief. A great power, at least the equal of our own, long pent-up, had at last sprung into daylight in Germany. [57]

According to G. M. Young, one of these officials thought it right to offer his resignation for having misled the Lord President. Young does not state who he was – it may possibly have been Sir Christopher Bullock – but he does give Baldwin's comment: 'I misled myself.' That may well be. 'I know nothing about the air,' Baldwin afterwards admitted to Londonderry's son in the course of a private conversation. Londonderry himself subsequently denied that Baldwin had been misled. 'He was continually being informed by me, not only of German rearmament in the air but of *the approximate rate of that rearmament.*' [58]

Whatever the merits of the matter, Londonderry was 'a man of un-questionable loyalty and patriotism', to quote Churchill again, and he did try hard during a period of severe financial retrenchment to keep a nucleus of an air force in being and get as much as he could from 'a severe and arbitrary Chancellor of the Exchequer'. It was therefore 'an odd and painful experience' for him, 'after having gone through several years of asking for more to be suddenly turned out for not asking enough. But apart from all this his political standing was not sufficient to enable him to head a Department, now at the very centre and almost at the summit of our affairs. Besides, everyone could see that in such times the Air Minister must be in the House of Commons.'

Earlier the same month (May 1935), Churchill had met Londonderry at a dinner in Buckingham Palace to mark the Silver Jubilee of King George V's reign, and had warned him that there was very strong opposition to his continuing as Air Minister. 'Look out, they are going to kick you out,' he said. 'I should resign if I were you.' Before they parted, Churchill gave Londonderry a further piece of advice. 'You ought to have a great campaign all over the country on the subject of rearmament. It has got to come to that.' But Londonderry did not see it in that light. He argued that now that the Government had agreed to a programme for the expansion of the RAF, as he had been urging for some time, surely this was the time for him to stay on. As events were very soon to show, it would have been better for Londonderry to have done as his kinsman suggested.[59]

Londonderry put forward his official apologia during a defence debate in the House of Lords on 21 May. He spoke to a ministry brief and so far as this went he put up a convincing case. Most unfortunately for himself, he spoiled it by the addition of a sentence of his own composition, which was to be widely used against him both before and during the General Election later that year, although when read in its proper context it could fairly be justified.

I have held the responsible position of Secretary of State for Air for nearly four years, and during that period I have seen, and had to prepare myself for some strange changes in public opinion and public policy in regard to the air arm, which must ultimately depend upon that opinion in a democracy like ours.

In 1931 the National Government assumed office to guide the country through what is known as 'the economic blizzard'. That was certainly not the time in which Ministers in charge of the Defence Forces in this country could bring forward any policy of expansion or could do anything more than avoid the most perilous decreases in the strength of the forces for which we were responsible.

In 1932 the Disarmament Conference assembled, and almost its earliest discussions were centred round the possibility of the total abolition of the artillery of the air – the bombing aeroplane, which is the weapon of the Air Force and to which it owes its separate existence. Throughout that period, difficult for any Air Minister, and particularly for one who like myself has always been convinced of the prime importance of an effective arm to the security of this country, I kept impressing on my colleagues and upon the country generally the vital place and nature of the Royal Air Force in the scheme of our defence.

I had the utmost difficulty at that time, amid the public outcry, in preserving the use of the bombing aeroplane, even on the frontier of the Middle East and India, where it was only owing to the presence of the Air Force that we have controlled these territories without the old and heavy cost of blood and treasure.

I felt certain that, when the ideals of abolition of Air Forces were examined practically, they would be found to be inapplicable in the state of the world today. We could not put the clock back. Limitation, not abolition, was all we could really hope for. Limitation was the ultimate policy; the policy which I and my advisers at the Air Ministry were constantly preparing; and I am gratified to find in Herr Hitler's words a definite acceptance of this doctrine.[60]*

Curiously enough, the statement contained in the italicised passage above had been made by Londonderry in the House of Lords before, but it had passed unnoticed. Now it raised a howl from Labour and was immediately seized upon as a stick to beat the Government with. 'My name became forthwith associated with air bombing and all its attendant horrors,' Londonderry afterwards admitted wryly.

It was soon made clear to me that my statement of fact had been unfortunate, however much it was justified. It was not calculated to catch votes, and after all a General Election was in the offing. From a purely political point of view my statement of fact had made me an embarrassment. My personal position was not made easier by certain intrigues against me in the Government, intrigues which became so apparent that they were the subject of comment in the public Press.

'It was all very unfortunate,' Baldwin subsequently told Londonderry's son. 'I feel now that your father should have offered his resignation at

* In a speech the same day Hitler had promised to hold by the Treaty of Locarno and pledged his willingness to accept parity in the air with Britain and a fleet only 35 per cent the strength of the British.

once. As you know, there was an outcry. The opposition seized the opportunity and made it the spearhead of their election and pre-election campaign, but a far bigger outcry came from the Conservative Party. Members were beginning to look to their seats and here was a Cabinet Minister giving the enemy ammunition free and for nothing.' Hence the demand which Baldwin had to face at the time – 'the Air Minister must go'.

As will be seen, Londonderry did go. He was unlucky as the advocate of air rearmament in the Cabinet and in the country. His unfortunate reference to the bombing aeroplane was to dog him for the rest of his life. Shortly before the outbreak of the Second World War, he was to remind Baldwin of the case he had tried to put forward with such unfortunate results for himself:

> I think looking back that you, Ramsay and Neville, lost confidence in me because you were frightened by the propaganda of Winston and Rothermere in 1935, which asserted that the Germans were overwhelmingly strong in the air and were ready almost at a moment's notice to bomb all the great cities in this country. You had refused to listen to our advice on rearmament, and I am sure you became anxious lest the propaganda might be correct and that you might be confronted with the charge of having failed in your duty of establishing the security of this country. I think that is why you threw me to the wolves . . .
>
> Of course, I was perfectly right all through. It was vitally necessary to re-arm, as Monsell, Hailsham and myself continually told you, but the Germans instead of having at that time an overwhelming air force had nothing but a few formed squadrons. Of course, training and organisation were proceeding very rapidly. My information had to be right, as I had all the ordinary opportunities of gauging the strength of Germany in the air, and if I wanted to get to know anything more, I was able to get it through the Secret Service; but you, Ramsay and Neville brushed all this on one side and immediately assumed that I was wrong and did not know my job.
>
> I really believe that that was the turning point. If we had begun to re-arm in earnest and at the same time had tried to make friends with Germany, we should then have been able to find out all we wanted, and at the same time we should have been in a position to stop any attempt by Germany to create an overwhelmingly armed strength, which she has been gradually acquiring ever since that time.[61]

7

In spite of his visibly failing health, Ramsay MacDonald had shown no inclination to relinquish the Premiership until it was plainly hinted to him that his continuance in Downing Street was hindering his son Malcolm's chances of promotion. By this time, 'Ramshackle Mac', as his friend Lady Londonderry had come to call him, was a pathetic figure mentally and physically. 'Poor old Ramsay was a doughty fighter in his early days,' Baldwin remarked. 'It was tragic to see him in his closing days as PM, losing the thread of his speech and turning to ask a colleague why people were laughing – detested by his old friends, despised by the Conservatives.' Eventually, on 16 May 1935, he saw the King and informed him that his doctor had advised that, though his eyes and body were fairly sound, it was 'imperative that he should be released from the heavy responsibilities of the office of Prime Minister'. Some post without departmental responsibilities such as Lord President and possibly Chairman of the Committee of Imperial Defence, he said, would help him to recover his strength and keep him in the National Government which 'it would break his heart to leave'. The King entirely agreed that he should resign as soon as possible and offered him a peerage. Ramsay MacDonald declined the honour, and on the King then offering to confer the Order of the Thistle upon him, he declined this also since it involved being knighted. 'Although I cannot actually accept the Thistle,' he said, 'I shall feel that I have the decoration as Your Majesty has offered it to me.'[62]

Four days later, Baldwin was also received by the King whom he told that he too had been examined by his doctor, 'who said that organically he was quite sound, but required rest'. According to Wigram, who noted their conversation, they talked about 'the probable reconstruction of the Government' when Baldwin became Premier again.

Mr Baldwin said that he had not yet seen the Prime Minister but understood the latter wished to resign. The King asked what position Mr Ramsay MacDonald was likely to hold in the new Government? Mr Baldwin replied that Mr Ramsay MacDonald had offered him any position he liked in 1931 and that he should do the same now to him. The King suggested that probably Mr Ramsay MacDonald would like to be President of the Council and Chairman of the Committee of Imperial Defence, to which Mr Baldwin said that he would be delighted for him to occupy these positions.

The King then said to Mr Baldwin that he, His Majesty, was a great Cabinet maker and made various suggestions regarding the Offices. With regard to the Foreign Office, Mr Baldwin was inclined to think that we ought to have a permanent Minister at Geneva and for wandering round the various capitals, while the Foreign Secretary stayed at home and did the work of a Foreign Secretary. Mr Baldwin said that Anthony Eden would probably fill the post of the Wandering Minister, but was not sure who to put into the Foreign Office, as Sir John Simon would vacate this post.

Mr Baldwin told the King that Sir Samuel Hoare was very keen to go to India as Viceroy. The King deprecated this, as a Secretary of State for India had never been Viceroy. His Majesty said he would prefer Lord Linlithgow, with which Mr Baldwin was inclined to agree.

Other Cabinet appointments and resignations were discussed. Mr Baldwin said that it was imperative that he should go away for two months rest and the King asked who would be Prime Minister in the interim. Mr Baldwin replied that Mr Ramsay MacDonald would probably take it on.

The King told Mr Baldwin that he hoped the reconstruction would be done before the 1st July [Race] Meeting at Newmarket, and Mr Baldwin replied that he hoped everything would be finished by then.[63]

'The King again saw the Prime Minister this morning,' Wigram noted on 24 May, 'and told him that HM had discussed the whole situation with Mr Baldwin who had been most complimentary about the PM. Mr Baldwin would try to meet his wishes in every way.'[64] Ramsay MacDonald seems to have been under the impression that they would both serve in a reconstructed ministry under the Premiership of Neville Chamberlain. Consequently it may have come as something of a shock to him when he learned that Baldwin had become Prime Minister for the third time. It has been said that he blamed Baldwin for having deceived him, as he thought; indeed, according to Londonderry: 'Ramsay did not forgive S.B. to his dying day.'[65]

Baldwin had been thinking over the possible changes he would make for a week or more. He mentioned his difficulties during the previous week-end to Tom Jones, when Baldwin and Jones and their respective wives were members of a large house party which the Astors entertained at Cliveden. 'I told L.G. yesterday that I could now sympathise with him in forming a Coalition Cabinet . . . Today I've had to part with an old colleague* . . . It's the balancing which is such a nuisance. Most would agree that Jimmy Thomas ought to go, but then Ramsay clings to him and he must therefore be kept on.'

'I hope you'll keep Edward Wood in the Cabinet,' said Jones.†

'When he was in India,' Baldwin replied, 'he wrote to me saying that on his return he wanted nothing better than to go pig-breeding or fox-hunting in Yorkshire. I've persuaded him to stay on to the end of this Parliament in order to see the India Bill through the Lords.'

After lunch on the Sunday, Jones and Baldwin went for a walk in the grounds of Cliveden with its superb views above the upper reaches of the Thames. Afterwards Jones noted:

He wants to keep as much of the 1931 façade as possible just now and is undecided as to the date of the election. New register will be ready in October and there are to be party gatherings at Bournemouth in that month.

Sam Hoare goes to the FO with Eden in the Cabinet definitely assigned to the League of Nations . . . Ernest Brown to Labour . . . Betterton sore because he thinks he should now be made a Secretary of State. When I told S.B. this he observed that few of us realise our limitations.

The week-end had its lighter moments when Lady Astor received her guests on their arrival and began with a speech addressed to Lucy Baldwin on the subject of maternal mortality. 'When I see the sort of children we're all having, I'm for letting the mothers die.' To which Lucy played up well: 'My dear Nancy, every child is born a bomb.'

Noticing that Baldwin was wearing an Old Harrovian tie, several of the other guests asked him whether there was any truth in the story of an incident which was said to have occurred in a railway carriage in which Baldwin was travelling during his previous Premiership. Baldwin admitted that it was quite true that he had been wearing the old school tie on that occasion and that the other occupant of the carriage had asked him: 'Were you not at Harrow in my time? What have you been doing since?'

On this occasion Baldwin also amused the company by his description

* Probably Sir John Gilmour, the Home Secretary, who retired in favour of Simon. 'He [Baldwin] told me yesterday,' Austen Chamberlain wrote on 1 June 1935 to his sister Hilda. 'I can well believe that it is about as hateful a task as man can have to undertake, especially when it is complicated by the fact that it is a coalition government and you have got to balance among parties as well as among men.' Chamberlain Papers AC5/1/702.

† Wood (Lord Irwin) had become Viscount Halifax on his father's death in 1934.

386

Baldwin

of a luncheon he had given in Downing Street earlier in the year for the French Premier Pierre Laval. 'I gave him good English food, and plenty of it,' he remarked. 'I didn't attempt to compete with French cooking. We had salmon trout, mixed grill – very mixed – Kentucky ham which tasted like crystallised nectar, plum pudding and brandy sauce. But for that luncheon we should never have got the important Declaration of February 3.'

> Upon which Elliot said that the historian of the future should study not the Cabinet Minutes but the Downing Street menus. And then we heard the praises of haggis and whisky as a possible diet for Hitler should he ever risk a luncheon over here! [66]

Ramsay MacDonald presided over the Cabinet for the last time on 5 June. At the conclusion of business, he referred to his imminent resignation. The reasons for this were known to his colleagues, he said, and 'had nothing to do with policy or co-operation'. He thanked them for 'the splendid co-operation and friendship they had given him'. Baldwin replied on behalf of himself and the rest of the Cabinet in the kind of short speech at which he excelled. His remarks were summarised in the Cabinet minutes. He began by paying a tribute to the loyalty displayed by Mac-Donald after the events of 1931:

> This had made loyalty to the Prime Minister by his colleagues easy, the more so owing to the Prime Minister's personality. All had learned to admire his unfailing courtesy and kindness. The Prime Minister had never shown himself to be a Party member of the Cabinet but always a National member, with the result that all members of the Cabinet had worked as a National body for National ends. The Prime Minister's fairness to everyone was conspicuous. All those present would admire his courage in carrying on his work, especially when his eyesight was affected. The Lord President felt he could say with confidence that the Cabinet would continue its work in the same spirit as heretofore. [67]

Two particular ministerial changes which Baldwin had in mind to make, at the Foreign Office and the Air Ministry, caused him some concern. Simon had not been a success as Foreign Secretary, and his transfer to another department had already been decided upon. The handsome and debonair Anthony Eden had done well as Simon's understudy with the nominal office of Lord Privy Seal and he had some reason to believe that he would succeed his chief. Accordingly when Baldwin touched him on the shoulder after questions in the House of Commons on 5 June and asked him to come to his room, Eden thought that he was to get the job. However, even before Baldwin had closed the door, Eden learned that it was to be Hoare. 'Sam is to go to the Foreign Office and I want you to stay on and help him there,' said Baldwin, speaking quickly and with some embarrassment, according to Eden. As compensation Eden was to have a seat in the Cabinet and to be designated by some such title as Minister for League of Nations Affairs. Eden objected, as he did not like the idea of two ministers in the Cabinet with responsibility for foreign affairs, and he asked to be allowed to serve elsewhere, possibly in a service department. But Baldwin would not hear of it. 'Sam is most anxious to have your help,' he said. Then, in an attempt to reassure him, the Prime Minister added: 'After all, it isn't everyone who has the chance to be in the Cabinet before he is thirty-eight.' Finally Eden agreed to go and talk it over with Hoare, although he remained unhappy about the prospect. In the event it was understood that his acceptance of the office was only to be on a temporary basis, and Baldwin was informed accordingly. As things turned out, it was to be shorter than either Eden or Baldwin anticipated at the time.[68]

The problem with the Air Ministry was not the choice of Londonderry's successor – Cunliffe-Lister was the obvious choice – but how Londonderry could be disposed of with the least amount of trouble and with some consideration for his feelings which were bound to be wounded. Neville Chamberlain was for dropping him altogether on the ground that his continued membership of the Cabinet would prove a serious election liability, and his dismissal was widely forecast by the newspapers. 'I could not do that,' Baldwin afterwards told Londonderry's son. 'To me it is all wrong. Your father had given years of devoted service to his country, and you cannot summarily fire a man with such a record . . . Instead of asking him to resign as I was advised to do, I actually promoted him to the leadership of the House of Lords, thinking this would be a very appropriate wind up to an honourable career.'[69]

This move seems to have originated with Hailsham, who was Leader of the Lords besides being War Minister in the MacDonald Cabinet. As a close friend of Londonderry, Hailsham had written to Baldwin on 28 May, after reading in the papers that Londonderry was likely to be dropped:

> I would only urge as a friend that he has worked very hard and loyally for four years, and under him the Air Ministry was able to

produce a vast scheme for expansion, which most of the Cabinet professes to believe a reasonable one at short notice.

That argument would not justify me in writing. The real reason for this letter is that I am not sure whether you are informed about the position in the House of Lords, and that it had seemed to me, after some considerable anxiety that it was perhaps not fair to you that I should not tell you what I gather as its Leader.

Just now the good will of the House of Lords may be very import-ant to us as a government. The old hereditary nobles of the House of Lords do not really regard myself or Sankey [the Lord Chancellor] as their representatives. We have come to them and they treat us always very kindly and are very good friends, but we are not born of them. Edward Halifax is, to some extent, suspect as being advanced in his views; the one real hereditary peer in the Government is Charley Londonderry who, incidentally, is the great host to the Conservative Party and is the representative of a family which has long been dis-tinguished in British politics. For that reason he has been able to do things for the government, such as the passing of the Petroleum Act, which I doubt if any of us could have done without him.

If he is dropped, I cannot help fearing that there will be a good deal of resentment – inarticulate, no doubt – but which will show itself in those who do not take a very keen interest in the National Government and who normally would be likely to support us, staying away or joining Salisbury.[70]

On the same day as he saw Eden, Baldwin sent for Londonderry and told him that it was essential for the Air Minister to be in the House of Commons, and that he was appointing Sir Philip Cunliffe-Lister who had the necessary qualifications for 'hustling' in the department. He then asked Londonderry if he would continue in the Cabinet as Lord Privy Seal and at the same time take on the leadership of the House of Lords, which entailed responsibility for government business there. According to Londonderry, Baldwin added: 'You can remain Leader of the House of Lords for as long as you wish.'[71]

Londonderry replied that he would like to think it over and would let Baldwin know his decision next day. He did so in a letter written in his own hand:

Air Ministry, Gwydyr House, Whitehall, SW1. 6 June 1935. You will understand it is a bitter disappointment to me to give up at this point the work of development which after a long struggle is now decided upon, to say nothing of leaving those in the Ministry who have never spared themselves all the years to help me in what at times in these three and a half years has been a desperate work.

With regard to the reasons which you give for the change, I have, as I think you know, had in my mind the possibility of the Air Ministry being in a stronger position if the Secretary of State were a member of the House of Commons, and you laid very strong emphasis on this yourself yesterday, so there is that measure of agreement between us on the question of change at the Air Ministry. I cannot help saying, however, that on the point you made, so far as 'hustling' is necessary, I think I can claim to be as capable of that as any one, and the record of my work here, especially when as recently the occasion has demanded it, will prove what I say.

In view of the very kind terms in which you have offered me Lord Privy Seal and Leader of the House of Lords I am willing to accept, but I must confess with certain misgivings, because I shall miss the definite character of the work and the interest of the administration of a great Department. However as you are good enough to attach importance to the services which I can render in the offices you propose, and as you have conveyed to me that it is your wish and the wish of your colleagues that I should continue to work with you, I shall certainly do my best to justify your confidence.[72]*

The change-over in Downing Street, which took place during the afternoon of 7 June 1935, just before the Whitsun recess, was one of the most rapid in modern English politics. At 4.10 Ramsay MacDonald drove to Buckingham Palace and surrendered his seals of office. He was followed twenty minutes later by Baldwin who kissed hands on his appointment as Prime Minister for the third time. At five o'clock Baldwin was back in Downing Street and asking his colleagues, who had been specially summoned to meet him in the Cabinet Room, to place their offices at his disposal in order that the Government might be reconstructed. This disposition was done by word of mouth, and an hour later the outgoing Ministers handed over their seals of office. At 6.30 the King held a Council at which the new ministers received their seals and took the oaths.[73]

The youngest newcomer to the Cabinet was the retiring Prime Minister's son Malcolm, who at the age of thirty-four became Colonial

* Londonderry subsequently wrote: 'My wife was against my accepting this offer from the very first, feeling instinctively that it was merely another stage in the plot of squeezing me out altogether. She said I ought to refuse office under the new PM and begged me to retire. However, I was unfortunately persuaded to the contrary by several of my intimate political friends.' *Wings of Destiny*, p. 144.

Secretary in place of Cunliffe-Lister; the latter now took Londonderry's place at the Air Ministry. Three Cabinet ministers retired – Sir John Gilmour, who yielded the Home Office to Simon, Sir Hilton Young who surrendered the Health Ministry to Sir Kingsley Wood – neither Gilmour nor Young was considered a success – and Sankey, who was believed to wish to retire, although (according to Austen Chamberlain) 'when told by S.B. that he must go, showed the yellow streak in him, turned on MacDonald and has made it a personal quarrel'.[74] At all events his place on the Woolsack was taken by Hailsham and his seat in the Cabinet Room by Malcolm MacDonald. Oliver Stanley entered the Cabinet as Minister of Education, taking over from Halifax, who went to the War Office in place of Hailsham. Hoare replaced Simon as Foreign Secretary, while Lord Zetland went to the India Office in Hoare's place, and Eden became Minister for League of Nations Affairs. Ernest Brown, an enterprising Simonite Liberal, was appointed Minister of Labour in place of Sir Henry Betterton, who was consoled for his loss of office with a seat in the Upper House and the title of Lord Rushcliffe. A seat in the Cabinet was also found for Lord Eustace Percy, who was brought back as Minister without Portfolio with responsibility for the 'special areas' of unemployment. Simon became Deputy Leader of the House of Commons in addition to Home Secretary, a solace to his wounded pride at losing the Foreign Office, while Londonderry became Lord Privy Seal and Leader of the House of Lords. Finally, as had been previously agreed, Ramsay MacDonald moved into the office of Lord President of the Council previously occupied by Baldwin. The other Cabinet ministers carried on as before. However, the addition of Eden and Percy enlarged the body to twenty-two compared with MacDonald's Cabinet of twenty. 'It must be a unique source of pride,' the King wrote to Ramsay MacDonald at this time, 'to feel that your family have the unique record of father and son being Members of the same Cabinet.' To which MacDonald replied: 'He has been well tested before responsibility came to him, and I can only pray that he may give to the State everything that is best in him.'[75]

Baldwin held his first Cabinet as the new Prime Minister on 19 June, when he welcomed his new colleagues. A few days later, he wrote from Downing Street to his old Aunt Edith at Wilden:

It is a curious thing coming here for the third time. If my health lasts, I hope to do a couple of years, but I don't want a longer time. I think by then I shall have given out all I have to give and I should like to retire whilst still in possession of such faculties as I have! So I shall do my best with the time that is left.[76]

TEN

THE
THIRD TERM

I

The first problem which Baldwin and his reconstructed Cabinet had to face was how to reconcile the rearmament programme with the public demand that the Government should lend support to the policy of collective security. This was reflected in the result of the misleadingly named Peace Ballot, which was declared on 28 June 1935. For some months the League of Nations Union had been carrying out a public opinion poll on the lines of the American Gallup Polls then becoming fashionable. Question 5 asked whether an aggressor should be stopped by economic measures and, if necessary, by war. Over ten millions answered yes to every question except the second half of the fifth – whether the aggressor should be stopped by force – and to this 6,750,000 answered yes, while over two millions said no and another two millions did not reply. Thus, the ballot, which had been originally designed as a ballot for international disarmament and collective security, was in effect a substantial vote for the enforcement of collective security by all means short of war, and even in some measure for war in the final resort.

One afternoon at this time, Churchill was in the smoking-room of the House of Commons, when Baldwin came in and sat down beside him. 'I have a proposal to make to you,' said the Prime Minister. 'Philip [Cunliffe-Lister] is very anxious that you should join the newly formed Air Research Committee, and I hope you will.' Churchill replied that he was a critic of the Government's air preparations and he must reserve his freedom of action. 'That is quite understood,' rejoined Baldwin. 'Of course you will be perfectly free except upon the secret matters you learn only at the Committee.' When Baldwin went on to explain that the Tizard Committee had become a technical sub-committee of the new body, Churchill made it a condition that his friend Professor Lindemann should at least be a member of the sub-committee, as he depended on his aid. Baldwin concluded by asking Churchill to see Hankey, and so the matter was arranged.

This led to a resumption of the amicable correspondence between Baldwin and Churchill which had ceased when Churchill left the Shadow Cabinet over India five years previously. On 8 July 1935 Baldwin wrote to Churchill:

> I am glad you have seen Hankey, and I take your letter as an expression of your willingness to serve on that Committee.
>
> I am glad, and I think you may be of real help in a most important investigation.
>
> Of course, you are free as air (the correct expression in this case!) to debate the general issues of policy, programmes, and all else connected with the Air Services.
>
> My invitation was not intended as a muzzle, but as a gesture of friendliness to an old colleague.

Churchill replied from Chartwell, his country home in Kent, where he spent much of his time at this period:

> Believe me, I recognise and value the 'gesture of friendliness' – especially considering our disputes about various things.
>
> You have gathered to yourself a fund of personal good will and public confidence which is indispensable to our safety at the present time. But there lies before us a period of strain and peril which I do not think has been equalled – no, not even in the Great War, certainly not in the years preceding it. Naturally this will never fail to govern my action.[1]

According to the new Air Minister, Baldwin only secured Cabinet agreement to Churchill's joining the Air Defence Research Committee in the teeth of considerable opposition, led by Neville Chamberlain. Cunliffe-Lister, soon to be created Lord Swinton, was most grateful to have Churchill in the Committee, as he was also for Baldwin's backing in the decision to turn all fighters and the fighter training on to radar technique, which meant superseding the old patrol practice, an innovation which did not commend itself to some of the senior officers on the Air Staff. Indeed, as Cunliffe-Lister later wrote:

> All of us at the Air Ministry who set out to achieve a revolutionary programme of expansion and innovation, the ordering of thousands

of aircraft off the drawing board, the Shadow Factories, the integration of leading scientists with the Air Staff which gave us radar, could not have achieved what we did without Baldwin's support; we knew it and were grateful.[2]

Lord Butler, who as R.A. ('Rab') Butler was Under-Secretary for India in Baldwin's Government at this time, has recalled a visit by the Prime Minister to a Conservative fête which was held in the grounds of Stanstead Hall, Butler's country house in Essex, in July 1935. When one of the Butler family dogs, whom the Prime Minister had approached sympathetically, nipped his finger, Baldwin said calmly: 'I quite understand how you feel; I want to do that to every supplementary question in the House at this time of year.' He then took an iodine pencil out of his pocket and painted the scratch. Although he declined to attack Lloyd George as his host wished ('That is exactly what he wants me to do') and also avoided the subject of the agricultural tithe ('Too controversial') nevertheless, according to Butler, he delivered 'a masterly speech which greatly complimented our neighbourhood because it addressed itself to all our local problems and showed his usual uncanny knowledge of the countryside, including the novels of Mary Webb, which in his idiosyncratic fashion he had both fingered and sniffed in my library'.

As Butler saw his guest off at the local railway station, the Prime Minister gave him some characteristic advice which the thirty-three-year-old junior minister never forgot:

> I am so glad to have seen you at home in the country. You must go on coming down every week-end. Life in the country makes you see things whole and will enable you, like me, to steer between Harold Macmillan and Henry Page Croft.* Then you will be on the path to Leader of the Conservative Party.[3]

MacDonald's last trip abroad as Prime Minister had been to Stresa in April, when he was accompanied by Simon and had a 'summit' meeting with Mussolini and Laval, the French Premier. At this gathering, in a well-known beauty spot on the western edge of Lake Maggiore, the representatives of the three powers pledged themselves to preserve a common front in the light of Hitler's violation of the Versailles Treaty

---

* Sir Henry Page Croft, later Lord Croft, was a right-wing Tory who sat for Bournemouth in the House of Commons, where he delivered nearly 300 speeches against the India Bill in 1935.

and to oppose any further breaches of international order *in Europe*. The limitation, which was inserted at Mussolini's request, was designed to facilitate the Italian dictator's designs on Abyssinia, as Haile Selassie's African empire of Ethiopia was then generally called. The 'Stresa front' was a gesture of solidarity against Hitler's ambitions and it was endorsed by the League, while Germany saw herself isolated and, on the conclusion of a Franco-Soviet non-aggression pact immediately afterwards, encircled. Unfortunately Stresa was soon undermined. The original blunder there, as Tom Jones put it, was 'when MacDonald and Simon funked talking straight out to Mussolini because they wanted his support in Europe'.

Towards the end of June, Eden went to Rome with the Cabinet's approval in an attempt to buy off Mussolini. Italy could have the Abyssinian lowlands, he told the Duce, and Britain would try to secure Abyssinia's agreement by surrendering to her part of British Somaliland containing an outlet to the Red Sea. But Mussolini rejected the offer, since he considered that the lowlands were economically worthless; what he coveted was the territory bordering Kenya and the Sudan with its mineral wealth.[4]

Eventually, after further fruitless meetings between Eden and the Italians, also the French, the dispute was referred to the League Council which had been summoned to meet in Geneva on 4 September. 'Mussolini is out for blood,' *The Times* predicted. 'He means to have a war.' Meanwhile Hoare and Eden, along with Vansittart, had managed with some difficulty to catch the Prime Minister before he left on his annual holiday and warn him that it looked as if the Italians would be 'entirely unreasonable' and as a result there would be 'a first-class crisis in the League' when it met. According to Hoare, in a letter to Neville Chamberlain written on 18 August, 'Stanley would think about nothing but his holiday and the necessity of keeping out of the whole business almost at any cost.'[5] On 23 August, in response to an urgent telephone call from Eden, Baldwin returned to London from Aix, and the Cabinet met next day. It was decided 'to uphold the obligations of Great Britain under the Covenant'. Eden spoke in this sense at Geneva, followed a few days later by Hoare.

Hoare's speech, which was made before a plenary meeting of the League Assembly, had been composed jointly by the Foreign Secretary and Vansittart, the Permanent Under-Secretary, in the hope (as Hoare afterwards wrote in his account of the period) of 'putting new life' into the League's 'crippled body'. Armed with a copy, Hoare hurried off to Chequers, before leaving for Geneva, to show it to Baldwin, who was in residence there. When Hoare arrived, as he recalls, they talked of the delights of Aix and the English countryside. They walked round the garden together and they had tea. Then, 'remembering something about Geneva', the Prime Minister said to his visitor: 'You have got a speech to make and you have brought me the draft. Let me have a look at it.' When Hoare gave the draft to him, he gave it a quick glance and said, handing it back to him: 'That is all right. It must have taken you a long time to make it up.'

That was all. Although the answer seemed to Hoare 'scarcely adequate to the importance of a comprehensive statement of policy, and his casualness damped any personal vanity that I possessed, on second thoughts I was not dissatisfied. At least his perfunctory acquiescence showed confidence in his Foreign Secretary and enabled me to go ahead on the lines that I had set out. That was what I wanted, and the way was open for the next chapter.'[6]

The speech, duly delivered on 12 September 1935, created an immense impression which echoed round the world. Britain meant to fulfil her obligations. The message was clearly expressed in these terms:

> It is to the principles of the League, and not to any particular manifestation, that the British nation has demonstrated its adherence . . .
> In conformity with its precise and explicit obligations, the League stands, and my country stands with it, for the collective maintenance of the Covenant in its entirety, and particularly for steady and collective resistance to all acts of unprovoked aggression.

The British Foreign Secretary repeated the last phrase, putting particular emphasis on the word '*collective*' and striking the desk of the rostrum with his hand as he did so.[7]

The general reaction at Geneva to Hoare's apparently unequivocal declaration was expressed by the Belgian Foreign Minister Paul Hymans: 'The British have decided to stop Mussolini, even if that means using force.' Indeed this was the only possible interpretation if the words meant what they said. Afterwards Eden took the view that there was an element of bluff in the speech and even Hoare himself claimed that if this were so the bluff was both 'legitimate and inescapable'. This is supported by Hoare's own admission that when he met Laval in Paris on his way to Geneva, 'both excluded the idea of war with Italy as too dangerous and double-edged for the future of Europe', and they also agreed that they 'must, if possible, avoid provoking Mussolini into open hostility'. But two days after Hoare's speech a large part of the British Home Fleet was moved to Gibraltar, an act which Laval was later to denounce as provocative, thus absolving France from common action with Great Britain against Italy. At all events the bluff, if bluff it was, failed to work, since the Italian army and air force attacked Abyssinia on 3 October.

Economic and financial sanctions were immediately applied by all members of the League except Albania, Austria and Hungary, who were in effect Italy's satellites. Italian credits were cut off, a trade embargo was imposed, with other measures designed to have an adverse effect upon Italy's economy. Collective security seemed to be in action at last, although a discordant note was sounded by Winston Churchill who declared that 'no one can keep up the pretence that Abyssinia is a fit, worthy, and equal member of the League of civilised nations', while his fellow-backbencher Leo Amery came out openly on Italy's side. [8]

Meanwhile, Baldwin had warned the Conservatives at their annual conference in Bournemouth on the day the invasion began that 'the Government have not, and have never had, any intention of taking isolated action in this dispute . . . The responsibility for any action that may be taken rests on all and must be faced squarely by all.' It was the first time he had addressed the conference for seven years. He spoke for an hour and had a great ovation. According to Tom Jones, he 'denounced the isolationists, reconciled the Party to the League by supporting rearmament, and reconciled the pacifists to rearmament by supporting the Covenant'. He also 'spoke strongly in favour of Trade Unions – all with an eye to the Election, on the date of which he was inscrutable'. [9]

On 16 October the Cabinet met in the disquieting shadow of Laval's backsliding and intrigues with Mussolini which were now apparent. Baldwin began to question whether Britain could rely on the French at all. He still remembered Chanak and he reminded his Cabinet colleagues that 'we must be careful not to be drawn into a quarrel with France as well as Italy', following the activities of the sanctions committee at Geneva. This latest development seems to have finally determined him upon an autumn election, since at this same meeting a Cabinet committee was set up to draft an election programme in the light of the worsening international situation. [10]

Londonderry saw this as the writing on the wall so far as his own future political prospects were concerned, and he immediately addressed an urgent note to the Prime Minister asking to see him 'as we are now committed to an election and a new Parliament'. They met later that afternoon.

Their interview was far from reassuring for Londonderry, who wrote to Baldwin next day:

Londonderry House. 17 October 1935. Thank you for yesterday. I always regret that I see you so seldom and perhaps I am now diffident in these matters. I am writing in case I did not put before you my exact point of view and the reason after long cogitation that I asked to see you.

Since I left the Air Ministry I told you that I had done no work which is literally true. You will remember my asking you if I could be on Committees and you asked me to let you know which Committees I wanted to serve on. I wrote to you and named the Committees but received no answer to my letter.

As Leader of the House of Lords I feel that my position is an impossible one unless I am able to be closely in touch with yourself and those who control policy. Rightly or wrongly I have felt that there is an influence which has the effect of excluding me from participating in those matters which even as a member of the Cabinet and certainly as Leader of the House of Lords I ought to be fully aware of . . .

You asked me if I should be happy in a different kind of life. Happy is a relative term. I am happy in all work, the more strenuous the better: but I am uneasy in the position in which I stand now because I bear full responsibility and have neither power nor knowledge.[11]

On 18 October Baldwin asked the King for a dissolution, with effect from the following week, 'to obviate uncertainty and particularly interference with Christmas trading', polling to take place on 14 November and the new Parliament to assemble on 3 December. This was agreed to and Parliament was duly dissolved on 25 October.[12]

2

Baldwin opened his election campaign with a remarkable speech in which he asked for no votes and announced no policy. The occasion was the annual meeting of the Peace Society and it provided him with an opportunity to display his eloquence on a subject on which, as he told his audience, he could see no difference between the political parties – the love of peace. For the ordinary folk of the country it was not a question of deep moral and legal issues, grouping of Powers and 'huge cloudy symbols', but of something 'far more intimate, much more dear, the lives of our children and grandchildren, of the familiar sights and institutions of our own land, all the boundary stones of our spiritual estate'.

We live under the shadow of the last war and its memories still sicken us. We remember what war is, with no glory in it but the heroism of man. Have you thought what it has meant to the world to have had that swathe of death cut through the loveliest and best of our contemporaries, how public life has suffered because those who would have been ready to take over from our tired and disillusioned generation are not there?

Perhaps we avert our thoughts from these terrors and send them roaming over this 'dear dear land'. We think perhaps of the level evening sun over the English meadow with the rooks trundling noisily home into the elms; of the ploughman 'with his team on the world's rim creeping like the hands of a clock', one of those garnered memories of the long peace of the countryside that a wise man takes about with him as a viaticum. To what risks do we expose our treasures, for you cannot build up beauty like that in a few years of mass production? Make no mistake: every piece of all the life that we and our fathers have made in this land, every thing we have and hold and cherish, is in jeopardy in this great issue.

He concluded with an assurance that the Government would stand by the League of Nations in the Abyssinian business:

Judgement may lead to action, cautionary action, restraining action, at the extreme to coercive action. We mean nothing by the League if we are not prepared, after trial, to take action to enforce its judgement. Look at the alternative. When I spoke, so inadequately, of the horrors of war, was it not clear that we must be prepared to take risks to prevent that evil thing stalking again across the world?

. . . Do not fear or misunderstand when the Government say that they are looking to our defences . . . do not fear that it is a step in the wrong direction. You need not remind me of the solemn task of the League – to reduce armaments by agreement. But we have gone too far alone and must try to bring others along with us. *I give you my word that there will be no great armaments*. We are 'bound over to keep the peace', and it may not be an easy task. But we accept it.[13]

This speech must rank as one of Baldwin's most effective public performances. 'It was like the first hearing of a great symphony,' wrote one listener to him afterwards. Professor Harold Laski, the Socialist academic, was positively ecstatic, describing it as 'the greatest speech a Prime Minister has ever made'. Even the prosaic Neville Chamberlain, who was sometimes irritated by what he called Baldwin's 'poetic temperament', was sufficiently moved to write to the Prime Minister: 'I will frankly confess that at times I have felt some transient impatience when it seemed difficult to bring your thoughts down to the earthy decision I wanted. But when I read a speech like that I can only think of our good fortune in having a leader who can raise us so far above ourselves, and can express what we should like to believe we had thought ourselves, in such moving words.'[14]

'The fact is you and I are complementary,' Baldwin replied to Chamberlain. 'Each puts into the pool his own contribution and we make a jolly effective unit!' That Chamberlain, on whose shoulders as chief of the Prime Minister's political staff fell the brunt of organising the campaign, fully appreciated this, is clear from what he told his sister Hilda shortly before polling day: 'I am bound to recognise that if I supply the policy and the drive, S.B. does also supply something that is perhaps even more valuable in retaining the floating vote.'[15]

Conservative Central Office estimated the Tory majority at 100, perhaps somewhat higher. In the event the Conservatives won 432 seats, which gave them a majority of 247 over the combined Opposition. Unfortunately both the MacDonalds lost their seats to official Labour, which increased its representation to 154.

'I am not biased by friendship when I say that the triumph is a personal one for S.B.,' wrote Tom Jones on learning the results.

He has made no mistakes. He timed the election correctly in his Party's interest. Six months hence and it is certain the results would be less favourable to him. He has only very slowly and with obvious reluctance proclaimed the need for more armaments; he has avoided all trace of the *Daily Mail*'s lust to arm the nation to the teeth and has also kept clear of Winston's enthusiasm for ships and guns. He has strictly confined the extent to which he was prepared to move against Italy and distinguished Mussolini from the Italian people . . . Over all he has thrown that halo of faith and hope, free from meretricious ornament, which inspires confidence. The effect is to gather to the Tories a large voting strength of Liberals and unattached folk who like his sober and sincere accents, and who are afraid of the menace to small owners and investors associated with Socialism.[16]

Baldwin's first task on the morrow of electoral victory was to review the composition of his ministerial team. He had previously hoped to make considerable changes, but this had been ruled out by the size of his majority since each member of the Cabinet tended to regard the result as a vote of confidence in himself as well as in the Cabinet as a whole. There was also the consideration whether it would not be preferable in a time of international crisis to keep the Cabinet substantially intact with the balance of parties unaltered. The changes, which in the event he did make, Baldwin reduced to a minimum. He even retained the two MacDonalds, though well aware that the problem of finding them seats in the new Parliament would not be easy. In the Government, however, Malcolm MacDonald changed places with J. H. Thomas, whose removal from the Dominions Office was necessitated largely by the general dissatisfaction with his handling of Anglo-Irish relations.

The only one of his former colleagues whose services Baldwin dispensed with was Lord Londonderry, whose notorious 'bombing' speech had been widely exploited by Labour during the election. Since Halifax now needed little or no pressing to stay on rather than retire to hunt the fox in his native Yorkshire, and Baldwin set considerable store by the moral weight which his presence lent to the Government, Halifax agreed to take Londonderry's place as Lord Privy Seal and Leader of the House of Lords, thus enabling Duff Cooper, the Financial Secretary to the Treasury, whom Baldwin wished to promote, to become War Minister with a seat in the Cabinet. There was some talk of bringing in Churchill; but due to the opposition of the Government Whips, and also probably of Neville Chamberlain, Baldwin decided to exclude him. 'As for Winston,' Baldwin told Davidson in a strangely prophetic letter at this time, 'I feel we should not give him a post at this stage. Anything he undertakes he puts his heart and soul into. If there is going to be a war – and no one can say that there is not – we must keep him fresh to be our war Prime Minister.'[17]

'Internally S.B.'s main troubles are over the defeat of the MacDonalds,' wrote Tom Jones at this time. 'S.B. has "dropped" Londonderry and kept out Winston, but it is not quite easy to preserve the "National" façade and get rid of Ramsay.' In the event, MacDonald remained Lord President of the Council, though he was by now politically of little account as well as being pathetically senile.[18]

Londonderry was given his quietus in a letter which it must have caused Baldwin some pangs to write:

> 10 Downing Street
> Whitehall
> 21 November 1935

My dear Charley,

I have been working for three days on one of the most difficult problems with which I have ever had to contend, and I am profoundly distressed that I find myself unable to offer you a place in the new

Government. The refusal of Ramsay to serve unless accompanied by Malcolm and Thomas and the desire of Halifax to continue have upset my calculations and I have more men than places.

You remember our talk in the House: you know what I feel. You have ever been a loyal and trusted friend: I think I know what you will feel. Yet I have faith to believe that our friendship is too firmly based to be broken by a cruel political necessity that obliges a PM – and none have escaped it – to inflict pain on those they hold not only in regard but in affection.

Always yours,
S.B.

At the same time he addressed a consolatory letter to Londonderry's wife:

My dear Lady,

I have written Charley a letter which I fear will distress him. I have never before written on such matters to the wife of a colleague. But you have always been so kind and understanding to me that I cannot refrain from sending a line to you. It is on such occasions that I understand in the depths all that Lord Salisbury meant and felt when he said, 'Politics is a cursed profession.'

And he did not use words lightly.

Next morning, Londonderry's son Castlereagh, who had heard the news the evening before from his brother-in-law Oliver Stanley, went round to Londonderry House with his sister to see their father. 'He was a tragic sight,' Castlereagh later recalled. 'I never really knew before the meaning of the phrase: "A broken man". He was sitting sideways in his chair with his legs dangling over the arm. Holding a letter in his hand and with the tears running down his cheeks, he kept muttering: "I've been sacked – kicked out." The letter was from Baldwin giving a number of reasons for not including him in the Cabinet.'

Later the same day Londonderry pulled himself together and replied to Baldwin, but with less than his usual warmth:

Londonderry House,
Park Lane, W
22 November 1935

My dear S.B.,

I have received your letter and I need not say that I acquiesce in your decision, but I have received it with some surprise because I recollect that you very expressly said that if I joined your Government in June I might retain the leadership of the House of Lords as long as I wished to do so. This hardly corresponds with your present decisions: nevertheless I quite recognise that you must only look at public considerations in determining the composition of your Government.

As to personal friendships I can warmly assure you that nothing will be changed in that respect.

> I am,
>
> Yours very sincerely,
>
> LONDONDERRY

Baldwin subsequently denied that he had given Londonderry any such assurance with regard to the leadership of the House of Lords. 'No PM is in a position to make such a promise,' he told Castlereagh in answer to the complaint that his father had been badly treated by Baldwin. 'No Minister could ever take such a promise as valid. It does not make sense. He must have misunderstood something I said. I know that I never wittingly said anything of the sort and that in his disappointment he must have got hold of the wrong end of the stick.' [19]

Whatever may be the truth of the matter, there is no doubt that Londonderry was under the impression that he could continue to lead the Lords if he wished and if it was within Baldwin's power to enable him to do so; his letter quoted above certainly lends some confirmation to this. At all events his sense of injury did rankle with Londonderry for long afterwards, and it was the increasing bitterness he felt towards Baldwin that eventually prompted his son, who was one of the Prime Minister's supporters at that time in the House of Commons, to complain about the manner in which his father had been treated. Londonderry's feelings suffered further hurt when it was announced that Cunliffe-Lister, his successor as Air Minister, had accepted a peerage with the title of Lord Swinton, particularly when one of the reasons which Baldwin gave Londonderry for shifting him from the Air Ministry was the need for the Minister to be in the Commons. 'But no one can foretell the results of an election and the ensuing complications,' Baldwin explained to Castlereagh. 'I found it more convenient to make Cunliffe-Lister a peer. But the reason he was chosen to replace your father was that with his wider experience of business and industry in general he would be better qualified to deal with expansion.' Apparently the reason he went to the Lords was that this would leave him freer to get on with the job in hand. However, in his case, history was to repeat itself, since in May 1938 Swinton was obliged to resign because

Neville Chamberlain, who by this time had succeeded Baldwin as Prime Minister, 'felt he must have a Secretary of State in the House of Commons who could pacify the House'. Swinton was offered another Cabinet post, but not wishing to make the same mistake as Londonderry, he wisely declined. 'I think I was right,' he wrote afterwards.[20]

It was hardly surprising that there should have been no eve-of-the-opening-of-Parliament reception at Londonderry House when the Prime Minister stood beside the host and hostess at the top of the grand staircase shaking hands with a thousand or more guests, whose political allegiance was supposed to be largely Conservative. Nor was the King able to deliver his speech in person – owing to the death of his sister Princess Victoria. His health was already failing and he did not feel equal to the strain, so that the Lord Chancellor read the Speech on the King's behalf.

Among the recently elected MPs was the writer Harold Nicolson, who belonged to the small National Labour group and indeed was the only one who did not have a Government job. He too kept a diary and on his first day in the House he recorded how the Prime Minister appeared at the Despatch Box:

There is something very strange about Stanley Baldwin. At first sight he is a solid English gentleman but then one observes odd nervous tricks. He has an extraordinarily unpleasant habit of smelling at his notes and licking the edges slightly as if they were the flap of an envelope. He scratches himself continuously. There are russet patches across his head and face. And a strange movement of the head, with half-closed eyes, like some tortoise half-awake smelling the air – blinking, snuffy, neurotic.[21]

Baldwin's publishers had planned to bring out a further collection of his speeches and addresses covering the previous seven years under the title *This Torch of Freedom*, which was the theme of the Prime Minister's speech of welcome to the delegates at the conference of the Empire Parliamentary Association during the King's Silver Jubilee celebrations. The publication was deferred by a few weeks, so as to include Baldwin's speech to the Peace Society, which he delivered at the outset of the election campaign. It finally appeared on 2 December, the day before the new Parliament assembled. 'Throughout this volume,' in the words of the publisher's introductory note, 'he speaks as the statesman and the Englishman, not as the party leader concerned with immediate issues.' These words were echoed by Tom Jones, who had helped considerably in the composition of the book's contents:

The PM's new collection of speeches came out on Monday and is having a good press and it will help to establish confidence in his, or what people think is his, typical Englishness. The speeches are professedly non-party – about Scott, Burne-Jones, John Wesley and so forth, but really about Stanley Baldwin – by the time you are through the book it is his character which emerges.[22]

Unfortunately the public confidence in Baldwin's character, which *This Torch of Freedom* stimulated, was to receive a violent shock within a few weeks of its publication.

3

Naturally enough the Abyssinian question came up in the initial debates of the new Parliament as it had already done in Baldwin's reconstructed Cabinet. Mussolini had refused to be bluffed, so that either some more drastic move would have to be made against Italy or else some compromise solution must be found. The League Council favoured cutting off oil supplies to Italy. This was approved in principle by the Cabinet and intimated by the Foreign Secretary when he spoke in the House of Commons on 5 December. At the same time, Hoare made it clear, also with Cabinet backing, that there would be 'an intensive effort to bring about a peaceful settlement' in the short time before the League Council was due to meet. 'The French and we intend not only to go on trying but to redouble our efforts,' he said.

Hoare was suffering from the effects of prolonged strain and overwork, and his doctor had advised him to have a winter sports holiday away from political harassments. Accordingly he had planned to leave for Switzerland immediately after the debate was over, having first obtained the Prime Minister's permission which was readily given. He told Baldwin, whom he saw for a few minutes in his room in the House while the debate continued, that he had been in touch with Laval and the French Premier had suggested that he should break his journey for a few hours in Paris and have a further discussion. According to Hoare, Baldwin was 'fully occupied with the many details connected with the new Government' and had little time for discussing with him the implications of his Paris visit. 'Have a good leave and get your health back,' the Prime Minister advised him simply. 'That is the most important thing. By all means stop in Paris and push Laval as far as you can, but on no account get this country into war.' Many years later Baldwin told Eden that he had no idea that Hoare would sign anything.

'When he went off, I had only one idea,' said Baldwin. 'It was a relief to see him going. I knew he was very tired and thought his skating holiday would do him good. I could not tell that he was going to fall on his nose.' [23]

The ailing Foreign Secretary arrived in Paris during the afternoon of Saturday, 7 December, and went straight to the Quai d'Orsay where the wily Laval was waiting for him. Here he was joined by Vansittart, who had been in Paris trying to counter the virulence of the anti-British articles in the local press against which the French Government had taken no action. The talks lasted until late in the evening and were continued next morning. The basis of discussion was the offer which Eden had made to Mussolini five months previously, but which was now made considerably more attractive so as to secure the Duce's acceptance. Briefly, Italy would receive the fertile plains, while Haile Selassie would keep his old kingdom in the mountains but would still have an outlet to the sea – 'a corridor for camels' Geoffrey Dawson was to call it in *The Times*.

The heads of the 'Hoare–Laval Peace Plan' were initialled by the parties on Sunday evening, and at the same time a communiqué was issued to the effect that they were subject to the approval of the British and other interested governments and to discussion by the League. As Hoare drove away with Vansittart and Sir George Clark, the British Ambassador, the two latter congratulated him on having re-established the Anglo-French front. [24]

Meanwhile Baldwin who had been spending the week-end at Chequers received a somewhat cryptic message from Hoare saying it would be necessary to have a Cabinet on Monday. He returned to London on Sunday evening and immediately sought out Eden, who had received a similar message but was none the wiser as to why a Cabinet should be summoned. Eden thereupon telephoned the Embassy in Paris and asked for Hoare. A secretary replied that the Foreign Secretary was resting and that Vansittart, who was at the Ritz Hotel, where he preferred to stay when in Paris, was likewise not available. In response to a request from Eden for some indication of what had been going on, the secretary went away to inquire and returned a minute or two later with the information: 'The Secretary of State and Sir Robert Vansittart are well satisfied with the day's work.' Eden was also told that Hoare was shortly leaving for Switzerland and that Maurice Peterson, another Foreign Office official, would be arriving in London early next morning with full details.

Peterson duly turned up at Eden's house at breakfast time on Monday morning with a four-page document in French, bearing the initials 'S.H.' and 'P.L.'. It had evidently been typed in a French Government Office and, according to Eden, bore signs of hasty drafting. Eden was surprised that

Hoare had not insisted on a translation, and his surprise quickly turned to astonishment when he read the text and realised that his chief had exceeded his instructions. Later in the morning Baldwin came into Eden's room in the Foreign Office and Eden explained the proposals with the aid of a map. On Baldwin asking him what he thought of them, Eden bluntly stated that two things were clear – Haile Selassie would not accept these terms, nor would the League. Baldwin looked unhappy and commented: 'That lets us out, doesn't it?' At the same time he agreed that the Cabinet must meet that evening, although he still seemed as uncertain as Eden 'why Hoare had suddenly done this thing'.[25]

Meanwhile, the contents of the document which Hoare and Laval had initialled were 'leaked' from the Quai d'Orsay, probably by an official who had been bribed, and they appeared in a hostile light in two papers, the *Oeuvre* and the *Echo de Paris*, which for different reasons were bent on destroying Laval. What happened next was described by Lord Zetland in one of his weekly letters from the India Office to the Viceroy:

> A Cabinet meeting was hastily summoned and was held in the House of Commons on the Monday evening. Meanwhile not only had the proposals appeared in the Paris press, but an official communiqué had been issued in Paris saying that the discussion had taken place and that Laval and Hoare had reached a programme of conciliation. The Cabinet consequently were in a most embarrassing position. We all disliked the proposals when we were shown them, but it was made clear to us that in the circumstances, if we refused to endorse them, our refusal would involve a repudiation of our own Foreign Minister. We were given no time for thought, since we were told that Paris must be informed immediately of our decision and in the circumstances we agreed, most of us, I think, very reluctantly to accept responsibility for them.
>
> A very brief period of reflection was sufficient, however, to make us regret our action and our regret was speedily reinforced by the storm of indignation which broke out not only in the country but throughout the world; and it really became a question whether the Government should attempt to compel the acquiescence of Parliament in a course of action of which they themselves disapproved, or whether they should accept the resignation of the Foreign Secretary . . . The whole thing has been most unpleasant . . .

Zetland's account of the Cabinet reaction was confirmed by Baldwin in a private talk with Tom Jones:

Before the Cabinet met the proposals were out, dressed up in a lot of preliminary frills. We had either to ratify or disown Sam. If we disowned Sam, the French would be angry and would say we had let them down, so we backed him. We did not like it at all, but the alternative seemed to us to be worse.

I know that Laval is like L.G. and normally Sam would have been a match for him, but he had become so obsessed with the fear of war that he thought this alternative better. I had repeatedly told Sam, 'Keep us out of war, we are not ready for it.' We could cut Italy's communications, but if Mussolini broke out there would be more killed in Valetta in one night than in all the Abyssinian campaign up to date, and until we get agreement with the French we should have to go singlehanded fighting the Italians for a month or so. French mobilisation would have led to riots. They are not ready in the air without mobilisation. Malta is the only harbour apart from those of the French where you can take ships that are wounded.

Sam was ready therefore to spring more than he ought to have done, and so was Van. Van is very tired and was excited, and on that subject holding views too similar to those of Sam.[26]

The public outcry was considerable, although it was confined to a relatively small but extremely vocal section of the community led by *The Times*, the two archbishops, the League of Nations Union, Austen Chamberlain and many of the younger Conservatives, including Oliver Stanley, Walter Elliot and Ormsby-Gore in the Cabinet. At all events the Government's stock slumped sharply. 'If we had to fight the election over again,' noted Neville Chamberlain at the time, 'we should probably be beaten.' Eden wrote afterwards that the reaction of public opinion was indignant and ashamed. 'It was said that we should have no part in rewarding aggressors. Many felt that the Government had won the election on false pretences and Members of Parliament were swamped by a tide of indignant letters.'[27]

Baldwin eventually realised that he was mistaken in not recalling Hoare from his holiday; but at first he had thought this was unnecessary as the situation was under control and later he was reluctant to do so as Hoare had fallen on the ice rink and broken his nose in two places. However, Vansittart returned on 12 December and immediately went to see Baldwin in his room in the House of Commons. He advised the Prime Minister to 'ride it out' and to take the press into his confidence, which Baldwin had hitherto refused to do. As Vansittart left the room, Baldwin was seen through the open door to throw a bunch of protesting letters and telegrams into the air where they floated for a moment or two like a flock of pigeons. 'Tell the press that we must have more aeroplanes,' he called after the departing visitor. In the event he himself only saw Dawson, *The Times* editor, who considered that Baldwin was 'probably more culpable than Sam'.

Meanwhile Baldwin talked mysteriously of facts that, if they were fully known, would convince the Commons and the country at large of the wisdom of what had been done. 'My lips are not yet unsealed,' he told the House in what he subsequently admitted to be one of the stupidest things he ever said. 'Were the troubles over, I would make my case and I guarantee that not a man would go into the lobby against me.' (One of the facts he could not or would not disclose was the information supplied by the Secret Service that Laval had been taking money from Mussolini.) The admission was a wonderful gift for the political cartoonists, and for weeks afterwards David Low of the *Evening Standard* invariably depicted him with a piece of sticking plaster across his mouth.[28]

On 16 December Hoare returned of his own accord to face the mounting storm. Next day Neville Chamberlain went to his house in Cadogan Gardens, where his doctor kept him in bed, and told him he would defend the unfortunate 'plan'. Baldwin called the same afternoon to reassure him. 'We all stand together,' he said. Hoare had given Chamberlain the draft of the speech he intended to make in the House of Commons, and Chamberlain sat up that night making an abstract of it so that he could tell the Cabinet.[29]

When the Cabinet met on 18 December, Baldwin prefaced Chamberlain's summary by observing that 'the Foreign Secretary was probably feeling on trial and must be allowed to make his speech in his own way'. He added that it was essential to know what other nations would do in the event of war and how far Laval was prepared to go in the event of a sudden Italian attack upon Britain. Chamberlain then indicated what Hoare would say – that the terms were the best that could have been got, that the rest lay with the League, and unless the League expedited sanctions, including oil sanctions, Mussolini would win.[30]*

Cunliffe-Lister, Kingsley Wood, Runciman, Elliot, Percy, Thomas, Zetland, Simon, Ormsby-Gore and Halifax all rejected this version of events and said they thought Hoare should resign. Otherwise they made it clear that they would do so. Cunliffe-Lister called it 'a staggering and

---

* The Minutes of this meeting were considered so secret at the time by the Secretary of the Cabinet Sir Maurice Hankey that they were not circulated. Only one copy was made with the principal arguments inserted by Hankey in his own handwriting. The original is preserved with the rest of the Cabinet conclusions in the Public Record Office.

demoralising episode', while Ormsby-Gore expressed the view that 'the Foreign Secretary had been caught by M. Laval in Paris and had involved the Cabinet in a humiliating crisis – in the circumstances he was unlikely to remain'. Baldwin said he did not wish to express a view at this Cabinet as he had not settled his opinion. All he could say was that, 'though he was not rattled, it was a worse situation in the House of Commons than he had ever known'.

It was left to Halifax to press home the attack. It was clear that Hoare must go, he said. But much more was at stake than a colleague's resignation, namely the whole moral position of the Government before the whole world. 'If the Prime Minister were to lose his personal position, one of our national anchors would have dragged.'

Baldwin concluded the meeting by saying that he would 'stand or fall by what he said [in the debate] on the morrow'. He added that 'he had found the present conversation very useful' and 'it was essential that everyone should state his mind'. Finally, Chamberlain said he was going straight round to see Hoare and would put their views to him.

When he saw Hoare, Chamberlain said that he had been asked to tell him that his proposed statement did not go far enough, and that it was necessary for him to say that the plan was bad, that he had been mistaken in accepting it and that in view of the general opposition he withdrew his support of it. 'I told him at once that I was not prepared to make any such recantation,' wrote Hoare afterwards. 'I was convinced that nothing short of the proposals would save Abyssinia and prevent Mussolini from joining the Hitler front. This being so, resignation, not recantation, was the only course open to me.' [31]

Chamberlain took Hoare's message back to Downing Street, and in the afternoon Baldwin called at Cadogan Gardens accompanied by Eden, who was on his way to the station to catch the boat train *en route* for Geneva. 'How do you feel?' Baldwin asked Hoare who was looking thoroughly miserable. 'I wish I were dead,' was the reply. His decision to resign rather than recant was final, he added. The same night his resignation was submitted to the King and accepted. [32]

Meanwhile Baldwin had learned that the spearhead of Conservative opposition to the Hoare–Laval plan was the veteran Austen Chamberlain, who had voiced the general feeling on the back benches in saying as he did that, when Baldwin and Hoare had told the House 'all that they must now tell it and the world, it is still impossible to regard Hoare's action in allowing himself to be associated with the French proposals and to recommend them as other than a bad blunder'. No one knew how Austen Chamberlain would vote in the debate – indeed he did not know himself –

but Baldwin realised that if he chose to do so he might bring down the Government. He therefore sent for him and said: 'Austen, when Sam has gone, I shall want to talk to you about the Foreign Office.' However this remark was intended, it was taken by Austen Chamberlain to be a hint that he might expect to return to that office which he had held in the previous Baldwin administration.[33]

Hoare duly delivered his resignation speech from the traditional place for such occasions, the corner seat on the third bench below the gangway on the Government side of the House. 'The best of the debate', Austen Chamberlain called it, adding that 'he did not convince many, but he won general sympathy and respect'. He was followed by Clement Attlee, who had succeeded to the leadership of the Labour Party on Lansbury's resignation and now proceeded to launch a strong attack on Baldwin:

> There is the question of the honour of this country, and there is the question of the honour of the Prime Minister. If, as is suggested in some quarters, the Prime Minister won an election on one policy, and immediately after victory was prepared to carry out another, it has an extremely ugly look.

In his reply Baldwin could only repeat the great Lord Salisbury's dictum, which he had already used with the Londonderrys, about politics being a cursed profession. He had misjudged the feeling of the House and the country, he said; he had also been at fault for letting a sick man go to Paris and for not immediately summoning him back to explain his proposals. 'It is perfectly obvious now that the proposals are absolutely and completely dead,' he added. 'This Government is certainly going to make no attempt to resurrect them.'

It was not one of Baldwin's happiest efforts, although in the event the House accepted his apology as it always did. 'Had I thought it compatible with the public interest,' Austen Chamberlain later admitted in private, 'I believe that, after S.B.'s miserably inadequate speech and the initial blunder, I could have so reduced his majority as to force his resignation.' Instead of adopting such a course, however, Chamberlain took advantage of the opportunity which Attlee had given him and declared that he would vote for the Government, not on account of what the Prime Minister had said but because the Opposition Leader had impugned his honour. This saved the day for the Government, which had a majority of 397 votes to their opponents' 165.[34]

Next day, Baldwin asked Chamberlain to call upon him again. 'Austen,' he began, 'I said I wished to see you about the Foreign Office after Sam

Hoare's resignation. If you had been ten years younger, there would be no doubt in my mind that you should have it. As it is – and I am sure you will admit my choice – I have decided to offer it to Anthony.' Baldwin went on to ask him what he thought of Eden, and Chamberlain replied that he had always thought that he 'had the making of a Foreign Secretary'.

'He told me I was ga-ga,' Chamberlain said to Eden afterwards.[35] Nevertheless he did go to see Baldwin again at the latter's request the following afternoon, when the Prime Minister invited him to join the Cabinet as Minister of State to advise on foreign policy and defence. He could do as much or as little as he liked, said Baldwin, and if he felt tired any time he could go away for a fortnight. On these conditions and without a department, there was no reason why the ex-Foreign Secretary 'should not last out the Parliament'.

Chamberlain asked for a little time to think over the invitation, but he wrote the same evening declining it. 'You laid so much emphasis on my age and health,' he told Baldwin with a hint of sarcasm in his letter, 'both when I saw you yesterday and again this afternoon, that I am compelled to add that anxiety about my health has played no part in my decision.' At the same time he unburdened himself to his sister Hilda:

> I certainly feel under no obligation to him for his offer. After he had taken such pains to explain and emphasise that he thought me physically unfit for hard work and that he feared I might become as much of an incubus as MacDonald, I could only infer that what he really wanted was not my experience or my advice but the use of my name to patch up the damaged reputation of the Government. He could scarcely have put it more plainly.[36]

This experience prompted Austen Chamberlain to return to the subject of the Prime Minister a few days later in a passage of devastating frankness in a letter to his sister Ida who had urged him to write something about Baldwin for publication. As an opinion of a political leader by one of his most senior followers – and one whose introduction to the House of Commons he had originally sponsored – it must be unique in political annals:

> Yes, I should like to write about S.B. but it is wiser not to do so, for the S.B. whom we know does not fit in at any point with the picture which the public have made of him for themselves. They think him a simple, hardworking, unambitious man, not a 'politician' in the abusive sense in which they so often use the word, whom nothing

but a stern sense of duty keeps at his ungrateful task, a man too of wide and liberal mind who has educated his party.

And we know him as self-centred, selfish and idle, yet one of the shrewdest politicians, but without a constructive idea in his head and with an amazing ignorance of Indian and foreign affairs and of the real values of political life. 'Sly, Sir, devilishly sly!' would be my chapter heading and egotism and idleness the principal characteristics that I should assign to him.[37]

While he was on his way back from Geneva, Eden received a message at Calais that the Prime Minister wished to see him as soon as he reached London. Eden accordingly went straight from Victoria Station to 10 Downing Street, where a highly nervous Baldwin received him in the little library at the front of the house. He began by putting a question to him. Who was the best man to be appointed Foreign Secretary? Eden promptly replied suggesting Austen Chamberlain. Too old, said Baldwin. To Eden's next suggestion that Halifax should be appointed, Baldwin replied that a Foreign Secretary in the Lords was not the answer just now. There was a silence. Eden had no more names to suggest, nor apparently had Baldwin. Eventually the Prime Minister turned to Eden and said: 'It looks as if it will have to be you.' Afterwards Eden confessed to feeling somewhat hurt at this eliminative method of being appointed, and he made this clear to the Prime Minister. Baldwin nodded understandingly, 'And so', as Eden was to recall in his memoirs, 'this strange interview ended with my words being taken as a tacit acceptance'.[38]

By this date the King had gone to Sandringham for Christmas and on 22 December Eden travelled there to kiss hands on his new appointment. The King looked ill and was coughing painfully, but otherwise he was in good spirits and even cracked a joke about Eden's predecessor whom he had told when he delivered up the seals of office what he thought of the Hoare–Laval peace plan. 'You cannot drive a train full steam in one direction, and then without warning suddenly reverse without somebody coming off the rails.' He added:

I said to your predecessor: 'You know what they're all saying – no more coals to Newcastle, no more Hoares to Paris!' The fellow didn't even laugh.[39]

As usual the Baldwins spent Christmas at Astley, where they also saw in the New Year. On 7 January 1936, when Tom Jones called on the Prime Minister in Downing Street, he had just returned, and Jones noted that 'he showed no signs of the crisis through which he had passed'. In fact, he was reading an essay on the use of words written by an Eton master for the Ascham Society. After thanking Jones for his Christmas gift of the Loeb edition of Virgil containing the Georgics, Baldwin went on to speak about the recent crisis. 'One thundering good thing we have got out of it is the realisation of what sanctions mean,' he said. 'They mean that we have got to be much more self-contained. Europe has to be rearmed and to be ready – that is the conclusion which follows upon collective security.'

'What did you mean by the sentence in your speech when you said, if only you could tell all you knew no vote would be cast against you?'

'That was not a very wise sentence,' the Prime Minister replied.

It shows the danger of rhetoric. I had in mind the menace of war; our fleet would be in real danger from the small craft of the Italians operating in a small sea. Italian bombers could get to London. I had also Germany in mind. Had we gone to war, our anti-aircraft munitions would have been exhausted in a week. We have hardly got any armament firms left . . . I had a deputation of the League of Nations Union the other day consisting of Gilbert Murray, Austen Chamberlain, Bob Cecil, Clifford Allen and Maxwell Garnett, and I let them realise a few of these things.[40]

4

On the afternoon of Thursday, 16 January 1936, the Prince of Wales was out shooting in Windsor Great Park, when an urgent note was handed to him. It was from his mother at Sandringham and began: 'I think you ought to know that Papa is not very well.' Queen Mary went on to suggest that, although she did not consider the danger immediate, the Prince should 'propose' himself for the following week-end, but that he should do so in such a way that the King should not suspect that she had warned him of his condition.

Rather than wait until the Saturday, the Prince flew to Sandringham next morning in his private aeroplane. He found his father in his bedroom dressed in an old Tibetan dressing-gown, 'a faded relic of his visits to India', and dozing in his favourite chair in front of a crackling fire. He was barely conscious of his son's presence in the room, but he did recognise his daughter the Princess Royal who had come down from Yorkshire, since he roused himself sufficiently to ask her if she had been skating. There had been a sharp frost during the night and the pond below the house was covered with ice. His mind had wandered back into the distant past and to the skating parties which he had enjoyed so much at Christmas time. A few minutes later he dozed off again and his two children left the room. The same evening the King's doctor Lord Dawson of Penn arrived. 'I saw him and feel rotten,' the King just managed to write in the last, almost illegible entry in his diary.[41]

Next day the King's condition grew worse and it was clear both to his family, and to Dawson and the other doctors who had been called in, that he could not be expected to live beyond the next few days. On Sunday the Prince motored to London in order to warn the Prime Minister that his father would not last much longer.

The relations between the dying monarch and his forty-one-year-old son and heir, as Baldwin knew, had never been particularly happy. The Prince was afraid of his father and the King never succeeded in winning the Prince's confidence. There is some evidence that both the King and Queen Mary were concerned by the 'latest friendship' which their son had formed with Wallis Simpson, a vivacious American *divorcée*, who was now married to an English businessman named Ernest Simpson. At this time she was in her late thirties and had previously been the wife of an officer in the United States Navy named Earl Winfield Spencer, who was an alcoholic and used to lock her in their bathroom, sometimes for hours on end, while he was out drinking with his cronies. Although she came of a respectable American family in Baltimore, in the circumstances she could hardly be regarded as a suitable consort for a future King of England. The only occasions on which King George and Queen Mary ever set eyes on Mrs Simpson was when she was presented at court with a long line of other women in trains and feathers shortly after her first arrival in England, and some years later at the Jubilee Ball in Buckingham Palace in May 1935, to which she and her husband were invited on the Prince's initiative. As she danced with the Prince she thought she sensed the King's eyes rest searchingly on her. It made her feel uneasy. 'In spite of David's gaiety and the lively strains of a foxtrot,' as she was later to recall, 'the sense of foreboding refused to lift; in that moment I knew that between David's world and mine lay an abyss that I could never cross, one he could never bridge for me.'[42]

Neither the King nor the Queen ever raised the possible implications of the Prince's attachment to Mrs Simpson with him, although the King is known to have expressed his apprehensions to the Archbishop of Canterbury and to the Prime Minister not long before his death. 'After I am dead,' he is said to have remarked to Baldwin, striking a remarkably prophetic note, 'the boy will ruin himself in twelve months.'

The stories which began to reach the King about the Prince's affair with Mrs Simpson were a cause of worry and anxiety, and before he was taken ill the King is known to have expressed the fervent hope that his eldest son would never marry and have children, so that 'nothing will come between Bertie and Lilibet and the throne', which he prayed would one day be occupied by the Duke and Duchess of York. ('The Yorks will do it very well,' Baldwin is said to have replied.) Indeed the view had been expressed by some in a position to judge that, if the King had lived a few months longer, the Prince of Wales would have renounced the succession in his determination to marry Mrs Simpson and so have avoided the acute constitutional crisis which in the event ensued. Indeed in his memoirs, *A King's Story*, the Prince was to hint at this possibility when he should have discussed the matter with his father. Unfortunately the opportunity for such a talk never presented itself owing to what he later described as 'a remarkable concatenation of events' – the Jubilee, his brother Henry's wedding, the General Election, the Abyssinian crisis, the death of his aunt Princess Victoria which much affected the King and, finally, the King's ultimate fatal illness. [43]

On the other hand, the Prince's relations with Baldwin, whom he had known for the past dozen years, had always been easy, and their friendship had been cemented by their visit together to Canada in 1927. When the Prince was summoned back to England from East Africa on account of his father's illness in December 1928, Baldwin went down to Folkestone to meet him and they talked all the way in the train to London. As they parted, the Prince said to him: 'Now you do understand, don't you, that you can always talk to me about everything?'

'Sir, I shall remind you of that,' Baldwin replied. According to his son, a most curious feeling came over him, a feeling of certainty that one day he should have something to say to him, and that it would be about a woman. And then, as suddenly as it had come, the feeling was gone. [44]

Shortly before Baldwin became Prime Minister for the third time, the Prince had given him an original drawing by Max Beerbohm which he had bought some years previously at a sale on behalf of the British Legion. Entitled 'The Old and the Young Self', it showed the 'young self' addressing the old: 'Prime Minister? *You?* Good Lord!!' In the letter which accompanied the gift the Prince wrote:

> I have always had it in mind to send it to you on the chance that you might find a place for it amongst your political souvenirs. I will not express an opinion on the truth of the likeness, but I think it is amusing and anyway I hope you will accept it with my best wishes. [45] *

* The drawing had originally formed part of a Beerbohm Exhibition at the Leicester Galleries in London in April 1925. It now hangs in the Athenaeum Club.

Sunday, 19 January, happened to be Mrs Baldwin's birthday and when the Prince of Wales called at Downing Street she invited him to join the Prime Minister and herself at tea which he was glad to do. When she left them to their talk, Lucy Baldwin said simply: 'We have faith in you.' The Prince was touched by this remark, and as she took her leave of him he pressed her hand and held it for a noticeable moment. Then, after the Prince had told the Prime Minister the latest news from Sandringham, Baldwin expressed his sympathy, adding almost wistfully, as the Prince was later to recall: 'I wonder if you know, Sir, that another great Englishman, a contemporary of your father's, died yesterday?' The Prince looked blank, whereupon the Prime Minister went on: 'But of course, Sir, you have a great deal on your mind. I should not have expected you to know. It was Rudyard Kipling, my first cousin.' To the Prince Mr Baldwin 'seemed a little resentful of the injustice of a situation that allowed the death of one of our great writers to go unnoticed while the nation was absorbed in the passing of a Sovereign'. This impression was not altogether fair to Baldwin. It was natural that he should have been saddened by the death of a near kinsman whom he had known since childhood. Nor had Kipling's death by any means gone unnoticed in the obituary columns of the newspapers. What had disappointed Baldwin, as Tom Jones put it, was 'to see so much stress in the obituary notices on Kipling's politics to the neglect of his literary genius'.

On the strength of their long acquaintance, as the Prince subsequently wrote of the Prime Minister on this occasion, 'he was inspired to say that both of us had good reason to contemplate the future with confidence. I replied in like spirit. We parted, giving voice to those reassurances of mutual esteem that in constitutional society show the hereditary and representative systems at their harmonious best.' He also told Baldwin that he was glad he was Prime Minister. However, the latter's feelings were more accurately expressed by him to Tom Jones when they met the following afternoon in response to a message from Baldwin for help in composing the talk he planned to broadcast as soon as the news of the King's death was announced.

'You know what a scrimshanker I am,' he told Jones when they were ensconced together in the library at No. 10. 'I had rather hoped to escape the responsibility of having to take charge of the Prince as King. But perhaps Providence has kept me here for that purpose. I am less confident about him than Lucy is. It is a tragedy that he is not married. He is very fond of children.' Baldwin went on to tell Jones that the Prince had been to see Mrs Simpson in her flat before he came to Downing Street. But the subject of their relations had never been mentioned between the Prince and the Prime Minister. 'Nor is there any man who can handle him,' Baldwin added. Certainly neither Sir Lionel Halsey, his Comptroller and Treasurer, nor Sir Godfrey Thomas, who had been his Private Secretary for the past seventeen years, could do so. Maybe they both scented trouble, since Thomas was to decline to carry on as Private Secretary in the new reign, preferring to act as an assistant, while Halsey was to retire altogether.

Jones, according to himself, 'put the other side of the new Monarch: his quick intelligence, his freedom from humbug, his social sympathies and sense of duty when on a job, e.g. visiting unemployment centres', and he pressed the view that 'he'll rise to the new responsibilities though he may discharge them in his own way'.

But Baldwin was not so sure. 'What I am wondering is whether he and the Queen will live in the Palace for a year or two,' he mused aloud. 'That is what I should like. When I was a little boy in Worcestershire reading history books, I never thought I should have to interfere between a king and his mistress.' [46]

Later that day, the BBC announcers began to intone at hourly intervals: 'The King's life is moving peacefully to its close,' the words of the bulletin composed by Lord Dawson of Penn to prepare the public for the news for which they had been waiting. This came shortly before midnight.

After receiving the homage of the Sandringham household, the new sovereign, as the Archbishop of Canterbury was quick to observe, began his reign at once by giving directions that the clocks, which by long custom at Sandringham were kept half an hour in advance of the real time, should be put back. ('I wonder what other customs will be put back also!' the Archbishop speculated.) King Edward then telephoned Mrs Simpson. 'It's all over,' he told her. 'I can't tell you what my own plans are, everything here is so upset. But I shall fly to London in the morning . . .' [47]

By mid-day the newspaper placards were proclaiming the King's characteristic gesture ('Edward VIII flies to London'), unlike his father who had never flown in his life. 'There was no affection between the two, but the son admired the father,' Tom Jones noted the same day. 'S.B. is distinctly nervous about him. One wonders whether it is going to be a case of the Prince in Shakespeare's *Henry IV* and the King in *Henry V*.' [48] Baldwin's uneasiness was reflected in a remark which the Prime Minister made to Clement Attlee, the parliamentary Labour leader, at the Accession Privy Council which assembled in the Banqueting Hall of St James's Palace that afternoon, when Baldwin admitted that he had grave doubts whether the new King would 'stay the course'. The purpose of this council, presided over by a somewhat rejuvenated Ramsay MacDonald as Lord President, was to swear allegiance to King Edward VIII and to hear the new sovereign declare, as he did, his intention to uphold constitutional government. 'In this I am determined to follow in my father's footsteps and to work as he did throughout his life for the happiness and welfare of all classes of my subjects.'

In the evening Baldwin broadcast to the nation from the Cabinet room. After paying a tribute to the late King, he went on to speak of his successor:

All eyes are upon him as he advances to his father's place, and, while he is no stranger to public duty, he is now summoned to face responsibilities more onerous, more exacting, more continuous, than any he has hitherto been asked to discharge . . .

The young King knows the confidence we all repose in him. He knows that he commands not only the allegiance, he knows that the understanding, the affection and the prayers of the countless multitudes of his subjects are with him at this hour. May God guide him aright and God save the King.

The broadcast was relayed overseas and Baldwin was astonished by 'the wonderful reception at immense distances'. For example, he had letters from places as far apart as Kenya and Seattle saying that it could be heard as though he were talking in the same room. 'That is a wonderful tribute to the perfection of your work,' Baldwin wrote to Sir John Reith, the Director-General of the BBC. 'A commonplace to you, I dare say, but it is new to me and very marvellous.' Indeed, broadcasting was a technique for reaching the widest audience which Baldwin had rapidly mastered and was able to use with dramatic effect.[48]

5

Next morning, 22 January 1936, the new Sovereign's accession, in accordance with tradition, was publicly proclaimed by the Garter King of Arms at Friary Court in St James's Palace and by the other Heralds at Charing Cross, Temple Bar and the Royal Exchange. The King invited a few close friends including Mrs Simpson to witness the ceremony from a room in the Palace, where they were joined at the last moment by the King himself. An enterprising press photographer was able to snapshot the group at the window, and the resultant picture showed Mrs Simpson standing beside the King. She had been photographed before with the King when he was Prince of Wales, on a skiing holiday in Austria and on a Mediterranean cruise with a party aboard Walter Guinness's yacht

Rosaura during the previous summer, but Ernest Simpson was always present as well. The proclamation ceremony was the first intimate occasion on which she was seen in animated conversation with the King, and this immediately set tongues wagging, although apart from publishing the photograph the press continued to maintain a discreet silence about Edward VIII and his woman friend. Nevertheless some public curiosity was aroused, and Baldwin for one made some inquiries about her. Apart from information supplied by the Secret Service to the effect that she was friendly with the German Embassy people, he did not learn very much.

So far as Mrs Simpson's relations with her husband went, it appeared that Ernest Simpson was still in love with her, although his suspicions had been aroused and she was not always very kind to him. One friend who knew them well was Bernard Rickatson-Hatt, the editor-in-chief of Reuter's, who gave some interesting particulars to Walter Monckton, the King's legal adviser, who had asked Rickatson-Hatt about her attitude towards her husband.

> He said that Simpson was extremely fond of her. She was extremely attractive to men, amusing and kind on most occasions but capable of hardness. She had often made Simpson extremely unhappy, and then overwhelmed him with kindness and affection in making up the difference.
>
> Rickatson-Hatt says that she likes the good things of the earth and is fundamentally selfish. He thinks her intention was to have her cake and eat it. She was flattered by the advances of the Prince of Wales and the King and enjoyed his generous gifts to her to the full. She thought that she could have them and at the same time keep her home with Simpson.

It also appears from what Rickatson-Hatt told Monckton that her husband had tackled her on several occasions in the past about her relations with the Prince. But hitherto she had always succeeded in allaying his suspicions. 'She had always told him that he could trust her to look after herself; she enjoyed the attention she received and there was no harm in it.'

Rickatson-Hatt's character sketch of Wallis Simpson has been strikingly supplemented by the report of a graphologist, to whom a member of Baldwin's entourage submitted a specimen of her handwriting:

> A woman with a strong male inclination in the sense of activity, vitality, initiative. She *must* dominate, she *must* have authority, and

without sufficient scope for her powers can become disagreeable . . . She needs a large field of organisation, of influence . . . primarily all she does comes from her wish to be important.

In the pursuit of her aim, she can be inconsiderate and can hurt – but on the whole she is not without some instinct of nobility and generosity. She is ruled by contradictory impulses; there is a certain restlessness in the writing, a sign that the satisfaction she gets is not strong enough to harmonise her life. She is ambitious and demands above all that her undertakings should be noted and valued.[49]

What with Kipling's funeral and the King's Lying-in-State in Westminster Hall, and the eulogy of the late monarch which custom required the Prime Minister to deliver in Parliament ('Do I need to say a word in this House of how his power and influence were enhanced in a million ways by that rich companionship he shared with the Queen?'), Baldwin had much to think about and settle in these trying days. For instance, the Queen wished to be known as Queen Mary and not the Queen Mother, but for some reason unclear to most people the two Archbishops objected to this style. The Prime Minister thereupon consulted Simon, the Home Secretary, and Sir Thomas Inskip, the Attorney-General, and they ruled against their Graces, following the precedent of Edward VIII's grandmother Queen Alexandra. From the point of view of Baldwin and his Government the interlude of nation-wide grief at George V's passing had one good result; it served to distract public attention from the folly of the Hoare–Laval affair by giving the Baldwin Cabinet a breathing space in which to recover its political balance.

Then there was the question of Mrs Simpson and her relations with the new King. At this date Baldwin did not believe that the King had formed any idea of marrying her, in spite of some curious information to the contrary which reached him within a few days of the late monarch's being laid to rest at Windsor. On 4 February, Sir Maurice Jenks, a former Lord Mayor of London, came to see Baldwin with a strange story. Some time before, Mrs Simpson's husband had been put forward for admission to a Masonic Lodge of which Jenks was the Worshipful Master. In spite of the fact that Mr Ernest Simpson's candidature was supported by the Prince of Wales, who belonged to the same Lodge, it was rejected. On the Prince demanding an explanation from the Worshipful Master, Jenks told him frankly that they could not admit a candidate whose wife was believed on good grounds to be the mistress of another member of the same Lodge without breaching Masonic law; whereupon, according to Jenks, 'the Prince promised that there was nothing between himself and Mrs Simpson', with the result that

Simpson was subsequently admitted. Since then, said Jenks, he had been told by Simpson that he had found out that the King wished to marry his wife as soon as possible after she had divorced him. Simpson had gone on to say that he would like to leave England, only he felt that this would facilitate the divorce, and that what he really desired for himself was to have his wife back. 'The *mari complaisant*,' Jenks remarked, 'is now the sorrowing and devoted spouse.' Jenks added that he had suggested to Simpson that he should see the Prime Minister, and he now asked Baldwin whether he would be willing to receive him.

Baldwin flatly refused to do so, pointing out that he was the King's official adviser and not the Simpsons'. Nevertheless he considered that what he had learned was sufficiently important for him to consult Lord Wigram, who for the time being was carrying on as the King's Principal Private Secretary. This he did the same evening in company with Davidson. Evidently they considered that the idea of the King marrying a *divorcée* whose previous husband was still living was unthinkable, since no further action was taken by Baldwin following the Jenks disclosure.[50]

Having failed to move the Prime Minister, Ernest Simpson decided that the only thing for him to do was to have it out with the King. What happened next was subsequently revealed by Bernard Rickatson-Hatt to Walter Monckton:

> He told me that in February 1936 he had been at York House with the King and Ernest Simpson. Rickatson-Hatt got up to go but Simpson asked him to stop, and in Rickatson-Hatt's presence, Simpson told the King that Wallis would have to choose between them, and what did the King mean to do about it? Did he intend to marry her?
>
> The King rose from his chair and said: 'Do you really think that I would be crowned without Wallis by my side?'

Monckton concludes his account of this incident by stating that it fitted the date 'when Mr Baldwin was approached – so it was said – by Sir Maurice Jenks with the story that the King meant to marry Mrs Simpson, which was alleged to have come from Mr Simpson'.[51]

Meanwhile, much to Baldwin's relief, Mrs Simpson had gone off to the United States on a visit. 'Rumour credits Nancy [Lady Astor] with this achievement,' noted Tom Jones. 'If so, she ought certainly to be made a Privy Councillor and join Margaret Bondfield.'[52] But Mrs Simpson did not remain out of the way for long. She was soon back in London, entertaining and being entertained by the King. Although they could no longer be seen in public places during the six-month period of Court mourning, they continued to meet privately; she and her husband were invited to spend most week-ends at Fort Belvedere, 'a castellated conglomeration' in the gift of the Crown near Sunningdale in Windsor Great Park, which the King had begged and obtained from his father some years previously and which he continued to make his principal home. When he had to spend the night in London, he used his old quarters in York House and merely kept a small office on the ground floor of Buckingham Palace, where for the time being his mother continued to reside.

Baldwin's anxiety about the King was shared by Neville Chamberlain. 'I do hope he ''pulls up his socks'' and behaves now he has such heavy responsibilities,' Chamberlain had noted in his diary after the Accession Council, 'for unless he does he will soon pull down the throne.' It shortly appeared, at least to Neville Chamberlain, that Edward VIII was not 'doing the boxes', that is reading the state papers, which were submitted to him daily in the traditional red boxes, with the patient care that his late father had shown. Indeed Chamberlain drafted a memorandum for Cabinet circulation, urging that the King should 'settle down', wear conventional dark clothes, work at his 'boxes' and not make remarks in public, which were apt to be reported, about such topics as the slums and unemployment. Baldwin thought it wise to suppress this memorandum. Nor did he think the time was opportune to warn the King about the stories which reached him through Wigram of the King's extravagances and indiscretions, not to mention the unhappy relations with the members of the royal household, some of whom were summarily dismissed after years of loyal service. Wigram himself only consented to remain as Private Secretary until a suitable successor could take over, and before he left he begged the Prime Minister to impress on the King the danger he was running, although (in the words of Baldwin's official biographer) 'at the same time he made it clear that against a passion so overmastering it was very doubtful whether words of reason would be of any avail'. So it came about that in his regular audiences with the King in the early months of his reign Baldwin preferred to keep his counsel and say nothing of what he and the rest of the Cabinet were thinking on the subject of the '*affaire* Simpson'.[53]

On 27 May 1936 the Baldwins obeyed the King's command to dine with him at St James's Palace. The other guests, all of whose names the King directed should appear in the *Court Circular* next day, included the Mountbattens, the Wigrams, the Duff Coopers, the Simpsons, Lady Cunard and two other Americans, and the aviator Colonel Charles Lindbergh and his wife, who had just returned from seeing Hitler in Germany. The prime object of the dinner party was to bring Mrs Simpson together with Baldwin at the same table. 'It's got to be done,' the King had told her one day at Fort

Belvedere when he was planning the party. 'Sooner or later my Prime Minister must meet my future wife.' According to Mrs Simpson, this was the first time that the King had directly raised the subject of their marrying and it took her by surprise. 'The idea is impossible,' was her initial reaction. 'They'd never let you.' [54] Nevertheless she had agreed to come to the dinner and to bring her husband if he was agreeable. Somewhat surprisingly he was, though it was to be the last time.

'My wife was well-placed,' Baldwin remarked afterwards, 'but I own it surprised me to see Mrs Simpson at one end of the table and Lady Cunard at the other.' Mrs Baldwin's comments, then and after, were less bland, according to G. M. Young. 'For her, and for women like her throughout the Empire, Mrs Simpson had stolen the Fairy Prince.' [55]

At the next dinner which the King gave, six weeks later, only Mrs Simpson's name appeared in the *Court Circular*. In the interval she had told her husband that she was starting divorce proceedings and he had moved out of their flat in Bryanston Square to a temporary residence in the Guards' Club. Baldwin noted the absence of Ernest Simpson's name from the *Court Circular* on 9 July and drew the obvious conclusion.

6

With the resumption of normal political activity after King George V's funeral, Baldwin's main preoccupation was with the question of national defence, particularly in the light of Germany's growing military strength on land and in the air. There was a perceptible demand on the Government back benches in the Commons for the appointment of a separate ministry responsible for defence, and this was expressed in a debate on the subject on 14 February when Austen Chamberlain chose to deliver a powerful attack upon Baldwin. Afterwards he wrote to his sisters:

> Having done much to save him [Baldwin] in December when an adverse vote would have been a direct vote of censure and necessitated his resignation, I decided to use this non-party debate to tell him what not only the older but many of the younger members are privately saying.
>
> If there is any truth in the rumour – I don't believe there is – that he proposes to hand over Defence to Ramsay MacDonald there will be a howl of indignation and a vote of no confidence, nor is Eustace Percy the man for that job. In my view there is only one man who by his studies and his special abilities and aptitudes is marked out for it, and

that man is Winston Churchill! I don't suppose that S.B. will offer it
to him and I don't think that Neville would wish to have him back,
but they are both wrong. He is the right man for that post, and in such
dangerous times that consideration ought to be decisive.[56]

A week later, Tom Jones breakfasted with Baldwin in Downing Street
and found him 'rather sorry for himself'.

He has lost the fresh vigour he gathered at Astley at Christmas and is
tired. Dawson has been to overhaul him. There is nothing wrong beyond an inclination to get tired sooner than usual – due, of course, to
the recent tribulations, Hoare–Laval, death of the King, anxiety about
the probable behaviour of Edward VIII, and Austen's castigation last
Friday.
    In these moods he naturally reflects upon his latter end, the danger
of repeating Ramsay's example and repeating your utility and
welcome. He recalled to me the disastrous effect of Milner's senility
in the Egyptian negotiations as a warning of what happens when old
and tired men carry on too long.* And there was Gladstone's case who
put the Tories in power for many years. S.B. wants to hand over to his
successor when his own prestige has not too far declined and with the
Party good in heart. That cannot be today or tomorrow, and may not
be until the summer of 1938, when God willing and political weather
permitting, Neville will take over.
    In the meantime, Neville having refused, Sam [Hoare] will act as
Deputy in the urgent matter of Defence. Those who desired Winston
will be disappointed and those who dreaded Eustace Percy will be
pleased. Defence, the King, and our relations with Germany are the
subjects which fill the PM's mind today.[57]

In the event Hoare was not made responsible for defence, owing largely
to the opposition of Eden who told Baldwin that 'the appointment would
make things much more difficult for him during the next few months',
although he had no objection to his ultimately returning to the Cabinet,
which in fact he was to do in June as First Lord of the Admiralty on Eyre-
Monsell's retirement. Various other names were canvassed including

* As Colonial Secretary in 1919 Lord Milner was entrusted by the Cabinet with the task of
reporting on the future of Anglo-Egyptian relations. His report, following protracted negotiations with the Egyptian Government, was rejected by the Cabinet, and his consequent resignation early in 1921 brought his official career to a close. He was sixty-seven at the time, a year
younger than Baldwin was in 1936.

W. S. ('Shakes') Morrison, who had succeeded Duff Cooper as Financial Secretary to the Treasury. However, Captain Margesson, the Government Chief Whip, pressed for the appointment of Sir Thomas Inskip, the Attorney-General, as 'the safest man', and Neville Chamberlain agreed. 'Every name involves risks and I should play for safety,' Chamberlain argued on 11 March. 'The events of the week-end (occupation of the Rhineland by Hitler) afforded excellent reason for discarding both Winston and Sam since both had European reputations which might make it dangerous to add to the Cabinet at a critical moment. Inskip would create no jealousies. He would excite no enthusiasm but he would involve us in no fresh perplexities.' [58]

So Sir Thomas Inskip, the future Lord Caldecote, was appointed Minister for the Co-ordination of Defence at a salary of £5,000 a year.* The news was greeted with some astonishment to say the least. 'Baldwin has to find a man of inferior ability to himself,' Churchill was credited with saying at the time, 'and this Herculean task must require time for its accomplishment.' The pseudonymous writer 'Cato', generally believed to be a young journalist named Michael Foot, made the unoriginal but acute observation that no such surprising appointment had been made since the Emperor Caligula had appointed his horse a consul. Even the editor of the *Annual Register* felt obliged to put on record that 'Sir Thomas's abilities had never been regarded as more than mediocre, nor could he lay claim to any great administrative experience'.[59] It was stated that the new minister's functions were to exercise, on behalf of the Prime Minister, day-to-day supervision of the Committee of Imperial Defence. He was also empowered to consult with the Chiefs of Staff, and to convene the Chiefs of Staff Committee under his own chairmanship whenever he or they thought it desirable. Inskip's task was certainly Herculean, and it was not made any easier by Hailsham's admission in the House of Lords that the staff of the new ministry consisted of only two civil servants, though there was a right to ask for more. War Office reaction was epitomised in the remark of an elderly General: 'Thank God, we are preserved from Winston Churchill!' Nevertheless the appointment did not by any means deserve the scorn which was heaped upon it at the time. Working in a quiet way as he did through a lengthy series of committees, relatively free from publicity, Inskip may well have achieved more than the publicity-conscious Churchill

---

* Although his new office carried an increase of £500 a year compared with that of Attorney-General, Inskip had to give up the fees which a Law Officer was allowed to take in those days and which in his case amounted to between £15,000 and £20,000 a year. He was succeeded as Attorney-General by Sir Donald Somervell, whose place as Solicitor-General was filled by Sir Terence O'Connor.

would have done with his more flamboyant methods of preparing for possible war which might have unduly alarmed the public.

Hitler's week-end coup in despatching 30,000 German troops, reinforced by police, into the demilitarised Rhineland, was a further violation of the Versailles Treaty and called for immediate action by the other Locarno signatories. As soon as Eden heard the news of the occupation, he telephoned Baldwin who was at Chequers and went off to see him. When they met, Eden warned that there was a chance that France might mobilise her forces and invade the Rhineland, but on the whole he was inclined to think, as indeed events turned out, that she would appeal to the League Council and ask for an early meeting of the Locarno powers. The Foreign Secretary went on to speak of 'the danger that would now beset the unity of the former war-time allies'.

Italy would not help, it was essential that we and the French should stay together, but this would not be easy.

Baldwin said little, as was his wont on foreign affairs. Though personally friendly to France, he was clear in his mind that there would be no support in Britain for any military action by the French. I could only agree. I told him of the earnestness with which Hitler had spoken to me of Locarno. I could not believe him any more. Baldwin did not dissent and accepted that we must now await the French reaction calling the Cabinet for Monday morning.[60]

The Cabinet, which met on 9 March, agreed that Eden and Halifax should go to Paris for discussions with Flandin and Van Zeeland, the French and Belgian Foreign Ministers. The truth was that the French army was only equipped for defence and the French politicians were only concerned with extracting a promise of future support from the British, since their army was incapable of invading the demilitarised zone and evicting Hitler's forces, although at the first signs of opposition Hitler would probably have given the order to withdraw. Britain and Italy, it is true, were the Locarno guarantors, but with the Italian armies fully engaged in Abyssinia and no prospect of any backing from that quarter Baldwin had to admit that his country had insufficient forces with which to implement her guarantee. When Flandin came to London, he told him bluntly: 'Britain is not in a state to go to war.' The facts and figures which he put before Flandin convinced France's Foreign Minister that he was right. There was also the consideration that British public opinion was opposed to the taking of any hostile action against Germany, even to the length of economic sanctions. People asked: 'Why shouldn't a man walk into his own back yard?' Surely that did not amount to 'flagrant aggression' in the sense of Locarno? Thus the case against Hitler was allowed to go largely by default. The most that the British Government could offer France and Belgium was a renewed guarantee against German aggression, to be reinforced by tripartite staff talks.

Fritz Hesse, a young journalist who was Press Attaché at the German Embassy in London, relates a curious story about the Rhineland crisis at this time. According to Hesse, he was with the Ambassador, Leopold von Hoesch, one day at the height of the crisis when the telephone rang in the Ambassador's study. The caller turned out to be the King, and von Hoesch who took the call handed another receiver to Hesse so that he could listen in to the conversation. The Ambassador, a career diplomat of the old school, had been on close terms with the King for some years; they had recently discussed Hitler's intentions, and von Hoesch had told the King that Hitler was ready to replace the Locarno Treaty with a new treaty and that if the Rhineland question were solved Germany would be willing to return to the League of Nations. The telephone call concerned the crisis. 'I sent for the Prime Minister and gave him a piece of my mind,' the King is stated to have said to the Ambassador. 'I told the old so-and-so that I would abdicate if he made war. There was a frightful scene. But you needn't worry. There won't be a war.' Upon which von Hoesch was delighted with himself. 'I've done it,' he exclaimed. 'I've outwitted them all, there won't be a war!' Hesse's conclusion was that the conflict which was already developing between Baldwin and the King over Mrs Simpson 'may already have been playing its part in the background of world events'.

If the story is true – and Hesse is hardly likely to have invented the telephone conversation – it shows how intimate the King was with the German Ambassador, whom he addressed as 'Leo'. On the other hand, he must have been joking if he threatened to abdicate, since at this date there was no need for him to have made a serious threat of this kind. Certainly, whether serious or not, the King's intervention in the sphere of Anglo-German relations was far from welcome to Baldwin, who was already worried by reports which had been reaching him from the head of the secret intelligence service about leakages of the contents of state papers which had been traced to the King. Indeed the matter came before the Cabinet, although like other matters concerning the King at this time there is no reference to it in the Cabinet minutes as circulated.[61]

The Council of the League now met in London and resolved that the Versailles Treaty had been breached, although the resolution was not unanimous. The only Council member to propose the application of sanctions against Germany was the Soviet Union through the mouth of its Foreign Minister Maxim Litvinov, but this was brushed aside in favour of an invitation to Hitler to renegotiate a new arrangement for European security. Hitler responded with a declaration that he had 'no more territorial claims in Europe', and he proposed a twenty-five year non-aggression pact with the Western Powers. In order, so he said, to expose Hitler's intentions, Eden drew up a questionnaire for submission to the Fuehrer, which he cleared with Baldwin at the end of April. It was handed to the German Foreign Minister, von Neurath, shortly afterwards by the British Ambassador in Berlin. Unfortunately a week elapsed before Hitler would receive the document, which had in the meantime been 'leaked' to the press. Hitler was naturally annoyed and did not reply, which in turn annoyed Eden. 'He had asked Hitler a number of perfectly reasonable questions which in fact he could only fail to answer if his intentions were bad,' Eden told Baldwin. 'It was therefore most important that he should be given no occasion to cloud the issue.' Eden was even more anxious that the Prime Minister should not do so either, in view of the strong warning he had given him that the object of German foreign policy was to divide Britain from France. ('I think S.B. saw the force and was rather alarmed.')

Meanwhile Mussolini was as defiant as ever and seemed confident of his ability to subjugate Abyssinia, largely by drenching the unfortunate natives with poison gas, in spite of the sanctions so far imposed by the League. In a speech to his constituents at Worcester on 18 April, the Prime Minister defined the attitude of Great Britain to the League of Nations and sanctions in the face of the new situation which had arisen. He began by pointing out that there did not seem to be as yet any effective machinery for stopping a war before it began, if one party was determined to go to war and not to submit the differences in dispute to discussion and arbitration. As for sanctions, these were slow in action and lost a great deal of their force unless they could be supported by the ultimate sanction which was blockade or force. He felt it was difficult to see how, under the existing membership of the League, a policy of blockade could be agreed to inside the League. So far as collective action could be secured, Britain would continue with it as she had done, 'neither going faster or slower than other countries, but all together'.

Although Eden was to follow this course when the League Council reconvened at Geneva two days later and to declaim vehemently against Italy, the British Foreign Secretary made no suggestion that existing sanctions should be strengthened. Indeed it was generally felt that they could not save Abyssinia from being conquered, and when this came about a fortnight later it only remained for Neville Chamberlain to deliver the *coup de grâce* by describing the idea of continuing sanctions, let alone of intensifying them, as 'the midsummer of madness'.

On 1 May the Emperor Haile Selassie withdrew from Abyssinia with his family on a warship thoughtfully provided by the British Government, and a week later the Italians entered Addis Ababa, having previously sprayed their half-naked opponents with mustard gas, while the King of Italy was proclaimed Emperor of Ethiopia. Haile Selassie took refuge in England and after several fruitless appearances in the League assembly chamber at Geneva he settled down in Bath. In the House of Commons the rising Labour member Hugh Dalton led a strong attack on the Government for its Abyssinian policy. He was skilfully answered by the Foreign Secretary who chided the Opposition for professing to support the League of Nations with horse, foot and artillery, whereas they really only meant to support it with threats, insults and perorations. At the end of the debate, Churchill intervened briefly to criticise Baldwin for not having taken part. The Prime Minister, he said, had all the power and therefore great responsibility. He should not have sat silent. Churchill was cheered by the Labour benches, but the Conservatives reacted with angry shouts.[62]

Baldwin took note of this and Churchill's other utterances at this time, particularly on the subject of defence. 'One of these days I'll make a few casual remarks about Winston,' he told Jones later the same month.

Not a speech – no oratory – just a few words in passing. I've got it all ready. I am going to say that when Winston was born lots of fairies swooped down on his cradle gifts – imagination, eloquence, industry, ability, and then came a fairy who said 'No one person has a right to so many gifts,' picked him up and gave him a shake and twist that with all these gifts he was denied judgement and wisdom. And that is why, while we delight to listen to him in this House, we do not take his advice.[63]

Baldwin was getting noticeably deafer, and at Question Time in the Commons, Captain Margesson, who sat beside him on the Treasury Bench, often had to repeat the questions to him. 'The PM frowns as he listens,' noted 'Chips' Channon. 'Like all deaf people he is a little annoyed when he has happened to hear and the remark is nevertheless repeated to him.' On the other hand, Baldwin could still make an effective speech, as he did when he addressed the 1922 Club at a dinner which its members, Conservatives who had been returned at the General Election following the downfall of the Lloyd George Coalition, gave him in the House. 'I think I had a great success,' he told Jones, and went on to retail some of the things he had said:

> There were from 130 to 150 present, and I spoke for three-quarters of an hour. I had just a note or two to keep me right. I said there were some who doubted whether I was a dyed-in-the-wool Tory. I told them I wore the Tory colours in my pram in the 1868 election. My father voted Whig then, but our cook was a Tory and she saw to my politics. For ninety-four years a Tory had represented Bewdley.
>
> I told them of my fight at Kidderminster, how I had come back from my visit to the United States a protectionist, how we were stirred by Joseph Chamberlain's tariff campaign, how we blundered badly over the Taff Vale decision. How when the war ended we were in a new world and how class conscious and revolutionary it was; how I felt that our Party was being destroyed and how I determined to do what I could to rescue it. I did not mention L.G. or Winston. Then in 1931 we conformed to the King's wish and all my colleagues agreed with me in doing so.
>
> I then touched on German rearmament and claimed that we could not have got this country to rearm one moment earlier than we did.

Baldwin redelivered the speech, for the benefit of Tom Jones, marching up and down the Long Gallery at Chequers, 'happy to recall it and to know in his bones that it had been a success'. He was particularly pleased that *The Observer* should have described it as 'Mr Baldwin's best'.

On the other hand, he had off days in the House and could strike a new-comer to the parliamentary scene as 'ineffectual and boring', particularly when he had to speak to a subject in which he himself had no strong interest. 'He is ageing and seems worn out, and one wonders whether he has lost his grip,' noted 'Chips' Channon after he had heard the Prime Minister reply to a foreign affairs debate. 'Will his strength survive or will it tide him over next year?'[64]

7

As has been seen, Baldwin's action in transferring Malcolm MacDonald to the Dominions Office was designed to improve Anglo-Irish relations, which had deteriorated badly owing to the 'economic war' consequent upon President de Valera withholding the disputed land annuities. The new minister was determined to achieve a comprehensive understanding with the Irish Free State, and with Baldwin's assent he began by persuading de Valera to meet him in secret. Such a settlement as MacDonald had in mind would, in the words of a confidential memorandum which he circulated to his colleagues on the Irish Situation Committee, 'greatly strengthen our position in world affairs, would increase our security from the point of view of defence and would materially assist British trade and industry'. The Dominions Secretary also pointed out that Mr de Valera was preparing a new constitution for the Irish Free State and that he intended in the process to remove the Crown entirely from his country's domestic affairs and to confine recognition of the King solely to external purposes. When a constitution of this nature was adopted, MacDonald predicted that all hope of keeping the Free State in the Commonwealth would be at an end unless some settlement was reached which would *inter alia* preserve the link with the mother country.

On 12 May 1936 the Irish Situation Committee met in Baldwin's room in the House of Commons to hear a progress report from Malcolm MacDonald and to consider his recommendations. The main one, on which the discussion hinged, was expressed in these words:

> The bases of any political agreement should be proper recognition by the Irish Free State Government of the position of the Crown in the Irish Free State Constitution, and acquiescence by the Irish Free State Government in the present position whereby the consent of Northern Ireland is essential to the establishment of a United Ireland.

Baldwin, who was in the chair, asked Malcolm MacDonald whether in his capacity of Dominions Secretary he was satisfied that it was well worth while making an attempt to reach a settlement because, as the Prime Minister pointed out, 'in certain respects the circumstances were more propitious than in 1932, and because to have made an attempt and failed would be better than to have taken no action at all'. MacDonald agreed that this was so.

Baldwin then inquired whether the Dominions as a whole took a different view of the Irish situation from what the mother country did. If there was a real chance of the Irish Free State leaving the Empire, said Baldwin, 'might we not have serious trouble with the other Dominions if we could not justify our attitude and policy by showing that we had done everything in reason and had made every practicable concession in order to secure a comprehensive settlement?'

To this question, the Dominions Secretary replied that he thought de Valera's position was now viewed with some sympathy in South Africa and to a lesser extent in Canada.

With his shrewd commercial sense, Baldwin went on to say that they would in particular have to make up their minds whether the concessions the British Government would have to make to the Irish Free State might not be too heavy a price to pay for the concessions which President de Valera might be prepared to give in return.

The opposition to Malcolm MacDonald's initiative was led by Lord Hailsham, who felt there should be no further truck with de Valera whom he was convinced was pursuing the objective of an all-Ireland Republic and he advanced his arguments with an expert lawyer's skill. What Malcolm MacDonald was proposing, said Hailsham, 'was destined to failure and could produce no good result either at home or abroad'. As MacDonald was considering how to answer Hailsham, the division bell rang and everyone went off to vote, a pretext which the Prime Minister seized on to adjourn the discussion.

Malcolm MacDonald has recalled in his book *Titans and Others* that while he was on his way to the division lobby he was overtaken by Neville Chamberlain, the Chancellor of the Exchequer, who was a member of the Committee. Chamberlain asked the Dominions Secretary to meet him in his room after the division and when MacDonald did so he was invited to rehearse the arguments with which he would have answered Hailsham if they had not been interrupted. The outcome was that Chamberlain told MacDonald he could count on his support in all future discussions, an important step forward since as Baldwin's successor-designate as Prime Minister, Chamberlain had considerable influence with Baldwin. The only point which worried Chamberlain was MacDonald's proposal that an appropriate lump sum payment by the Irish Free State should be accepted in settlement of the financial dispute, since he understood that the Free State could not be expected to raise more than £10 million at any one time, whereas the capital value of the sums on which de Valera had defaulted stood at nearer £100 million.[65]

At the next meeting of the Committee, thanks largely to the support from Baldwin and Chamberlain, MacDonald was given leave to go ahead and negotiate a settlement with de Valera. On 7 July 1936 he reported that he had had an encouraging four-hour meeting with de Valera, who seemed keen to preserve a Commonwealth link for the sake of ultimate Irish unity. 'It is an indication of his present practical mood,' MacDonald told the Committee, 'that in the course of the meeting he never mentioned Oliver Cromwell or any character or event which troubled Ireland prior to 1921.'

The Dominions Secretary went on to explain the significance of de Valera's proposal for 'external association', that is that the King would only be recognized as Head of Commonwealth for matters of 'common concern' such as accrediting Irish diplomatic and consular representatives to foreign states, and the oath of allegiance would be modified in this sense.

This produced quite a lecture from the Home Secretary, Sir John Simon, to the effect that the result might be, as he put it, 'something resembling the structure of the old North German Confederation'. Upon which Baldwin dryly observed that the new conception of allegiance would be 'very hard to explain to the man in the street' who had never heard of the North German Confederation.

The Committee's general conclusion, which Baldwin shared, was that the whole position turned on allegiance – 'not on the acceptance of a Governor-General or on the Crown's assent to legislation' – and Mr de Valera should be asked 'if he were willing to make an unambiguous declaration, on some prominent position in the new Free State Constitution, containing the substance of the doctrine of allegiance. For example, if the King visited Dublin, would he be given precedence over the President?' [66]

Fortunately for de Valera, time was on his side, and Baldwin and his Government were shortly to be overtaken by events in which Edward VIII was to play the central role, and which were to give de Valera a wholly unlooked-for opportunity to secure his objects unimpeded by the British Prime Minister and the Irish Situation Committee.

8

Baldwin wanted better relations with Hitler as well as with de Valera. 'We must get nearer to Germany,' he told Eden, the Foreign Secretary, on 20 May 1936. 'How?' asked Eden. 'I have no idea,' was the reply. 'That is your job.' [67]

Baldwin's desire to improve Anglo-German relations had been stimulated by Tom Jones who had breakfasted with him in Downing Street the same day. Jones was just back from Munich, where he had been received by Hitler, who was accompanied by Ribbentrop. According to Jones, the Fuehrer stressed the importance of an alliance with England and his 'great desire' to meet the British Prime Minister. Jones pointed out that 'Mr Baldwin was a shy and modest statesman who had never entirely got over his astonishment at finding himself Prime Minister'. When this was translated, Hitler smiled and remarked: 'And I also.' [68]

Baldwin was so fascinated by what he heard ('Go on. This is like an Oppenheimer story') that he invited Jones to come to Chequers for the week-end, where they could continue their talk. When Jones arrived on Friday evening he was offered a drink which turned out to be a glass of Baldwin's favourite Malvern water. He thought the Prime Minister was showing signs of suppressed excitement. The cause turned out to be much nearer home than Hitler. It was J. H. Thomas, the Colonial Secretary, and a member of the Cabinet, who had been shown to have been responsible for the leakage of some of the secrets of Neville Chamberlain's current Budget, 'the biggest fish ever caught by the machinery of a judicial inquiry', as the historian A. J. P. Taylor has described him.

'You'll see in the papers tomorrow Jim Thomas's letter of resignation and my acceptance,' Baldwin told Jones. 'I'm sorry for him. He wanted to make a fighting farewell speech in the House but we got him off that by a slight alteration in his letter – not important. He has fallen a victim to the two weaknesses of his class . . . he has been a terrific gambler. They say the turf agents' clerks had to work overtime to make an inventory of his bets . . . I don't think Jim deliberately gave anything away. What he most likely did was to let his tongue wag when he was in his cups.'

Baldwin's letter to his erring colleague was as follows:

10 Downing Street
Whitehall, SW1
21 May 1936

My dear Jim,

You have acted as I should have done in your place.

I accept your resignation with deep regret, which I know will be shared by all my colleagues.

The loyal support you have given through five strenuous years to the National Government will be always remembered by those who have worked with you.

With all good wishes,
I am sincerely yours,
STANLEY BALDWIN

It was a quiet week-end, which the Prime Minister spent mostly playing patience in the Long Gallery, when he was not talking to Jones. As the latter noted, 'his strained nervous condition showed itself in the ferocious energy he put into the game, banging the tiny cards on the table, venting on them the pent-up wrath which should have been poured on his colleagues . . . Throughout the week-end there was one telephone call, and

Chancellor of Cambridge University.

Electioneering with Lucy.

The Cabinet of the first National Government, August 1931.
Back row: Cunlife-Lister, J. H. Thomas, Reading, Neville Chamberlain, Hoare.
Front row: Snowden, Baldwin, MacDonald, Samuel, Sankey.
From a photograph taken in the garden of 10 Downing Street.

'PLANE SPEAKING.
Mr. Baldwin: "Ah! as I said long ago – 'Safety first'."
Mr. MacDonald: "And as I've said ever since – 'England is going up and up!'."
Cartoon by Sir Bernard Partridge. *Punch* 20 March 1935.
From the artist's proof in the possession of Mr D. Pepys-Whiteley.

ondonderry at home, with Hailsham
d MacDonald at Mount Stewart.

ondonderry abroad, with Hitler and
obentrop in Berlin.

The Rt. Hon. Sir Samuel Hoare, Bart, M.P., Secretary of State for Foreign Affairs.

The Rt. Hon. A. Duff Cooper, M.P., Secretary of State for War.

The Prime Minister arriving at No. 10
Downing Street after his holiday in
France for the special Cabinet meeting
called to discuss the Abyssinia crisis,
September 1935.

'You know you can trust me!'
This cartoon by David Low appeared in
the *Evening Standard* on 20 December
1935 following the abortive Hoare-Laval
agreement designed to end the war
between Italy and Abyssinia. Hoare,
who resigned as Foreign Secretary, is
shown as having assaulted the League of
Nations, while Baldwin appeals once
more for public confidence.
By permission of the Evening Standard.

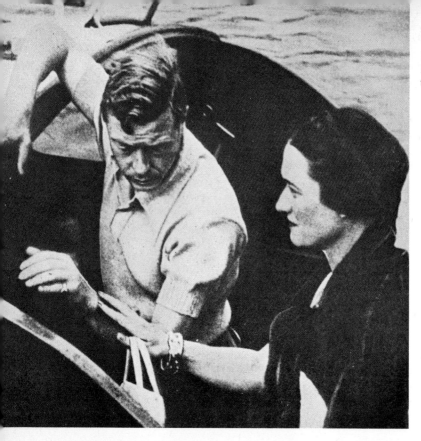

King Edward VIII and Mrs Simpson on holiday the summer of 1936.

Fort Belvedere. The crucial discussions between Baldwin and the King on the Abdication took place here, December 1936.

The Prime Minister leaving 10 Downing Street during the Abdication crisis, followed (*above*) by Sir John Simon and (*below*) by Mr Walter Monckton, the King's legal adviser.

Geoffrey Dawson, editor of *The Times*, and Lady Astor during the Abdication crisis.

Cosmo Gordon Lang, Archbishop of Canterbury.

THE CHOICE.
The Prime Minister: "All the peoples of your Empire, Sir, sympathise with you most deeply;
but they all know – as you yourself must – that the Throne is greater than the man."
Cartoon by Sir Bernard Partridge, *Punch*, 16 December 1936.
From the artist's proof in the possession of Mr D. Pepys-Whiteley.

"Happily ever after."
The Duke and Duchess of Windsor at the time of their wedding in France, June 1937.

...ceiving a farewell gift from his ...cessor, Neville Chamberlain, May ...7.

...ce I leave, I leave. I am not going to ...k to the man on the bridge, and I am ...going to spit on the deck.'

With his wife and Anthony Eden in the South of France, March 1938.

Addressing members at the Dr. Barnardo's Home meeting at the Central Hall, Westminster in 1943. Also on the platform are Lady Baldwin and the Bishop of Salisbury.

it was from Oliver Baldwin proposing himself for lunch on Sunday. One bag came from No. 10 and it had one letter in it. It was from Halifax and dealt with the Cabinet reshuffle consequent on Jim Thomas's resignation.' On the question of Cabinet changes, Baldwin intimated that these would be kept to a minimum, having seen Neville Chamberlain on the subject just before he left for Chequers. 'We both agreed we do not want a big reshuffle of offices now. There'll have to be one within a year. To do so now would mean a pack of troubles then. Of course, the Whips are always wanting jobs for our fellows. Margesson wants to move Ormsby-Gore to Colonies and put Philip Sassoon at the Office of Works because he's not strong enough for the Air Ministry. But we can't do that now. He'll have to hold on.' In the event Ormsby-Gore did immediately follow Thomas at the Colonial Office, being himself succeeded as Works Minister by Earl Stanhope, one of the Under-Secretaries at the Foreign Office, who now entered the Cabinet, while Sassoon continued to be Under-Secretary for Air as before. Baldwin's Cabinet now consisted of fifteen Conservatives, four Liberal National Members and two National Labour.

Baldwin also spoke of his own future and told Jones that he intended to retire after the Coronation, which had been fixed for 12 May 1937.* 'The 13th had been proposed,' he said, 'but the superstitious Queen [Mary] got it changed. The Czar Nicholas was crowned on a 13th.' He went on:

Ramsay will cling on till then. He floats around like a wraith. He held on as PM till the Jubilee and will hold on now as Lord President till the Coronation. I have heard of carrying on with a sack of flour fastened to your back; Ramsay is an eiderdown round my head . . .

After the Coronation, Lucy and I will go for a rest to France, perhaps to Brittany, and then we might go and see John Buchan in Canada, and I'd like to see South Africa. Australia and New Zealand are too far.

Religion still played a great part in his life, Baldwin told Jones, and he spoke 'quite simply but intensely of his belief that God could still make use of him', although 'as one grew old, one's prayers became shorter – just sighs and interjections'. The thought kept recurring to him that so far at least he had kept the country out of war. 'For three days I had terrible anxiety when Germany re-entered the demilitarised zone, and there were people clamouring that we should occupy the Rhineland.' He had found

* The date was approved by the King at a special meeting of the Privy Council held at Buckingham Palace on 28 May 1936.

that Halifax and Bridgeman 'talked the same language' as he did. 'My other colleagues don't.'

Jones begged him to realise that 'there was one big thing more he could do before he went – achieve an understanding with Germany', urging him to leave home affairs to Neville Chamberlain and 'give his whole mind to this foreign business'.

'What are we to do?' asked Baldwin.

First of all, said Jones, it was a mistake to underestimate Ribbentrop's influence and write him down as an ass because he did not adopt orthodox procedure. 'At the very least he is a reliable telephone from Hitler and the likelihood is that he is much more.' Secondly, if it was British policy 'to get alongside Germany', the sooner the Francophile ambassador Sir Eric Phipps was transferred from Berlin elsewhere the better. 'He should be replaced by a man of the D'Abernon or Willingdon type, unhampered by professional diplomatic tradition, able of course to speak German, and to enter with sympathetic interest into Hitler's aspirations.' As for the Fuehrer, Jones assured the Prime Minister: 'Hitler believes in you, and believes that only you in this country can bring about the reorientation of England, France and Germany which he desires. He wants to meet you to tell you this face to face. This secret visit should be arranged without too much delay, and a communiqué issued shortly after saying it had taken place.' The fact was that Hitler 'felt quite unequal to standing up alone to Russia', he was worried by the way in which the Soviet Union and Czecho-slovakia were concerting a joint air policy, and 'he is therefore asking for an alliance with us to form a bulwark against the spread of Communism'.

Baldwin seemed impressed by these arguments and, as Jones put it, 'not indisposed to attempt this as a final effort before he resigns after the Coronation next year to make way for Neville Chamberlain'. He asked his guest to repeat for Mrs Baldwin's benefit the story of his visit to Hitler. ('My wife and I are one.') This Jones did 'with gusto', seizing the op-portunity to stress some of the points in Hitler's message so that Baldwin interrupted his game of patience to listen.

Discussion followed on the projected meeting of the two leaders. Would Hitler be willing to fly and land at Chequers or in Thanet? S.B. did not fly and did not like the sea. Could the meeting wait till August when S.B. could go by car to some mountainous rendezvous? Then some more Malvern water, and to bed.[69]

While Tom Jones was enjoying a frugal week-end at Chequers, Lord Winterton, who had been a junior minister in the first two Baldwin governments and, having been excluded from the National Government, had become somewhat discontented – 'a finicky goat', 'Chips' Channon called him – was entertaining a party at his country house in Sussex, which included several other critical back-bench friends, Austen Chamberlain, Winston Churchill, Henry Page Croft and Edward Grigg. News of the party leaked out to the press, and on the Monday morning several sensational news stories appeared to the effect that the 'House Party', as its members were dubbed by the parliamentary lobby correspondents, had constituted themselves into a kind of Shadow Cabinet for the purpose of plotting the downfall of the Baldwin Government. These stories were greatly exaggerated, but they had some effect upon the Prime Minister since shortly afterwards he was moved to remark in the House that it was 'the time of year when midges come out of dirty ditches'.

During the succeeding days there were some hectic comings and goings between Jones and Ribbentrop in an endeavour to fix up a secret summit meeting between Baldwin and Hitler. Ribbentrop assured Jones that he could arrange for Hitler to come quite close to the south coast, two or three miles from Dover or Folkestone and the meeting could take place on board ship. At the same time Jones emphasised that Baldwin would wish to have Eden with him in order to balance Ribbentrop. Baldwin also toyed with the idea of going to Berlin accompanied by Eden, as he favoured an open rather than a secret meeting. On Ribbentrop pressing for a decision, Jones got hold of Horace Wilson, who had been seconded by the Treasury for service with the Prime Minister, and persuaded him to fix a meeting with Baldwin and Eden. The four men met late on the evening of 16 June in the Prime Minister's room in the House of Commons. Eden did most of the talking and it was quite plain from the outset that he resented the use of unofficial rather than the normal Foreign Office channels.

'The Prime Minister sat almost silent throughout,' noted Jones. 'But what little he did mutter showed a faint desire not to let slip altogether the chance of meeting Hitler. I caught sight of him one moment and thought he looked an incredibly old man.' Jones had learned from Ribbentrop that the answer to the British questionnaire was now with Hitler and it could easily be handed to Baldwin at the meeting. Also Ribbentrop was going to stay with the Fuehrer and wished to know what he could say to him. 'He was afraid Hitler would think we were playing with him and delaying the reply for some sinister reason,' said Jones.

In view of Eden's strongly expressed objections to the idea of a summit, the project was dropped and nothing further came of it. 'I have taken the matter as far as I can, without damage I hope to the cause we both have so much at heart,' Jones wrote to Ribbentrop two days later, 'and my task is done.' However, he did attempt to revive it when he heard that Baldwin was wondering whether it would be safe in view of the prevalent Popular Front troubles in France to go to Aix for their usual holiday in August. 'I suppose Lucy could find a good place for her treatment in Germany,' Baldwin remarked to Jones. The latter jumped at the idea and told the Prime Minister that if he could say the word he 'would have everything arranged at once, hotel, car, etc.'. But Baldwin shied away from this when it came to the point. 'He would have to ask our Ambassador in Paris,' Jones noted. 'I said the answer was a foregone conclusion.' [70]

Towards the end of June, Baldwin was told by his doctor that if he wished to last out until the summer recess he must have an immediate week's complete rest. Accordingly he went down to Chequers. While he was there, the faithful John Davidson wrote to him that even among his 'most devoted supporters' in the House of Commons there was a vague feeling that there was some truth in the accusation of 'lack of Cabinet control by the PM.' Davidson thought too there was a feeling that 'the inactivity of your colleagues in your support' confirmed this criticism. 'Every mongrel is yapping, believing that a very tired fox has gone to ground at Chequers, with no fight left in him,' Davidson went on. 'It must be remembered that the attack has developed on a wider front than hitherto because all the critics, from the extreme Socialist to the disgruntled elements in the Conservative Party, are combining their various motives to bring you down either in order to force an election or to get a reconstruction under Neville more favourable to the Right Wing of our Party.' [71]

The Prime Minister's temporary withdrawal to Chequers was widely noticed in the press and gave rise to an abundant crop of rumours that he was contemplating an early retirement, possibly before the summer recess and certainly in the autumn. However, he soon showed that he was not yet at the end of his resources. On 2 July he returned to London in order to be entertained with a dinner by the City Conservative Association. The same afternoon he put in an unexpected appearance in the House of Commons when he received a great ovation on taking his place on a crowded Treasury Bench between Chamberlain and Simon.

He was immediately questioned by a Labour Member about a speech made during his absence by Lord Londonderry at a Conservative meeting at Newcastle upon Tyne to the effect that the statement made by Baldwin in Parliament in November 1934 that he had been misled by Londonderry and his advisers at the Air Ministry with regard to the pace of German rearmament in the air was incorrect. All he had meant, the Prime Minister explained in a characteristically deft reply, which incidentally had been drafted for him by Londonderry with Simon's help, was that the acceleration of Germany's air armament had exceeded even the expert Air Ministry estimates. ('A reference to the statement made by Lord Londonderry in another place at the same time as my statement in the House of Commons shows that both of us meant that the German acceleration had been far greater than we and our advisers had anticipated.') There was therefore no foundation for any supposition that he (Baldwin) had disregarded warnings given by his advisers in 1934; on the other hand, in saying that he and the Government had been misled, he had not intended to cast any reflection upon any department or individual. The matter was closed with a statement from Londonderry later the same day to the effect that he was 'satisfied' with what the Prime Minister had said and did not wish to say any more himself.*

However, there was one member of the House of Commons who was far from satisfied, and that was Winston Churchill, who wished the House to go into secret session for the purpose of discussing the whole defence situation. 'Baldwin seems to have recovered and entered the lists again,' he wrote on 3 July to Austen Chamberlain, 'and there can be no reason why the necessary public action should not proceed.'

> We do not wish to know all the secrets of defence. Indeed all I want is to be able to debate the defence position with the same freedom as was possible in less dangerous years, and to receive answers from the Government which they would certainly give in ordinary times. I think I can make a considerable case that a secret non-reported session would enable a far more searching debate to take place upon defence, particularly air defence, than is possible in public, and that little more would be known than what is current talk in the Smoking Room and the Lobbies.

However Churchill's request was turned down by Baldwin and Neville Chamberlain on the ground that 'it would cause endless alarm'. Acting with Austen Chamberlain, Churchill then set about organising a deputation of senior Conservatives to the Prime Minister, which Neville Chamberlain told his brother he would look on sympathetically.[72]

---

* Recalling the incident three years later, Londonderry wrote to Baldwin (20 May 1939) about his speech at Newcastle: 'There was a hue and cry, as perhaps you will remember, and a question in the House. You were ill at Chequers and Simon sent for me. I was rather truculent as I felt I had been infamously treated; however, after some conversation, I eventually drafted a colourless reply with Simon. You came up from Chequers and just read out the reply I had drafted. That was an opportunity when you could have helped me a lot, but somehow you have never given me a thought unless just comparatively lately, when I have forced myself upon you.' Londonderry Papers.

Both Londonderry's attack and Davidson's letter were probably on his mind when Baldwin lunched alone with Tom Jones in Downing Street a few days later and complained to him of 'the day-to-day badgering' to which he was subjected in Parliament.

'Why do you attend so much?' asked Jones.

'It is very important that I should do so,' Baldwin replied. 'The House is very jealous. You remember how L.G. lost touch with it. I cannot very well go to the Lords and lead from there after keeping Curzon out.' He added that he had read a letter which Amery had written to *The Times* pleading for a small Cabinet whose members should be free of all departmental responsibilities; he sympathised, but at this stage in his political career he felt powerless to do anything about it.

I have told Neville he may be able to do something. I cannot. In the War those outside the inner group were restive and rebellious. I've urged Neville to get rid of all the tired men when he succeeds me. Ramsay is useless . . . A Prime Minister for the first time can do all sorts of things that later he will not be able to do. I am too tired for any fresh effort.[73]

9

By this time Baldwin was on the verge of a nervous breakdown. The secretaries in Downing Street complained that it was impossible to get a decision on anything out of him and with Jones's help they conspired with Lord Dawson of Penn to pack him off for a quiet holiday as soon as Parliament rose. To accommodate him for the first month Jones was able to borrow Gregynog Hall, a comfortable mansion in Montgomeryshire and the headquarters of a private press of the same name in which Jones was the moving spirit. After this Lord Lothian offered to put Blickling, his place in Norfolk and one of the finest Jacobean houses in the country, at Baldwin's disposal. Lunching at No. 10 on 27 July, Jones found the Prime Minister 'extraordinarily cheerful' at the prospect of a holiday in Wales. 'He had bought half a dozen of Bartholomew's maps, had been studying roads and contours, reading up the early history of the county, which is called Baldwinshire in Welsh, and planning visits to the Bridgemans, and Clement Davies, MP, at Meifod. Were there any books at Gregynog? Any shockers – as he liked to start off his holiday with them?'[74]

Two official matters particularly engaged Baldwin's attention before he left London three days later for Chequers *en route* to Wales. The first was the

unfortunate affair of Sir Christopher Bullock, the brilliant Permanent
Secretary to the Air Ministry. Early in July Baldwin had been obliged
to appoint a board of inquiry consisting of three senior civil servants to
investigate allegations that Bullock had misused his official position to
carry on discussions with representatives of the Imperial Airways Corporation including the chairman Sir Eric Geddes with a view to his eventually succeeding to the latter's position. The board worked at speed,
holding a dozen meetings inside a month and examining various witnesses
including Londonderry, Swinton, Geddes and Sir Warren Fisher, the head
of the civil service. The board's findings, published as a Government White
Paper, were to the effect that Bullock's conduct was 'completely at
variance with the tenor and spirit of the code which in their view precludes
a member of the Civil Service from interlacing public negotiations entrusted to him with the advancement of his personal or private interests'.
These findings were endorsed by Neville Chamberlain and Swinton before
the file reached Baldwin who could only do likewise. Baldwin then had to
decide what was to happen to Bullock. Sir Warren Fisher, whom Baldwin
naturally consulted since he was technically Bullock's superior, advised
that he should be dismissed from the service, and to this the Prime
Minister agreed, as he subsequently admitted, 'with considerable misgivings'. At the same time he added in the minute directing Bullock's
dismissal that he was 'glad to observe that, grave as was the offence from
the service point of view, no question of corruption was involved'.[75]

No doubt, in giving the advice he did, Fisher considered that he was
acting in the best interests of the civil service. On the other hand, he was
known to dislike Bullock intensely and it is difficult to resist the conclusion
that his advice was not wholly disinterested. Londonderry, who had been
Bullock's political chief, felt strongly about this and he also blamed
Baldwin for the way in which he used to send for Bullock when Londonderry was Air Minister.

> Incidentally, you destroyed little Bullock, because you gave him an
> entirely wrong idea of his own importance, which eventually brought
> him to grief. That story is a very sad one, and I do think that Swinton
> and you should have saved him, because he was most unjustly treated
> and was the victim of the inveterate hatred of a civil servant [Sir
> Warren Fisher] who never should have been allowed to encompass his
> downfall as he undoubtedly did.[76]

The incident affords an example of an unfortunate decision being made
by a man who was too tired 'to probe below the surface at the time', as

his Parliamentary Private Secretary Geoffrey Lloyd subsequently put it. 'Many years afterwards he did so,' Mr Lloyd was to say at Bullock's memorial service in 1972, 'and being one of the fairest and most honourable of men, wrote to one of his successors,' probably Clement Attlee, since an attempt was made without success after the last war to reopen the case and clear Bullock's name. What Baldwin wrote was:

> I feel it only right to say that, if I had had the full evidence before me which has now been made available, I should not have taken the decision I reluctantly did.[77]

The second business matter with which Baldwin had to deal before his holiday was a large parliamentary deputation consisting of senior Conservative members of both Houses, mostly Privy Councillors who sat on the back benches, led by Austen Chamberlain from the Commons and Salisbury from the Lords, with the purpose of putting forward their views on the relative state of British and German armaments. However, the moving spirit behind the deputation was Churchill who, as has been seen, really organised it in default of the secret session of the Commons he had wanted. In addition, he had appealed to Attlee in the Labour Party and Archibald Sinclair among the Liberals with the object of making it an all-Party affair, but they had declined to be represented. Besides Churchill and the two nominal leaders, the deputation, eighteen strong in all, included FitzAlan, Trenchard and Lloyd from the Lords, and Horne, Amery, Moore-Brabazon, Admiral Sir Roger Keyes, and Winterton and the other members of the 'House Party' from the Commons. They were formally introduced by Austen Chamberlain, and their case was put by Churchill who spoke for over an hour. With Baldwin were Halifax and Inskip, as well as representatives of the Committee of Imperial Defence, but unfortunately not Neville Chamberlain, who had already gone on holiday.

'This was a great occasion,' was how Churchill was to describe it in *The Gathering Storm*.

> I cannot recall anything like it in what I have seen of British public life. The group of eminent men, with no thought of personal advantage, but whose lives had been centred upon public affairs, represented a weight of Conservative opinion which could not easily be disregarded. If the leaders of the Labour and Liberal Oppositions had come with us, there might have been a political situation so tense as to enforce remedial action. The proceedings occupied three or four

hours on each of two successive days. I have always said Mr Baldwin was a good listener. He certainly seemed to listen with the greatest interest and attention.

Churchill drew a lurid picture of the strength of the German air force which he put at nearer 2,000 than 1,500, the British Air Ministry's estimate of German first-line strength, and he believed that German industry was so organised that it could certainly produce 'at full blast' 1,000 machines a month and increase the number as time went on. Then there was the menace of the incendiary or 'thermite' bomb, 'little bigger than an orange'. A single medium aircraft could scatter 500 of these incendiaries and 'one must expect in a small raid literally tens of thousands of these bombs which burn through from storey to storey', with consequent dislocation of essential services such as water, gas, light and telephones. There might be a vast exodus of the population which would present the Government with problems of public order, sanitation and food supply. 'We must accelerate and simplify our aeroplane production and push it to the largest scale,' he concluded. 'We are in danger, as we have never been in danger before – no, not even at the height of the submarine campaign [in 1917].' [78]

After everyone had had his say, Baldwin invited the delegation to meet him and Inskip again after the recess when he promised them a considered statement on the situation. At the same time he reminded his listeners of the 'pacific' if not 'pacifist' feeling in the country after the war, as expressed by the East Fulham election and the Peace Ballot, and what his own policy had been. His remarks can perhaps best be described as a brief but masterly exposition of the art of the possible.

It was a question in 1934 whether, if you tried to do much, you might have imperilled and more than imperilled – you might have lost – the General Election when it came. I personally felt that very strongly, and the one thing in my mind was the necessity of winning an election as soon as you could and *getting a perfectly free hand with arms*. That was the first thing to do in a democracy, and I think we did it at the first moment possible . . .

We fought the election, and we won it and won it more handsomely than anyone in this room, I think, would have expected before the election. That was a great thing done. It was done, and you had the support of the democracy for your armaments.

'I am not,' Baldwin concluded, 'going to get this country into a war with anybody for the League of Nations or anybody else or for anything else. If there is any fighting in Europe to be done, I should like to see the Bolshies and the Nazis doing it.'

'I certainly do not consider war with Germany inevitable,' said Churchill by way of summing up, 'but I am sure the way to make it much less likely is to afford concrete evidence of our determination in setting about rearmament.'

'I am with you there wholeheartedly,' Baldwin agreed as the deputation dispersed.[79]

Next morning, Baldwin left Downing Street for Chequers to begin the long holiday he had been ordered by his doctor to take. Before continuing his journey to Wales, Dawson came down to examine him and make a cardiograph. 'It was a funny performance,' he wrote to Mimi Davidson.

> I sat as if I were going to be electrocuted, in a chair with wires attached to both arms and one leg. Anyway my heart is sound and doesn't show any signs of one of the sixty-five ailments which may be revealed by the instrument.
>
> But I am to go very easy and try to lose sense of time, and he forbids me to go to any Cabinet committees this month or to Cabinets in September. He says three months is the least time I ought to have, and if I go to any meetings of that kind it will undo all the good of the rest . . .
>
> I'm quite all right, but tired right out with no desire to move.[80]

After a week in Wales, he wrote ecstatically to Jones:

> What a country! What peace! And what a healing air! I am soaking in the Welsh spirit and if I don't make a lovely speech about 'em one day, I'll eat my hat.
>
> I am not bothering about excursions for there will be time enough, if I live, later on. But I am going about a bit, chiefly to lunch with any-body who has a beautiful garden or view . . . Eden is coming for a night and two or three old friends singly. I am quietly happy and only worry at intervals.
>
> I spent a good hour at your Press yesterday . . . They seem such a jolly family: I told the binder I wish we could change places but he seemed content with his own lovely vocation . . .

'I wrote to Lothian,' Baldwin concluded this letter. 'What a parasite I am! But I like it.' Thus when Jones saw him at Blickling in the middle of

September, Baldwin spoke of Gregynog as 'the most peaceful holiday in his life'. Although he was walking with the aid of a stick, due to lumbago – his masseur had paid him three visits from London, which was expensive, he complained – he admitted to being much better. 'Now I see that I shall shortly be shouldering things again,' he told Jones. 'It is responsibility that kills. That is where you are lucky. It broke Bonar in 1921. I'll stay here until the end of the month, then we go to Hatfield and on to stay with Edmund Talbot [Lord FitzAlan] at Cumberland Lodge, Windsor, and back to town about [October] the 12th. I've got four good administrators – Neville, Sam, Swinton and Kingsley [Wood]. I'm doubtful about Duff Cooper. Must try him out for a year, and then Neville can decide whether to carry him on.'[81]

Baldwin's need to rest served as a good excuse for not attending the annual Conservative Party Conference which met at Margate. His place was taken by Neville Chamberlain, who had been deputising for him during the recess. Addressing the customary mass meeting at the end of the conference, he eulogised his ailing leader who, he said, had 'raised the whole tone of our political life'. Chamberlain also spoke of the need for intensified rearmament and of the civil war which had broken out in Spain, and in which, unlike Germany and Soviet Russia, the British and French Governments refused to intervene. 'The main result [of the party conference] appears to be a general acceptance of my position as heir-apparent,' Chamberlain noted in his diary, adding that he was 'sending for people and endeavouring to conduct business as if I were PM'.[82]

On leaving Blickling, Baldwin and his wife travelled north to spend a few days with two old friends Lord Richard and Lady Moyra Cavendish. The Cavendishes lived on the borders of Lancashire and Westmorland at Holker Hall, Cark-in-Cartmel, which was set in fine scenery overlooking Morecambe Bay. His companion on one of his walks in the neighbourhood thought that he seemed worried about the future, since he interrupted a talk about the beauty of the Westmorland fells to say: 'I cannot think what is happening to me. I seem to be losing the use of my legs.' Then he expressed the same feeling that he had confided some months previously to Tom Jones. 'It's the unbearable responsibility that gets me down.'

As he spoke, the Prime Minister stood gazing at the hills, 'so that his companion began to feel like an intruder'.[83]

ELEVEN

'THE KING'S MATTER'

I

Baldwin returned to Downing Street on 12 October 1936. To his surprise he found a pile of correspondence and cuttings from American newspapers awaiting his attention. They were all concerned with the King's association with Mrs Simpson and they included a large number of unconventional photographs of the King and his friend taken on a recent holiday cruise in the Mediterranean for which purpose he had chartered the millionairess Lady Yule's luxury yacht *Nahlin* and had invited the Duff Coopers and other friends as well as Mrs Simpson. The photographs showed the King and Mrs Simpson constantly together, one of them with her hand on his arm; they were also seen in the midst of cheering crowds at the various ports of call or bathing together on the secluded beaches of the Dalmatian coast. The Hearst newspapers ran a serialised version of her life story, while *Time* magazine crudely called her 'Queen Wally'. These accounts were interlaced with a good deal of spicy gossip, it being said that as soon as the Simpsons had been divorced the King intended to marry her. By contrast the British press generally maintained a discreet silence, although there was no knowing how long they would continue to do so.

On his return to England in the middle of September, the King had continued the royal tradition of spending some weeks at Balmoral; but instead of inviting Cabinet ministers, archbishops, admirals and the like, as had previously been the custom, he had filled the castle with his personal friends, whose stay including that of Mrs Simpson was duly published at the King's wish in the *Court Circular*. Declining to open a new wing of a hospital in Aberdeen on the pretext that he was still in mourning for his father, the King delegated the task to his brother the Duke of York, who was presumably also in mourning, and while this ceremony was taking place he was seen meeting Mrs Simpson off the London train at Ballater station.

His behaviour caused considerable offence in local circles, besides being commented upon most unfavourably in some of the letters which accompanied the American news cuttings.

One of the first people Baldwin saw on his arrival in London was the Foreign Secretary Anthony Eden, who called to bring him up to date on the international scene, particularly the civil war in Spain where Eden acting on his own initiative had applied an embargo on the supply of arms and aircraft from Britain. Baldwin listened for a while to what Eden had to say and then his attention began to wander, an attitude of apparent unconcern which exasperated the Foreign Secretary. At one point in Eden's dissertation, Baldwin interrupted by asking: 'Have you had any letters about the King?'

'No, not so far as I know,' answered Eden somewhat taken aback. 'Why should I have?'

'Well,' Baldwin went on, 'I wish you would inquire. I expect that you have had some. I fear we may have difficulties there.' Then, after a moment's pause for reflection, he added: 'I hope that you will try not to trouble me too much with foreign affairs just now.'

Eden was astonished, suspecting, as he subsequently recalled, that 'it was another example of Baldwin's reluctance to face the unpleasant realities which were our daily fare at the Foreign Office'. However, he was wrong. When he got back to his private office, Eden found that there had been letters from overseas similar to those addressed to Baldwin in critical strain, and these were now shown to him.[1]

On 14 October the King sent for Baldwin, who went to Buckingham Palace for what turned out to be an ordinary routine audience. The King discussed a visit which he intended to make to the Home Fleet at Portland in the following month and they had some talk about the unresolved controversial question of whether the Fleet Air Arm should be under the control of the Admiralty or the Air Ministry. The King did not mention Mrs Simpson and his intentions with regard to her. Nor did Baldwin raise the subject. However, before he left the Palace he confided his anxieties to the King's Private Secretary, Major Alexander Hardinge, later Lord Hardinge of Penshurst. Hardinge, son of a former Viceroy of India, and an Old Harrovian like Baldwin, was a courtier of the old school, who had been Assistant Private Secretary to the late King for fifteen years, after serving in the Grenadier Guards during the First World War. When Wigram resigned as Private Secretary, which he did early in the new reign because (so he told Baldwin) he found the King's 'temper and habits so irregular', he was succeeded by Hardinge after Godfrey Thomas had declined the post.[2] Hardinge now told Baldwin that sooner or later he would as the

King's Prime Minister have to intervene. Baldwin agreed but hoped that it could be 'staved off until after the Coronation'.

In view of the charge which was subsequently made against Baldwin, and widely believed, that he was the leading figure in a conspiracy to remove the King from the throne – the other two alleged conspirators being Geoffrey Dawson, the editor of *The Times*, and Cosmo Lang, the Archbishop of Canterbury – what Hardinge wrote looking back nineteen years later is of some interest:

> The fact is that, throughout the summer of 1936, far from Mr Baldwin plotting to get rid of King Edward VIII, it was seemingly impossible to persuade him to address his mind at all to the serious position which we, who were in the King's personal service, knew to be developing. At that time the Prime Minister's natural reluctance to interfere in the private life of the Sovereign, in spite of pressure that was always considerable, was reinforced by the fact that no constitutional issue could arise as long as Mrs Simpson remained married to Mr Simpson. Moreover, it had to be admitted that there was as yet nothing concrete on which any representation could be based.[3]

The very next day after Baldwin saw Hardinge, the sense of urgency was considerably increased by the news that the divorce petition which Mrs Simpson had filed against her husband, on the grounds of his misconduct with another woman at a hotel in Bray, near Windsor, was due to be heard at Ipswich Assizes within the next fortnight. The choice of this small county town as the venue for the hearing was not due to the petitioner's desire to avoid publicity, as has often been wrongly stated, but simply because the court lists in London were full for a year or more, and Mrs Simpson and the King were both anxious to have the matter disposed of before the Coronation. It is true that, had the petition been filed in the London divorce registry, the hearing could have been 'expedited', but this would have involved a special application to a divorce court judge and might well have led to embarrassing questions. At all events the case was set down for hearing on 27 October at Ipswich, and Mrs Simpson had already installed herself in a small house in nearby Felixstowe so as to fulfil the court's jurisdictional requirements of local residence.

With Baldwin's return to London, the weekly Wednesday meetings of the Cabinet were resumed. Ministers' social engagements were rarely allowed to interfere with these meetings, so that when Sir Samuel Hoare received an invitation from the King to spend several days at Sandringham for partridge shooting, he went to Baldwin, assuming that the Prime Minister would wish him to refuse. To Hoare's surprise, Baldwin told him that he must certainly accept the invitation. 'Your visit may be very helpful,' he went on. 'Do what you can to convince the King that the divorce proceedings that are due at Ipswich at the end of the month must be dropped, and try to persuade him to give up the idea of marriage altogether.'[4]

Hoare agreed, but 'with the uneasy feeling that the lady's divorce and the King's marriage were very unsuitable subjects for conversation at a friendly shooting party'. To Hoare's relief, he was spared this distasteful task by the initiative which Baldwin himself took shortly afterwards.

The visit which Baldwin had planned to pay Lord FitzAlan at Cumberland Lodge, in Windsor Great Park, took place during the weekend of 16–19 October. Also invited were Lord Salisbury, Lord Kemsley, the newspaper proprietor, and the Duke of Norfolk, FitzAlan's nephew and like him a leading Roman Catholic layman, who as hereditary Earl Marshal was responsible for the arrangements for the Coronation. Not unexpectedly the main topic of conversation was what came to be known as 'the King's matter', a phrase which originated with the Archbishop of Canterbury.

Shortly after his arrival on the Friday evening, Baldwin received a request from Hardinge to see him. They met next morning, when the King's Private Secretary urged the Prime Minister to approach His Majesty without delay so that he would not be able to say that he had not been warned of the implications of the pending divorce suit. Hardinge begged Baldwin to try and stop the divorce and tell the King not to flaunt his association with Mrs Simpson in public. Baldwin promised to think it over; and, although he did not relish the prospect of broaching the subject with the King, he finally agreed to do so. The same night he told Hardinge that he would try to see the King next morning. However, when he telephoned Fort Belvedere he learned that the King had already left for Sandringham, although he had not been expected to do so until Sunday afternoon. Baldwin therefore asked the Private Secretary to fix up an appointment. Repeated calls to Sandringham throughout Sunday elicited the reply that His Majesty had not arrived. In fact, he did not do so until four o'clock on Monday morning, having (so Baldwin correctly surmised) spent the intervening period with 'the lady' at Felixstowe.

Before leaving Cumberland Lodge, Baldwin asked Lord Kemsley if he could have a word with him. They retired to the library where Baldwin, having gone over the ground, asked Kemsley what he thought the effect of the King's intentions would be upon public opinion when they became known.

'Prime Minister,' Kemsley replied, 'the Nonconformist conscience is not dead.'

Baldwin laughed. 'I believe you ought to be in charge of this, not I,' he told Kemsley as they parted.[5]

Meanwhile Hardinge had left an urgent message at Sandringham for the King to telephone him at Windsor as soon as possible. When the King eventually got through to his Private Secretary, on the Monday morning, he learned that the Prime Minister wished to see him 'on an important and urgent matter'. The King's immediate reaction was one of surprise, since they had met only a few days previously and Baldwin had raised nothing of any particular urgency then. 'Well,' said the King, 'if it is all that important, let him come here – to Sandringham.' After a few moments' hesitation, Hardinge told the King that Mr Baldwin was quite prepared to do this, but his sudden appearance in the midst of a shooting party was almost certain to excite comment and speculation, and he thought it wiser if they could meet at Sunningdale. 'The Prime Minister regrets putting Your Majesty to this inconvenience,' Hardinge added. 'But he stresses the importance of secrecy, and hopes you will be able to receive him at The Fort on Tuesday.'[6]

The King agreed and told Hardinge to fix the meeting for 11.30 on Tuesday, 20 October, as he intended to leave Sandringham early the same morning. But on second thoughts he decided to fortify himself for the interview with a good night's sleep at Fort Belvedere, and accordingly he drove back there on Monday afternoon, having told his Private Secretary to change the time of the appointment to 10.30.

2

Baldwin motored over from Chequers to Fort Belvedere. 'It was a most beautiful morning, and St Luke's Day,' he afterwards told Tom Jones, to whom he gave a full account of the meeting, 'and I felt like a physician.'[7] When he reached The Fort, in the King's words, 'crunching up the drive in a tiny black car which did not seem half big enough for him', Baldwin found His Majesty talking to one of the gardeners. This gave the Prime Minister his opening cue. 'Friendly, casual, discursive,' the King recalled afterwards, 'he might have been a neighbour who had called to discuss a dispute over a boundary fence. He complimented me upon the beauty of the grounds, the arrangement of the garden, the silvery radiance of the birch trees, and the delicacy of the autumn tints.' The King then led the way to the octagonal drawing-room, where they sat down in front of the fire, Baldwin in an armchair and the King on a sofa.[8]

Warned in advance by Hardinge what to expect, the King sat and listened, while the Prime Minister did most of the talking. Although outwardly calm and composed, Baldwin occasionally showed some nervousness and at one stage in the conversation asked, almost apologetically: 'Sir, do you think I could have a whisky and soda? I do not find this conversation exactly an easy one to carry on.'

The King was somewhat startled by the request for a drink so early in the day. However, he rang the bell and when the butler answered it he told him to bring some whisky. A minute or two later the butler reappeared with a tray containing a decanter and two glasses which he placed on a table behind the sofa. Baldwin got up and went over to the table where he picked up the decanter and began to pour some whisky into one of the glasses. Looking inquiringly at the King, he asked: 'Sir, when?'

'No, thank you, Mr Baldwin,' the King replied gravely and, as he hoped, even severely. 'I never take a drink before seven o'clock in the evening.'

According to the King, the Prime Minister seemed to give a slight start, then went ahead and poured his own drink. A little later the Prime Minister produced his pipe and tobacco pouch. The King followed his example. Soon both men were puffing away, and, as the King noted, the familiar reciprocal action seemed to put Baldwin at his ease.

Baldwin began the conversation by reminding the King that when they met in Downing Street on the eve of the late King's death, the King had been good enough to say he was glad that Baldwin was his Prime Minister and counsellor. Did he still think so? The King nodded his assent. Baldwin then recalled their earlier meeting during George V's illness in 1928. 'You remember, Sir, when we came up from Folkestone together, you said I might speak freely to you about everything. Does that hold good when there is a woman in the case?' Again the King replied: 'Yes.'

The Prime Minister went on to tell the King that he liked him as a man, altogether apart from his qualities as a king. Indeed, he regarded him as an admirable monarch for the transition period the country was going through. 'You have all the advantages that a man can have,' said the Prime Minister. 'You are young. You have before you the example of your father and you are fond of your home. You are fond of your house and you like children. You have only one disadvantage. You are not married and you should be.'

The King made no comment, upon which Baldwin remarked that since the war morals had gone to pieces a good deal in every country. 'You may think me Victorian, Sir,' he said. 'You may think my views are out of date, but I believe I know how to interpret the minds of my own people; and I say, although it is true that standards are lower since the war, it only leads the people to expect a higher standard from their King. People expect more from their King than they did a hundred years ago.' Then, after a short pause, during which the King said nothing, Baldwin added: 'People are talking about you and this American woman Mrs Simpson.'

The King continued silent, so Baldwin went on: 'I get a large correspondence at Downing Street. Usually I see very little of it unless my secretaries draw my attention to anything unusual. Before I went away there was little or nothing about your relations with Mrs Simpson. On my return I found the position changed, and there was a great deal. Samples of it I have with me in this folder.'

He indicated the folder which he had been carrying and continued: 'I have had many nasty letters written by people who respected your father but who don't like the way you are going on. The American newspapers are full of it and even the Chinese vernacular newspapers are carrying stories about your behaviour.' The effect of such comment in the American press, he remarked, would be to sap the position of the throne in the world unless it were stopped.

Finally, Baldwin came to the point. 'I don't believe you can go on like this and get away with it.'

This prompted the King to break his silence. 'What do you mean, not get away with it?' he asked.

Baldwin, who had deliberately used the phrase, as he knew it to be a favourite of the King's, replied: 'I think you know our people. They'll tolerate a lot in private life, but they will not stand for this kind of thing in the life of a public personage, and when they read in the *Court Circular* of Mrs Simpson's visit to Balmoral they resented it.'

The King bridled at this remark. 'The lady is my friend and I do not wish to let her in by the back door, but quite openly.' It was now Baldwin's turn to be silent, so the King added: 'I hope you will agree that I have carried out my duties as King with dignity.'

'I do agree,' the Prime Minister assured him, 'and all the more as I know that the duties of royalty are not much to your liking.'

'I know there is nothing kingly about me,' said the King almost pathetically, 'but I have tried to mix with the people and make them think that I was one of them.'

At that moment Baldwin felt sorry for the King. But this did not deter him from pressing home the point of his visit. 'Cannot you have this coming divorce put off?'

'Mr Baldwin,' the King again spoke gravely. 'That is the lady's private business. I have no right to interfere with the affairs of an individual. It would be wrong were I to attempt to influence Mrs Simpson just because she happens to be a friend of the King's.'

The Prime Minister pointed out 'the danger of the divorce proceedings', since, if Mrs Simpson was granted a decree *nisi*, the necessary six months period before the decree could be made absolute 'might be dangerous, because then everyone would be talking . . . and there might be sides taken and factions grow up in a matter where no faction ought ever to exist'.

Baldwin then told the King he understood that the English newspapers would by 'a gentleman's agreement' report the divorce in the normal way, briefly and without comment. 'But you cannot keep them quiet for long, and when they do start to give tongue it will be a grave situation for the country. It will be an even graver situation for you, Sir.'

The Prime Minister went on to urge that Mrs Simpson should be asked to leave the country for six months. In this way Baldwin hoped, as he subsequently admitted to Tom Jones, that 'in the meantime the King's passion might cool and that other influences might be brought into play upon him'. Otherwise he felt the King might 'do something very foolish', such as either marrying Mrs Simpson before the Coronation or else abdicating and then marrying her.

Baldwin also emphasised two particular anxieties he had. The first was, as he later summarised it, 'the effect of a continuance of the kind of criticism that at that time was proceeding in the American Press, the effect it would have in the Dominions and particularly in Canada, where it was widespread, the effect it would have in this country'. The other anxiety was the importance of preserving the integrity of the Crown, 'being as it is not only the last link of Empire that is left, but the guarantee in this country so long as it exists in that integrity, against many evils that have affected and afflicted other countries'. Once it had been lost, he doubted if anything could restore it.

Nothing at this interview was said about marriage, although Baldwin had the possibility in his mind. Perhaps it might have been better if he had asked the King outright how far he intended to go with Mrs Simpson, although he must have had a shrewd idea of this when the King admitted as he did during their conversation that Wallis Simpson was 'the only woman in the world' for him and he 'could not live without her'.

Baldwin concluded the interview by saying that he would leave the file of letters with the King so that he could judge for himself. He did not want him to give an answer on the spot to anything he had said, but to think it over and then let him know what his considered view was.

'You and I must settle this matter together,' the King said in conclusion. 'I will not have anyone interfering.'

So the King and his Prime Minister parted, 'perhaps not with lively expressions of mutual esteem, but certainly without bitterness', as the King afterwards put it. 'In fact, as he took his leave he complimented me again on the beauty of my garden, and volunteered an excellent suggestion for replanting the herbaceous border in the coming spring.'

Baldwin did not take the Cabinet into his confidence at this stage, although he told Neville Chamberlain and Tom Jones about the interview. Afterwards Chamberlain wrote briefly in his diary:

> S.B. told me it had passed off in a friendly manner. The King however disclaimed all knowledge of the [divorce] proceedings and declined to interfere in what was not his business. He listened carefully to S.B. on the danger to his throne if he did not observe greater precaution but gave no promise or undertaking.[9]

Both Hardinge and Geoffrey Dawson hoped that Baldwin would take advantage of Mackenzie King, the Prime Minister of Canada, spending a night at Chequers, which he did on 23 October, to persuade him to indicate the nature of popular feeling in Canada, when he had an audience with the King which he was due to have four days later. But the Canadian Premier did not do so. Indeed, as Dawson noted, when he went to Buckingham Palace, he 'made matters worse by discoursing on the King's popularity in the Dominions'.[10]

Mackenzie King had his audience in Buckingham Palace immediately after the King had held a Privy Council on the morning of 27 October. Although the King strove to carry out these duties with his 'usual punctiliousness', as he put it, he was thinking all the time of what was taking place in the Assize Court at Ipswich. Finally, to his great relief, he got a telephone message shortly after lunch that Mrs Simpson had been granted a decree *nisi* with costs by Mr Justice Hawke because of her husband's adultery with an unnamed woman.

Next morning the result was briefly noticed without comment in the newspapers. *The Times* for example prefaced its report with the innocuous heading:

UNDEFENDED DIVORCE SUIT
CASE AT IPSWICH ASSIZES

The rest of the British press showed similar restraint. It was otherwise in America where one of the less inhibited journals headlined the story:

KING'S MOLL RENO'D IN WOLSEY'S HOME TOWN

'What exactly to do about the press isn't easy,' Baldwin told Tom Jones at this time.

> I wish now it had not kept quiet but had quoted the foreign press. Geoffrey Dawson has been looking up all the precedents and has an opening article ready on the lines that contents of American and foreign press have been percolating more and more in this country; no one has taken notice of these calumnies hitherto, but they are so persistent and widespread that the time has come to ask His Majesty what he is going to do about it.

On the whole Jones felt that the Prime Minister was in a much more decisive mood about this than about other political questions. Nor was the connection between Ipswich and Cardinal Wolsey, who was said to have been the son of a local butcher, lost upon Baldwin. According to Jones, the Prime Minister said 'he could quite understand why people were put in the Tower in the old days, and he would gladly put Mrs S. there if he could'.[11]

3

The new parliamentary session was opened by the King in state on 3 November with the traditional reading of the 'Most Gracious Speech from the Throne' in the House of Lords. In place of the usual crown, the King wore the cocked hat of an Admiral of the Fleet, since his Coronation had not taken place. First, the King made the statutory declaration of the Protestant faith, a duty which he subsequently admitted to finding repugnant. ('In spirit it seemed wholly inappropriate to an institution supposed to shelter all creeds.') Then he delivered the Speech with vigour and confidence. ('It was all very solemn and not a word of it was mine.') He was determined to play his part well and he succeeded, as The Times reported with satisfaction next morning. But as he discoursed upon the various subjects on which the Government proposed to introduce legislation in the coming season, ranging from rearmament to the unification of coal royalties under national control, the King was conscious that he was the centre of much curiosity, since the senior ministers knew what the Prime Minister had said to him about his behaviour with Mrs Simpson, and the press barons were only too well aware of what was being published in the American newspapers and journals. Indeed Mr Randolph Hearst had already announced in his papers that the King definitely intended to marry Mrs Simpson, and it was widely believed that Hearst had got the news if not from the King himself then from someone in his intimate circle.

Baldwin now reported the details of his conversation with the King on 20 October to three more of his senior Cabinet colleagues besides Neville Chamberlain – Ramsay MacDonald, Runciman and Halifax. The meeting of Parliament facilitated the extension of his consultations with other prominent politicians, and the Prime Minister consequently took Attlee and Sinclair, the two Opposition Party leaders, into his confidence. Since their talk was confidential, Attlee had to give the Prime Minister what in his judgement he felt would be the reactions of his Party.

> I said that while Labour people had no objection at all to an American becoming Queen, I was certain that they would not approve of Mrs Simpson for that position . . . I found that I had correctly gauged the Party attitude. Despite the sympathy for the King and the affection which his visits to the depressed areas had created, the Party – with the exception of a few of the intelligentsia who can be trusted to take the wrong view on any subject – were in agreement with the views I had expressed.

Attlee added that 'he knew the temper of the industrial constituencies was much stricter than that of London' and that 'opinion in the Commonwealth was likely to coincide with that of the provinces rather than of the metropolis'.[12]

Baldwin also received a deputation on the subject consisting of four senior backbenchers – Salisbury, Derby, FitzAlan and Austen Chamberlain – who urged the Prime Minister to decide on a policy and acquaint the King with it. 'Winston was asked but would not join them,' Baldwin told Tom Jones afterwards 'and you may be sure he is in with Beaverbrook on this and does not feel about it as we do.'[13] However, the deputation got little change out of Baldwin. He merely said he would think it over.

Meanwhile Warren Fisher and other senior civil servants like Horace Wilson were becoming apprehensive that the Prime Minister's waiting game might result in the English press breaking silence, and so they devised a plan to make Baldwin take some action. This took the shape of a draft submission to the King embodying formal 'advice' from the Prime Minister that His Majesty should put an end to his association with Mrs Simpson forthwith. The draft was shown to Hardinge in Buckingham Palace, and since it appeared to him to be 'very drastic' – it did not mention marriage at all – the King's Private Secretary made some suggestions for toning it down. It was then sent to Neville Chamberlain, who further amended it and drafted in addition an informal letter for Baldwin's signature intimating that should the formal advice be rejected

> only one result could follow in accordance with the requirements of constitutional monarchy, that is, the resignation of myself and the National Government. If Mrs Simpson left the country forthwith, this distasteful matter could be settled in a less formal manner.[14]

Baldwin now had to consider the question in its legal aspects and for this he turned to the lawyers in the Government. Unfortunately Hailsham, the Lord Chancellor, had suffered a slight stroke during the summer and had been given temporary leave of absence. However, the Prime Minister had the advice of Sir Donald Somervell, the Attorney-General, as well as that of Simon, the Home Secretary, who was an ex-Attorney-General. One evening shortly after the opening of the new Parliament, the Prime Minister sent for Somervell.* Baldwin told him that he would be seeing the King shortly and he wished to have his advice on three matters, which he had noted on a slip of paper in front of him – namely, Marriage, Abdication and the King's Proctor.

On the first of these, Somervell said that in his opinion the King's marriage was outside the Royal Marriages Act of 1772, which required members of the Royal Family to obtain the sovereign's consent before contracting a legal marriage, but that it would be unconstitutional for the monarch to marry contrary to the advice of his ministers. Somervell quoted Queen Victoria's sentence announcing her engagement to Prince Albert to the effect that she had throughout consulted Lord Melbourne 'who approves'. Thus, if the King did marry contrary to or without advice, he would be acting unconstitutionally just 'as if he did any other public act without or contrary to advice'.

Nor in Somervell's view was there any difficulty over abdicating. This could be done with the King's assent by Act of Parliament. However, the matter of the King's Proctor was more complicated. The King's Proctor was the officer of the court who was charged with intervening in divorce proceedings to show why a decree *nisi* should not be made absolute by reason of certain facts unknown at the trial, such as the petitioner's own misconduct or that the action was a collusive one. His duties were carried out by the Treasury Solicitor, at this time Sir Thomas Barnes, who acted either on evidence which had come to his notice or on direct instructions

* For a fuller account of this and subsequent meetings, see Appendix.

from the Attorney-General. No one had suggested to Somervell at this stage that the Simpson divorce was collusive. Indeed such evidence as he had from Walter Monckton, the King's official legal adviser, pointed in the opposite direction. 'According to Walter,' Somervell told Baldwin, 'the co-respondent was a woman whom Simpson (whose married life had ceased to have much attraction for him owing to the King) was anxious to marry and had been "caught".' At the same time the Attorney-General had made it clear that if evidence of collusion was forthcoming he would intervene at once.

On the other hand, as Somervell pointed out, 'it was suggested that the King had probably lived with Mrs Simpson in circumstances of which evidence would be available'. On this the Attorney-General took the view, which he admitted was debatable, that it would be contrary to the constitutional position of the King for the King's Proctor to invite the King's Courts to investigate allegations against the King. He based this view partly on the fact that the King cannot give evidence in his own courts and he would therefore have no opportunity of denying allegations made involving his conduct. There was also a wider ground, namely the fact that the King cannot be indicted for a crime or sued for a civil wrong or cited as a co-respondent, being thus in many respects above the law. Somervell felt that he was so in this instance.

> It seemed to me quite wrong that I should, assuming I had the evidence, bring allegations, which in an ordinary sense could be met and denied, against the King who could not by law go into the box and deal with them. I had no doubt a feeling that whatever else was to be the solution of the problem the King's Proctor appearing with a bevy of valets and chambermaids before Merriman* to prove that the reigning Monarch had been seen going down the passage, etc., was not the right one – assuming that the chambermaids were available.
>
> Some people took the other view, and Robert Horne, assuming contrary to the fact that evidence was available, regarded this apparently as a step which would have kept Edward on the throne and the monarchy unsullied. I may not do him justice, he may have thought the threat would have made the lady withdraw. However . . . I am myself quite sure that, in so far as I gave no encouragement at this stage to the idea that the King's Proctor was a way out, I was right.

Not only was Baldwin busily engaged in testing private opinion in Parliament at this time, but as Prime Minister and Leader of the Commons

* Sir Boyd Merriman, later Lord Merriman, President of the Divorce Division of the High Court.

he had to watch the debate on the Address which continued for a week and afforded an opportunity for discussing every aspect of Government policy as outlined in the King's speech. An amendment moved from the Liberal benches regretted the absence of any proposed legislation for Government control of the manufacture of arms as recommended by a recent Royal Commission. This led to a general discussion on the Government's rearmament policy, particularly in the air, which was once again strongly attacked by Churchill, and to which Baldwin felt bound to reply. Consequently Neville Chamberlain decided to wait until the rearmament debate had been concluded before showing the Prime Minister the two draft documents for his approval and submission to the King.

Churchill used the opportunity which the debate provided to reproach Baldwin for having failed to keep his pledge that his Government would 'see to it that in air strength and air power this country shall no longer be in a position inferior to any country within striking distance of our shores'. Taking it for granted that Germany was the potential enemy, he asserted that that country had a marked superiority over Britain in first-line bombing aeroplanes, and that its lead was likely to increase rather than diminish unless the Government made greater efforts. 'The Government simply cannot make up their minds, or they cannot persuade the Prime Minister to make up his mind,' he said in a speech full of brilliant invective. 'So they go on in strange paradox, decided only to be undecided, resolved to be irresolute, adamant for drift, solid for fluidity, all-powerful to be impotent. So we go on preparing for months and years – precious, perhaps vital, to the greatness of Britain – for the locusts to eat.'

In his reply, Baldwin did what he had often done so successfully in the past when he wished to take the House into his confidence.[15] He discarded his official brief, or at least the greater part of it, and spoke largely without notes. Unfortunately certain passages in the speech, when taken out of context, were capable of being used against him, and in fact were subsequently so used with damning effect – not only by political opponents but by supposedly impartial political commentators and academics such as Professors L. B. Namier, Harold Laski, Ivor Jennings, Max Beloff and Keith Feiling (in his biography of Neville Chamberlain), not to mention Stanley Morison's anonymous contribution to *The History of the Times* which with the speech in mind referred to 'Baldwin's subservience to party expediency and his indifference to State security'.[16] None of these writers apparently took the trouble to study the complete text of the speech. Even Churchill himself has blurred the record, no doubt unintentionally, in the account of the speech in *The Gathering Storm*, when he writes that 'it carried naked truth about his motives into indecency', thereby occasioning the notorious reference under Baldwin in the Index – 'confesses putting party before country'.[17]

The Prime Minister began by admitting that they had 'started late' in the matter of rearmament and he went on to speak of 'the years the locusts have eaten'. During the period 1924–9, there had been no difference of opinion on the need to cut down the fighting services between himself and Churchill, who was Chancellor of the Exchequer at the time and had himself initiated many of the cuts. 'We did it,' said Baldwin, 'because we still had hopes of disarmament, and because we believed that there was no danger of a major war within a decade and because we were very anxious to conserve the finance of the country.' These reasons also held good during the period of financial crisis in 1931–2. It was in the years 1933 onwards that there was a difference of opinion between Churchill and himself, he said. He recalled that Churchill had 'spoken more than once about the anxieties caused after the events in Germany in 1933, and the neglect of the Government to do anything or make any preparations in 1933–4'. It was in the nature of democracies to be a couple of years behind dictatorships in preparing for war, but when they did commence they could act with at least equal vigour. 'I believe that to be true,' he added. 'It has been true in this case.'

I put before the whole House my own views with an appalling frankness [Baldwin continued]. From 1933, I and my friends were all very worried about what was happening in Europe. You will remember that at that time the Disarmament Conference was sitting in Geneva. You will remember that at that time there was probably a stronger pacifist feeling running through this country than at any time since the War. I am speaking of 1933 and 1934. You will remember the election at Fulham in the autumn of 1933, when a seat which the National Government held was lost by about 7,000 votes on no issue but the pacifist. You will remember perhaps that the National Government candidate who made a most guarded reference to the question of defence was mobbed for it.

That was the feeling in the country in 1933. My position as the leader of a great party was not altogether a comfortable one. I asked myself what chance was there – when that feeling that was given expression to in Fulham was common throughout the country – what chance was there within the next year or two of that feeling being so changed that the country would give a mandate for rearmament?

Supposing that I had gone to the country and said that Germany was rearming and that we must rearm, does anybody think that this pacific democracy would have rallied to that cry at that moment? *I cannot think of anything that would have made the loss of the election from my point of view more certain.*

The passage in italics was to be frequently used by Baldwin's detractors to support the charge that he had deliberately kept quiet about the need for rearmament until after the General Election of 1935. This charge is completely baseless. It is clear from the whole context that what he had in mind was not the 1935 election but a purely hypothetical election in 1933 or 1934 which the National Government could not have succeeded in winning if it had sought a mandate for rearmament from the electorate at that time. Apart from the slightly increased air programme, for which the reasons were given when it was announced, Baldwin waited until public opinion had in some measure been alerted by Hitler's actions before going to the country. 'All I did was to take a moment perhaps less unfortunate than another might have been,' he said in conclusion, 'and . . . we got from the country – with a large majority – a mandate for doing a thing that no one, twelve months before, would have believed possible.'

Harold Nicolson, who was in the chamber, noted that the Prime Minister spoke slowly and with evident physical effort. 'This will take three months' energy out of him,' one of the Whips whispered to Nicolson, who thought that by the end of the speech Baldwin's voice and thought were limp as if he were a tired walker on a long road. ('The House realises that the dear old man has come to the end of his vitality.')[18] No doubt fatigue must be held accountable for the fact that the Prime Minister's story might have been better told. Yet when the speech is studied and analysed, the message is clear enough. In essence it was the same as he had already given the Conservative Party deputation in July. Six days later in Glasgow, he underlined it again when he described the autumn of 1935 as 'the earliest moment' at which the massive electoral verdict in favour of rearmament 'might have been given'. It is only fair to add that at the time no one thought that 'the election' which Baldwin thought might be lost on the rearmament issue referred specifically to the one which took place in 1935 instead of a hypothetical one in 1933 or 1934. It was not until some years later that the damaging legend gained currency, and unfortunately for Baldwin's reputation it was to stick.

'The critics have no historical sense,' Baldwin remarked to Tom Jones, after Jones had told him some years later of the widespread criticism of his failure to prepare for the Second World War when he was in office. He went on:

Remember that Ramsay's health was breaking up in the last two years [of his Premiership]. He had lost his nerve in the House in the last year. I had to make all the important speeches. The moment he went I prepared for a General Election and got a bigger majority for rearmament. No power on earth could have got rearmament without a General Election except by a big split . . . I had to lead the House and keep the machine together with those Labour fellows.

In 1940 Baldwin was to receive a reassuring letter from Austin Hopkinson, the Independent MP who took a particular interest in air matters. Hopkinson challenged the initial statement which Churchill had made about German air strength:

Winston's case against you is easily refuted. The critical year was 1936, and it was largely owing to his activities that you were fully engaged during the year with the Edward VIII business, so were obliged to leave rearmament in the hands of Tom [Inskip], and the Service ministers. His assertion in November 1934 that Germany had a large number of first-line aircraft was subsequently shown to be incorrect – he got muddled up between training machines and military types. The latter were not in full production till 1937. By the way, I believe that Winston's secret source of information was Rothermere's German mistress who subsequently turned out to be in Ribbentrop's pay.

Taking a broad view of the matter, it is safe to say that the historians of the future will make it all right as far as your reputation is concerned, though we may have to wait some years.[19]

4

On the same evening as Baldwin made his speech in the defence debate which subsequently became so controversial, Alexander Hardinge, the King's Private Secretary, had a momentous meeting with the Prime Minister. This meeting appears to have been at Hardinge's request and was for the purpose of consulting Baldwin on the desirability that he (Hardinge) should address a letter to the King, warning him that the silence of the British Press on the subject of his 'friendship' with Mrs Simpson was not going to be maintained and urging that the only course to avoid a dangerous clash between the King and his ministers was for Mrs Simpson to leave the country as quickly as possible.

Baldwin agreed that Hardinge should write in formal terms. After spending a sleepless night pondering its contents, Hardinge drafted a letter next day and despatched it by special messenger to Fort Belvedere the same afternoon. The King's Private Secretary, however, did not make any allusion to the Simpson divorce case or the possibility of intervention by the King's Proctor.

After a preliminary caution that it was 'probably only a matter of days' before an outburst in the newspapers might be expected, Hardinge continued:

> The Prime Minister and senior members of the Government are meeting today [13 November] to discuss what action should be taken to deal with the serious situation which is developing. As Your Majesty no doubt knows, the resignation of the Government – an eventuality which can by no means be excluded – would result in Your Majesty having to find someone else capable of forming a government which would receive the support of the present House of Commons. I have reason to know that, in view of the feeling prevalent among members of the House of Commons, this is hardly within the bounds of possibility.
>
> The only alternative remaining is a dissolution and a General Election, in which Your Majesty's personal affairs would be the chief issue – and I cannot help feeling that even those who would sympathise with Your Majesty as an individual would deeply resent the damage which would inevitably be done to the Crown, the cornerstone on which the whole Empire rests.

There was only one step which held out any prospect of avoiding this dangerous situation, Hardinge concluded, and that was 'for Mrs Simpson to go abroad *without further delay*'. He begged the King 'to give this proposal your earnest consideration before the position has become irretrievable', since, 'owing to the changing attitude of the Press, the matter has become one of great urgency'.[20]

The King received the letter that night on his return to The Fort from Portsmouth after a successful visit to the Fleet. He had invited Mrs Simpson and her aunt Mrs Merriman, who was now acting as chaperon, for the week-end, and he was in high spirits when he welcomed them. His mood changed to one of depression and anger when he read Hardinge's letter, though for the time being he kept the matter to himself. Indeed, as he afterwards admitted, he was angry and hurt by what he felt was the cold formality with which so personal a matter affecting his whole happiness had been broached. On the other hand, Geoffrey Dawson, to whom

Hardinge showed the draft at the time, considered it 'an admirable letter, respectful, courageous and definite'.[21] But that was not the light in which the King viewed it. Although he had told the King where he could be quickly reached during the week-end, since he was 'of course entirely at Your Majesty's disposal if there is anything at all you want', Hardinge never had the slightest response to his letter either in writing or by word of mouth.

Excusing himself after lunch on Sunday on the pretext that he had some work to do in Windsor Castle, the King drove there in the afternoon for a secret talk with Walter Monckton. Afterwards he described the meeting:

> Walter was waiting in my old rooms on the second floor. I showed him Alec Hardinge's letter. He read it slowly. His expression left me in no doubt that it had shocked him as much as it had me. He agreed that it could hardly have been written without some discussion with Mr Baldwin. And he also agreed that time would not wait.
>
> 'The first thing I must do,' I said, 'is to send for the Prime Minister – tomorrow. I shall tell him that if, as would now appear, he and the Government are against my marrying Mrs Simpson, I am prepared to go.'
>
> 'He will not like to hear that,' said Walter gravely.
>
> 'I shall not find it easy to say.'[22]

In the account which he subsequently wrote of the events of these days, Monckton states that he advised the King not to take any immediate action to bring matters to a head, as Hardinge's letter seemed designed to do. ('I advised him not to dismiss Major Hardinge – as this would at once indicate a breach over Mrs Simpson – and I wanted him once more to wait and be patient.') At the same time, the King asked Monckton if he would act as his personal adviser and liaison with 10 Downing Street, and this Monckton agreed to do, thus temporarily taking over Hardinge's principal duty as the constitutional link with the Prime Minister and the Cabinet.[23]

On his return to Fort Belvedere, the King let Mrs Simpson read Hardinge's letter. Her immediate reaction was to say she would adopt Hardinge's suggestion and leave the country. According to her account, the King told her almost peremptorily: 'You'll do no such thing. I won't have it. This letter is an impertinence.' He added that he would send for Baldwin next day and tell him that he intended to marry her regardless of the possible consequences.

Afterwards Mrs Simpson was to reproach herself for being deflected from her original inclination to leave England immediately. She attributed her decision partly to what she understandably called 'the fundamental inability of a woman to go against the urgent wishes of the man she loves', and partly to her 'failure to understand the King's true position in the constitutional system'.

> The apparent deference to his every wish, the adulation of the populace, the universal desire even of the most exalted of his subjects to be accorded marks of his esteem – all this had persuaded me to take literally the ancient maxim that 'the King can do no wrong'. Nothing that I had seen had made me appreciate how vulnerable the King really was, how little power he could actually command, how little his wishes really counted for against those of his Ministers and Parliament. David did nothing to disabuse me of these misconceptions. And, too, right to the end it seemed utterly inconceivable to me that the British people and the Dominions would ever allow anybody who had served them so well to leave them.[24]

Meanwhile Baldwin had been spending the week-end at Chequers. He had with him the two draft documents for submission to the King, one of which was the informal letter intended to bear the Prime Minister's signature and informing the King that if the advice tendered in the formal document was not taken, it would mean the resignation of the Cabinet. Baldwin, who had not been given the documents until he was leaving London after the defence debate, was deeply shocked by their tone. He felt he could not show them to the King, since if he did so and the King saw fit to publish them there would in all probability be an immediate public outcry against what appeared on the face of it to be a form of blackmail by the Government.

On the Sunday, Stanley Bruce, the level-headed Australian High Commissioner in London, was invited to lunch at Chequers. After he had heard Baldwin's account of his meeting with the King at Fort Belvedere he told the Prime Minister that, if the King really intended to marry Mrs Simpson and persisted with his intention, Baldwin would have to advise him that 'the people of this country and of the Dominions would not accept this woman as the Queen and would demonstrate both against her and the King himself'. Bruce went on to say: 'You would have to tell him that unless he was prepared to abandon any idea of marriage . . . you would be compelled to advise him to abdicate, and unless he accepted such advice you would be unable to continue as his adviser and would tender the resignation of the Government.'[25] This was precisely the same advice contained in Neville Chamberlain's draft letter.

Bruce's opinion had already been endorsed by Lord Tweedsmuir (John Buchan), the Governor-General of Canada, who wrote to Baldwin on 9 November:

> Canada is the most puritanical part of the Empire and cherishes very much the Victorian standards of private life . . . She has a special affection and loyalty for the King, whom she regards as one of her own citizens. This is strongly felt particularly by the younger people, who are by no means strait-laced; and they are alarmed at anything which may take the gilt off their idol.
>
> Canada's pride has been deeply wounded by the tattle in the American Press, which she feels an intolerable impertinence. She is very friendly to America, but she has always at the back of her head an honest chauvinism.

If the King could only be brought to realise how much he and the monarchy meant to Canadians, Tweedsmuir argued, he would surely discontinue a course of action which would reluctantly line them up against him. The only man to make the King see this was Baldwin – 'the Archbishop should be kept out of it'. In addition, representative Canadians with whom the Governor-General had been in touch were concerned about Beaverbrook's assuming the role of interpreter of Canadian opinion, and it was felt that his enthusiasm for the King stemmed in part at least from his vendetta against Baldwin. These points were reinforced by Lady Tweedsmuir who happened to be in England at the time and was specially bidden to lunch at Chequers so that the Prime Minister could talk to her privately. In particular, she emphasised the French Canadians' opposition to divorce. Baldwin had formed a romantic attachment for Canada which dated from his visit to the Dominion with the King when he was Prince of Wales. As G. M. Young later put it to Geoffrey Dawson, this 'keyed him up' during the period of crisis. 'If Canada goes – Canada, the eldest child of the Commonwealth – then everything goes. And he knew from his study of the Canadian press that Canada was alarmed and angry over the figure which the Crown was cutting in American eyes.' [26]

On Monday morning, 16 November, the King told Hardinge to summon the Prime Minister to Buckingham Palace that evening at 6.30 and to bring Chamberlain and Halifax with him, adding that he would be glad if Baldwin would allow Hoare and Duff Cooper, his two particular friends in the Cabinet, to come as well. Baldwin replied through Hardinge that he preferred to see the King alone, and, as the matter had not yet been before the Cabinet, he could hardly single out two of his ministers at random. The King reluctantly agreed.

When Baldwin was shown in, the King at once came to the point. 'I understand that you and several members of the Cabinet have some fear of a constitutional crisis developing over my friendship with Mrs Simpson?' Baldwin admitted that this was so.

There is some doubt as to whether it was the King or the Prime Minister who first raised the marriage question. The point is not of great importance. But there is no dispute about the substance of the conversation which was carried on with complete frankness on both sides. The King in his memoirs claims that it was Baldwin who brought up the subject of his possible marriage, but this may well be due to a misreading of the account subsequently given by the Prime Minister to the House of Commons which the King appears to have followed, writing many years after the event. On the other hand, Baldwin gave his wife the details later the same evening and this would appear to be the more likely version. According to this, it was the King who first raised the matter by asking whether the marriage he had in mind would be approved by the country at large. Both this account and that which he later gave the House of Commons agree that Baldwin said emphatically that it would not. 'I believe I know what the people would tolerate and what they would not,' he added. 'Even my enemies would grant me that.'

Speaking later in the House of Commons, Baldwin put it in these words:

That marriage would have involved the lady becoming Queen. I did tell His Majesty once that I might be a remnant of the old Victorians, but that my worst enemy would not say of me that I did not know what the reaction of the English people would be to any particular course of action, and I told him that so far as they went I was certain that that would be impractical . . .

I pointed out to him that the position of the King's wife was different from the position of the wife of any other citizen in the country; it was part of the price which the King has to pay. His wife becomes Queen; the Queen becomes Queen of the country; and, therefore, in the choice of a Queen the voice of the people must be heard.

Then, according to Baldwin, the King remarked that he wished to tell him something that he had long wished to tell him. 'I want you to be the first to know that I have made up my mind and nothing will alter it,' he went on. 'I have looked at it from all sides – and I mean to abdicate to marry Mrs Simpson.'

'Sir, this is a very grave decision and I am deeply grieved,' Baldwin replied. 'It is impossible for me to make any comment on it today.'

In between puffs at his pipe, Baldwin went on to say that 'according to some legal opinion the divorce ought not to have been granted, that there were some aspects of it that in any ordinary case would not have gone through'.

His Majesty, I gather, did not exactly like that [noted Lucy Baldwin]. Stan put to him the feelings of the Empire, how he had seen Mackenzie King of Canada and Bruce of Australia, both agreeing that it would break up the Empire: the throne was the one thing that held the Empire together.

Again the King said, 'I have made up my mind and I shall abdicate in favour of my brother, the Duke of York, and I mean to go and acquaint my mother this evening, and my family: please don't mention my decision, except to two or three trusted Privy Councillors until I give you permission.'

All the time the King was most charming, but S. said the King could simply not understand and he couldn't make him. On leaving the King held Stanley's hand for a long time and there were almost tears in his eyes when he said good-bye.[27]

In fact, the King escorted the Prime Minister to the Garden Entrance to the Palace and saw him into his car, 'the same undersized little black box in which he had first made his descent upon The Fort'. In the King's eyes, the vehicle 'began to take on the guise of a sinister and purposeful little black beetle'. 'Where was it off to now?' he asked himself.

By this date Queen Mary had moved out of Buckingham Palace and established herself and her household in Marlborough House, where the King's grandfather Edward VII had lived when he was Prince of Wales. After Baldwin had left him, the King put on evening dress, white tie and tails, customary for the male members of the royal family even when dining *en famille* with Queen Mary. On this occasion she had Mary, the Princess Royal, with her, so that the King was spared the painful duty of repeating the story to his sister. Both women at first listened sympathetically to what the King had to say, but when they heard that he was prepared to give up the throne in order to marry Mrs Simpson, they were deeply shocked. Queen Mary, as she was to recall in a letter she wrote to her son eighteen months later, implored him not to do so for their sake and for the sake of the country. But 'you did not seem to take in any point of view but your own'. The discussion ended in deadlock, unhappily for the King, since his mother and his sister both refused to meet Mrs Simpson when he asked if he could bring her to Marlborough House. 'It was not, I was sure, because they were wanting in understanding,' the King reflected afterwards: 'it was rather because the iron grip of Royal convention would not release them.'

The King told his mother that he was going off to South Wales next evening for a two-day tour of this 'distressed area'. Before he left Buckingham Palace, he received a note from Queen Mary:

> As your mother I must send you a line of true sympathy in the difficult position in which you are placed. I have been thinking of you all day, hoping you are making a wise decision for your future. I fear your visit to Wales will be trying in more ways than one, with this momentous action hanging over your head.

Earlier the same day, Queen Mary had received the Prime Minister, who called at Marlborough House to talk over the King's action with her. 'Well, Mr Baldwin!' she greeted him, as she stepped briskly into the reception room, extending her hands in a gesture of despair. '*This* is a pretty kettle of fish!'[28]

5

The King returned to London on the evening of 19 November after meeting the unemployed Welsh miners. ('Something must be done to meet the situation in South Wales,' he had told one of them, 'and I will do all I can to assist you.') His mail contained a letter from Monckton, who had been collecting the views of a wide range of contacts in the House of Commons, the Bar, the Stock Exchange, the Press, 'and in other places where this problem is the one topic of discussion'. The consensus of opinion Monckton had gathered was that, as he put it, 'you cannot throw up the job without letting the whole side down irretrievably in the eyes of the whole world'. There was also the feeling that the Simpson divorce suit was for the King's convenience and that he was getting advantages which the ordinary private person would not have. 'Some even say that the present association is enough to justify an intervention in the suit,' Monckton added. To avoid 'any risk about the final success of the suit', he tactfully suggested 'a purely temporary separation for the immediate future in order to secure our real objects'.[29]

The King saw Monckton next day. 'He was very glad that we have met and discussed the problem,' Monckton wrote to Baldwin the same evening; 'he trusts us both, I'm sure.'

You will find his decision unchanged on the main question. And he is facing the rest and, considering all that is involved, with a real appreciation of the interests which you would wish him to have in mind. I think he will want to see you about Tuesday or Wednesday. I shall no doubt see him before then and I will let you know anything worth reporting. At present his ideas are a little fluid, but I shall remember what you said to me and do my best. He will not do anything precipitate or selfish, saving *il gran refiutto*.

There is not much about all this that makes one cheerful, but at least it has given me the real pleasure of meeting you, if it isn't impertinent to say so. At least, after what we have told each other, you will recognise this as genuine.[30]

Meanwhile the King had gone off to spend the week-end at Fort Belvedere, where he was joined by Mrs Simpson and her aunt. Mrs Simpson remarked that he looked exhausted and harassed, so that it was with some misgivings that she brought up a new idea which had been put to her as a possible solution of the problem. This had occurred during the King's absence in Wales, when Lord Rothermere's son Esmond Harmsworth had invited Mrs Simpson to lunch at Claridge's. The idea was for a so-called morganatic marriage, a practice not uncommon in royal families on the Continent whereby the wife though legally married did not take her husband's rank nor did any issue of the marriage inherit their father's possessions or hereditary titles. This suggested compromise, as subsequently reported by Baldwin to the Cabinet and the House of Commons, was 'that the King should marry' and 'that Parliament should pass an Act enabling the lady to be the King's wife without the position of Queen', but with some such title as Duchess of Cornwall.*

The King's immediate reaction was one of distaste. But on second thoughts he agreed with Mrs Simpson that it might be worth trying as a means of keeping him on the throne. 'I'll try anything in the spot I'm in now,' he said. Accordingly he sent for Esmond Harmsworth, and on learning from him that the idea had originated with his father, he authorised Harmsworth to go ahead and try it out on the Prime Minister.†

Harmsworth saw Baldwin in Downing Street on Monday evening 23 November and found him 'surprised, interested, and non-committal'

---

* Some members of the British Royal Family, such as the Duke of Cambridge and the Duke of Sussex, who 'married' commoners, are sometimes described as having contracted morganatic marriages. However, since they had not obtained the consent of the reigning sovereign as required by the Royal Marriages Act, they were not legally married at all.

† In fact, the idea is said to have come from Collin Brooks, the City editor of Lord Rothermere's newspaper the *Sunday Dispatch*.

when the plan was put to him. The Prime Minister promised to refer it to the Cabinet. In fact, Baldwin was not as surprised as he appeared to be, since he had already been forewarned what to expect by Davidson who was actually talking to Baldwin when Harmsworth was shown in and trying 'to picture the scene in the House of Commons when S.B. had to explain why Mrs Simpson was good enough to be the King's wife but not good enough to be Queen'. Davidson returned after Harmsworth had left and asked Baldwin whether he was right. According to Davidson, Baldwin replied that he was and added: 'He wants Mrs Simpson to be a Duchess – not to be royal, but less than royal, but rather better than the ordinary Duchess.'[31]

Baldwin was equally forthcoming with Tom Jones who breakfasted with him two days later. On this occasion he said he could not carry the Commons with him on the project of a morganatic marriage, and did Jones see him attempting to do so? 'Is this the sort of thing I've stood for in public life? If I have to go out, as go I must, then I'd be quite ready to go out on this.'[32]

Meanwhile Somervell, whom Baldwin had earlier asked to get an Abdication Bill drafted and in readiness for possible rapid use, confirmed to Baldwin what he already knew, namely that 'the wife of the King is Queen' and that 'it would require an Act of Parliament to prevent this result'. It would be an odd Act, Somervell added, since if it had an honest recital it would start:

> Whereas the wife of the King is Queen and whereas the present King desires to marry a woman unfit to be Queen, Be it hereby enacted etc.

At their meeting on 16 November, the King had asked Baldwin whether he had any objection to his seeking the independent advice of two Cabinet ministers, who were also personal friends, namely Hoare and Duff Cooper. Certainly, said Baldwin, he could see any minister he wished. In the event he saw them on 21 November.

The King, who hoped to win Hoare over as an advocate of his cause with the Cabinet, found the First Lord of the Admiralty against the marriage in any form. 'Mr Baldwin, he warned me, was in command of the situation,' the King recorded later; 'the senior Ministers were solidly with him on this issue. If I were to press my marriage project upon the Cabinet, I should meet a stone wall of opposition.'[33]

Duff Cooper, whom the King saw at the Palace later the same day, was more encouraging. As an alternative to abdication Duff Cooper suggested that he postpone the marriage on which he seemed to have set his heart.

In any event it could not take place for at least five months, that is until after the divorce decree had been made absolute, and during this period the Government could not press him into a decision on a constitutional issue that did not exist. The War Minister's advice was that the King should be patient, that he should ignore the furore, go ahead with the Coronation, and in due time, after the people had become accustomed to see him as King, raise in a calmer atmosphere the question of his right to marry whom he pleased. 'It was a solution that I had known to work in the case of humbler folk and I had accepted it in my own case,' Duff Cooper later recalled. 'I thought that if they would agree not to meet for a year, during which he would be crowned and perhaps attend a Durbar, of which there seemed some possibility at the time, he would at the end of that period have grown more accustomed to his position and more loth to leave it.' Duff Cooper also secretly thought, as he afterwards was to admit, that the King might in the interval meet someone whom he would love more than Mrs Simpson.

But the King rejected what he called this 'counsel of a sophisticated man of the world'. To his credit, he did so on religious grounds, since at the Coronation he would have to take the oath as Defender of the Faith to uphold the doctrines of the Church of England which did not approve of divorce.

> For me to have gone through the Coronation ceremony while harbouring in my heart a secret intention to marry contrary to the Church's tenets would have meant being crowned with a lie on my lips. The Archbishop of Canterbury might then justifiably have reproached me for being wanting not only in Christian spirit but in sincerity. My soul contained enough religion for me to comprehend to the full the deep meaning attached to the Coronation service. Whatever the cost to me personally, I was determined, before I would think of being crowned, to settle once and for all the question of my right to marry.[34]

The King waited for a couple of days after Esmond Harmsworth had reported back to him, and having had no sign from Downing Street he summoned Baldwin to a further audience in the Palace on the evening of 25 November. That morning, unknown to any of his colleagues except Neville Chamberlain, Baldwin had invited Attlee, Sinclair and Churchill to No. 10 and put the question to them – would they be for or against the Government if it came to resignation? The Labour and Liberal leaders both pledged loyalty and said they would not try to form a Government if asked by the King. Churchill, on the other hand, according to Chamberlain, gave an assurance that, 'though his attitude was a little different, he would certainly support the Government'. Nevertheless, as Chamberlain also noted, Churchill was 'moving mysteriously in the background and, it is suggested, expressing willingness to form a Government if there should be any refusal on our part to agree'.

The inner Cabinet of senior ministers met again the same afternoon when Baldwin reported that, influenced by Mrs Simpson and Esmond Harmsworth, 'the King had now swung round and had taken up the position that he would contract a morganatic marriage to be legalised by Act of Parliament'. The general feeling was summarised by Neville Chamberlain in his diary:

> It was agreed that we must act cautiously, and find out the attitude of Opposition and Dominions before committing ourselves. S.B. should point out various difficulties but not turn anything down. I have no doubt that if it were possible to arrange the morganatic marriage this would only be the prelude to the further step of making Mrs S. Queen with full rights.[35]

Before leaving Downing Street for the Palace, Baldwin received a letter from the Archbishop of Canterbury who had evidently not heard of the morganatic marriage proposal. Written earlier the same day and hitherto unpublished, this contradicts the statement by the Archbishop's official biographer that he never sought to influence the course of events during the constitutional crisis or impose a point of view upon the Government.

> *Lambeth Palace. 25 November 1936.* Forgive me if in this letter I seem to intrude unasked into your many responsibilities about The Affair.
>
> 1. I gather that it is becoming more and more difficult to prevent leakage into the press. If so, the leakage will soon become a flood and burst the dam. This makes it most important that if any announcement is made of the kind you indicated to me [i.e. of the King's intention to abdicate], it should be made as soon as possible. The announcement should appear as a free act.
>
> 2. I have reason to think that He does not fully realise that if the course indicated is to be taken, he should leave as soon as possible. It would be quite out of the question that he should remain until the decree is made absolute. It is needless to dwell on this necessity. I understand you are seeing him tonight, and doubtless you could make this plain.[36]

The audience began with the King asking Baldwin whether the Harmsworth proposal had been put to him. He believed that he would have the support and sympathy of a very large part of the people, the King said, and while he realised that they might be unwilling to accept Mrs Simpson as Queen, he felt they would accept a morganatic marriage if the Government were willing to introduce legislation authorising it. Slowly and with careful attention to his words, according to the King, Baldwin replied that he had not considered the question.

Noting the King's surprise, Baldwin immediately explained what he meant. 'I can give you no considered opinion,' he said. But if he were asked informally for his immediate reaction, he went on, it was that Parliament would never pass the necessary legislation. Or, as he subsequently put it to the Cabinet in less courtier-like language, he told the King bluntly that 'if he thought he was going to get away with it in that way he was making a huge mistake'.

On the King then asking whether he was sure that Parliament would not pass the necessary Bill, Baldwin said that if he desired it he would examine the proposition formally. 'Yes, please do so,' answered the King.

'It will mean my putting it formally before the whole Cabinet and communicating with the Prime Ministers of all the Dominions. Do you really wish that, Sir?'

The King replied that he did. Before he left, Baldwin said he would try to find out the prospects in the House of Commons of such a measure being carried. He also urged upon the King the advisability of Mrs Simpson leaving the country before the formal decision was arrived at. Finally, he told the King that he would summon a special meeting of the Cabinet within the next forty-eight hours.

As the Prime Minister was leaving, the King remarked that he would like to consult some of his own friends, particularly Lord Beaverbrook.

That the King should contemplate calling in Baldwin's principal political enemy came as a considerable surprise to the Prime Minister, since Beaverbrook had hitherto not been known to enjoy the King's confidence. Beaverbrook's previous acquaintance with the King was slight, he had never at any time moved in royal circles, and he had only been to Buckingham Palace once in his life. This was at the time of the Simpson divorce hearing, when the King asked him to use his influence with the press to keep the case out of the headlines, which Beaverbrook had succeeded in doing. Since then, the King had been thinking of asking him to come and see him again but delayed doing so until after Beaverbrook had sailed for America, hoping to find a cure for his asthma in Arizona. The King then pursued him with telegrams and telephone calls, with the result that

Beaverbrook spent only a few hours in New York and returned to England by the same ship in response to the King's urgent messages that his advice was needed on much wider issues than the handling of the press.

The story subsequently got about that Beaverbrook responded to the King's appeal solely with the object of overthrowing Baldwin. This is not so and rests on little more than what A. J. P. Taylor calls 'late-night gossip by Randolph Churchill, not the most reliable of authorities'.[37]* Of course, Beaverbrook always enjoyed playing the role of 'fixer', but to be fair to him he could seldom resist a call for help, as he had already demonstrated in the case of Randolph's father and had more than once shown that he was a true foul-weather friend. 'I did not enter the struggle to dislodge the Prime Minister from Downing Street,' he was later to write. 'That would be a welcome by-product of my efforts. But I was striving to help the King because I believed he had a right to command support and because his cause was just. My efforts would be primarily directed to helping safeguard the Throne and trying to secure for the King freedom to marry the woman of his choice, a freedom enjoyed by the humblest of his subjects.'

Beaverbrook landed at Southampton on the morning after Baldwin's audience and drove straight to Fort Belvedere where the King was waiting for him. 'You have done a fine thing for me,' the King exclaimed as he grasped his hand, 'and I shall always remember it.' Over luncheon the King brought his guest up to date on the situation. But when he heard that the King had asked Baldwin to lay the morganatic marriage proposal before the Cabinet, Beaverbrook's face darkened. Such an idea, he said, would appeal neither to the British Cabinet nor, in his opinion, to the British people. He strongly advised the King to withdraw it at once. The King appeared to be convinced, but the same evening he telephoned Beaverbrook in London that Mrs Simpson preferred the morganatic marriage to any other solution and that therefore he intended to go on with it.

There was little that Beaverbrook could do in the face of the King's set determination. It was clear that the Government had only to reply that a morganatic marriage was impossible, and the King must either abandon Mrs Simpson or abdicate. As the King had made it abundantly clear that the former course was out of the question, it now looked as if there was no alternative to abdication.

* In a review of *The Abdication of King Edward VIII* by Lord Beaverbrook, which he wrote in the *Sunday Times* (24 April 1966), Randolph Churchill stated: 'It was not until four or five years ago that by chance one day I asked Lord Beaverbrook why, if he was so far from being a monarchist and one who scarcely knew the King, he had put himself to so much trouble on his behalf. He replied laconically: "To bugger Baldwin." So much for charity.'

'Sir, you have put your head on the execution block,' Beaverbrook told the King next day on hearing that the Cabinet had met. 'All that Baldwin has to do now is to swing the axe.' [38]

6

The minutes of the historic Cabinet which sat for three hours in the morning of 27 November 1936, together with those of nine subsequent Cabinet meetings concerned with the 'King's Matter', are officially closed until the year 2037. Fortunately a number of ministers who were present, such as Neville Chamberlain, Samuel Hoare and Lord Zetland, kept some private record of the proceedings, and from these sources it has been possible to put together a fairly accurate account of what took place behind the locked doors of the Cabinet Room in Downing Street and Baldwin's room in the House of Commons.

Since the first Cabinet was summoned at short notice to meet on a Friday at 11.30 in the House, several ministers who had left London to fulfil engagements in the provinces had to be hastily recalled. At the same time, the Government let it be known among the parliamentary lobby correspondents that this hurried summons was due to a new turn of events in the civil war in Spain, and one or two newspapers proceeded to speculate upon this topic.

Baldwin spent about an hour describing in considerable detail what had transpired at his three meetings with the King on 20 October, and 16 and 25 November. 'I have seldom listened to a more dramatic narrative,' wrote Zetland afterwards. At the end of it, when Baldwin had outlined the morganatic proposal, he told his colleagues that he was not asking them for an immediate decision. They could think it over until the next regular Cabinet, on the following Wednesday, 2 December. Meanwhile telegrams would be sent to the Dominion Prime Ministers asking them for their views. He hoped to see the King again, said Baldwin, but the King's 'present intention seemed to be to refuse to withdraw from his position'. Zetland's account continues:

It was pointed out at the Cabinet that this might involve the resignation of the Government and that in this case it would give rise to a Constitutional issue of the first magnitude, viz. the King *v.* the Government. It seems that the King has been encouraged to believe that Winston Churchill would in these circumstances be prepared to form an alternative Government. If this were true there would be a grave risk of the country being divided into two camps – for and against the King. This clearly would be fraught with danger of the most formidable kind.[39]

Another point which was raised in this Cabinet, notably by Simon and Malcolm MacDonald, was the constitutional propriety of Baldwin communicating directly with the Dominion Prime Ministers. Under the recent Statute of Westminster, the Dominions had become fully independent of Whitehall, the sole remaining link with the mother country being the Crown. Thus it would have been open to the King as sovereign ruler of Canada and the other self-governing Dominions to consult the various Prime Ministers through his personal representative on the spot, that is the Governor-General. Baldwin now explained that the King was loath to employ this channel, since he felt that 'the matter was much too personal, too delicate to be handled by the King himself'. Hence his instructions to the Prime Minister to act as his intermediary, an action which some of his friends were afterwards to argue was a serious tactical error, although he himself never regretted his decision. The possibility of the matter being raised in Parliament was thoroughly discussed – in fact it never was so raised – and it was agreed that if Baldwin or the Dominions Secretary were questioned about the precise replies received from the Dominions, the answer would be that the Government was not prepared to disclose this information, since in accordance with constitutional practice the replies though addressed to Baldwin were intended for the King.

Baldwin was to be accused of having slanted the telegrams in a sense adverse to the King's case, notably by Beaverbrook, and even the King himself afterwards remarked that 'with Mr Baldwin composing the cables they were hardly likely to be compassionate pleas on behalf of my proposal'. This charge is wholly without foundation. Although the cables bore Baldwin's signature and the texts were approved by him, he did not compose them. They were drafted in the Dominions Office, as were all the subsequent cables which passed between Whitehall and the Dominions, by Malcolm MacDonald, the Secretary of State, and Sir Henry Batterbee, the Permanent Secretary, with occasional help from Simon and Neville Chamberlain, following the directives of the Cabinet committee.

Three possible courses were indicated, and each Dominion Prime Minister was invited to indicate his preference with any particular comments he might wish to make. No attempt whatsoever was made to sway the individual judgements of the respective Prime Ministers, and (as Eden put it) they were 'worded with a scrupulous impartiality, which would have defied the reader to guess the judgement of the Government at home'. The three courses were:

(1) that Mrs Simpson be recognised as Queen;
(2) that she should not become Queen but that the King need not abdicate;
(3) that the King abdicate in favour of the Duke of York.

At the same time it was made clear that whichever course was favoured would require the Dominion Parliament concerned to pass separate legislation to implement it.*

Having failed to persuade the King to drop the morganatic marriage proposal, Beaverbrook tried to get him to hold up the telegrams. But he refused to do so and the telegrams were duly despatched on 28 November, that to Mr de Valera in Dublin taking the form of a letter delivered by Batterbee in person next day. By 3 December all the replies had been received in London. With the exception of de Valera, all the Prime Ministers were opposed in varying degrees of intensity to a 'morganatic' marriage as envisaged by the second course which would allow the King to marry Mrs Simpson without her becoming Queen and without his abdicating the throne. De Valera, who as will be seen had his own axe to grind in the matter, explained that the Irish attitude was one of detachment and that his preference for the second course was 'based on the assumption that divorce was a recognised institution in England'. The United Kingdom and the older Dominions must settle the matter as they thought best, but whatever happened Edward VIII could not remain King of Eire.[40]

The strongest reply came from Mr Joseph Lyons, the Prime Minister of Australia and a Catholic like de Valera, 'stating that in his view His Majesty could not now re-establish his prestige or command confidence as King'. As for Mrs Simpson becoming Queen, said Mr Lyons, this 'would provoke widespread condemnation, and the alternative proposal, or something in the nature of a specially-sanctioned morganatic marriage, would run counter to the best popular conception of the Royal Family'. Hertzog of South Africa thought that, while abdication would be 'a great shock', a morganatic marriage would be 'a permanent wound'. When Mackenzie King received the telegram in Ottawa, his reaction was: 'What Baldwin says is good enough for me,' and a reply was sent in this

---

* According to Hoare, the Cabinet committee originally favoured putting the second course only in the draft telegram. 'I got this altered and the three alternatives inserted,' wrote Hoare in the notes he made at the time. Templewood Papers, IX, 7.

sense. An even more bizarre communication came from Mr Michael Joseph Savage, the New Zealand Prime Minister, to the effect that his country 'would not quarrel with anything the King did nor with anything his Government in the UK did to restrain him'. In fact, until he received Baldwin's telegram, Mr Savage had never heard of Mrs Simpson and had to go to the Governor-General in Wellington for enlightenment.*

When the Cabinet met again on Wednesday morning, 2 December, the national papers all carried a report of an address to the Diocesan Conference in Bradford by the local Bishop, Dr A. F. W. Blunt, in which he expressed the hope that the King was aware of his need for God's grace at his Coronation and wished that 'he gave more positive signs of his awareness'. When he composed his address, which he had done six weeks previously, the Bishop of Bradford knew nothing of Mrs Simpson, and, as he subsequently explained, he had no intention of referring to current rumours which linked the King with her, but only to His Majesty's negligence in church-going. The national press simply printed the substance of the Bishop's address as an ordinary news item, although *The Times* extracted the significant reference to the King for the main page. On the other hand, the northern provincial papers, led by the *Yorkshire Post* and the *Manchester Guardian*, went a good deal further and ran editorials dealing with the gossip which had been current in certain sections of the American press and even quoted some typical extracts. Some editions of the London evening papers, which were on the streets while the Cabinet was still in session, followed suit, and it was evident that the long self-imposed silence of the English press was about to be broken.

It was later suggested that the Archbishop of Canterbury knew in advance of Dr Blunt's speech and had even instigated it. This has been denied by the Archbishop's official biographer, who has stated that on the contrary the Archbishop was extremely annoyed by it, since it looked as though the leakage had come from Lambeth Palace. 'Actually the Bishop's words merely anticipated something that was bound to have happened within two or three days. The newspapers were waiting for a cue and the Bishop of Bradford gave it them.' [41]

Baldwin duly reported to the Cabinet the views of the Dominion Prime Ministers and a general discussion followed. With the exception of Duff Cooper, who pleaded in vain for delay, everyone present agreed that the

---

* In India, which enjoyed a more limited measure of self-government than the other Dominions, opinion was divided between the two sections of the population largely on religious grounds. The Muslims favoured the King-Emperor's marriage and the Hindus took the view that he should abandon Mrs Simpson just as their former monarch Ram Chandra had banished Queen Sita for the sake of the public weal. But politically the crisis was of little account in the sub-continent.

morganatic plan was 'impracticable and undesirable' and it was formally vetoed. As for Duff Cooper, he put forward much the same argument as he had used with the King, and suggested that the question be dropped for the time being, that the King be crowned as planned in May 1937, and the question raised again in a year's time. Baldwin thereupon intimated that he was to see the King again that evening, and he was accordingly authorised to convey the views of the Cabinet to him and those of the Dominion Prime Ministers that had been received to date.

In the afternoon Baldwin went to the House of Commons, where Geoffrey Dawson saw him briefly in his room before Baldwin went to the Palace. 'He was going to see the King at 6, and had nothing much to tell me yet beyond reporting a solid front in the Dominions and the House of Commons,' Dawson noted in his diary. 'He seemed to be nearly at the end of his tether and sat with his head in his hands on the table, probably just glad to have someone with him till the time that his interview came.' [42]

The King has described the ensuing audience in his memoirs, remarking that his first concern was to ask about the answers from the Dominions, but before he could do so he judged by the Prime Minister's demeanour that they were unfavourable. Incidentally, Baldwin had brought with him the reply from Mr Lyons of Australia, and he handed this to the King. Although the inquiries were still incomplete, Baldwin added, 'it was already clear to him that the necessary legislation for a morganatic marriage would not be forthcoming'.

'What about Parliament?' I asked.

'The answer would, I am sure, be the same.'

'But Parliament has not been consulted,' I persisted. 'The issue has never been presented.'

He answered, unruffled. 'I have caused inquiries to be set afoot in the usual manner. The response has been such to convince my colleagues and myself that the people would not approve of Your Majesty's marriage with Mrs Simpson.'

Almost pedantically he summed up for me the three choices that had faced me from the outset:

(1) I could give up the idea of marriage.
(2) I could marry contrary to the advice of my Ministers.
(3) I could abdicate.

The Prime Minister prayed that I would take the first course. The second course, he continued, watching me closely, was manifestly impossible; if I married in the face of the advice of my Ministers, I could not hope to remain on the Throne. Never taking his eyes off me, he went on to say that if I would not abandon the project there was really no choice for me but to go.

'So, Mr Baldwin,' I said, 'you really leave me with only one choice.'

With undeniable earnestness, he said, 'Believe me, Sir, it is my sincere hope – and the hope of the Cabinet – that you will remain our King.'

'Whether on the Throne or not, Mr Baldwin,' I answered, 'I shall marry; and however painful the prospect, I shall, if necessary, abdicate in order to do so.' [43]

'He behaved there as a great gentleman; he said no more about it,' Baldwin afterwards told the House of Commons. 'The matter was closed. I never heard another word about it from him.'

The King had already seen some of the provincial papers and resented their unrestrained comments on his private life. Picking up a copy of the *Birmingham Post*, he showed it to Baldwin as an example of what he meant, saying: 'They don't want me!'

After the audience the King drove down to The Fort, whence he telephoned Beaverbrook at Stornaway House, telling him that the Cabinet decision against a morganatic marriage was known in Fleet Street and that the London press would come out with 'sensational disclosures' next morning, from which the King gathered that the attack on Mrs Simpson would be led by *The Times*, 'under the fluent and pitiless pen of Geoffrey Dawson'. The King thereupon got on to Downing Street and 'instructed' the Prime Minister to stop it.

In vain Baldwin pointed out that the press was free, and that he had no control over *The Times* or over any other newspaper. However, he immediately put through a call to Printing House Square and spoke to Dawson – 'the only time, I think, that I ever heard his own voice on the telephone', the editor remarked afterwards – saying that 'His Majesty was worrying him to find out, and if necessary stop, what was going to appear in *The Times*'. A little later, Dawson had another call from Baldwin, 'full of apologies . . . it was to say that the King would now be satisfied, and leave the Prime Minister alone, if the latter would read the leading article for him'. Could the editor possibly let him see it 'for the sake of peace'? 'You know, Geoffrey,' said Baldwin finally, 'the trouble is that the little man hasn't the faintest notion of the way this country is governed.'

By this time, as Dawson told Baldwin, the paper was just going to press. But towards midnight the editor despatched a messenger to Downing

Street with a proof of the leader, and he heard no more about it. By the time the messenger arrived, the Prime Minister had gone to bed, as he had done at a critical stage of the General Strike, and he did not see the text until he read it at breakfast next morning.

7

On 3 December, 'Chips' Channon, who was friendlily disposed towards Mrs Simpson, noted in his diary:

> The country and the Empire now know that their Monarch, their young King-Emperor, their adored Apollo, is in love with an American twice divorced, whom they believe to be an adventuress. The whole world recoils from the shock; but very few know that she is a woman of infinite charm, gentleness, courage and loyalty, whose influence upon the King, until now, has been highly salutary. *The Times* has a strong leading article, every other newspaper follows suit, though both the Beaverbrook and the Rothermere press is favourable. There is talk of abdication; of the King sticking to his guns, and marrying her; of a morganatic compromise.[44]

The leading article in *The Times* of 3 December was headed, 'King and Monarchy'. It contained some account of the American press campaign and admitted its solid basis of fact. Mrs Simpson was not mentioned by name but reference was made to the suggestion of 'a marriage incompatible with the Throne'. Since the institution was greater than the individual, it was argued, the time had come for a reassuring act or statement from the Monarch if the Monarchy was not to be damaged. In any coming trial of strength between Monarch and Government, the editor left the paper's readers in no doubt as to which party *The Times* would back. The other London morning papers all expressed belief that a grave constitutional crisis had arisen between King and Cabinet over the Sovereign's proposed marriage, but there were no disclosures of the kind that Beaverbrook had anticipated. The Liberal *News Chronicle* was the most specific on the morganatic plan, suggesting that if the King chose a wife whom public opinion considered unsuitable as Queen, then His Majesty could marry her in his private capacity as Duke of Cornwall, but she would only be his consort and her issue could be excluded from the succession. The Labour *Daily Herald* carried a clearly-reasoned signed article on 'Crown and Cabinet' by Professor Harold Laski, which stressed the salient fact that under the British constitution the Cabinet and not the King was politically supreme. That being so, the King must accept the Cabinet's 'advice' in everything, as they were responsible for his acts. Royal opposition to the established Government, if carried to a logical conclusion, Laski pointed out, could only end in one of two things – abdication or monarchical dictatorship.

When the daily papers were brought to him at his room in Fort Belvedere, the King was deeply shocked by what he read. 'Could this be the King or was I some common felon?' he asked himself. 'The Press creates: the Press destroys. All my life I had been the passive clay which it had enthusiastically worked into the hackneyed image of a Prince Charming. Now it had whirled around, and was bent upon demolishing the natural man who had been there all the time.' He was particularly incensed by what he described as 'the bitter unanimity with which the so-called "quality" newspapers lashed out' and which left little doubt that they reflected the Government's attitude towards him. He now took up an idea, which Mrs Simpson had put into his mind a short time before, that he should deliver a radio broadcast setting out his side of the story, since so far no clear and commanding voice had been publicly raised on the King's behalf. After he had sent urgent telephone messages to Walter Monckton and George Allen, his solicitor, to come to The Fort with all haste, he sat down to compose the broadcast. What he would tell his subjects was that it had taken him a long time to find the woman whom he wished to make his wife and that, having found her, he was determined to marry her. There was no question of Mrs Simpson becoming Queen and he spelled this out in a couple of sentences:

> Neither Mrs Simpson nor I have ever sought to insist that she should be Queen. All we desired was that our married happiness should carry with it a proper style and dignity for her, befitting my wife.

So as to give time for quiet and calm reflection on the part of the people, 'but without undue delay', he felt it best if he were 'to go away for a while', leaving the discharge of his constitutional functions to Counsellors of State.

His labours were interrupted by the appearance of Mrs Simpson with a picture paper in her hand. 'I had no idea it would be anything like this,' she said. She added that she had made up her mind to leave England that very afternoon. 'I cannot stay here another day, with all this going on.'

The King agreed, and arrangements were immediately made that she should stay with two American friends, Mr and Mrs Herman Rogers, at their villa in Cannes. The King's Lord-in-Waiting Lord Brownlow was thereupon summoned to escort her on the journey. They left the same night, to be hotly pursued by reporters across France.

Helped by Monckton and Allen, the King finished the draft broadcast during the afternoon. Monckton then returned to London with a copy to show Baldwin, whom the King summoned to meet him in Buckingham Palace after dinner that night. Meanwhile in the House of Commons Attlee put a private notice question to the Prime Minister, asking whether any constitutional difficulties had arisen and whether he had any statement to make. Baldwin, whom Harold Nicolson thought looked 'ill and profoundly sad', replied in a brief statement to the effect that, while there did not then exist any constitutional difficulty, the situation was of such a nature as to make it inexpedient that he should be questioned about it at that stage. Pressed by the Labour leader for an assurance, 'in view of the prevailing anxiety', that he would make a statement as soon as possible, Baldwin said that he had that very much in mind. Churchill then rose to ask the Prime Minister for an assurance that before he made his statement 'no irrevocable step' would be taken. 'I have nothing to add to the statement I have made, at this present moment,' Baldwin answered coldly. 'I will consider and examine the question my right honourable friend has asked.'

To put in the hour or so before his evening audience with the King, while at the same time escaping from the mounting pressures to which he was being subjected in Parliament and Whitehall, Baldwin borrowed an old police car and drove with Major Dugdale, his Parliamentary Private Secretary, to Hyde Park where they stopped and took a walk. Unfortunately their car was in collision with another vehicle, but somehow the Prime Minister was not recognised. Afterwards Dugdale took him for a quiet dinner at Bucks Club where he also escaped recognition, although he lit up his pipe at the end of the meal and was asked to put it out.

In spite of Baldwin's mollifying words in Parliament, the world press was now alerted to the gravity of the crisis. Although Baldwin went into Buckingham Palace shortly before nine by the side entrance through the Royal Mews, his visit was observed by reporters who had virtually surrounded the Palace. The King was waiting for him in his usual room on the ground floor. He began by reading the draft of the broadcast he proposed to deliver to the Empire on the following night, and when he had finished he asked his Prime Minister what he thought of it. Baldwin replied that he must consult his colleagues, but speaking for himself he had no doubt of their answer – 'that the proposal was thoroughly unconstitutional'.

'You want me to go, don't you?' the King interjected. 'And before I go, I think it is right, for her sake and mine, that I should speak.'

'What I want, Sir, is what you told me you wanted,' said Baldwin: 'to go with dignity, not dividing the country, and making things as smooth as possible for your successor.'

To broadcast would be to go over the heads of your Ministers and speak to the people. You will be telling millions throughout the world – among them a vast number of women – that you are determined to marry one who has a husband living. They will want to know all about her, and the press will ring with gossip, the very thing you want to avoid.

You may, by speaking, divide opinion; but you will certainly harden it. The Churches are straining at the leash. Only three papers would be on your side, the *News Chronicle*, the *Daily Mail*, and the *Daily Express*.

Besides this, there was a point of great delicacy which, Baldwin went on, he felt bound to mention. Mrs Simpson's divorce decree was not due to be made absolute until the following April when she should be free to remarry, but in the meantime 'it was not at all unlikely that some muddle-headed busybody would seek to delay the proceedings by an unjustified intervention'. So long as the King remained on the Throne, the divorce could not be upset in law by reason of Mrs Simpson's association with the King, and he had been advised that on the existing evidence this possibility was extremely remote, and that the decree could not be rescinded for collusion. But if the King were to abdicate, the situation might change, conceivably to Mrs Simpson's disadvantage.*

Finally, the King asked Baldwin whether he minded his seeing Churchill, 'as an old friend with whom he could talk freely'. Momentarily off his guard, Baldwin agreed, though he subsequently regretted it. ('I have made my first blunder,' he told the Cabinet next day, at the same time confiding to one of his private secretaries that it was 'the only way I could carry it off – owning up to a mistake'.)[45]

* Baldwin had just received a letter from Simon, in which the Home Secretary wrote (3 December): 'I think that intervention by the King's Proctor in this case on the present materials may be ruled out. The King's Proctor never acts except upon the express instructions of the Attorney-General, and though the Attorney-General in exercising this duty acts on his own responsibility and quite apart from Government advice, I as an old Attorney-General am quite satisfied that intervention by the Attorney-General in the present circumstances would not take place, at any rate unless some new and glaring evidence of collusion was forthcoming hereafter.' Baldwin Papers 176 f. 97.

Later that night the King drove back to The Fort, where he was to stay for the remainder of the crisis, accompanied by the faithful Monckton. In the event, he was never to return to Buckingham Palace as King.

'I do not find people angry with Mrs Simpson, but I do find an enraged fury against the King himself,' wrote Harold Nicolson in his diary the same night, after he had got home from giving a lecture in Islington where only about ten out of four hundred had joined in the singing of the National Anthem. 'In eight months he has destroyed the great structure of popularity which he had raised.' [46]

The Cabinet, hastily summoned, met again next morning, 4 December at 10.30. There were three items on the agenda – the King's proposed broadcast, the statement which the Prime Minister should make to the House of Commons on the morganatic marriage project, and what further representations he should make to the King on his future course of conduct.

First, the draft broadcast, described by Neville Chamberlain as 'an appeal to the people of the Empire to allow him to make a morganatic marriage', was read to the Cabinet. The Cabinet conclusion was summed up by Chamberlain in his diary:

> It was unanimously decided that it would be impossible to allow the King, while he was King, to broadcast or make any public utterance which had not been approved by his Ministers, since constitutionally they must be responsible for his words. [47]

Secondly, it was decided that 'it was essential that a statement should be made before the House rose for the week-end, at least on the question of a morganatic marriage, in the hope that the publication of the Government's decision not to introduce legislation for the purpose might stem the tide of propaganda which it was now realised was being organised in favour of such a course'. Accordingly, Simon as Home Secretary, as well as being a legal expert, was asked to draft a suitable statement for the Prime Minister to make in the afternoon, and this he undertook to do.

Discussion of the third item on the agenda was summarised by Lord Zetland in a private letter to Lord Linlithgow in New Delhi:

> There was a strong feeling in the Cabinet that the King should be asked to give his decision on the question of renunciation of the intended marriage or abdication without undue delay, since it was obvious that the crisis could not safely be permitted to exercise the public mind for an indefinite period; and the Prime Minister was

urged to lay before the King the desirability of his being placed in a position to make a definite statement to Parliament not later than Monday [7 December].[48]

Later the same day Baldwin wrote to the King informing him of the Cabinet's decision about the proposed broadcast:

In the case of broadcasting (as in the case of any other form of public address) there is a fundamental distinction between the position of the King and the position of a private person. As long as the King is King he can speak only in public in that capacity. If a Sovereign takes the formal action which is necessary to renounce the Throne, and if he becomes a subject of the reigning Sovereign, his claim to broadcast stands on quite a different basis. But the suggestion that the King should broadcast in the terms proposed is a suggestion that he should broadcast as King and while occupying the Throne. Such a broadcast could only be given on the advice of his Ministers, who would be responsible for every sentence of it. In these circumstances Mr Baldwin cannot advise that the King should broadcast as proposed.

The letter was accompanied by a memorandum apparently drafted by Simon in which the principles of ministerial responsibility were summarised. Such an intervention as the King wished to make, it was pointed out, would be calculated to divide his subjects into two opposing camps.

Moreover a Royal broadcast of the nature contemplated could only be given on the advice of *all* the King's Governments. Even if there were a change of Government in this country, and new Ministers could be found prepared to authorise such a proceeding, this would avail nothing unless all the Dominion Governments also approved the project.

Friday, on which the House meets at eleven in the morning and rises at 4.30 in the afternoon, is normally reserved for private members' bills and motions, and on this particular Friday, it looked as if business would be over shortly after lunch and the House would rise early. However, the Government Whips put up a backbencher to keep the debate going until Baldwin arrived just before four o'clock to make his statement on 'certain possibilities in the event of the King's marriage', as drafted by the Home Secretary with his usual skill. 'There is no such thing as what is called a morganatic marriage known to our law,' the Prime Minister announced.

The King was not himself bound by the Royal Marriages Act of 1772, which only applied to other members of the Royal Family who wished to marry, with the result that his wife automatically became Queen. The only possible way in which this result could be avoided would be by legislation dealing with a particular case. 'His Majesty's Government are not prepared to introduce such legislation,' Baldwin declared emphatically. Moreover, such a change could not be effected without the assent of all the Dominions, to whom it was a matter of common concern. 'I am satisfied from inquiries I have made,' he concluded, 'that this assent would not be forthcoming.'

This came as a real body blow to the King. 'I always thought I could get away with a morganatic marriage,' he was afterwards to remark. [49]

The Prime Minister read his statement to a hushed House, while the members of his Cabinet on the Treasury Bench beside him, 'looking like a picture by Franz Hals, a lot of grim Elders of the Kirk, squirmed uneasily'. When he sat down he was cheered from all sides. Churchill, in his usual place on the corner seat below the gangway on the Government side of the House, appeared to be scowling, and when the cheering persisted on the benches behind him he looked round as if in irritation. However, when he rose to repeat his previous question about no 'irrevocable step' being taken, he was greeted with some counter-cheers, which suggested support for a 'King's party'. The mood was reflected outside, where crowds began marching in the streets and assembled outside Buckingham Palace singing 'God Save the King'.

As soon as the House adjourned for the week-end, Baldwin and Major Dugdale drove off to Fort Belvedere to inform the King that his proposed broadcast had been turned down by the Cabinet. In fact, he had already heard the unpalatable news from Monckton, who sat in at this and all the subsequent audiences. At the same time, Baldwin handed the King a copy of an expert legal opinion supporting the Cabinet's decision which had been drafted by the indefatigable Simon.

After he had looked through this document, the King got to his feet, assuming the audience was at an end. But Baldwin had not finished. He went on to speak about 'the continued uncertainty', which 'if allowed to persist, was certain to create a dangerous constitutional position not only in this country but throughout the Empire'. Could the King give the Government his decision without further delay, if possible during the week-end? Perhaps even before he started back to London?

The King replied that the Prime Minister knew his views and he had not altered them. 'You will not have to wait much longer, Mr Baldwin,' he assured him.

It should be emphasised that, in spite of this dialogue, Baldwin did not press the King on the point, realising (as he afterwards told the Cabinet) that 'however great the inconveniences and even risk, the decision when taken must be the spontaneous decision of the King'. However, before he left The Fort, he did make a last appeal. 'There is still time for you to change your mind, Sir. That is indeed the prayer of Your Majesty's servants.' 'Mr Baldwin,' the King repeated as he showed his visitors out, 'I will let you know as soon as possible.'

The King had invited Churchill to dinner and shortly afterwards Churchill presented himself. During the meal he begged the King most strongly not to abdicate. He should ask for time – time to see what measure of support was forthcoming in Parliament and the country. 'We must have time for the big battalions to mass,' he said. 'We may win; we may not. Who can tell?'

Next morning, Churchill wrote to Baldwin, telling him that the King appeared to be under a very great strain and near breaking point, having had two marked and prolonged blackouts during the evening when he completely lost the thread of his conversation. Indeed, Churchill had strongly urged his staff to call in a doctor. 'I told the King that if he appealed to you to allow him to recover himself and to consider, now that they have reached their climax, the grave issues, constitutional and personal, with which you have found it your duty to confront him,' so Churchill concluded his letter, 'you would, I am sure, not fail in kindness and chivalry. It would be a most cruel and wrong thing to extort a decision from him in his present state.' [50]

At the same time, Zetland wrote to the Viceroy in New Delhi, indicating the danger of the situation as he saw it:

> India Office
> 5 December 1936
>
> The King is being advised by two different sets of people – first by his constitutional advisers, the Prime Minister and the Cabinet, and secondly by a body of unofficial advisers whose advice is having the effect of stiffening him against the advice of the Prime Minister and the Cabinet. He is being encouraged to believe that the Cabinet do not by any means reflect the united view of the people in their refusal to introduce legislation to legalise a morganatic marriage, and this theme is being harped on by certain sections of the press which is notorious for its habitual hostility to Baldwin. Among those working on these lines is undoubtedly Winston Churchill, who is said to be in close touch with Beaverbrook over the matter.
>
> The danger of the situation will be apparent to you. Supposing that

the King refuses to give a decision on either of the only two alternative courses which are open to him so long as the present Government remain in office, namely, to give up his intention of marrying Mrs Simpson or to abdicate, what will happen? The Government may be forced to resign. The Labour Party would almost certainly refuse to form a Government; but the King has undoubtedly been encouraged to believe that Winston would.

Winston could not survive in the present House of Commons, but it would be open to him to demand a dissolution. And therein lies the supreme danger, for the country would be divided into opposing camps on the question whether or not the King should be permitted to marry a woman – I say nothing about the antecedents of the woman, but you can imagine the sort of things that would be said in the heat of controversy on the platform and on the pavement – without making her Queen.

The Dominion Prime Ministers are strongly opposed to a morganatic marriage and legislation would be necessary not only here, but in every Dominion as well and it would not, so far as I can judge, be forthcoming. On this issue it might well be that the Empire would disintegrate, since the throne is the magnet which at present keeps it together, while there might arise a situation in this country which would not be far short of civil strife.

For a short time indeed the danger seemed very real. But even by that Saturday morning the King had already made up his mind. He would have nothing to do with any 'King's Party' as the Beaverbrook–Rothermere press called it. Shortly after breakfast, he sent for Monckton and said to him: 'I want you to go to London immediately and warn the Prime Minister that when he comes to The Fort this afternoon I shall notify him formally that I have decided to abdicate.'

Monckton pointed out that in this event, as soon as the King became a private citizen, he would still have to face the prospect of a prolonged separation from Mrs Simpson before her divorce decree became absolute and they were free to marry. Accordingly he suggested that, in addition to the Abdication Bill, he should ask the Government to present a second Bill simultaneously to Parliament which would make the divorce absolute forthwith.

Gratefully the King welcomed his friend's proposal; 'A lifeline thrown across a crevasse,' was how he described it.[51]

8

By the time Monckton reached Downing Street, the Cabinet had dispersed after meeting briefly to hear Baldwin's account of the inconclusive audience on the previous evening. However, Monckton had a word with Dugdale and Horace Wilson, and he invited them to join him and the King's solicitor George Allen for lunch at the Windham Club, which he and Allen had made their temporary London headquarters for dealing with the 'King's Matter'. Both Wilson and Dugdale conceded the justice of the proposed Divorce Bill and Wilson promised to lay it before the Prime Minister before the evening's audience. Wilson was as good as his word. Baldwin appeared favourably impressed and called in Simon who pronounced the proposed Bill to be 'practicable' and the legal difficulties 'not insuperable'. Neville Chamberlain also appeared to accept it. But they warned Baldwin that it would be certain to encounter opposition on religious grounds from ministers like Halifax, MacDonald, Inskip and Kingsley Wood. Baldwin repeated this warning when he met the King again that evening and the suggestion was formally raised by Monckton on the King's behalf. Baldwin added that he had called a meeting for Sunday morning of about a dozen of his Cabinet colleagues, whose opposition to the proposed Simpson Divorce Bill he anticipated and hoped to overcome. According to the King, Baldwin said he would resign if the Cabinet refused to approve this Bill. This is confirmed by the account which Monckton subsequently wrote of the Abdication.[52] ('S.B. said he would resign if he could not carry his colleagues. He would see the possibly awkward ones on Sunday.')

'Mr Baldwin was a cautious man,' wrote the King in recollecting the incident in his memoirs, 'and I never understood what persuaded him to make this handsome but rash promise. But it was made, I am sure, in good heart, although I do recall exchanging a wondering glance with Walter Monckton.' On the other hand, Monckton is also on record as having admitted under questioning that 'he did not recall any promise and that, if there was, certainly neither he nor the King attached any importance to it *at that time*'.

Monckton and Allen left The Fort shortly after Baldwin and went back to London to see the Treasury Solicitor who was preparing the two Bills. After they had seen and approved the drafts, Monckton arranged with Wilson to come to Downing Street next morning for the ministerial conference which Baldwin had summoned. Meanwhile Churchill was dining for the second night in succession with the King and discussing the appeal for delay which he had issued to the press earlier in the day, 'a masterly and objective exposition', as the King called it.

> I plead for time and patience. The nation must realise the character of the constitutional issue. There is no question of any conflict between the King and Parliament. Parliament has not been consulted in any way, nor allowed to express an opinion.
> The question is whether the King is to abdicate upon the advice of his Ministers of the day. No such advice has ever been tendered to a Sovereign in Parliamentary times.[53]

He went on to assert that no Ministry had the authority to advise the abdication of the Sovereign, nor had the Cabinet the right to prejudge the question 'without having ascertained at very least the will of Parliament'. If the King refused to take the 'advice' of his Ministers, they were of course free to resign. But they had no right whatever to put pressure upon him to accept their advice by soliciting beforehand assurances from the Leader of the Opposition that he would not form an alternative administration in the event of their resignation and thus confronting the King with an ultimatum.

Churchill's arguments, which were of doubtful constitutional validity, aroused deep resentment in the Cabinet and Parliament, as he was soon to discover. Also his plea came too late, since, although the King was temporarily affected by his friend's zeal in his case, he had no intention of changing his mind once it had been made up. Nevertheless Churchill still refused to believe that the die had already been cast for abdication, although Beaverbrook who had heard the news from Simon earlier in the day had told Churchill bluntly: 'Our cock won't fight.'

At 9.30 next morning, Sunday, 6 December, Baldwin saw those of his colleagues whom he had summoned to meet him in the Cabinet room for a discussion on the Simpson Divorce Bill. These were Neville Chamberlain, MacDonald, Simon, Oliver Stanley, Runciman, Inskip, Halifax, Kingsley Wood and Hoare. According to Hoare, Baldwin declared 'he was sure he could carry it through' and 'that he could not be responsible for any other policy'. Shortly afterwards the Prime Minister left the room and passed through the adjacent office, where Monckton was waiting. After greeting him pleasantly, Baldwin announced that he would shortly inform him of his colleagues' decision. But he did not reappear for two hours, having in the meantime gone off to Marlborough House to see Queen Mary and acquaint her with the latest development. When he returned to the Cabinet room, he found that the sense of the meeting was strongly against the Bill. Apparently the only real support for it came from Hoare, who observed that in his view it was not a moral issue but 'a choice between a ramp now or in five months' when the divorce decree was due to be made absolute. In view of the general feeling, Baldwin said he could only agree that the Bill should be dropped.

He then rose and, going to the door leading to the ante-room, opened it. 'Come in, Monckton,' he said. When he entered the Cabinet room, Monckton immediately sensed that the atmosphere was strained, as he glanced round the green baize table. It was left to Neville Chamberlain to make the announcement.

The Simpson Divorce Bill, Chamberlain told Monckton, was unacceptable on four grounds:

(1) it could not be denied that the King regarded the Bill as a condition of abdication, and it would therefore be denounced as an unholy bargain;

(2) it would irretrievably damage the moral authority of the Government at home and in the Empire;

(3) it would be looked on as an injury to the marriage law in general; and

(4) it would injure the respect for the monarchy.[54]

Someone asked Monckton what would be the King's reaction to the decision. Monckton replied that His Majesty had hoped that both Bills which the Prime Minister 'had looked upon with favour' would be acceptable. 'This decision will greatly disappoint him,' he added. 'In the light of the present circumstances, he will undoubtedly ask for additional time for further thought.'

At this point, Ramsay MacDonald spoke up. 'How much time will the King ask for? How many days?'

'Hardly days,' answered Monckton. 'I anticipate he will require weeks.' It would be necessary for him to consult his advisers, he went on, since 'a divergence of view had arisen'.

Baldwin who had hitherto been silent now interjected. 'This matter must be finished before Christmas.' Some other ministers remarked that this was too long to wait and the matter should be settled immediately. One minister was heard to say that the continued uncertainty was hurting the Christmas trade. According to Monckton, this observation emanated from Neville Chamberlain.

Finally Monckton said he would report to the King what had happened. When he did so later that day it was with some feeling. 'I was more philosophical,' the King admitted, 'although it did seem to me that the Chancellor of the Exchequer was being a trifle more mercenary than his office demanded.' According to Monckton, 'Baldwin was ready to resign but I told him the King would not wish that.' [55]

There was a full meeting of the Cabinet at 5.30 that evening. According to the index of Cabinet conclusions, which unlike the conclusions themselves have not been closed, possibly due to an official oversight, the first item to be discussed was the proposed Simpson Divorce Bill, which the Cabinet now formally declared it was 'unable to proceed with'. Also on the agenda was the question of the opinions of the Dominion Prime Ministers in response to the telegrams from the British Government and the action to be taken in the event of parliamentary questions being asked about them. Finally there was the interim statement which Baldwin would be expected to make in the Commons next day. After the Cabinet, Zetland wrote to Linlithgow:

> The statement will not contain anything very definite but will make it clear that we are not trying to rush the King into a hurried decision which is one of the charges now being brought against us by the Beaverbrook–Rothermere–Churchill combination and will point out, indeed, that he must be given time in which to come to a decision in a matter of such gravity.
>
> The King is, in fact, in a difficult position. He cannot be certain that the decree will be made absolute. He has asked, indeed, if the Cabinet could give him any guarantee that if he abdicates there will be no risk of anything happening to prevent the divorce becoming effective. The Cabinet are unable to give such a guarantee and it now remains to see how the King will react to this reply. Until we know, the matter rests much where it was. But if the agitation against the Government gains impetus from delay, something will have to be done. [56]

Baldwin felt confident that the opportunity which the week-end provided for contact with their constituents would rally the House of Commons behind him in spite of the continued outpourings of the Beaverbrook and Rothermere press in favour of a morganatic marriage. In the event his confidence was fully justified. 'I believe,' G. M. Young said to him afterwards, 'you were the only man on Friday who knew what the House of Commons would be thinking on Monday.' According to Young, he replied with a smile half-shy and half-triumphant, 'I have always believed in the week-end. But how they do it I don't know. I suppose they talk to the station master.' [57]

What Austen Chamberlain wrote privately to his sister Hilda on Sunday may be taken as typical of senior Conservative backbench opinion:

> It has been bad enough for months, but until a few weeks ago I thought the King had so strong a sense of public duty that there could be no question that he would subordinate his personal feelings to the needs of the State and to the dignity and usefulness of the Crown. I still hoped this even after the Aberdeen escapade and perhaps it would be better for him and for us if criticism had come earlier and he had been less sheltered.
>
> His grandfather as Prince heard some very plain speaking and learned his lesson. He at least knew what could and what could not be permitted to the wearer of the Crown, Ah me! What a tragedy it is! He seemed so pre-eminently fitted by temperament and training to be the King of the new age – if only he had known how to be King!
>
> . . . It looks now as if he was so much in the toils of this woman that he would abdicate rather than leave her . . . whatever happens it will take long to repair the damage done here and throughout the Empire.[58]

Another Tory backbencher, much less politically orthodox than Austen Chamberlain, who wrote to Baldwin, was Harold Macmillan. He had recently resigned the Government Whip, but he now assured the Prime Minister of his support 'for what it is worth'.

> As one who has criticised – perhaps wrongly but at least sincerely – some of the decisions of your Government, may I be allowed to send you a word to express my deep admiration of your handling of the present constitutional crisis . . .
>
> The slightest weakness now would be a shattering blow to the whole basis of Christian morality, already gravely injured during recent years. May God help you at this painful and difficult time.[59]

Another encouraging letter came from the late Lord Oxford and Asquith's daughter, Lady Violet Bonham-Carter:

> I feel I must write to send you, for what it is worth, the sympathy and the *gratitude* which I am feeling every hour and tell you, what you know already, that all the forces of decency are with you in solid loyalty.
>
> I think so often of my Father and thank Heaven for his sake that he didn't have your task to perform. But I also thank Heaven that you are there to do it.[60]

Even Londonderry, who had by this time made up his quarrel with the Prime Minister, sent him a few lines after seeing Churchill on Sunday, which seemed to suggest that some delay, 'a very short one', might be an advantage.

> My desire, and of course my knowledge is very imperfect and scanty, is that no charge could possibly be brought with any justice against you and the Government by any hostile section that an abdication was forced on the King during a week-end, as the general public are wholly unaware that this matter has been the subject of anxious consideration for several weeks. I myself have only realised it in the last few days.[61]

Baldwin's statement to the Commons on Monday afternoon that no decision had been reached and the monarch was still making up his mind was well received. Then Churchill, who tried to speak, was rudely shouted down amid cries of 'Drop it' and 'Twister' and was obliged to resume his seat but not before he had managed to shout at Baldwin: 'You won't be satisfied until you have broken him, will you?' The temperature was lowered immediately afterwards by George Lambert, an ex-chairman of the Liberal Parliamentary Party, who evoked wild applause by rising and asking: 'Does the Prime Minister realise the deep sympathy which is felt for him in all sections of the House?' Lord Winterton, afterwards the 'Father of the House', considered the Churchill incident one of the angriest manifestations he had ever heard directed against any man in the House of Commons. Indeed, it came as such a shock to Churchill himself that for a while he thought his political career was at an end.

'S.B. is on top of the problem and on top of his Cabinet,' Tom Jones remarked next day. 'Lambert's friendly intervention in the House yesterday and the prolonged cheers which followed bucked him up a lot. He'll go through with it but I expect a big reaction after it's over. Horace Wilson is invaluable to him in this sort of trouble and Walter Monckton and Simon ditto.'

A curious incident now occurred which formed as it were a plot within the plot of the main drama which was now approaching its climax. Theodore Goddard, Mrs Simpson's solicitor in the divorce, learned that another affidavit was about to be served by a private individual on the King's Proctor to the effect that the intervener was in a position to show why the decree should not be made absolute, 'by reason of material facts not having been brought before the court and/or by reason of the divorce having been obtained by collusion'. Goddard, who naturally felt he had a duty towards his client and that he ought to see her immediately, thereupon told Monckton. The latter passed on what he had heard to the King, who asked to see the solicitor and when Goddard appeared at The Fort forbade him to go to Cannes. Goddard then hastened to Downing Street, where he found the Prime Minister holding a copy of a statement which Mrs Simpson was going to release to the press next morning, 8 December. This was not a plain renunciation of the King but an offer, 'if such action would solve the problem, to withdraw forthwith from a situation that has been rendered both unhappy and untenable'. Baldwin, who was anxious to find out what Mrs Simpson's intentions really were, accordingly encouraged Goddard to go to Cannes, which he told him that it was his duty to do.

Goddard flew off to Cannes next morning accompanied by his doctor, since he suffered from a heart ailment, as well as his law clerk. However the doctor also happened to be a gynaecologist, and when this fact became known in the newspapers it gave rise to the unfounded rumour that Mrs Simpson was already pregnant, particularly as the law clerk was incorrectly described as an anaesthetist. ('I was shocked to the core of my being,' Mrs Simpson later recalled. 'Gynaecologist? Anaesthetist? Had the Prime Minister and my solicitor taken leave of their senses? Somebody had obviously gone mad.') On reaching Cannes, the solicitor conferred with his client, who assured him that 'she was, and still is, perfectly willing' to instruct him 'to withdraw her petition for divorce' and was also willing to do anything to prevent the King from abdicating. Having heard what she had to say, Goddard pronounced himself 'satisfied beyond any doubt that this is Mrs Simpson's genuine and honest desire'. Meanwhile, in London, the intervener, who turned out to be an elderly solicitor's clerk named Francis Stephenson employed in a London firm, decided not to proceed further with his application. Later the King's Proctor was to conduct his own investigation.[62]

Mrs Simpson's press release had been read over the telephone to the King who approved it, not realising that Mrs Simpson was ready to break off their engagement and withdraw her divorce petition. Indeed, several newspapers proclaimed that the crisis was over. However, the King soon cleared up the misunderstanding by assuring Mrs Simpson that if she were forced to throw him over he would follow her to the ends of the earth and get her back. She must not listen to Goddard, he insisted, and she must not be influenced by anything he said. Eventually Mrs Simpson assented.*

* According to Davidson, who later told Hoare, Goddard was also charged by Baldwin with the delicate task of recovering Queen Alexandra's emeralds, which the King had inherited from his grandmother.

For his part Baldwin was desperately anxious that the crisis should not be prolonged and when he saw Monckton on Tuesday morning, 8 December, the same day as Mrs Simpson's statement appeared, he suggested that he should go down to The Fort and make one last effort to persuade the King to remain. 'He must wrestle with himself in a way he has never done before,' said Baldwin, 'and if he will let me, I will help him. We may even have to see the night through together.' (G. M. Young thought that something of the old Wesleyan strain was perhaps audible in this utterance.) 'Hasn't everything been said that needs to be said?' the King queried, when Monckton telephoned the news of the proposed visit. In the light of the rebuffs he had suffered, particularly the rejection of the Simpson Divorce Bill by the Cabinet, this sudden solicitude, as he put it, struck the King as 'a trifle odd, if not gratuitous'. However, since 'it would have been ungracious not to receive him', the King said he could come.

Leaving Simon to answer any questions which might be put in the Commons, Baldwin set off for Fort Belvedere shortly after lunch, accompanied by Monckton and Dugdale. It was the first experience that Monckton had of motoring with the Prime Minister and he never forgot it. The journey was made in Baldwin's small black car, into which the three passengers and the driver were tightly squeezed. The recent collision had evidently made Baldwin more nervous than ever when being driven, since the driver had instructions to keep to a steady twenty-five miles an hour, with the result that overtaking drivers, unaware of the car's distinguished occupants, set up a furious honking in its wake. Meanwhile Baldwin was puffing away at his pipe and practising all the little habits which Monckton had learned by this time, particularly humming and snapping his fingers, as the vehicle became so full of smoke that the others literally gasped for air. 'I was praying for the journey to end,' Monckton later recalled, 'because I was so anxious about what was happening on the telephone with Cannes, and I knew that the King must be more tired than ever, and might hate the prospect of the Prime Minister staying the night.'

Indeed, when the King spotted Dugdale in the act of depositing Baldwin's suitcase in the hall he detailed a member of his staff – Sir Edward Peacock, who looked after the revenues of the Duchy of Cornwall – to explain to the Prime Minister that he was worn out and while of course he was welcome to stay to dinner he felt he could not have him for the night. Peacock duly explained this and Baldwin said he quite understood and would return to London after dinner, although Peacock offered to put him up in his own house.

The audience which took place in the drawing-room, with the large windows looking out on the gardens and the woods beyond, was to be the last that Baldwin had with King Edward VIII. The King sat in his usual chair by the fire with Baldwin on a sofa at right-angles to him, while Monckton was in a chair between them. Baldwin's deafness increased with fatigue and on this occasion it had a curious result, as when 'he urged once again all that he could do to dissuade the King, for the sake of the country and all that the King stood for, from his decision to marry', and 'the King wearily said that his mind was made up and he asked to be spared any more advice on the subject'. To Monckton's astonishment, Baldwin returned to the charge with increased vigour and, as Monckton thought, put the case even better than before. Then, turning to Monckton he asked him if he thought he had done all he could, and when Monckton explained that he thought 'he had done even more, it was plain that he had not heard the King's request to him to desist'.[63]

When the audience was over, the King appeared so exhausted that Monckton suggested that they should dine alone in his bedroom, leaving Baldwin and the other guests, eight in all including the King's brothers the Duke of York and the Duke of Kent, to have dinner by themselves downstairs. But the King made a supreme effort and eventually walked into the panelled dining-room dressed in his favourite white kilt and sat down at the head of the table with Baldwin at his right hand. By contrast with a short time before, he seemed in excellent spirits, the conversation never flagged and the topic which had brought them all together was never once mentioned. 'Look at him,' the Duke of York whispered to Monckton. 'We simply cannot let him go!' But both of them knew, as did Baldwin and everyone else at the table, that there was nothing that they could now say or do to stop him.

Towards the end of the meal, under the candlelight, the King looked at his Prime Minister, whose 'heavy face seemed pasty and lifeless', and he realised that the strain had also taken a heavy toll of him.

Shortly after dinner, the Prime Minister took his leave. As they parted in the hall, the King shook hands and said: 'I know that you and Mrs Baldwin do not approve of what I am doing, but I belong to a different generation.'

'Sir, it is quite true that there are no two people among your subjects who are more grieved at what has happened than we are,' Baldwin answered, 'but you must always remember that there are no two people who hope more sincerely that you may find happiness where you believe it to be found.'

'Although I never saw Mr Baldwin again,' the King was to recall many years later, 'I believe that he took from The Fort, that evening, the recollection of an unbowed, unresentful if somewhat whimsical Sovereign.'[64]

9

When the Cabinet assembled in Downing Street for the usual weekly meeting on Wednesday morning, 9 December, Baldwin reported that the King had requested him to say that it was his fixed intention to relinquish the Throne. The Prime Minister had spent seven hours at Fort Belvedere the evening before. 'It was like a mad house,' he said, and 'on the subject of marriage with Mrs Simpson the King was adamant.' He went on to describe the dinner, remarking (according to one account which reached The Fort) that 'the King appeared happy and gay, as if he were looking forward to his honeymoon'. It was useless doing anything more, Baldwin added. However, Hoare and Elliot took a different view and insisted, first, that they must ask the King to reconsider his decision, and secondly, that they must see, as a Cabinet, the message embodying this request. According to Hoare, 'Simon drafted the message, and put into it a lot about abdication', but 'I got this deleted'. Eventually the Cabinet officially passed a minute, and in accordance with it Baldwin addressed a message to the King 'with his humble duty', which stated that the Cabinet had received the statement of His Majesty's intentions 'with profound regret' and 'wished Mr Baldwin to convey to Your Majesty immediately the unanimous feeling of Your Majesty's servants'.

> Ministers are reluctant to believe that Your Majesty's resolve is irrevocable, and still venture to hope that before Your Majesty pronounces any formal decision Your Majesty may be pleased to reconsider an intention which must so deeply distress and so vitally affect all Your Majesty's subjects.*

In a second letter, likewise approved by the Cabinet, Baldwin reminded the King that in the event of his abdicating, since no higher constitutional authority existed, he would be obliged as Sovereign to provide Parliament with his own Royal Assent to his own Act of Abdication.

Only the first of these two communications which were rushed to The

---

* According to Hoare's view, 'S.B. would have destroyed himself if (1) he had not changed the Monday House of Commons statement into a friendly agreement for more time; (2) if the Cabinet had not sent this last request for reconsideration.' Hoare MS. 'King Edward's Marriage 35/36 Very Secret.' Templewood Papers IX, 7.

Fort required an answer, and the King immediately provided it with a brief statement in his own hand.

> The King has received the Prime Minister's letter of the 9 December 1936, informing him of the view of the Cabinet.
>
> His Majesty has given the matter his further consideration, but regrets that he is unable to alter his decision.

The Cabinet further directed that the Dominion Prime Ministers should be kept informed of the latest developments and the King was also advised of this. In this context an unusual situation had arisen in Dublin where for the past few days Mr de Valera had been urgently pleading for delay. However, the Free State Premier was not actuated by the same motives that had inspired Churchill. What de Valera wanted was sufficient time to introduce legislation of his own in the Dail, amending the Irish Free State Constitution by removing all references to the King and the Governor-General, thus taking advantage of the fact that England's difficulty was Ireland's opportunity. And this in the event he was to do.

During the afternoon of Wednesday, 9 December, a heavy fog descended on the Thames valley, so that it was not until several hours after he had left The Fort that Monckton reached Downing Street with the King's letter. The Cabinet was hastily called together and assembled in Baldwin's room at the House of Commons shortly before eight o'clock. 'We were informed that the King had received our message,' Zetland noted, 'but was unable to alter a decision which he had already intimated to the Prime Minister was irrevocable. He proposed, he said, to communicate a message to Parliament the following day. This, so far as we were concerned, at least had the merit of bringing the period of doubt to an end and the steps necessary to complete the arrangements for the relinquishment of the Throne by one individual and the accession to it of another were immediately put in hand.'[65] The terms of the short Abdication Bill, which had already been drafted by the Treasury Solicitor, were approved, and Baldwin intimated that he had told Monckton that everything must be completed by Friday, so that the new monarch, who was to be known as George VI, could hold his Accession Council on the following day. The Cabinet also passed a minute to the effect that the King must be absent from England for a period of not less than two years after he had abdicated, and this decision from which he did not dissent was duly communicated to him.

The King also let Baldwin know through Monckton that he intended to leave the country on the same day as the Abdication Bill became law and that before he did so he would make a farewell broadcast. Since he would then no longer be King, the Government would have no authority to seal his lips. However, out of courtesy, as he put it, he informed Baldwin through Monckton of the 'principal points' of the proposed broadcast, and these were considered by the Cabinet at this meeting. 'Some in the Government looked coldly upon the idea of my supplying an epilogue to a drama upon which the curtain had already descended,' he was to write in *A King's Story*. 'And even my mother tried to dissuade me.* But I was determined to speak. I did not propose to leave my country like a fugitive in the night.'⁶⁶ Apparently some ministers feared that he would use the opportunity provided by the broadcast to make an appeal calculated to divide the country. But they need not have worried. As Baldwin afterwards remarked to G. M. Young, 'whoever writes about the Abdication must give the King his due. He could not have behaved better than he did.'⁶⁷

After the Cabinet meeting most of the ministers including Baldwin and Duff Cooper dined together in their dining-room in the House. According to Duff Cooper, Ramsay MacDonald came in later than the others. 'Hullo,' said Baldwin. 'You look pretty glum!' 'Yes,' MacDonald replied, 'my body is here but my soul is elsewhere.' 'Well,' said Baldwin, 'I hope it's not at Cannes.' Afterwards Harold Nicolson, whom Duff Cooper had told about this encounter, noted in his diary: 'To do J.R.M. justice, he laughed at this.'⁶⁸

It was an especially gruelling day for Monckton. After the Cabinet he took Simon to dinner at his club, where together they drafted the King's Message to Parliament. They returned to Downing Street at ten for a meeting with representatives of the Dominions Office and the India Office, also Hardinge and Alan Lascelles, the King's Assistant Private Secretary, in order to co-ordinate the arrangements for abdication documents to be properly distributed throughout the Commonwealth at the right time and place. Afterwards Monckton noted that he had seen many staff officers but 'none so competent' as the Home Secretary showed himself to be on this occasion. Then, while the conference was still proceeding, Monckton was called to Marlborough House to show Queen Mary and the Duke of York the text of the Instrument of Abdication. Thus it was 1 a.m. before he arrived back at The Fort and was able to telephone Dugdale, who had

* Queen Mary wrote to her son on 11 December: 'Don't you think that as he the Prime Minister has said everything that could be said . . . it will now not be necessary for *you* to broadcast this evening, you are very tired after all the strain you have been and are going through, and surely you might spare yourself this extra strain and emotion – Do please take my advice.' James Pope-Hennessy, *Queen Mary* (1959), p. 580.

waited up with Baldwin in Downing Street, that the King had approved the document and would sign it at Fort Belvedere in the presence of his three brothers next morning.

Apart from Baldwin's few brief replies to Attlee's questions in the House of Commons, Parliament and the country were still largely in ignorance of the inner history of the crisis. Consequently there had been considerable relief when Baldwin announced on Wednesday afternoon that he would at length have a definite statement to make to them next day. There was no time to prepare a set speech and he knew that he would have to rely largely on the few scribbled notes he had made from time to time to refresh his memory at the various Cabinet meetings, to which he added one or two more notes on small slips of paper as different points occurred to him. Then he had to go off to Marlborough House during the morning to give Queen Mary some idea of what he was going to say.

He lunched quietly at No. 10 with his wife and Dugdale. The conversation did not flow very readily, as Dugdale has recalled, and Baldwin showed increasing signs of trepidation which his wife noticed. 'Just be yourself, Stan, and you'll be all right,' she told him. Then, as he and Dugdale were about to leave for the House of Commons, his notes could not be found. Eventually some odd bits of paper were recovered on the staircase and these were to form the sole basis of a speech the faithful Dugdale afterwards described as a masterpiece. As they drove along to New Palace Yard, Baldwin's nervousness disappeared and he turned to his companion and said: 'This is making history, and I am the only man who can do it.' [69]

By the time Baldwin had squeezed himself past his tightly wedged colleagues and taken his accustomed place on the Treasury Bench, during Questions, the chamber was overflowing with members, some sitting on the steps between the gangways and others crowding into the galleries. As often happens on such occasions, the solemnity was interrupted by touches of comedy. Baldwin wore a black tail-coat with a blue handkerchief protruding from the breast pocket, and he carried a red despatch box with him; but on sitting down was unable to find the key. However, after some rummaging in his pockets he retrieved the key and unlocked the box, from which he extracted several sheets of paper bearing the royal monogram embossed in red, together with his own scrappy notes. Harold Nicolson has described the scene after Baldwin had arranged 'these sheets of bromo carefully, and rather proudly, on the box in front of him'.

Questions proceed. There is one to Sam Hoare. He advances pompously to the box and places a file of Admiralty papers on the top of Baldwin's notes. He answers his question, then raises his Admiralty notes, which sends Baldwin's bromo fluttering to the floor. The old man collects them hurriedly and the next minute seizes his red-monographed sheets, walks firmly to the Bar, turns round, bows, and advances to the Chair. He stops and bows again. 'A message from the King,' he shouts, 'signed by His Majesty's own hand,' he then hands the papers to the Speaker.

The latter rises and reads out the message of Abdication in a quavering voice. The feeling that at any moment he may break down increases our own emotion. I have never known in any assemblage such accumulation of pity and terror.[70]

Indeed, according to one observer, when the Speaker came to the words 'irrevocable determination to renounce the throne', contained in the Instrument of Abdication, his voice broke and there were stifled sobs in the House. Baldwin then rose and moved formally: 'That His Majesty's most Gracious Message be now considered.'

'No more grave message has ever been received by Parliament,' he began, 'and no more difficult – I may almost say repugnant – task has ever been imposed upon a Prime Minister. I would ask the House, which I know will not be without sympathy for me in my position today, to remember that in this last week I have had but little time in which to compose a speech for delivery today, so I must tell what I have to tell truthfully, sincerely and plainly, with no attempt to dress up or adorn.' On the face of it his tale was largely a simple account of what had passed between him and the King. In reality it was an extremely adroit and subtle presentation of the facts, full of tributes to the King for his behaviour throughout the crisis, and designed to protect and preserve the Crown as the central feature of the constitution. He hesitated once or twice and got muddled due to his notes being in disarray. Once he turned to Simon, who was sitting beside him and asked in an audible aside: 'It was a Monday, was it not, the 19th?' To Harold Nicolson it seemed that the artifice of such asides was so effective that one imagined it to be deliberate. 'There is no moment when he overstates emotion or indulges in oratory. There is intense silence broken only by the reporters in the gallery scuttling away to telephone the speech paragraph by paragraph.'

In describing his audience with the King on 16 November, when he told him that the position of the King's wife was different from the position of any other citizen of the country, and that 'in the choice of a Queen the voice of the people must be heard', Baldwin quoted a few appropriate lines from *Hamlet*. Here again he was indebted to Simon who had suggested this particular Shakespearian quotation:

> His will is not his own;
> For he himself is subject to his birth,
> He may not, as unvalued persons do,
> Carve for himself; for on his choice depends
> The safety and the health of the whole State.[71]

When Monckton saw Baldwin earlier in the day, he had given him two small rectangular slips of paper on which the King had scribbled in pencil and which he hoped he would use in his speech. One of them referred to the King's confidence in his brother as his successor, and Baldwin quoted it with considerable effect:

Duke of York. He and the King have always been on the best of terms as brothers, and the King is confident that the Duke deserves and will receive the support of the whole Empire.

In the other note the King declared how 'the other person most intimately concerned' had consistently tried to dissuade him from the decision which he had taken. Baldwin did not make any reference to this note in his speech. It is possible that he mislaid it among his papers, but it is more likely that the omission was deliberate.* To have introduced it would have emphasised that the King and the King alone was responsible for his decision, and as he told Monckton he was anxious to present the King's action in the best light, and it would hardly have helped his case if he had added that, although Mrs Simpson had offered to give him up, the King still insisted on putting her before every claim of the Crown and every expression of his subjects' loyalty. As it was, he did succeed in bringing in Mrs Simpson with consummate tact and at the same time carrying the House with him when he said:

The King has told us that he cannot carry these almost intolerable burdens of Kingship without a woman at his side, and we know that this crisis, if I may use the word, has arisen now rather than later from that very frankness of His Majesty's character which is one of his many attractions.

Baldwin's last words on the 'King's Matter', before commending his successor to the House and the country, embodied a justifiable claim. 'I am convinced that where I have failed no one else could have succeeded.

---

* There is no trace of this note in the Baldwin Papers, although the first was carefully preserved.

His mind was made up, and those who know His Majesty will know what that means.'

Attlee, who was to reply for the Opposition, immediately asked that the sitting should be suspended until six o'clock, and this was done. Then, to quote Harold Nicolson, members filed out of the chamber, 'conscious that we have heard the best speech that we shall ever hear in our lives. There was no question of applause. It was the silence of Gettysburg.'

Shortly afterwards, Nicolson happened to bump into Baldwin in the corridor. It was impossible not to say something and Nicolson murmured a few kind words. The Prime Minister took him by the arm. 'You are very kind,' he said, 'but what did you really think of it?'

'It was superb,' answered Nicolson. 'I regretted only that Hitler, Mussolini and Lord Beaverbrook had not been in the Peers' Gallery.'

'Yes, it was a success,' Baldwin agreed. 'I know it. It was almost wholly unprepared. I had a success, my dear Nicolson, at the moment I most needed it. Now is the time to go.'

Nicolson made no reply, since there was nothing more he could say. Then Baldwin got on to the subject of Churchill. 'Do you know, my dear Nicolson,' he continued, 'I think Winston is the most suspicious man I know. Just now I said that the King had said to me: "Let this be settled between you and me alone – I don't want outside interference." I meant to indicate by that the reasons why I had not made it a Cabinet question from the start. But Winston thought it was a thrust aimed at him, and he has been at my Private Secretary within the last five minutes.'

Nicolson suggested that Churchill had put himself in a false position. Baldwin flung up his hand. 'We are all in false positions!' he exclaimed.[72]

The subsequent speeches were described by Lord Zetland as being 'of great dignity and pathos in our House and of mingled excellence and bad taste in the House of Commons'.

In the Commons, Winston Churchill, who recalled that as Home Secretary, more than a quarter of a century before, he had stood beside the King at his investiture as Prince of Wales amid the sunlit battlements of Caernarvon Castle, now gracefully bowed to the inevitable. He agreed with Baldwin that 'the decision taken this week, has been taken by His Majesty freely, voluntarily and spontaneously, in his own time and in his own way'.

I should have been ashamed if, in my independent and unofficial position, I had not cast about for every lawful means, even the most forlorn, to keep him on the throne of his fathers, to which he only recently succeeded amid the hopes and prayers of all. In this Prince there were discerned qualities of courage, of simplicity, of sympathy, and, above all, of sincerity, qualities rare and precious which might have made his reign glorious in the annals of this ancient monarchy.

It is the acme of tragedy that these very virtues should, in the private sphere, have led only to this melancholy and bitter conclusion. But, although our hopes today are withered, still I will assert that his personality will not go down uncherished to future ages, that it will be particularly remembered in the homes of his poorer subjects, and that they will ever wish from the bottom of their hearts for his private peace and happiness and for the happiness of those who are dear to him.

Less happy were the contributions from James Maxton, the left-wing chairman of the Independent Labour Party, who described the monarchy as the symbol of a class-ridden society and expressed the hope that its prestige had that day received a shock from which it would not recover, and his fellow-Clydesider George Buchanan, who accused the Government of having one law for royalty and another for the working man by being accessory to collusive divorce proceedings, a charge which the Government had been most anxious to avoid. 'A divorce case was taken when everyone of you knows it was a breaking of the law,' Buchanan fulminated at the Treasury Bench. 'You are setting aside your laws for a rich and pampered royalty.'

In his speech Baldwin had emphasised the importance of the Abdication Bill being passed into law next day. This was facilitated by the Commons sitting at eleven o'clock, as it normally did on a Friday, when the measure was rushed through all its stages.

In moving its Second Reading, which was carried by a majority of 403 to 5, Baldwin reminded the House that the Bill also concerned the Dominions, and stated that four of them (Canada, Australia, New Zealand and South Africa) desired to be associated with it in its present form. Only the Irish Free State took a different line, said Baldwin, and Mr de Valera was immediately calling his Parliament together to pass legislation dealing with the situation there.* The Bill's remaining stages were carried without

---

* De Valera had earlier made it clear to the Dominions Secretary that he and his Government could not follow the example of the other Dominions and introduce identical legislation in Dublin, so that the abdication of Edward VIII and the succession of the Duke of York would take place simultaneously throughout the Commonwealth. ('It was unthinkable that they should make themselves responsible for putting one British King off a throne in the Irish Free State only to elevate another.') Therefore, whatever the British Government did, he and his colleagues would do nothing. With Baldwin's assent Malcolm MacDonald pointed out to de Valera what the consequences would be of his proposed inaction – the Duke of York would become King as George VI in every part of the Commonwealth except the Irish Free State,

a division. When he moved the Third Reading, Baldwin remarked in a final tribute to the departing monarch that 'we shall always remember with regard and affection the whole-hearted and loyal service that His Majesty has given to the country as Prince of Wales and during the short time he has been on the Throne'.

Shortly before 1.30 p.m. the Bill was sent to the Lords and passed through all its stages there in a quarter of an hour. Fortunately it had been pointed out just in time by the First Parliamentary Counsel Sir Granville Ram that an Act of Parliament, in the absence of words to the contrary, takes effect from the first moment of the day on which it receives the Royal Assent.[73] Thus if the Bill had remained as drafted, Edward VIII would have ceased to be King some hours before he purported to give the Royal Assent. In these circumstances the Royal Assent could only properly be given by his successor King George VI, who would have been most reluctant to do so as the first official act of his reign. The matter was put right at the last minute by an addition specifying that '*immediately upon the Royal Assent being signified to this Act* the Instrument of Abdication executed by his present Majesty . . . shall take effect, and thereupon His Majesty shall cease to be King and . . . accordingly the member of the Royal Family then next in succession to the Throne shall succeed thereto . . .'

The Commons led by the Speaker with Baldwin and Attlee walking immediately behind him were duly summoned to the Bar of the Upper House to hear the Royal Assent being formally given by a Commission of three peers after the Clerk of the Parliaments Sir Henry Badeley had solemnly read out the text of 'His Majesty's Declaration of Abdication 1936' Act. 'I do not suppose,' wrote Lord Zetland later that day, 'that many of us who were present will live through a more dramatic moment than we did when Sir H. Badeley turned from the three noble lords seated in front of the throne to the Speaker and members of the House of Commons standing at the Bar and uttered the words, "*Le Roy le veult.*" Thus at eight minutes before two o'clock did Edward VIII cease to be King.'

---

where Edward VIII would continue to be the sovereign, while Mrs Simpson when she married him would presumably become Queen of Southern Ireland.

'This must have shaken de Valera,' MacDonald wrote afterwards. At all events he reacted very quickly by immediately introducing the constitutional legislation which removed the Crown from domestic affairs but preserved its functions in relation to external affairs. See Malcolm MacDonald, *Titans and Others* (1972), pp. 66 ff.

10

On his return to Downing Street, Baldwin received a handwritten letter from Queen Mary, who had gone the previous day to hear him from the gallery of the House of Commons.[74]

> Marlborough House,
> 11 December 1936

Dear Prime Minister,

We all listened to your wonderful speech yesterday and I feel I must write and thank you for the kind way you spoke of the King. Your speech has had a quieting effect on people and has helped us all very much to face the future with faith and courage.

Thank you gratefully and with all my heart for the kindness and patience you have shown towards the King during these long and anxious weeks . . .

I fear you must be dreadfully tired.

> Believe me,
> Yours very sincerely,
> MARY R

Meanwhile Churchill had been lunching with the King at Fort Belvedere, helping to put the finishing touches to the historic broadcast which the King was to make later the same day from Windsor Castle, when he confessed to his former subjects that he had found it impossible to carry the heavy burden of responsibility and to discharge his duties as King 'without the help and support of the woman I love'. It later became part of the Abdication Legend that the speech had been written by Churchill. This was not so. In fact it was largely drafted by Monckton, who incidentally persuaded the King to agree to the insertion of a statement to the effect that the ministers of the Crown, 'and in particular Mr Baldwin', had always treated him 'with full consideration'. Sir John Reith, the head of the BBC, intended to introduce him on the air as plain Mr Windsor, until the new Sovereign pointed out that by abdicating he had not forfeited the style of Prince, which he had acquired by birth as the son of a royal duke, and so in the event he was correctly announced as 'His Royal Highness Prince Edward'. After the broadcast he drove to Portsmouth Harbour where he embarked on a destroyer of the Royal Navy which was to convey him to a long and, at any rate at first, lonely exile. On reaching France, he sent a telegram to Mrs Baldwin thanking her for a letter of sympathy which she had written him and for her husband's 'great understanding at this difficult time'. He later remarked that 'the Prime Minister is the only person who has said any kind word to me about the future and wished me good luck'.

Next morning, Saturday, 12 December, Baldwin attended the Accession Council in St James's Palace and heard the new sovereign declare his 'adherence to the strict principles of constitutional government' and his 'resolve before all else to work for the welfare of the British Commonwealth of Nations'. At the same time he heard him announce that his first act on succeeding his brother would be to confer a Dukedom on him and that henceforth he would be known as 'His Royal Highness the Duke of Windsor'.

Baldwin also broadcast during the week-end on the subject of the abdication, as did the Archbishop of Canterbury. Both broadcasts were heard by millions of listeners at home and overseas. But whereas Baldwin's, framed in his usual felicitous language, was marked by the same friendly sympathy as he had shown in the House of Commons, the Archbishop launched an ill-conceived attack on the late King, which was keenly resented by many who heard it. His Grace recalled that it was on the 11th day of December 248 years ago that King James II fled from Whitehall and by a strange coincidence it was on the same day of the same month that King Edward VIII left Windsor Castle, the scene of all the splendid traditions of his ancestors and his throne, and went out an exile. ('In darkness he left these shores.') The Archbishop then went on to condemn the monarch for having surrendered the high and sacred trust he had received from God.

> With characteristic frankness he has told us his motive. It was a craving for private happiness. Strange and sad it must be that for such a motive, however strongly it pressed upon his heart, he should have disappointed hopes so high and abandoned a trust so great. Even more strange and sad it is that he should have sought his happiness in a manner inconsistent with the Christian principles of marriage, and *within a social circle whose standards and ways of life are alien to all the best instincts and traditions of his people. Let those who belong to this circle know that today they stand rebuked by the judgment of the nation which had loved King Edward.*

'I have shrunk from saying these words,' the Archbishop declared. 'But I have felt compelled for the sake of sincerity and truth to say them.' The real truth is that the Primate's allocution was an extraordinary compound of ignorance and prejudice. The social circle so roundly condemned in this notorious broadcast consisted of people like the Duff Coopers, the Brownlows, the Marlboroughs, the Sutherlands, the Channons, the Edens, the Mountbattens, Sir Samuel Hoare, Lady Cunard and various foreign ambassadors, besides many more whose 'personal reputations', in Channon's words, were 'quite unsullied'. It is true that some of them, such as Lady Cunard, Lady Furness and Mrs Simpson herself, were American by birth, but they were or had been married to members of the English aristocracy and upper classes – even the unfortunate Ernest Simpson, who worked in the City, had been a Guards officer – and they had thoroughly assimilated English 'standards and ways of life'. Certainly they were in no sense 'alien to the best instincts and traditions' of Edward VIII's subjects. When Lord Brownlow called at Lambeth Palace and civilly demanded an apology for the false construction which had been placed on his loyalty to his sovereign and which incidentally had done him incalculable harm, the Archbishop flatly refused. 'The innocent must suffer with the guilty,' he remarked. Pressed by Brownlow to name the members of the late King's allegedly disreputable social circle, the Primate was at a loss for a reply. The fact was that he did not know.[75]

The Archbishop's broadcast attracted a large and overwhelmingly hostile mail. One correspondent, widely believed to be the writer Gerald Bullett, was moved to communicate in verse and his composition secured a wide currency. A copy eventually reached Baldwin's desk:

> My Lord Archbishop, what a scold you are!
> And when your man is down, how bold you are!
> Of Christian charity how scant you are!
> And, auld Lang swine, how full of cant you are!

A more kindly if slightly ambiguous letter of praise came from the Prime Minister, in which the Archbishop's effort was described as 'the voice of Christian England'. To this the Primate sent the following reply:

Lambeth Palace. 14 December 1936. I cannot tell you how greatly encouraged I was by your kind and generous letter. I felt acutely the difficulty of my task, and when I went to the BBC last night I was oppressed by a sense of the inadequacy of my words. I am the more thankful to hear from many today whose opinion is worth having that I did not wholly fail. But of course your letter was to me of far greater value than any other. I cannot but thank you with all my heart for having written it.

I like to think that at least your Christian shoulders have been eased of this burden. But how well you carried it! The universal testament of Parliament and People must be some reward for all those weeks of toil and strain. You have lived to play a decisive part in English history.[76]

One person who was greatly disturbed by the Archbishop's public rebuke was Sir Patrick Gower, who had been a member of Baldwin's secretariat and was now Chief Publicity Officer at Conservative Central Office. He wrote to Geoffrey Fry, his former colleague in Downing Street, on 16 December:

If there are repetitions of statements of this kind I am afraid that they will undo a great deal of S.B.'s work. He succeeded in convincing the country that there was no Constitutional crisis, that there was no attempt on the part of the Government to force him [the King] to abdicate, and that the whole issue arose because the King had expressed a desire to marry Mrs Simpson . . .

If now that he has abdicated, attempts are made to criticise his behaviour, I feel that the consequences may be disastrous from many points of view. The public may begin to think that after all there was a definite desire in high quarters to get rid of him because of his moral conduct. Their sympathies will be intensified because any attacks on him will be contrary to the good old British instinct that you do not 'kick a fellow when he is down'. These sympathies may be increased by the thought that he is out of the country and, therefore, not in a position to defend himself. What is more, criticisms of this kind would make it easier for the Rothermere and Beaverbrook Press to keep the subject alive.

From every point of view the less we hear about the late King and his activities in the newspapers the better. The public will soon forget him if he ceases to be an object of popular interest in the papers, but nothing will do more to complicate matters than to throw brick bats at him now that it is all over.[77]

The subject of the ex-King's social circle prompted another writer, Osbert Sitwell, to compose a scathing poem entitled 'Rat Week', in which the author castigated those, admittedly not many, who on the morrow of the Abdication proclaimed that they had never really liked Mrs Simpson or else that they scarcely knew her. A copy of the poem, like Gerald Bullett's lampoon, duly reached Baldwin's hands. 'He read it to me at Chequers,' the art connoisseur and former Tory minister Lord Crawford reported to Tweedsmuir in Ottawa. 'This is one of his week-end re-laxations and the best entertainment he can give his guests.'

'We have a PM who sees some things quite simply and of this business he has been master throughout and quite calm,' wrote Tom Jones by way of summing up. 'There was no rough word between him and the King. And in the Cabinet S.B. was easily supreme. Fortunately there was among his colleagues a strong Nonconformist element. And in the Dominions there were Prime Ministers who knew the personal and moral qualities of our Prime Minister. Lyons and Hertzog were firm and prompt; Mackenzie King less forthcomingly prompt. But there has been no ministerial crisis. De Valera goes his own tortuous way almost unnoticed here. All who know the new King say he will grow into the likeness of his father.' [78]

'S.B. as I anticipated,' wrote Neville Chamberlain, 'has reaped a rich harvest of credit which has carried him to the highest pinnacle of his career.' Although this remark was made in a private letter to Hilda Chamberlain, which he could not possibly have seen, it is worth noting that it should have been confirmed by Winston Churchill who used the same word a dozen years later in *The Gathering Storm*.

> The Prime Minister proved himself to be a shrewd judge of British national feeling. Undoubtedly he perceived and expressed the pro-found will of the nation. His deft and skilful handling of the Abdication crisis raised him in a fortnight from the depths to the pinnacle. [79]

Of the mass of letters – the majority congratulatory, others abusive – that flowed in to Downing Street and were carefully sifted by his secre-taries, Baldwin kept more than a hundred. Only a very few can be noticed here. 'What a debt of gratitude I think the nation and Empire owe you,' wrote J. R. M. Butler, the historian son of his old master at school and university. 'I hope they will not forget it. I am sure Harrow and Trinity will not.' [80] One letter which must have particularly touched his heart came from Phyllis Broome, a boyhood flame and neighbour in Worcester-shire. 'Dearest Stan,' she wrote:

> I do want to add my small local squeak to the immense Hallelujah Chorus of gratitude and admiration that goes to you from all Britain and beyond. *What* a life to look back on! If the memory of your father has been a trumpet call to you (a remark of yours that always sticks in my mind) what a grand fanfare it sounded. I wish he could have heard it in the distance the last afternoon I had tea with him and your

mother so many years ago. Thank you, Stan dear, for all you have done for, and been to, England – for those who are gone as well as for ourselves.[81]

A veritable *cri de cœur* came from Baldwin's literary friend Helen Waddell:

I began many letters to you and could not go on, for there was so much bitterness in my heart. Never against you, but against mankind. Their cruelty, their fickleness, their smugness in the face of tragedy. Your final speech was like a mountain. But the days before it were poisoned to me by the slow distilled venom of the leaders in *The Times*. What blackness of heart was in Geoffrey Dawson, wounded vanity or secret spite, that made him pursue that haunted figure, that 'Love in desolation masked'? It was anguish to me to read them. But three people in that tragedy redeemed it: the lad that is gone, the brother who succeeded him with such heartbroken chivalry, and you that were father to them both.[82]

Finally, the new monarch wrote from Sandringham on New Year's Eve:

I do want to tell you how much I admired the dignified way you carried out a very difficult and very delicate task in that most unfortunate affair, and to congratulate you on the way that all parties rallied to you in the House of Commons during those fateful days.

I am new to the job, but I hope that time will be allowed to me to make amends for what has happened.

I am very grateful for what you have done, and that the country and Empire appreciate it too.[83]

'Sir, if I may say so,' Baldwin replied to this last letter, 'you need have no fear for the future, so far as you are concerned. The whole country is behind you with a deep and understanding sympathy.'[84]

As was their wont, Baldwin and his wife went to Astley for the Christmas holiday, much of which the Prime Minister spent answering his huge mail by hand. To Tom Jones who had sent him several volumes of Seneca, he wrote on Boxing Day:

We had a wonderful day yesterday for Christmas. The sunrise was as the opening of the gates of heaven itself and the glow it threw on the western hills transfigured the whole landscape for half an hour. The strange unearthly light lasted for nearly all day . . .

I am feeling quietly content and very thankful.

That *was* good of you to send me the Senecas for Christmas. I have only his letters. I value them. Bless you.[85]

Baldwin had sent a signed Christmas card to the Duke of Windsor, as also (he was astonished to learn) had Ernest Simpson. 'I don't want our old friendship to die on my hands,' he told Walter Monckton. 'Of course, she will look over his shoulder and say: "That old b——?" (or whatever may be the Baltimore equivalent!) But I must take the risk of that.'[86]

'Up to the waist in letters,' he wrote to the Davidsons on New Year's Eve. 'They are still pouring in from all over the Empire and the personal ones I feel I *must* answer myself. I have done about sixty and am still spending a good slice of every morning writing till I am in a dream.'[87]

After Lord Brownlow had returned from the Continent, where he left Mrs Simpson in the care of her friends at Cannes and had also arranged for Baron and Baroness Eugene de Rothschild to offer the Duke of Windsor the hospitality of their castle, Schloss Enzefeld, on the shore of an Austrian lake, during the months of waiting before he could be reunited with Mrs Simpson, the ex-King's faithful courtier was invited to Chequers to report on his mission. He told Baldwin, whom he found 'interested and sympathetic', that his late master was 'quite pathetic and highly nervous'.

He sleeps in a room at Enzefeld entirely devoid of anything personal except several large photographs of Wallis. No bibelots, nothing personal at all except a little yellow pillow on his bed that was once hers. Everything belonged to the palaces which are entailed 'on the King'. All that he has is twenty-six suits of clothes and a Cairn terrier . . .

Brownlow added that he was 'desperately sorry for him' and did not know which of his moods was more tragic, 'when he is angry, and delighted to have cut the painter thinking only of his marriage with Wallis, or when he is gayer and chatters of old days and of his intention of keeping his Colonel-cies, etc., in various regiments'.[88]

Afterwards Brownlow lost his job of Lord-in-Waiting, a mean and shabby reward for his loyalty to the late sovereign, for which Wigram and Hardinge appear to have been responsible. But Brownlow, though greatly hurt by this treatment, bore little if any malice, and he did not complain in the letter which he subsequently wrote to Baldwin, thanking him and his wife for their hospitality at Chequers.

> I do not wish to go any further into the tragic events of last month, except to say that the Archbishop was very kind, but equally firm! and while for obvious reasons would withdraw nothing, was good enough to say that he did not regard me as an 'exotic' in any shape or form!! and never had.
>
> May I, Sir, in conclusion thank you once more for your personal kindness and sympathy to me on my return from perhaps the saddest and most difficult journey ever undertaken. I shall never regret it in any way, for like you I was, and *still* am, devoted to my late master, in spite of his tragic folly.[89]

Although the interfering busybody Mr Francis Stephenson had announced that he was taking no further proceedings to stop the Simpson divorce, his intervention still remained on the file of the Divorce Registry. This posed a problem for Somervell and Barnes, the King's Proctor. Should they make *all* inquiries or not? Somervell took a little time to make up his mind. Assuming there was some evidence of adultery, he argued, if brought to the notice of the court, Mrs Simpson and the Duke of Windsor might well return to England to give evidence and deny it. 'Even if proved, would not the Court on ordinary principles grant a discretion, particularly as Mrs Simpson could plead the difficulty of informing the Court of her misconduct with the then ruling Sovereign? Result a first-rate and squalid sensation and the divorce allowed as if I had never intervened.'

However, during the Christmas holidays, the King's Proctor, who had been bombarded with abusive letters urging him to intervene and stop the divorce, wrote to Somervell suggesting that he should follow up inquiries on adultery as well as collusion. He had already with the Attorney-General's approval seen some of the apparently more responsible of his correspondents, who admitted that 'they had no evidence but were repeating the gossip of the Clubs or the Temple'. Somervell wrote back agreeing, and Barnes as a result interviewed countless people, members of the crew of the yacht *Nahlin*, servants, hall porters and the like. 'It was more than in most cases,' commented Somervell, 'because people wrote suggesting suspicious events which on examination turned out never to have happened.' In the end the King's Proctor was convinced that they would get nothing in the way of credible evidence. 'Whether or not they ever committed adultery,' Somervell added in his account of the matter, 'is a question on which I believe those who know him well differ.'

It became however obvious that if they had done so they had not done so openly and had also not publicly indulged in the familiarities which normally indicate cohabitation. Our inquiries also confirmed the view that the divorce, even if it had some collusive factor, e.g. the willingness of Mrs Simpson that her husband should be unfaithful, was not a collusive divorce in the ordinary or any provable sense.

At all events the President of the Divorce Court, Sir Boyd Merriman, duly dismissed Mr Stephenson's intervention in the suit of Simpson v. Simpson, and the divorce decree was made absolute on 27 April, exactly six months after the original hearing at Ipswich.*

A few days before this, Baldwin saw Brownlow and suggested that he should write to the Duke of Windsor on the subject of his future conduct. This Brownlow did and sent Baldwin a copy of the relevant passage in his letter:

(a) In the interests of all concerned, you should postpone any plans to return for as long as possible. You know the reasons and difficulties, Sir, and I am sure that the future and ultimate happiness of both of you is already interlocked with this decision; a premature or ill-timed visit might well leave a scar of sorrow and disappointment you might find difficult in removing from your memory.

(b) While you are abroad, prolonged visits and close contacts in Fascist countries would be unwise from your point of view, as it might create suspicion and hostility in the Left Wing in England, which would react against you and your ultimate return.[90]†

The announcement shortly afterwards of the Duke's forthcoming

* Writing twenty-five years later to a biographer of Edward VIII, who had sent him the first draft of his book and can only have been Robert Sencourt, whose *Reign of Edward VIII* appeared in 1962, Somervell remarked: 'You half suggest that the divorce case was brought on at Ipswich because Hawke [Monckton's predecessor as the King's legal adviser] was the Judge: You half suggest that the divorce was collusive; you say that the witnesses were "suborned". I have quite good grounds for believing that all these gross accusations are untrue. The result is that I would not wish to be associated in any way with your book. I feel that Baldwin would have felt the same objection.' Draft letter in the Somervell Papers.

Sencourt's belief that the Simpson divorce had been a collusive action was apparently formed as the result of an interview he had with the *maître d'hôtel* of the Hôtel de Paris in Bray where Ernest Simpson had stayed with the unnamed woman in the case, afterwards sending the bill to his wife's solicitors as evidence of his adultery. According to the *maître d'hôtel*, whom the present writer has also consulted, he had been asked by Simpson's solicitors to keep their client and the lady under careful observation during their stay, particularly when breakfast was brought to their room. But such a precaution, which was then customary in divorce cases, did not necessarily imply that this one was collusive, although Robert Sencourt appears to have formed the impression from what the *maître d'hôtel* told him that it was.

† The Duke disregarded this advice, since later the same year he and his wife visited Germany, where they were received and entertained by Hitler, Goering, Hess and other Nazi leaders.

marriage made it necessary for his style and title to be given legal form. This King George VI proposed to do by the issue of Letters Patent, which would also indicate whether Mrs Simpson on becoming Duchess of Windsor would thereby acquire the right to be styled Royal Highness like her husband. Letters Patent were issued under the Great Seal which was affixed by the Lord Chancellor and therefore required the approval of the Cabinet, and in this instance of the Dominion Cabinets too. First the King informed Baldwin how he and his family felt on the subject.[91]

Since he was on the point of handing over to Neville Chamberlain at this time, Baldwin did not relish the idea of sounding out the Dominion Ministers and he told Simon that he wished Chamberlain to do it. Chamberlain grumbled but did as he was asked, with the result that the Dominion Ministers unanimously came down in favour of the issue of the Letters Patent in the form desired by the King. In fact the Letters Patent were approved by the Cabinet on 26 May and immediately issued under the Great Seal; they accorded the Duke of Windsor the title of 'Royal Highness' but precluded his wife and any descendants they might have from using it. The reaction of Mr Savage of New Zealand was characteristic of all the Dominion Prime Ministers. On being informed that on her marriage Mrs Simpson would henceforth be known as 'Her Grace the Duchess of Windsor', Mr Savage observed to Baldwin: 'And quite enough too!'[92]

Monckton had previously written to Simon warning him that to deprive the Duke's wife of the title that would otherwise have been hers was bound to create an intense bitterness in the Duke which should not be underestimated. Since the minutes of the Cabinet which considered the question are closed with the rest of the Cabinet papers relating to the Abdication, it is impossible to say with any certainty how all the members felt individually. Monckton thought that if it had been left to them, the Letters Patent might not have been issued at all, but that it was the Dominions, particularly Australia and Canada as he had been informed, that tipped the scale against Mrs Simpson. Certainly if the matter had been left to Baldwin alone, it is quite possible that he would have allowed Mrs Simpson to become 'royal' and to have enjoyed the bows and curtsies which by convention accompanied this style. But from his place in the Prime Minister's chair in the Cabinet room, the last occasion on which he was to occupy it, Baldwin could not do other than accept the majority view in the light of the messages from the Dominions. His feelings were shared by Ramsay MacDonald, who was also on the point of retiring. MacDonald had to leave before the meeting concluded, but he wrote to Baldwin next morning to let him know that he was 'perfectly willing to fall in with the Cabinet's decision'. By an ironic coincidence, which was not lost upon the Duke of Windsor, the Cabinet decision formally embodied in the Letters Patent was announced on the same page of the *London Gazette* as the King's decision to confer an earldom on Mr Stanley Baldwin to mark his retirement as Prime Minister.[93]

The unpalatable news was contained in a letter from King George VI to his brother which was brought by hand of Walter Monckton when he arrived with George Allen and Randolph Churchill at the Château de Candé, near Tours, where the Duke's wedding took place in the following week.

'This is a nice wedding present!' exclaimed the Duke, on reading the letter. 'I know Bertie – I know he couldn't have written this letter on his own.' The Duke's immediate reaction was to declare his intention of giving up the royal title for himself rather than continue to use a style different from his wife's. But with her help Monckton dissuaded him from this course. It would have been openly offensive to the King, Monckton pointed out, and would have meant giving up something for very little. Nevertheless, according to the Duchess, nothing in the aftermath of the Abdication hurt the Duke of Windsor more than his brother's action. 'In his eyes it was an ultimate slur upon his wife, and, therefore, upon himself. He could not bring himself wholly to blame his brother, who, he knew had bowed to strong pressure. But his action made for a coolness between them thereafter.' As it was, the Duke could neither forgive nor forget a decision, for which he was to consider Baldwin partly responsible, since he had presided at the Cabinet which had ratified it. Thirty years later it still rankled with him, when he wrote in a New York newspaper that 'this cold-blooded act, in its uprush, represented a kind of Berlin wall alienating us from my family'.[94]*

* Monckton greatly sympathised with the Duke of Windsor over this. 'When he had been King,' Monckton wrote after his return from the wedding, 'he was told he could not marry Mrs Simpson because she would have to take his status and become Queen, so he gave up his Kingdom and Empire to make her his wife. He could not give up his royal birth, or his right to be called "His Royal Highness" which flowed from it. It was a little hard to be told, when he did marry her, that she would not have the same status as himself.' Birkenhead, *Walter Monckton*, p. 166.

The Duke raised the question with Monckton at the time, and Monckton advised him to consult Sir William Jowitt who produced a closely reasoned opinion which had been drafted by his junior Walter Wigglesworth and was to the effect that the act depriving the Duchess of the style of HRH was illegal. No further action was taken until after the war when Jowitt became Lord Chancellor in the first post-war Labour Government and the Duke reminded him of his opinion. But Jowitt did nothing and the matter was finally dropped although not forgotten by the Duke. The arguments questioning the validity of the Letters Patent of 26 May 1937 restricting the royal title to the Duke have been persuasively advanced by Philip M. Thomas in the 1967 edition of *Burke's Peerage* and by Patrick Montague-Smith in his editorial preface to the 1972 edition of *Debrett's Peerage*. For the contrary argument, see letter by the present writer in *The Times*, 20 September 1972.

Monckton also brought with him a letter from Baldwin which was handed to the Duke just before the wedding. Baldwin had ceased to be Prime Minister a few days before, and he now wrote as 'a private English citizen', asking the Duke to regard his letter 'as a renewal of confidence in one who was for so short a time his master, and affection for a prince who honoured him with his friendship'.

Sir, do you remember that last evening at The Fort when I told you how my wife and I hoped from our hearts that you might find the happiness that you desired in the course you were proposing to take? I cannot at this moment refrain from saying again what I then said to you, and I hope you will accept my message in the spirit in which it is sent.

I do want also to say this: I realise that in your new life there must be difficulties inherent in the situation, not all of which could have been foreseen. I am convinced that you will triumph over them, but I want to assure you of an understanding and sympathy.

Through all that time in the early winter, you ran dead straight with me and you accomplished what you said you would do: you maintained your own dignity throughout: you did nothing to embarrass your successor, nor anything, as might so easily have happened, to shake the monarchy more than was inevitable in the circumstances. I am confident your mind today is as it was then.[95]

There is no record in Baldwin's carefully preserved papers of the Duke of Windsor having sent any reply to this letter, and it must be assumed that he did not do so. They never met again. Nor, so far as is known, did any further communication pass between them.

TWELVE

OLD AGE AND FRIENDSHIP

I

'I am going roundabout Whitsun,' Baldwin told Tom Jones in discussing his retirement over tea in Downing Street at the beginning of the New Year. The Prime Minister and his wife were just back from a week-end at Sandringham with the King and Queen. It was a small family gathering, at which Mrs Baldwin sat next to the King at all meals. On the Sunday a crowd of several thousand spectators cheered the royal party on its way to church, singling out the Prime Minister for a particular ovation. This heartened him greatly, since (as Lucy Baldwin put it) 'the last seven or eight weeks have been so full of acute anxiety and sorrow for the author of it all that it has been a perfect nightmare (interspersed with the real thing at night!) and one is more than thankful that it has lifted.'

> Stanley has seen his duty so plainly through all this that in that way it has not worried him, but the anxiety and tension of trying to get things to work out as they have, have been nerve-wracking and exhausting in the extreme. Now what we all have got to do is to set to work to repolish the Throne!

With this last objective Baldwin whole-heartedly agreed, as also with Jones's suggestion that the new King should extend his range of public acquaintances. 'Oddly enough I was talking over this very matter with the King,' he told Jones. 'I asked him if he would be willing to meet some members of the House if Lucy and I fixed up some small dinner parties after my resignation.'[1]

Shortly afterwards the King sounded out Baldwin as to whether he would accept an earldom traditionally offered by the sovereign to a retiring Prime Minister. Baldwin intimated that he would and the King was delighted. 'In these difficult days,' the King told him, 'I cannot, and the country cannot, afford to lose a man with all your wisdom and understanding, and your wise knowledge and experience gained in the public service.'

As his principal title, he decided on Earl Baldwin of Bewdley, with Viscount Corvedale from the nearby Shropshire valley of his ancestors as the second title, which his son Oliver would use by courtesy. 'The old King told me how he liked the familiar names retained,' Baldwin remarked to Tom Jones, confiding in him the news of his future elevation. 'I have a dismal prospect before me,' he added half-jokingly. 'Look at the flotsam and jetsam of political life thrown up on the beach – L.G., Winston, Horne, Gilmour.' According to Jones, 'his decision to take a house in London and an earldom must be put down largely to Mrs Baldwin's account. Eighteen months ago he was saying firmly that all he needed was a bedroom in London and the Benchers of one of the Temples were providing him with this.'2*

In this twilight period of his premiership, in which he was really acting as caretaker for Neville Chamberlain, Baldwin alternated between bursts of energy and fits of lassitude, the natural reaction to the Abdication crisis, which Jones had predicted, as well as his doctor. 'You will pay for this,' Lord Dawson of Penn told him with some truth. It was not merely the rheumatic pains in his right leg of which Baldwin complained to Jones, who merely asked one of the servants at No. 10 to get the Prime Minister some Iodex. The machine was clearly showing signs of running down. One afternoon 'Chips' Channon happened to look in to the chess room in the House of Commons and saw Baldwin sitting alone, absorbed in *The Field*. When Channon returned an hour later, he was still reading it. 'He often sits alone in the window seat of this room and stares out at the river,' noted Channon. 'He was not at his wife's "At Home" this afternoon, which I dutifully attended.' On another occasion, when Jones lunched alone with him in Downing Street, he found Baldwin counting the hours like a schoolboy within sight of the holidays. 'When I get out of here, I'll sleep for a week,' he declared. 'Here I've been for fifteen years going down to the House to answer fatuous questions.'3

Foremost among the matters of state which claimed Baldwin's attention at this time was the constitutional position of the Irish Free State as reflected by de Valera's recent legislation affecting Anglo-Irish relations. When the question was discussed in the Irish Situation Committee, a few days after the Abdication, Baldwin agreed with Simon that the legislation which removed the King and the Governor-General from the

* Presumably the Inner Temple, of which he was an Honorary Bencher.

constitution, while at the same time in effect nominating the King to act as the state's agent in the matter of accrediting Irish diplomatic representatives abroad, might well be criticised as insulting and derogatory, which indeed it was. But from de Valera's point of view it was a cleverly constructed milestone along the road of complete and unfettered political independence for his country. Meanwhile the Irish Free State remained within the Commonwealth and continued to enjoy all the advantages of membership. 'What Mr de Valera wanted,' Baldwin bluntly observed, 'was the finest possible line with which successfully to wangle Unemployment Insurance and Old Age Pensions for persons of Irish Free State origin resident in the United Kingdom.' And, needless to add, he got it. In the result Baldwin and his Cabinet colleagues acquiesced in the disappearance of the Crown from the Irish constitution except as an anonymous and convenient 'organ' for international relations. Thus for the second time in half a century a divorce shaped the course of Irish history and, in A. J. P. Taylor's words, 'the private life of an English king sapped the Irish Treaty of 1921, or what remained of it'.[4]

The next meeting of the Irish Situation Committee took place on 20 January 1937 and was the last over which Baldwin presided, although thirteen more meetings were to be held under Neville Chamberlain before the eventual settlement was reached in April 1938 and the economic war called off. The only statement which Baldwin is recorded as having made at the last meeting which he attended was in answer to Malcolm MacDonald who inquired whether he had any information as to the Northern Ireland Premier Lord Craigavon's view on de Valera's latest constitutional measures. According to the minutes Baldwin thought that 'Lord Craigavon did not worry about what was happening in the south of Ireland so long as the boundary was not touched and no question of a United Ireland was raised'.[5]

On the other hand, the other members of the Commonwealth, notably Australia, New Zealand and Canada which possessed considerable Irish minorities, had a particular interest in the settlement of the Anglo-Irish dispute. When the economic war began in 1932, these Dominions had some sympathy for Britain's action over the land annuities, but as the dispute dragged on they gradually came round to the view, appreciated by Baldwin and Chamberlain, that the dispute was basically political and the sooner it was settled the better for the general Commonwealth image. Pressures that it should be were apparent when the Dominion Prime Ministers met in London for the Imperial Conference in May 1937 and Baldwin was on the point of handing over the reins of office to his successor. The eventual settlement came ten months later in the agreement which generally restored the trading position to what it had been before 1932, accepted the payment by Eire (as the Free State was now officially known under the new Constitution) of £10 million in settlement of the financial differences – the maximum sum which Chamberlain felt she could pay at any given moment – and finally provided for the return of the 1921 Treaty ports which could only have been put in order and maintained at enormous cost by the British in time of war.

Like Chamberlain, Baldwin realised that sanctions were a mistake and merely increased mutual hostility and caused mutual impoverishment. If one British politician more than any other deserves the major share of the credit in achieving the settlement of the dispute which bedevilled Anglo-Irish relations in the nineteen-thirties, it was the Dominions Secretary Malcolm MacDonald. But at least some measure of credit goes to Baldwin for appointing him in the first place and then encouraging him to initiate the lengthy and tortuous series of negotiations which were eventually crowned with success. After all, Baldwin was a man of peace, and his Irish policy gave peace in his time, which it was designed to do, although in the event it was unable to provide the ultimate solution of the Irish question which has eluded every Englishman who has been concerned with the administration of Ireland or any part of it from Strongbow to Whitelaw.

Besides serving as a sounding board for the Irish question, the Imperial Conference gave Baldwin a final opportunity of impressing upon the Dominion Prime Ministers the threat both to the Commonwealth and the mother country posed by the Nazi and Fascist dictators, just as he also tried to shock the House of Commons into a just appreciation of the dangers from the same quarter. 'We want to put ourselves in a position to deter aggression,' he had said in a debate on the service estimates.

> Deterrence is our object, and if you believe that deterrence is pos-
> sible you will believe that ineffective deterrence is worse than
> useless. We shall neither assure our own safety and that of the
> Empire, nor play our part in securing peace in the world, unless we
> bring our forces up to the necessary standard. That, and that alone,
> is what this expenditure is for.

At one of the Imperial Conference sessions, Baldwin was sitting next to Eden, and as the meeting was about to adjourn Baldwin said to Eden: 'I don't often say anything on foreign affairs. Do you mind if I do so now?' 'Of course not,' the Foreign Secretary replied, 'please do.' Whereupon Baldwin treated the delegates to a brief, pessimistic account of the dangers in Europe, which he attributed to Hitler and Mussolini. 'We have two madmen loose in Europe,' he concluded. 'Anything may befall.' Although Eden was afterwards to blame Baldwin for not putting enough drive behind the rearmament programme, he had to admit that, so far as he knew, Baldwin never had any illusions about the dictators. It was otherwise with most of the Dominion Prime Ministers, who apart from Savage of New Zealand favoured a policy of appeasement, being more apprehensive of Japan than of Germany or Italy and the possibility of being involved in a war on two fronts. As for himself, Baldwin resisted another attempt at this time on the part of Ribbentrop who came down to Chequers to persuade him to visit Germany, although he envied the Labour politician George Lansbury 'the faith which enabled him to go and tackle Hitler'.[6]

On 16 March 1937, Austen Chamberlain died suddenly at his London home while taking a book from its shelf. 'Austen happy in a sudden death,' wrote Tom Jones to a friend, 'and I think you will agree that whatever S.B. cannot do, he can speak a funeral oration.' This was delivered along with other tributes in the House of Commons. 'It is the sort of thing he does magnificently,' noted 'Chips' Channon, 'and he reduced many Members to actual tears.' In his speech Baldwin described the departed statesman as 'above all a very great Parliamentarian', who 'loved this House . . . and the life of it', recalling his kindness to young men, notably himself, whom Austen had introduced as a new MP twenty-nine years before.

The spoken word often loses much of its effect when translated into the form of cold print. But it is difficult to believe that those who heard Baldwin on this occasion, particularly from the floor of the House, were not moved by his peroration.

> When our long days of work are over here, there is nothing in our oldest customs which stirs the imagination of the young Member as the cry which goes down the Lobbies, 'Who goes home?' Sometimes when I hear it I think of the language of my own country-side and my feeling for those who have borne the almost insupport-able burden of public life; there may well be a day when they will be glad to go home.
>
> So Austen Chamberlain has gone home. The sympathy of this House from the heart of every one of us will go out to those who are left. The relationship of father and son is not a thing on which I shall touch here, except to say that no more beautiful relationship ever existed. In all his domestic relationships it was the same – with

his wife, with his brother. There is not a soul in this House but will give that sympathy from the bottom of his heart . . . He always maintained that public service was the highest career a man could take. In that belief he fitted himself for it and in that belief he worked and died. Let us renew our efforts from today to take further pride in this work to which we have been called.

'I listened to your most beautiful tribute to Austen,' his brother Neville wrote to Baldwin the same evening, 'and rejoiced profoundly that it had fallen to you to express what the House felt. Thank you.'[7]

2

One of the last government measures which Baldwin sponsored in Parliament was the Ministers of the Crown Bill, which revised the existing inequalities in ministerial salaries, due to historical circumstances which could no longer be justified, and broadly speaking provided that all ministers of Cabinet rank should be paid £5,000 a year. In addition, the Leader of the Opposition, whose time under modern conditions was entirely taken up by his parliamentary duties, should receive £2,000. In his speech supporting the Bill, which was duly passed into law, Baldwin emphasised the importance of placing men in high office in a position where they would be free from temptation, an example which he thought might with advantage be followed by foreign countries.

The statute also gave ex-Prime Ministers a pension of £2,000 a year. Baldwin told Tom Jones that he had decided to take it for himself, reversing his earlier decision.* 'It would be unfair to poorer Prime Ministers not to do so,' he said, no doubt with Ramsay MacDonald in mind. He added that it would also enable him to continue to live in London, for which purpose he had leased a house in Eaton Square.[8]

Appropriately enough Baldwin's last speech in the House of Commons was on his favourite subject of industrial relations, in which he once more successfully played the role of peace-maker. A national coal strike was threatened following a dispute in the Harworth colliery in Nottinghamshire where the Miners' Federation had accused the owners of practising intimidation and victimisation against the men, in order to prevent them from joining this trade union. After a ballot had been taken favouring strike action by an overwhelming majority, Attlee brought up the matter in Parliament, describing the conditions which prevailed in the Harworth

* See above, p. 235.

colliery as a travesty of industrial democracy. Baldwin, who replied for the Government at the special request of the Labour Party, agreed with the necessity for collective bargaining and made what he called 'my last appeal in this House to that little handful of men who can decide whether it is to be peace or strife'. For several days he had thought carefully about what he would say and in his peroration he adroitly brought in the approaching Coronation with dramatic effect.

The whole world has its eye today on London . . . In the Abbey on this day week our young King and his Queen, who were called suddenly and unexpectedly to the most tremendous position on earth, will kneel and dedicate themselves to the service of their people, a service which can only be ended by death. I appeal to that handful of men, with whom rests peace or war, to rend and dissipate this dark cloud which has gathered over us and show the people of the world that this democracy can still at least practise the arts of peace in a world of strife.[9]

The appeal had its effect both inside and outside the House. A Labour member immediately stood up and said: 'I am of the opinion that it would be folly to continue this debate.' In the coalfields, pending further negotiations, the strike was put off, and shortly afterwards a satisfactory settlement was reached between the parties.

Wednesday, 12 May 1937, was the date which had been fixed for the coronation of Edward VIII, and it was felt that the ceremony for George VI should take place on that date rather than be postponed. The cheers for Baldwin and his wife from the crowds lining the streets as they drove in the procession were particularly marked. If Oliver Baldwin had proved a sore trial to his parents in the past, that was over now, and they were reconciled in the father's hour of triumph. Next day Oliver wrote to him in terms which must have touched his heart:

> Little Stoke House,
> North Stoke,
> Oxon.
> 13 May 1937

My dear Father,

As yesterday was, outwardly, the greatest day in your life, may I say how thrilled I was to hear of the real affection with which you were greeted during your passage through these streets of the West End yesterday – and I say West End purposely because I know had it been the East End your reception would have been as great, and because of many political differences, the greater.

You have indeed had a glorious ending to your rule, which has been of so much more importance to our people than that of any British king, and I am glad for your sake. All of which means that I hope you are happy and do not regret for one moment the events at the end of last year, which rid us of one who I am sure would have caused civil strife in our midst before many years had gone by. And don't we both take off our hats and bow low before mother whose faith in you has been so really grand, and without which neither you nor I would know our possibilities or (in my case only) superfluity?

If we only had the sentimental grandeur of the French, I would urge the erection of a tablet for you, '*S.B. qui a bien merité de sa patrie*', and I shouldn't mind either if an American would add '*et comment*', which the French might not understand but we should.

God bless you,

OLIVER[10]

A few days later, Baldwin made his last public speech as Prime Minister, which he afterwards entitled 'The Torch I Would Hand On'. The occasion was the Empire Rally of Youth at the Albert Hall, and his words, which Tom Jones among countless others at home and overseas heard over the radio, were delivered with emotion and passionate earnestness. 'I have had my hour,' he said. 'I pass soon into the shade . . . You are the governors of the future. We are passing on to you the duty of guarding and safeguarding what is worthy and worth while in our past, our heritage and our tradition, our honour and all our hopes.' His message was a simple one:

You are trustees in every sense of that noble word. What is coming to you is a trust, and not merely a benefit which devolves upon you, a trust you hold for future generations. Unless you rise to the trust there will be little benefit for you or your children to enjoy.

It will be for you to protect democracy in whatever part of the Empire you may live. It must be defended from without, and equally it may have to be defended from within. And it may well be that you will have to save democracy from itself . . .

The torch I would hand to you, and ask you to pass from hand to hand along the pathways of the Empire, is a Christian truth rekindled anew in each ardent generation. Use men as ends and never merely as means; and live for the brotherhood of man, which implies the Fatherhood of God. The brotherhood of man is often denied and derided and called foolishness, but it is, in fact, one of the foolish things of the world which God has chosen to confound the wise, and the world is confounded by it daily.

We may evade it, we may deny it; but we shall find no rest in our souls, nor will the world until we acknowledge it as the ultimate wisdom.[11]

A week later, on 26 May, Baldwin took the chair in the Cabinet room for the last time. He would have preferred not to do so, certainly for the first item on the agenda, which was to confirm the Duke of Windsor in the title of 'Royal Highness', while at the same time denying it to his future wife and any possible children of their marriage. It was at the same Cabinet that the decision was taken to raise the salaries of MPs from £400 to £600. Some ministers argued, as has frequently been done since, that the proposed rise would breed a class of 'professional politicians', but Baldwin, who had been convinced by the Labour Party leaders that hardship existed due to the fall in the value of money, was able with Chamberlain's support to overrule the objectors. The following afternoon, his last in the House of Commons, wearing a summer cream waistcoat with pearl buttons, he announced the rise amid loud applause. With what Harold Nicolson called 'characteristic subtlety' he did this in the form of an answer to a parliamentary question, 'so that his final words are to give us all £200 a year more. This means a lot to the Labour members and was done with Baldwin's usual consummate taste. No man has ever left in such a blaze of affection.' The same evening, standing in front of the fire in the Members' Lobby, he confessed to Robert Boothby that his chief regret was that he had not taken a greater interest in foreign affairs. Nevertheless, as he told a press photographer who was waiting for him in Downing Street, he was glad to be a gentleman of leisure. 'Beaverbrook has been trying to hound me out of public life for fourteen years,' he told another friend, 'but I go of my own choice, in my own time, and on the top of my form.'

Next morning, 28 May, Baldwin went to Buckingham Palace and formally tendered his resignation to the King. A few minutes later Neville Chamberlain took his place as Prime Minister.

It was fourteen years to the day since Baldwin had been elected leader of the Conservative Party in succession to Bonar Law. During his audience the King made him a Knight of the Garter and his wife a Dame Grand Cross of the British Empire. For a few days he was Sir Stanley

Baldwin, until on 8 June it was announced that he had been created Earl Baldwin of Bewdley and Viscount Corvedale in the county of Salop. He did not very much want to go to the House of Lords, he told Inskip, but his royal master was anxious that he should. 'There is perhaps a certain retributive justice in it,' he added, 'as I have sent so many others there hoping I should never see their faces again.'

The other 'Resignation Honours' included a Viscountcy for Baldwin's faithful henchman John Davidson and lesser distinctions for the staff at 10 Downing Street. 'In these matters there is nothing to choose between L.G. and S.B.,' noted Tom Jones. ('S.B. sent me a charming photograph of himself, sitting at ease with his pipe, signed "T.J. with gratitude and affection", and I sent him the Loeb edition of Cicero's *Old Age and Friendship*.') His secretaries past and present, about a score in all, clubbed together to give him a writing desk similar to the one in the library at No. 10 for his new house in Eaton Square, while his old constituents presented him with some fine wrought-iron gates for the main entrance to Astley Hall. At the same time the historian Arthur Bryant wrote a graceful biographical 'tribute' which Hamish Hamilton published in conjunction with the National Book Association.

Considering that Bryant's 'tribute', which ran to nearly two hundred pages, was written in three weeks, it was a remarkably accurate piece of work. 'My only hope is that, in however imperfect a way, I have managed to do what I set out to do,' the historian told his subject at the time: 'to make people see the consistent purpose underlying everything you have said and done. Part of the book at least is very good, for it was written by you!' Bryant was reassured by Baldwin's words of thanks. 'I think it made me happier than any letter I ever received.'

Of the contemporary diarists who noted Baldwin's departure, Donald Somervell has given as good a brief assessment of his political career as any:

His achievements have been, I think, first in freeing our politics from the seeds of corruption and press domination which the war plus L.G. had planted, and which (particularly the latter) have grown. Secondly, so directing the policy of the Conservative Party that class bitterness and class unrest had no justification. Third, as an example that real power has its foremost foundation in a complete absence of personal selfseeking and striving for position. Unselfishness is not only the way to heaven but also to political success.[12]

The Baldwins' new house, 69 Eaton Square, had a large study on the first floor at the back, and Jones remarked that it was 'already in apple-pie order' when he called a fortnight later and was given an affectionate welcome. He found Baldwin 'very tired', as he had been toiling for hours and hours answering letters of congratulations in his own hand. 'Neither Beaverbrook nor L.G. has sent me one,' he observed wryly. Those who did included King George VI, who wrote of the 'real sadness' with which he had accepted his resignation, of 'the high standard which you have always set in public life', and of his 'deep gratitude for your great service to my Father and myself'.

> You take with you into retirement the abundant goodwill of our people – and, heavy as their loss will surely be, I regard it in one sense as my gain – for in my inexperience I shall look to you for guidance and advice in the difficulties with which I know that I shall from time to time be faced.[13]

Of the letters he received from his late Cabinet colleagues, that from Lord Halifax touched him deeply. 'I shan't try to say what I feel about your going,' Halifax wrote. 'A good deal of the savour of political life so far as I am concerned goes out with you, for the main pleasure of the last year's work was that it was being done with you. I think you have taught me more about life than anybody except my father – and that I hope will remain.' Baldwin replied in terms which appeared to Halifax to give 'a glimpse of the romantic, almost mystical streak, in his composition.'[14]

60 Eaton Square, SW

8 June 1937

My dear Edward,

    I shall value your letter as long as I live. Our friendship has been a very real thing to me and a real influence which I treasure.

    This last ten days has been a strange time: a time that comes only once and cannot recur.

    All hearts seem open at the moment: most will close again, some perhaps be kept ajar, but it is very wonderful. I feel tired, happy and at peace: and mighty humble. I wish my dear Dickens hadn't destroyed what is really a very beautiful word: but you will know all I mean by it.

    I still have that sense of wonder that the Blessed Damozel shewed in her face as she leaned over the golden bar of Heaven. It wore off: so will mine. But it leaves something good, I hope, behind.

I hope indeed we may see something of each other: it will be a joy to me.

I won't say more: I am sitting among stacks of letters, but they are diminishing: but may all good be with you for long years.

Ever yours,

S.B.

A few days later, he paid a farewell week-end visit to Chequers with his wife and their children Betty and Windham and the latter's American wife. Before leaving the place for the last time – they were never to go there again – Lucy Baldwin did not forget to write to Lady Lee and thank her and her husband 'for all that it has been to us on and off for over fourteen and a half years'.

Two matters concerning his ennoblement required the new Earl's attention. The first was the formal grant of a fresh coat of arms by the College of Heralds, embodying 'supporters' in addition to the Baldwin family crest of 'a cockatrice sejant'. After a visit to the College, he asked Tom Jones whether he thought two owls would do as supporters, notwithstanding that Lady Baldwin had 'mentioned a number of superstitious incidents in the family history in which owls had played a minor accompaniment'. What Jones replied is not on record, but when the grant of arms was made two white owls 'proper' appeared, 'that on the sinister side holding in the beak a sprig of bloom also proper'.[15]

The second matter was Baldwin's introduction to the House of Lords. This ceremony took place on 10 June, his two sponsors being Derby and Londonderry. The latter, somewhat surprisingly, in view of their past differences, had proposed himself for the role, and Baldwin gratefully accepted his offer as proof of their reconciliation.* It was an ancient and picturesque ceremony. Wearing ermine robes and carrying his coronet and flanked by his two sponsors, Baldwin followed Black Rod, Garter King of Arms and the Lord Great Chamberlain into the chamber of the House. After the Clerk had read the Letters Patent and the writs of summons, the new peer took the oath in a low voice and signed the roll. He and his sponsors then seated themselves on the Opposition Front Bench and directed by the Garter King of Arms they rose and bowed thrice to the Lord Chancellor. The procession then reformed and moved along to the Woolsack where Hailsham was sitting ready to greet his old colleague which he did with a warm handshake. The galleries as well as

---

* New peers are introduced in the House of Lords by fellow-peers of the same rank. Londonderry, although a titular Marquess, was able to act in this capacity, since his Marquessate was an Irish creation and he sat in the Upper House by virtue of his United Kingdom peerage of Earl Vane.

the chamber itself were crowded by those who had come to watch the proceedings and it is on record that the newly ennobled Earl showed some surprise at the numbers of those present.

When Earl Baldwin of Bewdley took his seat in the Upper House, it was with the fixed resolve never to make another political speech. 'Once I leave, I leave,' he said. 'I am not going to speak to the man on the bridge, and I am not going to spit on the deck.'[16]

3

The round of social visits and hospitality in the summer of 1937, which followed Baldwin's resignation and to which he cheerfully submitted with his wife, quickly proved too much for him, and for the second time in twelve months he experienced a nervous breakdown. Early in July, Lord Dawson of Penn packed him off to Astley with orders to rest absolutely quietly in the country, not to get up for breakfast and to go to bed early. 'I had to cancel all my engagements and undertake nothing for the next few months,' he explained to Queen Mary, apologising for being unable to meet her at a country house party to which they had both been invited. 'It is only nerves, but not surprising after the strain of many years. But for the time being it is real and unpleasant.'[17]

In August he was well enough to make the slow motor journey with his wife to Aix-les-Bains. But he now suffered from increasing pain in one of his legs due to arthritis, and this prevented him from taking the walks in the Savoy mountains which he had once enjoyed. The result was that he quickly became bored and he and his wife moved on to Switzerland where they completed their holiday. Back in London, Tom Jones thought he was much better though in some danger of relapsing into an 'old man'. ('He has arthritis in the hip, but the doctors say that it has been taken in time.') Jones also fed him with titbits of political gossip such as that Eden thought the Chamberlain Cabinet 'very weak and the armament programme far in arrears'. Jones had met the Foreign Secretary the previous week-end at Lady Astor's. 'I told him about my Sunday at Cliveden,' noted Jones. 'He thought it most foolish of Eden to tire himself out at the week-ends by going to such crowded parties and said he would talk to Eden, this because I remarked on Eden's obvious fatigue.'[18]

Baldwin went on to tell Jones that he was making a new will and proposed to leave all his personal and political papers to Cambridge University. Did Jones think that was appropriate? Jones agreed that it was. So also did the Cambridge historian G. M. Trevelyan, who seems to have originally suggested it. 'I gave Macaulay's Journal to Trinity Library and have not regretted my choice,' he wrote to Baldwin at this time. 'But your papers will be more worked at and more voluminous and should be in the University Library.'[19]

One document in the collection caused Baldwin some concern and he consulted Jones as to its disposition. Jones noted the matter in his diary on 26 October 1937:

> He raised the question of a paper which Neville Chamberlain had drafted some months before the Abdication in the form of an appeal to the King to mend his manners – in fact a memorandum of censure. This was discussed by an inner group of Ministers, and S.B. had dissuaded them from sending it to the King. 'It would have sent him sky-high and, I am sure, would have been a mistake.' What was to be done with it? Should he destroy it?
>
> I said: 'No, put it with the others. Someone is sure to be in possession of a copy of it, and you may as well have yours preserved for future historians.'[20]

Whether or not Baldwin followed his friend's advice is unclear. At all events there is no trace of the document in the Baldwin Papers as at present preserved.

Ramsay MacDonald had retired at the same time as Baldwin, giving up his office of Lord President of the Council and refusing a peerage. However, though he was less than a year older than Baldwin, his health was much poorer, and it was in the hope of recovering it in some measure that he planned a holiday voyage to South America. 'I should so much like to see you before I go,' he wrote to Baldwin on 17 October. Baldwin responded by spending several hours with him at his house in Hampstead shortly before he sailed on 3 November. Five days later the news came that the once all-powerful but now sadly neglected ex-Labour leader had died suddenly at sea. 'It was a mercy he died when he did,' Baldwin remarked afterwards, 'because he was always talking of returning to public life in some way when he came back from the cruise.' He added that 'MacDonald's powers of control had entirely gone and that when he came to exert himself he would realise it and suffer very much'.

At the end of November the Athenaeum Club entertained Baldwin to dinner, limited to 160 places for which the members had to ballot, so 'packed with celebrities' was the gathering. Lord Macmillan took the chair and in introducing the honoured guest recalled that in 1889 a candidate for election to the club who had been dead for six years was elected with the backing of some twenty supporters. Fortunately Baldwin, who had been elected under the club's special rule as a person of public distinction, was now able to exhibit himself to his fellow-members as being alive and in comparatively good health. While the chairman described him as a scholar and a humanist, the Archbishop of Canterbury eulogised his magnanimity as that of a man who belonged to all parties because he represented the spirit of England which was confined to none. Then, in a speech of thirty-five minutes, the guest of the evening treated his audience to what Leo Amery, who was among those present, called 'a most artlessly artful tale, largely romance', in which he explained the whole of his career from the break with Lloyd George in 1922 onwards in the light of his philosophy of the last few years towards the Labour Party and the need for winning them to the Constitution. He said little of his own Party, and though he mentioned India was completely silent on foreign affairs. 'It was an apologia for his political career and was well received,' noted Tom Jones. 'He had delivered it already at least once to the junior Conservative members when saying farewell some months ago.' Afterwards Lord Macmillan declared that it was the most memorable after-dinner speech to which he had ever listened. 'As Ben Jonson said of Bacon, "the fear of every man that heard him was lest he should make an end".'[21]

A few days after the Athenaeum dinner, Harold Nicolson was invited to breakfast at 69 Eaton Square. When he arrived, he found Baldwin seated at the breakfast table opening his morning mail. He limped a little from his arthritis, but otherwise Nicolson thought he looked well. He told him that he had 'only just got out in time and that a few weeks more would have led to a real collapse similar to that of Ramsay MacDonald'. According to Nicolson, he said he had always looked forward to his retirement as a time to read and think, but that for the first three months he had been quite unable to think and only able to read detective novels. He was now beginning to recover, and was reading Froude on Erasmus. This led him to speak of his mother's family and the artistic and literary circle of his Burne-Jones and Kipling cousins. They went on to discuss the Abdication, on which Baldwin considered Mrs Simpson to be 'an admirable woman within her circle of conscience, but to have no conception of proportions outside that circle'. He showed Nicolson the original of one of the notes the King had sent him at the time, but whether this was the one about the Duke of York which Baldwin had used in his speech to the House of Commons, or whether it was the one about Mrs Simpson which he did not use, Nicolson does not relate.

He talked of Winston Churchill and said he lacked soul. I suggested that Winston is very sympathetic to misfortune in others. He answered, 'I don't deny that Winston has his sentimental side.' He then goes on: 'And what is more, he cannot really tell lies. That is what makes him so bad a conspirator.'

I was alone with him for an hour, and nothing could have exceeded his mellow charm.[22]

Politics still interested Baldwin, but only from the sidelines, as he had given up most of his political interests, including the Primrose League. Although he prudently held his tongue, he was far from happy about the way his successor was shaping as Prime Minister. 'The real tragedy of the situation was that Baldwin wasn't able to carry on after the Abdication,' said Lord Davidson looking back on this period.

He could have formed a National Government and got the Labour Party in, and persuaded the trade unions to agree to put industry on a war footing, which they would have done had Baldwin been Prime Minister. It was common talk in the lobby that they greatly disliked Neville Chamberlain . . .

Baldwin was adored by the trade union element and he always understood why they felt like that, and they would have served under him with the greatest delight. But there were two or three of them in the lobby who said: 'We'll kill Neville,' and they did. They never felt he understood them; nor, of course, did he.[23]

Like Davidson, Baldwin was dismayed by the stories which reached him of Chamberlain's interference in his Cabinet colleagues' departments, particularly the Foreign Office, and he was hardly surprised when he heard that Eden had resigned, which he did on 20 February 1938, along with the Under-Secretary Lord Cranborne. There was some talk that, if the Government broke up as a result of these resignations, Baldwin might be called back. However, the latter told Eden that in the event of his being consulted by the King he would advise him to send for Eden and invite him to form an administration. But the contingency did not arise, since apparently no one in the Cabinet supported Eden, though a few wished to hush up the dispute. 'The parting of Anthony and the PM was inevitable and in all the circumstances the retiring ministers were right to go,' wrote Baldwin at the time.

Whether Anthony could have been brought along with tact and

understanding I don't know, nor is it of any use wondering now. But the loss of any other colleague would have passed without a ripple on the surface, for Anthony was the only minister who had got across in the country . . . What worries me is the wider strategy of politics over the whole country. I fear the growth of an impression that the government is swinging to extreme right.[24]

In the spring of 1938 the Baldwins spent a month in the south of France, where they met Eden. Afterwards Baldwin wrote to J. P. L. Thomas who had been Eden's PPS at the Foreign Office:

Anthony, now that he is out of the Government, will naturally see much of Winston as their minds are moving in the same direction. W. is a very forceful character and if war should come, the country will want him to lead them. If war is avoided and we remain at peace, the country might well in the future turn to A. as peace PM. Tell A. therefore not to be dominated by W. and play second fiddle to him.

Both Baldwin and Eden were the guests at this time of Sir Sidney Herbert, the popular member for the Abbey Division of Westminster, who had formerly been Baldwin's PPS. Possibly as the result of Baldwin's advice, Eden did not immediately ally himself with Churchill, but formed his own group of Tory backbenchers for the purpose of encouraging Chamberlain and Halifax, who had succeeded Eden as Foreign Secretary, to stand up to the European dictators. Known variously as 'The Eden Group' and (by the Government Whip's Office) as 'The Glamour Boys', its members included Amery, Cranborne, Herbert, Thomas, Harold Macmillan, Bonar Law's son Richard, and Harold Nicolson. Duff Cooper joined them after he had resigned on the issue of the four-power Munich agreement which resulted in Hitler's dismemberment of Czechoslovakia. 'What disturbs me most about the present position,' Duff Cooper confided in Baldwin at this time, 'is that the Prime Minister has now the unanimous support of all that element in the Party which was once so false to you – whereas the people who are feeling your doubts are the very people who were your most loyal supporters in evil days.'

Oswald Birley had recently finished painting Baldwin in his robes as Chancellor of Cambridge University for his old college, where it hangs today. Halifax who had seen it in Birley's house was enthusiastic about it. 'I would rather take his verdict than anyone I know,' the artist told his sitter afterwards. 'So I am much relieved! I have so much enjoyed painting his portrait and am very grateful to you for your patience and for "playing up" so well.' Birley looked forward to painting a 'Conversation Piece' of Baldwin and Lucy which he admitted he would much like to do. Unfortunately he was never able to do it.

The crisis over Czechoslovakia developed while the Baldwins were enjoying what was to prove to be their last holiday at Aix, and they hurried home fearful for the peace of Europe. Baldwin occupied a seat in the Peers' Gallery of the House of Commons on the momentous night of 28 September when a note was passed along the Treasury Bench as Chamberlain was speaking on his efforts for peace and handed by Simon to the Prime Minister. When Chamberlain announced that Hitler had invited him to meet him in Munich next morning and that Mussolini had accepted a similar invitation, the hysterical demonstration which followed was such as Baldwin had never before seen in the chamber. Members cheered wildly and waved their order papers, others in tears crossed the floor of the House and with what Simon described as 'unrestrained emotion' grasped Chamberlain by the hand. There was an outburst of clapping in the galleries, in which Baldwin joined, momentarily forgetting the rule which forbids this kind of applause. Two days later, when he heard the first news of the settlement over the radio, Baldwin sat down and penned his message to the Prime Minister: 'You have everything in your hands now – for a time – and you can do anything you like. *Use that time well, for it won't last.*' [25]

On reflection Baldwin distrusted the Munich settlement and doubted whether it would last. Nor was he at all favourably impressed by the way in which it was carried out. Privately he criticised Chamberlain for his emotional outburst on his return to Downing Street. 'Peace with honour,' he considered a most unfortunate phrase. 'I should have done it very differently,' he admitted to Lord Hinchingbrooke, who had been one of his Private Secretaries. 'I love a crisis.' But he did not reveal exactly how he would have dealt with this one except to say that he would not have gone to Munich. 'Can't we turn Hitler east?' he asked Hinchingbrooke with remarkable prescience. 'Napoleon broke himself against the Russians. Hitler might do the same.' [26]

Tom Jones urged him to speak in the Lords, and as a result he was persuaded to break his self-imposed silence in the debate which took place there on the Munich settlement on 4 October. He repeated that he would not himself have gone to Munich – 'I know I could not have done it' – but he praised Chamberlain's courage in doing so and said that no Prime Minister should commit his country to war until he was sure that it was ready to fight. That did not mean having sufficient forces to outnumber everyone else's but rather every precaution of foresight, skill, knowledge and science. He saw one straw of hope: in the last week all the peoples of Europe had 'looked down into the volcano' and had begun to ask questions as to where they were going. He recalled to mind 1914 and the face of Sir Edward Grey when all seemed dark. 'And the children of men, the children of all nations, have their part to play in the fleeting hours that are before us.' [27]

The only jarring note amid the paeans of praise which followed Baldwin's contribution to the debate came from Lord Lloyd, who had been one of Churchill's most vocal supporters in his campaign for rearmament. 'After all,' he said, 'my noble friend Earl Baldwin ought to know better than any man his responsibility for failure to rearm.' Indeed Baldwin did know, and soon the whole nation was to be informed of it in abundant measure.

Jones saw Baldwin immediately after his speech. 'His notion of re-constructing the Cabinet is to bring Swinton, Runciman, and Eden back,' he noted at the time. 'I was shocked.' But Eden would only join a Government based on national unity. 'His position is difficult. He is popular with the left but does not want to bang the door against his return to the right.'

Baldwin and Halifax are sympathetic to Eden's attitude. Eden is more clearly interpreting the mood of this country than Chamber-lain, though all are grateful to Neville for keeping us out of war. Lord Macmillan remarked to me at a Pilgrim Trust meeting that if there were a John Wesley about today he could produce another religious revival. Neville does not sense this, Eden and S.B. do. [28]

4

Perhaps this is the most convenient point in the narrative to revert to the difficult question of Londonderry's relations with Baldwin. After he had been so ignominiously 'dropped' by Baldwin from his Cabinet after the 1935 Election without a word of public explanation, Londonderry had found himself in what he described as 'a position of great freedom and less responsibility'. Accordingly he determined to utilise it in order to visit Germany and meet some of the country's leaders, particularly in the aviation field. He spent about a month there early in 1936 and was welcomed with lavish hospitality by Hitler, Goering, Ribbentrop and the other leading Nazis as well as the *Luftwaffe* chiefs. Not everyone at home approved of his visit, and among the critics was Harold Nicolson who met Londonderry on his return to London at the house of his daughter Lady Maureen Stanley. 'Now I admire Londonderry in a way, since it is fine to remain 1760 in 1936; besides, he is a real gent,' Nicolson wrote at the time. 'But I do deeply disapprove of ex-Cabinet Ministers trotting across to Germany at this moment. It gives the impression of secret negotiations and upsets the French.' [29]

During his talks in Germany Londonderry did succeed in gathering a certain amount of useful information, particularly on the German air force and the German aircraft industry. But with the exception of his son-in-law Oliver Stanley, then Education Minister, who listened politely, and a few top service people like Hankey and Ellington, nobody took much interest in what the unfortunate Londonderry had to say. 'When I returned from Germany after the most valuable contacts which our diplomats had not had,' he complained to Baldwin several months later, 'so much was I personally wiped out of your mind that neither you nor Anthony (but the attitude of the FO is consistent) bothered to hear what I had to say. I could have told you a good deal which may be common knowledge now but which our Foreign Office did not seem to know at that time.'

Londonderry also complained that he had been shabbily treated by Baldwin, who had 'kicked him out' of two Cabinet posts inside five months without indicating any reasons. Although the reasons were fairly widely known – Londonderry having allegedly 'misled' Baldwin on German air strength and his notorious 'bombing' speech having made him an electoral liability – it would have been better for him if he had resigned to the accompaniment of the usual exchange of platitudinous letters customary on such occasions. As it was, Londonderry nursed a grievance for the rest of his life. This was epitomised in a formal letter dated 18 May 1936 and two informal ones written a few days later, in which he set out his case as he saw it.

The first letter concluded with these words:

Nobody realised more than I did the difficulties of a Prime Minister but I felt that I could quite safely leave myself in your hands. But as I naturally took no steps to safeguard my public position, all the damage that could be done to it has been done. I have felt it necessary, therefore, to write to you on these matters because I consider it imperative that my position in the form of this letter should be placed on record amongst my papers, not only for my own satisfaction but for those of my family who will follow me and will be wholly ignorant, as most people are, as to why I was practically removed from public life without any reason whatsoever being given by the Prime Minister of the day.[30]

Baldwin returned a brief acknowledgement, asking for a little time to digest and reply to this letter. 'I am more than usually busy,' he wrote, 'and with more accumulated and accumulating difficulties than usual.' But he never sent any further reply, and although he saw Londonderry during the Abdication crisis he did not mention the letter. Londonderry wrote again several times but his letters remained unanswered. Meanwhile he had paid a further visit to Germany and afterwards produced a short book, *Ourselves and Germany*, in which he described his meetings with Hitler and Goering and other leaders in the light of the failure to come to an understanding with Germany and the deterioration in Anglo-German relations which had begun when Germany had been denied a place at the Disarmament Conference at Geneva. The book, which appeared in the spring of 1938, had a modest success, it was serialised in the *Evening Standard*, and Londonderry received numerous letters from a wide range of correspondents to whom he had sent copies, both in England and abroad. These included King George VI, Queen Mary and the Duke of Windsor who had recently visited Germany with the Duchess, most of Londonderry's former Cabinet colleagues, experienced British diplomats who had served in Berlin like Sir Horace Rumbold and leading Germans who had entertained Londonderry such as Goering, Von Papen and Hitler himself. This encouraged Londonderry to reissue the book as a paperback, one of the first to appear under the imprint of Penguin Books, bringing the story down to Munich and also adding a selection from this interesting correspondence.

Londonderry was still feeling sore at Baldwin's failure to answer his letters. Shortly before Christmas 1938 he sent Baldwin a copy of the paperback, 'as you expressed so much interest in the original edition', together with a copy of his letter of 18 May 1936, and again reproached Baldwin for his seeming neglect.

I still repeat that if only I had a little more power, and could have induced the Government first, and the Press next, to take some notice of my activities, we should be in an entirely different position to that in which we find ourselves at the present moment...

You will understand, therefore, that it has been most disappointing to me to have felt most completely impotent during this crisis, when I know I was right, owing to my weakened political position to get anything across.[31]

Londonderry's gesture finally brought forth a characteristic reply in Baldwin's own hand:

> Astley Hall,
> Stourport
> Christmas Eve, 1938

Dear Charley,

You are a faithful friend. The little book arrived last night and I shall read it with care. It is tragic how the Germans seem to do everything to neutralise all the efforts of men like yourself who have done everything in your power and risking all kinds of mis-understandings to obtain understanding, and through understanding, Peace.

I am distressed if I ever failed to answer any letter of yours. I don't think I have a record of much of my own correspondence. It is large: I write all private letters myself and rarely keep a copy. It is perhaps not wise but I am too old to change now! I was never methodical and I must have been the despair of my secretaries. But you are the last man I would wittingly offend and I have always regarded you as a true friend in good times and bad, and I have had my share of both as you have.

Bless you and all good be with you in this dark world.

> Yours ever,
> S.B.[32]

To this Londonderry rejoined with another long letter, of some fourteen typewritten pages, in which he went over the ground again. 'I could not refrain from smiling when you associated me with your ups and downs,' he concluded. 'I had never experienced any downs that I could complain of with any justification, until with one stroke you wiped me off the political map, whereas notwithstanding the downs which you may have experienced, you retired from an active part in public life in a blaze of glory.'[33]

It had always been Londonderry's ambition to become Viceroy of India, and he had been very disappointed when Baldwin chose Edward Wood, later Lord Halifax, in 1926, particularly as he felt that Lady Londonderry was 'made for the job' of Vicereine, which indeed she was. Then, as he reminded Baldwin when they met in London in May 1939,

'Ramsay was frightened of criticism and sent Willingdon, and you sent Linlithgow, the result, I am told, of the best bit of lobbying ever done. So my star was properly set.'

> What I mind is that you left me under a stigma which has done me personally and publicly untold harm; but I believe one only really minds things if one thinks they can be rectified. I have long since realised no one can rectify them now. I sometimes feel rather shame-faced *vis-à-vis* my ancestors. I feel that they are murmuring: 'Well, he might have done better than that,' and with the motto I have always had graven on my heart: 'Luck is the superstition of the incompetent', I find I have no answer to make.

At their meeting, Baldwin had cautiously observed that time would tell whether Londonderry was right in his attitude to the Germans. 'It will not take fifty years to discover whether I was right or wrong,' Londonderry wrote back next day. 'I was obviously right and the Government obviously wrong and I am enclosing two letters I wrote to a Committee to consider German rearmament in November 1934. You were on the Committee, but you all brushed me on one side.'[34]*

Baldwin had just returned from a trip to Canada where he had stayed with the Tweedsmuirs in Ottawa, which he always wished to do, and had delivered three lectures at Toronto University on the well-trodden path of the English character and the English system of democracy, and the ways in which they had reacted to events at home and abroad since the last war. At what was to be one of their last meetings, Baldwin told Londonderry about his visit and how he found the Canadians. On one point at least Londonderry was in agreement with him, namely his belief, as he told his Canadian audience, that the Chamberlain Government had been 'wholly right' in undertaking to defend Poland if she were attacked.

---

* The letters marked 'secret and personal' and written from the Air Ministry were addressed to Hailsham, who was then War Minister. The originals were returned to Londonderry at the latter's request when he was writing his book, as he wished to quote from them in justification of his policy. Direct quotation was not possible since they were technically official papers, but Londonderry was allowed to summarise them in part in *Ourselves and Germany* (original edition, pp. 62–5). Londonderry's object was to persuade Germany to return to the League of Nations and to reach an accommodation with her which would restore her lost prestige and at the same time render her secure from attack by the French on the west and the Poles on the east. This should be done, he argued, while the Germans were still 'not in a position to challenge the world'. Otherwise 'this situation will be entirely altered in a comparatively short space of time, and we shall find ourselves up against ultimatums from Germany and a power behind those ultimatums which will plunge the world once more into the catastrophe of war'. Londonderry to Hailsham, 22 November 1934: Londonderry Papers.

And now we know that should the challenge come, we shall be there. In Luther's words, 'we can no other'. We were there when the Spanish galleons made for Plymouth: we were on those bloody fields in the Netherlands when Louis XIV aimed at the domination of Europe: we were on duty when Napoleon bestrode the world like a demi-god, and we answered the roll-call, as you did, in August 1914. We can no other. So help us, God.[35]

In August 1939 Baldwin crossed the Atlantic again to deliver a similar address at Columbia University in New York. He also spoke to an audience of 7,000 in the Waldorf-Astoria Hotel on democracy and industrial relations, and he visited the New York Fair, where he emphasised that the issue of war or peace lay with Hitler, and whatever happened Britain would do her duty. 'Lothian* thought he would do more good seeing a lot of people privately for three weeks,' wrote Tom Jones at the time, 'but the fact is that S.B. is no longer equal to this sort of active talking and dining existence and moves about with some difficulty and his lady must be with him and she is accustomed to attention and comfort.'[36]

On 20 August, Baldwin and his wife sailed from New York for Southampton intending to go on to Aix-les-Bains for their usual holiday. But their ship was diverted to Le Havre to pick up stranded British tourists as the result of the news received over the radio that German panzer troops had begun to invade Poland and that the conflict was likely to spread. After docking in Southampton they immediately hurried off to Worcestershire. 'Of course my cure and holiday are off,' he wrote to Tom Jones, 'and we go to Astley to prepare for an invasion of Black Country children.'[37]

5

'What wouldn't I give just now to be ten years younger!' Baldwin confessed to Miss Watson, his old and faithful secretary in Downing Street. 'The first time I have ever wished it.' To the Davidsons he complained of 'being of so little use'. By this date he was 'very lame' and hobbled about the house, finding it 'quite a tiring business' to get to the Broad Walk in the grounds of Astley and back.[38] ('It is a weird time just now, cut off from the world, useless and knowing nothing.') However, there were the evacuee children to be looked after, and Lucy Baldwin immedi-

* Then British Ambassador in Washington.

ately made over part of the large but thinly-staffed house for their feeding and accommodation. Unfortunately the evacuees were followed by a burglar who ransacked Lucy Baldwin's bedroom and made off with most of her jewellery.

'He has now no private secretary and has to wrestle with his private correspondence unaided,' noted Tom Jones after a visit to Astley at this time. 'His desk was littered with papers and he keeps a lot of his more private papers in an OHMS official box which belonged to his father and had stamped on it, "Railway Rates Committee, Alfred Baldwin, MP".' Jones also noticed a signed photograph of Lloyd George, the result of Lloyd George having written to ask Baldwin for one of himself, in return for which he sent his own – 'a rather fierce one in which L.G. was looking straight into the eyes of the beholder and giving the impression of the most positive and direct and honest statesman in Europe'.[39]

Windham Baldwin has given a characteristic pen-picture of his father at this time:

> He still sped through books as the whim took him; but more often now he would sit, puffing his pipe, in his armchair, meditating; still occasionally snapping his fingers, or screwing up one eye, or picking up a book and putting it to his nose, or making short grunting noises deep in his throat; less now than when his nerves were jangled by great affairs. When energy allowed he would re-read old letters and records of younger days, destroying some. His father's locked diaries in many volumes, though they would have been surely interesting to him, he had never opened, for it seemed to him indelicate, disloyal, or somehow improper for him to do so, so they lay piled on chairs in the library, as they had lain since his mother's death at Wilden twenty years before.[40]

He was glad of an excuse to make an occasional brief visit to London with his wife. He was there in November 1939 when he saw the King, Halifax and others, and 'had a peep at old friends at No. 10'. He found Neville Chamberlain in bed, 'but *very* well in himself'. They looked back together on the recent past and found it difficult to see how they could have acted otherwise than they did. 'Who could in 1934–1937 have foreseen Hitler's development?'[41]

Baldwin was in London again in January 1940 when he asked Sir John Reith, the BBC chief whom Chamberlain had just appointed Minister of Information, to come and see him. After expressing disquiet at the arrangements which had been made for the control of information and organisation of propaganda, he told Reith that he was 'unhappy about many of Chamberlain's appointments'. He himself had kept the Conservative Party 'left centre', but Chamberlain was undoing much of that. Reith gave him a lift in his official car to an oyster bar off St James's Square, where was he joined by Lady Baldwin. As they parted, Reith, whose appointment had involved his election to the House of Commons, remarked that he would be glad of any advice Baldwin could give him. Baldwin replied that he would have to think about it.

Reith did not expect to hear any more, but a few days later, on his return to Astley, Baldwin sat down and wrote Reith a long and helpful letter in his own hand. The letter, which was later quoted by Reith in his autobiography *Into the Wind*, is too long for reproduction here. But a few salient points may be noted in passing since they hold equally good today. 'Patience first and last all the way' and 'Be yourself' were the things which should always be remembered both for Minister and Private Member.

Every House has its own distinctive character and every man of position has to make good (or not!) in a new House. You come in like a new boy at a new school and you must learn its ways. Time will soon show you what instinct you possess in understanding it . . .

Make the acquaintance of the Smoking Room: your PPS or a Whip should arrange this for you. Look in and let them get a few of the right men to sit with you. A pipe and a chat and get them to talk. You want to get it about that you are accessible; that you are ready to hear complaints and to meet them when reasonable. You can often avoid questions in the House by personal contact in time and a debate in which you are the principal figure will often go much more smoothly if you can create an impression of yourself – which I am sure you can . . .

One thing the House will NEVER forgive and that is if a Minister misleads it. If you find you have given an answer that isn't true, acknowledge it at once and express your regret. The blame is always on you and *not* the Civil Service . . .[42]

'That great, that unfortunate, that much-maligned man,' as Sir Alan ('A.P.') Herbert called Baldwin, had always been a great believer in the efficacy of personal contact in the House. 'We had many a gossip in the Smoking Room (where I don't think I ever saw Mr Neville Chamberlain),' Herbert was to recall after Baldwin's death. 'I remember one day when I came from the Chamber exhausted and cross after an afternoon failing to catch the Speaker's eye, he gave me a philosophical and practical talk about "bumping" as he called it. How often, after all, when an eager young Member did "get in" he afterwards regretted it.'[43]

Baldwin was at Astley when the Chamberlain Government fell in May 1940 and Churchill became Prime Minister. 'The country wanted Winston, just as it wanted Lloyd George in 1916,' he told Tom Jones who visited him a fortnight later. 'Did I tell you I had quite a nice letter from Winston?' he wrote to the Davidsons at this time. 'I thought I ought to send him a line but I wasn't sure whether I should get an acknowledgement! I think he is the right man at the moment and I always did feel that would be his opportunity. He thrives in that environment.'[44]

Churchill had invited Chamberlain to join his new Government and the War Cabinet, which he did as Lord President of the Council. Unhappily an operation which he underwent during the summer revealed that he had incurable cancer of the bowel, but he struggled on gamely until the beginning of October knowing that he only had a short time to live. When at last he resigned, he declined all titular honours including the Garter, preferring to die 'plain Mr Chamberlain' like his father before him. Baldwin wrote him a long letter, full of sympathy and affection, in the light of his own experience of painful readjustment. Let him not worry over the past, he counselled him; those who had done their best must be content to await the sentence of history. Although Chamberlain was in considerable physical discomfort and indeed was to die within a matter of weeks, he sent Baldwin by return of post a remarkable handwritten apologia for the most controversial chapter in his political career, which Baldwin (according to Tom Jones) 'did not relish'.[45]

Never for one single instant have I doubted the rightness of what I did at Munich, nor can I believe that it was possible for me to do more than I did to prepare the country for war after Munich, given the violent and persistent opposition I had to fight against all the time.

You remember how I, as Chancellor of the Exchequer, asked leave of the Cabinet to review the programmes put up by the Service Ministers, and submitted a programme which was accepted by you and the others which provided for a larger Air Force than Charley Londonderry had ventured to propose. After Munich I still further increased that programme, and inaugurated all the A[ir] R[aid] P[recautions] measures which have developed since. I also introduced Conscription, but I had to fight for every one of these things. In September '38 we only had sixty fire pumps in London, which would have been burnt out in a week. Some day these things will be known. My critics differed from me because they were ignorant, it is only fair to add wilfully ignorant in many cases.

So I regret nothing in the past. I do regret that I should be cut off when I feel capable of doing much more were it not for physical disability. But I accept what I can't help and hope I shan't cumber the earth too long. I doubt if I shall ever visit Brum again.[46]

Neville Chamberlain never did see Birmingham again. He died on 9 November 1940 and five days later his ashes were placed beside those of Bonar Law in Westminster Abbey. Afterwards Churchill delivered the customary tribute in the House of Commons, which had been bombed out and now met in Church House. Someone complimented him on his speech. 'No,' said the Prime Minister, 'that was not an insuperable task, since I admired many of Neville's great qualities. But I pray to God in his infinite mercy that I shall not have to deliver a similar oration on Baldwin. That indeed would be difficult to do.'[47]

Tom Jones came to Astley regularly, usually on Pilgrim Trust business, and kept the Baldwins in touch with what their mutual friends were doing. He was there in January 1941, and noted that Lucy Baldwin was 'full of vigour' but her husband 'while mentally fresh in the forenoon grew visibly fatigued by the evening, when he frequently flicked his fingers and his face twitched restlessly as it used to do at No. 10 when he was tired'. The Trust Committee, which had already given away nearly a million pounds, met at Astley at Easter, the other members thoughtfully bringing their butter rations with them. In July there was another meeting at Harlech in Merionethshire. 'This was Baldwin's first visit, age seventy-four, to a county only one remove from his native Shropshire,' Jones remarked. 'He attributed this to a servant girl at his home in Bewdley who always spoke of the Welsh (and all foreigners) as savages, a sentiment which long clung to him and which still lingers in remote, and not so remote, corners of his mind.'[48]

In June, the Baldwins spent a few days with the Davidsons near Berkhamstead. R. A. Butler appeared one evening. 'I hadn't seen him since the war began and I was delighted with our talk,' Baldwin afterwards wrote to Halifax, who had been Butler's chief at the Foreign Office. Butler has described his visit in his memoirs:

S.B. was sitting in the porch rather like an old villager outside his cottage. He stood up for a while when we arrived, but then said he felt his arthritis too much and we all sat down and talked before dinner. His first agonised question was: 'Did any of you foresee the collapse of France?' I had been told that he had been suffering from a very serious depression, and so I took as optimistic a view of the situation as I could.

After dinner I noted that S.B. had lost none of his old habits. He sniffed the knives and forks and curled up his eyes and clicked his fingers exactly the way he used to do. But his conversation had declined in vigour, point and quality.

At 9 p.m., this being a typical British household there was a rush to hear the news. S.B. pulled out an old turnip watch and asked if he need really participate in this ritual. Joan Davidson gave way and the women went off to hear the BBC. We then talked for more than an hour, and the theme to which S.B. continually returned was that his military advisers had told him Germany would not be fully prepared until 1942; he had therefore felt that by starting re-armament when he did, in 1935, he was just in time.[49]

In December Baldwin heard the unexpected news of Lord Lothian's death in Washington. Lothian, who had lent Baldwin his great house in Norfolk, Blickling Hall, during his convalescence in 1936, had later been appointed British Ambassador to the United States by Chamberlain and in the short time he was there had proved himself an outstandingly able diplomatic representative, his work being aided by his intimate knowledge of the country and its people. When he was quite a young man and known as Philip Kerr, his great friend Lady Astor had converted him from Roman Catholicism to Christian Science, which may have accounted for Baldwin's description of him as 'a queer bird' and 'a rum cove'. True to his accepted beliefs, Lothian refused the services of a doctor when he became ill in the Embassy and, instead of submitting to a simple operation which would undoubtedly have saved his life, he was ministered to without effect by a 'faith healer'. Knowing how upset Lady Astor would be by the fatal news, Baldwin penned a characteristic note to her in her grief. 'My dear Lady Nancy,' he wrote. 'This needs no acknowledgement but I think I know what this means to you and I just want to grasp your hand for a moment. With affection and regard. S.B.'

Tom Jones urged Baldwin to make himself heard in the House of Lords and he received other invitations to speak, all of which he turned down. On 30 September 1941 he wrote to Lionel Curtis:

The time may come when I may speak again, but at present I fear the last person many people want to hear is a survivor from the days of 1931–1937. We are out of date and I am widely supposed to be responsible for all that has happened since. The M[inistry] of I[nformation] did ask me informally if I would do a broadcast a month or so ago. But after consideration and consultation with two of my wisest and most intimate friends (one was T.J.), I declined on the grounds that it would arouse a controversy that would do no good and might do harm.[50]

He also continued to say no to requests for his memoirs. 'When I left office, I decided to take no further part in political activity,' he wrote in reply to one such request: 'and, in my view, to write or say anything about any of my old friends and associates still in active politics would be a breach of that resolve which I am not prepared to make.' At the same time he was not ashamed of what he had attempted to do in the Party political field. For instance, he wrote to Derek Pepys-Whiteley:

I tried hard in those confused years immediately following the [last] war to get a re-orientation as it were of the Tory party i.e. to give it a national rather than a party outlook. If such a spirit should animate those who undertake the great adventure of government after the [present] war, then I could feel that I had not worked in vain.

Baldwin had continued to meet and correspond intermittently with Eden, who was now back at the Foreign Office. After dining together in the autumn of 1941, Eden wrote: 'I felt very sorry for S.B. He has grand things about him. He attempts no self-justification. I believe that history *will* treat him more kindly than his contemporaries do now. He did much to kill class hatred and to unite the country.'[51]

6

In September 1941, the Ministry of Supply caused all local authorities to carry out a survey of all iron gates and railings in the country for requisitioning as scrap to aid the war effort, the only exception being those 'of special artistic merit or of historic interest'. There were a dozen or so such gates at Astley, most of them lightly wrought and containing in their design dates of peculiar significance to their past owners; they were of little or no value for melting down as scrap. 'Men are measuring our lovely iron gates which our District Council will commandeer,' Baldwin wrote to the Davidsons: 'about £400 worth of beauty to be sold to the Government at 27 shillings a ton and gates don't make up much weight!'[52] Thereupon Baldwin appealed on the grounds of artistic merit, and the Council appointed an architect to examine the gates and assess their merits. In December 1941 the architect recommended that the gates should be spared. It would be a tragedy if such ironwork were allowed to disappear, he reported, as some of it certainly could not be replaced. The Ministry of Public Buildings and Works, which was responsible for carrying out the requisitioning orders, then stepped in, and two months later Baldwin was officially informed that the Ministry's Headquarters Appeal Panel had 'given their utmost careful consideration' to the matter and had decided that all the gates must go with the exception of the modern pair at the entrance to the main drive, 'which the Local Authority considers are necessary'. These were the gates which had been presented to Baldwin by the Worcestershire Conservative Association on the occasion of his retirement in 1937.

At the time the requisitioning order was made, Lord Beaverbrook was the Minister of Supply, and the story was later widely circulated that he had deliberately engineered the removal of Baldwin's gates as part of his personal vendetta. There was no truth in this. Sir John Reith, by this time Lord Reith, and not Beaverbrook, was responsible as Minister of Public Buildings and Works. Baldwin wrote privately to Reith and received a negative reply in brief magisterial terms, contrasting strongly with the long and helpful letter of advice which Baldwin had sent Reith on his first becoming a minister two years before.

The matter now became public knowledge, and the *Daily Mirror* sent its well-known columnist William Connor ('Cassandra') to Astley to investigate it. Baldwin refused to see him, and 'Cassandra' got his own back by writing a virulent article in which he described Astley as 'this National Park of Failure' and demanded that the gates be left 'as a national monument to the attitude of mind that has put us in the desperate peril in which we now find ourselves'. On his way from London a stranger had given him the poisonous fruit of a tomato tree. How 'Cassandra' disposed of it was thus:

At the bottom of the field on the south side of the Hall, I dug a shallow hole. The ground was hard and frosty, but I pierced it with a stout stick. In it I placed the fruit of the tomato tree and I planted it well. Grow up, little tree. Blossom and flower and bring forth many fruit. For you are on famous ground.

On 4 March 1942 Mr George Hicks, the Parliamentary Secretary to the Works Minister, was asked in the House of Commons whether he could state the position with respect to the railings on the property of Lord Baldwin. Mr Hicks replied that 'with the exception of the pair of gates at the entrance to the main drive . . . all railings and gates have now been safely gathered in'. Whereupon Captain Alan Graham, a Conservative backbencher, inquired: 'Is the Honourable Member aware that it is very necessary to leave Lord Baldwin his gates in order to protect him from the just indignation of the mob?'

It was ironic that this supplementary question should have been put by a Conservative, while the official view was expressed by a Labour Member who now held office in Churchill's war-time Coalition Government, and had previously stated as a Private Member on the eve of the General Election in October 1935 that 'the path to war and disaster lies in the strengthening of national armaments and in relying on armaments for security'. Certainly, the civil servant in the Works Ministry who was able to overrule the recommendation of the local authority architect in Worcestershire was guilty of a mean-spirited action, although of course the ultimate responsibility lay with the Minister Lord Reith.[53]

Early in 1942 the Baldwins received a visit from an unusual relative who spent some weeks at Astley. This was Monica Baldwin, a granddaughter of George Baldwin, who it will be recalled had once lived in Wilden House and shared the control of the family business with his brother Alfred (Stanley's father) and another brother, until they had been bought out.* Shortly before the outbreak of the First World War, Monica had become a nun and remained in her convent, almost completely cut off from the outside world, for twenty-eight years, until she decided to make a figurative 'leap over the wall', being inspired to do so by the actual leap out of the Tower of London made by her ancestor Thomas Baldwin of Diddlebury in Queen Elizabeth's time. Stanley Baldwin had occasionally visited her in the convent, at Bruges, and when she came out it was natural that she should turn for help among others to her cousin and his wife, whom she always referred to as 'Uncle Stan' and 'Aunt Cissy'. One of the things which she most enjoyed during her stay at Astley, which she was later to describe in her best-selling autobiography *I Leap over the Wall*, was breakfasting alone with 'Uncle Stan', whose wife and daughter Diana, who was staying at Astley for the duration, did not

* Monica's father Arthur Baldwin, a son of George, had died young.

appear until later in the morning. 'At that hour the average Englishman is apt to be morose and taciturn,' Monica wrote. 'Not so Uncle Stan. He was then at his wittiest and best. I could have listened to him indefinitely held captive by the interest and fascination of his talk.'

It took Monica a little time to become acclimatised to her new surroundings. Her convent training had taught her to open doors so quietly that at Astley she would make people jump when they encountered her unexpectedly. In the result 'Uncle Stan' spoke to her about it and she thereupon made a habit of stamping up and downstairs, rattling door handles and banging doors. Afterwards she admitted that she found this extremely difficult as she had spent the greater part of her life trying to be noiseless. Margaret, another of the Baldwin daughters who lived near by and was married to Sir Maurice Huntington-Whiteley, suggested to Monica that she should become a 'Land Girl', which she did. However, she found 'digging for victory' rather too strenuous for her liking after the quiet convent life, and she moved on to a variety of other occupations of which being a temporary assistant in the London Library was probably the most congenial.[54]

On 12 September 1942 the Baldwins celebrated their golden wedding at a large family reunion at the Dorchester Hotel at which all their children and most of their grandchildren were present. The occasion was also marked by a simple service at Rottingdean Parish Church, where their gift of an oak chair was dedicated as a thank-offering for fifty years of happy married life.

On 15 February 1943 Baldwin lunched with Churchill and James Stuart, the Government Chief Whip, in the 'dug-out' which served as a dining-room at 10 Downing Street. The meeting, which had been tactfully arranged by Stuart, happily put an end to the strained relations which had existed between Churchill and Baldwin for some years. Their talk, which was continued in the Cabinet room, lasted for almost three hours. Baldwin called Churchill 'PM', a form of address to which Churchill demurred. But Baldwin insisted – it was due to the greatness of his office, he said. With considerable tact, the Prime Minister asked the older man his advice. Should he speak out against Southern Ireland's neutrality in the war and the de Valera Government's refusal to let Britain use the old treaty ports as anti-submarine bases? He handed the notes of his intended speech to Baldwin, and while Baldwin read them Churchill sipped his brandy and smoked a large cigar. 'I wouldn't make that speech,' said Baldwin, and in the event Churchill did not. Baldwin refused the offer of one of Churchill's famous cigars and lit up his pipe, explaining that he had given up cigars long ago as he could not afford them. 'Oh,' said Churchill, puffing away, 'I flatter myself that I have democratised cigars!'

Their conversation was interrupted by the arrival of a Guards Officer to demonstrate the use of a new beret for the troops. Churchill took a keen interest in such military details and when he heard that some of the troops were drawn up outside in the garden, he immediately went off to see for himself how they looked in their new headgear, which incidentally had encountered some opposition among the men. 'Don't go out without you coat, PM,' said Baldwin. 'It is very cold and this room is very hot.' However, Churchill chose to disregard this advice with near fatal results for himself and the country. The first of the berets to be demonstrated blew off and during the time it took to retrieve it and try it on again, Churchill stayed in the garden and in the event caught pneumonia. Next day he was in bed with a high temperature and was obliged to stay there for the rest of the month.[55]

A few weeks later, Baldwin met Walter Citrine, the General Secretary of the TUC, who called at the Dorchester Hotel, where Baldwin now stayed on his occasional visits to London. 'I feel I still have a young brain, but I am dreadfully out of things,' he remarked in response to Citrine's inquiry about his health. 'I get to know nothing in the country. You remember I had pretty heavy going; I had to face all that Abdication trouble by myself for a time. Even some of the members of my own party didn't agree with me but I never wavered because I knew what the British people would do.'

'You had the good sense to retire at the height of your prestige,' said Citrine. 'I don't know whether Winston will do the same. I rather thought he would up to a few days ago but now it is pretty clear that he intends to carry on into the post-war period.'

'My prestige is all gone now,' Baldwin answered a little sadly, 'but Winston stands at a higher peak than any man in the world. Lloyd George never rose to the same heights in the last war.' Baldwin added that Churchill had 'thought and dreamed of war all his life', and recalled that at their last meeting he had remarked that some of the things Churchill had said reminded him of his ancestor the first Duke of Marlborough. 'He seemed immensely pleased with that.'[56]

Baldwin also wrote of this meeting to his young grandson Colin Munro:

A few weeks ago I was happy enough to have three hours with the PM whom I hadn't seen since the war began. I was very impressed by him: the war has brought out all that is best in him and all that is BIG. It was always there but nothing less than the war would have brought it out.[57]

Shortly after this, Harold Nicolson had breakfast with Baldwin at the Dorchester, when they talked of Kipling, Ramsay MacDonald and Churchill. They had last met over the same meal six years ago, but this time the fare was one of war-time austerity. Nicolson wrote in his diary:

> We sit at opposite ends of a tiny table, with a kipper in front of each of us. He is lame and slightly deaf, but I see no diminution of his curiosity or his memory . . . He talks of human ambition and endeavour, and says that in his long life he has found always that in the end men and women are as good as one thinks them . . . He lives in a sort of pool or ambient water of forgiveness. He said the only man he could never forgive was Beaverbrook.
>
> I did not notice much change in him. His nose has got squarer and more bulbous, and now really looks like what Low made him look like years ago. His face is still that strange colour, as if lightly dusted by ginger-powder.[58]

G. M. Young, who stayed at Astley in 1943, remarked that he used to contrive his uprising and downcoming so that he entered the breakfast room as nine was striking. He always found his host either helping himself at the sideboard or just spreading his napkin – never by a quarter of a minute behind or in front. One day was very much like another. The morning in the library with his books and pipes – Young counted fortyseven of them – reading the papers, listening to the news on the 'wireless', talking, writing letters, lunch, a brief turn in the garden, solving the cross-word, followed by an early dinner and bed. American troops would sometimes come over to tea from a neighbouring camp.

During one visit Tom Jones found Lucy Baldwin 'formidable and overwhelming in laying down the law, almost as if we were in the Albert Hall'.

> She would be horrified to be dubbed a Feminist, but she does battle manfully for women's rights and wants far more training for girls as home-makers, and finds little of that in Butler's Education Bill. She came down to dinner in a one-piece seamless robe of gorgeous golden brocade, for which there is doubtless a name, but one unknown to me.

We all drank a little Burgundy as it was Windham's birthday. He is in Algiers and at last commissioned. They are certain that for a long time after he enlisted his promotion was blocked because he was his father's son.

All Jones saw in the way of servants on the occasion of this visit, in March 1944, was 'the antique butler and a pantry boy from some orphan school near Hereford, a cheerful lad who was heard the other day singing the following jingle'.

> I am very happy,
> I am full of joy,
> I am Lord Baldwin's
> Pantry Boy!

Tom Jones again visited Astley in February 1945 when he found Baldwin recovering from an attack of shingles, 'brought on no doubt by long and unacknowledged war worry'.

This house is too large in old age, miles from a railway station, petrol is scarce, and their loneliness and separation from friends complete. Travelling is no pleasure and as likely as not you may have to stand for hours in a crowded corridor and reach an hotel which has not enough coal to feed its heating system. Lady B. keeps vigorous and voluble but he is quiet and more than ever given to silent ruminating, broken now and again by a gurgle in the throat.

Fortunately Baldwin liked reading, and during the war he got through all Jane Austen and Scott – although he admitted to skipping some of Scott – as well as *War and Peace*, *The Dynasts* (twice), Thomas Hardy's novels, Horace Walpole's *Letters* and sundry works on Roman Britain and the history of the Anglo-Saxons. When Jones happened to mention Lytton Strachey, Baldwin expressed strong disapproval of this writer. 'I would not have his books in my house,' he said.

Arthur Bryant had recently seen Jones in Wales, and when he heard Jones was going to stay with the Baldwins he said to Jones: 'Please give my very kindest regards to S.B. and Lady Baldwin. He never says a word for himself, but History, I am sure, will place him where he belongs with Walpole and Harley and Clarendon.' Jones duly delivered the message, and Baldwin observed: 'To be with Clarendon will be good enough for me.' [59]

Jones's final glimpse of the regime of 'rather austere war-economy' at Astley was of his host and hostess in the morning room 'trying to keep warm by a fire of peat and logs, and no child or presence of cat or dog to warm the hearth'.

7

Tom Jones happened to be staying with the Baldwins at Astley in 1941 when they heard the news of Dame Margaret Lloyd George's death. Mention of the subject at dinner prompted Baldwin to bring up the place of his own burial. Turning to his wife, he put the question deliberately, adding 'Wilden?' by way of a possible place. 'No, Worcester,' she replied. 'We want to be together.' Jones rightly took this to mean Worcester Cathedral, and no more was said.[60]

For both husband and wife the end was to come swiftly and unexpectedly. Lucy was the first to go, on 17 June 1945, a few weeks after the end of the war in Europe. She had been playing on the lawn at Astley with two of her grandchildren, throwing and catching a ball. Later the same evening she suddenly collapsed in the house and died.*

For the surviving partner it was a terrible shock, from which he never fully recovered. 'I have been stunned by what has happened, and realisation only follows later,' he wrote to the Davidsons a week afterwards. 'I am not a hermit and I perform little duties towards my neighbours, but I have not yet got that control of myself that I must have before I venture forth even amongst my intimate friends.' 'I am still stunned and am automatically answering some five hundred letters,' he told Helen Waddell, whose translation of the mediaeval Latin lyric 'Thou hast come safe to port' he found 'of great comfort' at this time. 'But my friends are wonderfully kind,' he added, 'and I cling to them.' For a time he was kept occupied in answering the inevitable letters of sympathy which poured in from old colleagues and friends. To Lord Salisbury, for example, he wrote from Astley: 'I always dreaded that I might go first. I doubt if she could have kept this house up, as a good slice of my income dies with me and she might have seen the home she made broken up.' Indeed, as he told Tom Jones, he was now paying surtax out of capital or borrowings, and he recalled that during the great slump in 1929–30, when the £1 ordinary shares in Baldwins which had once stood at £3 were written down to 4s., he had lost £140,000. Thus the man who had once handed over £120,000 of his personal fortune to the Exchequer, as

* The cause of death was officially certified as coronary thrombosis.

a free gift, was obliged to sell the library in his London house to meet his immediate post-war liabilities.[61]

Meanwhile his daughter Diana, always his favourite, stayed on at Astley and kept house for him. She had also suffered a grievous blow when her husband George Kemp-Welch, who was a captain in the Grenadier Guards, was killed by the flying bomb which struck the crowded Guards Chapel one Sunday morning in June 1944. In the circumstances she was probably the best kind of companion-housekeeper for her father. Nevertheless, as she was to write after his death, 'he was dreadfully lonely without mother and though I looked after him entirely for two and a half years, I could not possibly make up for him what he had lost. I think his lameness was a secret source of great regret to him, though he never complained, as he was such a walker in the old days.' Nor could he really afford to keep up Astley. In the result part of the house was shut off and the place assumed a sad and neglected air, as the gardens and grounds lacked the staff necessary to maintain them.

The great Labour victory at the General Election in the summer of 1945 was an interesting reflection on Baldwin's statesmanship as Prime Minister between the wars. 'If this Government shows itself ready to govern constitutionally, it will be because you taught them to be a parliamentary and not a revolutionary Party,' a friend wrote to him at this time. 'It was, as I know from talks we had in those days, your constant and conscious aim, and I believe that history will credit you, more than any man of our generation, with having saved Parliamentary Government.'[62]

In January 1946 Tom Jones spent a week-end at Astley on his way from Wales to London. Afterwards he wrote from Aberystwyth of his host to a friend:

He was fairly well physically, but I noticed a great inability to concentrate on any one topic; he quickly got tired, and we must have touched on a couple of hundred topics during the week-end. It has now been arranged, to my great relief, that G. M. Young shall do his *Life*, and I sent to Geoffrey Fry's a lot of S.B.'s papers from the National Library here where they had been stored since I brought them from Harlech. S.B.'s memory is still very good and he possesses a most interesting collection of old letters from Burne-Jones, Kipling, William Morris and that period.

This was the last occasion on which Jones recorded any of Baldwin's table talk, although they continued to meet from time to time. Among other revelations, Baldwin told Jones that he had dissuaded Eden from accepting the Viceroyalty of India, which had been suggested to him in 1943 by Amery, then Secretary of State. If Eden now went to New York as the Permanent British Representative at the United Nations, an idea which had also been mooted, Baldwin supposed that R. A. Butler would lead the Conservative Party after Churchill had gone. Another topic which Baldwin touched on was the quality of French political life. 'One of the things that comforted me when I gave up office was that I should not have to meet French statesmen any more,' he said. 'Not more than a few are said to be incorruptible. Caillaux's wife shot the editor who had attacked him. Not the sort of support you want from your wife!' 63

The choice of G. M. Young as Baldwin's official biographer had been strongly urged by Jones and Fry. Unfortunately it was to prove far from successful. Although Young, an able historian and Fellow of All Souls, was a fairly frequent visitor to Astley during the last years of Baldwin's life, he was never really in sympathy with his subject. At the very outset he was to state that Baldwin's invitation to him to become his biographer was extended 'somewhat languidly' and accepted by him 'with misgiving', not the happiest frame of mind in which to embark on such a literary undertaking. Admittedly Young was handicapped in his work by the paucity of personal letters, since Baldwin seldom kept copies of anything he wrote of this kind, but the biographer was unable or did not take the trouble to get in touch with those intimates such as Tom Jones and the Davidsons to whom Baldwin had unburdened himself over the years both orally and on paper. In his interviews with Baldwin, Young misunderstood his subject's silences which occurred with some frequency during their conversations and he failed to draw him out as Jones and others were in the habit of doing. The result was a relatively brief and inadequate as well as in places unfair and inaccurate memoir, which greatly disappointed Baldwin's family and friends when it appeared five years after his death. Jones, who was to write an excellent short sketch of Baldwin for the *Dictionary of National Biography*, would have been a much better choice if he could have been persuaded to do it.

Maybe Baldwin had some inkling of what to expect at Young's hands, as he was aware of the risks attached to contemporary biography. While Professor Keith Feiling was engaged on his life of Neville Chamberlain, which was published in 1946, Baldwin had many talks with him. 'The Chamberlain is well done and there are some thick stabs for me in it!' he remarked to his son Oliver after reading it.

At the end of 1946 he attended his last Garter Chapter at Windsor. 'I am glad I made the effort, effort though it was,' he said afterwards. 'But the kindness of everyone to an old crock warmed my heart.' He still visited old friends like the Davidsons, whose home he 'hated leaving', as 'I always have to screw myself up to coming back to Astley'. He also carried on with his relatively mild duties at Cambridge, although he had found the programme which had been planned for the visit of the King and Queen in June too much for him, and he had to cry off. ('I dread the day when they say they want a younger Chancellor.') However, he was still able to attend the quarterly meetings of the Pilgrim Trust. But, in July 1947, when the Committee dined together afterwards at the Athenaeum, Jones noted that Baldwin was 'very conscious that his end could not be far off'. To Sir James Irvine, another committee member, he spoke intimately on this occasion of the 'desolation of crippled age and the depression which comes from the thought that one's days of service are done'. But he added, as Irvine thought, solemnly and confidently: 'It is my belief that we are called away only when we are ready, and the fact that I have to endure so much means that I am not ready yet.'[64]

A few days later, Baldwin celebrated his eightieth birthday. The event went unnoticed outside his family except for a brief reference in *The Times* with other birthdays which fell on 3 August. A few like Lord Macmillan and Phyllis Broome wrote to congratulate him. 'I have been fortunate in my friends,' he replied to Macmillan.[65] To Phyllis Broome he wrote that, inadequately as he acknowledged her message and others like it, he could still say, ' "Thank God for my friends!" while still feeling gratitude for so much human kindness.'

'One never hears of Baldwin nowadays,' someone remarked to Winston Churchill at this time. 'He might as well be dead.'

'No, not dead,' said Churchill, 'but the candle in that great turnip has gone out.'[66]

During one of his visits to London in 1947, Baldwin heard that Londonderry was lying ill in hospital, the result of a flying accident when the tow-rope of his glider broke and he sustained serious injury to his spine, which was eventually to prove fatal. Baldwin thereupon called at the hospital and had a friendly talk with his old protagonist, a meeting which ended in a complete reconciliation after years of bitterness on Londonderry's part.[67]

Baldwin was in London again for the unveiling of the statue of King George V by his son George VI in Old Palace Yard opposite the Houses of Parliament on 22 October 1947. It was a cold, wet day, and Attlee who was then Prime Minister, afterwards remarked how frail Baldwin looked, as he watched the ceremony in front of the memorial for which he had himself launched the public appeal when he was Prime Minister eleven years earlier. Lord Macmillan, as chairman of the Executive Committee, formally invited the King to unveil the statue, which Macmillan described as 'the spontaneous tribute of the people of the United Kingdom and of the Commonwealth and Empire beyond the seas to a beloved Sovereign who for a quarter of a century reigned not only on the throne but in the hearts of all'.[68] Then as the King pulled the cord, the Union Jack which draped the statue fluttered to the ground revealing the distinguished work of Sir William Read Dick, the band of the Grenadier Guards played the National Anthem, and the bells of St Margaret's Church rang a peal. 'Chips' Channon, who was present, described the scene in his diary:

> The ceremony itself was over in twenty minutes, but then followed that interminable pause whilst the Royalties greeted each other, inter-kissed and chatted. It is only in England that a crowd of several thousands can stand happily in the rain and watch one family gossip . . .
>
> When the King, Queen and the Princesses had driven away, there was a pause of nearly two minutes, as the Queen Mary, tall, magnificent and sad, stood at the foot of the Memorial as she waited for her car to come up. The crowd sensed the pathos of the moment, and I wondered what were her thoughts as she looked up at the King, her husband. Then she was much cheered, as was Winston. No one cheered Attlee, or even recognised Baldwin.[69]

In fact, although Channon evidently did not see them, a few people did recognise Baldwin and as his car moved off in the rain they managed to raise a feeble cheer. Hearing the noise and accustomed to being the target of popular abuse, Baldwin mistook the purport of the demonstration, and turning to his companion beside him inquired pathetically: 'Are they booing me?'

Before returning to Astley, he went to the Davidsons for a few days. It was his last visit to them and his letter of thanks was the last they received from him. 'I was very happy at Norcott, as I always am, and I am grateful for much that you said,' he wrote on 28 October. 'There are not many left to tell an octogenarian his faults in the spirit of love and not of criticism. I hope that I may improve and be asked again.' But it was not to be.[70]

One piece of news about his son Oliver, to whom he was now closer than he had ever been, gave him particular pleasure during the next weeks. 'I have thought a lot of you,' he had recently written to Oliver, 'and have scoured the papers to see if your Party are doing anything for you. It would cheer me to learn that there is a chance of your getting a bit of work that would appeal to you.' He now learned that Oliver would shortly resign his seat in the House of Commons to become Governor and Commander-in-Chief of the Leeward Islands. Although it was not the greatest public appointment with which the then Labour Prime Minister might have rewarded a devoted follower for many years of conscientious service, it was well suited to Oliver's particular talents and his unconventional and eccentric character. At all events, as his younger brother has recorded, their father was quite delighted that the one who had always been regarded as something of a black sheep in the family should be honoured in this way. 'His delight was affecting to see,' Windham Baldwin recalled some years later, 'and I seem still to hear the happiness in his voice when he told me of the good news that was imminent. But he did not live to see it fructify.' [71]

The evening of 13 December 1947 was spent with Diana, like many others at Astley since his wife's death. According to his son, his humour was particularly lively and he went to bed at his usual hour, shortly after ten o'clock. 'I am ready,' he had remarked not long before. And so it turned out. When his servant came to call him next morning, he did not stir, having apparently died in his sleep. As his daughter remarked, 'his end was so blessedly peaceful and painless'.*

The Times, as might be expected, devoted its first leader to his passing, as well as giving him a five-column obituary, most of which had been written some years before by Tom Jones. ('Our unpreparedness for war was blamed on him alone; posterity will be more just, but it is certain that the man who was thrice Prime Minister between the French occupation of the Ruhr and the visit of Chamberlain to Munich will have to bear a large share.') The leader writer repeated the oft-quoted sentence which had previously appeared on the same page, that 'his spiritual home was the last ditch', in attempting a historical judgement of the kind which Baldwin's old colleagues in the House of Commons deliberately avoided when they came to offer their tributes later the same day. ('For his failure in a supreme moment he had himself to pay a heavy and bitter price, but there will be lasting gratitude for all that he gave to English public life.')

'This is not the time nor the occasion to appraise his work – that is a matter for the historian,' said the Prime Minister Mr Attlee in moving

* The cause of death was officially certified, like his wife's, as coronary thrombosis.

the adjournment of the House as a mark of respect to Baldwin's memory. 'We are too close to those events to pass a fair judgment. A statesman must be judged, not only by what he accomplished, but by what he sought to achieve. Account must be taken of the conditions in which he worked and the possibilities of the situation as it appeared to him at the time.'

> I always felt myself, when he was speaking, that although he disagreed with us, he understood better than any man on the other side, the reasons and emotions that inspired our actions . . . He seldom adopted a controversial tone. He always appeared to be putting his point of view in a disarming spirit of reasonableness, which is much more difficult to controvert than any amount of invective; yet in fact no one more shrewdly judged the temper of the House or selected with more skill the most effective line of argument for his purpose.
>
> It was, I think, this quiet manner of speech which made him such an effective speaker when broadcasting. He was, indeed, the first statesman to realise the particular technique required by this new means of approach to the electorate. But he could, on occasions, be both moving and eloquent. He was a great lover of the English language and he was deeply versed in our literature.

Eden spoke for the Conservative Opposition, followed by the Liberal Party leader, the 'Father' of the House (Lord Winterton), and several other backbenchers. Perhaps the most remarkable as well as one of the briefest tributes came from Willie Gallacher, the only Communist Member. 'History will judge him and his life work. Some may praise, some may blame, but here nothing should be said that could disturb the minds of those near and dear to him who are mourning his passing . . . let him sleep in everlasting peace.' One voice which was not heard on this occasion was that of Winston Churchill, who was on a working holiday in Morocco, painting and putting the finishing touches to *The Gathering Storm*, the first volume of his history of the Second World War, in which he was to deal at some length with what he called 'the years of the locust' and the part played by Baldwin in those years. Churchill's public tribute was to come later.[72]

In accordance with his wishes and those of his wife, Baldwin's ashes mingled with hers were buried in Worcester Cathedral, beneath a stone bearing a simple inscription near the West Door.* This was done at a

* 'Here lie the Ashes of Stanley 1st Earl Baldwin of Bewdley Knight of the most noble order of the Garter Privy Counsellor and three times Prime Minister of Great Britain 1867–1947 and of his wife Lucy Dame Grand Cross of the most excellent order of the British Empire 1869–1945.'

short ceremony during evensong in the Cathedral.[73] A similar plaque was erected in the public gardens at Aix-les-Bains by the municipality '*en souvenir des nombreux séjours*' made by the town's most distinguished honorary citizen from abroad.

When the details of his will were published, they showed that he may have worried unduly over his personal finances: in fact he left over a quarter of a million pounds. Besides his political papers, which went to Cambridge University Library, he bequeathed to Trinity College a replica of a silver flagon which his ancestor Richard Baldwin had presented to Munslow Church in 1689. His Worcestershire property was divided between his two sons, Oliver inheriting Astley along with his father's titles.* The dozen or so gold and silver caskets, with which he was presented when he received the freedom of various cities and boroughs, were designated as family heirlooms. His favourite, from Winchester, bore the inscription: 'To a lover of England who bears the burden of her greatness.'

An appeal launched through the press for the cost of a simple sandstone memorial to Baldwin in a roadside garden near Astley was embarrassingly under-subscribed. However, when he heard of it, Winston Churchill sent a generous sum which made up the difference and furthermore came down and spoke at the ceremony, when he handed over the deeds of the memorial to the trustees.

As the years roll by and the perspective of history lengthens and reduces so many of our disputes to their due proportion, there will be many who will not pass this place without giving their respectful salute.

Of the man who gave him high office ('my old chief') and later excluded him from his Cabinet, Churchill also remarked on this occasion: 'He was the most formidable politician I have ever known in public life.'[74]

'The reason for his long, tenacious, successful hold over the electorate,' one of his juniors has conjectured, 'is probably to be found in the simple fact that he was, fundamentally, a nice man: and the country knew it.' Lord Boothby, who began his own political career in Baldwin's secretariat, confirmed this when he recently remarked in the course of an interview that of all the men in high political office whom he had encountered in his life, 'he was the nicest'. This view had already been most fittingly expressed by G. M. Trevelyan, the historian and master of Baldwin's old

* The second Earl Baldwin of Bewdley later sold Astley Hall to Birmingham Corporation, to become a school for educationally subnormal children: *The Times*, 2 May 1950.

Cambridge college, on the occasion of the first Trinity Commemoration dinner after Baldwin's death. 'Stanley Baldwin was an Englishman indeed, in whom was much guile, never used for low or selfish purposes. In a world of voluble hates, he plotted to make men like, or at least tolerate, one another. Therein he had much success, within the shores of this island. He remains the most human and lovable of all the Prime Ministers.'[75] This may well be his fairest epitaph and the one above all others by which he would have wished to be remembered.

APPENDIX

Extracts from the unpublished Journal of the Attorney-General Sir Donald Somervell relating to the Abdication of King Edward VIII.*

I was sent for by the PM one evening. He told he me was seeing the King shortly and wanted my advice on three matters. Marriage, Abdication, King's Proctor. He had written them out on a slip of paper. I wrote out a memorandum in my own hand of which I did not keep a copy. I said that the King's marriage was outside the Royal Marriages Act but that it would be unconstitutional for him to marry contrary to the advice of his Ministers. I quoted Victoria's sentence to Leopold announcing her engagement to the effect: Lord Melbourne '*whom I have of course consulted throughout and who approves, etc.*' If he did marry contrary to or without advice he would be acting unconstitutionally as if he did any other public act without or contrary to advice. Abdication I said could be done with the King's assent by Act of Parliament.

The King's Proctor: at that time the only suggestion was of possible adultery between the King and Mrs Simpson. On this I took the view that it would be contrary to the constitutional position of the King for the King's officer to invite the King's Courts to investigate allegations against the King. This is a debatable point. I base my view on (1) the King's general immunity to legal process – he cannot be indicted for a crime or sued for a civil wrong or cited as a co-respondent. This is based I imagine partly on the fact that they are his Courts and partly on the necessity of preserving his unique and supreme position. (2) He cannot give evidence. This

* From the original MS in the possession of Mr Robert Somervell.

is in accordance with an opinion supported by much learning given by Simon at the time of the Mylius trial and is I have no doubt right.* It seemed to me wrong that I should, assuming I had the evidence, bring allegations, which in an ordinary case could be met and denied, against the King who could not by law go into the box and deal with them. I had no doubt a feeling that whatever was to be the solution of the problem the King's Proctor appearing with a bevy of valets and chambermaids before Merriman to prove that the reigning Monarch had been seen going down the passage etc. was not the right one – assuming that the chambermaids were available.

Some people took the other view and Robert Horne assuming contrary to the fact that evidence was available regarded this apparently as a step which would have kept Edward on the throne and the monarchy unsullied. I may not do him justice, he may have thought that the threat would have made the lady withdraw. However I am anticipating; the full tale of the King's Proctor and the Simpson divorce comes later and is not fully revealed at the time of writing. I am myself quite sure that in so far as I gave no encouragement at this stage to the idea that the King's Proctor was a way out I was right. I might add that at this stage a month or so before the abdication no one had suggested to me that the divorce was collusive – and such evidence as I had from Walter Monckton pointed in the opposite direction. According to Walter the co-respondent was a woman whom S. (whose married life had ceased to have much attraction for him owing to the King) was anxious to marry and had been caught.

My next interview with the PM was after the visit to the King told of in his speech. He said the King is determined to marry Mrs Simpson and is prepared to abdicate, so you had better send for Gwyer and get a bill in draft.† I sent for Gwyer and I shall never forget his reaction. Gwyer is one of those men who never go up in

---

* In 1911, Edward Mylius, a journalist of republican sympathies, was convicted of criminally libelling King George V, who was stated prior to his marriage with Queen Mary to have married a daughter of Admiral Sir Michael Culme-Seymour in Malta in 1890. After the jury had found Mylius guilty, without leaving the jury box, the Attorney-General Sir Rufus Isaacs read out a statement in open court which the King had signed to the effect that he had never been married except to the Queen and that he 'would have attended to give evidence to this effect had he not received advice from the Law Officers of the Crown that it would be unconstitutional for him to do so'. Simon was Solicitor-General at the time.

† Sir Maurice Gwyer, First Parliamentary Counsel to the Treasury. 'He was a very good constitutional lawyer and a wise man,' wrote Somervell, 'and I could not have had a better draftsman and adviser.'

the air, but he had a great many other things on hand and he very nearly rose a little way.

The next occasion was when S.B. sent for me and told me of the proposal for a morganatic marriage. I confirmed what of course he knew that the wife of a King is Queen, that it would require an Act of Parliament to prevent this result. I remember adding it would have been an odd act. If it had an honest recital it would start Whereas the wife of the King is Queen and whereas the present King desires to marry a woman unfit to be Queen – be it hereby enacted etc.

When the crisis started Simon took over the major constitutional issue. At the time I rather felt he might have called me in to co-operate on one or two occasions when he didn't. However, the main legal lines were pretty clear, and I've no doubt he felt as I should have in his position that he knew as much or more about it than I did and things had to be done fairly quickly.

In the crisis I spent most of my time with Malcolm MacDonald over the intricate problem of getting the Dominions to agree a course of action. Canada was the most nervous (Mackenzie King). S. Africa the most troublesome (Bodenstern). Irish Free State the most enigmatic. New Zealand the least familiar with Mrs Simpson. Australia the easiest.

Baldwin was the man who enabled the crisis to be surmounted with the minimum of discredit. He finally decided the following as soon as they appeared for decision.

(1) That Mrs Simpson could never be Queen.
(2) That the King would not give up the chance of marrying Mrs Simpson.
(3) That a morganatic marriage was impracticable.
(4) That the decision must be the King's own decision.

He may have realised earlier than most of us that the King was in the long run unfitted to be King. If so it is all the greater tribute to his qualities that he never took a step to force the issue or encourage abdication.

I think the King showed undue hesitation in going, after the press, released by the Bishop of Bradford's inadvertence, had brought matters to a head. From the point of view of the country his hesitation was a good thing. It gave public opinion time to form and incidentally showed I think how much better it was he should go.

It was a dramatic scene when Winston, digging his own grave, as usual appeared to be attacking Baldwin. Shouts of Sit down, etc. Winston lost his head, let his supplementary develop into a speech and was called to order. Everyone longing for some legitimate means of showing their dislike of W. and their confidence in B. were given the opportunity by the most apt of all supplementary questions. George Lambert. 'Is the Right Honourable Gentleman (S.B.) aware that there is a deep feeling of sympathy for him in all quarters of the House?' – loud and prolonged cheers.

We shall never know all the facts. I think the King had always had a claustrophobic repugnance to the throne. He is a man I imagine with few 'spiritual' resources in religion or imagination. He is happy if the passing moment is fair – otherwise and therefore generally very unhappy. Such a character would be more than most at the mercy of an infatuation such as he obviously has for Mrs Simpson. Semi-consciously it may have been a bolt hole . . . To surrender a kingdom because it's a bore is unimpressive, to surrender it for Love seems on a bigger scale and may or may not be. I think that with many gifts and obviously a lot of character the whole proceeding from the outset showed an extraordinary insensitiveness. The ordinary man will do a good deal not to disappoint those who expect something of him. *Noblesse oblige*. Few if any men have had such hopes and such affection to recompense them, but they seemed to pass him by. That is why I think the explanation may be that for years he had got into the centre of his being the very natural feeling that it was unjust that the accident of birth should so inexorably determine his life and limit the scope of his inclinations.

After the abdication the position changed. Should we make *all* inquiries or not? I took a little time to make up my mind which I finally did with Barnes's help quite definitely.* I took time to think over this aspect. Assume there was some evidence of adultery. If brought to the notice of the Court Mrs S. and the D. of Windsor might well return to the country to give evidence and deny it. Even if proved would not the Court on ordinary principles grant a discretion, particularly as Mrs S. could plead the difficulty of informing the Court of her misconduct with the then ruling Sovereign? Result a first-rate and squalid sensation and the divorce allowed as if I had never intervened.

There were three outside factors:

* Mr (later Sir) Thomas Barnes was the Treasury Solicitor and King's Proctor.

(1) A very considerable body of opinion with no basis that the King's Proctor or the Judge or I (presumably to those who knew I controlled the KP) had been got at corruptly to abstain from administering justice.
(2) Those who felt it essential in the public interest that the divorce should be stopped.
(3) Those who felt it would be outrageous if the King having abdicated to marry was prevented from doing so.

Barnes who was bombarded with abusive letters wrote to me about Christmas suggesting that he should follow up inquiries on adultery as well as collusion. He had already with my approval seen some of the apparently more responsible of his correspondents who admitted they had no evidence but were repeating the gossip of the Clubs and the Temple. I wrote back agreeing. I decided we'd go ahead as if this was an A.B. [i.e. ordinary] case. We'd make all the usual inquiries on information and suggestions in our own practice. Barnes as a result interviewed countless people, members of the crew of the yacht, servants, hall porters, etc. It was more than in most cases because people wrote suggesting suspicious events which on examination turned out never to have happened.

While this was proceeding Merriman* who was troubled about the allegations against the Court referred a private intervention which had not been followed up by affidavits to the KP. By this time Barnes was convinced we should get nothing. Whether or not they ever committed adultery is a question on which I believe those who know him well differ. It became however obvious that if they had done so they had not done so openly and had also not publicly indulged in the familiarities which normally indicate cohabitation. Our inquiries also confirmed the view that the divorce – even if it had some collusive factor – e.g. the willingness of Mrs S. that her husband should be unfaithful – was not a collusive divorce in the ordinary or any provable sense.

* Sir Boyd (later Lord) Merriman was President of the Divorce Court.

BIBLIOGRAPHY

A. MANUSCRIPT SOURCES

Baldwin bequeathed his political papers and correspondence, together with his press cutting books, consisting in all of 233 volumes, to Cambridge University. They are the most important source of his life, particularly his public career, although they contain little before 1922 and copies of few letters from him, since he usually wrote to correspondents in his own hand and did not keep copies. The collection includes his confidential correspondence with the Royal Family and important papers relating to the Abdication of King Edward VIII, access to which is subject to restriction and requires the Queen's permission.*

Most of Baldwin's private family correspondence is in the possession of his second son, the present Earl Baldwin of Bewdley, also his private letters to his closest friends, Lord and Lady Davidson. These have been extensively used by Lord Baldwin in *My Father: The True Story* (1955) and *The Macdonald Sisters* (1960), and by Robert Rhodes James in *Memoirs of a Conservative* (1969).

The MS of G. M. Young's official biography *Stanley Baldwin* is also in Cambridge University Library (Add. 7799). It contains some passages, relatively unimportant, which do not appear in the published version.

The following are the principal archival collections which have been consulted:

Asquith Papers. Official and private papers of the first Earl of Oxford and
    Asquith. In the Bodleian Library, Oxford.
Baldwin Papers. Political papers, memoranda and correspondence of the
    first Earl Baldwin of Bewdley. In the Cambridge University Library.

* Full details, with a useful Introduction, are given by A. E. B. Owen of the University Library, in his *Handlist of the Political Papers of Stanley Baldwin, First Earl Baldwin of Bewdley* (Cambridge, 1973).

Bonar Law Papers. Papers and correspondence of Andrew Bonar Law. In the Beaverbrook Library.

British Broadcasting Corporation Archives. In Broadcasting House.

Carson Papers. Papers and correspondence of Lord Carson. In the Public Record Office of Northern Ireland, Belfast.

Cabinet Minutes and Papers. In the Public Record Office, London.

Chamberlain Papers. Papers and correspondence of Austen and Neville Chamberlain. In Birmingham University Library.

Crozier Papers. Political and biographical sketches written by W. P. Crozier when Editor of the *Manchester Guardian*. In the Beaverbrook Library.

Davidson Papers. Papers and correspondence of the first Viscount Davidson. In the Beaverbrook Library.

Lee Papers. Papers and correspondence of Viscount and Viscountess Lee of Fareham. In the Beaverbrook Library.

Londonderry Papers. Papers and correspondence of the seventh Marquess of Londonderry. In the possession of Lady Mairi Bury.

Ramsay MacDonald Papers. Papers and correspondence of James Ramsay MacDonald. In the Public Record Office, London.

Royal Archives. Papers and correspondence of King George V. In Windsor Castle.

Somervell Papers. Papers and journals of Sir Donald Somervell. In the possession of Mr Robert Somervell.

Templewood Papers. Papers and correspondence of Sir Samuel Hoare Viscount Templewood. In Cambridge University Library.

Weir Papers. Papers and correspondence of the first Viscount Weir. In Churchill College, Cambridge.

Zetland Letters. Private letters of the first Marquess of Zetland to Lord Linlithgow. In the India Office Library.

B. PUBLISHED SOURCES

Baldwin wrote no autobiography, but during his lifetime he published five volumes of speeches and addresses, which contain some interesting autobiographical matter and throw a revealing light on his character. The nearest he had to a Boswell was Thomas Jones, the Deputy Secretary of the Cabinet and later Secretary of the Pilgrim Trust, who has recorded Baldwin's informal conversation and table talk on numerous occasions in his own diaries and letters.

Shortly before he died, Baldwin asked G. M. Young to become his official biographer and arranged that all his papers should be put at his disposal for this purpose. 'What happened to G. M. Young was the worst thing that can happen to any biographer,' wrote Sir Rupert Hart-Davis when he presented the MS of Young's work, which his firm had published, to the Cambridge University Library in 1969, 'that is to say, he fell out of love with his subject – even began to dislike him – before the book was finished. He wanted to give it up, but I persuaded him that he must bring it to a conclusion.' Young's biography produced various hostile reactions, notably from the historian D. C. Somervell and from Baldwin's second son, then the Hon. Windham Baldwin, who both wrote considered replies. Since then, the process of rehabilitation has continued with the publication of a monumental biography by Keith Middlemas and John Barnes in 1969.

Shorter appreciations, which should be particularly mentioned, have been written by Sir Arthur Bryant, on the occasion of Baldwin's retirement in 1937, by Thomas Jones for *The Dictionary of National Biography 1941–1950*, and by Robert Blake in his essay, 'Baldwin and the Right', in *The Age of Baldwin*, edited by John Raymond (1960).

The following major printed authorities have been used:

Amery, L. S. *My Political Life.* 3 vols. London, 1953–5.
Annual Register.
Attlee, C. R. (Lord). *As It Happened.* London, 1954.
Avon, Earl of. *The Eden Memoirs. Facing the Dictators.* London, 1962.
  The Reckoning. London, 1965.
Baldwin, A. W. (3rd Earl Baldwin of Bewdley). *My Father: The True Story.* London, 1955.
  The Macdonald Sisters. London, 1960.
Baldwin, Monica. *I Leap Over The Wall.* London, 1949.
Baldwin, Oliver (2nd Earl Baldwin of Bewdley). *The Questing Beast.* London, 1932.
Baldwin, Stanley (1st Earl Baldwin of Bewdley). *On England.* London, 1926.
  Our Inheritance. London, 1928.
  This Torch of Freedom. London, 1935.
  Service of our Lives. London, 1937.
  An Interpreter of England. London, 1939.
Bassett, Reginald. 'Telling the Truth to the People: The Myth of the Baldwin "Confession" ', *Cambridge Journal*, November 1948.
Beaverbrook, Lord. *Politicians and the War 1914–1916.* 2 vols. London, 1928–32.
  Politicians and the Press. London, 1926.

Men and Power 1917–1918. London, 1956.

The Decline and Fall of Lloyd George. London, 1963.

The Abdication of King Edward VIII. Edited by A. J. P. Taylor. London, 1966.

Birkenhead, 1st Earl of. *Contemporary Personalities*. London, 1924.

Birkenhead, 2nd Earl of. *The Life of F. E. Smith First Earl of Birkenhead*. London, 1959.

The Prof In Two Worlds. The Official Life of Professor F. A. Lindemann Viscount Cherwell. London, 1961.

Halifax. The Life of Lord Halifax. London, 1965.

Walter Monckton. The Life of Viscount Monckton of Brenchley. London, 1969.

Blackett, Monica. *The Mark of the Maker: A Portrait of Helen Waddell*. London, 1973.

Blake, Robert. *The Unknown Prime Minister. The Life and Times of Andrew Bonar Law*. London, 1955.

Blumenfeld, R. D. *All in a Lifetime*. London, 1931.

Boothby, Robert (Lord). *I Fight to Live*. London, 1947.

'The Baldwin I Knew', *Sunday Telegraph*, 16 July 1967.

Boyle, Andrew. *Montagu Norman*. London, 1967.

Trenchard. London, 1962.

Broad, Lewis. *The Abdication Twenty-Five Years After*. London, 1961.

Bryant, Arthur. *Stanley Baldwin*. London, 1937.

Butler, J. R. M. *Lord Lothian*. London, 1960.

Butler, R. A. (Lord). *The Art of the Possible*. London, 1971.

Carr, J. C., Taplin, W. and Wright, A. E. G. *A History of the British Steel Industry*. Oxford, 1962.

Carrington, Charles. *Rudyard Kipling*. London, 1955.

Channon, Sir Henry. *Chips. The Diaries of Sir Henry Channon*. Edited by Robert Rhodes James. London, 1967.

Churchill, Randolph S. *Lord Derby 'King of Lancashire'*. London, 1959.

Churchill, Winston S. *The Second World War*. Vol. I. *The Gathering Storm*. London, 1948.

Citrine, Walter (Lord). *Men and Work. An Autobiography*. London, 1964.

Colvin, Ian. *Vansittart in Office*. London, 1965.

Cooper, Diana. *The Light of Common Day*. London, 1959.

Cooper, Duff (Viscount Norwich). *Old Men Forget*. London, 1953.

Coote, Colin R. *A Companion of Honour: The Story of Walter Elliot*. London, 1965.

'Baldwin: The Image and the Man', *Daily Telegraph*, 14 July 1967.

Cowling, Maurice. *The Impact of Labour 1920–1924*. Cambridge, 1971.

Cunliffe-Lister, Sir Philip. *See* Swinton, Earl of.

Curzon of Kedleston, Marchioness. *Reminiscences*. London, 1955.

Dalton, Hugh (Lord). *Memoirs*. Vol. I. *Call Back Yesterday*. Vol. II. *The Fateful Years*. London, 1953–7.

Driberg, Tom. *Beaverbrook*. London, 1956.

Dugdale, Blanche E. C. *Arthur James Balfour*. 2 vols. London, 1936.

Eden, Anthony. *See* Avon, Earl of.

Elletson, D. H. *The Chamberlains*. London, 1966.

   Chequers and the Prime Ministers. London, 1970.

Feiling, Keith. *The Life of Neville Chamberlain*. London, 1946.

Fitzroy, Sir Almeric. *Memoirs*. 2 vols. London, 1925.

Green, John. *Mr Baldwin. A Study in Post-War Conservatism*. London, 1933.

Grigg, P. J. *Prejudice and Judgment*. London, 1948.

Halifax, Earl of. *Fullness of Days*. London, 1957.

Hardinge of Penshurst, Lord. 'Before the Abdication', *The Times*, 29 November 1955.

Harkness, David. *The Restless Dominion: The Irish Free State and the British Commonwealth of Nations 1921–31*. London, 1969.

   'Mr De Valera's Dominion: Irish Relations with Britain and the Commonwealth 1932–1938', *Journal of Commonwealth Political Studies*, November 1970.

Herbert, Sir Alan. *A.P.H. His Life and Times*. London, 1970.

Heuston, R. F. V. *Lives of the Lord Chancellors 1885–1940*. Oxford, 1964.

Hewins, W. A. S. *The Apologia of an Imperialist*. 2 vols. London, 1929.

Hoare, Sir Samuel. *See* Templewood, Viscount.

Hyde, H. Montgomery. *Carson. The Life of Sir Edward Carson Lord Carson of Duncairn*. London, 1953.

Inglis, Brian. *Abdication*. London, 1966.

James, Robert Rhodes. *Memoirs of a Conservative. J. C. C. Davidson's Memoirs and Papers 1910–37*. London, 1969.

   Churchill. A Study in Failure 1900–1939. London, 1970.

   'Reappraising the reviled Prime Minister', *The Times*, 14 July 1967.

Jenkins, J. Gilbert. *Chequers. A History of the Prime Minister's Buckinghamshire Home*. Oxford, 1967.

Jones, Thomas. *Whitehall Diary 1916–1930*. Edited by Keith Middlemas. 3 vols. London, 1969–71.

   A Diary with Letters 1931–1950. London, 1954.

   Article on Baldwin in *The Dictionary of National Biography 1941–1950*. London, 1959.

Kinnear, Michael. *The Fall of Lloyd George*. London, 1973.

Lee of Fareham, Viscount. *A Good Innings*. 3 vols. Privately printed, 1941.

Lloyd George, Frances. *The Years that are Past*. London, 1967.
　Lloyd George. A Diary by Frances Stevenson. Edited by A. J. P. Taylor. London, 1971.

Lockhart, J. G. *Cosmo Gordon Lang*. London, 1949.

Londonderry, Marquess of. *Ourselves and Germany*. London, 1938.
　Wings of Destiny. London, 1943.

Longford, Earl of, and O'Neill, T. P. *Eamonn De Valera*. London, 1970.

MacDonald, Malcolm. *Titans and Others*. London, 1972.

Mackenzie, Compton. *The Windsor Tapestry*. London, 1938.

Macleod, Iain. *Neville Chamberlain*. London, 1961.

Macmillan, Harold. *Winds of Change, 1914–1939*. London, 1966.

MacMillan, Lord. *A Man of Law's Tale*. London, 1953.

Middlemas, Keith, and Barnes, John. *Baldwin. A Biography*. London, 1969.

Mosley, Leonard. *Curzon. The End of an Epoch*. London, 1960.

Mosley, Sir Oswald. *My Life*. London, 1968.

Nabarro, Sir Gerald. *Severn Valley Steam*. London, 1971.

Nicolson, Harold. *Curzon: The Last Phase*. London, 1934.
　King George V. His Life and Reign. London, 1952.
　Diaries and Letters 1930–1961. Edited by Nigel Nicolson. 3 vols. London, 1966–8.

Owen, Frank. *Tempestuous Journey. Lloyd George His Life and Times*. London, 1954.

Percy, Eustace (Lord Percy of Newcastle). *Some Memories*. London, 1958.

Petrie, Sir Charles. *The Life and Letters of the Rt. Hon. Sir Austen Chamberlain*. Vol. II. London, 1940.

Pope-Hennessy, James. *Queen Mary*. London, 1959.

Raymond, John (editor). *The Baldwin Age*. London, 1960.

Reader, W. J. *Architect of Air Power. The Life of the first Viscount Weir of Eastwood*. London, 1968.

Reith, J. C. W. (Lord Reith). *Into the Wind*. London, 1949.

Roberts, Bechhofer. *Stanley Baldwin: Man or Miracle?* London, 1936.

Ronaldshay, Earl of. *The Life of Lord Curzon*. Vol. III. London, 1928.
　See also Zetland, Marquess of.

Roskill, Stephen. *Hankey Man of Secrets*. 2 vols. London, 1970–2.

Rowse, A. L. *All Souls and Appeasement*. London, 1961.

Salvidge, Stanley. *Salvidge of Liverpool*. London, 1934.

Samuel, Viscount. *Memoirs*. London, 1945.

Sencourt, Robert. *The Reign of Edward VIII*. London, 1962.

Shakespeare, Sir Geoffrey. *Let Candles be Brought In*. London, 1949.

Simon, Viscount. *Retrospect*. London, 1952.

Smith, Janet Adam. *John Buchan*. London, 1965.

Somervell, D. C. *Stanley Baldwin. An examination of some features of G. M. Young's Biography*. London, 1953.

Steed, Wickham. *The Real Stanley Baldwin*. London, 1930.

Stuart, James (Viscount Stuart of Findhorn). *Within the Fringe*. London, 1967.

Swinton, Earl of. *I Remember*. London, 1948.

Sixty Years of Power. London, 1966.

Sykes, Christopher. *Nancy: The Life of Lady Astor*. London, 1972.

Taylor, A. J. P. *English History 1914–1945*. Oxford, 1965.

Beaverbrook. London, 1972.

Teeling, Sir William. *Corridors of Frustration*. London, 1970.

Templewood, Viscount. *Nine Troubled Years*. London, 1954.

Empire of the Air. London, 1957.

'The Other Side of the Abdication Story', *Sunday Dispatch*, 30 September, 7 October, 14 October, 1951.

The Times. The History of the Times. Vol. 4. Part II. London, 1952.

Vansittart, Lord. *The Mist Procession*. London, 1958.

Waterhouse, Nourah. *Private and Official*. London, 1942.

Wheeler-Bennett, John. *King George VI. His Life and Reign*. London, 1958.

Whyte, Adam Gowans. *Stanley Baldwin. A Biographical Character Study*. London, 1926.

Windsor, Duchess of. *The Heart Has Its Reasons*. London, 1956.

Windsor, Duke of. *A King's Story*. London, 1951.

Winterton, Earl. *Orders of the Day*. London, 1953.

Wood, Edward. *See* Halifax, Earl of.

Wrench, Sir John Evelyn. *Geoffrey Dawson and our Times*. London, 1955.

Young, G. M. *Stanley Baldwin*. London, 1952.

Young, Kenneth. *Arthur James Balfour*. London, 1963.

Churchill and Beaverbrook. London, 1966.

Zetland, Marquess of. *'Essayez' Memoirs*. London, 1956.

NOTES

CHAPTER 1 FATHER AND SON

1 Thomas Jones. *A Diary with Letters 1931–1950*, p. 154. S. Baldwin. *On England*, pp. 11–12.
2 Jones, p. 289.
3 Jones, p. 154.
4 T. F. Dukes. *Antiquities of Shropshire* (Shrewsbury, 1841), p. 220.
5 S. Baldwin. *On England*, p. 15. Jones, p. 154.
6 Sir Gerald Nabarro. *Severn Valley Steam*, pp. 23, 48.
7 A. W. Baldwin. *My Father: The True Story*, p. 31.
8 Jones, p. 154.
9 Speech on Welsh Disestablishment Bill 8 July 1913: Wickham Steed. *The Real Stanley Baldwin*, p. 20. A. W. Baldwin. *The Macdonald Sisters, passim.*
10 Jones, p. 204. Speech on receiving the Freedom of Bewdley, 8 August 1925: S. Baldwin. *On England*, p. 8.
11 A. W. Baldwin. *My Father: The True Story*, pp. 35–6.
12 A. W. Baldwin. *The Macdonald Sisters*, pp. 216–17.
13 S. Baldwin. *This Torch of Freedom*, p. 141.
14 S. Baldwin. *Our Inheritance*, p. 295; *On England*, p. 16.
15 Georgiana Burne-Jones. *Memorials of Edward Burne-Jones* (1904), I, p. 49.
16 A. W. Baldwin. *My Father: The True Story*, p. 39.
17 S. Baldwin. *On England*, p. 189.
18 Earl of Birkenhead. *Life of F. E. Smith First Earl of Birkenhead*, p. 21.
19 E. D. W. Chaplin. *Winston Churchill and Harrow* (1941), p. 87.
20 A. W. Baldwin. *My Father*, p. 44.
21 Sir Arthur Bryant. *Stanley Baldwin*, p. 28.
22 Jones, p. 155.
23 A. W. Baldwin. *My Father: The True Story*, pp. 53 ff.
24 S. Baldwin. *On England*, p. 104.
25 ibid., p. 92.
26 G. M. Young. *Stanley Baldwin*, p. 21.
27 Keith Middlemas and John Barnes. *Baldwin. A Biography*, p. 23.
28 S. Baldwin. *On England*, p. 34.
29 Charles Carrington. *Rudyard Kipling*, p. 193.

30 Middlemas *and* Barnes, p. 28.
31 Young, p. 23.
32 Rudyard Kipling. *Something of Myself* (1937), p. 137.
33 A. W. Baldwin. *The Macdonald Sisters*, p. 201.
34 Bryant, p. 36.
35 J. C. Carr, W. Taplin *and* A. E. G. Wright. *History of the British Steel Industry*, p. 269. Kenneth Warren. *The British Iron and Steel Sheet Industry since 1840*, passim.
36 S. Baldwin. *Our Inheritance*, p. 281; *The Torch of Freedom*, p. 119.
37 Robert Rhodes James. *Memoirs of a Conservative: J. C. C. Davidson's Memoirs and Papers 1910–37*, p. 105. Baldwin Papers 205 f. 193.
38 Angela Thirkell to Sir Donald Somervell 6 October 1953. Communicated by Mrs David Somervell.

CHAPTER 2   THE POLITICAL APPRENTICE

1 Alfred Baldwin to Bonar Law 9 August 1902: Bonar Law Papers 23/1/11.
2 16 June 1905: Baldwin Papers 175.
3 Bechhofer Roberts. *Stanley Baldwin: Man or Miracle?*, p. 21 ff.
4 Baldwin Papers 35. G. M. Young. *Stanley Baldwin*, p. 23.
5 S. Baldwin. *On England*, p. 89.
6 Roberts, p. 26.
7 ibid., p. 27.
8 ibid., p. 29.
9 Young, p. 24.
10 Alfred Baldwin to Bonar Law 28 January 1906: Bonar Law Papers 21/1.
11 A. W. Baldwin. *My Father: The True Story*, p. 76.
12 Roberts, p. 31. A. W. Baldwin. *The Macdonald Sisters*, p. 202; *My Father: The True Story*, p. 73.
13 S. Baldwin. *Service of Our Lives*, p. 97.
14 Roberts, p. 31.
15 S. Baldwin. *Service of Our Lives*, p. 84.
16 Keith Middlemas *and* John Barnes. *Baldwin, A Biography*, p. 43.
17 Election Address, 31 December 1909. Communicated by Lord Baldwin.
18 Hansard. Parl. Deb. H of C, 22 June 1908. 4th Series. Vol. 190, Cols. 1433–8.
19 A. W. Baldwin. *My Father: The True Story*, p. 74.
20 ibid., p. 74.
21 W. A. S. Hewins. *The Apologia of an Imperialist* (1929), I, p. 245.
22 Hansard. Parl. Deb. H of C, 17 March 1909, 5th Series, Vol. II, Cols. 1146–52.
23 A. W. Baldwin. *My Father: The True Story*, p. 74.
24 Hansard. Parl. Deb. H of C, 15 July 1909. 5th Series. Vol. 13, Cols. 2091–7.
25 John Green. *Mr Baldwin. A Study in Post War Conservatism*, p. 106.
26 Election Address, 31 December 1909. Communicated by Lord Baldwin.
27 Middlemas *and* Barnes, p. 48.
28 A. W. Baldwin. *My Father: The True Story*, p. 75. Bonar Law Papers 24/3/38 (15 November 1911).
29 Cited Wickham Steed. *The Real Stanley Baldwin*, p. 22.
30 Hansard. Parl. Deb. H of C, 12 June 1912. 5th Series. Vol. 39, Cols. 955–8.
31 S. Baldwin. *On England*, p. 35.

32 Bonar Law Papers 30/4/12 (8 November 1912).
33 Baldwin to Bonar Law 15 November 1909: Bonar Law Papers 1/2/5 (7).
34 Middlemas *and* Barnes, p. 59.
35 Roberts, p. 39. A. W. Baldwin. *My Father: The True Story*, p. 75.
36 Hansard. Parl. Deb. H of C, 25 June 1914. 5th Series. Vol. 58, Cols. 2091–7.
37 Viscount Simon. *Retrospect* (1952), pp. 273–4.
38 A. W. Baldwin. *My Father: The True Story*, p. 78.
39 Middlemas *and* Barnes, p. 52. Roberts, p. 42.
40 The MS notebooks are preserved with the Davidson Papers in the Beaverbrook Library. See also James, p. 54 ff.
41 Middlemas *and* Barnes, p. 56.
42 Thomas Jones. *Whitehall Diary*, II, p. 195.
43 Robert Rhodes James. *Memoirs of a Conservative*, p. 78.
44 Hewins, II, pp. 11, 63.
45 ibid., p. 66. Middlemas *and* Barnes, p. 57. Sir Arthur Bryant. *Stanley Baldwin*, p. 60.
46 Hansard. Parl. Deb. H of C, 7 November 1916. 5th Series.
47 A. W. Baldwin. *My Father: The True Story*, p. 84.
48 S. Baldwin. *On England*, p. 50.
49 Lord Beaverbrook. *Politicians and the Press*, p. 62.
50 Middlemas *and* Barnes, p. 59.
51 James, p. 36. Baldwin's appointment as Law's PPS was announced on 22 December 1916.
52 *The Times*, 30 January 1917.
53 A. W. Baldwin. *My Father: The True Story*, p. 81.

CHAPTER 3   ASCENT TO THE CABINET

1 Bechhofer Roberts. *Stanley Baldwin: Man or Miracle?*, pp. 43–4.
2 A. W. Baldwin. *My Father: The True Story*, p. 81.
3 ibid., p. 81. Robert Rhodes James. *Memoirs of a Conservative*, p. 78.
4 Keith Middlemas *and* John Barnes. *Baldwin, A Biography*, p. 65.
5 ibid., p. 65. Davidson, p. 79.
6 Lord Beaverbrook. *Men and Power*, p. 99 ff.
7 Robert Rhodes James. *Memoirs of a Conservative*, pp. 94–5. Wickham Steed. *The Real Stanley Baldwin*, pp. 32–3.
8 Middlemas *and* Barnes, p. 65. S. Baldwin. *On England*, p. 135.
9 James, p. 79.
10 ibid., p. 64. A. W. Baldwin. *My Father: The True Story*, p. 82. Middlemas *and* Barnes, p. 67.
11 Middlemas *and* Barnes, p. 68.
12 ibid., p. 66. A. W. Baldwin. *My Father: The True Story*, p. 81.
13 Lord Beaverbrook. *Men and Power*, p. 295 ff. A. W. Baldwin. *My Father: The True Story*, pp. 96–7.
14 Lord Beaverbrook. *Men and Power*, p. x.
15 A. W. Baldwin. *My Father: The True Story*, p. 89.
16 ibid., p. 82.
17 Sir Charles Petrie. *Life and Letters of the Rt. Hon. Sir Austen Chamberlain*, II, pp. 133, 137.
18 Lord Beaverbrook. *Men and Power*, p. xiii.
19 G. M. Young. *Stanley Baldwin*, pp. 25–6.

20 A. W. Baldwin. *My Father: The True Story*, p. 94.
21 ibid., p. 82. James, p. 81.
22 James, pp. 81, 83.
23 ibid., p. 198.
24 A. W. Baldwin. *My Father: The True Story*, pp. 81, 101.
25 Steed, p. 27.
26 James, p. 94.
27 Middlemas *and* Barnes, p. 74 note.
28 W. A. S. Hewins. *Apologia of an Imperialist* (1929), II, p. 197.
29 A. W. Baldwin. *My Father: The True Story*, pp. 82, 95.
30 James, p. 95.
31 A. W. Baldwin. *My Father: The True Story*, pp. 95, 97.
32 James, p. 112.
33 Lee to Law 10 February 1921: Bonar Law Papers 100/2/16.
34 Young, p. 27.
35 Baldwin to Law 2 April 1921: Bonar Law Papers 107/1/10. Lord Beaverbrook. *Lloyd George*, p. 244.
36 James, p. 112.
37 Roberts, p. 51. *The Times*, 21 April 1921. A. W. Baldwin. *My Father: The True Story*, p. 89.
38 Sir Herbert Llewellyn Smith. *The Board of Trade* (1928), *passim*. Viscount Swinton. *I Remember*, p. 26.
39 James, p. 107.
40 Thomas Jones. *Whitehall Diary*, I, pp. 143, 153.
41 Young, p. 29.
42 Sir Arthur Bryant. *Stanley Baldwin*, p. 79.
43 Middlemas *and* Barnes, p. 81.
44 Swinton, p. 15.
45 Hewins, II, p. 231.
46 James, p. 113. A. W. Baldwin. *My Father: The True Story*, p. 113.
47 Bryant, p. 78.
48 *John Bull*, 15 July 1922.
49 Jones, III; Frank Pakenham, *Peace by Ordeal* (1935); H. Montgomery Hyde, *Carson* (1953) *passim*.
50 Robert Blake. *The Unknown Prime Minister*, p. 435. S. D. Waley. *Edwin Montagu* (1964), p. 261.
51 Bonar Law Papers 107/2/2A. Partly quoted, Blake, p. 437.
52 Middlemas *and* Barnes, pp. 103–4.
53 Petrie, II, p. 176.
54 Petrie, II, p. 183. Lord Beaverbrook. *Lloyd George*, p. 155.
55 Steed, p. 35. James, pp. 113, 114.
56 Maurice Cowling. *The Impact of Labour 1920–1924*, p. 131. Middlemas *and* Barnes, p. 108.
57 Earl Winterton. *Orders of the Day*, p. 115.
58 Chamberlain to Hilda Chamberlain 20 November 1922: Chamberlain Papers AC/5/1/251.
59 L. S. Amery. *My Political Life*, II, pp. 233–4.
60 Middlemas *and* Barnes, p. 109. Winterton, p. 116.

CHAPTER 4   CHANCELLOR OF THE EXCHEQUER

1 Robert Rhodes James. *Memoirs of a Conservative*, pp. 113–14.

2 Lucy Baldwin. 'The Recollections of a Cabinet Breaker's Wife on the Government Crisis October 1922': Baldwin Papers 42 ff. 3–10. Lucy Baldwin's account is most informative on the details of the crisis as she saw it.

3 Earl Ronaldshay. *Life of Lord Curzon*, III, p. 309.

4 Robert Blake. *The Unknown Prime Minister*, p. 448.

5 Lucy Baldwin, loc. cit.

6 A. W. Baldwin. *My Father: The True Story*, p. 116.

7 Blake, p. 451.

8 Ronaldshay, III, p. 314.

9 Viscount Templewood. *Empire of the Air*, p. 21.

10 Sir Charles Petrie. *The Life and Letters of the Rt. Hon. Sir Austen Chamberlain*, II, p. 200.

11 L. S. Amery. *My Political Life*, II, p. 236.

12 ibid., p. 237.

13 Templewood, p. 24.

14 S. Salvidge. *Salvidge of Liverpool*, p. 238.

15 Templewood, p. 25.

16 Lucy Baldwin, loc. cit. A. W. Baldwin. *My Father: The True Story*, p. 116.

17 Amery, II, pp. 237–8.

18 Petrie, II, p. 202.

19 James, p. 123.

20 Templewood, pp. 27–8.

21 Lord Beaverbrook. *Lloyd George*, p. 199.

22 Salvidge, p. 238. James, p. 124.

23 James, p. 125.

24 James, p. 126. Wickham Steed. *The Real Stanley Baldwin*, p. 40.

25 Salvidge, pp. 239–40. James, pp. 127–33, gives full details of the voting. See also accounts by Beaverbrook, Blake, Templewood, Middlemas *and* Barnes, etc.

26 Beaverbrook, p. 200.

27 G. M. Young. *Stanley Baldwin*, pp. 40–2.

28 Lucy Baldwin, loc. cit. A. W. Baldwin. *My Father: The True Story*, p. 117.

29 ibid. See also Stephen McKenna. *Reginald McKenna* (1948), *passim*.

30 Stephen Roskill. *Hankey*, II, p. 306.

31 *The Times*, 24 October 1922.

32 James, p. 134.

33 Petrie, II, pp. 207–9.

34 Keith Middlemas *and* John Barnes. *Baldwin, A Biography*, p. 125. Beaverbrook, p. 219.

35 Baldwin Papers 140 ff. 110, 127, 213.

36 James, p. 10. Sir Almeric Fitzroy. *Memoirs*, II, p. 788.

37 James, pp. 138–9. Thomas Jones. *Lloyd George* (1951), p. 94.

38 Andrew Boyle. *Montagu Norman*, p. 155.

39 P. J. Grigg. *Prejudice and Judgement*, p. 98.

40 Middlemas *and* Barnes, p. 137.

41 Grigg, p. 99. See also Baldwin Papers 233 for detailed account of the mission.

42 Thomas Jones. *Whitehall Diary*, I, p. 230.

43 Middlemas *and* Barnes, p. 138.

44 Jones. *Whitehall Diary*, II, p. 227.
45 Grigg, p. 102. Bechhofer Roberts. *Stanley Baldwin: Man or Miracle?*, p. 98. See also recollections of Horne and Burnham in their letters to *The Times*, 20, 21 January 1931.
46 Baldwin Papers 159 f. 99.
47 *The Times*, 30 January 1923. Young, p. 46.
48 Steed, p. 53.
49 Young, p. 46. Middlemas *and* Barnes, pp. 146–7.
50 R. Churchill. *Lord Derby*, pp. 494 ff. James, p. 142 note.
51 Nourah Waterhouse. *Private and Official*, p. 252.
52 Roberts, p. 99.
53 Young, p. 47. A. W. Baldwin. *My Father: The True Story*, p. 120.
54 The history and associations of the Chequers estate are fully recounted by J. Gilbert Jenkins in his *Chequers: A History of the Prime Minister's Buckinghamshire House* and by D. H. Elletson in his *Chequers and the Prime Ministers*. See also Viscount Lee of Fareham. *A Good Innings*, 3 vols, privately printed. A copy of the latter work together with a photostat reproduction of the Chequers Visitors' Book from 1910 to 1945 are preserved among the Lee Papers in the Beaverbrook Library.
55 Lee, II, pp. 938–41.
56 Elletson, p. 68. Lee, II, pp. 1071–2.
57 Jones. *Whitehall Diary*, I, p. 243. Boyle, pp. 191, 299.
58 Lee MSS. Communicated by Mr D. H. Elletson.
59 Baldwin to Bernard Partridge 15 April 1923: communicated by Mr D. Pepys-Whiteley. Middlemas *and* Barnes, pp. 155–7. A. W. Baldwin. *My Father: The True Story*, p. 121.
60 Blake, pp. 512–15. Middlemas *and* Barnes, pp. 159–60. *The Times*, 23 May 1923.
61 James, pp. 150–2.
62 Ronaldshay, III, p. 350. Chamberlain Papers AC/35/2/11b.
63 'How Mr Baldwin became Premier': *Evening Standard* 12 February 1924.
64 Blake, p. 518.
65 Stamfordham to Revelstoke 31 May 1923: RA K 1853/37.
66 A. W. Baldwin. *My Father: The True Story*, p. 122.

CHAPTER 5   PRIME MINISTER

1 Sir John Evelyn Wrench. *Geoffrey Dawson and our Times*, p. 217.
2 RA K 1853/17. *Baldwin, A Biography,*
3 Harold Nicolson. *King George V*, p. 377.
4 Robert Rhodes James. *Memoirs of a Conservative*, pp. 154 ff. RA K 1853/4–5. Robert Blake. *The Unexpected Prime Minister*, p. 520.
5 Marchioness Curzon. *Reminiscences*, p. 179. W. Churchill. *Great Contemporaries* (1937), p. 287. Nourah Waterhouse. *Private and Official* (1942), p. 259.
6 Harold Nicolson. *Curzon: The Last Phase*, p. 354.
7 *The Times*, 23 May 1923.
8 Thomas Jones. *Whitehall Diary*, I, p. 237.
9 Keith Middlemas *and* John Barnes. *Baldwin. A Biography*, p. 169.
10 Baldwin Papers 42.
11 Earl Ronaldshay. *Life of Lord Curzon*, III, p. 353.
12 N. Chamberlain to Baldwin 23 May 1923: Baldwin Papers 42. Keith Feiling. *Life of Neville Chamberlain*, pp. 106–7.

13 Iain Macleod. *Neville Chamberlain*, p. 93.

14 CAB 23/46/15.

15 Sir Almeric Fitzroy. *Memoirs*, II, p. 807.

16 A. W. Baldwin. *My Father: The True Story*, p. 122.

17 Lee. *A Good Innings*, III, p. 1068.

18 Chamberlain Papers AC/35/2/11b.

19 Chamberlain Papers AC/35/2/18. Sir Charles Petrie. *Life and Letters of the Rt. Hon. Sir Austen Chamberlain*, II, p. 225. Baldwin to Carson 16 June 1923: Carson Papers D 1507/1/1923/4.

20 Baldwin Papers 60.

21 G. M. Young. *Stanley Baldwin*, p. 58.

22 CAB 23/46/2. Baldwin Papers 60.

23 James, p. 175.

24 ibid., p. 222.

25 Young, p. 50. Jones. *Whitehall Diary*, I, p. 243.

26 Jones. *Whitehall Diary*, I, p. 237.

27 Sir F. Maurice. *Viscount Haldane* (1939), II, p. 149. James, p. 170. Jones. *Whitehall Diary*, I, p. 244. Young, p. 52.

28 A. W. Baldwin. *My Father: The True Story*, p. 122.

29 Jones. *Whitehall Diary*, I, p. 242.

30 Wrench, p. 219. Middlemas *and* Barnes, p. 168.

31 Chequers Visitors' Book.

32 Jones. *Whitehall Diary*, I, p. 241. *Glasgow Herald*, 27 July 1923.

33 A. W. Baldwin. *My Father: The True Story*, p. 122.

34 N. Chamberlain to Baldwin 16 August 1923: Baldwin Papers 42. Feiling, pp. 107–8.

35 S. Baldwin. *On England*, p. 190.

36 20 June 1923: Cabinet Papers 32 (23).

37 *The Times*, 27 August 1923. Middlemas *and* Barnes, p. 320. Young, p. 60.

38 Nicolson, pp. 368–70.

39 Middlemas *and* Barnes, p. 196. R. Churchill. *Lord Derby*, p. 516.

40 Jones. *Whitehall Diary*, I, p. 249. Middlemas *and* Barnes, p. 198.

41 Middlemas *and* Barnes, p. 206.

42 Jones. *Whitehall Diary*, I, p. 244. Macleod, p. 96.

43 Jones. *Whitehall Diary*, I, p. 249.

44 Curzon, p. 183.

45 Jones. *Whitehall Diary*, I, p. 254.

46 Robert Blake. *The Unknown Prime Minister*, p. 531.

47 Birkenhead to A. Chamberlain 15 August 1923: Chamberlain Papers AC/35/2/24.

48 Wickham Steed. *The Real Stanley Baldwin*, p. 61. Jones Papers 25 November 1943, cited Middlemas *and* Barnes, p. 249.

49 R. Churchill, pp. 527–8. L. S. Amery. *My Political Life*, II, pp. 280–1.

50 Petrie, II, p. 229.

51 Wrench, p. 222. Baldwin Papers 42.

52 S. Roskill. *Hankey*, II, p. 342.

53 CAB 23/46/50. Jones, II, p. 250. E. F. C. Wood, 'Record of some events preceding the dissolution and General Election'.

54 *The Times*, 26, 27 October 1923.

55 Petrie, II, pp. 230–2.

56 R. Churchill, p. 525.

57 S. Salvidge. *Salvidge of Liverpool*, p. 253.
58 Wood: Baldwin Papers 35.
59 Curzon, p. 184.
60 CAB 23/41/53.
61 Feiling, p. 109. Chamberlain Papers AC/35/3/21a.
62 Amery, II, p. 280.

CHAPTER 6   OPPOSITION LEADER

1 Chamberlain Papers AC/35/3/21b.
2 L. S. Amery. *My Political Life*, II, p. 281.
3 Chamberlain Papers, loc. cit.
4 Harold Nicolson. *King George V*, p. 380. RA K 1924/2–3.
5 R. Churchill. *Lord Derby*, p. 534.
6 CAB 23/46/54.
7 Marchioness Curzon. *Reminiscences*, p. 187.
8 Wood: Baldwin Papers 35.
9 *The Times*, 14, 15 November 1923.
10 Baldwin Papers 42 f. 130.
11 *Glasgow Herald*, 8 November 1923.
12 Chamberlain Papers AC/35/3/21C. Curzon, p. 191.
13 Baldwin Papers 35 f. 92 ff. K. Feiling. *The Life of Neville Chamberlain*, p. 110.
14 Curzon, p. 190.
15 CAB 23/46/57.
16 Curzon, p. 191.
17 Thomas Jones. *Whitehall Diary*, I, pp. 254, 255. *Beatrice Webb's Diaries, 1912–1924*. Edited by Margaret I. Cole (1932), p. 251.
18 Jones, I, p. 257.
19 S. Salvidge. *Salvidge of Liverpool*, p. 255.
20 Lord Beaverbrook, *Politicians and the Press*, pp. 72–3.
21 Salvidge, p. 255. R. Churchill, p. 541. Curzon, p. 203.
22 Jones, I, pp. 258–9.
23 R. Churchill, pp. 551–2. Curzon, p. 205. Memoranda by Stamfordham, 8–10 December 1923: RA K 1918/14, 25, 34. Harold Nicolson, p. 382.
24 Robert Rhodes James. *Memoirs of a Conservative*, p. 191. R. Churchill, p. 558. Baldwin to Carson 16 December 1923: Carson Papers D 1507/1/1923/8.
25 James, p. 192.
26 Chamberlain Papers AC/35/4/1.
27 Nourah Waterhouse. *Private and Official*, p. 295.
28 A. C. Benson. *The Diary of Arthur Christopher Benson*. Edited by Percy Lubbock (1926), p. 302.
29 Feiling, p. 111. Macleod, p. 102.
30 Chamberlain Papers AC/35/4/5.
31 R. Churchill, p. 365. Amery, II, pp. 289–90. W. A. S. Hewins. *Apologia of an Imperialist*, II, p. 282.
32 Sir Charles Petrie. *Life and Letters of the Rt. Hon. Sir Austen Chamberlain*, II, p. 240. Chamberlain Papers AC/35/4/14.
33 Jones, I, p. 262.
34 A. Chamberlain to Birkenhead 28 February 1924. Chamberlain Papers AC/35/4/9.

35 James, p. 194.
36 Amery, II, p. 292. James, p. 195.
37 Davidson Papers, cited Keith Middlemas *and* John Barnes. *Baldwin, A Biography*, p. 263.
38 Wickham Steed. *The Real Stanley Baldwin*, p. 71.
39 Jones, I, pp. 275–6.
40 S. Baldwin. *On England*, p. 5.
41 *The People*, 18, 25 May 1924.
42 Jones, I, p. 280. Tom Driberg. *Beaverbrook*, p. 181.
43 Chamberlain Papers AC/5/1/319.
44 Chamberlain Papers AC/5/1/322.
45 Chamberlain Papers AC/5/1/324.
46 Petrie, II, p. 241.
47 R. Boothby. *I Fight to Live*, p. 36.
48 Chamberlain Papers AC/5/1/325.
49 Chamberlain Papers AC/35/5/1.
50 Chamberlain Papers AC/35/5/2a.
51 Chamberlain Papers AC/5/1/327.
52 James, p. 196.
53 Jones, III, pp. 234–5.
54 Hickleton Papers cited Middlemas *and* Barnes, p. 270.
55 James, p. 196. A. W. Baldwin. *My Father: The True Story*, p. 129.
56 RA K 1958/13. On the Campbell case, see particularly H. Montgomery Hyde. *Sir Patrick Hastings* (1960), p. 141 ff.
57 Nicolson, p. 400.
58 Amery, II, p. 296. Middlemas *and* Barnes, p. 275.
59 James, p. 199. On the Zinoviev letter, see generally Lewis Chester, Stephen Fay *and* Hugo Young. *The Zinoviev Letter* (1967).
60 Asquith Papers 33 f. 310. A. J. A. Spender and Cyril Asquith (1932), II, p. 351.
61 Iain Macleod. *Neville Chamberlain*, p. 109.
62 Chamberlain Papers AC/35/5/3.

CHAPTER 7   THE SECOND TERM

1 Harold Nicolson. *King George V*, p.403. Memorandum by Lord Stamfordham 4 November 1924: RA K 1958/44.
2 G. M. Young. *Stanley Baldwin*, p. 88. Ronaldshay. *The Life of Lord Curzon*, III, p. 369.
3 Tyrell to Baldwin 1 November 1924: Baldwin Papers 42 f. 226.
4 Thomas Jones. *Whitehall Diary*, I, pp. 301–3.
5 Jones, II, p. 295. Earl Birkenhead. *Contemporary Personalities*, p. 140.
6 A. Chamberlain to Baldwin 6 November 1924: Chamberlain Papers AC/35/5/4.
7 Robert Rhodes James. *Memoirs of a Conservative*, p. 205. Iain Macleod. *Neville Chamberlain*, p. 110. Chamberlain Papers, loc. cit.
8 Young, p. 88.
9 Keith Feiling. *The Life of Neville Chamberlain*, p. 117. C. P. Scott. *Political Diaries 1911–1918*. Edited by Trevor Wilson (1970), p. 486.
10 Jones, I, p. 303.
11 Chamberlain Papers, loc. cit., to Baldwin 6 November 1924; Churchill to Baldwin, n.d. Baldwin Papers 42 ff. 252, 215.

12 Baldwin Papers 159 f. 214.

13 Jones, I, p. 304.

14 Chamberlain Papers AC/5/1/340; partly quoted Sir Charles Petrie. *The Life and Letters of the Rt. Hon. Sir Austen Chamberlain*, II, p. 243. Stamfordham to Baldwin 6 November 1924: Baldwin Papers 178 f.55

15 Viscount Lee. *A Good Innings*, III, p. 1022. Jones, I, p. 305.

16 Cited D. H. Elletson. *Chequers and the Prime Ministers*, p. 73.

17 Edith Marchioness of Londonderry. *Retrospect* (1938), p. 223. Londonderry to Baldwin 7 November 1924: Baldwin Papers 42 f. 263.

18 CAB 23/49/59. Eustace Percy. *Some Memories* (1958), p. 127.

19 Baldwin Papers 159 ff. 214–15; partly quoted Young, p. 99.

20 Birkenhead to Baldwin 16 October 1928: Baldwin Papers 163.

21 Percy, p. 128.

22 Jonathan Cape Archives *re* Nourah Waterhouse, *Private and Official*, in the first draft of which this story appeared.

23 Jones, I, pp. 306, 307.

24 ibid., p. 306. Petrie, II, p. 338. Chamberlain put through his call to Chequers while his colleagues were still with him: CAB 23/49/63. According to the minutes of the meeting it was agreed that 'Lord Allenby had not been justified in acting in defiance of the express instructions of the Secretary of State for Foreign Affairs, but that any advantage that might now attach to the note as approved by the Cabinet would altogether be outweighed by the appearance of hesitation and loss of prestige which would be involved in disavowing Lord Allenby's action by revoking a document which had already been communicated by our representative and that they had no option but to support the authority of Lord Allenby in dealing with a critical situation'.

25 Jones, I, p. 312.

26 Halifax. *Fullness of Days*, p. 102. Young, p. 91.

27 S. Baldwin. *On England*, p. 33 ff. Young, p. 94.

28 Young, loc. cit. Chamberlain Papers: AC 52/80/11b.

29 S. Baldwin. *On England*, p. 138.

30 A. W. Baldwin. *The Macdonald Sisters*, p. 204.

31 S. Baldwin. *On England*, p. 100 ff. *The Times*, 20 May 1925. Jones, I, p. 314. A. F. Tschiffely. *Don Roberto* (1937), p. 402.

32 A. W. Baldwin. *My Father*, p. 134. Jones, I, p. 315.

33 Baldwin to King George V 2 July 1925: Baldwin Papers 60.

34 Nicolson, p. 428.

35 ibid., p. 429. James, pp. 276–7. Earl Birkenhead. *The Life of F. E. Smith First Earl of Birkenhead*, p. 544.

36 Jones, I, p. 316.

37 L. S. Amery. *My Political Life*, II, pp. 506–7.

38 Baldwin Papers 43 f. 48; partly quoted Young, p. 101.

39 Churchill to Baldwin 1 November 1925: Baldwin Papers 160 f. 26. Baldwin to Churchill 11 August, 30 November 1928: Churchill Papers. Communicated by Dr. Martin Gilbert.

40 Young, p. 90.

41 Jones, I, pp. 325–6.

42 ibid., p. 330.

43 Baldwin to Stamfordham 3 October 1925: RA K 2025/1–2.

44 James, p. 198. Chamberlain Papers AC/52/82.

45 Petrie, II, pp. 285 ff. Feiling, p. 152. Nicolson, p. 409.

46 Jones, III, pp. 236 ff. See also Baldwin Papers 99 for Baldwin's correspondence with President Cosgrave and other documents concerning the Boundary Commission and its eventual settlement.

47 St John Ervine. *Craigavon Ulsterman* (1949), p. 501 ff.

48 Birkenhead to Reading 3 December 1925: Birkenhead Papers. Communicated by the Earl of Birkenhead.

49 Ervine, pp. 503, 507.

50 Jones, III, pp. 245, 246.

51 Young, p. 60 ff. James, p. 232.

52 Jones, II, p. 10.

53 ibid., p. 33.

54 Young, p. 116.

55 James, p. 232.

56 Jones, II, p. 36. James, p. 238.

57 Young, p. 116.

58 Young to Baldwin 20 October 1939: Baldwin Papers 174 f. 253.

59 Jones, II, pp. 38–9.

60 *British Gazette*, 6 May 1926. Jones, II, p. 43.

61 *British Gazette*, 13 May 1926.

62 Jones, II, p. 44. Baldwin Papers 176 f. 2.

63 *British Gazette*, 13 May 1926.

64 Jones, II, p. 53.

65 Young, p. 121.

66 Baldwin to George V 18 February 1927: Baldwin Papers 62.

67 BBC feature 'Personality and Power: Stanley Baldwin' presented by Dr Norman Hunt 13 October 1970.

68 Young, p. 122. Harold Macmillan. *Memoirs*, I, p. 229.

69 Trenchard Papers CII/3/214. Roskill. *Naval Policy between the Wars*, ch. XIII. Boyle. Trenchard, ch. 18. James, p. 220 ff.

70 Jones, II, pp. 64, 142. Baldwin to George V 23 August 1926: RA K 2066/5 Baldwin to Stamfordham 11 April 1927: RA K 2101/2. Nourah Waterhouse. *Private and Official*, p. 342.

71 Communicated by Mr Neville Ford.

72 W. P. and Z. K. Coates. *A History of Anglo-Soviet Relations* (1945), p. 267 ff. Birkenhead, p. 538. S. Baldwin. *Our Inheritance*, p. 138.

73 Baldwin to George V 24 August 1927: Baldwin Papers 177 f. 13. RA J 2123/11–12.

74 S. Baldwin. *Our Inheritance*, p. v.

75 ibid., p. 307. Young, p. 52. Asquith Papers 18 ff. 127–8. Baldwin to Beaverbrook 1 January 1929: Baldwin Papers 163.

76 Jones, II, p. 179.

77 ibid., p. 23. Lee to Baldwin 7 July 1925; R. Waterhouse to A. E. Messer 10 March 1927: Baldwin Papers 179.

78 Edward Garnett. *Selected Letters of T. E. Lawrence* (1938), p. 216. Baldwin Papers 159 f. 134.

79 James, pp. 199, 203, 277, 285.

80 Jones, II, p. 167. Baldwin to Hoare 28 October 1926: Templewood Papers V, 2. Sir Alan Herbert. *A.P.H. His Life and Times*, p. 296.

81 Baldwin Papers 62.

82 Young, p. 129.

83 Macleod, p. 129. RA K 2155/1.

84 Birkenhead, p. 545.

85 Londonderry Papers (Memorandum by Lord Castlereagh March 1936) partly quoted by Keith Middlemas *and* John Barnes. *Baldwin, A Biography*, p. 806. Duke of Windsor. *A King's Story*, p. 228. Baldwin Papers 171 f. 48.

86 Jones, II, pp. 176, 180.

87 Amery, II, p. 505.

88 Sir John Evelyn Wrench. *Geoffrey Dawson and our Times*, p. 274. *The Times*, 13 April 1929.

89 Jones, II, pp. 176–7.

90 Feiling, p. 166.

91 Jones, II, p. 177.

92 Baldwin to George V 11 May 1929: Baldwin Papers 62.

CHAPTER 8   THE PARTY REVOLT

1 Thomas Jones. *Whitehall Diary*, II, p. 191. Robert Rhodes James. *Memoirs of a Conservative*, p. 303.

2 James, p. 302.

3 Memorandum by Lord Stamfordham 31 May 1929: RA K 2223/24.

4 Jones, II, p. 192.

5 A. W. Baldwin. *My Father: The True Story*, p. 146.

6 Keith Middlemas *and* John Barnes. *Baldwin, A Biography*, p. 528.

7 Jones, II, p. 192.

8 Memorandum by Lord Stamfordham 2 June 1929: RA K 2223/30.

9 Keith Feiling. *The Life of Neville Chamberlain*, p. 168.

10 Jones, II, p. 194. *The Times*, 29 June 1929.

11 Iain Macleod. *Neville Chamberlain*, p. 132.

12 James, p. 322. A. J. P. Taylor. *Beaverbrook*, pp. 268, 288.

13 30 June 1930: Chamberlain Papers AC/5/1/508.

14 James, p. 342.

15 7 July 1930: Chamberlain Papers AC 5/1/508.

16 4 October 1930: Chamberlain Papers AC 5/1/508.

17 Macleod, p. 136.

18 Bridgeman to N. Chamberlain 3 October 1930: Chamberlain Papers NC/8/10/6.

19 A. Chamberlain to N. Chamberlain 9 October 1930: Chamberlain Papers NC/8/10/10.

20 N. Chamberlain to A. Chamberlain 9 October 1930: Chamberlain Papers AC/39/2/39.

21 Jones, II, pp. 273–5.

22 Baldwin to Davidson 6 November 1930: Davidson Papers, cited Middlemas *and* Barnes, p. 579.

23 Bridgeman to N. Chamberlain 3 November 1930: Chamberlain Papers NC/8/10/19. R. Churchill. *Derby*, p. 583.

24 Jones, II, pp. 276–7.

25 Introduction by Stanley Baldwin to the illustrated edition of *Precious Bane* (1929), p. 9. Jones, II, pp. 98, 244. Michael S. Howard. *Jonathan Cape, Publisher* (1971), p. 100.

26 Davidson Papers cited Middlemas *and* Barnes, p. 574.

27 Birkenhead to Baldwin 8 May 1930: Baldwin Papers 165 f. 32. S. Baldwin. *This Torch of Freedom* (1935), p. 233. W. Churchill. *Great Contemporaries* (1937), p. 183.

28 *History of The Times*, IV, Part 2, p. 818. Jones, II, p. 278.
29 Baldwin Papers 165.
30 Harold Nicolson. *Diaries and Letters*. Edited by Nigel Nicolson. I, p. 56.
31 Macleod, p. 138.
32 Derby to N. Chamberlain 25 February 1931: Chamberlain Papers AC/8/10/21.
33 ibid., 9 March 1931.
34 Macleod, p. 140.
35 A. Chamberlain to I. Chamberlain: Chamberlain Papers AC/5/1/532.
36 James, pp. 357 ff. Davidson Papers cited Middlemas *and* Barnes, pp. 588–90.
37 Macleod, p. 142.
38 Memorandum by Sir Clive Wigram 3 March 1931: RA K 2324/1.
39 Feiling, p. 187. A. Chamberlain to I. Chamberlain 13 March 1931: Chamberlain Papers AC/5/1/534.
40 Chamberlain Papers NC/8/10/28.
41 ibid., NC/8/10/27, 31.
42 Diana Cooper. *The Light of Common Day*, p. 100.
43 A. Chamberlain to N. Chamberlain 22 March 1930: Chamberlain Papers NC/8/10/29. Feiling, p. 187. Macleod, pp. 143–5.
44 James, p. 362.
45 Duff Cooper. *Old Men Forget*, p. 176.
46 Feiling, p. 189. Macleod, p. 148. Stephen Roskill. *Hankey*, II, p. 548.
47 James, p. 368.
48 Macleod, p. 149.
49 Chamberlain Papers cited Middlemas *and* Barnes, p. 621.
50 Viscount Templewood. *Nine Troubled Years*, p. 18.
51 Sir John Evelyn Wrench. *Geoffrey Dawson and the History of our Times*, pp. 291–2.
52 Viscount Samuel. *Memoirs*, p. 204. Harold Nicolson. *King George V*, p. 461.
53 Macleod, p. 151.
54 James, p. 370.

CHAPTER 9 THE NATIONAL GOVERNMENT

1 Stephen Roskill. *Hankey*, II, p. 549.
2 G. M. Young. *Stanley Baldwin*, p. 167. Robert Rhodes James. *Memoirs of a Conservative*, p. 368.
3 A. Chamberlain to I. Chamberlain 31 August 1931: Chamberlain Papers AC/5/1/551; partly quoted Petrie, *The Life and Letters of the Rt. Hon. Sir Austen Chamberlain*, II, p. 382. A. Chamberlain to Hilda Chamberlain 3 October 1931: Chamberlain Papers AC/39/3/30.
4 Roskill, II, p. 548. CAB 68/48/1 ff.
5 RA K 2330(1)/19. A. Chamberlain to H. Chamberlain 3 October 1931: Chamberlain Papers AC/39/3/30.
6 Keith Feiling. *Neville Chamberlain*, p. 195.
7 Memoranda of Sir Clive Wigram 28 September, 2 October 1931: RA K 2331(1)/18, 24.
8 Iain Macleod. *Neville Chamberlain*, p. 154.
9 Thomas Jones. *A Diary with Letters*, p. 20.
10 A. W. Baldwin. *My Father: The True Story*, p. 153.
11 CAB 23/69/1 ff.

12 *Daily Telegraph*, 4 November 1931. Memorandum by Lord Stamfordham 2 November 1931: RA K 2331(1)/48. Harold Nicolson. *King George V*, p. 494.

13 John Evelyn Wrench. *Geoffrey Dawson and our Times*, p. 295. Wigram 4 November 1931: RA K 2331/50.

14 Young, p. 167.

15 Viscount Samuel. *Memoirs*, p. 215. Somervell Papers ('Politics').

16 Hansard. Parl. Deb. H of C, 5th Series, Vol. 260, Cols. 342–7.

17 Jones, pp. 25–6.

18 Young, p. 171.

19 Jones, p. 56.

20 Royal Archives, cited Harold Nicolson. *King George V*, p. 498.

21 Sir Henry Channon. *Chips. The Diaries of Sir Henry Channon*. Edited by Robert Rhodes James. p. 131.

22 Crozier Papers: Beaverbrook Library.

23 Baldwin Papers 169 f. 59.

24 Young, p. 175. Chamberlain Papers AC/40/5/13.

25 W. Churchill. *Second World War*, I, p. 88.

26 James, p. 398.

27 Ian Colvin. *Vansittart in Office*, p. 31. James, p. 399.

28 W. Churchill, I, p. 89.

29 Crozier Papers: Beaverbrook Library. Somervell Diary, pp. 19, 25, 63.

30 Marquess of Londonderry. *Wings of Destiny*, p. 112.

31 ibid., p. 115.

32 Young, p. 180. Feiling, p. 239.

33 Londonderry Papers.

34 Londonderry to Baldwin, 29 December 1938: Baldwin Papers 171 f. 178.

35 James, p. 405.

36 Crozier Papers: Beaverbrook Library.

37 Jones, pp. 65, 93, 101. Monica Blackett. *The Mark of the Maker: A Portrait of Helen Waddell* (1973), p. 112.

38 ibid., pp. 122–4.

39 ibid., p. 140.

40 ibid., p. 144.

41 Frank Owen. *Tempestuous Journey*, p. 729.

42 Frances Lloyd George. *Lloyd George. A Diary by Frances Stevenson*. Edited by A. J. P. Taylor, p. 299.

43 Jones, p. 138.

44 W. Churchill, I, p. 116.

45 Earl Birkenhead. *The Prof in Two Worlds*, p. 176.

46 CAB 80/245–6.

47 Keith Middlemas and John Barnes. *Baldwin, A Biography*, p. 789.

48 Birkenhead, p. 178.

49 ibid., pp. 179 ff.

50 Baldwin Papers 1.

51 'Air Parity in Western Europe', Memorandum by Londonderry 31 May 1935: PRO: CP 116 (CAB 24/255).

52 Baldwin Papers 1.

53 'German Air Programme and its bearing on British Air Strength', 15 April 1935: PRO: CP 85 (CAB 24/254).

54 Londonderry, p. 163.
55 Reports of Air Parity Sub-Committee 8 May, 17 May 1935: CP 100(35), 103(35). Baldwin Papers 1 ff. 186–9. W. J. Reader. *Architect of Air Power*, p. 198 ff.
56 W. Churchill, I, p. 99.
57 ibid., p. 100.
58 Young, p. 101. *The Times*, 27 June 1936.
59 Londonderry, p. 134.
60 ibid., pp. 140–3.
61 Londonderry to Baldwin 29 December 1938: Baldwin Papers 171 f. 185.
62 Memorandum of Sir Clive Wigram 16 May 1935: RA K 2473/1.
63 ibid., 20 May 1935: RA K 2473/2.
64 ibid., 24 May 1935: RA K 2473/3.
65 Londonderry, p. 4.
66 Jones, pp. 150 ff.
67 CAB 23/81/465.
68 Earl Avon. *Facing the Dictators*, p. 217.
69 Londonderry Papers (Memorandum by Lord Castlereagh March 1936).
70 Hailsham Papers, cited R. F. V. Heuston. *Lives of the Lord Chancellors*, p. 478.
71 Londonderry, p. 144.
72 Baldwin Papers 171.
73 CAB 23/81/468.
74 A. Chamberlain to H. Chamberlain 11 June 1935: Chamberlain Papers AC/5/11/703.
75 RA K 2473/23, 26.
76 CAB 23/82/1. Middlemas and Barnes, p. 825.

CHAPTER 10 THE THIRD TERM

1 W. Churchill. *The Second World War*, I, p. 117. Baldwin Papers 170 f. 66.
2 Earl of Swinton. *Sixty Years of Power*, p. 89.
3 Lord Butler. *The Art of the Possible*, p. 29.
4 Thomas Jones. *A Diary with Letters*, p. 187.
5 Viscount Templewood. *Nine Troubled Years*, p. 164.
6 ibid., p. 166.
7 ibid., p. 170.
8 Robert Rhodes James. *Churchill. A Study in Failure*, p. 258.
9 Jones, p. 155.
10 CAB 23/82/285.
11 Baldwin Papers 171.
12 RA K 2497A/2–3.
13 S. Baldwin. *The Torch of Freedom*, pp. 319 ff.
14 G. M. Young. *Stanley Baldwin*, p. 215.
15 Iain Macleod. *Neville Chamberlain*, p. 185.
16 Jones, p. 155.
17 Robert Rhodes James. *Memoirs of a Conservative*, p. 410.
18 Jones, p. 157.
19 Baldwin Papers 171. Londonderry Papers (Memorandum by Lord Castlereagh March 1936).
20 Earl Swinton. *I Remember*, p. 147.

21 Harold Nicolson. *Diaries and Letters*, I. Edited by Nigel Nicolson, p. 228.

22 Jones, p. 157.

23 Templewood, p. 178. Earl of Avon. *Facing the Dictators*, p. 298.

24 Templewood, p. 182.

25 Avon, p. 302.

26 Zetland to Linlithgow 20 December 1935: India Office Library. Jones, p. 159.

27 Macleod, p. 188. Avon, p. 306.

28 Ian Colvin. *Vansittart in Office*, p. 81. Sir John Evelyn Wrench. *Geoffrey Dawson and our Times*, p. 327.

29 Templewood, p. 185.

30 CAB 23/90B/53–67.

31 Templewood, p. 185.

32 Avon, p. 309.

33 Colvin, p. 83.

34 Sir Charles Petrie. *Life and Letters of the Rt. Hon. Sir Austen Chamberlain*, II, p. 406.

35 Avon, p. 316.

36 A. Chamberlain to H. Chamberlain 22 December 1935: Chamberlain Papers AC/5/1/718.

37 ibid., 28 December 1935: Chamberlain Papers AC 5/1/719.

38 Avon, p. 316.

39 Avon, p. 319.

40 Jones, pp. 158–60.

41 Duke of Windsor. *A King's Story*, p. 261. Harold Nicolson. *King George V*, p. 530.

42 Duchess of Windsor. *The Heart Has Its Reasons*, p. 216.

43 Duke of Windsor, p. 259.

44 A. W. Baldwin. *My Father: The True Story*, p. 299.

45 Prince of Wales to Baldwin 8 March 1935: Baldwin Papers 177 f. 13.

46 Duke of Windsor, pp. 262–3. Jones, pp. 163–4.

47 J. G. Lockhart. *Cosmo Gordon Lang*, p. 392. Duchess of Windsor, p. 219.

48 Jones, p. 162. J. C. W. Reith. *Into the Wind*, p. 240.

49 Earl Birkenhead. *Walter Monckton*, p. 157. Robert Sencourt. *The Reign of Edward VIII*, p. 160.

50 Davidson Papers cited Keith Middlemas *and* John Barnes. *Baldwin, A Biography*, p. 980 note.

51 Birkenhead, p. 128.

52 Jones, p. 169.

53 Macleod, p. 195. Young, p. 233.

54 Duchess of Windsor, p. 225.

55 Young, p. 233.

56 Petrie, II, p. 408.

57 Jones, p. 175.

58 Macleod, p. 193.

59 *History of the Times*, IV, Part 2, p. 902 note. *Annual Register* (1936), p. 16.

60 Avon, p. 343.

61 Hesse. *Hitler and the English* cited Brian Inglis. *Abdication* (1966), p. 70.

62 Avon, p. 374. Hugh Dalton. *The Fateful Years*, p. 93.

63 Jones, p. 204.

64 Sir Henry Channon. *Chips. The Diaries of Sir Henry Channon*. Edited by Robert Rhodes James, pp. 61, 67.

65 CAB 27/5213. Malcolm MacDonald. *Titans and Others*, p. 56 ff.

66 CAB 27/524.

67 Avon, p. 374.

68 Jones, p. 201.

69 ibid., pp. 203–8.

70 ibid., pp. 224, 228. Middlemas *and* Barnes, p. 958.

71 James, p. 411.

72 *The Times*, 3 July 1936. Chamberlain Papers AC/41/3/105. Keith Feiling. *The Life of Neville Chamberlain*, p. 285.

73 Jones, p. 228.

74 ibid., p. 231.

75 'Report of the Board of Enquiry appointed by the Prime Minister to investigate certain discussions engaged in by the Permanent Secretary to the Air Ministry', *The Times*, 6 August 1936.

76 Londonderry to Baldwin 29 December 1938: Baldwin Papers 171 f. 184.

77 *The Times*, 16 June 1972.

78 W. Churchill, I, pp. 178–9, 538–43.

79 PRO: Premier 1/193.

80 James, p. 412.

81 Jones, pp. 237, 266–7.

82 Feiling, p. 287. Macleod, p. 195.

83 Middlemas *and* Barnes, p. 964.

CHAPTER 11 'THE KING'S MATTER'

1 Earl Avon. *Facing the Dictators*, p. 410.

2 Duke of Windsor. *A King's Story*, p. 312. Thomas Jones. *A Diary with Letters*, pp. 305, 306.

3 Lord Hardinge of Penshurst. 'Before the Abdication': *The Times*, 29 November 1955.

4 Viscount Templewood. *Nine Troubled Years*, p. 217.

5 G. M. Young. *Stanley Baldwin*, p. 234.

6 Duke of Windsor, p. 316.

7 Jones, p. 284.

8 The account of this and Baldwin's subsequent interviews with the King is based on the notes which Baldwin kept at the time and which are now preserved in the Baldwin Papers 176 ff. 23–7, 31, 35, 36, supplemented by what Baldwin told the House of Commons in his speech on 10 December 1936, the diaries kept by Lucy Baldwin, Neville Chamberlain and Tom Jones, and the King's version in his memoirs *A King's Story*.

9 Chamberlain Papers, partly quoted in Iain Macleod, *Neville Chamberlain*, p. 196 (Communicated by Mr Stephen Lloyd).

10 Sir John Evelyn Wrench. *Geoffrey Dawson and our Times*, p. 343.

11 Jones, p. 289.

12 Lord Attlee. *As It Happened*, p. 86.

13 Jones, p. 288.

14 Hardinge Papers, cited Keith Middlemas *and* John Barnes. *Baldwin, A Biography*, p. 988.

15 Baldwin's speech and its implications have been carefully analysed by Reginald Bassett

in an illuminating article in the *Cambridge Journal* ('Telling the Truth to the People: The Myth of the Baldwin "Confession" '), Vol. II, pp. 84–95 (November 1948).

16 *History of the Times*, IV, Part 2, p. 1023.
17 W. Churchill. *The Second World War*, I, p. 169.
18 Harold Nicolson. *Diaries and Letters*. Edited by Nigel Nicolson, I, p. 279.
19 Jones, p. 482. Hopkinson to Baldwin 25 October 1940: Baldwin Papers 174 f. 184.
20 The complete text of this letter, parts of which were quoted by the Duke and Duchess of Windsor in their respective memoirs, was first published by Hardinge in *The Times*, 29 November 1955.
21 Wrench, p. 345.
22 Duke of Windsor, p. 328.
23 Earl of Birkenhead. *Walter Monckton*, p. 134.
24 Duchess of Windsor. *The Heart has its Reasons*, p. 247.
25 Baldwin Papers 176 ff. 61–71.
26 Janet Adam Smith. *John Buchan*, p. 402. Wrench, p. 339 note.
27 Cited Middlemas *and* Barnes, p. 995.
28 James Pope-Hennessy. *Queen Mary*, pp. 575–6.
29 Birkenhead, p. 136.
30 Monckton to Baldwin 20 November 1936: Baldwin Papers 176 f. 75.
31 Robert Rhodes James. *Memoirs of a Conservative*, p. 417.
32 Jones, p. 288.
33 Duke of Windsor, p. 340.
34 Duff Cooper. *Old Men Forget*, p. 201. Duke of Windsor, loc. cit.
35 Iain Macleod. *Neville Chamberlain*, p. 197.
36 Baldwin Papers 176 f. 76.
37 A. J. P. Taylor. *Beaverbrook*, p. 370.
38 Lord Beaverbrook. *The Abdication of King Edward VIII*. Edited by A. J. P. Taylor (1966), p. 42 ff.
39 Zetland to Linlithgow 27 November 1936: Zetland Correspondence, India Office Library; cited Zetland. '*Essayez*', p. 213.
40 Earl of Longford *and* Thomas P. O'Neill. *Eamonn De Valera*, p. 291.
41 J. G. Lockhart. *Cosmo Gordon Lang*, p. 401.
42 Wrench, p. 349.
43 Duke of Windsor, p. 355.
44 Sir Henry Channon. *Chips. The Diaries of Sir Henry Channon*. Edited by Robert Rhodes James, p. 89.
45 Young, pp. 239–40, 242.
46 Nicolson, p. 282.
47 Macleod, p. 197.
48 Zetland to Linlithgow 5 December 1936: India Office Library. Baldwin to Edward VIII 4 December 1936: Baldwin Papers 176 ff. 38–41.
49 Tom Driberg. *Beaverbrook*, p. 225.
50 Baldwin Papers, cited Middlemas *and* Barnes, p. 1009.
51 India Office Library. Duke of Windsor, p. 387.
52 Birkenhead, p. 145.
53 Robert Rhodes James. *Churchill: A Study in Failure*, p. 273.
54 Templewood Papers IX, 7. Macleod, p. 198.
55 Birkenhead, p. 146.
56 Zetland to Linlithgow 6 December 1936: India Office Library.

57 Young, p. 242.
58 Chamberlain Papers AC/5/1/729.
59 Baldwin Papers 176 f. 103.
60 ibid., f. 102.
61 ibid., f. 91.
62 Jones, p. 291. Duchess of Windsor, p. 274. Compton Mackenzie. *The Windsor Tapestry*, p. 490.
63 Birkenhead, p. 148.
64 Duke of Windsor, p. 402.
65 Zetland to Linlithgow 9 December 1936: India Office Library.
66 Duke of Windsor, p. 409.
67 Young, p. 241.
68 Nicolson, p. 286.
69 T. Dugdale to Sir Donald Somervell, 8 October 1935 (Communicated by Mrs D. C. Somervell). Robert Sencourt. *The Reign of Edward VIII*, p. 192. Information from Lord Crathorne.
70 Nicolson, p. 285.
71 Viscount Simon. *Retrospect* (1952), p. 222.
72 Nicolson, p. 286.
73 Private information.
74 Baldwin Papers 176 f. 17.
75 Lockhart, p. 405. Channon, p. 103.
76 Baldwin Papers 176 f. 115.
77 ibid., 172 f. 68.
78 Smith, p. 403. Jones, p. 296.
79 Chamberlain Papers (Communicated by Mr Stephen Lloyd). Churchill, I, p. 171.
80 Baldwin Papers 172 f. 41.
81 ibid., f. 34.
82 Blackett, p. 134.
83 Baldwin Papers, 177 f. 13.
84 J. W. Wheeler-Bennett. *King George VI*, p. 298.
85 Jones, p. 287.
86 Birkenhead, p. 161.
87 Davidson Papers cited Middlemas *and* Barnes, p. 1018.
88 Channon, p. 102.
89 Baldwin Papers 176 f. 117.
90 ibid., f. 124.
91 ibid., f. 21.
92 Communicated by Lady Lorna Howard.
93 MacDonald to Baldwin 27 May 1937: Baldwin Papers 173 f. 80. Birkenhead, p. 166.
94 Duchess of Windsor, p. 198.
95 Middlemas *and* Barnes, p. 1015.

CHAPTER 12   OLD AGE AND FRIENDSHIP

1 Thomas Jones. *A Diary with Letters*, p. 303. Colin Coote. *A Companion of Honour*, p. 177.
2 George VI to Baldwin 29 March 1937: Baldwin Papers 177 f. 68. Jones, pp. 324, 329.
3 Sir Henry Channon. *Chips. The Diaries of Sir Henry Channon*, p. 116. Jones, p. 314.

4 Irish Situation Committee Minutes 15 December 1936: CAB 27/523. A. J. P. Taylor. *English History 1914–1945*, p. 403.
5 Irish Situation Committee Minutes 20 January 1937: CAB 27/523.
6 Earl Avon. *Facing the Dictators*, p. 444. Jones, p. 330.
7 Jones, p. 325. Channon, p. 117. S. Baldwin. *Service of our Lives*, p. 84. Baldwin Papers 173 f. 32.
8 Jones, p. 330.
9 S. Baldwin. *Service of our Lives*, p. 141.
10 Communicated by Mr Richard Paine.
11 S. Baldwin. *Service of our Lives*, p. 156.
12 Harold Nicolson. *Diaries and Letters*. Edited by Nigel Nicolson, I, p. 301. Lord Boothby, 'The Baldwin I Knew': *Sunday Telegraph*, 16 July 1937. Sir Donald Somervell, MS Journal 1934–7: communicated by Mr Robert Somervell. Jones, p. 347. Baldwin Papers 173 f. 26.
13 Jones, p. 353. Baldwin Papers, cited J. W. Wheeler Bennett. *King George VI*, p. 318.
14 Baldwin Papers 173 f. 58. Earl of Halifax. *Fullness of Days*, p. 182.
15 Jones, p. 353.
16 *The Times*, 11 June 1937. Sir Percy Starris. *Forty Years in and out of Parliament*. (1947), p. 133.
17 RA CC47/1671.
18 Jones, p. 371.
19 Trevelyan to Baldwin 27 October 1937: Baldwin Papers 173 f. 143.
20 Jones, pp. 370, 371.
21 L. S. Amery. *My Political Life*, II, p. 223. Jones, p. 381. Lord Macmillan. *A Man of Law's Tale*, pp. 212–13.
22 Nicolson, I, p. 314.
23 Robert Rhodes James. *Memoirs of a Conservative*, p. 420.
24 Keith Middlemas *and* John Barnes. *Baldwin, A Biography*, p. 1043.
25 Keith Feiling. *Neville Chamberlain*, p. 382.
26 Middlemas *and* Barnes, p. 1046.
27 Hansard. Parl. Deb. H of L, 4 October 1938.
28 Jones, p. 414.
29 Nicolson, I, p. 245. Londonderry's account of his visit based on notes he made at the time is contained in his book *Ourselves and Germany*, which was published in the spring of 1938 and was reprinted as a paperback with additional material later the same year. He further described his visit in *Wings of Destiny* (1943).
30 Londonderry to Baldwin 18, 19 May 1936: Baldwin Papers 171 f. 171.
31 Londonderry to Baldwin 19 December 1938: Londonderry Papers.
32 Londonderry Papers.
33 Londonderry to Baldwin 29 December 1938: Baldwin Papers 171 ff. 178–91.
34 Londonderry to Baldwin 20 May 1939: Londonderry Papers.
35 S. Baldwin. *An Interpreter of England*, p. 118.
36 Jones, p. 435.
37 Jones Papers cited Middlemas *and* Barnes, p. 1053.
38 Jones, p. 427.
39 ibid., p. 446.
40 A. W. Baldwin. *My Father: The True Story*, p. 331.
41 Jones, p. 447.
42 J. C. W. Reith. *Into the Wind*, p. 363.

43 Sir Alan Herbert. *A.P.H. His Life and Times*, p. 295.
44 Jones, p. 549. James, p. 427.
45 Jones, p. 482.
46 Feiling, p. 456.
47 Harold Nicolson. *Diaries and Letters*, II, p. 129.
48 Jones, p. 490.
49 Lord Butler. *The Art of the Possible*, p. 87.
50 Christopher Sykes. *Nancy, The Life of Lady Astor* (1972), p. 449. Jones, p. 491.
51 Baldwin to F. W. Pick 2 April 1940 and D. Pepys-Whiteley 15 February 1941: communicated by Mr Michael Pick and Mr Derek Pepys-Whiteley. Avon, p. 446.
52 James, p. 428.
53 A. W. Baldwin. *My Father: The True Story*, pp. 319–22. A. J. P. Taylor. *Beaverbrook*, p. 520.
54 Monica Baldwin. *I Leap over the Wall*, p. 40 ff.
55 William Barkley. 'Baldwin and Churchill': Davidson Papers A6.
56 Lord Citrine. *Men and Work*, p. 354.
57 19 April 1943. Communicated by Mr Colin Munro.
58 Nicolson, II, p. 306.
59 Young, p. 251. Jones, pp. 515–16, 527, 529.
60 ibid., p. 483.
61 ibid., p. 538. James, p. 428. Salisbury Papers cited Middlemas *and* Barnes, p. 1068. Blackett, p. 198.
62 Young, p. 254.
63 Jones, pp. 538, 540.
64 Jones, p. 545. Middlemas *and* Barnes, p. 1071.
65 Macmillan, p. 289.
66 Harold Nicolson. *Diaries and Letters*, III, p. 193.
67 A. W. Baldwin. *My Father: The True Story*, p. 324.
68 Macmillan, p. 205.
69 Channon, p. 415.
70 James, p. 428.
71 Middlemas *and* Barnes, p. 1069 note. A. W. Baldwin. *My Father: The True Story*, p. 331.
72 *The Times*, 15 December 1947. Hansard. Parl. Deb. H of C, 5th Series. Vol. 445, Cols. 1466–74.
73 *The Times*, 23 January 1948.
74 ibid., 22 May 1950.
75 *Dictionary of National Biography 1941–1950*, sub. Baldwin.

INDEX

Street, 199; Shadow Cabinet meets in his house, 202; 'not a good leader of Opposition', 203; on worries as Party leader, 207; interview with *The People*, 209 ff; and Ulster boundary dispute, 220; wins 1924 election, 223; becomes Prime Minister for second time, 225; his Cabinet, 237; writes to Canadian namesake, 238; on object of life in politics, 239; and Political Levy Bill, 242–4; on death of Curzon, 244; on King's objection to his parliamentary report,, 248–9; visits Glasgow slums, 255; at Chequers conference on Irish boundary dispute, 259–63; and General Strike, 265 ff; on the Labour Party, 274; 'out of gear', 276; tours Canada, 283–5; loneliness of, 285; accepts £25,000 charity donation from Beaverbrook, 290; takes Londonderry into Cabinet, 295 and note; watches boat race practice, 300; would not serve with Lloyd George, 301

'Safety First' Election (1929), 302–3; resigns after defeat, 306; criticism of, 308, 310; asks Derby whether he should resign party leadership, 312; Chancellor of Cambridge University, 314; his leadership criticised, 317–19; prepared to 'go down fighting', 321; praises Irwin's work as Viceroy of India, 323; denounces Rothermere and Beaverbrook for press campaign, 326–7; rejects idea of a national government, 329–30; on Labour Government's financial difficulties, 332; meets King with MacDonald and Samuel, 336

joins National Government as Lord President, 338; on Statute of Westminster, 347; 'the bomber will always get through', 354; on air policy, 354, 358, 361, 370, 377; uneasy relations with Londonderry, 361; deafness, 364, 429; on Londonderry's bombing speech, 381–2; talks to George V re MacDonald and future of Government, 383; story of his encounter with fellow old Harrovian in railway carriage, 385; what

he gave Laval for lunch, 386; tribute to MacDonald, 386; appoints Londonderry Lord Privy Seal and Leader of House of Lords, 388

succeeds MacDonald as Prime Minister, 389; asks Churchill to join Tizard Committee, 390–1; visits R. A. Butler in Essex, 393; asks King for dissolution, 397; assures Peace Society Government will stand by League of Nations and that 'there will be no great armaments', 397–8, and 1935 election, 399; drops Londonderry, 400–2; and Hoare–Laval pact, 405 ff; 'my lips are not yet unsealed', 408; on meaning of sanctions, 413; refuses to see Ernest Simpson, 401; dines with King, 422; and Hitler's Rhineland coup, 426, 435; wishes to get nearer to Germany, 433; on Ramsay MacDonald, 435; declines to meet Hitler, 438; on Bullock affair, 442; receives parliamentary deputation on defence, 443; on his holiday in Wales, 444

learns about King and Mrs Simpson, 446; audience with King at Fort Belvedere on Mrs Simpson, 450–4; controversial speech on rearmament, 460–2; audience with King at Buckingham Palace re Mrs Simpson, 466–8; on morganatic marriage proposal, 471, 474, 487–8; tells Cabinet of 'King's Matter', 476; puts three choices before King, 480; opposes King's broadcasting while still King, 484, 487; goes to Fort Belvedere, 488; summons colleagues to discuss proposed Simpson Divorce Bill, 492; final visit to Fort Belvedere, 498–500; tells G. M. Young that the King 'could not have behaved better than he did', 502; speech on Abdication to House of Commons, 504–6, and Abdication Bill, 507; broadcast on Abdication, 510; sends Christmas card to Duke of Windsor, 515; intention to retire, 521

accepts peerage, 522, 530; on de Valera's constitutional legislation, 523; on deterring aggression, 524; tribute to